The Beginnings of Russian-American Relations

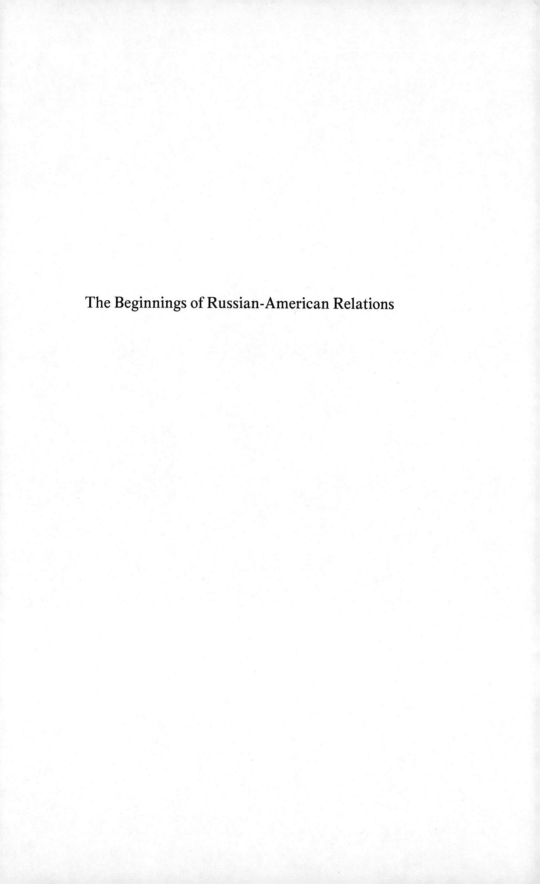

The Beginnings
of
Russian-American Relations
1775-1815

Nikolai N. Bolkhovitinov

translated by

Elena Levin

Harvard University Press
Cambridge, Massachusetts
and London, England
1975

Contents

PREFACE vii

INTRODUCTION by L. H. Butterfield xi

Part One: Russia and the War of Independence in North America . . .   1

  I Russian Diplomacy and the War of 1775-1783   3

  II The Attitude of Russian Society to the American Revolution . . . 30

  III Russians in the United States and Americans in Russia
     at the End of the Eighteenth Century. 56

Part Two: Russian-American Relations during the Late Eighteenth
     and Early Nineteenth Centuries 79

  IV Trade Connections Between Russia and the United States 91

  V The Development of Scientific, Cultural, and Socio-
     Political Connections. 116

  VI Russian Colonization of the Northwest 146

Part Three: Russian-American Rapprochement 1802-1812 187

  VII The Establishment of Diplomatic Relations 195

  VIII The Expansion of Trade Contacts 218

  IX Relations in the Northwest and the Agreement of
     20 April 1812 255

Part Four: The War of 1812 and Tsarist Russia 279

  X The War of 1812 and Its Evaluations by Russian
     Diplomats 283

  XI Russia's Attempted Peace Mediation 304

  XII Cultural Contacts and American Attitudes toward the
     Russian War of 1812 334

CONCLUSION 349

APPENDIX: Writings and Sources on Early Russian-American
     Relations 357

NOTES 387

INDEX 473

PREFACE

The present study was first published in Moscow by the Nauka Press in 1966. Since that time important changes have taken place in the world and especially in the relations between the United States and the Soviet Union. Long years of the cold war, more than once threatening to develop into a new thermonuclear catastrophe, gave way to a detente, constructive negotiations and businesslike cooperation. The Cuban crisis of the autumn of 1962, and the winter of 1965 when the escalation of the long tragedy of the Vietnam war began, were succeeded by May 1972 and the summer of 1973. A new period has begun in the history of relations between our two countries.

Although the period reviewed in this book is separated by some two centuries from the present time, the analysis of the events of that time has proved instructive. It was in those distant years that the first contacts between Russia and America were established. Friendly and mutually beneficial ties were formed and developed despite great geographical distances and social, political, and ideological barriers. The experience and the history of these contacts, as I see it, deserve close attention and study.

This work not only deals with diplomatic relations between Russia and the United States but also investigates their trade, social, political, scientific, and cultural ties as well as the history of Russian America and the development of business contacts between Russian settlers and American traders and navigators in the North Pacific.

In the past historians of international relations rarely turned to the study of social-political, scientific, and cultural ties. Their attention was focused on inter-state, especially, diplomatic relations, on the activity of

outstanding political figures and statesmen, famous generals and diplomats, tsars and presidents. Thus, the principal element, the people, as
represented by the finest, most educated, and active spokesmen—scientists, public figures, writers, and journalists—dropped out of the history
of international relations. Again and again historians recounted well-
known documents and entertaining episodes of diplomatic struggle,
almost completely ignoring the contacts between distinguished representatives of science and culture and also between social-political,
scientific, and cultural institutions. Yet the history of Russian-American
relations opens with the direct and indirect contacts between Benjamin
Franklin and other American scholars, and their Petersburg colleagues
—M. V. Lomonosov, G. W. Richmann, F. U. Epinus in the middle of the
eighteenth century. Probably the most original parts of the book are the
investigation of the American theme as reflected in the *pages of* Russian
journals and magazines, and its analysis of the attitude of advanced
representatives of the Russian society—N. I. Novikov, F. V. Karzhavin,
A. N. Radishchev—toward the American Revolution and the Constitution
of 1787, as well as its concrete study of the development of trade and
cultural ties in the eighteenth and the beginning of the nineteenth
centuries.

Though the content and conclusions of the 1966 publication have
remained basically unchanged, some corrections and additions have been
made in the original text and especially in the notes on the basis of recent
studies, documentary publications, and archive sources with which I
became acquainted during my visit to the United States in 1968. Some
new materials found reflection in my research articles and reviews published in Soviet periodicals (see page 472). At last, in the spring of 1975,
the second volume of the history of relations between Russia and the
United States, covering the period from 1815 to the 1830's, was published
in Moscow (N. N. Bolkhovitinov, *Russko-amerikanskie otnosheniia*,
1815-1832 [Moscow, 1975].) Of course, even taking into account these
new publications, I cannot lay claim to an exhaustive study of the long-
standing and many-sided ties between the United States and Russia.
However, I would be gratified if my work stimulated further studies and
promoted, if only to a small degree, understanding between the Soviet and
American peoples and the strengthening and broadening of the cooperation between our two countries.

Nearly twenty years have passed since I came for the first time to a
comfortable reading room in an old Moscow house on Bolshaya Serpuk-
hovskaya Street, where the Archive of the Foreign Policy of Russia is

located. Since that time I have worked in at least twenty different Soviet and American archives. Everywhere I have met with unfailing attention, kind cooperation, and valuable assistance. The number of persons who at different times and in different ways helped me in my work is too great to enumerate here without defeating the purpose of this preface. I cannot, however, refrain from mentioning my close colleagues in the American sector of the Institute of General History of the USSR Academy of Sciences and the staff of the Archive of the Foreign Policy of Russia. It was their benevolent attitude, support, and help that in many ways promoted the consummation of the present work. For a number of years valuable advice was offered to the author by Academicians M. P. Alekseev, A. A. Guber, E. I. and N. M. Druzhinin, A. L. Narochnitskii, and Corresponding Member of the USSR Academy of Sciences A. V. Efimov. I recall with deep gratitude the attention and help given to me by Professors Richard B. Morris, Oscar Handlin, Dexter Perkins, Assistant Librarian of Congress Elizabeth Hamer Kegan, Director of the Oregon Historical Society Thomas Vaughan, as well as Drs. Robert V. Allen, Whitfield J. Bell, Jr., David M. Griffiths, Patricia Kennedy Grimsted, Daniel Clarke Waugh, and many other American historians.

My special acknowledgments are due to everyone connected with the English edition of this book; first of all, to the Editor in Chief of the Adams Papers L. H. Butterfield, the translator Elena Levin, and my editor at the Harvard University Press, Ann Louise McLaughlin, who spent a great deal of time and energy in order to give the American reader an opportunity of becoming acquainted with the work in its present form. At last, the exceptional patience and kind-heartedness of my wife, L. A. Bolkhovitinova, created the genial atmosphere which enabled me to finish this long work.

N. N. B

Moscow, August 1975

INTRODUCTION
by
L. H. Butterfield

In the spring of 1802, Alexander I, the new young Tsar of All the Russias, let it be known to a liberal friend that, being interested in the American experiment in republicanism, he would like "information on the internal government of the United States." This wish was meant to reach President Jefferson, who had come to office in the same year as the Tsar; and it did. In response, again through intermediaries, Jefferson furnished a little reading list, which included among other items *The Federalist.* In a respectful manner, he pointed out that if Alexander was considering some measure of self-government in Russia, certain preparatory steps would be desirable, such as "diffusing instruction and a sense of their natural rights through the mass of his people, and . . . relieving them in the meantime from actual oppression." A year and a half later, with the help of further intermediaries and the Tsar's intercession to free the crew of an American vessel stranded in Tripoli, Jefferson opened a direct correspondence. His first letter was on a lofty level and had a curiously avuncular tone. "What has not your country to hope," he wrote, "from a career which has begun from such auspicious developments: Sound principles, pursued with a steady step, dealing out good progressively as your people are prepared to receive and hold it fast, cannot fail to carry them and yourself far in the improvement of their condition, during the course of your life." To which Alexander replied that his intercession had been intended to promote both trade and friendship between their two countries. "I have always felt a great esteem for your nation which knew how to make noble use of its independence by creating a free and wise constitution assuring the well-being of each and all."

There was more in this vein. The two heads of state exchanged gifts of books about Russia and the United States, and the Tsar also sent a sculptured bust of himself. But by far the most consequential result was the establishment of full consular and diplomatic relations. Levett Harris, an American merchant, served as American consul in St. Petersburg from late in 1803. Andrei Dashkov came to America in 1809 to serve as consul general in Philadelphia and as chargé d'affaires until the arrival of a minister, Fedor Pahlen, already appointed. One of the most observant and articulate among all the able diplomats sent from Russia to the United States from that time until this, Dashkov reported touchingly on his reception by President Madison and his first impressions of the young republic. He must have suffered inwardly when the formal address he had prepared was pocketed by the President without being read. It contained these sentences: "Living among your fellow citizens I shall often feel I have not changed my residence. I shall always admire the native creations of genius, the rapid progress of civilization, and a wilderness once more yielding in every respect to the enterprises of men protected by laws, guided by science, and successfully cultivating the arts."

On the American side there had been some false starts, but when in June 1809 Madison for the second time named John Quincy Adams (by far the best qualified man in the country) as minister, the Senate voted approval next day, and Adams sailed soon afterward. He was able, in fact, to carry Dashkov's first dispatches back to St. Petersburg with him; and he arrived *there* in time to be consulted by the Russian court on the final instructions to his counterpart, Pahlen, waiting in Paris for word to proceed to Washington.

These exchanges of cordial sentiments, followed by exchanges of representatives under the most auspicious circumstances imaginable, have all been taken from Professor Bolkhovitinov's narrative. The intention has not been to steal his thunder—there could be no way one could do that!—but to suggest the richly detailed character of this book, constructed as it is from published and unpublished sources in both the Soviet Union and the United States. From now on, *The Beginnings of Russian-American Relations,* as revised and enlarged by the author in the light of the most recent scholarship and translated from the Russian by Mrs. Levin, will serve as the standard reference work for the important subject it treats.

Antithetical in their institutions of government and geographically remote, there was no reason for either Russians or Americans to suppose in 1776 that they would have much to do with each other for some time to come. Catherine II felt more satisfaction than concern over the rebellion of England's American colonies, not because she liked rebels but because she disliked George III and thought the British government deserved the chastisement it was about to receive. (She refused the British request for mercenary troops without a second thought: the embattled Americans were no threat to the Russian Empire.) A little flurry of diplomatic activity did take place after a few years when Russia promulgated the Armed Neutrality of 1780. This attempt by "the northern powers" to curb Great Britain's arbitrary rule of the seas greatly interested Americans and led the Continental Congress to send Francis Dana to St. Petersburg (accompanied by the fourteen-year-old John Quincy Adams as secretary and French interpreter) in the hope of recognition. The Tsarina had her own complicated and cogent reasons for not recognizing the United States or its envoy, and the mission failed—though it is the author's contention that it did not fail so entirely as is commonly supposed. There was occasional talk but no really serious move toward diplomatic *rapprochement* before 1802, when Alexander I asked his old Swiss tutor, La Harpe, to put him in touch with President Jefferson.

These facts have long been on record, though Professor Bolkhovitinov has related them in greater depth and with fuller archival documentation than anyone else hitherto. At the same time he has broken ground well beyond the narrow confines of diplomacy, and he demonstrates that the roots of early Russian-American entente lie deep in economic and cultural ties that were in process of formation from the 1770's on. He derives his evidence from a wide variety of sources: N. I. Novikov's *Moskovskie Vedomosti* (Moscow Gazette), the verse and prose of the radical writer Aleksandr Radishchev, trade statistics, travel literature, the correspondence and memoirs of diplomats and consuls, and the fragmentary but cumulatively impressive records of international cooperation, or at any rate reciprocal recognition, in such scientific fields as electricity and linguistics. The author has found and now first printed from the William David Lewis Papers at the Historical Society of Pennsylvania a letter from Benjamin Franklin to the Russian physicist Epinus in 1766. And he has also furnished new and important evidence on the reason for John Ledyard's expulsion from Siberia in 1788. Jacoby, governor general of Irkutsk, was virtually sure that Ledyard, a former member of Captain Cook's crew, "is sent here by the English Crown for reconnaissance of the local situation."

Although Professor Bolkhovitinov does not suggest it, it is perhaps a measure of the insignificance of the young United States in Russian eyes that the wary Russian officials did not guess that Ledyard could be acting for *American* interests, public or private, overt or covert, in attempting to penetrate the American continent from across the Pacific. But the two illuminating chapters in this volume devoted to Russian America show that, thanks to the seamanship and commercial enterprise of the "Bostonians" (long the generic name for Americans among Russians on Pacific shores), the United States soon had most decidedly to be taken into account. Realizing that the Bostonians could be neither ignored nor warned off, the Russians eventually tried to join what they could not suppress. After all, American provisions were badly needed in the distant Russian settlements. And so one of the Russian aims in seeking formal diplomatic relations was to "regularize" American trade in the Northwest—that is, to confine it to Russians and stop American trade in guns, spirits, and furs with the natives. But despite the agreement between Astor's American Fur Company and the Russian-American Company in 1812, these hopes proved futile, and nothing was resolved in the Oregon country before the issues arose in a new and intensified form in the 1820's, as part of the background of the Monroe Doctrine.

New and unpredicted forces changed the face of things in Europe in the years following 1809. The Tsar, the President, and their emissaries in each other's capitals confronted a world hurtling toward Armageddon as allies became adversaries, enemies became friends, and the "Tilsit system" collapsed. These changes cannot even be summarized here, but Professor Bolkhovitinov has sketched them with skill and clarity to provide the necessary setting for the first years of Russian-American *rapprochement*. It suffices to say that a single element in the emerging entente between the two powers remained stable despite so many other changing relationships in the final phase of the Napoleonic wars. Madison called it an "affinity between Baltic and American ideas of maritime law." This was a high-sounding way of saying that Russia hoped American trade and carriers would diminish if not eliminate her dependence on Great Britain; and the United States, now that ports throughout western Europe were barred, viewed Russia as her only friend in, and her only access to, the Continent.

The new partners played their game of state skillfully. Upon his arrival in what he pronounced "the most magnificent city of Europe, or of the world," John Quincy Adams successfully protested, through Tsar Alexander, the impoundment of American vessels and goods held in Danish ports under the French Continental System. As Adams' grandson Henry was later to write, he could have chosen no better way to bring about a rupture between Alexander and Napoleon, and as Professor Bolkhovitinov comments, he was thus "unsuspectingly . . . helping to intensify an enormous conflict" that was in the making. Adams was to watch the whole

Tolstoyan drama played to its end. Most of it he saw and brilliantly reported from the Russian capital. But when the British government declined the Tsar's offer to mediate England's war with America, Adams went to Ghent for protracted peace negotiations, on to Paris during the Hundred Days, and back through Belgium on his way to London shortly before the battle of Waterloo. His Russian experience had been excellent training for the future secretary of state and chief author of the Monroe Doctrine.

In St. Petersburg, Adams had served as a cultural ambassador par excellence, acquiring Russian works of learning for his own library and transmitting other books to and from the United States. His lifelong study and patronage of astronomy owe much to his sojourn in Russia, which was a world center for the study of that science. At the same time, the evidence assembled in the present volume shows that Adams' counterparts in the United States, ministers and consuls alike, were quite as alert and almost as assiduous as he was in the cultural field, and they were more numerous and more widely located. The writings of such men as Dashkov, Pahlen, Svin'in (a gifted documentary artist as well as writer), Poletika, and Evstaf'ev make an impressive and informative record of early nineteenth-century American life when collectively considered. Parts of this record were made available for Russian and American readers contemporaneously. Much more of it has reposed in Russian archives and has now been brought to light as one of the chief contributions of this pathbreaking book.

For in the end it must be said that knowledge of each other was the most important result of the gradually achieved first *rapprochement* between Russia and the United States. The objectives that were so ardently hoped for on both sides disappeared in wars and in peace settlements that left few things as they were. The surprisingly cordial relationship between the northern autocracy and the transatlantic republic, as Professor Bolkhovitinov says, sprang more from coincidence than sentiment. It was a "union of convenience," the fragility of which was evidenced by its rapid breakdown.

Such sensible judgments are characteristic of this study as a whole. It is written in a truly and not merely an ostensibly scientific spirit (to use an adjective much favored by Soviet scholars). Aside from occasional remarks and epithets showing the writer's distaste for certain "Western" historians and for almost everything about the Russian *ancien régime,* the interpretation is little marred by ideological bias. Professor Bolkhovitinov even points out one thoroughly enlightened, though in the end frustrated, figure in the inner circle of the tsarist court whom he says history has not sufficiently honored. This is Nikolai Rumiantsev, who told John Quincy Adams, "Je puis dire que j'ai les entrailles Américaines," and sincerely meant it. The author has described his own stance as an interpreter of the events he narrates in his moving conclusion:

> I do not intend to present an idealized picture and create an impression that no disagreement or antagonism existed between Russia and America. . . . To ignore class contradictions, to write about "sincere" and "forgotten" friendships of Tsars and Presidents, . . . is just as inaccurate as to spread propaganda about "age-long hostility." The lesson of Russian-American relations consists not in the absence of differences and conflicts, but in the fact that history testifies to the possibility of overcoming them—not with the help of weapons, but peacefully, by means of negotiation.

Another means to this great end is by replacing mutual ignorance with mutual knowledge. Here the role of scholarship is vital, and Professor Bolkhovitinov's career and writings show how vital. It would appear to be literally the case that he is the first Russian or American scholar to have systematically studied the archival documentation and interpretive writing relating to the wide field of his interest in both countries and in both languages. Exceptions that might be pointed to—and a number of them are listed and interestingly discussed in the comprehensive bibliographical appendix to the present work—are so partial as to be almost if not entirely negligible. Even such magisterial works of scholarship as Bemis' biography of John Quincy Adams and Morris' *Peacemakers* were produced without benefit of access to original materials in Soviet archives —which, it must be kept in mind, embrace *all historical manuscripts*, not just official records.

Thus there was a great gap to be filled, in fact a whole panorama of diplomatic, economic, social, scientific, and literary relations to be delineated, when the Americanist N. N. Bolkhovitinov began his professional career in the 1950's. His first book, *Doktrina Monro (Proiskhozdenie i kharakter)* [The Monroe Doctrine (Origin and Character)], was published in 1959 and drew respectful though belated and rather wary comment from American scholars. The earliest form of the present volume was as a dissertation which won him a doctorate in historical sciences at the Institute of History of the Soviet Academy of Sciences and was published by the Academy in 1966. The work received highly favorable reviews in American scholarly journals, primarily on the grounds of its objective historical judgments and the stores of fresh information it furnished from original sources. By this time Dr. Bolkhovitinov had already done much research for a sequel, which in 1975 appeared in print as *Russko-amerikanskie otnosheniia, 1815-1832* (Russian-American Relations, 1815-1832) and constitutes an even more formidable volume than its predecessor. He has served meanwhile as one of the editors of the multivolume *Vneshniaia politika Rossii XIX i nachala XX Veka. . . . Seriia pervaia, 1801-1815* (Russian Foreign Policy in the Nineteenth and Beginning of the Twentieth Centuries. . . . First Series, 1801-1815), and has published more than fifty articles on many aspects of American (including Latin American) history, a number of which have been translated and published in American journals. In the spring of 1975, at a Library of Congress symposium on the impact of the American Revolution abroad, he delivered a learned paper tracing the influence of American political ideas in the following decades, most notably on the Decembrist movement. In short, although no one could be said to have preempted so large and diverse a field of scholarly endeavor (and he himself would be the last to make such a claim), Professor Bolkhovitinov bestrides it.

In the winter of 1964-1965, one of the articles translated and published in English drew my attention to Professor Bolkhovitinov's work. The article dealt with Russian diplomacy and the American Revolution, sketching the first faint and fumbling beginnings of a relationship that has become all-absorbing two centuries later. In addition to its lucid treatment of a complex subject, what struck me was its meticulous citation of sources by *fonds* and file and sheet in the old tsarist archives. The present book had not yet appeared, but the footnotes in the article confirmed at every point that the early records relating to the United States, listed in guides prepared by Frank A. Golder before the Russian Revolution, survived intact in the Archives of Russian Foreign Policy, though no longer in Peter's or Lenin's city but in Moscow. This confirmation sent me to Moscow in the spring of 1965, where with helpful advice and encouragement from Professor Bolkhovitinov I found and arranged to have copied on microfilm the files covering John Quincy Adams' mission to Russia in 1809-1814, including both his notes exchanged with Chancellor Rumiantsev and the instructions and dispatches sent by and to the Russian Foreign Office and its representatives in the United States. In return, and in the hope that further exchanges might follow on a systematic basis, a considerably larger body of material, both official and personal in character but all relating to Russia, was furnished on film from the Adams Papers in the Massachusetts Historical Society for the use of scholars in the U.S.S.R. In the enlarged and translated text of the present book, use has been made of this material, but unhappily no further exchanges of scholarly materials have taken place. Nor have the Soviet archival authorities instituted any copying program comparable to those of our National Archives and the Library of Congress which have made millions of pages of American historical records and manuscripts available on a nonprofit basis to anyone in the world who wishes to order them.

In 1968, as an exchange scholar in the cooperative program of the American Council of Learned Societies and the Soviet Academy of Sciences, Professor Bolkhovitinov investigated other sources relevant to his field in a broad sweep from coast to coast in the United States. An incident in his mission turns up in one of his pleasantly copious footnotes and is worth reporting here. The precise date and archival history of Tsar Alexander's earliest letter to President Jefferson in 1804 have long been uncertain because of the wanderings of the original, the existence of a duplicate, and inconsistent citations in the scholarly literature. One reference noted by Professor Bolkhovitinov was to "the private Morgan Library in New York [which] was so far away I could not even imagine working in it." But being in New York City in 1968, he presented himself at the imposing building on East 36th Street, "found the Library administration very amiable, and in a few minutes" held in his hand the authentic recipient's copy, properly dated at St. Petersburg and characteristically endorsed "Recd May 21 [1805]." The situation was as fraught with paradox as the early epistolary exchanges between Tsar and President or the intimate conversations of the Tsar with the strait-laced republican minister, John Quincy Adams, as they walked together on the Nevsky Prospekt a few years later.

Of course Professor Bolkhovitinov could have sent a written inquiry to the Pierpont Morgan Library in the first place, and he would have received a speedy, nonbureaucratic, and satisfactory response, probably accompanied by electrostatic prints of the imperial communication. When shall we achieve a veritable détente, running unobstructedly in both directions, in archival and historical activities which will parallel that which has now at least begun in space science? The benefits to knowledge on both sides are manifest everywhere in the pages of this book. The product of indefatigable labor, fine organizational skill, and acute scholarly judgments, it throws beams of light on obscure chapters in the history of two nations still struggling to understand each other.

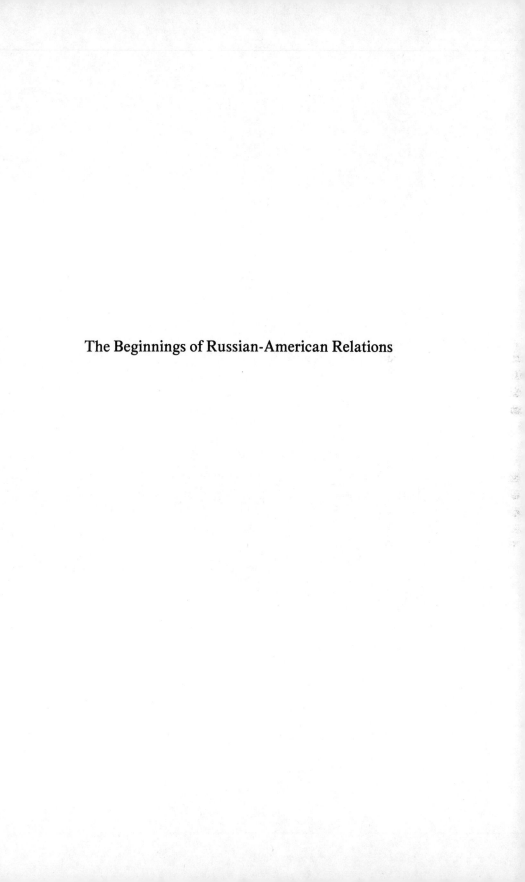

The Beginnings of Russian-American Relations

Part One

Russia and the War of Independence in North America

Almost two centuries ago, in the heat of a revolutionary war for independence, a new nation—the United States of America—was born. "The history of modern, civilized America," V.I. Lenin wrote, "opens with one of those great, truly liberational, truly revolutionary wars, of which there were so few among the vast number of predatory wars." Rating the historical significance of the War of American Independence especially high, the great founder of the Soviet state noted that the American people gave to the world "a model of revolutionary war against feudal slavery."[1]

The basic events, causes, and character of the war of England's North American colonies for independence, 1775-1783, are well known; hundreds and thousands of large and small books, documentary publications, articles, and reviews have been devoted to the theme.[2] Marxist historiography in the United States, which includes well-known general works by William Z. Foster, H. M. Morais, and Phillip Foner, has recently been enriched by a specialized book by Herbert Aptheker.[3] A number of general and specialized works dealing with the War of Independence have appeared also in Soviet literature.[4]

Aside from the general history of the American Revolution, its international aspect—the politics of the major European powers, above all, France—has been subjected to detailed investigation.[5] Much work has been devoted to the study of the positions of Spain, Holland, and other countries, and a publication dealing with the relation of Prussian diplomacy and United States independence also has appeared.[6]

Russia's position has been much less fully investigated, although one cannot maintain that no specialized works dealing with Russian-American relations for these years exist. A note by Frank A. Golder describes the policies of Catherine II[7] and specialized books by Francis P. Renaut and William Cresson cover the Francis Dana mission to St. Petersburg.[8] Nevertheless, on the whole Russia's attitude has not received extensive treatment in historical literature. Even in a work considered as reliable and authoritative as the official publication of the diplomatic history of the War of Independence edited by Francis Wharton, minimal attention is devoted to Russian policy; the account of it in the extensive Introduction, encompassing the entire first volume, occupies less than two pages.[9] Many general surveys of United States foreign policy pay no serious attention whatsoever to Russia's position at the time of the American Revolution,[10] although an exception is the text by Samuel Flagg Bemis, who was too well acquainted with documentary materials to ignore completely Russia's role.[11]

Detailed investigation of the Russian position during the American Revolution is seriously hindered by the lack of a suitable documentary foundation. The basic Russian diplomatic correspondence of the end of the 1770's and the beginning of the 1780's is scarcely known to most specialists. Publication of the "Political correspondence" of Catherine II was carried only to the end of the year 1777.[12] Publication of the correspondence of the French, English, Austrian, and Prussian ministers to St. Petersburg was interrupted at an even earlier date, while a valuable collection of Russian documents dealing with the history of the promulgation of Armed Neutrality[13] long ago became a bibliographical rarity, and it was surprisingly difficult even to uncover a copy in the Soviet central libraries.

As a result, during the research for this book major attention had to be focused on the search for new archival sources, so as to construct on their foundation a true documentary portrayal of the operation of Russian diplomacy in a difficult and complex time for the United States of America: the years of the heroic war for independence.

I

RUSSIAN DIPLOMACY AND THE WAR OF 1775-1783

Events in the English colonies in North America from the sixth decade of the eighteenth century on attracted the attention of Russian diplomats abroad, who informed their department of foreign affairs about the developing conflict between the colonists and the mother country in a detailed and rather objective manner. Even before military hostilities broke out, the belief that a rupture was unavoidable became more and more certain. A characteristic report of the Russian minister to London, A. S. Musin-Pushkin, of October 31/November 11, 1774, stressed the firm intention of the American colonists to defend their rights against the encroachment of their English rulers. "Letters received here yesterday from America," Musin-Pushkin informed Nikita Panin, senior member of the College of Foreign Affairs, "confirm convincingly the firm and almost unanimous intention of the inhabitants there not to obey any orders which might in the slightest lead to the consolidation of the right of legislation over them stemming from here . . . The General Congress of Philadelphia has already decided not to export any more American goods to this country, and not to accept any from here."[1]

The Russian minister not only correctly evaluated the situation taking shape at the time, but also managed with enviable penetration to foresee the consequences of the conflict with the colonies for England's internal life as well as for her international position. In the same report to St. Petersburg, Musin-Pushkin wrote:

> Such a situation justifiably alarms the government here, all the more so since they are aware of all the advantages the market and the factories here receive both from unfinished goods transported into the country from America and from the finished goods exported. The yearly

3

import of goods from there generally reaches a value of not less than three million pounds sterling, of which New York Province yearly sends out goods to the amount of six hundred thousand pounds sterling, and Philadelphia a little more than seven hundred thousand. Any cessation of such imports will at least harm very perceptibly, if not completely undermine, manufactures here. France and Spain are concerned, and will not refrain from interfering in the discord between England and her colonists. Two frigates flying the flag of the former, one hears, have appeared near Boston loaded with various military supplies; the latter has sent five more military ships from Ferrol, probably to America.[2]

Subsequent events confirmed the accuracy of these suppositions: the conflict with the American colonies not only "very perceptibly" affected the economy of Great Britain but led to war with France and Spain, then striving to take advantage of the "discord" for their own interests.

What appeared so obvious to a foreign diplomat patently was not grasped by George III and the members of his conservative government. The English ministers exhibited no desire to pay any attention to commercial "respect" and proceeded to "the awful declaration of the Americans as rebels."[3]

The shortsighted policy of Great Britain's ruling circles left the colonists no alternative to armed struggle. "A civil war seems so unavoidable," Musin-Pushkin wrote justifiably, "that they have been led to the extreme of either meekly obeying all the laws here or else opposing them as burdensome and restrictive to their natural and lawful rights."[4] Reporting that in various places in America "huge stores of all forms of military weapons with sufficient amounts of powder" were uncovered, he continued: "The people there, abandoning their usual occupations, voluntarily participate in military exercises. This enthusiastic spirit infects equally all grades and ranks; it begins to manifest itself in the Virginia Province even more strongly than until now it has been felt in New England itself."[5]

On April 19, 1775, at the battles of Lexington and Concord, shots rang out heralding the armed struggle of England's North American colonies for independence. Given the conditions under which war broke out, Russia's attitude took on special significance for Great Britain. The English government had counted on receiving from Russia the aid now needed so badly. On more than one occasion British ministers regretted that in the past they had been so unyielding in negotiations concerning the conclusion of a treaty of alliance. From the time of the creation of the Northern System by Panin (the idea for which was suggested by Baron Korf, the Russian envoy to Denmark), Anglo-Russian relations had evolved in a friendly direction, a fact partially explained by their joint opposition to French influence. In detailed instructions of July 26/August 4, 1768, to I. G. Chernyshev, the Russian envoy to London, it was pointed out: "By the Northern System we have in mind and mean the largest and closest possible union of northern powers in a direct focal point for our common interest, in order to oppose to the Bourbon and Austrian houses a firm counterweight among European courts, and a northern peace completely free from their influence, which has led so often to harmful effects."[6]

As early as 1762 Lord Buckingham, the English ambassador, had been instructed to arrange the conclusion of treaties of alliance and commerce with Russia.[7] An important trade treaty with Great Britain was signed June 20/July 1, 1766, in St. Petersburg,[8] but negotiations for the conclusion of a treaty of alliance brought no practical results. English diplomacy was disinclined to render decisive support to Russia in its relations with Sweden, Poland, and Turkey, and in particular stubbornly refused to agree to include Russian war with Turkey as a *casus foederis,* a provision which at the time interested the Russian government most of all.

During the Russo-Turkish War of 1768-1774, however, England's position was on the whole favorable to Russia, although she did not hasten to take on the obligations of an ally. On the other hand, she was not above interfering in the conflict to bring about her own mediation, an idea in turn rejected by Russia.[9]

The war in America very substantially influenced the subsequent development of Anglo-Russian relations, revealing contradictions which had not been evident up to that time, and changing to a certain extent even the very character of these relations. George III sent a personal message to Catherine II on September 1, 1775. Playing on the monarchical feelings of the Empress, the King in elevated tones "accepted" in form—but actually asked for—Russian soldiers to participate in the suppression of the rebellion of his subjects in North America.[10] The British envoy to St. Petersburg was given detailed instructions to obtain the dispatch of a corps of twenty thousand men and was sent the draft of an appropriate treaty.[11]

The reliance of the English king on Russian support proved unfounded. It was not a question of sympathy on the part of Catherine II for the rebellious colonists but of considerations of practical politics. The Empress, dreaming of "becoming ruler of Europe's destinies," was little disposed to send Russian soldiers to distant America to fight for the glory of His Britannic Majesty, whose virtues and abilities, it should be mentioned, she seriously doubted. In a letter to her friend Mme. Bielke in the summer of 1775 Catherine II caustically remarked that the loss of a sister, "who is of no importance,"[12] caused George III more grief than "the defeat of his troops in America." And, she continued, "his excellent citizens are very weary and often also . . ."[13] Catherine intentionally failed to finish, employing instead significant dots; she neither could, nor wanted to, recognize the legality and justice of the rebellion of George III's colonists, even in a private letter. At the same time the Tsarina took into account the prospects for war in America realistically enough when she finished her letter with the words: "I wish with all my heart that my friends the English would get along with their colonies; but so many of my prophecies have come true that I expect we may see America detach herself from Europe during my lifetime."[14] It is therefore not surprising that in a letter of September 23/October 4, 1775, Catherine replied to her august correspondent politely but firmly with a decisive refusal.[15]

All attempts by the English envoy Robert Gunning, through N. I. Panin and Aleksei Orlov, to obtain a favorable decision or simply to soften the refusal proved fruitless.[16] He attributed the failure to the intrigues of the all-powerful G. A. Potemkin and the Chernyshev brothers, but this was not where the main problem lay. In making her decision Catherine II first had to take into account Russia's internal and international situation: the war with Turkey (1768-1774) had ended only recently, and the memory of the menacing events of the peasant war led by Emelian Pugachev (1773-1775) was too fresh to think of defending the interests of the English king in America.

Failing to receive Russian support, the British cabinet hired soldiers from sovereign German princes.[17] These mercenaries, though, brought the English crown no special success: the separation of the colonies became a fact. The Declaration of Independence, signed on July 4, 1776, proclaimed the birth of a new nation: the United States of America. "The publication of this piece, as well as the proclamation of the formal declaration of war against Great Britain, shows all the courage of the leaders there," V. G. Lizakevich, adviser to the Russian embassy, reported from London.[18]

Although the outcome of the struggle was not yet obvious to European diplomats, it was already evident that English influence would be weakened significantly and that there would be important changes in international relations. "The strife occurring between England and her American colonies, and the war stemming from it," wrote N. I. Panin in a secret report to Catherine II in October 1776, "presages, apparently, significant and imminent changes in the present position of the European powers, and therefore in the whole system. Whether the colonies succeed in maintaining their already declared independence, or England in the end manages through exhaustive efforts to enslave them to its power—which cannot reasonably be assumed unless the colonies reach a state of exhaustion—in both cases one must probably reason that the London court will lose a great deal of its present significance."[19]

With the development of military affairs in America and the aggravation of antagonisms among European powers, Paris, capital of England's major rival in Europe, took on more and more significance as the center of the diplomatic struggle. It was here that Benjamin Franklin came in December 1776 to inaugurate secret negotiations with the French government. In noting his arrival in a detailed dispatch in cipher to Vice-Chancellor I. A. Osterman, December 1776, the Russian envoy to Paris, I. S. Bariatinsky, stressed the importance of Franklin's mission and the tremendous impression he created in France. "The public is so occupied with him," Bariatinsky wrote, "that nothing else is any longer talked about except the reasons for his arrival here."[20] Giving further information about "the sensation which he created" in the French capital and the probable goals of his mission, Bariatinsky noted that, according to the general opinion of the diplomatic corps, "Franklin's arrival here" constitutes "a significant event."[21]

News of the surrender of the English troops under the command of General Burgoyne at Saratoga, October 17, 1777, struck a severe blow at England's international prestige. It was with good reason that Musin-Pushkin viewed very skeptically England's new military preparations, justifiably supposing that they would result only in a further rallying of forces by the rebellious colonists. "Time has shown," he noted in December 1777, "that from the start of intentions here against America, the Americans gained strength precisely according to the size of the previous threatening measures undertaken."[22]

After long delays, on February 6, 1778, the French Minister of Foreign Affairs, Vergennes, together with the American envoy, Benjamin Franklin, signed two important treaties concerning trade and an alliance.[23] On February 26/March 9, commenting upon the unofficial news of the conclusion of the "treaty" and its provisions, Bariatinsky wrote to St. Petersburg:

> France took a false step in dragging out the conclusion so long, for it could have had more favorable conditions with the Americans had it decided last July. Then the Americans would have considered them-

7

selves obligated to France, with independence due to their aid. Now, however, the Americans feel they are receiving freedom through their own efforts; moreover, they know that France entered in only after being precisely informed of General Burgoyne's misadventures. According to all estimations it is assumed that the abovementioned treaty will be made public next April; they also say that a plan of war against England has been made here already. The Spanish will operate in the Mediterranean Sea, and France in the [Atlantic] Ocean.[24]

In the course of this phase of the war for independence, Paris remained one of, if not the most important, center of information—both for the tsarist government and Russian society—concerning international politics and, in particular, events connected with the war. Bariatinsky's dispatches contain extremely valuable information. Also, representatives of the Russian upper aristocracy and prominent cultural figures often journeyed to France from Russia. Among these, Princess E. R. Dashkova, Count A. P. Shuvalov, Count I. G. Chernyshev, and D. I. Fonvizin might be mentioned, with the last-named deserving special attention. A leading figure in Russian culture and famous eighteenth-century writer, Denis Ivanovich Fonvizin had served in the College of Foreign Affairs since 1769, where he was secretary and close aide and friend to Nikita Panin. In 1777-1778 he journeyed to Europe in a private capacity and spent a prolonged period of time in Montpellier and Paris.

During his stay in France, Fonvizin corresponded regularly with his sister and with P. I. Panin, brother of the head of the Department of Foreign Affairs. His letters, wonderful examples of eighteenth-century literary prose, are also valuable historical documents, describing important events in the international life of that time. Fonvizin repeatedly turns his attention to the increasingly aggravated relations between England and France caused by the war in America. "They cannot stand Englishmen here," he writes on December 31, 1777/January 11, 1778, "and although they conduct themselves civilly in their presence, they abuse them behind their backs and laugh at them. . . . Their American affairs are leading to the very extreme, and they are in such despair that one is led to think they will abandon America and declare war on France; for, since ancient days, every time England has reached a stage of extreme misfortune she has always resorted to the habit of declaring war on France."[25]

A while later, in March 1778, Fonvizin relates in a letter to P. I. Panin "that the state of affairs here is so bad that war is certainly unavoidable." France concluded "a treaty with the Americans, as with an independent power. . . . In a word, although war is not yet formally declared, this declaration is awaited from hour to hour. It is predicted that Franklin, the American chargé at court here, will be accredited minister plenipotentiary from the United American states any day now."[26] Fonvizin repeatedly mentions Franklin and, in August 1778, specifically reports his meeting with him. "They sent an invitation to me as well as to the famous Franklin who resides here as minister from the American United Provinces," he writes, "to the gathering founded this year under the name of the *rendez-vous des gens de lettres.* He, the famous English physicist Magellan, and I were received very well, even to the extent that the newspapers wrote of our visit the next day."[27]

In commenting upon the meeting of Fonvizin with Franklin in Paris, P. V. Viazemsky later wrote: "The representative of the young Russian enlightenment conversed with the representative of young America."[28] The very fact that such a meeting took place was without doubt quite significant, especially if it is juxtaposed with the "enlightened" Catherine's secret hostility to Franklin,[29] and the open tactlessness of the heir to the throne, Paul, who, when visiting Paris in 1782 under the title of Le Comte du Nord, rudely ignored the American envoy. An unpleasant incident which occurred when Franklin was mistakenly presented with the calling card of "Le Comte du Nord and Prince Bariatinsky" was, however, quickly settled, and had no political repercussions.[30]

On the whole, despite the obvious antagonism of monarchical circles toward the rebellious republicans, American diplomacy managed with rare success to use to its advantage the ancient antagonisms among the European powers. The young republic, Lenin noted, was able to use in its interests "the discord among the French, Spanish, and English"; the American people fought "alongside the troops of the French and Spanish oppressors against the English oppressors."[31]

The British position became more and more difficult. The broadening of the conflict caused by the entry of France and Spain into the war made the position of the mighty power to the north even more significant. It was precisely in this direction that the gaze of the London court turned; for in England they were still confident that Russian support could be obtained—at least against the European powers, if not against America. One of England's most capable diplomats, the young James Harris (later Earl of Malmesbury),[32] was sent to the Russian capital, and, at the beginning of 1778, renewed negotiations for the conclusion of an alliance. In transmitting the draft of an alliance treaty in April, Harris wrote of the necessity to destroy "the ambitious plans of the House of Bourbon." Stressing its "frankness" and "artlessness," the English government still did not forget to make the reservation—"strictly from commercial considerations"—that a *casus foederis* would not include a Russian war with Turkey. At the same time, it generously agreed not to enlarge the coverage of the treaty to include the war in progress in America.[33]

The reply of the Russian government, summarized in a May 6/17 note from Panin to Harris, proved of little comfort to the London court. Panin wrote that, "although Her Imperial Majesty understands the full significance of the adherence" of Great Britain to the Northern System, she "is forced with deep regret to recognize that the existing situation is totally inappropriate for the conclusion of an alliance between the two courts."[34]

Nor were later efforts of the English government, which now suggested the conclusion of a defensive alliance "without any conditions whatsoever," crowned with success.[35] In defining the Russian position in December 1779, Panin stressed "that the conclusion of a defensive alliance by its very nature cannot coincide in time with actual war, especially one such as the given war, the cause of which was brought about by circumstances which have always been excluded from alliance treaties between Russia and England as bearing no relation to the possessions of these countries in Europe."[36] With respect to negotiations for a treaty of alliance, it had been pointed out in the most categorical fashion even earlier, in July 1779, to I. M. Simolin, the new Russian envoy to Great Britain, that, given the London court's present "critical and delicate situation," "the very question cannot exist."[37]

Thus, from the very beginning of the war of the English colonies in North America for independence, the Russian government firmly and steadfastly carried out a policy of strict neutrality, decisively rejecting all attempts by England to bind it to alliance obligations.

The position taken by the Russian government was highly approved of in the United States. "We are not a little pleased to find from good authority," George Washington wrote the Marquis de Lafayette in the spring of 1779, "that the solicitations, and offers of the Court of Great Britain to the Empress of Russia have been rejected *with disdain*."[38] Again, in noting the decisive refusal of Catherine II to conclude any treaty of reciprocal aid with England, Washington stressed that the Russian government justified its position in expressions marked by "a generous regard to the rights of mankind."[39]

In considering mankind's well-being, the government of Catherine II proceeded primarily from state interests and a sober evaluation of the situation. A detailed analysis of the general international situation and the

Russian system of foreign policy with regard to England's war in Europe and America was presented to Catherine II during the summer of 1779 in a secret report of the College of Foreign Affairs. The report expressed the general opinion of the senior member of the College of Foreign Affairs, N. I. Panin; the Vice-Chancellor, I. A. Osterman; and the Bakunin brothers, members of the secret expedition of the College of Foreign Affairs, and was worked out at a session in July 31/August 11.[40] This document is of primary importance in understanding Russia's policy with regard to the war being waged by England. "Her American colonies," it points out, "becoming an independent and sovereign area through the very fault of the British government, do not and cannot fight against her in any other way than from within their dwellings and land, defending their new existence solely in response to her attacks."

From the excerpt cited it is evident that the Russian government not only considered the separation of the colonies from the mother country an accomplished fact, but viewed the cause of this as "the very fault" of the British cabinet. Moreover, the report points out specifically that the separation of the colonies from England would not be contrary to Russian interests but would be beneficial to them, inasmuch as Russian goods could successfully replace articles previously supplied to the English market from America and, in addition, mutually advantageous direct trade relations would develop with America itself. "The loss by England of her colonies on dry land," the report concluded, "would be not only unharmful, but might even prove advantageous to Russian commercial interests, inasmuch as with time a new direct area of commerce with America might open up and be established for the satisfaction of mutual needs directly."

It should be remembered that all this was expressed not as the personal opinion of some influential state figure but as the result of the collective work of men directing the foreign policy of the country. The very character of the document—a secret report to the Empress—lends its contents special significance.

The report's authors viewed the current British government with skepticism: "The true internal state of the court and the English ministry is not such as to be able to arouse national and outside confidence in it." They expressed particular dissatisfaction with England's actions on the seas: "Being surrounded by a great number of powerful enemies, she nevertheless does not halt the seizure of neutral ships, even with the most innocent cargoes, thus more and more embittering and irritating other nations."

In general the authors assume that, in defining the Russian position, "our own interests and the very basis of all our policy"—the Northern Sys-

11

tem—must be taken into account before all else. In adhering to a policy of strict neutrality, they recommend a simultaneous strengthening of the Northern System, and in particular "communicating and exchanging advice on general measures openly and in a timely fashion" with Denmark and Prussia. This, in their opinion, would prepare the way for Russia to assume the role of powerful arbitrator for the pacification of the warring parties. Subsequent actions of the Russian government in general correspond to the views expressed in the secret report.

An extremely important international act undertaken by Russia in connection with the war being waged by England against her American colonies and two European powers was the declaration of Armed Neutrality. Despotic measures on the high seas by the powers, especially by England, were undermining international commerce and leading to the seizure of neutral ships and the violation of elementary rights of navigation.[41] A. S. Musin-Pushkin continually sent in reports dealing with the brazen activities of English privateers, which attacked "all ships they came across, without any regard for various flags."[42] "Unpleasant explanations" in this regard took place regularly at the Court of London with representatives of the neutral nations. In a rescript from Catherine II of November 8/19, 1779, Simolin was ordered to make "the strongest representations" concerning the seizure of two ships belonging to the Riga merchants of Karl Berens and Company.[43]

Verbal explanations were of little help, however, and it became necessary to take more positive measures. On February 28/March 11, 1779, a note in the form of a declaration sent to the English and French governments announced Russia's intention to dispatch "a squadron of our ships-of-the-line and frigates, which will be ordered to defend in a proper manner trade and navigation, by chasing away from the coastal area any privateer which appears there, without exception, regardless of its nationality."[44]

Within a year, this time in connection with the Spanish capture of the merchant ship *St. Nikolai,* the Russian government recognized the necessity, "before insulting the Russian trade flag becomes a harmful habit," of informing London, Paris, and Madrid of a decision "to utilize all means available to us and all the power at our disposal for its complete protection and security with, however, the firm intention to harmonize them religiously and inviolably with the rules of the strictest impartiality and neutrality during the course of the present war."[45] It was resolved to send a new squadron into the North Sea in the summer "to chase out of those waters all privateers and to guarantee free navigation to our ports for all friendly peoples," and to prepare an additional fleet of fifteen ships and four frigates at Kronstadt.[46]

So that foreign nations, and primarily the warring powers, did not arrive at false conclusions, "through ignorance or unfounded impressions," and did not misinterpret Russian measures, the famous Declaration of Armed Neutrality was simultaneously promulgated, founded, as the same rescript pointed out, "on simple, clear, and indisputable concepts of natural law on the one hand, and on the explicit resolutions of our commercial treaty with Great Britain on the other."

The declaration provided: (1) neutral ships may visit freely the ports of belligerents; (2) property belonging to belligerents on neutral ships may pass inviolable, with the exception of military contraband; (3) only items listed in the 10th and 11th articles of the 1766 Russian treaty with England (that is, weapons, ammunition, and so forth) are recognized as military contraband; (4) only a port, the entrance into which is actually impeded by military-naval forces, falls under the definition of a blockaded port; (5) these principles will serve as standards in the determination of the legality of prizes.[47]

The promulgation of the Declaration of Armed Neutrality had great international significance: it established a firm basis for an international law protecting the sea trade of neutrals in time of war. As Friedrich Engels noted, with this act Catherine II "created for the first time in her name and in the name of her allies the principle of 'armed neutrality,' (1780)—a demand for the limitation of the rights on the high seas which England claimed for its warships."[48]

In the period from 1780 to 1783 practically all neutral European countries adhered to the declaration in actions made official through diplomatic agreements. France and Spain also recognized the principles put forth by Russia. A mountain of historical literature—books and documentary publications by German, French, English, Danish, American, and other foreign (not to mention Russian) authors, among whom can be found government figures, historians, lawyers, and professional diplomats—has been devoted to the history of the Armed Neutrality, the origin of the principles of the Russian declaration, and their significance. To the valuable 1859 Russian publication of documents and the recent monograph by Madariaga, already mentioned, must be added the research of the German lawyer Bergbohm,[49] the monograph by the French scholar Fauchille,[50] and the American publication of John Brown Scott.[51]

Despite the amount of investigation into Armed Neutrality, many problems connected with its history and significance have not yet been fully clarified, and widely varying opinions have been expressed, particularly about the identity of the author of the celebrated act. The names of N. I. Panin, Catherine II, the Danish Minister of Foreign Affairs Count Bernstorff, the Prussian King Frederick II, and the French Minister of Foreign Affairs Vergennes have been suggested. At one time von Dohm and and Count Goertz[52] created a version which ran that the promulgation of the Declaration of Armed Neutrality was almost accidental, the result of court intrigue and competition between Count Nikita Panin and Prince Grigory Potemkin. As for Catherine II, according to them she so little understood the actual significance of the declaration drawn up on Panin's initiative that she assumed it had been promulgated in the interests of England![53]

However, it had been correctly noted in earlier Russian works (by V. Leshkov and V. Danevsky) that the promulgation of Armed Neutrality was the natural result of events which preceded it, and that the domestic interests of Russia itself, coinciding at the time with the principles of the celebrated declaration of 1780, caused its promulgation.[54]

Russian sea trade in the second half of the eighteenth century was mainly in the hands of English merchants and was transported on English ships. It was only natual for Russia to strive to free itself from excessive reliance on England and to encourage the development of its own and other neutral navigation. In 1775, 414 ships (including 17 Russian and 236 English) were involved in foreign trade; in 1787 the number had increased to 2,015 (including 141 Russian and 767 English).[55]

The principles of the declaration of 1780 were in no way completely new: many of them could be found earlier in contractual acts (the declaration itself contains a reference to the 1766 trade agreement with England), diplomatic correspondence, and the works of legal scholars. Count Bernstorff's reply of September 29, 1778, to the Russian government on the question of the defense of naval navigation in accordance with a definite system of principles was based on materials presented to the Danish Foreign Office by the distinguished jurist Max Huebner.[56] Finally, it must be especially noted that the Russian declaration of 1780 in point of fact vindicated the very same principle which the Continental Congress in 1776 approved upon the recommendation of John Adams ("free ships, free goods"), that is, the right of neutral countries to trade freely in time of war in any goods with the exception of obvious contraband.[57] This principle was later reflected in the text of the aforementioned 1778 commercial agreement between France and the United States. It turned out that, in promulgating the Declaration of Armed Neutrality, the Russian government vindicated (in view of its own interests) one of the principles in whose name the rebellious colonies in America were fighting. It is therefore not coincidental that many years later President James Madison wrote of Armed Neutrality as "an American doctrine," stressed that its promulgation in 1780 comprised "an epoch in the history of maritime law," and noted that the United States "have a special interest" in its maintenance.[58]

The fact that the principles of Armed Neutrality had been prepared by preceding events, the development of a theory of naval rights, and the customs of commercial navigation explains its wide acceptance and its importance in the history of international relations. References in historical literature to the effect that the Russian government did not understand the meaning of the act it had undertaken and that Catherine II even assumed she would render a service to England by her declaration do not stand up to serious criticism. In reality the British Government had not abandoned throughout the preceding years the idea of possible support from Russia. No earlier than November 5, 1779, George III, Catherine's "most devoted Brother," had asked for a demonstration of Russian naval power which might, in his words, "restore and secure the peace of the whole of Europe by dispersing the league that has been formed against me, and by maintaining the balance which this league attempts to destroy."[59] Catherine carried out such a demonstration—sending a squadron into the North Sea and promulgating the Declaration of Armed Neutrality—but this demonstration was not in favor of, but opposed to, Great Britain. References are often made to the effect that Catherine herself noted in a conversation with James Harris, December 7, 1780: "mais quel mal vous fait cette Neutralité armée, ou plutôt Nullité armée?" (but what harm is done you by this Armed Neutrality or, rather, Armed Nullity?).[60]

In his reports to London, Harris expended a great deal of energy in trying to belittle Armed Neutrality and its significance. But, as Martens wrote, "the witty English diplomat failed to note that in terming her grandiose plan a trifle or a nonentity, Catherine II both pacified him and mocked him."[61]

Despite the large number of people given major, and sometimes exclusive, credit in historical writing for the preparation of the Declaration of Armed Neutrality, and the thoroughness of the investigations carried out, the actual roles of individual people (F. U. Epinius, for instance) are not completely clear to this day. The role Petr Bakunin played in the direct preparation of the draft of the declaration is little known, although we have the testimonies of S. R. Vorontsov and Catherine II herself on that score.[62] Until recently, the activities of the Russian ambassador in The Hague, D. A. Golitsyn, remained unacknowledged by scholars.[63] Nevertheless, to some extent he played a substantial role in the preparation of the Declaration of Armed Neutrality as well as in the establishment of the first Russian-American diplomatic contacts.[64]

The interesting and unusual figure of D. A. Golitsyn assumes a somewhat unconventional position in the history of Russian diplomacy. A person broad of mind and education, author of works on the theory of electricity, mineralogy, geography, political economy, and philosophy, Prince Dmitri Alekseevich Golitsyn filled the post of Minister to Paris from 1762 to 1768, and then was transferred to The Hague. He was an honorary member of several academies and scientific societies (including academies of science in St. Petersburg, Berlin, and Stockholm), was a friend of Voltaire, Diderot, and Mercier de la Rivière, and was especially close to the physiocrats. It is to him that the credit belongs for the posthumous publication in 1773 of the celebrated book *De l'homme* by the materialist philosopher Helvétius, and also for the working out of a plan, radical for the time although theoretically very limited, for the abolition of serfdom in Russia, envisaging freedom of the peasants by redemption without land.[65] Without dwelling in detail on the complicated, and to a large extent contradictory, views of Golitsyn, we can note that in their class nature they reflected eighteenth-century gentry liberalism.[66] He was an advocate of the development of agriculture by means of what today is called the "Prussian way." The limitations and contradictions in Golitsyn's views resulted from the fact that, objectively reflecting the development of capitalist formation in the midst of a feudal-serf-owning structure, he strove to turn it to the interests of the nobility to which he belonged.

At The Hague, Golitsyn maintained regular contacts with American agents, first C. W. F. Dumas and then John Adams, corresponded with Benjamin Franklin, and even received a reprimand from St. Petersburg for transmitting a portrait of Washington, which Catherine ordered sent back.[67] In May 1782 he was also given strict instructions to refrain from official recognition of John Adams as American minister.[68]

Unlike many of his colleagues—narrow-minded and complacent tsarist officials—Golitsyn had independent views on a number of important problems, and regularly submitted advice to Nikita Panin, I. A. Osterman, and the Empress herself in St. Petersburg, a practice rarely encountered in the diplomacy of the time.

Of particular interest for the history of the February 1780 declaration is a letter from Golitsyn to Panin in which the minister lays out in detail the project for a treaty of alliance between Russia and Holland, with the participation also of Denmark and Sweden, "solely in the interest of protecting the trade of the contracting powers and upholding neutrality and free navigation."[69] He presented this project as Holland's plan, calling it "just, sensible, and correct." "With regard to the benefit from this treaty," Golitsyn wrote:

> Your Excellency will understand it better than I. The English and Germans, by seizing all the Republic's ships, have hampered its trade to such an extent that the Dutch will find it necessary to relinquish it, with the result that the market for our goods will suffer, inasmuch as virtually from the beginning of the American war with England, Russia alone has had to supply the belligerent powers with hemp, sails, and ship timber. However it is just these goods that the English most zealously take away from the Dutch. I must also inform Your Excellency that I know from a reliable source that the Court of Versailles would not object to the formation of an alliance between the Republic and our court, and even among all the northern courts, and that at the present time it desires peace, if only such may be concluded on reasonable terms, chief of which would be freedom of trade and navigation for all European nations.

Detailing his ideas in a letter of March 1780 to Nikita Panin,[70] Golitsyn noted: "In my opinion, the major advantage which can be derived from this would be to step forward as mediator between the belligerent powers: they could not refuse this mediation: the Empress would compel them to peace and dictate its conditions, as she did at the Teschen Congress. Here then would be the basic goal which would have to be borne in mind when concluding the alliance."

It is difficult to reach a final verdict about Golitsyn's degree of influence on Russia's proclamation of Armed Neutrality, but his advice could not help hastening the development of events. Let us turn our attention to a curious chronological coincidence: Golitsyn's letter of February 7/18, 1780, was received in St. Petersburg on February 26/March 8 as witnessed by the inscription on it; the very next day the Declaration of Armed Neutrality was signed. The Russian government had come forward as instigator of the formation of a league of neutral powers for the defense of commercial navigation. One should not draw any categorical conclusions from this simple chronological concurrence. Golitsyn's letter was, so to speak, the last drop, overfilling the cup already full to the brim. But also there is no doubt that Golitsyn's activities at The Hague deserve special attention from historians.

Russia's actions had a great deal of importance for improving the international position of the United States by undermining England's sea power and isolating her diplomatically. Benjamin Franklin, writing to C. W. F. Dumas, American agent at The Hague, in June 1780, gave a high evaluation of Armed Neutrality:

> I approve much of the Principles of the Confederacy of the Neutral Powers, and am not only for respecting the ships as the House of a Friend, tho' containing the Goods of an Enemy, but I even wish for the sake of Humanity that the Law of Nations may be further improv'd, by determining, that, even in time of War, all those kinds of People, who are employ'd in procuring subsistence for the Species, or in exchanging the Necessaries or Conveniences of Life, which are for the common Benefit of Mankind, such as Husbandmen on their lands, fishermen in their Barques, and traders in unarm'd Vessels, shall be permitted to prosecute their several innocent and useful Employments without interruption or Molestation, and nothing taken from them, even when wanted by an Enemy, but on paying a fair Price for the same.[71]

In describing the favorable international situation evolving after the proclamation of Armed Neutrality, George Washington noted that the Russian declaration, to which all the European governments adhered, humbled "the naval pride and power of Great Britain."[72]

John Adams placed exceptionally high value on the Russian declaration, considering it almost a more unpleasant act for Great Britain than a declaration of war would have been. Judging from materials in English newspapers and debates in Parliament, Adams reported the great dissatisfaction in England caused by Russia's promulgation of Armed Neutrality, in a letter to the President of the Continental Congress. At the same time he thought that the reform of international law, for which the Russian government was striving, would be advantageous for all nations, and especially for the United States.[73]

In September and October of 1780 the Declaration of Armed Neutrality became the subject of special consideration by the Continental Congress. At the September 26, 1780, session Robert Livingston introduced a proposal to recognize the regulations contained in the Russian declaration as "useful, wise, and just." Along with members of that Congress, he thought the Russian declaration deserved "the earliest attention of a rising republick."[74] In accordance with the recommendation of a committee created to consider the question, the Continental Congress, on October 5, 1780, adopted a special resolution approving in full the declaration by Catherine II as based "upon principles of justice, equity, and moderation." The resolution stipulated the preparation of appropriate instructions for American warships,[75] and gave full powers to American diplomats abroad to adhere to the principles promulgated by Russia.[76]

In transmitting the decision of the Continental Congress to Golitsyn, John Adams wrote that he would be happy "to be the instrument of pledging, in form, the faith of the United States of America to a reformation in the maritime law of nations, which does so much honor to the present age."[77] This letter is considered by historians to be the first diplomatic document in the history of relations between Russia and the United States of America.[78] From the formal point of view this seems correct. It must be borne in mind, however, that this decision along with the debates preceding it in the Continental Congress had been sent to Golitsyn by Dumas still earlier, as witnessed by the inscription on the transmitted document: "C. W. F. Dumas, agent of the United States."[79] If we consider meetings of Russian diplomats with American representatives, then the most favorable opportunities were available to I. S. Bariatinsky, who on orders from Nikita Panin entered into "private" negotiations with Benjamin Franklin in late 1779 in connection with news of the appearance of foreign ships in the region of the Chukotsk peninsula.[80]

Taking into account the significance of Russia's favorable position in the American Revolution, and placing a high evaluation upon the promulgation of Armed Neutrality by Catherine II, the Continental Congress in the middle of December 1780 adopted a resolution concerning the necessity of sending an American diplomatic representative to St. Petersburg. To draw up the commission and instructions for the new minister a committee was created, consisting of John Duane, John Witherspoon, and James Madison; Francis Dana, Arthur Lee, and Colonel Alexander Hamilton were nominated for the newly created post.[81]

Francis Dana, "former delegate to Congress from the State of Massachusetts and member of the Council of said state," was elected to the post of minister on December 19, 1780.[82] That same day President of the Continental Congress Samuel Huntington signed the appropriate instructions, the commission and credentials for the new envoy.[83] "The great object of your negotiation," it was pointed out, "is to engage Her Imperial Majesty to favor and support the sovereignty and independence of these, and to lay the foundation for a good understanding and friendly intercourse between the subjects of Her Imperial Majesty and the citizens of these United States, to the mutual advantage of both nations."[84] In the event of a favorable reception at St. Petersburg, Dana was to sign a convention for the adherence of the United States to the Declaration of Armed Neutrality and to reach an agreement on a draft treaty of friendship and commerce.

Aside from the Declaration of Armed Neutrality, the suggestion of a peaceful mediation between England and her adversaries was a most important step in Russian diplomacy in these years. And it was not accidental that the aforementioned secret report of the College of Foreign Affairs to Catherine II of July 31/August 11, 1779, pointed out that it would be in Russia's interests to procure "the enviable role of mediation in the present war which is enveloping all parts of Europe."

In her ambitious plans Catherine II was not against becoming "arbitrator of affairs" at the conclusion of peace, which "would embrace all parts of the inhabited world."[85] One of the main purposes of the promulgation of Armed Neutrality was to strengthen Russia's international authority and to attach more significance to its peaceful initiative. In dealing with this question Nikita Panin notes in a March 1780 report to Catherine that a combination of neutral powers would "attach still more importance to our impartial endeavours to restore peace to Europe."[86] It was also characteristic that in the February 7/18 letter to Panin, D. A. Golitsyn, expounding a plan for the union of the neutral powers to defend commercial navigation, stressed that its basic goal was "to bring an end to the war between England and the Bourbon Houses by offering them the mediation of the Empress and the Republic."[87]

From December 1778 on, the question of peaceful mediation was discussed from time to time in diplomatic circles in St. Petersburg. On September 1, 1780, the Marquis de Vérac, new French minister at St. Petersburg, reported to his government that Panin regarded American independence as "something very advantageous for all nations, and in particular for Russia." According to Panin's plan, America would have "complete liberty to decide its own fate and . . . during the armistice it could conduct commerce freely with all nations." Throughout the autumn of 1780 the Russian government kept returning to the subject, producing very reasonable arguments for the courts of London, Versailles, and Madrid, pointing out that the expenditures of one company could prove to be greater than the advantages obtained in the end.[88]

Finally, on December 16, 1780, I. M. Simolin made an official offer of mediation (the famous "insinuation verbale"), couched in very vague terms, to the English government. That government expressed no particular enthusiasm for the Russian initiative, and suggested that the negotiations be conducted under the joint mediation of Russia and Austria. In general the arguments cited for conciliation were not readily accepted in London. Sober-minded and calculating British diplomats were little inclined to believe in Catherine's "love for mankind," and, most important, feared Russia's unexpected initiative and growing influence. Everyone remembered quite distinctly the result of the Teschen agreement of May 24, 1779, when Russia presented itself as powerful mediator in the negotiations and guarantor of the peace treaty between Prussia and Austria, and in return received the right to participate in German affairs.

Without entering into the complicated peripeteia of the prolonged negotiations concerning Russian (and soon Austro-Russian) mediation, we can note that in the future Russian diplomacy devoted special attention only to a conciliation between England and Holland; in this regard, on January 30/February 10, 1781, I. M. Simolin and D. A. Golitsyn were ordered officially to offer Russia's good offices and mediation.[89] Later a manifesto and credentials for the assignment of Golitsyn and A. I. Morkov as mediators for the cessation of war between England and Holland were signed.[90]

It was no secret to the Russian government that the real reason for England's attack on Holland was the adhesion of the latter to the system of Armed Neutrality. For this same reason England had no desire to conclude peace with Holland, fearing lest the republic take advantage of the fruits of "the new system in behalf of the trade and navigation of neutral nations," put forth by Russia.[91]

In the long run attempts to incline England to "greater pliancy" brought no important practical results. And, although satisfactory relations between the two nations were preserved externally, it was no secret that England was waging an open battle against the system of Armed Neutrality created by Russia. It is characteristic that D. A. Golitsyn became an object of English diplomatic intrigue. As he wrote to I. A. Osterman from The Hague: "The English party is conducting diabolical intrigues to frustrate everything and, in particular, to ruin me. It has quite openly declared that, although the intentions of the neutral powers are completely justified and founded on treaties with England, they do not suit the Court of London." Bitterly he reported further that all sorts of "nasty things" were being spread concerning him: he was being represented as an "intriguer," "a rash person," who had exceeded his commission, and so on.[92]

However unpleasant the rise of Armed Neutrality may have been for England, by the eighth decade of the eighteenth century this system had become a fact which had to be reckoned with in one way or another. It was also impossible to ignore completely Russia's persistent proposals for peace mediation. Although mediation eventually was refused, the very fact of its promotion and the repeated Russian proposals in the cause of a peace settlement could not help aiding to some extent the opening of peace negotiations.

A certain pressure was exerted on England in the delicate question of the war with her revolted colonies and the recognition of American independence. Thus, in the middle of March 1780 James Harris was informed through a third party of the Empress' desire that England renew its efforts to attain a truce with the Americans. At the beginning of April, Panin developed "vague and inadmissible plans of pacification" (according to Harris), and stressed the necessity of finding some sort of solution to the American problem. Somewhat later, in the summer and autumn of 1780, Panin expressed his approval of American independence as beneficial to Russia, in discussing various peace projects with the Marquis de Vérac, the French minister. Harris, who had termed Panin his "most dangerous opponent," clearly had no desire to heed his wishes. Soon, however, the Empress herself reinforced them. In the course of her celebrated discussion with the English minister in December 1780 Catherine II advised: "Faites la paix; traitez avec vos colonies en détail; tâchez de les diviser" (Make peace; negotiate with your colonies one by one; try to divide them).[93]

Finally, in February 1782, in transmitting to I. A. Osterman the "Imperial will," A. A. Bezborodko, all-powerful secretary to the Empress, wrote that, in line with her "friendly disposition toward the British King," the Empress "greatly desired that the affair between him and his colonies in America, which are separating from him, at this time the only obstacle to conciliation, might be ended by a voluntary and preliminary agreement between them, and that the present stay in Holland of Mr. Wentworth as well as the emissary of the abovementioned colonies, Adams, might present a suitable occasion." In this regard at the same time Arkady Ivanovich Morkov was similarly instructed to make certain that in dealing with this problem he act with great circumspection, "not giving England cause to conclude that this court desires to interfere in her affairs with the American colonies."[94]

The English government at first resolutely refused to make any concessions at all regarding the question of independence for the rebellious colonies.[95] In time, however, the question became more and more academic; the independence of the rebellious colonies was not only declared, but won in a long and difficult struggle against the mother country. And this struggle determined in the last analysis the complete victory of those fighting for independence. The surrender of the British forces under the command of General Cornwallis at Yorktown, October 19, 1781, in particular had great significance. The defeat of the British forces in America resulted in the fall of the old Tory cabinet and the bringing to power of the Rockingham-Fox Whig government in the spring of 1782. England had no alternative but to recognize American independence and open peace negotiations.

"When the former ministry revealed and repeated to me," reported Ivan Simolin from London on June 7/18:

> that the nation would sooner be buried under the debris of the state than go so far as recognition of American independence, as Your Excellency deigned to recall, it was speaking in an imposing tone and had at its disposal the votes of the electorate before the catastrophe when Cornwallis' army was captured . . . Events on the Chesapeake have created a new situation and have led to the dismissal of the ministry mentioned. If at that time chances for victory and defeat for British arms had been equal, I am inclined to think that the ministry referred to would have continued to exist and would not have renounced its plan to subdue America by force of arms, and with this goal in mind would have resorted to the most extreme measures.[96]

As a result of negotiations between the American delegation and English plenipotentiaries a preliminary peace treaty was concluded on November 30, 1782. On September 3, 1783, the text of the definitive treaty was signed at Versailles.[97] In connection with preparations for signing the act, the question of Austro-Russian mediation again arose. This time it was a matter of the strictly formal aspect of affairs: would the signatures of the Russian and Austrian representatives be found under the text of the agreement? This procedural aspect was of vital importance to the United States, inasmuch as official recognition of the independence of the new state by the governments of both powers would result from the signing of the treaty by Russia and Austria. It is therefore understandable that when French Minister of Foreign Affairs Vergennes asked the American plenipotentiaries if the United States wanted to sign the definitive peace treaty under mediation by the St. Petersburg and Vienna courts, they immediately assented.[98] But the English representative, David Hartley, decisively rejected the suggestion.

I. S. Bariatinsky, the Russian minister in Paris, reported to St. Petersburg, August 13, 1783, in this regard:

> Yesterday I met with Franklin; he always treats me with sufficient confidence. In conversations I extended him personal greetings on the occasion of a reference made by Adams concerning their intention to invite us and [Count] Mercy to sign the treaty with England . . . Franklin answered: We, of course, would always consider it a particular honor

that the foundation of our independence had been confirmed, and for our part we shall exert all our efforts toward this goal; but we are not yet certain if we shall have the honor, for Mr. Hartley, the English commissioner with whom we are now treating of the affair, is opposing us in this, responding that England has no need of any mediation."[99]

In deliberations which Franklin and Adams held with Hartley and Vergennes although pretending "strict neutrality," the French minister was in fact also opposed to mediation, and the question was finally abandoned. It was no secret to the American representatives that this opposition stemmed from British and French desire to prevent solidification of America's international position. "The signatures of the two Imperial Courts" (St. Petersburg and Vienna), Adams wrote, "would have made a deep and important impression in our favor upon full one-half of Europe as friends to those courts, and upon all the other half as enemies . . . From all the conversations I have had with the Count de Mercy and Mr. Morkov it is certain that the two courts wished, as these ministers certainly were ambitious, to sign our treaty. They and their sovereigns wished that their names might be read in America and there respected as our friends."[100]

It is not surprising that English diplomacy expended such effort to hinder the success of the Dana mission to St. Petersburg and to forestall the establishment of direct diplomatic relations between the two nations. As soon as the assignment of Francis Dana to St. Petersburg became known in London in the spring of 1781, British Minister of Foreign Affairs Lord Stormont hastened to inform I. M. Simolin that in England they "were completely undisturbed by this and thought it would be an insult to Her Imperial Majesty's friendly feelings for Great Britain if they were to suspect Her of the slightest desire to receive this minister at Her court."[101] Not counting only upon the "friendly feelings" of the Empress, James Harris applied direct pressure at St. Petersburg to hinder the success of the Dana mission, warning that, given the approach of war with the Turks "during the course of which she necessarily must want at least the influence, if not the assistance of Great Britain," Russia would hardly find it expedient to "adopt a measure that would alienate forever the affections of that nation."[102]

Under these circumstances Francis Dana could not count on much success for his mission to St. Petersburg, where he arrived on August 27, 1781, in the guise of a private citizen. John Quincy Adams, son of John Adams, accompanied Dana to St. Petersburg as secretary, and remained there more than a year.[103] Knowing a little French (unlike his patron), young John Quincy served as "translator" in conversations with Vérac, the French minister to St. Petersburg, and as much as possible (for he was at that time only fifteen years old) tried to make easier the unenviable position in which his superior found himself.[104]

Despite the length of his stay at St. Petersburg the cautious Dana did not distinguish himself by his activity, and for a long time undertook no official measures. It was not until February 24/March 7, 1783, after receiving news of the signing of the preliminary peace treaty, that he finally decided officially to inform the Russian government of his assignment to the post of American minister to St. Petersburg.[105] In a conversation with Dana on April 12/23, Vice-Chancellor I. A. Osterman made it clear that the Empress could not receive an American envoy before the signing of the definitive peace treaty, because this would be incompatible with the principles of neutrality and with the role she had assumed as impartial mediatrix. "As soon as this treaty is completed," Osterman revealed, Dana "could be certain there then would no longer be any difficulties in establishing these same direct relations with his superiors." Osterman referred also to the necessity of presenting a new set of credentials.[106]

The formal arguments of the Russian government were opposed decisively by Dana. The demand for a new set of credentials especially upset the American envoy. In a lengthy memorandum handed Osterman on April 27/May 8, Dana noted that the United States had been an independent and sovereign nation for seven years, and that independence did not depend on recognition by the English king.[107]

Dana's argumentation, based upon principles of popular sovereignty, could create no particular impression (unless negative) on the tsarist government. An official reply of June 3/14 confirmed that, although the Empress had received the news of the dispatch of an official representative of the United States, "with a feeling of satisfaction," she could recognize him only after the signature of the definitive peace treaty. However (and this is very important), it was pointed out in the reply that not only Dana but all of his fellow-countrymen who might come to Russia, "either on commercial or other affairs," would receive "the most favorable reception and the protection of the law of nations."[108] In effect this represented de facto recognition of American independence.

With regard to the ticklish question of the length of time which the United States had existed as an independent state from the legal point of view, the Russian government preferred to avoid consideration of "such a delicate matter." Osterman quite transparently hinted "privately" to Dana "that the less he entered into arguments and legal points the more pleasing his person would be and the sooner he would attain his desired goal in this affair."[109] Thanking Osterman for the "hopes" given him,

Dana promised to await the signature of the definitive peace treaty.[110]

By an irony of fate back in America a decision had been taken to recall Dana just when he had almost attained official recognition at St. Petersburg. On February 26, 1783, Robert Livingston had written the President of the Continental Congress that he could see no reason for Dana's remaining in Russia any longer, and thought it inadvisable to maintain a diplomatic representative at St. Petersburg even after the conclusion of the peace treaty.[111] Accordingly, on April 1, 1783, Congress adopted a resolution recalling Dana, if at the time he received said resolution he had not already entered into negotiations with the Russian government. In the case of the latter, the desire that the negotiations be completed before his return was expressed.[112]

At the time of his assignment to St. Petersburg in December 1780 Francis Dana had been empowered to sign a convention adhering to Armed Neutrality and to reach an agreement on the project for a treaty of friendship and commerce. Under the changed circumstances, with American independence to all intents and purposes secured and the preliminary peace treaty signed, there was less need to search for new allies; Congress even feared being drawn into the European political system, in particular in connection with the suggestion made by Holland that it adhere to Armed Neutrality. Dana's powers to conclude an agreement pledging the United States to Armed Neutrality were not renewed, because "the true interest of the States requires that they should be as little as possible entangled in the politics and controversies of the European nations." However, in this decision of June 12, 1783, it was noted that as a whole the liberal principles of the league of neutrals were favorable to the interests of all nations, and especially to those of the United States, and "ought, in that view, to be promoted by the latter as far as will consist with their fundamental policy."[113] Having received from Congress permission to return home, Francis Dana informed Osterman, July 28/August 8, of his intention to leave St. Petersburg. In order to avoid any "misunderstanding" concerning the cause of his unexpected departure, he thought it advisable to refer to poor health and personal affairs in a letter to Osterman of August 3/14.[114]

Francis Dana left St. Petersburg without awaiting the official recognition which was so very near at hand. (The definitive peace treaty was signed at Versailles on September 3, 1783.) But if one bears in mind the actual causes of his mission's poor results, this was not the chief cause. The success of the negotiations was hindered by the antagonism of the tsarist government, and primarily Catherine II herself, toward the revolting republicans. More than a minor role was played in this affair by the English minister with his open opposition. Dana's mission was not always aided by the "advice" of his ally, the Marquis de Vérac, who seems to have been interested primarily in restraining Dana as long as possible from any decisive measure.[115] Changes in the tsarist government were also far from propitious. After the removal in the spring of 1781 of Nikita Panin, whose favorable attitude toward American independence has been mentioned, A. A. Bezborodko exerted ever more influence on foreign policy. At the same time the attention of Russian diplomacy was directed chiefly to relations with the Turks, and in particular the annexation of Crimea. Given these conditions, it was inadvisable for the Russian government to exacerbate relations with Great Britain by an official recognition of American independence.

Finally, it seems to me that not the least role in the failure may have been played by mistakes committed by Dana himself, for he lived in St. Petersburg isolated not only from the tsarist government (which is understandable), but from Russian society as a whole, although the original instructions given him by the Continental Congress pointed out explicitly that "the great object" of his mission aside from winning Catherine's support was "to lay the foundation for a good understanding and friendly intercourse between the subjects of Her Imperial Majesty and the citizens of these United States, to the mutual advantage of both nations."[116]

Francis Dana did practically nothing to carry out this important part of his mission. This may have been his greatest mistake, or at least one that usually escapes the attention of historians. Remaining in St. Petersburg almost two years, Dana undoubtedly had opportunities to establish connections with those circles of Russian society which could to a certain degree promote the success of his mission. The brilliant example set by Benjamin Franklin in France was available, although naturally France on the eve of the Revolution was not the serfdom regime Russia was in the time of Catherine II, and there was no reason for the puritan diplomat to count upon particular success. It is quite obvious, however, that Francis Dana was no Benjamin Franklin, and it was much harder for the unknown citizen from Massachusetts to penetrate higher society in St. Petersburg than for his celebrated colleague—a renowned scientist and philosopher—the Paris salons. Dana's activity was further hindered because he knew not only no Russian, but no French—and this alone could not help telling in the most negative fashion during his stay in St. Petersburg.

In concluding any analysis of the position taken by Russian diplomacy with regard to the American war for independence, it must be noted that, although there was no formal recognition of the United States as an independent nation (after the conclusion of peace with England the American government itself expressed no interest in establishing diplomatic relations with St. Petersburg, fearing to be drawn into the European political system), one can with complete justification speak of de facto recognition of the new government. The Russian government's aforementioned reply to Dana of June 3/14, 1783, the activity of Russian diplomats abroad, and, finally, the official instructions they received somewhat later from St. Petersburg permit such a conclusion. Particularly significant is a report from I. S. Bariatinsky in the summer of 1783, relating that Franklin had made "his first visit to the whole diplomatic corps, and all the ambassadors and envoys had returned it."[117]

As noted, D. A. Golitsyn had at one point received strict orders to refrain from official recognition of John Adams as American minister to The Hague. When in June 1784 Adams informed Russian minister to The Hague S. A. Kolychev, together with the other foreign diplomats, of the recognition of American independence and the signing of the definitive peace treaty, the Russian diplomat did not avoid a return visit.[118] Finally, Catherine's government itself issued official instructions to Russian diplomats to be guided in their relations with American representatives by the generally accepted norms observed by other impartial powers, "all the more so since by the recognition of independence of the American provinces by England herself there is no longer anything to prevent dealing with them as with other republics."[119]

These are only the formal aspects. Much more important during the difficult, critical years of the struggle for freedom and independence was Russia's general position, which had positive significance for the improvement of the international situation of the rebellious colonies, for the diplomatic isolation of England, and, in the last analysis, for America's victory in its struggle against the mother country. A number of documents concerning Russia's peaceful mediation bear witness to its desire, admittedly very guardedly expressed, to persuade England to make peace with the rebels and recognize their independence. In 1780, during a difficult period of the war, Panin's mediation plan "seemed to be a way to cut the 'Gordian knot,' as Vergennes termed the problem of American independence, even if several of the colonies decided to retain their ties with Great Britain. It would be convenient for France, honorable for Great Britain, and advantageous for the Americans, who would be allowed to decide their own future."[120] There is clearly no question of "sympathy" on the part of Catherine II and her government for the rebellious colonists, but of considerations of practical politics: growing dissatisfaction with the policies of the British cabinet; the Empress' desire to play the role of arbiter in European affairs; comprehension of the inevitability of the separation of the colonies; and even Russia's stake in the creation of an independent United States, preservation of the European "balance of power," the strengthening of Russia's international prestige and influence, and so forth.

Russia's proclamation of the Declaration of Armed Neutrality in 1780 had great international significance. This declaration, directed against Great Britain, proved advantageous for all other nations, and especially for the United States. It was no accident that it was approved by the Continental Congress. Thereafter, and over a period of many decades, the defence of the right of neutral navigation became the firm basis for Russian-American rapprochement. The principles of freedom for neutral shipping, which were declared in 1780 and became one of the fundamentals of international maritime law, to a certain extent preserve their significance to this day.

II

THE ATTITUDE OF RUSSIAN SOCIETY TO THE AMERICAN REVOLUTION

The War of Independence in North America was closely watched not only by Catherine II, the tsarist government, and official diplomacy. To a far greater degree and for altogether different reasons revolutionary events in America excited progressive circles of Russian society, above all, writers and scholars representative of eighteenth-century Russian enlightenment.

Because of a number of objective reasons and favorable circumstances, the course of the American War of Independence (1775-1783) received more impartial, if not more complete, coverage in the Russian press than did the subsequent events of the French Revolution (1789-1794).[1] The facts that must be borne in mind are the strong differences in the attitude of the tsarist government toward the United States in 1775-1783 and toward the revolutionary France in 1789-1794, the special features of Russian internal development in the corresponding years, and not the least, the idiosyncratic methods of governing adopted by Catherine II herself during different periods of her reign.

In theory, the American War of Independence and the bourgeois revolution in France, phenomena of a similar nature, provoked a sharply negative reaction on the part of the ruling classes in Russia as well as in the other feudal-absolutist nations of Europe. In practice, however, the events in America infringed on the interests of England primarily; they took place far across the ocean and apparently did not present a threat to the existing system. By contrast, the stormy events in France (even disregarding the fact that they were much more radical in nature than the American Revolution) occurred not at the edge of the world, but in the center of Europe, and created in the eyes of European monarchs an immediate threat to the existing order.

30

To understand the more objective evaluation of the American Revolution in the Russian press one must consider the survival into the 1770's and 1780's of some remains of the "liberalism" of Catherine II, who with them sought to conceal the ugly form of Russian serfdom. By offering her patronage to representatives of European Enlightenment, Catherine hoped to strengthen her position within the country and, even more, to raise her prestige abroad. The Russian Empress used her correspondence with leading philosophes to disseminate information advantageous for her and to strengthen her authority in European public opinion. Although after the Pugachev uprising Catherine put an end to "legislative pranks," as she herself termed them, she did not sever her ties with the Enlightenment philosophes. Voltaire, "the sovereign of minds and fashions," corresponded regularly with the Empress until his death in 1778. Even livelier and more extensive (continuing until 1796) was Catherine's correspondence with the French critic Baron Melchior Grimm, who belonged to the circle of encyclopedists. Grimm was more than a constant correspondent; he became a confidential agent abroad whom Catherine consulted on miscellaneous questions and to whom she rendered financial support.[2]

Members of the high aristocracy were eager not to lag behind the "enlightened" Tsarina. While Catherine summoned Diderot and d'Alembert to St. Petersburg, Grigori Orlov and Konstantin Rasumovsky invited the exiled Rousseau to their estates. The Tsarina became engrossed in reading Montesquieu's *Spirit of the Laws*, while Pavel Potemkin translated Rousseau, and Princess Catherine Dashkov published excerpts from Helvétius' book, *On the Mind*, in the journal *Nevinnye uprazhneniia* (Innocent Exercises). While in Paris the Princess made the acquaintance of Benjamin Franklin, had breakfast with Abbé Raynal, and received in her home in the evening "the whole society," including Diderot.[3] One must not take the enlightened "pranks" of the Empress too seriously. Her infatuation with Western Enlightenment turned out to be superficial; where Russian matters were concerned her attitude changed abruptly. There is bitter irony in Pushkin's pointed remark in this connection: "Catherine loved the Enlightenment, but Novikov who spread the first rays of it was passed through Sheshkovsky's hands into the dungeon where he remained until her death. Radishchev was exiled to Siberia; Kniazhnin died under the birch rod, and Fonvizin, whom she feared, would not have escaped a similar fate were it not for his great fame."[4]

But the Empress' liberal "pranks" created some legal means for the dissemination of progressive literature and revolutionary ideas in Russia, and Russian progressive minds took full advantage of the opportunity. One may judge the degree of the Russian reader's familiarity with the ideas and literature of the eighteenth-century Enlightenment by the fact that approximately sixty individual works by Voltaire, mostly major, were translated during Catherine's reign; some of them went through several editions.[5]

Voltaire's popularity in Russia was incomparably greater than that of Franklin, and American influence was very small in comparison with French. Nevertheless, there are grounds to assume that Russian society (at least its educated portion) was reasonably informed about the situation in North America and the nature of the events taking place there in the seventies and eighties. A number of books in Russian (not to mention various foreign ones), a great many articles in the periodical press, and, finally, extensive and varied material which appeared regularly in the pages of *Moskovskie and Sankt-Peterburgskie vedomosti* (Moscow and St. Petersburg gazettes) were available.

The subject of America was not altogether new to the Russian reader of the last quarter of the eighteenth century. In one way or another, the theme of America, the history of its discovery and colonization, had been attracting attention for some time. Mikhail Lomonosov had touched upon various aspects of it. A poem (1759) by Aleksandr B. Sumarokov, "Ob Amerike" (About America), filled with heartfelt sympathy for the Indians, was widely known.

Kosnulis' evropeitsy sushi,
Kuda ikh naglost' privela,
Khotiat ochistit' smertnykh dushi
I porazhaiut ikh tela.[6]

The Europeans touched the land
To which insolence had led,
And sought to cleanse the souls of men
By smiting down their bodies.

Count Artemui Vorontsov became interested in the question of the origin of the first inhabitants of North America.[7] One of the earliest detailed books on North America was published in 1765.[8]

This list could go on; by the middle 1770's information had begun to accumulate in Russia, and some (although very limited) literature concerning America existed. However, it was only after the outbreak and as a result of the War of Independence that one encounters in Russian society a serious and increasing interest in America, making it possible to speak of a real awareness of American events on the part of the Russian reader. Nor was it only a matter of a significant growth in literature on the subject. Writings on American topics, formerly more or less haphazard, took on an entirely different tone, and were filled (indirectly, and at times even directly) with a new, revolutionary content. Stirring news from across the ocean aroused the interest of the Russian reader in the most varied works on America, even those which initially appeared to have no direct relation to current affairs.

The History of America by the prominent English historian William Robertson, published in England in 1777, enjoyed a considerable reputation since the late 1770's. *Akademicheskie izvestiia* (Academic News) in 1779-1780 published "A Review of the *History of America*, compiled by Mr. Robertson, historiographer to His Majesty the King of Great Britain."[9] It might be noted that the translator, Ivan Bogaevsky, expounded rather than translated the basic contents of Robertson's book, which was of special interest for the Russian reader "in the midst of Europe's attention, turned to affairs now taking place in the American Colonies separating from England, which are so firmly opposing British power."[10] Robertson's work came out in a separate edition in 1784.[11]

The first work by a Russian author devoted specifically to the new nation—the United States—appeared, significantly, in 1783, the year the War of Independence ended. This monograph by D. M. Ladygin gave the reader a general impression of the history of the colonization and the contemporary situation in the former English colonies in North America, which had proclaimed their independence.[12]

That same year American themes were especially well represented by the publisher Nikolai Novikov, who printed particular books by Jean Bernard Bossu[13] and F. B. Taube[14] in Russian translation. The very title of Taube's book called attention to the year of the declaration of American independence, 1776; it also pointed out the justice of the causes which had brought about the war. Unfortunately the author was inconsistent, and in the introduction termed "unnatural" the "strife between England and her American colonies." The text, however, contains these stirring words: "Freedom, that most noble natural right of thinking creatures. She populated these great lands [the English colonies in America] and made them powerful, rich and brave."[15]

The Russian reader's familiarity with books about America was not limited to translations. Many of the best foreign books about America failed to appear in the Russian language at that time because of censorship. But the educated circles of Russian society were well aware of their contents, ordered them from abroad, and read them in the original. A characteristic example is the celebrated work of the Abbé Raynal, *Histoire philosophique et politique des établissements et du commerce des Européens dans les deux Indes,* [16] which was reprinted several times in the seventies, and was enlarged in 1780 by chapters dealing with the American Revolution. The great variety of the subjects touched upon in the book, its political topicality, criticism of the feudal-absolutist system, and unmasking of the colonial policies of the European monarchies, combined with the author's brilliant literary style, insured Raynal's *Histoire des deux Indes* a place among the most popular works of the European Enlightenment. In this multivolume work the reader discovered along with propaganda for the American Revolution a merciless unmasking of the serfdom system in Russia. And, although Raynal might have erred in certain details, his passionate criticism of political and civil slavery rang out as a bold call for overthrow of the old order by force. [17]

It is therefore not surprising that the progressive public in Russia and the tsarist government reacted to Raynal's book in completely different ways. Catherine II received the chapters on the American Revolution in manuscript form in the summer of 1780, and noted in a letter to her regular correspondent Baron Melchior Grimm that "the American charter was full of declarations of little wisdom and much misplaced impudence," and that "I have less time than ever for almost useless reading." [18] Evidently she nonetheless found time to read Raynal, for in a letter of April 1/12, 1782, Catherine II again mentioned "the ineffectual outpourings of the Abbé Raynal against us" and several days later added with obvious irritation in her native tongue that the Abbé Raynal "quackt und lügt" (quacks and lies). [19]

The Russian public, however, appraised the Abbé Raynal's work entirely differently. In the opinion of that prominent literary figure, editor of *Akademicheskie Izvestiia* (Academic News), P. I. Bogdanovich, "nowhere is it possible to draw such unbiased and such well-founded information concerning these subjects as in the excellent *Philosophical and Political History of the Colonies and the Trade of Europeans in the Two Indies*, translated into Russian by Iv. Parf. Khmelnitsky." He expressed confidence that the book "without doubt will shortly be published." [20] It proved impossible to publish a translation of Raynal's book "shortly," for understandable reasons, and a number of attempts to bring about the publication of Raynal's book in Russian in the eighteenth century also miscarried. [21]

Although it was possible to forbid the publication of the translation of

Raynal's book, and even confiscate and burn copies that had already appeared, as was done in France in 1781 by the government of Louis XVI, it was impossible to stop the progress of revolutionary ideas. To some extent news of the prohibition of Raynal's book increased interest in it and made it all the more popular; and the punitive measures by the French authorities proved ineffective. "Almost no one was led to destroy this prohibited book, and the author was given the means to go to England," reported the *Sankt-Peterburgskie vedomosti* (St. Petersburg Gazette) in the summer of 1781.[22] The French text of Raynal's work (sometimes in several editions) was represented in all the major book collections in Moscow and St. Petersburg, and could be obtained on the open market. Thus, for instance, there was an advertisement in *Moskovskie vedomosti* (Moscow Gazette) November 13/24, 1781, that in St. Petersburg orders were being taken for "the work of the renowned Abbé Raynal . . . at the merchants Kurtener Reinber and Company."[23]

At approximately the same time an even more interesting advertisement concerned an opportunity to subscribe to a collection of American legal acts: "It is written from Philadelphia, July 28, that, at the request of the American Congress, a collection of the various acts of this congress relating to the new government of the thirteen United American provinces was recently published in that city; and namely: (1) the constitutions of the various independent states in America; (2) declarations of independence of the states mentioned; (3) the Articles of Confederation among these states; (4) treaties concluded between H. M. the King of France and the United American States. This collection consists of 226 pages, in octavo, and those desiring to do so may subscribe to it from Holland."[24]

Opportunities for the Russian reader to familiarize himself with the best foreign publications increased in these years. The number of book stores rose sharply: in 1768 there was only one in St. Petersburg; twenty-nine more opened in the next thirty years. By the end of the eighteenth century there were twenty bookstores in Moscow, and seventeen in the provinces.[25]

Although books played a large role in forming the Russian reader's idea concerning America and events occurring there, they were not the only, and not even the major, source of information. Much more important were the extensive materials published in the Russian periodical press of the time, journals to some extent, but especially newspapers (*Moskovskie and Sankt-Petersburgskie vedomosti*). These provided the reader's main source of information about events in America, and in them are found the most important materials on the progress of America's revolutionary war of independence.

Current information on the most important events in America, of primary interest to the reader of the times, quite naturally found its way into books belatedly.[26] In this respect the periodical press enjoyed greater opportunities. American subject matter attracted the attention of the most varied journals: *Sobranie novostei* (Collection of News), a journal with close relations to academic circles, published by I. F. Bogdanovich in 1775-76; the moderately liberal *Sankt-Peterburgskii vestnik* (St. Petersburg Herald) of G. L. Braiko, which came out from 1778 to 1781; *Akademicheskie izvestiia* (Academic News), edited by P. I. Bogdanovich; and, most important, Novikov's *Pribavlenie k "Moskovskim vedomostiam"* (Supplement to Moscow Gazette), 1783-84.[27] In the last decade of the eighteenth century, much material on the United States could be found in *Politicheskii Zhurnal* (Political Journal), published at Moscow University by P. A. Sokhatsky.

Bogdanovich's *Sobranie novostei* regularly contained surveys of foreign information, with a prominent place devoted to news of the rebellion then beginning in England's North American colonies. Although English reports predominated in the journal, occasional articles were based on materials from French, and even American, sources.[28]

In 1781 *Akademicheskie izvestiia* carried "Opisanie stran, voinoiu obiatykh" (A description of the nations engulfed in war), in which principal attention was devoted to the American war with England, and Catherine II and her system of Armed Neutrality were extolled in every possible way.[29] In the same year P. I. Bogdanovich, the editor of the journal, published over a period of six issues an extensive article "O Amerike" (About America),[30] evidently based on a number of French works, in particular, that of Raynal.

Although reports of the American War of Independence in the journals were incidental and appeared irregularly (actually the period of publication for most of the journals was limited to a few years, and in certain cases even a few months), from 1775 on the newspapers of the two capitals—*Sankt-Peterburgskie* and *Moskovskie vedomosti*—regularly carried a vast amount of material offering a systematic view of the progress of military affairs, the general international situation, and the internal condition of the rebels.

Soviet investigators, starting with A. I. Startsev and, more recently, M. N. Shprygova,[31] have already studied the rich materials in the Russian periodical press dealing with the American Revolution, a fact which substantially eases my task. Their valuable investigations, however, are not without some shortcomings and omissions. For instance, while Startsev—mistakenly, in my opinion— denies the existence of essential differences in the positions of the Moscow and St. Petersburg Gazettes and fails to single out the Novikov decade (1779-1789), Shprygova commences her investigation in 1779, excluding from her field of attention the preceding years. Utilization of materials for the years 1775-1779 would permit a more vivid delineation and analysis of the new element brought by Nikolai Novikov when he became editor of *Moskovskie vedomosti*, in 1779, without minimizing the significance of the preceding period.

In any evaluation of the contents of the two newspapers (and *Sankt-Peterburgskie* and *Moskovskie vedomosti* were Russia's only two newspapers at the time) it must be understood that, although one was published by the Academy of Sciences and the other by Moscow University, they were official government organs and not private publications, as was the case with many foreign newspapers—a fact that unavoidably left a distinct governmental imprint both on their contents and their make-up. In this respect the publishers of the St. Petersburg newspaper naturally had a particularly hard time. (In the years 1776-1782 it was edited by Ippolit Fedorovich Bogdanovich, the well-known literary figure already mentioned.)[32]

Another peculiarity of Russian newspapers and journals of the eighteenth and early nineteenth century was the predominance of translated material. It is difficult for today's researcher to ascertain when he is dealing with an original text and when with a translation, how to distinguish author from translator, and what is original from what is borrowed. The predominance of translations was of course not accidental: that which could not be written in one's name then in Russia could be expressed in veiled form under the name of a foreign author. The very choice of subject matter, and especially the selection of material for translation, permits in a number of cases a judgment concerning the general orientation of the given publication, and the views of the publisher or translator.

Each of the Russian newspapers devoted a great deal of attention to events in America even before the outbreak of the military struggle. This gave the reader an idea of the seriousness of the conflict between England and her American colonies and the inevitability of armed conflict. After having mentioned the irreconcilable position of Lord North's government in a dispatch from London of January 20, 1775, it was pointed out: "From the following one may easily conclude that one must almost inevitably await internecine struggle. Troops, numbering 3,000 men, in Ireland, have been ordered to prepare for shipboarding and conveyance to America; moreover another regiment of light dragoons received a similar command." And further: "All recommendations, all decisions and all instructions are directed toward subduing the Americans."[33]

As the conflict grew more exacerbated, and especially after the commencement of open military conflict on the part of England's colonies, information concerning events in America became more and more regular and more plentiful. Basic information, it is true, continued to stem from British sources. (Dispatches from London at this time, as a rule devoted to a large extent, and often entirely, to events in America, were printed in almost every issue.) And in a number of cases the reader found materials concerning events in America in dispatches from Paris, and also from American sources (already in 1775 there were dispatches from Boston, Philadelphia, and other cities). As a rule, material in Moscow and St. Petersburg newspapers concurred (right up to the end of the 1770's), although in Moscow the same dispatches were published somewhat later, and at times in abridged form.

Both newspapers devoted much attention to news of the beginning of military activities. Starting in June 1775 formerly unknown place names appeared—Lexington and Concord, where the shots rang out heralding the outbreak of the war of the English colonies in North America for independence. A dispatch from London of May 29, 1775, published in both St. Petersburg and Moscow gazettes, noted: "With the arrival here yesterday from America of a special messenger from General Gage,[34] it was learned that the emnity between royal troops and the inhabitants of Boston finally actually extended to hostile engagements."[35] A short description of a battle "not far from the village of Concord" followed. Several days later both newspapers mentioned a battle at Lexington on April 19.[36] Finally, a detailed description of the battles of Lexington and Concord, based on official English sources, was carried in *Sankt-Peterburgskie vedomosti* June 30/July 11, 1775. This was a dispatch "from Vitegal" (that is, Whitehall) of July 10, 1775, in which the Americans were termed "rebels," and their "inhumanity and barbarity" were extravagantly portrayed. The dispatch also noted that the London court "intended to hire ten thousand German troops and send [them] to Boston."[37]

The predominance of dispatches from the English sources naturally created a bias against the rebellious colonists in the general flow of the information concerning events in North America. Another unavoidable effect was caused by the class sympathies of Russian ruling circles, which viewed the rebellious colonists as "insurgents" against their legitimate monarch. The steps the patriots were forced to undertake against the internal enemies of American independence—open partisans of the English king, termed Tories or Loyalists—caused particular discontent. In the autumn of 1776 a Saint Petersburg Gazette dispatch on this question pointed out: "The provincial or local rabble . . . is pillaging and plundering everything, and many noble families have now been led to extreme ruin as a result."[38] However, even from these words filled with cruel class hatred for the rebels, the imaginative reader could draw his own conclusions about the nature of the events taking place in America, where war was waged not only for independence, not only against the external enemy—England—but against partisans of the old colonial regime within the country, against the "noble families," against Loyalists with ties to the British crown.

Reports of events in America gave the Russian reader food for thought. Despite the falseness of official English descriptions of military activities, the general impression was often far from favorable to the British. One could read that "all America has taken up arms," and "royal forces evidently have been reduced to extremity."[39] The reader learned of the people's dissatisfaction with the policies of North's Tory cabinet, the protests of British merchants about the war in America, the disagreements within the government itself, and so forth. A London dispatch of June 20, 1775, stated:

> Because of the very critical circumstances in which England finds herself, secret conferences are now taking place continually at court; and the court sees more clearly every day that a large portion of the people is extremely dissatisfied with the actions of the ministry in its reasoning on America. The Dublin petty bourgeoisie is again talking about sending deputies to the King with a resolution dealing with American affairs, . . . for it is being ruined by the cessation of trade with America. With a similar view in mind the London townsmen [meshchanstvo] will have a meeting on the 24th of this month in the city hall; and the merchants who trade with America will also soon do the same.[40]

As though summarizing the diverse material concerning events in America, both newspapers carried the following dispatch: "Much information has come from America, but it is all of the same nature. It announces the unanimity of all the settlements, the resolution of American strength against royal forces, General Gage's complaints that the whole country has taken up arms against him, and that he and the royal forces are being incapacitated and are denied provisions, although the whole country abounds in them."[41]

The English government and the conservative press strove insistently to represent the rebellious colonists in the darkest possible colors as "insurgents," "mutineers," and "bandits." The Russian reader, however, learned that the respresentative of these "insurgents" in France was the "celebrated Doctor Franklin," a name which had been well-known to the whole world since the middle of the eighteenth century. Although they formerly knew of him primarily as an outstanding scientist—the inventor of the lightning rod—in progressive public opinion he now embodied the new state stirring to battle against England for its independence. From late 1776 and early 1777 the name of the "celebrated doctor" was constantly on the pages of both Russian newspapers. The reader discovered interesting details about his arrival first in Nantes and then in Paris, about his friendship with leading French figures of the Enlightenment and his visit with the aged Voltaire, about his secret negotiations with the French government, and, finally, about the conclusion of the Franco-American alliance of 1778, the recognition of Franklin as official representative of "the American United Settlements," and his ceremonial reception at Versailles.[42]

Having been so informed, the perspicacious contemporary could naturally come to his own conclusions concerning the American "insurgents," whose representative in Europe was a world-renowned scientist, friend of Voltaire, Diderot, and other leading figures of the Enlightenment. Despite the falseness of the official English bulletins, in the long run the truth about the progress of the war in America became known to the Russian public in one way or another, and reports of greater defeats of the royal forces acquired an especially sensational character. This was true, for instance, when on December 29, 1777/January 9, 1778, *Sankt-Peterburgskie vedomosti* published news of General Burgoyne's surrender at Saratoga in the autumn of 1777. This report contained not only a detailed description of the military operations which concluded with Burgoyne's ignominious surrender, but noted that "the consternation of the English Parliament upon receiving this news equaled that of the Roman senators upon receiving the news of the defeat suffered at Cannae."[43] The mention of Cannae gave the reader a clear enough notion of the extent of the catastrophe experienced by the British, and of the strength and skill of the American forces.

Russian press coverage of the concluding stage of the War of Independence is bound up with the activities of the leading eighteenth-century Russian Enlightenment figure, Nikolai Ivanovich Novikov.[44] In the spring of 1779 Novikov signed a contract for the lease of the university press for a period of ten years (from May 1/12, 1779 to May 1/12, 1789). Along with the press the publication of *Moskovskie vedomosti* fell under his jurisdiction. This opened a brilliant new period, the true flowering of the newspaper and of the Moscow press generally. Himself a product of the "middle class," Novikov did much to destroy the exclusive and rigid class nature of Russian culture. At the time there had only begun to form in Russia "a class of middle people . . . between the *barin* and the *muzhik* . . . who everywhere comprise the true firm foundation of the state. This was the milieu that produced Novikov. . . . He was the first to establish a circle of educated young people of middle rather than high society."[45]

The talented and energetic man fundamentally reorganized the Moscow newspaper; attracted new contributors to the publication, primarily from among the alumni of the university (Likhonin, Rykachev, Popov, Stepanov, Davydovsky, Petrov, and Malinovsky);[46] and substantially increased the publication of international news. He added a series of supplements: *Ekonomicheskii magazin* (Economic Magazine), under the editorship of A. T. Bolotov; *Moskovskoe izdanie* (Moscow Edition) in 1781; and, in 1783-84, the celebrated *Pribavlenie k "Moskovskim vedomostiam,"* which carried articles of political importance.

As a result of the changes introduced by Novikov, the newspaper's popularity sharply increased, there was a notable increase in numbers of readers and subscribers, and toward the end of 1781 the publisher himself noted with satisfaction the favorable reception "by the esteemed public of *Moskovskie vedomosti*, which was presented in a completely new form."[47] Indicative in this regard is the testimony of N. M. Karamzin, who noted that, prior to Novikov, "Moscow newspapers were distributed in no more than 600 copies,"[48] but with his arrival the newspaper became "much richer in content. . . . The number of subscribers increased every year, and in about ten years climbed to 4,000." Of special interest is Karamzin's observation that "many nobles, even when well off, still do not take newspapers; however the merchants and townsmen love to read them. The poorest people subscribe, and the least literate want to know what is being written from other lands."[49] It is hard to suspect Karamzin of antipathy for the nobility, therefore his testimony about the social composition of the readers of *Moskovskie vedomosti* takes on additional value. Novikov's newspaper was read not only and not so much by the "enlightened nobility" as by the people, the merchants, townsmen, representatives of different estates, people of various substance and diverse cultural levels.

Amidst the extensive and diverse international news in *Moskovskie vedomosti*, a prominent place was occupied by dispatches connected with the war the English were waging against their former colonies in America, and lately also against France and Spain. From early 1781 it was full of news about England's increasing difficulties, and open dissatisfaction in the country with the policies of North's conservative cabinet, which stubbornly insisted upon a continuation of the American war. In particular, the newspaper cited the critical speeches of representatives of the Whig opposition in Parliament and often mentioned the names of the brilliant Whig orators, especially Fox. On January 8/19, 1780, informing its readers in detail about the speeches of the opposition leaders, *Moskovskie vedomosti* cited Fox's declaration that in the annals of English history "it was impossible to find a war more ill-fated and shameful for England than the present."[50] On the whole, in the years 1780-1782, *Moskovskie vedomosti,* unlike *Sankt-Peterburgskie vedomosti,* gave much space to the subject of the strengthening of the opposition in Parliament, the grave internal situation, the increase in the national debt, loans, and taxes, and the presentation by various groups of petitions demanding an end to the war in America and the conclusion of peace.[51] A prominent place was also devoted to the situation in Ireland, where the inhabitants were "exasperated," and where "respect for the English Parliament" was steadily declining.[52]

Although reports unfavorable to the rebels were still being published in St. Petersburg at the beginning of the 1780's, those in the Moscow newspaper usually led readers to think of an unavoidable and imminent English defeat. Thus, for instance, *Sankt-Peterburgskie vedomosti* devoted considerable attention to news of military failures by the American troops, the difficult domestic situation in the rebellious colonies, and the discontent of the soldiers in Washington's army, who claimed supposedly that "one may better obtain bread under one king than under numerous rulers."[53] The newspaper wrote of speeches made by Philadelphia inhabitants against Congress' authority and of the total anarchy ruling in the cities—the lamentable result of "insurgency and disorder."[54] On the other hand, with the arrival of Novikov the tone of *Moskovskie vedomosti* became more and more objective, and even favorable to America. Many dispatches gave the reader the impression that total victory for the rebels was near. On March 25/April 5, 1780, in a dispatch from Pennsylvania, *Moskovskie vedomosti* noted that "the refuge in America, proves their weakness and foretells a total freeing of America from the English."[55] A little later the newspaper reported that the American people "were never so unanimous as at present," that the army was in good condition and its "number reaches 35 thousand."[56] In the autumn of 1781 one could read on the pages of *Moskovskie vedomosti* a rousing speech by one of the supporters of American independence, summoning the Dutch stadtholder to declare against Great Britain: "All of Europe's striving," the author of the speech noted, "is turned to America. Let political figures learn from this great change and assure themselves that the independence of the Americans is the stumbling block by which all Great Britain's power will fall to the ground."[57]

In late 1782 and early 1783 *Moskovskie vedomosti* carried extensive news about the virtual conclusion to the war in America, the signing of the preliminary peace treaty, and recognition by the English King of the new government's independence.[58]

The newspaper reflected the apparent pro-American sympathies of its editor. In a September 1782 issue a fable entitled "The Bluebird in the Field," taken from the French journal *Courier de l'Europe*, dealt with "England and her former colonies." The moral was that, once having escaped to freedom, the bluebird would no longer return to its mistress, although the latter promised to set it free. To the servants whom its mistress had sent to it, the bird declared: "It is your fate to suffer under her power, but I enjoy my independence." In commenting on the fable the newspaper noted that its contents "have the ring of truth."[59] This was a way of saluting the idea of legitimacy of the right to liberty and independence, expressed by the fable.[60]

Of special interest is the publication of a series of short biographies of "famous people of the present century." Together with leading French Enlightenment figures (such as Montesquieu, Voltaire, and Diderot), *Moskovskie vedomosti* published "commentaries" on Washington, Adams, Franklin, Raynal, and Lafayette. One read that Raynal "taught people to think of their most important interests." Of Lafayette it was stated: "This young hero has one of those great minds that open up new paths for themselves. Overcoming all barriers, he was the first to enter the vast field where fame invited courage." Adams was characterized as the first "instigator" of American freedom, a decisive advocate of the republic. "The simplicity of his exterior appearance is combined with the keenness of his ideas which, directed solely toward the republic, have in no way lost their ardor in being expressed with pleasantness and accuracy, just as an army attacking the enemy nonetheless observes the law of tactics."

Most important were the vivid character sketches of Franklin and Washington. It was pointed out that Benjamin Franklin "will be revered as a god in several centuries. Electricity is transforming all physics, the English settlements are transforming all politics. Franklin was the leader in both these important changes and thus earned himself two of the best niches with posterity." A detailed characterization of George Washington (or "Vasginton," as he was then called in the Russian press) gave an occasion for outlining a harmonious conception of revolution, a necessary precondition for which was the unity of the people and their leaders.

General Washington, "was very much needed for the changes taking place in America." Revolution cannot be successful "when the people rebel," but its leaders "do not sympathize with that spirit of freedom with which they are animated"; and, when "the leaders arouse the people to insurgency," but "do not foresee from that the same benefits for themselves that the leaders expect. . . . But when the people and their leaders are driven in essence by the same spirit and inflamed by the same passions, then the first disturbance accomplishes a complete change; in such a case, the whole nation becomes one monolyth which crushes all with its weight and size, and against which nothing can stand in opposition."[61] The conclusion to be drawn from this "Commentary" was that the guarantee of the success of revolution lies in the unity of the people and their leaders, which no barriers can withstand.

The publication of such materials on the pages of *Moskovskie vedomosti* was a very daring act on the part of Nikolai Novikov: in Russia at that time it was no simple thing to write about revolution (even if taking place somewhere far across the ocean) and its leaders. And one may only admire the skill with which Novikov made use of the legal avenues open to him. An intelligent and cautious publisher, he avoided using his own name in any open approbation of the revolution, but the very choice of subject, the selection of the information published, and occasionally the nature of editorial comments bear witness to pro-American sympathies. Novikov forces the reader to think, to compare his reading about international events with Russian reality, and to draw his own conclusions. Although he seldom commented personally, the material he published spoke clearly and convincingly. In some instances the commentaries were made secondhand, that is, in an indirect manner. For example, an article entitled "A Discourse on War," from *Moskovskoe izdanie* (Moscow Edition) of 1781, which developed on a theoretical level the idea of just and unjust wars, might serve as such a peculiar "indirect" commentary on events in America. With all the "ill-fated actions produced by war, the author of the article considered it legitimate "to resort to arms when necessity demands it," when war is a "justified defense of the oppressed against the unjust oppressor." He noted that "the good resulting from a just war based on truth covers the evil resulting from it."[62] In analyzing contemporary events of the American war of independence, the objective reader could not help but arrive at an idea that this war was legitimate and just—and the abundant material published in Novikov's editions helped to strengthen this opinion.

Throughout 1783 both Russian newspapers carried detailed dispatches dealing with the conclusion of the American Revolution and the signing of the peace treaties. "Preliminary peace resolutions" between Great Britain and America, containing the signatures of "R. Oswald, I. Adams, E. Franklin, I. Jay, and H. Laurens" (sic), were made public in February 1783. In the history-making first article of the preliminary agreement Great Britain recognized "the American provinces as free, self-governing, and independent."[63] A report of September 23/October 3, 1783, concerned the signing on September 3 in Paris of the definitive peace treaty between England and "The United American States."[64]

Reports of the victorious conclusion of the war of independence, received sympathetically by Russian readers, aroused in them a great interest in international politics, and especially in American matters. Novikov's constant concern to increase the channels of information on international events led him in 1783 to undertake the publication of a political journal, *Pribavlenie k "Moskovskim vedomostiam,"* that gained immediate popularity among the broadest strata of the Russian public. Nikolai Novikov himself, in informing his readers of the new publication, stressed its special significance for the Russian merchant estate. "Russian merchants," he wrote, "may receive excellent benefits from these 'Supplements': for they will obtain information from this reading about all produce and goods, in what places one may obtain them in larger quantity and with greater profits ahead of other cities."[65] With the very first issue of the "Supplement" Novikov began to publish an extensive tract "On trade in general."[66] The interest in trade manifested by the leading figure of the eighteenth-century Russian Enlightenment was hardly accidental. The rapid growth in trade at that time was one of the most important indications of the establishment of new capitalist relationships ripening in the midst of the old feudal structure.

It is significant that the author of the tract devoted great attention to Holland and the republican form of government in general. "The freedom obtained by Holland in war against its oppressor Philip, the Spanish King, was the chief reason for its rapid rise."[67] "This republic," stressed the tract's author in another place, "contained within itself the very source of its wealth; it found credit among its own citizens, because commerce continually kept its forces in balance."[68] Characteristically, Novikov's sympathies in England's war against her colonies in North America from the very beginning of the conflict was clearly on the side of the rebels. "North America revolted: its taxes were too burdensome and unjust."[69]

The victorious conclusion of the American war brought forth the extensive publication of interesting and varied material by the new journal. In particular, a biography of George Washington contained enthusiastic praise of the leader of the rebellious colonists. According to the author of the article, the outstanding heroes of the past could not compare with Washington, because "he founded a republic which probably will become a refuge for freedom, which has been exiled from Europe by luxury and depravity."[70]

Because of the nature of its material the Supplement to *Moskovskie vedomosti* inevitably aroused the displeasure of the tsarist authorities. When Catherine found out that Novikov was publishing "an abusive history of the Jesuit order" in his Supplement she, pointing to her protection of the order, forbade "such writings."[71] Novikov issued the Supplement only two years, 1783 and 1784, but in this short period it carried a whole series of articles specially devoted to America.[72]

In his detailed elucidation of the War of Independence and its results Novikov did not neglect several negative features of American life. The 1784 Supplement contained an article entitled "The Concept of Trade in Slaves," written by an open defender of American slavery.[73] Praising the infamous institution, the article's author declared that, as a result of the "trade in slaves," the Negroes "are extracted from their ignorance and transformed into better people," and exposed to "the best of religions." While publishing this article Novikov simultaneously carried a special commentary which condemned slavery in a decisive manner and repudiated the pharisaical arguments of its defender. "We have communicated this letter," Novikov wrote, "primarily because it is written by a well-intentioned witness. Although we have published the previous defense of trade in slaves, we nevertheless do not agree with it, because it is based on many false conclusions. . . . The excuse that we in Europe commit similar injustices, that by means of trade in slaves much good is brought about that without it would have to be abandoned—all these excuses do not stand up before the court of reason and humanity, and still do not prove the justice of the right assumed by white men over their black brothers."[74]

With this comment Novikov juxtaposed the views of the American slave trader to his own opinion, that of the leading Russian intellectual of the time. His implacable position with regard to American slavery is fully understandable: the yoke of serfdom in Russia was already too heavy, and the Russian people had suffered too much from it, to view indifferently the spread of slavery anywhere, including even in America. In repudiating American slavery Novikov protested obliquely but unequivocally against

Russian serfdom which could not be justified before "the court of reason and humanity."

Before concluding my analysis of the attitude of the Russian press toward the events of the American Revolution I must comment on the treatment of Shays's Rebellion (September 1786-February 1787). Both *Moskovskie* and *Sankt-Peterburgskie vedomosti* gave generally hostile reports of it. The newspapers wrote of the "anarchy and confusion" in America and of the dispatch of government forces against the "rebels." On April 24/May 5, 1787, *Moskovskie vedomosti* reported, not without a certain satisfaction, that "the insurrection in Massachusetts province has been safely suppressed, and they are now trying only to catch its chief instigator: Shair."[75]

To write objectively of a poor people's rebellion in a nation which had undergone Pugachev's peasant war was of course impossible. Herein lay the prime reason for the unanimity of *Moskovskie* and *Sankt-Peterburgskie vedomosti* in their treatment of Shays's Rebellion. Novikov himself might not have been inclined to deviate from the official point of view, for the Russian philosopher was not an advocate of the revolutionary overthrow of the existing system or of peasant warfare. He sympathized with the American War of Independence, but this in no way signified that he would have sympathized with a rebellion directed against the established bourgeois power in America. The views of the great Russian revolutionary of the eighteenth century, Aleksandr Radishchev, were incomparably more radical.[76] More profoundly than anyone else in Russia, Radishchev comprehended the meaning of the American Revolution and, on the basis of his analysis, made profound theoretical generalizations. His remarkable ode "Liberty" is one of the most outstanding works of European literature of the time dealing with the subject of the American Revolution.

> My soul yearns for thee,
> For thee, O glorious land,
> Where once freedom lay trampled,
> Bent under the yoke.
> Thou rejoiceth now, while we still suffer!
> We all thirst for the same things,
> Thy example has revealed the goal,
> I have not partaken of thy glory
> But, since my spirit is not enslaved,
> Let my ashes rest on your shores.[77]

In these moving lines Radishchev expressed his admiration for the War of Independence and made revolutionary deductions for Russia.

Today, after a number of interesting and thorough investigations by our literary specialists, [78] it is quite simple to write of this; we take the allusions for granted. But there was a time when the very thought of a connection between the ode "Liberty" and the American Revolution seemed almost a fantasy; Radishchev's salute to the "glorious" country was thought by readers and historians of literature to be addressed to revolutionary France. [79] But, on the basis of a thorough analysis of the text of the ode, its juxtaposition with the progress of historical events and with the literature of the period, V. Semennikov established the direct connection between these lines and the War of Independence and traced the influence on Radishchev of Raynal's work on the American Revolution. [80]

Some pedant unimaginatively analyzing the text might point to some "borrowing" by Radishchev from Raynal or another Western author. There is nothing more absurd and dangerous than such a simplistic point of view. Analysis of Radishchev's work—for that matter, the work of any Russian or foreign author—can always unearth some degree of "Western" or, as the case may be, "Eastern" influence. [81] Radishchev himself repeatedly referred to and cited American legislative acts. A new generation of Russian revolutionaries, the Decembrists—Radishchev's descendants— also made use of the experience of the American Revolution. In Nikita Murav'ev's constitution project, for example, it is possible to discern a certain resemblance to the constitutional acts of the United States of America. The specific nature of my work causes me to pay attention precisely to this side of the question, but it does not provide a basis for asserting Radishchev's or Murav'ev's lack of originality, or their "borrowing" from Western sources.

Granted, Radishchev and later the Decembrists and other Russian revolutionaries were acquainted with the ideas, events, and basic documents of the American—and to an even greater extent, the French—revolution. But this is their merit and not a shortcoming. They were all highly cultivated and educated people, who were in step with the times and kept up with contemporary progressive literature. Thus, in defending his position on the need for civil liberties and, especially, freedom of the press, Radishchev displays a knowledge of the history of the question, witnessed, for instance, by the section on the "origin of the censorship." To support his point of view he cites the experience and documentation of all sorts of epochs and nations; beginning with the most distant antiquity, he analyzes the history of ancient Greece and Rome, and utilizes historical materials of the German states, England, France, Austria, Denmark, Spain, and, finally, the United States of America.

Since Radishchev gave his exposition of the problem on a high, modern level there was no need for him to disclose already long-established truths. In publishing their works and projects, and basing themselves primarily on the Russian experience, on Russian reality, our revolutionaries at the same time made use of all the best that had been accomplished in the West. Russian society and the revolutionary movement did not develop along their own specific, exclusive path apart from the mainstream of world progress. Russian revolutionaries valued and studied the experiences of other peoples. They had avant-garde views, and their works took into account the best that had been accomplished by the world revolutionary movement before their time.

In order to settle the question once and for all, let us return to the lines just quoted. Granted, Radishchev praises and admires the American Revolution. What else could one expect from the great Russian revolutionary? "Thou [America] rejoiceth . . . while we still suffer!" exclaimed Radishchev, joining in but one phrase the Russian and American experience. "Thy example hath revealed our goal": here is a model of true internationalism, and at the same time patriotism. What sort of patriotism? the skeptical pedant might ask, for in the conclusion of the forty-sixth stanza Radishchev dreams that his "ashes" might rest on the "shores" of America. It is probably impossible to reply to this any better than Radishchev himself did in these lines: "But no! Let the place where it was my fate to be born/Be the one where my days will end." The poet proudly sees the continuity between his first "prophecy" of freedom and the future generation of Russian revolutionaries.

> And a youth, hungering for glory,
> Thou shall come to my deserted grave
> To declare with emotion:
> Born under the yoke of tyranny,
> Enchained in gilded shackles,
> He was the first to prophesy liberty to us. [82]

When it comes to Raynal, Radishchev was of course familiar with his "Histoire des deux Indes" (as well as with many of the best works of the leaders of his day), and he himself testified at his trial: "I may consider this book the beginning of my disastrous situation." One must not, however, take this remark literally. Radishchev disclosed this at his trial, when it was in his best interest as a means of self-defense to bring forward the widely known work of the Western revolutionary man of the Enlightenment, and also to lead the investigation on a tangent, if not on a false trail (that would have been senseless), then at least on a secondary one.

In reading "Liberty," one must truly admire its unique contents, as a whole and in detail. Radishchev not only understood many of the most characteristic special features of the American Revolution, he succeeded in portraying them graphically, briefly, and expressively. With exceptional penetration he recognized the just nature of the American War of Independence and saw the advantages of the new, people's army over the old "conscript" forces of the feudal states. The famous thirty-fourth stanza of the ode illustrates this.

> Gaze on the boundless field,
> Where the host of brutality stands effaced:
> They are not cattle driven there against their will.
> It is not a chance that brings courage,
> Nor the crowd—
> Each soldier feels himself a leader.
> He seeks a glorious end.
> O steadfast soldier,
> Thou art and were unconquerable,
> Your leader Washington, is liberty.

Let us turn to two lines. First, "They are not cattle driven there against their will." How great a contempt for the old army, its conscript organization, and its militarism these few stark words convey! And further, "Each soldier feels himself a leader." This single phrase reveals how clearly and accurately Radishchev understood the chief feature of the American army, founded upon completely different, and progressive, principles of organization. In analyzing this stanza V. Semennikov concluded that the ode was composed during the period 1781-1783, inasmuch as the War of Independence is referred to as an event in progress, or at least contemporary, and Washington is still leader of the army.[83]

However, Semennikov did not pay sufficient attention to the following thirty-fifth strophe depicting the triumph of the republic which has just acquired freedom: "The temple of the two-faced god has been closed;/violence is discarded;/the god of triumph appeared amid us/and blew the horn of festivities."

We must remember that, according to established custom, the temple of the two-faced god Janus was open during war and closed once peace had been restored. In this instance, "the temple of the two-faced god has been closed" means that the war is over; "violence is discarded"; the time of triumph has come: "the god of triumph appeared amid us." Finally, in the address to the "glorious land" (forty-sixth strophe) quoted before Radishchev exclaims: "Thou rejoiceth now," that is, the United States are rejoicing. Hence the deduction: the ode "Liberty" was written not during, but soon after the end of the War of Independence, most likely immediately after news of the termination of hostilities. The unusual freshness of the impressions of the events described, which are not as yet obscured by anything, is another argument in favor of this deduction.

We shall also allow ourselves to note that Radishchev in his ode already had discerned the characteristic features of the new agrarian society in America, to some extent was able to delineate that which today we term the American, or farmer's, path to the development of agriculture. If the term sounds contemporary, the essence remains the same. Radishchev brilliantly disclosed the advantages of the farmer's free labor over the serf's slave labor.

> The spirit of freedom warms the cornfield,
> The field presently grows fertile without tears;
> Everyone sows for himself, reaps for himself.

How happy the life of the free cultivator seemed in comparison with the sad fate of the Russian bonded peasant (see strophes thirty-one, thirty-two, and thirty-three). For the free, "work is joy, sweat is dew," Radishchev wrote, and he believed that the time would come when the Russian peasant would find happiness in free work, on free land, and in a free country. The poet's faith in Russia's future and in the Russian people remained steadfast. While Raynal viewed the disintegration of the Russian Empire as a stroke of "fortune," Radishchev saw in it only the first stage of the revolution, which would be crowned by the formation of a republic constructed on federalist principles.

> From the depths of the huge ruins . . .
> New luminaries will arise,
> Their firm helms,
> Adorned with the wreath of friendship,
> Will guide the ship to benefit all.[84]

"Oh most chosen of days!" exclaimed Radishchev in conclusion, greeting the approach of revolution.

Radishchev constantly returned to the theme of America in the text of his *Puteshestvie iz Peterburga v Moskvu* (A Journey from St. Petersburg to Moscow),[85] revealing knowledge and understanding of his subject. He expounded on the freedom of the press in detail. "The American governments adopted freedom of the press among the very first statutes confirming civic freedom," he wrote, citing characteristic excerpts from constitutional acts of the states of Pennsylvania, Delaware, Maryland, and Virginia: "That people have a right to freedom of speech, and of writing and publishing their sentiments; therefore, freedom of the press ought not to be restrained" (Pennsylvania Constitution of 1776, paragraph twelve of the Declaration of Rights); "The freedom of the press is one of the great bulwarks of liberty and can never be restrained but by despotic governments" (Virginia Declaration of Rights).[86]

Radishchev's ideas on freedom of speech and the excerpts cited by him from the constitutions of various American states are of great interest. Their significance increases if one considers that these excerpts were apparently the first official American constitutional materials to appear in the Russian language. As a concrete example characterizing the democratic social structure in America, Radishchev cites an instance concerning that prominent figure of the American Revolution, John Dickinson of Pennsylvania, who openly refuted an unjust criticism directed at him. "The first town governor (gradonachalnik) of the province (Pennsylvania)," Radishchev wrote, "descended to the jousting ring, issued a defense of himself, justified himself, refuted the arguments of all his opponents, and put them to shame . . . This is an example to follow of how to avenge oneself by means of a printed work when someone accuses another person publicly."[87]

While praising political freedom in the United States, Radishchev did not hesitate to condemn the negative sides of American life. He angrily criticized social injustice, Negro slavery, and the annihilation of the Indians. "Once having slaughtered the Indians, the wicked Europeans, preachers of love of peace in the name of God's truth, teachers of meekness and love of humanity, graft upon the root of violent murder of conquest the cold-blooded murder of enslavement through the acquisition of slaves by purchase. These unhappy victims of the sun-drenched shores of Niger and the Senegal . . . work the bountiful cornfields of America which disdains their labor. And we call a country of devastation blissful, because its fields are not overgrown with thorns and its cornfields abound with a variety of plants. We call that country blissful where a hundred proud citizens roll in luxury, while thousands have neither reliable subsistence, nor their own shelter from the burning sun and the frost."[88]

The interpretation of Radishchev's attitude toward America is often one-sided. Some authors concentrate exclusively on the negative aspects of his characterization of American society; others are inclined to minimize the significance of the critical remarks and give prominence only to Radishchev's positive statements on the American Revolution. Even such a specialist as A. I. Startsev has not succeeded in avoiding this trap. Although thoroughly conversant with Radishchev's negative attitude toward slavery in America and the annihilation of the Indians (he even mentions his basic remarks on this subject), Startsev attempts to prove that these remarks refer "to America, outside the U.S.A.," that is, primarily to the nations of Latin America. He supports his argument by claiming that eighteenth-century Russian literature contained two distinct American themes: the new, connected with the revolutionary war of independence, and the old, connected with the conquest of the American continent and the annihilation of the Indians.[89]

Doubtless, these observations have some foundation in fact. It has been established that Radishchev's condemnation of slavery and the annihilation of the Indians applies not only to the United States, but to America as a whole, especially when he writes about sugar, coffee, and dyes (products primarily of Latin American origin), still not dry from "the sweat, tears, and blood by which they had been drenched in their tilling."[90] But in the last analysis this point of view seems not only unconvincing, but even mistaken. First of all, Negro slavery and the annihilation of the Indians in America, including of course North America, were bitterly condemned by leading Russian men of culture not only before Radishchev (Sumarokov, Novikov), but also after him (Pushkin, Chernyshevsky, and others). It is therefore obvious that in the nineteenth century it was a question primarily of Indians and slavery in the United States of America.

Thus, if one considers continuity, Radishchev's point of view should not be differentiated from that of other Russian cultural figures. Further, if we wish to be objective, why should we attribute all Radishchev's positive remarks to the United States alone, and the negative ones chiefly, even exclusively, to Latin America? Would it not be more equitable to attribute all remarks about America primarily to the United States (although some concern Latin America as well), inasmuch as major attention at the end of the eighteenth century was riveted on the new republic in North America?

Finally, condemnation of Negro slavery and the annihilation of the Indians is not evidence of any ill-will on Radishchev's part toward the United States. On the contrary: it was exactly because he valued the attainments of the American Revolution so highly that he so angrily condemned the preservation of ugly traces of the Old Order in the new republic.

The documentary material examined shows convincingly that the peals of the "alarm bell" of the American Revolution sounded clearly in Russia, and, most important, were heard quite sympathetically by progressive circles of the Russian public. The Russian reader's serious interest in events in America was neither accidental nor paradoxical.

The acute class contradictions of Russian reality, the cruel serf yoke combined with new bourgeois forms of exploitation related to the early capitalist economic structure arising in the midst of the feudal system, and the powerful tide of the spontaneous peasant movement which did not die down even after the brutal suppression of the Pugachev rebellion (1773-1775)—all created favorable soil for the sowing of revolutionary ideas. Although under autocratic Russian conditions it was impossible to speak of the right of the Russian people to revolt, the right to change the political regime in their own country, it was possible—because of acknowledged favorable circumstances—to write with some objectivity of the right to freedom and independence for the American people, and of the experience of their successful revolutionary war against Britain.

Publication in the Russian press, and primarily in Novikov's journals, of rich material dealing with the American War of Independence took on special meaning and significance vis-à-vis the conditions of the autocratic serf system in Russia. The reading of the dispatches concerning the successful military activities of the revolted colonists against the royal forces, the fact of the victorious conclusion of the war, and the consolidation of a republican state in America—all brought to the Russian reader's mind his own country, and forced him to examine critically the reality surrounding him, and to compare republican America with autocratic, serf-owning Russia. Thus, by its contents—aside from the wishes of the individual editor, translator, or author—the material dealing with the American War of Independence which was published in Russia took on to a certain extent a revolutionary political meaning.

It would be highly erroneous to view any given phenomenon of Russian culture and the Russian revolutionary movement as the result of Western European or American influence. But it would be just as inaccurate to suggest that the development of Russian society took place in some exclusive, isolated fashion, completely outside of contact with world progress. Russian society as a whole, and especially its progressive part, not to mention such figures as Novikov, Fonvizin, and Radishchev, attentively followed the development of the revolutionary movement in the West and, in particular, were thoroughly acquainted with the events and ideas of the American Revolution. This was, understandably, their service and their strength, and far from their shortcoming or weakness.

Without exaggeration it is possible to say that in depth of analysis of its events and ideas, in richness of thought and vividness of exposition, the appropriate sections of Radishchev's ode to "Liberty" and *Journey from St. Petersburg to Moscow* belong among the outstanding responses in world literature to the American Revolution. Characteristically Radishchev occupies the most consistently progressive position of his day regarding the very important questions of the liberation movement; he belongs in the vanguard of world revolutionary progress. Finally, the outstanding figures of the eighteenth-century Russian Enlightenment, while welcoming the revolution in America, did not ignore the negative sides of American life, and angrily condemned Negro slavery and the annihilation of the Indians.

III

RUSSIANS IN THE UNITED STATES AND AMERICANS IN RUSSIA AT THE END OF THE EIGHTEENTH CENTURY

Research on the earliest journeys of Russians to America and Americans to Russia is beset with difficulties. Little information is available, with the exception of a little material largely of an accidental or secondary nature; also, the actual number of such journeys in the eighteenth century could not have been significant. A journey to America by a Russian or by an American to Russia was neither easy nor safe. Travelers had to conquer enormous distances, assess complex political situations, and confront unknown conditions. No wonder that in overcoming all these difficulties, they rarely took care to preserve their impressions for historians. We know virtually nothing about some of them; others have left fragmentary, at times unreliable and self-contradictory, records.

Francis Dana's mission to St. Petersburg in 1781-1783 has been discussed. Earlier than that, in 1780-1781, one Stephen Sayre traveled in Russia on his own initiative. Persistently, although without marked success, he sought recognition from Benjamin Franklin and in St. Petersburg in an attempt to organize shipbuilding. Several years later John Ledyard arrived in Russia, and after him, John Paul Jones. Their experiences, for different reasons, had unfortunate endings, amid circumstances which have never been completely clarified.

The complex, contradictory, and original personality of Fedor Vasil'evich Karzhavin, Russian traveler and man-of-letters (1745-1812), has eluded the specialist's attention for a long time. It is true that in 1875 N. P. Durov published a lively autobiographical memoir of Karzhavin's with ample annotations and supplements in *Russkaia Starina* (Russian

Antiquity); for all practical purposes it has been hidden in the pages of a rare historical publication.[1] However, in recent years, scholars have shown a renewed interest in Karzhavin, and several studies have appeared in short succession by M. P. Alekseev, A. I. Startsev, and E. M. Dvoichenko-Markova.[2] These are useful in many ways, but extant materials are so scattered, contradictory, and fragmentary that it is impossible to determine Karzhavin's precise role in early Russian-American relations.

Karzhavin was born into the family of a rich St. Petersburg merchant. He received an encyclopedic European education, and a series of unique experiences led him, as he put it, "through fire, earth, and water." It was not without some foundation, albeit with obvious exaggeration, that he claimed to have "traversed three-quarters of the globe" as "no lesser Christopher Columbus." Fate was unjust to this daring, educated, and able man. There were too many abrupt changes, heavy losses, and family troubles in his life, and too few ordinary human satisfactions. An outstanding personality, he could not find his niche in serf-owning Russia and was obliged to spend many years wandering around in different countries. "It would have been better for me to have been a shoemaker than to spend my time studying and wasting my life in vain," he wrote bitterly in 1785.[3]

It is not always possible to ascertain the motives for Karzhavin's actions. He himself usually referred only to purely personal circumstances. To what extent this was correct, it is difficult to say. In any case it was easier and, more important, safer to put things that way. "In accordance with your permission," Karzhavin informed his father in September 1773, "I have departed for foreign lands, not because of any need, but solely in order to leave you in peace."[4] We learn from his memoir that, while in Paris in the beginning of 1774, he "thought to soften the severity of his fate by marriage, but has not found a real peace in marital state either."[5] Mlle. Rembour, although a poor orphan, judging by her correspondence, turned out to be a rather capricious person.

Soon financial difficulties and altercations with his wife led Karzhavin to seek happiness across the sea. Informing his father in 1775 about his intention to set out for Martinique and Santo Domingo in connection with his business, he wrote: "even though I have established there correspondence concerning American trade in sugar . . . cotton and coffee, it is far out of one's sight, and it would be better to observe it in person."[6] Only casually, almost as if by accident, did this letter refer to the "not unimportant" riots taking place in America.

Karzhavin started out for Martinique in September 1776. This was the beginning of his long American sojourn lasting until 1788. During this period he visited the United States several times: first, in the midst of the War of Independence, from May 1777 until January 25, 1780; a second time while he was staying aboard a Spanish vessel in the port of New York from May 12, 1782, until June 11, 1782; and, finally, after the cessation of hostilities, from September 4, 1784, until April 1787. The actual itinerary of his complex and tangled activities is well known primarily because of his memorandum to the College of Foreign Affairs in 1788.

The reliability of Karzhavin's information is confirmed by documents found among his papers, in particular by passports granted by various officials including the French minister to the United States, Conrad Alexandre Gérard, on February 27, 1779; the consul in Massachussetts, Joseph de Valnais, on March 13, 1779; the consul in Virginia, Chevalier d'Anmours, on January 8, 1780; and the vice-consul in Virginia, Martin Oster, on April 15, 1787.[7] E. M. Dvoichenko-Markova has shown that his memorandum accords quite accurately with American materials, including the statements in the local press. But while the chronological aspect of his journey is well established and does not cause any specific doubts, matters are much more complicated when it comes to understanding his motives and degree of participation in events of the period in America. Dvoichenko-Markova notes that, "in their struggle for freedom, the Americans were helped by the representatives of almost every European nation: the French Lafayette, the German Steuben, the Pole Kosciuszko, and others are listed among the participants of the American revolution, but no Russian was known by the American historians to take part in the American Revolutionary War."[8] She goes on to show that Karzhavin had been such a Russian.

Indeed, upon his arrival in America, Karzhavin found himself in the very midst of the revolutionary events. But what was his own role in these events? What political views did he adhere to? Where were his sympathies? It is difficult to answer these questions. A. I. Startsev, who is well acquainted with the available documentary materials, states that "what we know of Karzhavin's political views does not offer sufficient grounds to characterize him as an adherent of bourgeois revolution." At first glance this statement seems convincing. On a number of occasions Karzhavin sharply criticized American government as "ill-based and powerless," and, justifying his actions to his father, reminded him that "Karzhavins have never been Pugachevs." However, even Startsev had to admit that Karzhavin's assurances made in official documents and in censored letters must be taken with due regard for all circumstances demanding assertions of loyalty.[9]

Although "Karzhavins have never been Pugachevs," neither were they the usual loyal subjects of the Tsar. It was not for nothing that they were labeled "a family of freethinkers."[10] A political denunciation of the father and an uncle of Fedor Karzhavin, accusing them of atheism and of criticizing high tsarist officials including the Empress Elizabeth herself, was filed by the Secret Service Bureau back in 1755.[11] While refraining from rendering final judgment, I shall attempt to juxtapose and analyze the whole conglomeration of facts and circumstances connected with Karzhavin's life and activity. For instance, he was very close to the famous architect V. I. Bazhenov, and in his literary activities he had connections with N. I. Novikov.[12] Among Karzhavin's papers one finds the text of the *Marseillaise*, and a fragment of his own, censored poem, which is permeated by the hatred of "proud magnates" and by the sympathy for the poor;[13] "seditious" comments are written in the margins of books he read. In his printed works he expressed open sympathy for enslaved Negroes and Indians; he published an epitaph for Benjamin Franklin, called Montesquieu a "famous jurist," and so on.[14] On the other hand, in a memorandum to the College of Foreign Affairs, as well as in letters to his father and wife he emphasized the commercial motives for his actions.

The question naturally arises, if Karzhavin had such a strong interest in commercial affairs, was it really necessary for him to leave Russia and cross the ocean to a war-torn America? His quarrel with a father who dedicated his life to his business, developed an active foreign trade, and had even composed a special note for the government about enlarging Russia's commerce in European countries also remains unexplained.[15]

In justifying the reasons for his trip from Martinique to the United States, Karzhavin writes: "Wishing to double my capital, because of the critical circumstances of that period, through the New England trade, I entered a partnership with a Creole named M. Lasserre, who was sending a big vessel to America; having invested in it I have embarked on this ship on April 13, 1777."[16] What was the "New England trade" in which Karzhavin took part? Its character leaves little room for doubt. Martinique by this time had become an important supply base for the revolutionary colonists. It is true that in letters to his father, Karzhavin cites an innocent list of goods including wine, molasses, salt—he refrains from mentioning military equipment—but at the same time he reports that the ship was armed and that he had been directed by the shipowners to take charge of the military command. Events proved these precautionary measures far from superfluous. "We found ourselves unwittingly in a battle between an English privateer and a Philadelphian half-privateer-half-merchant, wherein we lost the vessel."[17] The adventure ended safely, for in the thick fog Karzhavin's ship managed to slip away from the English frigate and reach the Virginia coast. This is confirmed by a dispatch in the *Virginia Gazette* of May 16, 1777, announcing the arrival of the ship from Martinique with a cargo of "gunpowder, arms, salt, etc."[18]

Touching on his sojourn in Virginia, Karzhavin notes that he was engaged in trade in various cities and towns for a period of twenty-two months. Utilizing American sources, Dvoichenko-Markova pointed out his connection with Captain Laporte, in whose Williamsburg home Karzhavin lived in 1779, and his possible participation in the creation of a French military unit consisting of inhabitants of Martinique and Santo Domingo.[19]

Karzhavin's return trip to Martinique was extremely unlucky. Immediately following its departure from Virginia, the ship with its "rich cargo" was captured by the English. "Intending to seek help in Boston, and full of undaunted Russian spirit," Karzhavin, "to the surprise of all who knew him," started out on his long way home on foot, with a "sack upon his shoulders." Twenty-three days later, "with the passport of a French minister and consul," he reached Boston. However, he was not successful in his enterprise and was compelled to return to Philadelphia, "after experiencing great privations, being blinded for two days by the sun rays reflecting from the snow-covered fields, and being in danger both of the English and the Americans themselves."[20]

While describing vividly the misadventures of his American trip, Karzhavin is exceptionally reticent in political comments. In his papers there is no direct evidence of his political sympathies for the rebels, and certainly none of his participation in military actions. Nevertheless, accidental remarks, occasionally found between the lines, enable us to surmise his attitude to the American struggle for freedom and independence. Referring to his experiences in America, Karzhavin wrote to his wife bitterly:

> I lost three years, two ships, and everything that I possessed in New England. During this time I risked my life more than twenty times . . . and ahead of me there is no way out from this disastrous state. Why all this? It is all because of one fatal *no* said by the one who wanted to be a Mademoiselle Lami [the name which Karzhavin used while he lived in France] and would not agree to be Mme. Karzhavin. Remember, poor Lami, that you have lost her proud heart, and that you are nothing but a

miserable apothecary; keep mixing drugs for the brave people who will revenge your enemies, the English, for your ruination.[21]

Thus, it seems that for Karzhavin the English were the enemies, and Americans brave soldiers for whom he prepares medicines, utilizing his pharmaceutical knowledge. One can also guess at his sympathies on the basis of his cautious memorandum, which contains the following information about 1779 events in Virginia: "The English, under the command of John Goodrich, arrived at Chesapeake Bay and sailed up all the rivers for pillage and destruction." We also learn that Karzhavin had helped a French merchant, Venel, "to convey his goods by water to distant forests where we concealed ourselves until the enemy departed."[22]

The most important and interesting evidence of Karzhavin's close contacts with the rebelling colonists and their leaders was the plan to send him to St. Petersburg with the special diplomatic mission of the Congress of the United States. Reminiscing about this, Karzhavin wrote to his parents in Russia on September 1, 1785:

> Six or seven years ago I lived for about six months in Williamsburg in the service of Virginia's government, being intended to be sent by the American Congress to Her Russian Imperial Majesty as a public representative. At the same time they sent Dr. Franklin as Minister Plenipotentiary to the French King. But circumstances of war, some reverses in American affairs, my memory that I have not been in your good graces, the concern of the Russian minister Panin, that I, a Russian subject, might be sent to my Imperial Majesty as a public representative from a foreign crown, and so on caused me to prefer returning to Martinique aboard a French 74-gun ship *Le Fendent*.[23]

Karzhavin's announcement is startling, and at first implausible. Nor is there any confirmation of this statement in historical literature and documents. Nevertheless, there is no reason to deny the trustworthiness of Karzhavin's information. To begin with, one should attempt to establish the precise dates. From his memorandum we learn that Karzhavin "embarked on a 74-gun French ship under the command of the Marquis de Vaudreuil," on January 25, 1780, in "little York," and in twenty days "arrived in Martinique having endured upon the entry into the harbor the cannonade of the whole English fleet."[24] Thus, talk about sending him to St. Petersburg apparently took place in the end of 1779 or the beginning of 1780, at any rate no later than January 25. At that time the question of the diplomatic mission to Russia had not yet been resolved. Francis Dana's candidacy was not approved by the Continental Congress until December 1780. A. I. Startsev advanced a supposition that Karzhavin's candidacy could have been a subject of preliminary discussion in the circle of his Virginian acquaintances, which included Carlo Bellini, a professor at the College of William and Mary and a steady correspondent and a close friend of Thomas Jefferson. Bellini might have suggested Karzhavin's candidacy to Jefferson who in 1779-80 was Governor of Virginia. Startsev has called attention to the fact that, in 1778, Virginia authorities sent to Europe on a financial and diplomatic assignment, a close friend of Bellini's, an Italian physician and agronomist, F. Mazzei.[25]

On his return to the United States after the War of Independence, Karzhavin again settled in Virginia, first in Smithfield, then in Williamsburg. "Finally, having come to Virginia, I took up doctoring, did some merchandising, and served as an interpreter of the Anglo-American tongue in the office of the French consulate," he wrote about this period of his life in a biographical note presented as an exercise in translation in one of his special philological publications.[26] Here he had an opportunity to renew and enlarge his contacts with the personalities of American Enlightenment, and with Carlo Bellini first of all. It is of some purport that Karzhavin dedicated one of his books to "M. Bellini, Professor at Williamsburg University in Virginia."[27] In it he begs Bellini to "accept these lines as a sign of the close connection existing between fellow-believers [vrais-croyans] in spite of the boundless seas dividing them."

At a later date Karzhavin categorically denied having sympathized with ideas of "liberty and equality." He wrote his wife on April 27, 1797, from St. Petersburg: "I don't know why Madame chooses to ascribe to me sympathy for liberty and equality: if it were so, I wouldn't have left America; I could have become a professor, like M. Bellini, and every one there knew and liked me."[28] If his denials are taken at face value, his friendship and ideological closeness to Bellini become inexplicable. Nor would the friendly tone and content of their correspondence be comprehensible. Bellini's letter from Williamsburg of March 1, 1788, mentioning the federal constitution adopted by the Philadelphia convention in 1787, is of special interest in this connection. It can be deduced from this letter that Karzhavin was acquainted with such well-known personalities of the day as Bishop James Madison, and one of the best-educated representatives of American Enlightenment, professor at the College of William and Mary, George Wythe.[29]

Thus, the circle of Karzhavin's American and Russian friends bears witness to the direction of his views and sympathies. As a very young man he lived in Paris in the residence and under supervision of D. A. Golitsyn. In Russia, he maintained a lifelong friendship with V. I. Bazhenov, and his publisher was N. I. Novikov. In America, he counted among his acquaintances Madison and Wythe, and Bellini was a close friend. In view of this, it seems quite natural that Karzhavin, descendant of a "family of freethinkers" and a representative of the Russian "third estate," found himself from the very beginning of the revolutionary War of Independence allied to the American-French side.

From a conventional point of view, Karzhavin's American journey could not be called successful. "The Goddesses called by the Romans *Paupertas* and *Necessitas*"[30] constantly pursued him. He could not even manage to save enough money for a homeward voyage, and had to apply to the Russian embassy in Paris for the necessary 1200 livres.[31] On the other hand, his role in the formation of the very first Russian-American connections, especially cultural ones, appears to be rather substantial. His practical activity, his literary work, and his wide and varied acquaintance all undoubtedly led to increased understanding of the living conditions in both countries and stimulated reciprocal interest and exchange of experience. Also, one must not forget that Karzhavin was the first Russian who undertook a voyage to America upon his own initiative, and who lived in the United States for a considerable length of time both during and after the War of Independence.

During his stay in the United States, Karzhavin undoubtedly succeeded in learning a great deal about living conditions there. In his own words, he got to know "this huge country, and to know it well." The accuracy of information in his memoirs, numerous details, and especially the chronological dates lead one to suppose that he must have kept a journal during his stay. There are, indeed, some diary entries among his papers, in particular from March through August 1782. Bellini, in his letter of March 1, 1788, mentioned "the North-American journal of Karzhavin," and his interest in learning how soon it could be made available for the American public. Unfortunately, the book never appeared and the fate of the journal remains unknown.

On the other hand, Karzhavin's literary writings, including his manuscripts, abound in unexpected and often very interesting observations, directly connected with his North American travels. Thus, among his pedagogical materials the reader finds a general comment on his American voyage: "One of our countrymen, a knowledgeable and inquisitive man, set out in 1776 upon the Atlantic Ocean and, bearing Southwest, arrived at the shores of the West Indies . . . whence he proceeded to the American continent and did not return to his country until 1788 . . . This Russian is the first among our people to have had a residence of twelve years' duration in those remote countries and to have seen them with an observant eye."[32] It is also worth noting that Karzhavin signed the preface to one of his books as "Russian-American."[33] Perusing the contents of the book one finds, in an annotation to a table, some interesting details of Karzhavin's American journey, which show that in 1785 he published in Virginia a similar work in English, under the title *The Virginian Fortune-Teller*. The reader learns further that the table used in both books was copied from the "nineteenth issue of the *Havana News* of 1783, published in Havana, the capital city of the island of Cuba where F[edor] K[arzhavin] then lived."[34]

Karzhavin's condemnation of Negro slavery, so typical of the progressive circles of Russian society in that period, is especially interesting. The same book, which in its subject matter seemed very far from politics and constituted, according to the author, nothing but "an innocent exercise at the time of boredom for people not wishing for a better occupation," contains some wrathful lines about Negro slavery and its defenders: "All the African and American shores groan because of the inhumanity with which sugar manufacturers deal with black-skinned people."[35]

Democratic ideals and sympathy for Negroes and oppressed American Indians are evident in Karzhavin's comments on the so-called "savage" people:

> I have lived in various regions of America, both warm and cold, for twelve years, and have been away from my own country all in all for twenty-eight years . . . I have seen multitudes of people who live differently from us or other Europeans; I have encountered intelligent people, and I have encountered stupid people; I saw *human beings* everywhere, but I have never seen a *savage*, and I have to admit I have not found any one more savage than myself.[36]

These remarks, dropped by the author as if accidentally, throw definite light on his views, and it becomes clear why this unique and educated man could not find a place in Russia's serfdom-based regime. Having lived in Europe and America for a long time, and not belonging to the nobility, Karzhavin seemed politically unreliable, and his reiterated declarations of loyalty were not much help. Even his wife did not put much faith in them—let alone tsarist officials. It is not surprising that his application to the College of Foreign Affairs, for "service in foreign lands"[37] was not acted upon, and that until his death in 1812 Karzhavin never ceased to struggle with life's vicissitudes.

Karzhavin's manuscript and printed legacy have not yet been studied in detail; far from all of it appears clear, and far from all has artistic or intellectual value today. Much of what he wrote was of a casual or abstract nature and has little meaning for the modern reader. On the other hand, it was brought to light that his philological researches had considerable significance for their time, as did his works on the theory of architecture and his vivid realistic drawings. His literary works deserve special attention. A graduate of the University of Paris, "world traveler" Karzhavin, to quote M. P. Alekseev, "did a great deal of work for his country in his role of a teacher 'approved and privileged by Moscow University,' a translator and a writer, and it was not his fault that his achievement fell short of what he hoped for and was capable of."[38]

A different kind of problem arises in connection with the study of the first American visitors to Russia. As a rule there is no lack of attention on the part of their admirers. On the contrary, in the case of one of the first Americans to visit Russia, soon after the War of Independence, researchers encounter difficulties precisely because of his exceptional popularity. This was no other than the American naval hero John Paul Jones. Strictly speaking, he was not a "real American," since he was born in Scotland in 1747 and died in Paris in 1792. Recognition of the brave captain by his "grateful" fellow Americans was far from immediate; for many years they called him a "corsair," apparently in order to avoid the ruder word, "pirate"; he was, after all, a hero.

It was only when the United States began to compete for a leading place among the great naval powers, that John Paul Jones's reputation was restored. The mighty state's navy needed traditions and heroes. John Paul Jones's remains were quickly transported from Paris to America, and he became one of the most revered heroes of the War of Independence, acknowledged founder of the American Navy, and its "first captain."

Americans know how to honor their heroes. Every schoolboy knows about John Paul Jones, and the story of the brave captain can be found alongside the biographies of George Washington, Benjamin Franklin, Abraham Lincoln, and Franklin Delano Roosevelt. At first somewhat surprised to find John Paul Jones in such brilliant company, I finally decided that Americans know whom they should honor, and I have no desire to belittle the famous captain. It might be noted that in Russia he was awarded the rank of admiral, and was decorated for his participation in the Dnieper Liman engagement of June 1788. Some oversensitive biographers do not like to touch upon the details of his sojourn in Russia in 1788-89, because of its unfortunate ending, restricting themselves to abusing the "oriental barbarians." For Gerald White Johnson, the court of Catherine II is a "brothel," and Grigori Potemkin is not a man but "troglodyte." The touchy admirers of Paul Jones apparently assume that piling accusations and epithets on Catherine II, Potemkin, and, for good measure, Russian sailors can elevate their hero.[39] In reality incongruous accusations and abuse harm rather than help him, who was much more objective in his evaluations.

The basic reasons for his biographers' touchiness result from an unpleasant judicial investigation which completely wrecked the American's career in Russia. John Paul Jones was accused of a criminal offense (the rape of a minor, "virgin Catherine").[40] He resolutely denied the accusation, in particular in letters to the chief of St. Petersburg police, Major-General Ryleev; to Potemkin; Catherine II, and others.[41] Finally, with the help of the French Ambassador, Count Ségur, Paul Jones succeeded in breaking through the isolation in which he found himself and appearing at Court again,[42] although this was, so to speak, merely the Empress' granting of a farewell favor. Having received a two-year "leave," in the fall of 1789, Paul Jones left the Russian empire forever.

Certain authors are not averse to using the "Paul Jones affair" to stimulate hostility between Russians and Americans, piling up various incongruous accusations against "oriental barbarians." One could with greater reason attack "civilized America" by pointing to an analogous affair of the Russian consul in Philadelphia, N. Ia. Kozlov. Russian officials considered that, in his position of general consul, Kozlov was entitled to diplomatic immunity, and his "affair" almost caused the severance of diplomatic relations between Russia and the United States. However, this is no reason to claim damage from Americans for the Kozlov affair or from the Russians for the "Paul Jones affair." Incidentally, Paul Jones himself was inclined to blame his troubles on his long-time enemies, the English, and on Admiral Nassau-Siegen, although neither he nor Count Ségur was able to produce concrete evidence. The possibility that Nassau-Siegen clandestinely participated in the affair seems quite probable to modern historians,[43] since he was most interested in spoiling the reputation of the American sailor.

While this affair cannot be overlooked, I do not wish to cast a shadow on the memory of an American hero. But one cannot state that his visit to Russia ended unsuccessfully. John Paul Jones might have had his troubles with Potemkin, might have become an object of intrigues by the English sailors, and might have quarreled with Nassau-Siegen, but none of this would be reason enough to consider his stay in Russia an overall failure. Paul Jones stayed in Russia for a fairly long time and met a great many people. He served in the Russian navy with Russian sailors, for whom he had a very high regard. His encounters with A. V. Suvorov are especially remarkable. These aspects of his activity deserve detailed investigation, and that is why we shall pause on some details of Paul Jones's stay in Russia.

The question of employing Paul Jones in the Russian service was broached at the end of 1787 or beginning of 1788 by the Russian and American envoys in Paris, I. M. Simolin and Thomas Jefferson; it was made official in Copenhagen through the efforts of Baron Kruedener.[44] The proclamation of Catherine II to the Admiralty College on February 15/26, 1788, entered Paul Jones (in Russia he was called Captain-Commodore Pavel Jones) into Russian service with the title of "Captain of the Major-General rank" and assigned him to the Black Sea fleet.[45] Paul Jones himself expected the rank of rear-admiral and was perplexed as to why he was commissioned major-general.[46] It was decided in St. Petersburg not to bargain and on April 4/15, by a further proclamation he was appointed a rear-admiral.[47]

John Paul Jones arrived in Russia in April 1788, and instantly became the object of general attention and unusual imperial favor. "The Empress received me with a distinction the most flattering that perhaps any Stranger can boast of, on entering into the Russian service," he informed Lafayette in June 1788.[48] To the great annoyance of the English, the Empress' new favorite was enthusiastically received by St. Petersburg society: "His door was besieged with carriages, and his desk loaded with invitations."[49] Unlike his careful predecessor, Francis Dana, Paul Jones behaved quite boldly in the Russian capital and began by offering Catherine II the gift of a copy of the new American constitution signed by the secretary of the Continental Congress.[50] The autocratic Tsarina apparently had to "swallow" this unusual gift, although acquaintance with the constitution hardly could have provided her any special pleasure. On the other hand, according to Paul Jones himself, Catherine II frequently spoke with him about the United States and expressed a conviction that "the American Revolution cannot fail to bring about others, and to influence every other government."[51] In his talks with Catherine II, Paul Jones touched upon the question of Armed Neutrality and United States participation in this "famous association." Even earlier, in a letter to Thomas Jefferson, written from Copenhagen on April 8, 1788, he had noted that it would be highly advantageous for America with its increasing commerce to join the system of Armed Neutrality, which he called a "noble and humane Combination."[52]

His enthusiastic reception in St. Petersburg and the imperial benevolence apparently turned the brave sailor's head. In his letters he lavished extravagant compliments on Catherine II, and for a time turned from a defender of liberty and equality into an enthusiastic admirer and loyal subject of the Russian Empress. He expressed his delight in the Empress rather frivolously and naively to no other than Potemkin himself: "If her Imperial Majesty were not the Empress of all Russia (not to mention her other great qualities)," he wrote to His Highness the Prince on May 30/ June 10, 1788, "in my eyes she would have been the most amiable of all women."[53]

Grigori Potemkin knew the qualities of Catherine II well enough, and it was inappropriate for Paul Jones to express his raptures about the Empress to her all-powerful favorite. In a certain sense, the too-brilliant beginning of Paul Jones's career in Russia caused its sad ending. But that was still ahead, and for the time being, the American, full of hopes, raised his new rear-admiral flag on the ship *Vladimir* in the Dnieper Liman.[54]

The study of naval operations in the Dnieper Liman in the summer of 1788 and Paul Jones's role in them presents difficulties. The Russian fleet of this theater was under the command of Nassau-Siegen, who was in charge of the Flotilla, that is, craft propelled by oars; Paul Jones was in charge of the Squadron, which consisted of three ships of the line, five frigates, and six small craft. As a result of battles which had taken place near Ochakov on June 7/8 and 17/28, 1788, the Turkish fleet had suffered a heavy defeat. On the night of June 18/29, while trying to withdraw into the open sea, the Turkish fleet came under the fire of a Russian battery set up on the Kinburn peninsula by General Suvorov. Becoming confused, some Turkish ships ran aground and later were destroyed by the Flotilla. Turkish losses in the battles of June 17/28 and 18/29 amounted to six hundred casualties; in addition, almost eighteen hundred persons were taken prisoners.[55]

The opinion that the decisive role in these operations was played by the Flotilla, under the command of Nassau-Siegen, is firmly imbedded in official documents and military histories. On the other hand, documents emanating from Paul Jones give the main credit for destruction of the Turkish fleet to the Squadron, and Nassau-Siegen's actions are severely criticized. Later, the offended Paul Jones prepared for publication his own account of the operations in the Liman in which he intended to prove that it was precisely his own operations that "not only saved Cherson and the Crimea, but decided the fate of the war."[56]

Such obvious exaggeration of the significance of the naval battles in the

Dnieper Liman in June 1788 in which Paul Jones took part does not warrant detailed refutation. It is evident that, in spite of their importance, these victories had not and could not have exercised decisive influence on the outcome of the war, which continued for several years and was not terminated until 1791.

Although wounded self-esteem obviously prevented Paul Jones's ability to evaluate objectively the operations in which he participated, the materials he gathered deserve attention. Because the historian must take into account that Paul Jones was an interested party and that his documents give a one-sided view of the events, it has not always been possible to assess correctly the whole conglomeration of facts.

First, one should point out that, in his report of June 25/July 6, 1788, on military operations "to the members of the Black Sea Admiralty" in Kherson, Paul Jones had already expressed a very high opinion of his Squadron.[57] Later he was greatly distressed that the officers of his Squadron (as distinct from the officers of Nassau's Flotilla) were not promoted; and he petitioned Potemkin on their behalf.[58] Finally, the text of his account of the campaign of 1788 contains flattering estimates of the Russian seamen serving under his command.[59]

The person about whom Paul Jones expressed himself most sharply was his colleague, Rear-Admiral Nassau-Siegen; and in my opinion he was absolutely correct. A foreign adventurer who enjoyed the favor of the Russian court, Nassau-Siegen did not possess any ability for command of naval operations; he proved to be a mediocre, even dull, naval commander. The irony of fate made him a "principal" victor over the Turks in the Dnieper Liman and showered him with sovereign favors. However, later it was his fault that the Russian Flotilla suffered a cruel defeat from the Swedes in the second Rochensalm battle. Nassau-Siegen was determined to have a battle on the anniversary of Catherine's ascension to the throne (June 28/July 9, 1790), but his "gift" to the Empress proved to be a military disaster.[60]

Paul Jones's documents characterize Nassau-Siegen quite convincingly as a totally ungifted commander, unable to manage the operations of the ships under his command. Paul Jones was especially irritated by the excessive royal favors showered on Nassau-Siegen after the Dnieper Liman victory. The displeased American refused to salute the new vice-admiral flag raised by Nassau-Siegen, and their relations became extremely strained.[61] Paul Jones's vanity was badly wounded when he learned that his own reward for the battle of the Liman was limited to the award of the Order of St. Anna.[62] Later, writing to Potemkin from Paris, Paul Jones emphasized that it was himself who had commanded all the useful operations against the Captain Pasha in Dnieper Liman: It "was I and the brave men I commanded who conquered him on the 17th June . . . it was I who gave to General Suwarow, (he had the nobleness to declare it at court before me, to the most respectable witnesses), the first project to establish the battery and breast-works on the isthmus of Kinbourn, and which were of such great utility on the night of the 17-18 June."[63]

Paul Jones's statements about "the great utility" of Suvorov's guns deserve attention. Essentially, the fire of the battery set up by General Suvorov on Kinburn Peninsula determined the definitive defeat of the Turkish fleet endeavoring to escape into the open sea on the night of June 17-18. It is hardly necessary to prove in detail that Suvorov himself understood quite well the importance of the battery which he set up and foresaw its role in the destruction of the fleet. "In respect to the might of Her Majesty's naval forces, on our side a battery with thirteen guns is set up on Kinburn Peninsula," Suvorov informed Potemkin on June 8/19; "so far as it is possible we shall not offer a golden bridge [that is, allow the enemy to retreat] to the unfaithful."[64]

The need to set up guns on Kinburn Peninsula at the outlet of the Liman was evident to everyone except Field Marshal Potemkin himself. Paul Jones reports that he was "so struck at finding the tongue of land at Kinbourn without any battery or blockfort, that he instantly spoke of it to the Commandant, General Suwarow."[65] It is possible that this was the case; there is no reason to distrust Paul Jones's testimony. But one should call attention to an important circumstance. Suvorov was not only a genius as a general but also a brilliant tactician and diplomat. Apparently these were the very qualities which Paul Jones, who could not get along with either Potemkin or Nassau-Siegen, lacked. It was very hard for Suvorov to find himself under the command of Potemkin (and, let us admit, much harder than it was for Paul Jones). But how carefully and tactfully he conducted himself, even in this seemingly quite obvious matter of the setting up of the battery on the Kinburn Point! "For God's sake, do me a favor, show some patience," the wily man wrote His Highness the Prince on June 10/21, "it was not I who thought up the battery; I held out against *die Redlichkeit* and all the naval commanders for about two weeks, and, fearing Your Highness, was almost compelled to agree. So be it; it is already installed, and the other, the cross one, has arrived last night, as you will please see tomorrow on the plan. For goodness sake, Your Highness, if they are to be taken down, it will not look very good either for the Turks or for our own side."[66]

Suvorov's irony in this letter borders on open insult, nevertheless it never crosses the limits of the permitted. "His Highness" had to "show some patience" and become reconciled both with the established battery, upon whose removal he had insisted, and with the "cross" one. One should note, incidentally, that Paul Jones's relations with the great Russian general from the very beginning were of a friendly nature. According to Suvorov himself, they met on May 25/June 5, 1788 as "age-old friends."[67] Unfortunately, Suvorov, possibly out of caution, has not cited any details of his conversations, and in published documents, as a rule, limited himself only to a simple mention of Paul Jones.

The contact with Suvorov had little influence on the American's ability to get along with his superiors, and he had more than one occasion to regret the sharpness of his letter to Potemkin of 14/25 October 1788, written "under feelings highly excited."[68] In the fall of 1788 the Prince thought it best to get rid of the restless American by sending him on a plausible pretext to St. Petersburg. In the letter to Catherine II, handed to Paul Jones, Potemkin noted that the American had evidenced "ardor and devotion" in the imperial service.[69] On arriving at the capital, Paul Jones was granted a private audience by the Empress on the eve of New Year (old style), but had not received any new assignment. In the meanwhile, in the expectation of such an assignment, the possiblity of which was hinted to him by A. A. Bezborodko, Paul Jones thrust himself into a diplomatic activity somewhat unusual for his situation.

As can be seen from his letters to Thomas Jefferson in January 1789, Paul Jones was much preoccupied at that time by the idea of a close alliance between Russia and the United States for consolidated actions in the Mediterranean against Turkey and Algiers. He naturally presumed that he would be offered the command of the united forces. He also reported that he had already discussed the matter in St. Petersburg, and begged Jefferson to express his views on this subject as soon as possible.[70] In his memoirs Paul Jones states that in February 1789 he "gave to the Vice-Chancellor Count d'Osterman a project for forming an alliance, political and commercial, between Russia and the United States."[71] Soviet archives preserve an original of Paul Jones's interesting letter to Osterman of January 31/February 11, 1789, containing detailed grounds for the value of such an alliance between Russia and the United States. In particular, he pressed for the unification of Russian and American actions and proposed to create a special squadron in the Mediterranean. After the conclusion of peace Paul Jones hoped to secure freedom of navigation for the American vessels in both the Mediterranean and the Black seas. The letter developed in detail the presumed advantages from trade between Russia and the United States on the basis of the most-favored-nation principle, and expressed some curious considerations about Crimean colonization and the recruitment of American seamen into the Russian fleet. On the whole, it envisioned a broad program of military, political, and trade relations between the two countries.[72]

This daring and unexpected project of Paul Jones, who acted without any authorization from the American government, never could have materialized, even under very favorable circumstances. There is no need to argue that neither the United States nor Russia was prepared for such an alliance, and it is not surprising that Jefferson avoided any definite reply.[73]

The idea of an expedition into the Mediterranean could have seemed enticing to the Russian government. Earlier, in the summer of 1788, a project actually had been afoot in Russia to send a naval expedition to deal a blow to Turkey on the side of her vulnerable rear, utilizing for this purpose a revolt of enslaved Balkan peoples.[74] However, England undertook decisive measures to break up this expedition, by making it impossible to hire English sailors and to purchase provision and supply ships. From that time on relations with Great Britain continued to deteriorate. Sweden was drawn into the war against Russia in the summer of 1788, not without the participation of English diplomacy. Instead of planning a Mediterranean expedition, Russia had to ready its fleet for the defense of St. Petersburg.[75]

According to Paul Jones, some time after the transmission of the plan to the Field-Marshal Potemkin, the latter took him into his cabinet and said that "his plan contains some good ideas, but he did not think it expedient to adopt it at this time, as this might still further irritate the English against Russia, and that it was necessary first to make peace with the Turks."[76] Potemkin's misgivings in respect to the English reaction were quite justified. According to S. R. Vorontsov's report from England, English naval officers, ever since the acceptance of Paul Jones into the Russian service, had "lost all desire to serve in it," and "found it impossible to serve under his command."[77] Paul Jones was well aware of the hatred on the part of his old enemies. He knew that in St. Petersburg the English had been accusing him of all sorts of atrocities. (It was claimed, for example, that he was a contraband trader, and that he killed his own nephew.)[78] He saw in these intrigues one of the main causes of his persecution in Russia.[79]

The process served against Paul Jones in the spring of 1789 greatly complicated the already complex situation in which he found himself in St. Petersburg upon his return from the south. In spite of his formal acquittal, leaders of the Russian government preferred to avoid encounters with the American. Meanwhile, Paul Jones, with enviable persistence, continued to strive for the realization of his broad military-diplomatic projects. On June 6/17 he gave Count Bezborodko a secret note on the subject of sending a Russian fleet into the Mediterranean with a view to cutting off communications between Egypt and the coast of Syria with Constantinople. To encompass this end, he asked for carte blanche and five large vessels carrying from forty to fifty guns.[80] This suggestion, which under normal conditions would have been quite reasonable and feasible, was unacceptable. Both Bezborodko and Osterman tried, insofar as possible, to avoid meeting with the persistent seaman, and his letters went unanswered. "I could not have imagined," Paul Jones wrote bitterly to Count Bezborodko on 14/25 July 1789, "that these plans were so carelessly to be thrown aside and, in place of discussing and arranging them with you, I was very much astonished when his Excellency the Count de Bruce announced to me that the Empress had granted me a leave of two years."[81]

Unwilling to accept the idea that his proposals would remain unrealized, Paul Jones returned to the project of an alliance and trade agreement between Russia and the United States. "As the Vice-Chancellor spoke to me of going to America about this purpose, and as I shall soon again be connected with my old friends who constitute the present government of the United States, I would be extremely happy to learn, through your Excellency, the intentions of Her Imperial Majesty in this respect, and to be appointed to forward an alliance by which Russia must gain."[82]

Apparently Paul Jones's proposals were no longer taken seriously in St. Petersburg, and in September 1789 he was compelled to leave the Russian capital without having won approval of them. The French Revolution, which began in the summer of 1789, did not make the time auspicious for the project of Russian-American rapprochement.

At times Paul Jones evidently did not fully realize that he was in the capital of monarchist Russia rather than republican America. Having presented a copy of the new federal constitution of 1787 to Catherine II in the spring of 1788, he continued to inform the tsarist government about the constitutional development of the United States. In February 1789 he reported in particular that the constitution "which does so much honor to the most enlightened statesmen has already been adopted. It protects the rights of citizens beautifully, and at the same time the government which was recently created will become the most efficient of all existing in the world."[83]

Consolidation of the central power through the adoption of the constitution of 1787, and the forthcoming creation of a new government based on it, were deemed by Paul Jones the most important arguments in favor of the expediency of Russian-American rapprochement. It was not by chance, apparently, that in his letter to Osterman he began the justification of his project with these points. Naturally, his enthusiastic explanations about the republican form of government made no impression, other than a negative one, on the tsarist government.

In spite of his failure, Paul Jones never gave up the idea of returning to Russia and resuming his service in its navy. On 25 February/8 March 1791 he sent, via Baron Grimm, a new letter to Catherine II, still hoping to gain her favor. "I have in my hands the means to prove, incontestably, that I directed all the useful operations against the Captain Pasha," he wrote, and he begged the Empress to free him as soon as possible "from cruel uncertainty."[84] On July 9, 1791, he wrote Baron Grimm, mentioning a new construction of a 54-gun warship and asking him to acquaint Her Majesty with it.[85] The Russian Empress, who earlier had been little interested in Paul Jones's projects, was all the less disposed to accept his good offices at the time when the French Revolution was at its peak and the war with Turkey almost over (preliminary peace terms were signed in the summer of 1791).

Paul Jones died in Paris on July 18, 1792, without having succeeded in winning royal rehabilitation. The American Minister to France, Gouverneur Morris, did not consider it necessary to attend the funeral, which took place July 20, 1792. During this "busy day," one gathers from his diary, he occupied himself with more "important" affairs: having dined in pleasant society, Gouverneur Morris called on his neighbor, Madame de Narbonne, on the British Ambassador, on Madame de Gilbert, and finally on Madame Couteulx. But (and this is much more important) the National Assembly honored John Paul Jones by sending a deputation of twelve members to the funeral.[86] This evidently was the occasion about which Catherine II expressed herself sharply and definitely enough, writing "Ce Paul Jones était une bien mauvaise tête et très digne d'être fêté par un ramas de têtes détestables," to her learned correspondent Baron Grimm on 15/26 August 1792.[87]

In history words often reverse their meaning, and the Empress' abuse turned out to be praise for Paul Jones, since by "ramas de têtes détestables" she meant French revolutionaries. One might say that Paul Jones finally received his long-awaited "sovereign reward"—though posthumously.

Though the most conspicuous, Paul Jones and Fedor Karzhavin were by no means the only eighteenth-century travelers to have journeyed on both sides of the Atlantic, in tsarist Russia and the new transatlantic republic. Even before Paul Jones went there, Russia was visited by such well-known persons as Francis Dana, with the young John Quincy Adams, and John Ledyard, who sought to gather information about Russian possessions in the northern reaches of the Pacific Ocean and to traverse Siberia and the continent of North America (see Chapter VI). The entourage of the Field-Marshal Potemkin at Ochakov included the American Lewis Littlepage, chamberlain of the Polish king, who participated with Paul Jones in the expeditions in the summer of 1788.[88] It was through him that Paul Jones conveyed his letters to Thomas Jefferson and Marquis de Lafayette.[89]

But the most numerous group of Americans who stayed in Russia at the end of the eighteenth and the beginning of the nineteenth centuries was comprised of American merchant seamen. The first American ships to arrive in St. Petersburg soon after the end of the War of Independence were followed by dozens, and some years even hundreds, of ships bearing the flag of the far transatlantic republic, arriving in Baltic ports and later those of the White Sea. Each new ship meant new dozens of seamen, new business contacts between Russian and American merchants, new meetings and impressions.

The number of Americans who visited Russia grew steadily, and in the first half of the nineteenth century one can count among them such prominent men as Finance Minister Albert Gallatin, future President James Buchanan and Vice-President George Dallas, well-known journalist and diplomat Alexander Everett, and others. American military leaders who visited Russia included Generals William Sherman and George McClellan, who became famous during the Civil War period and Admiral Farragut.[90] By the beginning of the nineteenth century John Paul Jones had successors in the Black Sea service. Thus, on 13/25 March 1811, the head of the Ministry of the Naval Forces, Traverse, signed an order to enroll in the Russian fleet a "lieutenant Sontag, formerly of the American marine service." In the campaign of 1814 he entered Paris as colonel in a regiment, then successfully served in the Black Sea region, was promoted to general, married a Russian lady with a large estate, and for many years lived happily with his family in Odessa.[91]

The highest opinion of the Russian army was held by Allen Smith, who stayed in Russia in the early nineteenth century and maintained a friendly contact with the Vorontsov family for a long time. "Having visited in Russia and seen Russian soldiers, I do not fear any more that Europe might fall victim to unlimited vanity combined with enormous talents," he wrote from Sevastopol in the spring of 1804.[92]

The Archive of the Leningrad section of the Institute of History of the

Academy of Sciences preserves some letters written by Allen Smith between 1804 and 1821, in which on several occasions he mentioned enthusiastically the exploits of Russian soldiers in their struggle against Napoleon. In the summer of 1815 Smith recommended to the Vorontsovs General Scott, a young American who was going to Europe with two young aides-de-camp. "General Scott," he wrote on June 25th from Philadelphia, "is eager to see the Russian army, and his greatest ambition will be satisfied if he is permitted to meet Emperor Alexander. Give him, my dear Vorontsov, some friendly advice (les conseils d'ami) and remember that this is not simply General Scott whom I am recommending, but an interesting representative of our brave little American Army."[93] The American General's desire to become acquainted with the Russian troops was natural. The prestige of the conquerors of Napoleon I was very high at that time, and Russia was observed by the entire world, including faraway America.

The fragmentary and vague character of surviving information prevents us from forming a full and clear idea of the first Russian travelers and immigrants to America. Nevertheless, there is sufficient reason to believe that in the eighteenth century Karzhavin had both predecessors and followers. Incidental references in American literature name one Charles Thiel, a St. Petersburg pharmacist who came to Philadelphia in 1769. Assuming the name of Charles Cist, the enterprising apothecary soon became successful in the publishing business. His main claim to fame, however, results from the fact that he was one of the first to understand that coal could be used as fuel.[94] A curious fate befell another Russian wanderer, a Nizhegorod petty bourgeois called "Vasily Baranshchikov," who found himself in America in the beginning of the 1780's on the Danish island of Saint Thomas.[95]

Among the participants in the War of Independence was Estonian nobleman Gustave Heinrich Wetter von Rosenthal (1753-1829). The Gothic script of a poorly legible manuscript, *Information on the Family of Wetter von Rosenthal*, found in the Historical Archive of the Estonian Soviet Republic in Tartu states that he left Europe in 1775 in order "to take part in the struggle for liberation of the young American republic against England." One learns later that in America young Gustave Heinrich became aide-de-camp to Jackson, a mayor and a knight of the Order of Cincinnati, and even "was acquainted with Washington."[96] Through an entry in the *Encyclopedia of American Revolution* one learns that Gustave Henri, Baron de Rosenthal, known as Lieutenant John Rose in America, was made surgeon in 1777, and was aide-de-camp of General

Irvine in 1781-82. He maintained contact with Irvine long after his departure from the United States in April 1784. In return for his participation in the war, the federal government granted him some land in Ohio and Pennsylvania, but he never returned to America and died in Reval on June 26, 1829.[97]

In the United States, Wetter von Rosenthal is referred to as "the only Russian" to participate in the War of Independence on the American side.[98] This statement is not altogether accurate in view of the information about Fedor Karzhavin. Nor can we exclude the possibility that researchers might yet unearth more information about Russian participants in the events of 1775-1783. One can note in particular that Karzhavin mentioned in his diary (May 29, 1782) that among German soldiers in America he encountered a Russian, a native of Reval. On June 2 he specified that the name of this Russian was Zakhar Bobukh, and that at one time he had executed "for Her Majesty Catherine II and for the Counts Orlovs much diamond work on the garments, but instead of a reward he was compelled to flee Russia."[99]

The fate of the Russian specialist in diamond work, as possibly the fate of other obscure wanderers, is unknown. On the other hand, the life and activity of another Russian, of aristocratic background, who had moved to the United States permanently in the end of the eighteenth century, made a deep impression on his contemporaries and on later researchers. This was no other than the son of Prince D. A. Golitsyn, who came to Baltimore in 1792 under the name of Augustine Smith. Having renounced a great fortune and a princely title, young Demetrius Gallitzin became a Catholic missionary, Father Augustine, and founded in a remote part of Pennsylvania, about two hundred miles from Philadelphia, a settlement, Loretto, in which his monument is preserved to this day. Several works in English, German, and French about the life and work of Father Augustine exist, so it is not necessary to dwell on the details of his unusual fate.[100] However, it seems obvious that in his choice of America as a country of residence the young Golitsyn was in some measure influenced by his father's sympathy for the country.

In calling attention to the first Russian travelers and immigrants to the United States I do not intend to exaggerate their number and importance. Nevertheless, the preliminary information gathered, especially material about the participation of men of Russian origin in the American Revolution (including Fedor Karzhavin and Gustave Heinrich Wetter von Rosenthal) shows that this subject deserves study, and that a persistent researcher might be rewarded by some interesting discoveries.

Part Two

Russian-American Relations during the Late Eighteenth and Early Nineteenth Centuries

In order to understand the character of Russian-American relations, to estimate the significance of the earliest socio-political and commercial contacts, and especially to gauge the prospects of their further development, it is important to have some idea of the internal conditions of both countries, of their economic situations and particularly of the main trends of their foreign trade.

In the last quarter of the eighteenth century the serf-owning regime of feudal Russia attained its peak of development. Serfdom, supported by the power of the military-bureaucratic machine, controlled the whole national economy, with a complete grasp of agriculture and occupation of key positions in industry. At the same time every decade saw the growth of bourgeois phenomena. Handcrafts and manufacturing were developing; trade and the production of goods were on the increase. The rudiments of the capitalist system in industry were enlarging and strengthening; consequently, toward the end of the eighteenth and the beginning of the nineteenth century the process of disintegration of serfdom was becoming more and more tangible.[1]

The development of productive forces led to a significant population growth (from 19 million in 1762 to 45 million in 1815). Foreign trade had grown considerably: in the 1760's Russian foreign trade amounted to 20 million rubles, in the eighties 50.6 million, and in the nineties it topped 71 million rubles.[2] Russian exports were principally the products of feudal rent (produced by the peasants)—agricultural raw materials and half-finished products: flax, hemp, tow, as well as leather, lumber, bristle, tallow, furs, and so on. The export of grain (rye, wheat, barley, oats)[3] was considerable, although unstable because of frequent crop failures. Russian imports consisted primarily of objects destined for consumption by the gentry: sugar, woolens, silk and cotton goods, dyes, coffee, wine, fruit, perfume, and so on.

At the same time, an important part of the export was made up of Russian manufactured products, primarily iron and duck. Industrial products constituted about 44.5 percent[4] of total Russian exports. In 1790 Russia's percentage of the world production of black metal was 35, and in 1794 Russia exported 3,885 thousand poods of iron, apparently the highest figure in prerevolutionary Russian history.[5]

In considering Russia of the late eighteenth and early nineteenth centuries one should not blindly accept the notion of its economic backwardness in comparison with Western Europe and America which was commonly held in the second half of the nineteenth century and the early twentieth century. In a well-known article, "Was the Russia of Catherine the Great an economically retarded country?" E. V. Tarle called attention to the thriving state of Russia's foreign trade. The distinguished researcher was especially impressed by the size of individual textile mills, enormous for those days, which employed many hundreds and even thousands of workers. Thus, Goncharov in Moscow employed 3,479 persons, Demidov in Peremyshl employed 472, and in 1793 the Kaluga linen and sailcloth factories employed 8,860 persons working on material for export.[6] Comparing these figures with the numbers of workers in French factories, Tarle, in his characteristic graphic manner called them "monstrous indeed"; at the same time he made an important reservation that "far from all of these thousands of workers employed by the Russian enterprises worked in the buildings of the manufactories."[7] This article, which for Tarle himself was only an incidental episode in his wide and many-sided activity, occasioned a great many arguments among historians. By today the economic history of eighteenth- and early nineteenth-century Russia has been studied much more profoundly, and much that once seemed odd and even improbable has been understood and logically explained.

The nature of serf manufacture was the subject of prolonged and sharp discussion in Soviet historiography. However, in the end a certain approximation of the points of view took place, and most researchers admitted the existence of a "mixed" character of manufacuring with forced labor combining feudal and capitalist elements.[8]

The high level of development of the mining industry, above all metallurgical production in the Urals, has been studied in detail by S. G.

Strumilin, V. V. Danilevsky, B. B. Kafengaus, and others.[9] Soviet researchers have taken into account Lenin's well-known statement that the mining industry of the Urals and the manufacture of woolens in European Russia were an example of "an original phenomenon in Russian life which consists in using serf labor in industry."[10] At one time "serfdom was the foundation of the highest prosperity in the Urals and its dominance not only in Russia, but to some extent also in Europe."[11] On the other hand, at a later period of capitalist prosperity it was the main reason for the stagnation and decay in the Urals. An 1805 register of factories and plants gives the number of iron-manufacturing plants as 151, blast furnaces as 224, furnaces as 40,[12] and overall production of cast iron in the country as 12 million poods.[13] Although the volume of metallurgical output in the beginning of the nineteenth century seems impressive, the negative consequences of the serf system already had begun to be felt. Industrial growth began to slow down, and from the end of the eighteenth century on the export of iron decreased. The annual export of iron averaged as follows (in thousands of poods): 1767-1769, 1,951; 1793-1795, 2,965; 1800-1814, 1,771.[14] In the world market there was increasing competition from cheap English iron, which, according to G. Nebo'sin, although of poorer quality than the Russian or Swedish product, was preferred.[15]

On the whole the main place in Russian foreign trade, in some cases an exclusive place, belonged to England.[16] Thus, between 1793 and 1795 England's share of Russia's exports constituted 80 percent of iron, 58 percent of hemp, and more than 60 percent of flax trade.[17] One must remember that the construction of the English navy depended to a large degree on Russian ship timber, hemp, sailcloth, and pitch.[18]

The volume of English-Russian trade was so considerable that its effect, both in the economic and political sphere, had contradictory results. Trade expansion is usually followed by an expansion and strengthening of political relations between two countries. The degree of political influence as a rule is directly dependent on the development of business, particularly commercial contacts. However, in this case, the volume of Russian-English commercial connections became excessive, threatening to make Russian trade completely dependent on England, and evoked a reverse reaction: the desire to free the country from the clutch of British merchants and to expand contacts with other countries.

Most Russian goods were transported at that time on English and to some extent on Dutch and other foreign ships, so Russia was deprived of a considerable share of profits from her foreign trade. And, although trade with England was always active, Russian profits were diminished by the payment for transportation on English vessels. Consequently, it was no accident that Russia, striving to enlarge its own commercial fleet, took up decisive defense of the freedom of neutral navigation and encouraged the expansion of trade with other countries. As has been noted, in the early eighties there was formed a League of Neutrals, headed by Russia, for the safeguarding of free commercial navigation based on the principles of the declaration of 1780, which had an obvious anti-English bias. Following that, Russia concluded a whole series of commercial treaties with European countries: Denmark in 1782; Austria in 1785; France, the Neapolitan Kingdom, and Portugal in 1786-87. It was characteristic that, for goods imported in the vessels of the contractual parties a lowering of the import duty was stipulated.

Professor Tarle long ago noted that trade with France at that period was rather significant. Thus, in 1782 France's import from Russia amounted to 9,721 livres, while its export to Russia came up only to 4,802 livres.[19] According to the new commercial treaty, France was considered one of the "most favored nations." Consequently, it is not surprising that British diplomacy was quite irritated by this treaty, and Russian-English relations were strained again.

By the late eighteenth century the foreign trade of the United States was developing in a way that was in some respects analogous to Russian foreign trade—if one keeps in mind the predominant role of England in the foreign trade of the country. As a result of a prolonged and persistent struggle the former English colonies in North America had won political independence; however, it proved much more difficult to acquire economic independence, and it was taking much longer. We must recall that in 1866 Karl Marx viewed the United States in a certain sense as a European colony, and its economic development as a product of European, and especially British, heavy industry.[20] In the course of the War of Independence economic connections with the mother country were interrupted, but trade with England continued through direct and, especially, indirect channels: British, Dutch and Danish possessions in the West Indies, Nova Scotia, and so on. One should also note that part of the territory of the separating colonies remained in the control of English troops (New York, the Carolinas, and Georgia) for a considerable length of time.

The end of the war and international recognition of the new republic in 1783 resulted in the expansion of United States trade connections, but did not produce basic changes in the general direction and character of foreign trade. Without waiting for the conclusion of final peace terms, in the spring of 1783 enterprising American merchants had begun to send their ships to various lands, first of all to the familiar possessions of the British Crown. A dispatch from London dated July 18, 1783, in *St. Peterburgskie Vedomosti*, states: "Americans did not fail to take advantage, with the greatest alacrity, of the signing of preliminary peace terms and not only sent a multitude of their goods to China, to our islands [i.e. English] in West India, but also brought back from here a goodly quantity of different products. Similarly, they prepared a not inconsiderable number of ships for the opening of trade with East India."[21]

Quite soon the practical Americans discovered that in becoming independent they had forfeited many advantages they had enjoyed as a part of the British colonial empire. In particular, they found themselves automatically cut off from the direct trade contacts with British West India. Earlier these trade connections amounted to 3.5 million dollars a year and, according to the specialists, constituted "the cornerstone of American commerce."[22] Having turned into a foreign power, the United States lost the right of free entry of ships into the British West Indies. At the same time English merchants were growing rich transporting American goods to the West Indies.

England's refusal to sign a commercial treaty produced great discontent in the United States. The proud mistress of the seas preferred to regulate its relations with her former colonies by the publication of one-sided proclamations. Only on the 19 November 1794 a special deputy of the United States, Chief Justice John Jay, and the English Minister of Foreign Affairs, Lord Grenville, signed a treaty of "amity, commerce, and navigation"; however, it was not fully reciprocal.[23] Although England's policy could not help but annoy the newly independent Americans, the new republic still had to trade with the mother country first of all. The reasons for this lay in the economic character of both countries, in the division of labor formed during the colonial period, and in historical traditions. English and American merchants were well acquainted with conditions in both countries and could draw upon many years of experience with mutual connections.

On the whole the development of the foreign trade of the United States after the conclusion of the War of Independence did not proceed smoothly. A short postwar boom was followed in 1785 by a deep depression.[24] The country was flooded by foreign goods and credit was undermined. Difficulties were increased by the weakness of a central government which had no authority either to regulate the trade or to establish a general tax system and introduce a single firm currency. By the end of the 1780's the economic situation had improved somewhat. The contributing factors were the consolidation of federal power resulting from the adoption of the Constitution of 1787, and the activities of the federal government in 1789, with President George Washington at its head.[25] The value of United States imports in 1790 was 23 million dollars, and the value of exports amounted to 20 million dollars.[26] By this time trade connections with Great Britain were fully restored. England and her possessions accounted for three-quarters of American imports and about half of the exports.[27] The loss inflicted on the American shipping by the closing of the British West Indies was compensated for by the establishment and development of trade with new countries and regions: the Far East (Canton), Mediterranean countries, and, finally, Russia.[28]

Such were the first steps in the development of the foreign trade of the young republic. The true heyday of American trade arrived somewhat later. The reasons for it, naturally, lay not in the special wisdom of the Founding Fathers and the merits of the Constitution of 1787, not in the tariff and navigational act, which encouraged trade and shipping and was ratified by the first Congress in 1789, and not in the administrative talents of Alexander Hamilton, the able young minister of finance, who was the main initiator of the "federalist program" approved by the Congress in 1789-1792. No matter how paradoxical it seems at first, the actual basis for America's commercial success was war in Europe. The epoch of prolonged and bloody wars which began in 1792-93 and shook the whole continent with short interruptions until 1814-15 proved to be a period of profits for American trade which were unheard-of until that time. This unprecedented flourishing of trade was noted by all observant eyewitnesses and subsequent investigators. P. P. Svin'in's testimony deserves special attention: "The enterprising spirit of Americans in commercial affairs, the superiority of their shipbuilding, with the help of the European war, in the past twenty years put, one may say, the trade of the whole world in their hands. In the last thriving years the American trade turnover was 200 million dollars annually, and about five thousand ships left their ports and came there loaded with goods." "It is possible," Svin'in continued, "that England will put all possible obstacles in the way of American trade, since she sees clearly that this nation through its enterprise and skill in trade will forever be a feared rival for her."[29]

Later historians have justifiably called this period of 1793-1807 (until the introduction of the embargo on December 22, 1807) "the golden age"[30] of American mercantile shipping. The general tonnage of the American fleet increased from 202,000 in 1789 to 1,269,000 in 1807, that is, more than six times.[31] Such an increase was unprecedented either in world history or in the history of the United States.[32] American historians cannot point to another equally prolonged period when trade attracted such attention and exercised such a decisive influence on the economic life of the country as a whole.[33] The income from foreign trade produced the greatest fortunes of that period. Elias Hasket Derby, John Jacob Astor, William Gray, and Stephen Girard became the richest men in America. Already toward the beginning of the nineteenth century American exports and imports reached proportions never seen until that time (93 and 111 million dollars respectively in 1801). The wars in Europe were sowing death and destruction, ruining merchants and shipowners, flagrantly destroying the normal commercial ties between countries. But that which signified ruin for European merchants brought unprecedented success and profits for Americans.

No sooner did an unstable peace develop in Europe, after the signing on March 25-27, 1802, of the Amiens peace between France and its allies, Spain and the Batavian republic, on one side, and England on the other,[34] than the curve of American trade swung downward. Fortunately for the United States, this peaceful breathing spell proved of short duration, and in the next round of European wars the general volume of American trade reached a figure in 1807, gigantic for those days, of 247 million dollars. (The subsequent decrease is connected with the introduction of embargo and the Anglo-American War of 1812.)[35]

Military actions in Europe, the upkeep of enormous armies, and crop failures resulted in increased demand for agricultural products. The growth of flour prices is indicative. If in 1783-1793 the cost of a barrel of flour in Philadelphia averaged $5.41, in 1793-1807 (excluding the years 1802 and 1803, when Europe was at peace) its cost rose to $9.12. In the 1820's, when Europe returned to normal peaceful life, flour prices returned to their former level of $5.46 per barrel.[36]

In the first decade of the nineteenth century the main culture of the American South, the foundation of its power and prosperity, was cotton. In the early 1790's cotton manufacture had consisted of 3,000 to 4,000 bales. Since then, influenced by the industrial revolution in England and later in the Northeast of the United States, which created enormous demand for it in the world market, the production of American cotton rose swiftly, reaching 100,000 bales in 1801, 146,000 in 1805, and 178,000 in 1810.[37] Tobacco, which had been the main product of the South for almost two centuries, in 1803 yielded the lead to cotton, the new and much more powerful "king" of American exports. In 1803 cotton export surpassed 7.9 million dollars in value, and in 1807 it reached 14.2 million.[38]

However, the enormous increase in American trade during these years was produced not so much by the export of American goods as by extensive re-exporting. Although in 1793 goods of foreign origin constituted only a very insignificant part of the nation's exports (2 out of 26 million dollars), by 1797, their value had risen to more than half of the general export (27 out of 51 million dollars). Subsequently, in spite of a considerable increase in the export of domestic products (to 46 million dollars in 1801 and 49 million in 1807), the re-export of foreign goods, with the exception of the years 1802-1804, continued to account for more than half of the total export of the country, reaching its highest level of 60 million dollars in 1806-07.[39]

Taking advantage of their neutral position, Americans supplied Europe with goods from the West Indies, South America, and the Orient. A considerable part of the great quantity of foreign goods which arrived in those years in American ports was reshipped in American vessels to most diverse countries upon receipt of a certificate of "neutrality" after payment of import duties. Thus, in 1807 out of total imports valued at 139 million dollars, only 79 million dollars worth was retained for domestic consumption; the rest was exported.[40]

Taking a leading place in neutral navigation, American ships supplied Europe with foodstuffs, especially flour, and transported to the mother country from the French West Indies sugar, coffee, and chocolate. The English utilized American ships to export their industrial products to the United States and to import from America cotton, grain, flour, tobacco, as well as for the export of English goods into European ports.[41] The tonnage of foreign ships utilized in the American foreign trade in 1793 constituted 26 percent of the total tonnage in foreign trade; in 1807 it was 6.8 percent, and in 1811 only 3.4 percent.[42] Thus, the enormous foreign trade of the United States was conducted almost exclusively in American bottoms, and their tonnage in 1807 was greater than that of a hundred years later.[43]

The great dimensions of the mercantile navigation of the United States made that country especially concerned with the strict observance of the navigation rights of neutral nations, whose consistent defender Russia had been ever since 1780. Later, in December 1800, Russia concluded new conventions with Denmark, Sweden, and Prussia which formed what came to be known as the Second Armed Neutrality.[44] On the whole, the defense of the freedom of neutral navigation constituted the firm basis of Russian-American rapprochement ever since the War of Independence. Another important factor in the establishment of relations between the two countries was commercial contacts.

By the time of the Declaration of Independence in 1776 commercial ties between North America and Russia already had a rather solid, albeit indirect prehistory. Individual American ships made contraband runs into St. Petersburg,[45] but in the majority of cases the intermediary of commercial contacts between Russia and America was the mother country. The question of the export of Virginia tobacco to Russia has been studied in detail. In 1698, during Peter the Great's stay in England, an agreement was signed by which a quantity of American tobacco (1,216 thousand pounds in 1699, and 1,450 thousand pounds in 1700) was delivered to Russia. But the British exporters did not take into account that in peasant Russia the demand for overseas tobacco was extremely limited, and very soon the English had to worry, not about fulfilling the conditions of agreement and increase of the export, but about pulling out of their "tobacco adventure in Russia" without too great a loss. Only as a consequence of prolonged negotiations did the British envoy Charles Whitworth succeed in the spring of 1706 in winning Peter the Great's agreement to accept the unsold tobacco into the government treasury.[46]

Throughout the entire eighteenth century the export of American tobacco to Russia never even came close to attaining the 1699-1700 level, and only in isolated periods, for example, 1711-1713 and 1769, did it rise to 150-190 thousand pounds.[47] In the second half of the eighteenth century Russia herself became an exporter of tobacco to the European market, and toward the end of the War of Independence, because of the discontinuance of American exports, the export of tobacco from St. Petersburg and Riga reached millions of pounds.[48] Besides Virginia tobacco, the American products reaching Russia via England included rice, indigo, and furs. On the other hand, the English colonies in North America, again mainly via the mother country, imported goods needed for shipbuilding such as high quality hemp, flax, and Ural iron.

From the point of view of her trade interests, Russia's attitude toward the separation of the North American colonies from the mother country was mixed, and the perspectives of business contacts with the new republic were unclear. On the one hand, the United States Declaration of Independence seemed to create possibilities for the development of Russian trade and opened perspectives for the establishment of direct connections with the overseas republic. This point of view was held by the author of a memorandum on the advantages of direct commercial contacts with the United States. He pointed out that America, while still an English colony, imported via the mother country a considerable amount of cast iron and steel from Sweden, and that, having achieved independence, would undoubtedly be able to import these goods directly from Sweden or Russia.[49]

Another memorandum developed in detail the idea that if America achieved independence it would soon be able to supply southern Europe with "all the naval gear and all the products that at present are supplied by Russia and Baltic countries" and in a few years would become "the greatest mercantile power."[50]

Along with this memorandum other reports came from abroad at this period testifying to the possible competition of American goods. Specifically, Russian consul F. Brandenburg wrote from Cadiz on September 22, 1781, expressing apprehension that, "if North America establishes independence and the number of her inhabitants increases, they will undertake the cultivation of flax and hemp, and they already have timber, tar, pitch, wax, and other goods which come from the north, and will be able to supply all the southern regions with these goods at advantageous prices and with greater ease than it is possible for the north."[51] Referring to the geographic advantages of American ports and the convenience of year-round maritime communications, Brandenburg reported: "Ships from Boston arrive at Cadiz in twenty or thirty days, while the northern bottoms require for this voyage eighty or ninety days, and, on top of it, sometimes are forced to winter over in Norway."[52]

Some interesting information about American success in the cultivation of hemp and the desire to acquire the fertile lands contiguous to Mississippi was offered about ten years later by William Eton in his memorandum "Sur le Chanvre de l'Amérique," which is preserved among the papers of A. R. Vorontsov. Incidentally, it is interesting that Eton mentions in his memorandum some Americans who "took great pains to gather information on the means of processing hemp after harvesting."[53] This report is one of the early evidences of direct business contacts between Russians and Americans. Unfortunately, Eton does not mention the names of American citizens then in Russia. However, it is clear from the memorandum that Americans testified that hemp could be processed more cheaply than it was done in Russia, if the machines run by the energy of numerous American rivers were used. Eton concluded that, although Americans did not yet have sufficient hemp for their own consumption and for trade of any significant volume, nevertheless they did cultivate it and soon would no longer need to import it.

There was good reason to fear the competition of American goods on the European market; agricultural products predominated in both Russian and American exports. One must also take into account the mercenary influence and the opposition of England, which maintained a firm grasp on the Russian and American markets and was interested in preventing direct contact between Russia and the United States. However, on the whole, both in governmental circles and especially among the Russian public, the opinion prevailed that the emergence of a new independent state was advantageous for Russia and that it was desirable to establish and develop direct Russian-American mercantile connections.

In the summer of 1779 leaders of the Department of Foreign Affairs, in a secret report to the Empress pointing out the advantages of the separation of the English colonies in North America from the mother country, referred to the enlargement of Russian trade, "because England, having lost through the rebellion of her colonies the whole import of their products is compelled to replace them by ours, not only for re-export but also for their own consumption." The authors of the report stressed further that "American colonies undertook the cultivation of products suitable for their climate only when the British government imposed heavy duties on their importation from abroad, or, on the other hand, when it allotted substantial monetary rewards in their favor." Finally, presenting their well-known conclusion that in the long run the separation of the colonies from England, "may be not only not harmful, but on the contrary useful for Russian mercantile interests," the leaders of the Department of Foreign Affairs predicted that, in time, "a new direct branch of commerce" would open up between Russia and America.[54]

As has been noted, American trade was advocated by the Russian press (the Supplement to *Moskovskie Vedomosti, Politicheskii Zhurnal*, and others). D. M. Ladygin insistently recommended the new American market "to the attention and enterprise" of the Russian merchants.[55] His opinion about the expediency of the establishment and development of trade relations between Russia and the United States is especially interesting because it was based on information and experience gained in the course of his many years in the Department of Commerce. A book by Karl Snell on mercantile profits derived from the independence of the United States of North America by the Russian state was published in 1783 in Riga.[56] Its author predicted that American "productions" (masts, timber, pitch, tar, iron, and so on) would not lead to serious loss for Russian trade, "since they themselves are in need of a great part of it, especially of what pertains to the equipment of their fleet, and partly because these products are not as good a quality as the Russian ones, especially in respect to size, thickness, and firmness of masts." Similar considerations were expressed with regard to Russian iron. Snell noted that "Russia will not only retain her customers, but will get some new ones through disposing of canvas and duck which Americans use to clothe Negroes." On the whole, the Russian state, according to him, could hope to receive "great profits," and the Russians would "not be the last ones" to see in their harbors American ships with West Indian products. [57] The extent to which these considerations and prognoses were justified can be judged through a concrete analysis of the development of early Russian-American trade contacts.

IV

TRADE CONNECTIONS BETWEEN RUSSIA AND THE UNITED STATES

The first trade contacts between Russia and the young American republic are usually considered to have been established toward the end of the War of Independence. In his letter of July 13/24, 1783, Francis Dana wrote to Robert Livingston, the Secretary of Foreign Affairs, about the arrival in Riga of an American vessel.[1] A Boston ship of five hundred tons, under the command of Captain Daniel McNeill, had come up from Lisbon with a cargo of tropical goods (sugar, rice, fruit) and some salt and brandy. Earlier still, one Jeremiah Allen, an enterprising Boston merchant, had sojourned in Riga and in St. Petersburg and had shipped a valuable cargo of Russian linens, cordage, hemp, and iron to America aboard the *Kingston*, under the command of Captain Norwood. Officially, this ship's port of registry was St. Petersburg; she was probably an English ship operating under a Russian flag. Having returned to the United States in December 1783, Allen advertised his Russian goods in the *Boston Gazette,* and promised to offer "every possible information" on the Russian market "if any gentleman inclines to send a ship that way."[2]

Samuel Eliot Morison mentions that in May 1784 George Cabot of Beverly sent his ships the *Buccaneer* and the *Commerce* to the Baltic and to St. Petersburg. James Duncan Phillips has offered an interesting note on the plucky Salem merchants and seafarers who had opened a direct trade with Russia in those years.[3] It has been assumed that the Americans, whose ships by that time had begun to make their way to far-off countries, pioneered in establishing the first commercial contacts with Russia, and that the appearance of the Russian mercantile flag off American shores did not occur until the first decade of the nineteenth century. This arrival is connected with a courageous venture of the Russian merchant Kseno-font Anfilatov, who, in 1806-7 with the support of the government, sent two large vessels to America from St. Petersburg and Archangel.[4]

The role of the enterprising Massachusetts merchants and seafarers and of the Russian merchant from Archangel in initiating direct commercial ties between the two countries should not be underestimated. However, the perusal of documentary materials suggests the possibility that Russian-American contacts had been in existence as early as the period of the War of Independence. In a June 1782 secret report by the College of Foreign Affairs to Catherine II it is stated that "the whole aim of the famous system of maritime neutrality" consisted in "ensuring the safety of navigation and commerce of neutral nations, which would give tangible encouragement to our own trade. That this aim has been achieved in two years is evidenced by the appearance of the Russian merchant flag *even in America.*"[5]

Nonetheless, for a long time it was impossible to support this claim by means of direct documentary evidence. It is true that a significant work of the period on the subject of Russian trade does state that, "during the American war Russian vessels sailed from Bordeaux to America." However, the author, G. Nebolsin, does not supply any additional references which might have helped to confirm this statement.[6] Gradually, however, archival search led me closer to the goal. The fund of the College of Commerce of the Central State Archive of the Ancient Acts contains an interesting report of the Russian consul in Bordeaux, Arvid Wittfooth (in Russian documents, A. Vitfot), dated May 12, 1788 and entitled "On the benefits of establishing Russian trade with the United States." In those days Bordeaux served as one of the most important centers for supplying the rebellious colonists with necessary goods, which included, one learns from Wittfooth's report, some Russian products. "United American Provinces have sent a consul," he wrote, "who will remain here to manage the affairs of these provinces. Since various goods, including Russian produce, are sent to them, it would be desirable if some Russian goods were sent here for consignment,[7] especially duck, which is being bought in great quantities for American ships and imported there. I have already discussed the matter with the American consul, who assured me that it will also be very advantageous for America."[8]

Wittfooth's report concerning his contacts with the American consul in Bordeaux and shipment of Russian goods to America, was received by the College of Commerce without any censure, although this body could not sanction his proposals officially without prior consultation with the College of Foreign Affairs. On August 8/19, in accordance with the ukase of

Catherine II, the College of Commerce considered Wittfooth's report and reached the following decision. "Since the setting up of a consul in France for the American colonies is a new venture, and whereas Russian merchants have not so far been engaged in direct trade with American merchants, and whereas this might entail some difficulties with regard to political matters, the College of Commerce cannot advise the undertaking of such a trade by Russian merchants without first communicating with the College of Foreign Affairs; for which purpose a memorandum is being sent to that College, from whom notification is to be expected."[9]

This document, signed on September 5/16, 1778, is interesting not only for its general message. Alexander Radishchev is among its signatories. The attitude of the author of *A Journey from Petersburg to Moscow* toward America and the American Revolution is quite well known, but even most specialists are unaware of the fact that Radishchev was involved in establishing the earliest contacts with the new republic in the course of his practical activity. The great Russian revolutionary resolutely supported Russian-American ties, and made known his hope that ships of the United States "will not tire of visiting us."[10]

How long the College of Commerce had to wait for notification from the Department of Foreign Affairs and whether it was ever received has not been established. However, the extensive correspondence of Wittfooth with the Department of Foreign Affairs makes it possible to evaluate his actions as Russian consul in Bordeaux and provides a picture of general conditions there in the beginning of the 1780's. At that time lively contacts were maintained between the United States and France, and, as Wittfooth noted, American ships frequently docked in Bordeaux. In December 1778, the Consul reported "From now on Russian ships will find profitable carrying trade in this port," since the Russian flag "is respected by British privateers more than that of any other nation."[11] Respect for the Russian flag had grown significantly in the wake of the Declaration of Armed Neutrality in February 1780. Insurance companies, according to Wittfooth's reports of August 1780, began to insure Russian ships at 4 and 8 percent,[12] thus furthering still more favorable conditions for the development of trade.

Finally, new confirmation of the fact that Russian ships were being sent to America has been discovered among the extremely rich collection of the papers of the Vorontsovs in the manuscripts file of the Leningrad division of the Institute of History of the Academy of Sciences. It came in a form of a highly interesting report, dated July 30, 1782, to the College of Commerce, from that same Wittfooth. An excerpt of it runs as follows:

At present there are many Russian ships here, a number of which are loaded with cargo for America. The Russian flag under present circumstances is more advantageous than that of other nations, and because of that these ships can get very profitable freights, which is all the more flattering for me since I laid the beginnings of this very advantageous opportunity for the Russian ships. For this reason I try to the utmost of my ability to prevent any possible embarrassment, to inspect the shippers' documents and watch to make sure that they do not load any forbidden goods onto their ships. Although skipper Brand, who arrived here from St. Petersburg and was loaded hence for America, had indeed been taken by an English privateer, it is said that he has been freed upon the payment of 1500 pound sterling as the recompense for the loss. The aforesaid skipper's documents, which I examined upon his departure, were in complete order, because of which I hope that, if in the future Russian ships encounter a similar occurrence, they will be dealt with in England with equal justice.[13]

In evaluating Wittfooth's information, one should examine it from a perspective of the basic fact it establishes: the existence of the trade contacts between the United States and Russia and the sailing of Russian ships to the shores of the faraway republic during the period of the War of Independence. The document makes it evident that these commercial ties were neither an accidental episode nor a historical curiosity; they "blended" into the general international situation of that time and were quite explicable and even natural occurrences.

At that period the United Sates badly needed to establish commercial contacts with European countries and was striving to utilize every opportunity to develop them. At the same time, Russia was actively engaged in the struggle to safeguard the freedom of neutral navigation and was encouraging the enlargement of her own merchant fleet. By 1779 the number of Russian vessels passing through the Sound rose to sixty-two; esteem for the Russian flag by the maritime powers was growing; and even the proud mistress of the seas was forced to reckon with the head of the League of Neutrals. Therefore, it is not surprising that the Russian flag became "more advantageous than that of other nations," and that Russian ships received "very profitable freights" from the Americans too, since the safety of transportation was especially important for them.[14]

The United States continued to be vitally interested in developing trade contacts with Russia after the end of the War of Independence. On April 15, 1784, the Continental Congress passed a resolution pointing out the desirability for the United States to sign special treaties of amity and commerce with Russia, Austria, Prussia, and other European countries. John Adams, Benjamin Franklin, and Thomas Jefferson were commissioned to undertake the appropriate negotiations.[15] Referring to this resolution, John C. Hildt states that no such treaty was concluded.[16] This is correct, although, as the materials in Russian archives demonstrate, the Americans did attempt to open negotiations. On September 22, 1784, Adams, Franklin, and Jefferson sent a letter to I. S. Bariatinsky, the Russian minister in Paris, informing him that the American Congress, mindful that commerce between Russian subjects and American citizens, "founded on principles of equality, reciprocity, and friendship, may be of mutual advantage to both nations," had commissioned them (May 12, 1784) to begin negotiations for a treaty of amity and commerce with an appropriate Russian representative, provided that the Empress would grant him the necessary authority for this purpose.[17]

On the same day David Humphrey, secretary of the American commission for obtaining the treaty, asked for a meeting with Bariatinsky, in order to transmit to him the letter of the American deputies.[18] The meeting took place on September 26. However, "the American secretary for negotiation expressed himself with great difficulty in French," and the Russian minister "did not possess knowledge of the English tongue"; consequently, "their conversation could not have been very far-reaching." Accepting the letter, Bariatinsky could only promise to forward it to St. Petersburg, and Humphrey let it be understood that the American deputies were anxious and hopeful that Catherine II "might deign to grant them the favor of a reply."[19] So far as can be judged by the correspondence with Paris which I have perused (1784-85), Catherine II did not "deign" to grant a reply, although Bariatinsky's report with its accompanying documentation was received on October 9/20, 1784.

Two years later, however, Secretary of Foreign Affairs John Jay informed Congress that American "treaties with France, the United Netherlands, Sweden, Russia, etc. . . . stipulate to each 'the right of the most favored nation.' "[20] What Jay meant by "Russia" is difficult to surmise. Hildt supposes it to be Prussia, with which country a treaty containing such an article had been signed on September 10, 1785. Even without a treaty, however, trade relations between Russia and the new republic managed to develop quite normally in the aftermath of the War of Independence, with no special limitation imposed on either side.

On June 15, 1784, the bark *Light Horse*, belonging to Elias Hasket Derby and under the command of Captain Nehemiah Buffington, sailed from Salem, with a cargo of sugar destined for sale in Russia. Unfortunately, upon their arrival in Kronstadt, the Americans could not elicit any special interest in their cargo and had to sell it at a loss. To make up for this, they loaded the boat with a return cargo consisting of commodities necessary for shipbuilding and valuable for export: hemp, canvas, and iron. Derby was advised against sending large cargoes to Russia by the agents in St. Petersburg, Gale, Hill, and Carzalet, who recommended drafts on London as the best purchasing medium.[21]

Another pioneer in establishing direct connections with Russia was the brig *Hector*, under the command of John Little, which made the voyage to St. Petersburg from Salem with a stopover in Charleston in 1783-84, and another voyage in 1786-87. The *Light Horse* also returned to Russia, first in 1785, via Martinique, and in 1786 by a direct route. According to James Duncan Phillips, at least nineteen voyages to the Baltic were made before the end of 1790, some direct, and others with stopovers to collect cargo in the Southern states or the West Indies.[22] Naturally the accuracy of such information must remain relative, but it does at least indicate the minimal number of American vessels which voyaged to Russia in those years.

Somewhat more complete, though hardly systematic, data can be found in the Russian sources, namely, the so-called "Kronstadt reports" which recorded the arrivals of foreign ships in the port of St. Petersburg.[23] Unfortunately, there are many years for which the reports have not been preserved, and even some of the preserved materials have certain omissions. Reports for 1781-1784 have substantial gaps, and no notations of American ships were found for those years.[24] On the other hand, there were discovered, among the Kronstadt reports for the late 1790's, some general registers of Russian trade which had been signed by the President of the College of Commerce, A. R. Vorontsov, during the middle 1780's. From the register for 1785 it may be gathered that 2,145 vessels arrived in Russian ports. Of these 640 were English, 100 Russian, 18 French, 9 Spanish, 6 American, and many of Dutch, Danish, Swedish, and other nationalities.[25] During the following year, there were 2,155 vessels, including 705 English, 107 Russian, 14 French, 4 Spanish, and 10 American.[26]

Russian foreign trade in those years was carried principally through the port of St. Petersburg, which attracted more than 60 percent of the country's maritime commerce.[27] The other Baltic ports (Riga, Reval, Narva) also had substantial trade. In 1787, of the total number of 803 ships which docked in the port of St. Petersburg, 400 were English, 64 Russian, 17 French, 5 Spanish, and 11 American.[28] In 1792 there were 932 arrivals, including 517 British vessels, 98 Danish, and 22 American.[29] Obviously, American ships constituted only a negligible fraction of the total number of the foreign ships in Russian ports, but the very fact of their appearance and a budding of trade contacts with the overseas republic is significant. For it was precisely in those years that Americans had their chance to become acquainted with the Russian market and that the two countries engaged for the first time in commercial relations with any degree of regularity. These contacts demonstrated that former apprehensions regarding the potential competition of American goods in the European market had proved to be exaggerated. Arguing against such an opinion of "badly informed persons" in his letter to Osterman of January 31/February 11, 1789, John Paul Jones had called the attention of the Vice-Chancellor to the fact that every year since the end of the War of Independence, Americans had sent many vessels to Russian ports to collect cargoes consisting precisely of those commodities which Russia supplied to France and England.[30]

The earliest Russian-American commercial contacts were not in vain, for the number of vessels arriving in the Russian ports gradually increased. In 1792, 24 American ships arrived in St. Petersburg, in 1795 there were 42 (or 44), in 1798 there were 39, in 1801 there were 61, and so on.[31] In the course of the decade (1791-1800), 368 American ships arrived in Kronstadt, and according to some data (A. I. Dashkov's report), this figure can be raised to 500.[32] A more complete idea of the volume of Russian trade, and in particular of the number of the American ships in Russian ports, can be gained from the annual surveys of state trade. These were published from 1802 on, at the initiative of the new minister of commerce, N. P. Rumiantsev. These materials, in tabular form, give an idea of the number of American vessels and the significance of their role in Russia's commercial navigation.[33]

In 1807 the number of American vessels arriving in and departing from Russian ports was greater than 90. Although American vessels accounted for less than 4 percent of the total number of ships engaged in Russian

Year	Total of vessels arriving	Baltic ports			White Sea ports			Total of vessels leaving with cargo
		Arrived		Left with cargo	Arrived		Left with cargo	
		with cargo	without cargo		with cargo	without cargo		
1802	64	37	26	61	1	–	2	63
1803	85	27	58	85	–	–	–	85
1804	69	29	40	66	–	–	–	66
1805	69	26	43	68	–	–	–	68
1806	78	40	38	77	–	–	–	77
1807	91	36	54	90	–	1	2	92

commercial navigation (in 1807, 2,476 vessels with cargoes left Russia),[34] their presence becomes apparent. In fact, we may gather that the American flag at that time became a familiar sight, and, later, during the continental blockade, a welcome one, in Russian harbors.

The export of American goods to Russia presents a much more complex picture. The earliest sources of information that allow us to form any conclusions concerning the volume of American trade with Russia appeared in the American statistics in the 1790's.[35]

Year	Dollars	Year	Dollars	Year	Dollars	
1790	–	1796	47,381	1802	73,721	
1791	3,570	1797	3,450	1803	–	
1792	4,669	1798	60,732	1804	–	
1793	5,769	1799	46,030	1805	12,044[a]	59,328[b]
1794	90,388	1800	–	1806	3,580	8,827
1795	69,221	1801	9,136	1807	78,850	366,367

[a] American goods
[b] Foreign goods

The above data, quoted from official sources, show that the volume of American exports to Russia was extremely slight. No wonder, therefore, that the impression had long prevailed in historical literature that commerce between the two countries was insignificant. American researchers, largely preoccupied with diplomatic history, tended to neglect economic factors, observing at most, that the trade of the United States with Russia was "exceedingly small and unimportant."[36]

This point of view seems inaccurate and should be revised. Official data on American exports to Russia are indeed very slight. Moreover, the actual figures are so minute as to seem implausible to a modern researcher—especially when juxtaposed with the number of vessels entering Russian ports. It is hard to imagine that dozens of American ships crossed the vast Atlantic for the sole purpose of delivering to St. Petersburg goods whose value sometimes was below ten thousand dollars. It makes no sense, and there is an added incongruity in it being done by practical Yankees, with their business acumen.

The explanation for this apparent paradox lies in the fact that these ships brought to Russia fewer goods of American origin than foreign products from the West Indies and South America. "The United States," wrote Nebolsin somewhat later, "are the main intermediary between Russia and American domains, since it is known that sugar which is brought in American ships comes from Havana and Brazil, and that the Russian cordage and canvas are used not only in the United States proper, but are largely shipped to the West Indies, Brazil, and other countries on the American continent."[37]

In the table above, the United States export of foreign products is calculated separately only for the last three years (1805-1807). With the exception of 1807, when the continental blockade began to be felt ($366,000), the volume of re-export is also slight. This is explained apparently by the fact that only the re-export of foreign goods from the United States was subject to registry, and not the direct intermediary trade which might have been substantial before 1807.

In his general evaluation of Russia's commercial ties with America, Nebolsin noted that American ships brought two-thirds of the whole Russian consumption of raw sugar, and part of the coffee, cotton, sandalwood, indigo, and other commodities.[38] The following figures suggest some notion of the volume of this trade: in 1793-1795 total Russian imports of raw and refined sugar amounted to 341,356 poods, and in 1800-1814 the annual import averaged 244,715 poods of raw sugar, plus 172,760 poods of refined sugar. "In recent years the importing of sugar has much increased, as a result of North American mediation, while previously Russia was supplied primarily by Great Britain," Nebolsin wrote. There was also considerable importing of coffee (for the years 1793-1795, the annual average was 74,811 poods, and for 1800-1814, 91,829), "primarily from America, but also from Great Britain and Hanseatic towns."[39] Cotton imports rose sharply in these years: in 1793-1795 the average was 9,616 poods, and in 1800-1814, 50,615. "American ships which previously arrived in our ports with ballast," Nebolsin noted, "now besides sugar, import some cotton."[40]

Nebolsin's data and conclusions refer to the whole period of 1800-1814 and therefore give an exaggerated picture of the export of the United States to Russia for the first years of the nineteenth century. We shall have an occasion later to consider the sharp rise in Russian-American commerce in 1809-1811. Nevertheless, these figures do reflect to a degree a tendency toward an increase in trade with America which by 1807 was making itself felt, however weakly and dimly.

American statistics provide little information about goods exported to Russia before 1807. Numerous tables provided by Timothy Pitkin contain insignificant notations for these years indicating that in 1807 there was exported to Russia 149,271 pounds of coffee, 52,852 pounds of raw sugar, and 297,844 pounds of refined sugar, and, in scattered years, unimportant quantities of whale oil, rice, pork, and beef.[41] On the other hand,

Nebolsin's work and a survey of Russian-American trade, compiled by Dashkov in June 1808, indicate that sugar, coffee, cotton, indigo, peppers, spices, and other products were exported to Russia in rather large quantities.[42]

Until now we have discussed primarily the American re-export of foreign goods. This is a matter of common knowledge, long and well established. However, the researchers usually did not take into account that the goods of the United States and the Latin American countries were shipped to many European countries not directly, but via Great Britain, the Hanseatic towns, and so on. Friedrich Engels, summarizing Gülich's book *Geschichtliche Darstellung des Handels,* called attention to the fact that after the War of Independence Bremen came to occupy a central place in the European trade of American tobacco, and Hamburg in coffee and sugar. The scale of the trade can be judged by the fact that, in 1795, 236 vessels from the United States docked in Hamburg and the same number in Bremen. Both these towns became important continental entrepôts for colonial trade.[43]

These goods certainly reached the Russian market too, although formally they were not considered imports from America; as Nebolsin wrote: "The import of tobacco is largely American leaf, up to 30,000 poods, from Great Britain, the Hanseatic towns, and Holland." It is significant that the United States is not mentioned among supplying countries, even though it was their tobacco that was sold on the Russian market. As to England, the Hanseatic towns, and Holland, it is common knowledge that they never produced any tobacco and themselves purchased it from the United States. Nebolsin also mentions cotton—"American raw cotton," Russia's import of which (mainly from Great Britain, with small quantities from the United States) reached 70,000 poods.[44] Although cotton came mainly from England, it was never grown there; the cotton sold to Russia came from the United States.

American products were brought to Russia by the English and other intermediaries with "extra charges for import duty and profit,"[45] a situation extremely disadvantageous for Russian consumers. Touching upon this question, the Minister of Commerce, N. P. Rumiantsev, in a special memorandum of May 4/16, 1806, observed that the Hanseatic towns "grew rich while passing foreign goods into foreign hands." "If these causes are removed," he wrote, "we should be able to get raw sugar directly from America, the money which the Hamburgers extract from us for commission and profit would stay in the country, and the number of sugar refineries will increase." The Minister foresaw "special profits as soon as we enter the direct trade with places where the above-mentioned towns procure the goods for passing on to us," and he considered that Russian shipping should be increased for this reason.[46]

In the annual report of the Ministry of Commerce for 1805 Rumiantsev also set forward the advantages of "direct commerce with the United States in America." "Of colonial goods," the report pointed out, "sugar is a necessary staple among our foodstuffs. Cotton has become a similar necessity for our textile mills. These two items extract from us up to 8 million rubles, besides that cotton which is brought from Asia. In carrying these products from America to us, and our goods to America, England not only took the profits which by rights should belong to us, but knew how to take measures so that the Americans kept their goods at prices equal to those charged by other nations delivering their goods via Europe."[47]

Finally, in analyzing American exports to Russia, we must remember that a considerable percentage of American vessels arrived at Russian ports with ballast. In some years (for example, 1803) the number of American vessels without cargo (58) was more than double the number of ships with cargo (27). Obviously, these ships did not come to Kronstadt for pleasure, even if many had previously cleared in England or on the continent. In making an empty voyage they obviously counted on buying valuable and important goods on the Russian market. Apparently their hopes never proved vain: in any case, American ships as a rule left Russian ports with full cargoes. It is significant that, while American statistical information on exports to Russia before 1807 is of a symbolic rather than a practical nature, by the 1790's the importing of Russian goods to America had reached a substantial volume.[48]

Year	Dollars	Year	Dollars	Year	Dollars
1795	1,168,715	1797	1,418,418	1799	1,274,913
1796	1,382,878	1798	1,067,152	1800	1,524,995
				1801	1,672,054

Taken abstractly, these figures are not impressive. Nevertheless, they were many times—sometimes even hundreds of times—higher than the figures of American exports to Russia, and already were significant. Although the share of Russian goods rarely constituted more than 1 1/2 percent, and always less than 2 percent of total United States imports, one should not belittle its importance, especially since most American imports came from England, and the place left for all the other countries was not large.

Goods exported from Russia to America in significant quantities included such important ones as iron, hemp, cordage, duck, flemish linen, bristle, tallow, leather, and various kinds of cloth. Of iron and iron products alone exports from St. Petersburg to America were: 6,615 poods in 1783; 182,473 poods in 1793; and 414,076 poods in 1803. In the same years, figures for hemp of various sorts were 7,943, 160,276, and 362,067 poods; for sailcloth, 500, 13,391, and 32,190 bolts; for wide and narrow linen, 27,304, 13,288, and 318,643 archines.[49] In the early years of the nineteenth century the export of linen alone by American ships averaged 1,363,000 rubles. The total value of hemp, linen and cordage imported into the United States from Russia came close to 2 1/2 million rubles in value.[50] The United States' share of the total export of iron from Russia was increasing sharply. Although in 1797-98 England's share of Russian iron export was 85 percent, and that of the United States was 9.5 percent, in the years between 1801 and 1807 England's share decreased to 71.5 percent, and that of the United States increased to 21.5 percent.[51] According to official American data, in 1802-1804 the average value of Russian import commodities paying ad valorem duties (iron and goods of hemp and flax) constituted 1,302,217 dollars; in 1807 it increased to 1,804,860 dollars. According to the same data, in 1802-1804 the United States imported on the average 88,330 cwt. of Russian hemp at a cost of 779,473 dollars; in 1807 imports reached 135,775 cwt. In addition, the United States imported tarred and non-tarred cordage to the amount of 1,007,780 and 6,843 pounds, and cables to the amount of 57,579 pounds.[52]

The most complete idea of the volume of Russian-American trade between 1783 and 1806 can be gathered from information provided in the work of the Danish researcher Aage Rasch. During these years Americans imported from St. Petersburg 393,460 poods of iron; 365,503 poods of hemp; 27,986 poods of cordage; 369,365 bolts of sailcloth; and 333,027 bolts of duck.[53]

Although these figures might not seem impressive judged by modern standards, their significance for their period should not be underestimated. As Alfred Crosby noted, in those years "the American economy survived and prospered because it had access to the unending labor and rough skill of the Russian muzhik." Despite the extravagance of this statement, one must to some extent agree with Crosby: Russian hemp, linen, and iron "were prosaic but absolutely essential"[54] for the United

States. Of course Americans could grow flax and hemp and smelt steel and cast iron themselves, but according to contemporary opinion, their quality left much to be desired when compared to the Russian products. Small wonder that experienced American seamen preferred cordage made from Russian hemp even if it cost twice as much as the native Kentucky product! The decisive factor was quality: the strength of cables made of Russian hemp, metal lashings made of Zlotoust steel, and sails made of Russian flax.

It is also difficult to evaluate the real significance to Russia of ties with the United States. Unreliable official data on the value of American export to Russia has already been mentioned as has the role of England as an intermediary in eighteenth-century trade connections between Russia and North America. Although up to 1807, the volume of Russian-American trade gradually increased, its role in the country's total trade balance, even taking into account the export of Russian goods to America, was not great. But one should consider more than just the direct practical significance of early Russian-American trade connections. Business contacts with the American market were in their infancy, so naturally their volume could not have been very large. The political significance, however, should be emphasized: in the 1790's revolutionary France and Russia were at war, and republican America and Russia were engaged in trade. This alone indicates the basic difference between tsarist Russia's French and American policy. Let us keep in mind that the atmosphere of the feudal serfdom reaction, which in the last years of Catherine II's reign had been steadily increasing through fear of the menacing events of the great French revolutionary storm of 1789-1794, had reached its zenith during the reign of Paul I (1796-1801). The arrest of N. I. Novikov followed the ruthless punishment of Alexander Radishchev. Police persecutions of other representatives of the Russian intelligentsia were initiated. The government savagely repressed the peasant disturbances which during Paul I's reign involved thirty-two provinces. In foreign policy tsarist Russia was a violent enemy of the French Revolution from its very inception. However, because of her desire to preserve freedom of action in the East and in Poland, the government of Catherine II refrained from direct participation in the first anti-French coalition. Later, during Paul I's reign, Russian troops were sent to Europe and, in the last years of the eighteenth century, participated in the war against France as a part of the Second Coalition.

At the same time relations with the Americans, especially with the members of the ruling Federalist party, were not at all hostile. The friendly relations which Gouverneur Morris had established first with V. P. Kochubei and then with S. R. Vorontsov are colorful and curious illustrations. Young Kochubei made Morris' acquaintance in Paris, and as the latter's Diary shows, they had many social encounters.[55] There seems to be nothing surprising in the closeness of the young count to an American. Another future member of the Secret Committee (Neglasny Komitet), young Pavel Stroganov, a pupil of montagnard Gilbert Romme and a lover of one of the most outstanding women of the French Revolution, Téroigne de Méricourt, frequented sessions of the National Assembly and the Jacobin Club. The surprises came later. Introducing Morris in a letter to Vorontsov, the Russian ambassador in London, Kochubei wrote: "I asked Mr. Morris to present my letter in person, in the belief that you will not be displeased to make the acquaintance of a well-informed man, with a very good understanding of the affairs of this country: a rare thing, especially if one thinks of the exaggerated pictures both in England and elsewhere by men attached to prejudiced parties. It is not that I am always of the same opinion as this American, but I believe him to be, in spite of his attachment to the *ancien régime,* very reasonable."[56] Although on the whole Kochubei emphasizes Morris' moderation and impartiality, the phrase "in spite of" (malgré) says a great deal. "Malgré son attachement à l'ancien régime"—that is, feudal-absolutist France of Louis XVI. This is a not too flattering (but basically true) comment on a Founding Father whose signature adorns the federal constitution of 1787.

In that period the young Kochubei could be considered a "liberal," and in the eyes of many fanatical reactionaries he looked even like a revolutionary. Semen Romanovich Vorontsov was a quite different kind of person. This extremely conservative statesman of Catherinian times hated the French Revolution violently. Unlike in age, disposition, and views, Vorontsov and Kochubei had identical feelings toward Morris. With rare success Morris found the key to the heart of the noble ambassador, who in July 1795 wrote to his brother, future chancellor of the Russian empire A. R. Vorontsov as follows:

No doubt you will be surprised to learn that two days ago I encountered a very well-informed man. He is Mr. Morris, for three years American Minister in France, whom I knew here before he left for Paris. He detested the French Revolution, as he is a man of judgment and knowledge and professes the same principles as his compatriot, Mr. Adams. In Paris he could never conceal his scorn for all that took place there, and, far from aiding the Convention, which aimed only at embroiling America and England, he always wrote to Mr. Washington, who is his friend, in a sense quite contrary to the wishes of the odious regicides.[57]

This fond accord of the Catherinian nobleman and one of the Founding Fathers of the United States, which may seem an exaggeration, actually is historical fact and not as paradoxical as it may appear at first. Gouverneur Morris, who held the post of Minister to France during the most critical years of the Revolution (1792-1794), did not resemble his brilliant predecessors, Benjamin Franklin and Thomas Jefferson. His figure might have suited the Court of Louis XVI or the Prussian king, but he was out of place in Jacobin Paris. Morris' actions worsened relations between France and the United States, which already had deteriorated after the latter's refusal to support its former ally (Proclamation of Neutrality of April 22, 1793) and demand for the recall of the French minister, "Citizen Genêt."

Like his compatriots and confederates, Alexander Hamilton and John Adams, Morris was a Federalist. The conservatives had greater and greater influence in the American government in the 1790's. Their way of thinking and their actions could not help but win the approval of even the most conservative statesmen of monarchic Europe. Gouverneur Morris' case was no exception.

Vorontsov was on excellent terms with another Founding Father, the envoy extraordinary and minister plenipotentiary of the United States in Britain, Rufus King, "a sensible man who is universally respected for his principles." (King, who came from Massachusetts, was also a Federalist.) In one of his private and friendly conversations with Vorontsov, the American minister noted that, "so long as his country united with England, the Russian ally, and feels revulsion for the loathsome principles by which the French government is guided, he personally considers that direct connections between the United States and Russia could be useful for them, especially taking into consideration the ever-growing commerce between the two countries."[58] Such argumentation apparently produced a most favorable impression on Vorontsov, who remarked that he did not foresee any complications on condition that the first step would be taken from the American side. Since Rufus King talked only "on his own initiative," initially Vorontsov did not attach special significance to the conversation. It soon became clear, however, that the conversation had definite practical consequences. "Rufus King has just informed me," Vorontsov reported to St. Petersburg in March 1799, "that the United States would like to start a direct correspondence with Russia, and that he is likely to be authorized to conclude with me an agreement on the trade between the two countries."[59]

This procedure did not seem quite acceptable to the proud Russian aristocrat. After all, the question concerned the great Russian Empire, not some "Prussia and Portugal with whom Americans signed their treaties in London." The Tsar's dignitary, highly versed in diplomatic protocol, "explained" to Rufus King that the United States would first have to appoint an envoy to St. Petersburg; if that were done, he supposed that the Russian emperor, "taking into consideration the good conduct of the United States in matters concerning *La Bonne Cause* would also appoint a minister with Philadelphia as place of residence." Only then would it be time "to talk about commercial affairs." The treaty, Vorontsov supposed, could not be concluded anywhere but St. Petersburg.

There is nothing unusual in the procedure suggested by Vorontsov, and the modern reader, even were he a meticulous lawyer or a historian, should be able to understand Vorontsov's predilection for strict observance of diplomatic etiquette which was widely accepted in Europe of that day, especially since the Russian Ambassador not only had in essence approved the idea of starting direct relations, but even had offered some practical advice in this connection. In particular, Vorontsov recommended that, in selecting a candidate for the post of ambassador to faraway America, they look for a man who "would have fluent knowledge of the English tongue, and could read, write, and especially speak it, since in that country hardly one out of a thousand persons has any knowledge of French."

Although the direct contacts of Russian representatives abroad with American diplomats—among them, the talks between Vorontsov and Rufus King in London in the spring of 1799—are interesting indeed, the reaction of the tsarist government in St. Petersburg to the proposal of Rufus King is much more significant. Vorontsov's report from London was received in St. Petersburg on April 18/29, and in a very few days, on April 23/May 4, 1799, a reply was dispatched in which Paul I expressed the official consent of the Russian government to the establishment of diplomatic relations and the exchange of the appropriate missions. "We shall be all the more willing to establish reciprocal missions," the Tsar wrote to Vorontsov, "since in the present circumstances the behavior of their government has gained our utmost respect, and since they have such good relations with England, our sincere ally; therefore, as soon as the aforesaid States appoint the minister, we shall do likewise."[60]

The agreement of the Russian government to establish diplomatic relations with the United States is of a paramount importance, all the more so since the question concerns an official document approved by the Tsar. It is interesting to note that this tsar was the extremely reactionary Paul I, who not only did not see any obstacle to the establishment of the direct diplomatic contacts with the republican United States but even wrote that its government had gained his "utmost respect."

Russian-American rapprochement at the end of the eighteenth century was determined to a large degree by international factors. It was in this respect a derivative of the relations of both powers with France and England. Actually, ever since 1798 an undeclared war had existed between the United States and France, and hundreds of·American privateers were operating against French shipping. In this connection, Secretary of State Timothy Pickering had already, in February 1799, expressed the view that the President's nominating commissioners to treat with France would defeat King's negotiations with Russia. At the same time it was felt in the United States that the number of American foreign representatives should be curtailed rather than enlarged. As a result, when Vorontsov informed King in June 1799 of the Russian decision, the United States did not take advantage of the opportunity offered, and the American minister considered it best to avoid further negotiations.[61]

Meanwhile, the international situation underwent an abrupt change. Irritated by the treacherous policy of Austria, Paul I dropped out of the second anti-French coalition, recalled Russian troops from western Europe, broke relations with England, and seized English ships and goods. These anti-English actions undermined Russian trade and provoked extreme discontent among influential circles of Russian nobility, merchants, and officers of the Guard. During the night of March 11, 1801, Paul I was murdered by the participants of the Palace plot, and Alexander I ascended to the Russian throne. Although the new government did not have an immediate reaction on Russian-American connections, in the long run it created a more favorable atmosphere for rapprochement with America. Nikolai Petrovich Rumiantsev, who was appointed to the post of minister of commerce in 1802, was an active and consistent adherent of the Russian-American rapprochement.

A natural result of the development of Russian-American relations in the last decades of the eighteenth century and the beginning of the nineteenth was the appointment of American consuls, first to St. Petersburg and later to other Russian ports ((Riga, Archangel). President Washington appointed John Miller Russell of Massachusetts consul for the port of St. Petersburg on November 24, 1794;[62] however, Russell never reached his destination. In conversation with John Quincy Adams in March 1801, the tsarist minister in Berlin, Baron A. I. Krüdener, expressed his approval of the plan to send an American consul to Russia.[63] Adams himself requested that the minister free those American citizens who were detained in Russian ports because of the embargo on English vessels.[64] J. Q. Adams was also informed that the Russian ruling circles looked upon the enlargement of trade with the United States with utmost favor.[65]

An important event in the history of Russian-American relations was the appointment on April 4, 1803, of Levett Harris to the post of consul of the United States in St. Petersburg. Harris arrived in the Russian capital on October 19.[66] The very first meetings with state Chancellor A. R. Vorontsov and Minister of Commerce N. P. Rumiantsev indicated that Harris could count on a successful mission. The Chancellor assured the American that he did not foresee any special problems in the question of recognition since Alexander I contemplated the ever growing trade of the United States with his Empire with great interest and satisfaction.[67] Indeed, on October 16/28 Vorontsov had already announced to the College of Foreign Affairs the ukase of Alexander I on the recognition of Levett Harris as the consul of the United States. On October 29/November 10, 1803, an appropriate ukase was sent from the Ruling Senate to the College of Commerce.[68] On February 4/16, 1806, by the ukase of Alexander I, a foreign merchant, F. Küsel, was recognized as vice-consul of the United States in Archangel, and on 12/24 July 1808, Christian Rodde was recognized as a vice-consul in Riga.[69]

Levett Harris was destined to play a prominent role in the development of Russian-American relations. During his prolonged stay in St. Petersburg he not only managed the usual round of consular affairs, but virtually from the very beginning successfully performed some diplomatic functions, thus earning the good will of many statesmen and of the Tsar himself. In particular, he had great success early in 1804 with his petition for Russian mediation in the attempt to free from captivity in Tripoli the sailors of the American warship *Philadelphia,* which had run aground on North Africa on October 31, 1803.[70] "The Government of the United States of America," Harris wrote Vorontsov:

> . . . will undoubtedly employ the earliest and most efficacious means to their redemption; in the meantime, as their distressed situation may be ameliorated by the interference of some of the Courts of Europe and as the undersigned has the honor to find himself acknowledged as the public agent of America and the most powerful among them . . . impelled by duty and moved by the cry of humanity he has had no hesitation in addressing this note officially to Your Excellency in order to solicit . . . His Imperial Majesty to use his influence with the Ottoman Porte; his Majesty's mediation in such form as may be calculated to soften the fate of his unfortunate countrymen and contribute to releasing . . . them from their . . . captivity.

Harris assured the chancellor that the "President and People of the United States will not fail to appreciate an interposition so gracious and honorable."[71] Considering the character of Russia's relations with Turkey in the early nineteenth century, and the influence of the Russian minister in Constantinople, we must admit that Harris' appeal was quite timely and appropriate.

A. R. Vorontsov immediately brought Harris' petition to the notice of Alexander I, and it was fully complied with. "It gives me great pleasure," Vorontsov wrote Harris,

> to let you know that H. I. M., being well-disposed toward your government, ordered me to instruct his Minister in Constantinople to make most energetic representations to the Turkish Ministry demanding that the firman of the Porte be sent to the Bay of Tripoli, requesting that he set at liberty not only the crew but the vessel itself. These orders will be sent to Constantinople posthaste,[72] and I have no doubt that the representations of Mr. Italinsky will then prove effective.[73]

Other appeals of the American consul were also treated favorably. In connection with Harris' request to facilitate the obtaining of permission for the American vessels to navigate the Black Sea, Adam Czartoryski,[74] in February 1804 the new head of Russia's Ministry of Foreign Affairs, instructed A. Ia. Italinsky in Constantinople to "exercise utmost effort at the Turkish ministry for obtaining the requested permission for the American flag."[75]

In accordance with these directions, Italinsky presented to Reis Effendi (the Porte's minister of foreign affairs) a "proper statement." The minister, Italinsky wrote Czartoryski a month later, "promised to bring the same to the notice of His Majesty the Sultan and to give me a definite answer in the near future. The conversation I had with Reis Effendi on this occasion leaves me no doubt of the complete success of my memorandum." Reis Effendi assured the Russian minister that, as a token of "gratitude" to the emperor, the Porte would not refuse to permit "the American merchant flag free navigation" through the Straits; but along with this assurance he noted that, "accordance of the above advantage to the American flag will necessarily have to be accompanied by the enactment of a treaty of amity between the Ottoman Empire and the American States."

According to the Turkish minister, the Porte had earlier repeatedly declined similar addresses of the United States, and the change in her position resulted solely from "sincere friendship between Russia and Ottoman Empire."[76]

Much is implied in Reis Effendi's answer. Unfortunately, it has proved impossible to establish definitely whether the Sublime Porte gave due attention to this question "in the near future." Perusal of the relevant correspondence with Constantinople for the years 1804-5 did not reveal any additional material. The files of Parisian correspondence provided better results, although on a somewhat different plane. On April 7, 1804, Robert Livingston, the American minister to France, sent a letter to Russian chargé d'affaires P. Ia. Ubri (Oubril), in which he proposed to conclude a trade agreement between Russia and the United States, based on the most-favored-nation principle and granting the right of passage into the Black Sea to American vessels. Livingston's initiative was somewhat unexpected and Ubri was baffled. Before replying, Ubri visited the American minister. He called his attention to the fact that the right of navigation in the Black Sea had been granted to England and France only with great difficulties and said he was not sure whether Alexander I, "even if he agrees to sign the trade agreement with the United States, would include in it provisions concerning the trade in the Black Sea." "The objects exported from our ports to America," Ubri continued, "such as hemp, cordage, and sailcloth are not available in sufficient quantities in the Black Sea ports, whose trade consists of grain and timber."[77] Nevertheless, Livingston asked him to bring this project to the notice of the Russian government again. Ubri did so on April 16, 1804. In replying to Livingston he stated that, "although H. I. M. does not believe that commercial relations between his subjects and those of the United States require particular conditions at this time, he nevertheless appreciates your desire to work toward making them more active."[78]

Livingston's proposal through P. Ia. Ubri cannot be considered successful. This limited, second-rate diplomatic official, secretary of the Russian consulate in Paris, who became chargé d'affaires after the recall of A. I. Morkov, proved unable to assess fully all the possible consequences of the proposals made to him and saw only their negative features. Yet, what seemed so improbable to him had already become a subject of official action in Constantinople. Nor did official caution prevent Ubri from writing to Czartoryski that, in his opinion the agreement proposed by Livingston "will be useful only for the United States, who, while gaining great privileges for their trade with Russia, can give us in exchange only a seeming reciprocity, since not one Russian vessel sails in those waters." Ubri also feared that Livingston had made the proposal "on his own initiative," and suspected that it might have been "done under the influence of France, who in time of war would derive great profits from the coastal trade that Americans would undertake from the ports of the Black Sea to the Mediterranean ports belonging to France."[79]

In their day Ubri's doubts may have had grounds, but from our perspective they seem exaggerated. It is hard to say with any degree of certainty to what extent they could influence the decision of the Russian government. At any rate, no agreement with the United States was signed at that time; this, however, had little bearing on Russian-American trade relations, which continued to develop without any special obstacles and limitations. Following Adam Smith, Alexander I and his closest collaborators, including V. P. Kochubei and N. P. Rumiantsev, in the beginning of the nineteenth century inclined toward a free trade program and did not try to conclude new trade treaties.

In general, this apparently suited the government of the United States as well. Apart from the official expression of gratitude, made by Secretary of State James Madison,[80] for the mediation in the cause of liberating the command of the American frigate from Tripolitan captivity, President Thomas Jefferson, on June 15, 1804, sent Alexander I a personal message in which he also expressed satisfaction with the development of trade connections between Russia and the United States.

> I see with great pleasure the rising commerce between our two countries. We have not gone into the policy which the European nations have so long tried and to so little effect of multiplying commercial treaties. In national as in individual dealings, more liberality will, perhaps, be found in voluntary regulations than in those which are measured out by the strict letter of a treaty, which, whenever it becomes onerous, is made by forced construction to mean anything or nothing, engenders disputes and brings on war. But your flag will find in our harbors hospitality, freedom and protection and your subjects enjoy all the privileges of the most favored nation. The favorable reception of our consul at St. Petersburg, and the friendly sentiments conveyed through your minister of foreign affairs, is an earnest that our merchants also will meet due favor in your ports.[81]

As we have seen, the most-favored-nation principle was realized in practice without any contractual obligations, which did not diminish its effectiveness in any way.

The last important matter relating to the subject of trade relations concerns the shipping by Slobodsk merchant K. A. Anfilatov of Russian-built vessels to America in 1806-7. Anfilatov, who "engaged in foreign trade in the ports of Archangel and St. Petersburg" apparently was to some extent a unique personality. Although not always successful in his undertakings, it cannot be denied that he was farsighted, enterprising, and daring. His office in Archangel was in no way inferior to foreign offices. He took part in 1803 in organizing the "White Sea Company" for fishing, and in 1804 in the setting up of "bread reserve stores" in Archangel. Later, in 1810, Anfilatov founded in the town of Slobodsk in Viatka province, a public bank, one of the first in Russia, having donated to it 25,000 rubles.[82] However, the most important of his enterprises undoubtedly was the opening of direct trade with America.

In the beginning of December 1805 Anfilatov addressed a letter to the minister of commerce, N. P. Rumiantsev, informing him of his intention to "start the direct trade with North American provinces and supply there our products and goods, and in return to bring from there the products on hand in our own Russian ships." He intended to send to the United States three ships with Russian goods, and begged to "be granted great imperial favor," since "the first experiment entails many extra expenditures."[83]

The Minister of Commerce presented Anfilatov's case directly to Alexander I, without preliminary scrutiny by the Committee of Ministers, and provided a project of appropriate ukase. Rumiantsev well understood the importance of developing direct commercial ties between Russia and America, and even earlier had repeatedly called to the Tsar's notice the usefulness of direct trade relations with the United States. This time he called special attention to the considerable sugar (5 million rubles) and cotton imports.[84] Since "the western part of the United States has an abundance of these two products," it seemed obvious that "they would cost less if gotten first hand." Consequently, "so as to give our merchants a definite push toward the opening of American commerce," Rumiantsev suggested to Alexander I, "that the first three ships built in Russia and belonging to Russians which leave with cargo the ports of Archangel and St. Petersburg bound directly for the United States would be released from duties." Likewise, it was proposed to release from duty American goods brought back to Russia on these ships.[85] Alexander I agreed to these proposals, and on December 29, 1805/January 10, 1806, he instructed Rumiantsev to announce to Anfilatov his imperial "favor."[86] The next day the Minister of Commerce informed Anfilatov that the Emperor received his intention of sending three ships "to the United American States" with a "a special pleasure" and "has issued an ukase not to collect duties either from the goods you will be sending to the United States, or from those brought from there into the Russian ports."[87]

Although such "imperial favor" was not common, it was by no means "unparalleled in the chronicles of Russian foreign trade," as some overenthusiastic authors have stated.[88] In any case, it demonstrated the significance attached in those days to the direct trade with the United States. It is also meaningful that, by the special ukase of Alexander I, Anfilatov was granted a government loan to the sum of 200 thousand rubles, "without any pledge or guarantee."[89]

112

In 1806 Anfilatov sent to America only two ships, one from Archangel and one from St. Petersburg, with various Russian goods. The first returned safely from New York to Kronstadt with a rich cargo on October 8/20, 1807.[90] The second, *Archangel Michael,* though it lost a part of its cargo when it ran onto a shoal going through the Sound, eventually reached Reval in the fall of 1807.[91] Also, since in Boston this ship had been loaded with "3,600 bottles of liquor," which it was forbidden to import into Russia, Anfilatov again had to petition Rumiantsev,[92] who had to petition the Tsar, for these goods to be admitted without obstacles.

On the whole one can say that Anfilatov's enterprise of 1806-7 ended quite successfully. Among the goods brought from the United States were coffee, sandalwood, cloves, pepper, raw sugar, indigo, laurel, cinnamon, chocolate, and mahogany. The total sum of canceled duties and other collections on them totaled 900 thousand rubles, not counting the profits from their sale.[93] This figure gives an idea of the scale and importance of the voyages of Anfilatov's ships. There is reason to believe that vessels under the Russian flag entered the ports of the United States in other years. American statistics contain the following information on "Russian tonnage" in ports of the United States: 1792, 390 tons; 1804, 216 tons; 1805, 368 tons; 1806, 849 tons; and 1807, 293 tons.[94] Only the figures for 1806 can refer to Anfilatov's ships. As for 1792, 1804, and 1805, it is natural to suppose that in these years at least one ship a year entered the ports of the United States under the Russian flag, but so far no details have been uncovered. Although Anfilatov probably cannot claim for himself exclusively the opening of the American market, as G. A. Zamiatin would have him do[95] (he must be credited with sending the first Russian-built ships to the United States directly from Russian ports), his daring enterprise deserves a prominent place in the history of Russian trade. The importance which the Russian government attached to the subject of direct trade with the United States can be judged from the 1805 annual report of Rumiantsev for the Ministry of Commerce, which devotes a whole section to this problem.

In a detailed enumeration of the advantages of a "direct trade between Russia and the United States," Rumiantsev noted that he had entered into "appropriate negotiation with the American consul in St. Petersburg, Levett Harris, and had repeatedly petitioned the Tsar

for some indulgence for the Americans, as it happened concerning the release from confiscation of the forbidden goods marked for re-export; and then, so as to give our merchants a definite push toward opening American commerce, I begged . . . the favor . . . that the first three ships built in Russia and belonging to Russians which leave with cargo from the ports of St. Petersburg and Archangel, would be released from duties. . . . By means of this measure I hoped that such strong encouragement would attract not just three ships but many of our merchants to a new way; American goods, necessary for us, brought in directly, will be cheaper and extract less money from the government.[96]

Anfilatov himself, later evaluating the results of sending Russian ships to America in 1806, wrote that, first of all, "despite all foreigners' opinion," it was proved "possible to use pine ships, so long as they were firmly constructed, for distant sea voyages," and, second, "Americans themselves started sending their ships to Archangel and established offices there, something which had not happened before this enterprise. In this way, American goods come to us first hand, in Archangel, quite advantageously, and our goods reach them without intermediaries."[97]

In summarizing Russian-American trade relations in the last decades of the eighteenth and in the beginning of the nineteenth centuries it is possible to isolate the following features:

1. We now have documentary confirmation of the existence of commercial contacts between Russia and the young American republic as early as the War of Independence. The sailing of vessels under the Russian flag from Bordeaux to America, which Wittfooth, the consul in Bordeaux, had reported, was of definite assistance to the rebels and helped offset naval blockades and the disruption of normal trade contacts during the course of military actions.

2. The development of normal commercial ties between Russia and the United States after the termination of the War of Independence was just as essential. The very fact that normal commercial ties with republican America were developing, while Russia was at war with revolutionary France, attests to the fundamental difference between French and American policies of tsarist Russia, connected with a complex series of international and internal problems which have been discussed.

3. Although the overall volume of Russian-American trade was not great, contacts with America gradually began to assume a certain practical significance. Already in the first years of the nineteenth century American imports from Russia totaled more than 1.5 million dollars. Russia exported to America such important goods as high quality iron from the Ural Mountains, hemp, linen, and cordage, all essential to the shipbuilding industry of the United States. To Russia were shipped, both directly, and, especially through other countries (England, and the Hanseatic towns), various colonial products: sugar, coffee, tobacco, and, somewhat later, cotton. Of considerable interest is the sending by K. A. Anfilatov in 1806-7 of the first ships of native construction from Archangel

and St. Petersburg directly to America, accomplished with the support of the government, and, above all, of the minister of commerce, N. P. Rumiantsev, who took great interest in the development of the direct trade between Russia and the United States. In evaluating the general significance of the first Russian-American trade contacts, A. Ia. Dashkov stressed that "the advantages of our connections with Americans are already tangible, but if we look to the future, we shall realize the great importance for Russia of direct commerce with the United States."[98]

4. The development of trade relations between the two countries occasionally led to the establishment of diplomatic contacts and, in particular, to the discussion of direct diplomatic ties and signing of a trade agreement. For example, in the spring of 1799, as a result of unofficial negotiations between Russian and American envoys in London, S. R. Vorontsov and Rufus King, some preliminary agreement was reached on this subject, and St. Petersburg even gave official sanction to the exchange of diplomatic missions. Finally, a natural result of the development of commercial ties between Russia and the United States was the official recognition in the fall of 1803 of Levett Harris as the United States consul in St. Petersburg, and, somewhat later, the appointing of American vice-consuls in Archangel and Riga.

On the whole, trade connections between Russia and the United States were one of the major causes of the ensuing Russian-American rapprochement.

V

THE DEVELOPMENT OF SCIENTIFIC, CULTURAL, AND SOCIO-POLITICAL CONNECTIONS

The names of the two greatest scientists of their time, Mikhail Lomonosov and Benjamin Franklin, spring to mind when we approach the question of early scientific and cultural connections between Russia and America. Alexander Radishchev was the first to juxtapose these figures, in *A Journey from St. Petersburg to Moscow.* In this work Radishchev, although voicing a high opinion of Lomonosov, gave preference to Franklin because of the role the American played in the War of Independence. This was another way of underlining the revolutionary thrust of his book. Radishchev translated the Latin verse inscribed under Franklin's portrait, "Eripuit coelo fulmen sceptrumque tyrannis," in a pointedly anti-tsarist form: "from the hand of tsars" [iz ruki tsarei] (rather than "tyrants"), and noted that it was the highest praise "that a man could see beneath his portrait."[1]

This inscription conveys vividly and precisely the enormous significance of the great American's scientific work in the field of electricity. *The famous Experiments and Observations on Electricity Made at Philadelphia in America*[2] constituted a scientific event that in a sense can be compared with the revolutionary upheaval caused later in the field of politics by the revolt of the North American colonies against England and by the Declaration of Independence—another product of Philadelphia. The self-taught genius from far-off America understood the essence of electrical phenomena and pointed the way for further investigation—a feat which eluded his most educated colleagues on the other side of the ocean, armed though they were with all the experiences and knowledge of Newton, Huygens, and Euler.[3]

Naturally, general recognition was not accorded Franklin immediately. The Holy Church stubbornly assumed that bell-ringing, which in its enlightened opinion drove evil spirits away, was the only correct method for fighting thunderstorm phenomena. Ironically, those tall and solidly constructed church belfries provided the most vulnerable medium for lightning strikes; therefore it was far from safe to engage in bell-ringing during thunderstorms. In the end of the eighteenth century in Germany alone, one hundred twenty bell ringers were killed and four hundred church belfries destroyed in the course of thirty-three years.[4] And—as if to mock the Holy Church, evil spirits, and the Lord Himself, the temple of the wise King Solomon in Jerusalem—covered, it turned out, by polished metal plates which were good conductors of electrical current—remained invulnerable for many years.

But religious prejudices were not the only, nor the major, obstacle to the dissemination of new views on the nature of electricity. During the War of Independence the opposition to Franklin's scientific ideas and the introduction of the lightning rod assumed a political character. This was especially evident when English scientist Benjamin Wilson proposed that, instead of Franklin's rod with its sharp point, a blunt version be used in order to avert a dangerous flow of electrical current. The country's passions were enflamed, and any Englishman who provided his house with a pointed rather than a blunt rod was in danger of being considered politically unreliable.

Today such "scientific" arguments seem as meaningless as the conflict of Swift's heroes concerning the sharp or blunt end of an egg. But in the motherland of the great satirist the argument for the pointed end of the lightning rod proved unsafe for even John Pringle, president of the Royal Society and royal physician. His renowned reply to George III to the effect that he would always conform to His Majesty's wishes but could not change the laws of nature or the action of their forces proved costly for the obstinate author. He was dismissed from his post and had to resign the presidency of the Royal Society.

It might have been easy to dismiss the royal physician, and even, if necessary to imprison him, but it was much more difficult to halt the progress of science—even if Holy Church or the head of the greatest power on earth wished to do so. The Philadelphia Experiments, with their great simplicity and clarity, left no doubt about electricity and lightning, and the rod worked so faultlessly that it could convince the most distrustful skeptic.

In Russia, Franklin's experiments first became known to a wide circle of readers through an article in the *St. Peterburgskie Vedomosti* (St. Petersburg Journal) in June 1752. The paper announced that, "in Philadelphia in North America, Mr. Benjamin Franklin was so daring as to wish to extract from the atmosphere that awesome fire which destroys whole lands," and gave a detailed description of his experiments, which were subsequently repeated in France.[5]

The news of the Philadelphia Experiments fell on fertile ground in Russia. At that time in St. Petersburg, working fruitfully in an adjoining field, were Mikhail Lomonosov and his friend and sometime collaborator, Georg Wilhelm Richmann, who in 1745 constructed an "electrical indicator" for measuring the volume of charge in an electrified body. With the help of the "thunder machine," a metal pivot installed on the roof and connected with an electro-measuring device, Lomonosov and Richmann were investigating atmospheric electric discharges. In the summer of 1753, while experimenting with a "thunder machine" with Lomonosov, Richmann approached the conductor too carelessly, and was killed by an electric discharge. "Richmann died a beautiful death, performing a duty for his profession. His memory will never die," wrote Lomonosov about his friend.[6] Later, while arriving at some broad generalizations in the field of electric phenomena, Lomonosov created an ether concept of electricity which to some extent anticipated nineteenth-century theories in this field.

The works of Lomonosov and Richmann on physics indicate that they valued Franklin's works on electricity highly and referred to them repeatedly. At the same time, their own experiments of many years pointed out some shortcomings in Franklin's work, and they skillfully supplemented and developed his ideas. Many of their experiments had been carried out before the publication of the Philadelphia Experiments or before the time when they could have become acquainted with them; besides, they differed considerably from some of the ideas developed by Franklin.[7]

Responding to unfair criticisms of his famous "Address on air phenomena caused by electric power,"[8] Lomonosov stated that he interpreted "many phenomena connected with thunderstorms which Franklin does not touch upon."[9] Showing how his theory differed from Franklin's "guess," Lomonosov explained: "He tries to attract electric matter for northern lights from the torrid zone, while I suppose that there is enough of it in that place, that is, the ether is present everywhere. He does not define the place of electric matter; I suppose it to be above the atmosphere. He does not explain how it is produced; I explain it clearly. He does not confirm his suppositions with any arguments; I confirm mine by the interpretation of phenomena."[10] While pointing out the difference of his theory from the views of the American, Lomonosov emphasized his respect for the "famous Mr. Franklin," and insisted that "all this is affirmed here not because I want to see myself in a preferred position."[11]

Somewhat later, new ideas on the nature of electrical phenomena were studied and popularized in Russia through the works of Franz Ulrich Theodor Epinus, who determined the connection between electric and magnetic powers and made broad calculations in the theory of electricity. In his fundamental work, Essay on the Theory of Electricity and Magnetism, published in the end of 1759 or the very beginning of 1760, Epinus repeatedly refers to Franklin.[12] In the work's dedication he wrote: "The power inherent in bodies which is called electricity has been but recently discovered and hardly investigated sufficiently. . . . I am greatly satisfied by the theory of this power suggested by Franklin. . . . Nevertheless, I concluded that I had found some shortcomings in this remarkable theory; therefore, I made an effort to correct them and, with the help of these corrections, to adjust this theory so as to coordinate it fully with the phenomena."[13]

The scientist succeeded brilliantly. The importance of Epinus' work on the development of Franklin's ideas is sometimes compared with the significance which the work of Maxwell, in the nineteenth century, had on the development of Faraday's ideas. In both cases the experiments and observations of self-taught geniuses were given mathematical elaboration by trained professional physicists.[14]

D. A. Golitsyn, who published interesting works in this field himself, held the highest opinion of Franklin's work. In the annals of the St. Petersburg Academy of Sciences for 1777, he reported that Franklin was the first to establish the existence of two kinds of electricity, the positive and the negative.[15] In January 1777 Golitsyn wrote to Franklin:

> J'ose me flatter, Monsieur, que vous ne desapproverez pas la liberté que je prens de vous écrire sans avoir en aucune façon l'avantage d'être connu de vous. A titre d'un de vos plus sincères admirateurs, j'ai cru pouvoir me permettre cette demarche: celui d'aimer les Sciences et de m'interesser veritablement à leurs progrès, me donne même le droit de m'addresser à vous. Qui mieux que vous, Monsieur pourroit décider si les idées que je me suis faites des Electricités positive et négative et du pouvoir attractif des Points sont justes ou non.

He then gave a detailed account of his experiments in atmospheric electricity.[16]

A direct address to Franklin, who at that time was a representative in Paris of the rebelling colonies, with no official recognition from the French government, was a daring move on the part of the Russian minister in The

Hague. It should be said to Golitsyn's credit that in the interest of science he did not hesitate to forego the usual formalities, even though such a liberty could be viewed unfavorably by the Court in St. Petersburg.

The materials cited demonstrate that the Philadelphia Experiments were known in Russia from the middle of the eighteenth century and were highly esteemed in scientific circles. But what was Franklin's own attitude toward Russian work on electricity, if, indeed, he had any knowledge of its existence? Although a complete answer to this question cannot be given without studying American archives, the documents and research materials published so far indicate that Franklin knew about Russian experiments and valued them highly. In a letter to James Bowdoin of December 13, 1753, he wrote: "I have yet received no particulars of the unhappy gentleman's death at Petersburg, (whose fate I lament). One of the papers says, that all the letters from thence confirm the account, and mentions his name (Professor Richmann), but nothing farther. No doubt we shall have a minute account of the accident with all its circumstances, in some of the magazines of the Transactions of the Royal Society."

On March 5, 1754, Franklin's *Pennsylvania Gazette* published a detailed account of the experiment, which led to the death of Richmann. "Counsellor Lomonosov" was mentioned as a participant in the experiment. This seems to be the first appearance of his name in the American press.[17]

In 1759 Franklin performed some experiments to check the work of Epinus and concluded that "his account of the positive and negative states of the opposite sides of the heated tourmalin is well founded."[18] Franklin was well acquainted with the famous experiments of Joseph-Adam Braun on solidifying mercury which took place in St. Petersburg in 1759, as well as with Epinus' fundamental work on the theory of electricity and magnetism. Although in the opinion of American specialists Franklin did not possess sufficient knowledge of higher mathematics for a detailed reading of Epinus' monograph, there is no doubt that he was familiar with its general deductions. Besides, it was through Franklin that other American scientists, like John Winthrop, a professor of natural philosophy at Harvard, and Ezra Stiles, a clergyman who became President of Yale, became acquainted with these works.

"The Russian Philosophers have found," Franklin wrote Stiles on May 29, 1763, "that in extream Cold, Mercury itself becomes solid, and is malleable like other Metals. Hence it seems that in the State we have it, it is really a melted metal that melts with less Heat than other Metals.

"Æpinus, a Member of the Academy of Sciences at Petersburg, has lately published a Latin work in 4to. entitled, Tentamen Theoriae Electricitatis et Magnetismi, wherein he applies my Principles of Electricity to the Explanation of the various Phenomena of Magnetism, and I think with considerable Success."[19] Along with this letter Franklin lent Stiles "a little Piece of Æpinus's" requesting him to forward it, after he perused it, to John Winthrop, whose mathematical background would make full appreciation of the work possible.

The latter commented appreciatively on the learned work of the Petersburg mathematician, although he noted, not without malice, that the author suffered from "truly German verbosity," and that the reader had little patience to follow his formulas. At the same time Winthrop thought that Epinus' book contained many interesting ideas and that its author was a "man of bright ideas, many-sided and inquisitive mind . . . He throws a new light on the theory of magnetism, and his hypotheses correspond with many unexplained phenomena of this mysterious force, and explain them with a considerable degree of probability."[20]

In a letter to his friend, French scientist Barbeu Dubourg, Franklin himself expressed a still higher opinion of Epinus' book:

> a strong apparatus of magnets may charge millions of bars of steel without communicating to them any part of its proper magnetism; only putting in motion the magnetism which already existed in these bars.
>   I am chiefly indebted to that excellent philosopher of Petersburg, Mr. Æpinus, for this hypothesis, which appears to me equally ingenious and solid. I say *chiefly* because, as it is many years since I read his book, which I have left in America, it may happen, that I may have added to or altered it in some respect and, if I have misrepresented anything, the error ought to be charged to my account.[21]

Of greatest interest is the documentary material that indicates a possibility that there were direct contacts between American scientists and Epinus, Braun, and especially Lomonosov. Eufrosina Dvoichenko-Markova was the first to explore this idea in her interesting paper on the contacts between Benjamin Franklin and the American Philosophical Society with the St. Petersburg Academy of Sciences, which was published in 1947 and later developed at greater length and supplied with a valuable documentary supplement.[22] As proof, the observant researcher refers to a letter of February 20, 1765, from Ezra Stiles to Franklin.[23] Stiles had written to Lomonosov concerning some thermometrical observations which were made in Boston in 1764, and requested Franklin to pass this letter on to Russia, since Franklin, as he understood, was engaged in "Petersburg correspondence with Æpinus and Braunis." "If I make too free a use of your name and friendship," he wrote Franklin, "you have it in your power to prevent the abuse. At least, however, give me leave to ask from yourself an account of the discoveries of the Polar voyage, if such a one should be effected."[24] Stiles also wrote that "Upon reading in 'Annual Register' of 1762, an account of the congelation of mercury, by M. Braunius, with artificial cold in Petersburg, in December, 1759," he ventured on some of his experiments of refrigeration which led him to somewhat different results than the ones he expected from Braun.

Stiles's letter is a real find for researchers. It contains a mention of Lomonosov, indicative of the great interest in and the respect for his work in America; a request to be informed of the Russian Polar expedition which was being planned by Lomonosov; a reference to the possibility of Franklin's "Petersburg correspondence"; and a description of Stiles's attempted experimentation derived from the brilliant experiments of Joseph-Adam Braun and his colleagues in St. Petersburg. A letter, written in Latin, enclosed in the same envelope addressed by Stiles to the "much esteemed M. Lomonosov, citizen of Petersburg in Russia and member of Petersburg Academy of Sciences" is of even greater interest.[25]

> I have happened to read in a London newspaper of October 29, 1764, that believing in the possibility of opening up an access from Russia to America across the ice-bound sea, you have equipped two vessels which, after wintering in Kola, will head to the North Pole in the course of the next spring and will engage in a thorough investigation of the northern regions. This is a most laudable plan, truly worthy of a naturalist! In my turn I am convinced that the polar regions and arctic seas in proportion to the distance from the shores are lighted either by the northern lights or the tropical sun.[26]

The inquisitive American was at that time preparing some tables of thermometrical observations; in this connection he wanted Lomonosov to send him, either directly or through Franklin, "all the information concerning magnetism and temperatures registered or deduced in the polar lands and oceans" as well as some missing "information on temperatures in some regions of the Russian empire." In particular, Stiles asked for such observations to be made in Petersburg, Moscow, Kazan, and Tobolsk, and even in Archangel, Kola, Kamchatka, and Selenginsk.

On this occasion, E. M. Dvoichenko-Markova, who is exceptionally precise and cautious in her evaluations, was somewhat hasty with her categorical deduction that Franklin fulfilled this request.[27] In his reply to Stiles of July 5, 1765, Franklin wrote that in the near future he would send Lomonosov the enclosure intended for him; he was unaware that Lomonosov died on 4/15 April 1765. Obviously Lomonosov could not have received Stiles's letter. It is also quite possible that Franklin did not send the letter to St. Petersburg; thus, the document was preserved in the archives of the American Philosophical Society.

Although Franklin and Stiles did not succeed in establishing direct contact with Lomonosov, in the light of data now available it is possible to affirm that they knew the work of the Russian, and valued it highly. They were also well informed about the work of several other Russian scholars. One can deduce from the abovementioned reply to Stiles that Franklin was interested in Russian geographical discoveries and knew about the expeditions to the northwest coast of America and the unsuccessful attempts to cross the Arctic Ocean. Franklin considered the new polar expedition very significant and stated that "Lomonosov will set the matter straight."[28]

Until lately there were serious doubts about the existence of the correspondence, referred to by Stiles, between Franklin and Braun and Epinus. The editors of the Franklin Papers noted that there is no proof of the correspondence.[29] But I succeeded in finding, in the collections of the Pennsylvania Historical Society, a previously unknown letter from Franklin to Epinus, dated 6 June 1766. Because it is the earliest documentary evidence of direct contact between the great American and the Russian scientist, I quote in full:

London, June 6, 1766

Sir,
When last in America I received there your excellent Work on the Theories of Electricity and Magnetism, which I understand you did me the Honour to send me. I read it with infinite Satisfaction and Pleasure, and beg you to accept my best Thanks and Acknowledgements, which indeed are due to you from the whole Republick of Letters. Enclos'd I take the Liberty of sending you a little Piece of mine, that is to be in the next Transactions of the Royal Society, but is not yet publish'd:—Please to accept it as a small Mark of the great Esteem and Respect with which I am,

Sir,

Your most obedient
and most humble Servant
B Franklin

Monsr. Æpinus[30]

The first official contact between the American Philosophical Society of Philadelphia, founded by Benjamin Franklin in 1743, and the Russian Academy of Sciences in St. Petersburg took place in the early seventies. The groundwork for it was laid by reciprocal interest in scientific experimentation and by the first episodic connections, mainly through mutual acquaintance with the works in the field of physics and geographical discoveries.

At the meeting of the American Philosophical Society on February 22, 1771, it was decided that the first volume of the newly published *Transactions* should be sent to all important philosophical societies.[31] The Imperial Society of St. Petersburg was on this list.[32] The official inscription on the presentation copy of *Transactions* states that "The American Philosophical Society founded at Philadelphia, humbly desirous to cooperate with the Imperial Society at Petersburg . . . request . . . to accept this Volume as the first Fruits of its Labors in this New World." Copies of the *Transactions* were sent to Franklin in London for distribution among various European learned societies. An opportunity for contact with the St. Petersburg Academy of Sciences presented itself in the summer of 1772, when one of the members of the Academy, Baron Timotheus von Klingstädt, was staying in London. On July 31, 1772, Franklin presented him a personally inscribed copy of the *Transactions*. Somewhat belatedly, in the summer of 1774, Baron Klingstädt passed this copy on to the Academy, a fact recorded in its minutes for August 22/September 2, 1774.[33] On Franklin's recommendation, Baron Klingstädt was elected on January 15, 1773, as the first member of the American Philosophical Society representing Russia.[34] Some time later *Akademicheskie Izvestiia* (Academic News), published by the St. Petersburg Academy of Sciences, brought out a translation of the basic contents of the first volume of *Transactions*. Among the translated materials were two articles by Hugh Williamson, "An Attempt to account for the change of climate, which has been observed in the Middle Colonies in North America" and "An Essay on Comets."[35]

In the late 1780's, some interesting scientific contacts between Russia and America were initiated, if one may say so, on the top level, through the cooperation of Catherine II, Washington, Franklin, and Lafayette. These were the outgrowth of the interest the Russian Empress took at that time in the preparation of a comparative dictionary of all the languages of the world. Naturally, Catherine II had no cause to complain about the bad conditions for scientific work: an army of officials of all ranks throughout the country was at her disposal, ready to execute her commands or caprices. No wonder linguistic material was sent to St. Petersburg in abundance from all the corners of the Great Empire! It was more difficult to get information from America, but even here the Empress solved the question quite simply. As soon as she informed Lafayette of her project, he approached George Washington and Benjamin Franklin directly. "Enclosed I send you a vocabulary," Lafayette wrote, "which the Empress of Russia requests may be filled up with Indian words. You know her plan of a Universal Dictionary . . . Your commissioners for Indian Affairs, Colonel Harman and General Butler, will be able to superintend the business, which it is important to have well done, as the Empress, although I think to very little purpose, sets a great value upon it."[36]

Washington and Franklin, anxious to respond as soon as they could, contacted a number of persons in the United States who might be able to obtain the materials needed by Catherine.[37] The practical results of the "imperial request" were not long in arriving. In April 1787 Benjamin Franklin was able to return Catherine's questionnaire to Lafayette with the "words of Shawanese and Delaware languages."[38] In the beginning of 1788, similar materials were sent by George Washington, who expressed his hearty wish that the attempt of the Empress "to form a universal Dictionary, may be attended with the merited Success."[39]

Thus was performed, to put it in contemporary terms, the first scientific exchange between America and Russia on the top level. The documentation was published a long time ago but, as sometimes happens, has been overlooked among the countless documents in the multivolumed works of Washington and Franklin. Researchers apparently considered it too insignificant for serious attention, and it was quoted comparatively infrequently. But actually contemporaries—George Washington, first of all—saw this endeavor, not unreasonably, one must say, as an important step for achieving harmony among nations. In transmitting the material on Indian languages, Washington wrote:

> To know the affinity of tongues seems to be one step towards promoting the affinity of nations. Would to God, the harmony of nations was an object that lay nearest to the hearts of Sovereigns; and that the incentive to peace (of which commerce and facility of understanding each other are not the most inconsiderable) might be daily increased! Should the present or any other efforts of mine to procure information respecting the different dialects of the Aborigines in America, serve to reflect a ray of light on the obscure subject of language in general, I shall be highly gratified.[40]

Washington expressed a further desire that the plan of the Empress "lay the foundation for that assimilation of Language, which, producing assimilation of manners and interests, should one day remove many of the causes of hostility from amongst mankind."[41]

At the time, those dreams had a character of abstraction; nevertheless, the first practical step, participated in by Franklin and Washington, had valuable consequences for the development of linguistics both in Russia and in America. Materials from the United States were partially utilized for the second edition of the general comparative dictionary,[42] which exerted a considerable influence on the philological investigations in the United States. The act of collecting materials for Catherine II involved Americans in a comparative study of Indian languages. At a later date, dictionaries of various Indian tribes were prepared on the model of the Russian dictionary by Benjamin Smith Barton, J. Heckewelder, and Theodor Schults. E. Dvoichenko-Markova, who planned to devote a separate work to this subject, offers some interesting data for it. Although unfortunately this project has not yet been realized, the documents she has brought out so far, especially the correspondence between the well-known American philologist Peter S. Du Ponceau and his colleague in Russia, Friedrich Adelung, which took place in 1817, are of considerable interest.[43] Although the correspondence chronologically lies beyond the framework of this book, I cannot refrain from quoting an excerpt from it which sounds exceptionally timely in our day:

> The late general pacification has left the world at liberty to pursue without interruption the arts and sciences which unite mankind; the enlarged views of your August Sovereign, and the immense progress which your country has made in every branch of learning, point that Country out to us as a source from which our labours may derive considerable aid, permit us then, thro' you, to begin to unite the two hemispheres in joint efforts to promote a Science, the utility of which is equally felt by the learned of your Country and the Students of our own.[44]

In studying Russian-American scientific and cultural contacts in the 1780's and 1790's one should not disregard the correspondence and personal acquaintance between Benjamin Franklin and Princess Catherine Dashkov (Dasshkaw), Director of the St. Petersburg Academy of Sciences in 1783-1796, and president of a special Russian academy, which she herself founded in 1783 for the reform of Russian language. The first exchange of letters and an encounter between Princess Dashkov and Franklin took place in Paris in the winter of 1781.[45] At a later date Franklin sent her the second volume of *Transactions,* which the Princess thanked him for in a letter of August 30, 1788.[46]

On April 17, 1789, proposed by Franklin, Catherine Dashkov was unanimously elected a member of The American Philosophical Society. On May 15 she was sent an appropriate certificate, which stated: "Seeking to promote the interests of the Society by attracting prominent scholars to it, Madame la Princesse de Daschkaw, President of the Imperial Academy of

Sciences at Petersburg, has been elected a Member of the said Philosophical Society."[47] Princess Dashkov became the first woman and the second Russian member of the American Philosophical Society. On August 18/29, 1791, the Academy of Sciences was officially informed of this election by A. Iu. Kraft who presented to the Academy the copy of notification, "signed in person by the famous Dr. Franklin," as "testimony of high appreciation of the literary work of the Princess on the part of most distant learned societies."[48]

Touching on the circumstances of her election, Princess Dashkov wrote in her memoirs: "He [Franklin] bears me enough friendship and esteem to propose me as member of this respected and already famous Philosophical Society of Philadelphia. I was unanimously elected. I have already received the diploma and since that time the Society has never failed to send me all its published works."[49] Princess Dashkov continued more or less regular contacts both with the Philosophical Society and with individual American scientists, the physicist John Churchman[50] and the "father of the corps of engineers," Jonathan Williams. Her letter to Williams, acknowledging the receipt of his *Memoir of the Use of the Thermometer in Navigation,* of February 21/March 4, 1793, is significant.

> I am perfectly sensible of the great importance of this discovery which You have the merit to have established on so many troublesome observations, a merit that gives You a claim to the gratitude of Mankind, and especially of every trading nation. I should be very happy if I could contribute something towards the divulgation of so useful a knowledge, and I thank you for the opportunity You have given me to do it. Accordingly, I have not only delivered into our Marine Department a copy of Your memoir, but have also ordered to be drawn up an explication of the Method, and of its great usefulness in Navigation, in the Russian language.[51]

In such a manner contacts between the St. Petersburg Academy and the American scientific circle were developing quite successfully. The number of Russian members of the American Philosophical Society was increased in 1791 through the election of John Gottlieb Grosche, Professor of Natural History in Mitau, Courland, and Peter Simon Pallas, a well-known naturalist and academician. Understandably, it was primarily scholars of German origin who became the members of the American Philosophical Society. German professors, upon moving to Russia, kept up their extensive international connections, and it is through them that the West judged the state of Russian science. Among the professors who came to Russia there were some outstanding scientists like Leonard Euler (1707-1783); there were also, unfortunately, more than a few mediocre, sometimes simply chance individuals. It is not surprising, therefore, that it was not the most outstanding ones who became members of the American Philosophical Society. Among the very first members, perhaps only Pallas left a more or less significant trace in the history of world science. As to Baron Klingstädt, he probably owes his election mainly to acquaintance with Franklin. Nevertheless, the very fact of the election of Russians testifies to the respect of the American Philosophical Society for scientific achievements in Russia and to its desire to develop connections with the Petersburg Academy of Sciences. In a moving speech, delivered on May 21, 1782, Dr. Thomas Bond, vice-president of the American Philosophical Society, stressed Russian achievements in science and the great importance of international cooperation among scholars.

> If we look around the Nations of the ancient or modern World, we shall find that the most eminent Trait in their Character, and that which procured them Reverence abroad, was their love of Literature, Arts and Sciences. *Russia,* who but a few years ago was scarcely known in Europe, has risen, like the Morning Sun into luminous Greatness. She has searched the World for Men of Science; and given every generous Encouragement to the various Branches of Literature; and there is something so similar and corresponding betwixt the Circumstances of *Russia* and *America*, so far as relates to created Improvements and sudden Eminence, I cannot avoid earnestly recommending to the Society, to promote an Acquaintance with the Learned Persons and Societies of that distinguished Country. Science is Nurse of universal Friendship. She knows not what Enmity or Hatred is. She is at War with none—she is at Peace with all,—and the Line of Communication which she opens, is open to all Mankind. [52]

Another old learned society of the United States, the American Academy of Arts and Sciences, founded in Boston in 1780 at the suggestion of John Adams, made an excellent early choice in electing Leonard Euler to membership. Until recently even specialists were unaware of this significant fact, but the minutes of the St. Petersburg Academy of Sciences for February 28/March 11, 1782, settle it beyond dispute. There the secretary, Johann-Albrecht Euler, the son of Leonard Euler, states that he "unsealed the packet addressed to the Imperial Academy of Sciences, containing a letter of the Academy of Arts and Sciences, recently founded in Boston, in America, to M. Euler-senior, of June 1, 1781, and signed by the secretary Joseph Willard. This recently founded Society has elected M. Euler-senior to its membership and requested him to make known in the Imperial Academy its charter, entitled "Act to incorporate and establish a Society for the cultivation and promotion of Arts and Sciences." [53]

In making this excellent choice, the Academy of Arts and Sciences expressed its respect for the achievements of the St. Petersburg Academy, with which it had established contacts from the very beginning of its existence. Unfortunately, neither the Archive of the Academy of Sciences of the Soviet Union, nor Euler's manuscript collection[54] has yielded further material in connection with this election. But we know from a note of E. Dvoichenko-Markova, published in 1965, that on August 22, 1782, Euler's letter of acceptance was read in the meeting of the American Academy of Arts and Sciences.[55]

This same work shows that contacts between the American Academy of Arts and Sciences and Russia did not end with this election. Boston scientists expressed interest in studying Siberian wheat. On August 22, 1781, William Gordon presented some remarks on the subject, and on November 14, 1781, a letter from Daniel Little and Caleb Gannet on the cultivating of Siberian wheat in America was read at the Academy's meeting. On May 29, 1787, in connection with the publication of the first volume of the *Transactions* of the Academy[56] it was decided to send it to various literary societies, including the Imperial Academy in St. Petersburg. The receipt of these works, together with Joseph Willard's letter of September 25, 1787, was confirmed in the official publication of the St. Petersburg Academy. Some time later the same publication announced the news received from Boston of the death of the first president of the American Academy of Arts and Sciences, James Bowdoin.[57]

The choice of the first American foreign member of the St. Petersburg Academy was also excellent: Benjamin Franklin. According to the minutes of the Academy for November 2/13, 1789, Princess Dashkov, during her perusal of Academy papers, "realized with amazement that the name of the famous Franklin is not among foreign members. Her Highness proposed his candidacy, after which this respected and famous scholar was unanimously elected."[58]

In her letter to Franklin of November 4/15, written in English, Catherine Dashkov wrote:

> Having always supposed, and even cherished the idea, that you were a member of the Imperial Academy of Science, which is at St. Petersburg under my direction, I was greatly surprised, when, reviewing the list of its members, some days ago, I did not find your name in the number. I hastened therefore to acquire this honor for the Academy, and you were received among its members with a unanimous applause and joy. I beg you, Sir, to accept this title, and to believe that I look upon it as an honor acquired by our Academy.

The Princess closed the letter assuring Franklin of her "regard and veneration," and saying that she would "always recollect with pride the advantage I had to be personally noticed by You."[59] When sending Franklin his diploma of foreign membership in the St. Petersburg Academy, the "permanent secretary of the academic conferences," Johann Albrecht Euler, was fully justified in writing that, although the Academy "was one of the last to offer this official token of its esteem, it has not ceased for more than a quarter of a century to admire his rare achievement, more than that of any other academician."[60]

Franklin's election as a foreign member reflected more than respect for his scientific achievements; it was also a recognition of his broad political, social, and literary activity which had long been the subject of serious and growing attention of Russian society. Franklin was the first American author whose works were translated into Russian.[61] *Poor Richard's Almanack,* first published in 1784 and reprinted many times in various versions, was especially popular.[62] Franklin began to publish his almanac in 1732, under the pseudonym of Richard Saunders. He "filled all the little spaces, that occurred between the remarkable days in the Calendar, with proverbial sentences, chiefly such as inculcated industry and frugality." He observed that it is "more difficult for a man in want to act always honestly" or that "it is hard for an empty sack to stand upright." "These proverbs," Franklin wrote in his *Autobiography,* "which contained the wisdom of many ages and nations, I assembled and formed into a connected discourse, prefixed to the Almanac of 1757, as the harangue of a wise old man to the people attending an auction."[63] These clear, simple, and precise sayings reflected perfectly the ideals of the rising bourgeoisie and were enormously successful. New editions of the almanac, which became a handbook for the third estate, kept coming out. The author's Preface to the 1791 Moscow edition pointed out the necessity of "disseminating true principles for a wise behaviour in the course of a life and instilling the taste for civic and moral virtues to that precious class of people without whom we lacked almost everything."[64]

Franklin's *Autobiography,* which came out in a French translation in 1791, also enjoyed great popularity in Russia.[65] The book got immediate response from one of the most prominent literary figures of the day, N. M. Karamzin, who reviewed it in his magazine: "Anyone reading this remarkable book will marvel at the wonderful interweavings of human fate. Franklin, who wandered through Philadelphia in his working clothes, without money, without friends, knowing nothing but the English tongue and poor printer's trade—this Franklin in a few years became known and honored in two halves of the world, subdued British pride, gave freedom to almost all of America, and enriched science with great discoveries!"[66]

Several years later a characteristic "Excerpt from Franklin's Memoirs," devoted to various moral virtues and order of the day, was printed in a journal with the innocent title, *Pleasant and Useful Pastime,*[67] which enjoyed great popularity in the most diverse circles of Russian society.[68]

The modest image of Franklin who appeared in the brilliant Parisian salons in his plain brown coat, with his hair smoothly combed rather than wearing a powdered wig as the fashion of the day required, made an unforgettable impact on his contemporaries.[69] He was so to speak a live model of the moral rules and virtues of which he wrote so clearly and colorfully. This impact was strengthened by the unusual, even exceptional, fate of the American, in itself a striking example of the advantage of modesty, talent, and work over wealth, good birth, and idleness. "Having emerged from the poverty and obscurity in which I was born and bred to a state of affluence and some degree of reputation in the world," Franklin wrote proudly in his *Autobiography.*[70]

Not being a literary expert, I should refrain from judging Franklin's influence on Russian literature. However, the personal acquaintance of D. I. Fonvizin with Franklin probably played some part in the creation of Starodum's image in the immortal eighteenth-century comedy *Nedorosl'* (Ignoramus). There is no doubt that Leo Tolstoy studied Franklin's legacy,[71] but this is too distant a subject for us to dwell on.

The chronological limits of this book make it more important to define the degree of Russian society's acquaintance with Franklin's works and their dissemination in Russia on the eve of the nineteenth century. There is no doubt that Franklin's very name elicited great interest in Russian society, and that his works, both in French and in Russian translations, were widely read. In the end of the eighteenth and in the beginning of the nineteenth century the first collections of his works begin to appear. In 1799 a student of Moscow University, A. I. Turgenev, translated "An Excerpt from Franklin's Memoirs with an Addition of a Short Account of His Life and Some of His Works," and in 1803 the Beketov publishing house issued another, more complete, collection of Franklin's works.[72] Although these first, incomplete collections could not reflect all the wealth and variety of the American's literary, political, and scientific legacy, they included a number of his important works. Among them are some curious moral-philosophical parables with which he used to entertain his friends in Passy (such as the parable, "Morals of Chess," which developed the principle of wise egoism[73]), observations directed against reactionary, expansionist war and defending the role of farmers and merchants;[74] "Remarks concerning the Savages of North America,"[75] which contained an interesting analysis of the life and mores of Indians, and many others. A substantial part of the *Collected Works* of 1803, especially "The Way to Happiness or the Science of Kind-Hearted Richard" ("The Way to Wealth"), and the excerpts from the *Autobiography,* were already known to the Russian reader. Some parts, on the other hand, were printed for the first time. Important among these was "Benjamin Franklin's answer to Lord Howe" of June 30, 1776, which demonstrated the impossibility for the revolted colonists to submit to the mother country. Franklin compared the British Empire with the china vase, that, "once being broken, the separate parts could not retain even their shares of the strength and value that existed in the whole," and called England's war against the colonists "both unjust and unwise"—"unjust and insane," the Russian translation said.[76]

Franklin's works were printed not only in the pages of the Moscow and St. Petersburg publications. In 1786, the first Russian provincial journal, *Uedinennyi Poshekhonetz* (A Solitary Wise Man of Gotha), published in Iaroslavl', printed an "Allegorical and Philosophical Letter from M. Franklin to Mme. B—, written in English and translated from the French."[77] This short, witty piece, "The Ephemera; an Emblem of Human Life," written in French by Franklin for Madame Brillon in 1778 was entitled in Russian editions "The Conversation of the Ephemeras and a monologue of an old insect."[78] The letter, written in philosophically pessimistic tones somewhat unusual for its author, discoursed upon the meaning of human existence as exemplified by ephemeral insects whose life span was but a few hours. An old ephemera proclaimed that, judging by "the apparent motion of the great luminary that gives life to all nature, and which in my time has declined considerably toward the ocean at the end of our earth" (that is, the River Seine, the author comments), it must soon "leave the world in cold and darkness. . . . What now avails all my toil and labor, in amassing honey-dew on this leaf," he wonders, foreseeing that the world will end in universal "death and destruction."[79]

This picture of the destruction of civilization depicted by the old ephemera apparently seemed too gloomy to the optimistic Franklin, who could not refrain from expressing a certain satisfaction in his life and work, the aim of which he saw in "ceaseless desire to serve others."[80]

Ever since the start of the War of Independence, the Russian press had voiced the highest praise of the leaders of the young republic, which upheld its liberty in the struggle against the powerful mother country.

This opinion remained unchanged even in the nineties, years of extreme reaction magnified by fear of the French Revolution. Characteristically, in 1790 T. Voskresensky published in Tobolsk a speech by Condorcet which contained warm tributes to Benjamin Franklin and Leonard Euler.[81] Although the names of these two scientists were not mentioned, the text of the speech left no room for doubt whom the author had in mind.

In 1791 the *Moskovskii Zhurnal* (Moscow Journal), published by Karamzin, printed a poem, "To the current century," which praised the main achievements of the eighteenth century as it was nearing its end: "O century of marvels, of thought and inventions! / May I, this speck of dust before you / Bring to your altar reverent praise! / Was there ever an age of such luminous glory? / You have redeemed our corrupted mores, and / Opened a road to the temple of knowledge, / You gave birth to Voltaire, Franklin, Cook, / To Rumiantsev and to Washington, / Through you, nature's laws were made known to man."[82]

The names of Franklin and Washington were mentioned often in the Russian press of that period, usually accompanied by most flattering epithets. For example, in 1796, a note printed in a journal with the lyrical title *Muza* (The Muse) urged the imitation of "the renowned and the heroes," and in particular of "immortal Washington."[83]

On the whole, American subject matter received systematic and favorable treatment in journals and newspapers of the end of the eighteenth and early years of the nineteenth century, and the interest of Russian society in the new republic did not end with the victorious conclusion of the American Revolution. What were the results of the struggle of the colonies for their independence? What went on in the new state? What was the meaning of the changes that took place and what was their outcome? These were some of the more important questions which could not help but interest the Russian reader. "It now transpires," wrote *Moskovskie Vedomosti* in the fall of 1789, "that those politicians who in the very beginning of the American Revolution asserted that the United States with time will arrive at the most thriving state, were right, even though at present only a commencement of this state is to be seen."[84]

The reader learned from *Politicheskii Zhurnal* (Political Journal) that, "in respect to land, North America is the greatest republic in the world, and in respect to number of people it is stronger than seven United Provinces; but, proportionately, its army is smaller."[85]

In April 1797 the same journal provided an enthusiastic description of the sights of North America and the swift successes of the young republic. "North American free society has the qualities of a youthful body. The lively growth of the blooming youth is pleasing to the eyes of the observer. This is how most of the people today see the North American regions; people praise them and marvel at them."[86]

In 1802 N. M. Karamzin began to publish through the press of Moscow University a new journal, *Vestnik Evropy* (Europe's Messenger), which, in contradiction to its title, devoted considerable attention not only to Europe but also to America. In 1802, among other material on the United States, the journal printed a note on the swift increase of its population and commercial progress. "Nowhere did the number of inhabitants grow so fast as in the United American States. In 1784 there were 3,250,000, and, in 1802, 6,000,000 inhabitants in America. In other words, in eighteen years their number has doubled."[87] Further, information was offered on the swift growth of American export, from $19,000,000 in 1791 to $93,000,000 in 1801. On another occasion, an eyewitness who had lived in the United States observed that "the spirit of commerce is the main characteristic of America," adding that wealth is in marked contrast with poverty and slavery.[88]

Critical remarks about the United States were not infrequent. On the one hand, they were well-founded when slavery or the extermination of Indians was the subject, especially when the criticism emanated from a revolutionary position (recall Radishchev's remarks). On the other hand, and this was much more frequent, sharp criticism came from representatives of the most extreme circles of serf-owning gentry. I am thinking not only of the reactionary monarchist abuse of democracy and the republican regime. Matters are much more complicated when well-justified criticism came from the right, as for example, in these lines by Karamzin: "The brave man in discovering America / Did not discover a road to happiness; / He who chained the Indians / Was himself shackled in chains."[89]

The author was right in saying that Columbus in discovering America "did not discover a road to happiness," but the very idea of "happiness" in the understanding of the ideologist of nobility cannot but call forth serious doubts. New bourgeois customs did not suit the sensitive nature of the sentimental writer, therefore it is not surprising to find in the *Vestnik Evropy* rather harsh descriptions of American mores: "People are rich and crude, especially in Philadelphia where they live only for themselves, and eat and drink in dull monotony."[90] In general *Vestnik* illustrates well the complex and often contradictory views of its editor. The journal's second issue (January 1802) contained an interesting "Letter from the United American Provinces," which gave an enthusiastic appraisal of the democratic mode of government in the United States, and especially of the views and activity of their new president, Thomas Jefferson.

Our motherland presents a phenomenon rare today in the history of nations: the phenomenon of government directed solely toward society, toward supreme good. For this we are obligated to Thomas Jefferson (the president of the Congress), the faithful executor of law . . . This *philosophe,* known in Europe through his works on agriculture and botany, has equally good knowledge of the human heart. . . .

The aristocrats, who three or four years ago, in accordance with the wishes of foreigners, had taken charge of all elections, do not possess such power any more and have no influence.

Everything proceeds inconspicuously, since everybody strives for the same goal: true prosperity.

Independence of private opinions is limited here only by society's opinion; but we do not overstep the limits of reasonable freedom. . . .[91]

In publishing this panegyric to Jefferson, freedom, and democracy, Karamzin might seem not only a liberal, as he is occasionally called, but almost a revolutionary.

However, in the very next issue of the journal we encounter an infamous "Letter from Baltimore" with a frank defense of slavery. "American Negroes, left alone by the world rebels, accept their fate and their positions."[92] The writer attempted to convince the reader that "the Negro of North America is a happy laborer, possessing everything he needs for himself, his wife, and his children, and living without any worries." He proceeded to tell such obvious falsehoods as that on holidays one can see "gay crowds of Arabian women sprayed with perfume, dressed even fancier than their mistresses, wearing expensive rings, earrings, necklaces, lace, with painted feathers on their heads."[93] This hypocritical verbiage and fairy tales about "expensive rings," "silk stockings" and "satin shoes" could not fail to produce in the Russian reader, with his first-hand knowledge of serfdom, any feeling but disgust. At another time N. I. Novikov also published an article by an apologist of slavery, but in a note juxtaposed the author's views to his own, those of the progressive eighteenth-century enlightenment.

The sentimental liberal Karamzin, who considered himself a "republican at heart," did not think it necessary to make any explanations. It is hard to say whether he himself believed the fairy tales of his Boston "correspondent." We might suppose that he could not believe them, but printed the article anyway, as later he published articles defending serfdom, which presented the Russian nobleman almost as a benefactor of his peasants, "their defender in civil cases" and "helper in cases of calamity." We see at this point not a liberal writer-sentimentalist but a conservative defender of serfdom and autocracy, the future author of the Note on Ancient and Modern Russia (1811).

Although Karamzin's influence should not be underestimated, Russian society was not so homogeneous as to be affected by his ideas alone. During the so-called "Karamzin period," Russian literature was represented not only by Karamzin and his admirers, but also by Radishchev and his followers.[94] And, although the tsarist government exercised police repression over Radishchev and banned his book, it could not stop the dissemination of his ideas.

Soviet historians and literary scholars have dispersed the legend of Radishchev's complete solitude and demonstrated that his ideas are reflected in the work of I. Pnin, V. Popugaev, I. Born, A. Vostokov, and several others.[95] Although the modest writers belonging to "Free Society of Lovers of Letters, Science, and Arts," founded in the summer of 1801, did not reach the revolutionary heights of their great predecessor, nevertheless they continued his tradition, although sometimes inconsistently. Their popularity could not be compared with that of Karamzin, but in the long run the future belonged to them. It is significant that their stand on slavery differed radically from the views of the brilliant idol of Russian nobility. Popugaev's essay "The Negro" protested angrily against slavery and appeared as one of the more daring anti-serfdom thrusts in the open press in the beginning of the nineteenth century. Popugaev had first read his essay to the "Free Society" in 1801; he published it in *Periodicheskoe Izdanie* (Periodical Publication) in 1804; and later in an anthology, *Taliia* (Thalia; 1807).[96] "Who allowed you to make prisoners of your brethren?," wrathfully asked the hero of the essay, Negro Amru, in conclusion. "Freedom is not a saleable commodity; the gold of the whole world will not suffice to buy it, and no tyrant dispose of it."

While the subject of "Negro" or in some cases, "Indian" slavery was more often than not geographically linked with the former colonies in America, essentially it was an allegorical form of denouncing serfdom in Russia. Popugaev's essay was in this sense perhaps the most daring, but by no means an isolated phenomenon. The same issue of *Periodicheskoe Izdanie* that printed "The Negro" contained "A Sonnet of an Iroquois, Written in His Native Tongue," by another member of The Free Society, A. E. Izmailov; in this, although disguised as Canada, a reader could easily recognize the serfdom regime of Russia. Great popularity in Russia was enjoyed by the well-known drama of August Kotzebue, *The Negro Slaves*, Nicholas Gnedich's poem, "A Peruvian to a Spaniard" (1805), "Against sugar" by S. Bobrov, and others.[97]

In their daring denunciations of Negro slavery and of the living conditions of the American Indians, in their protests against injustice and inhumanity, the Russian radicals of the early nineteenth century, with Popugaev in the vanguard, continued the best traditions of Alexander Radishchev. Members of the "Free Society" were also definitely influenced by Abbé Raynal's *Histoire des deux Indes,* which was the subject of their special attention and study.

The beginning of the early nineteenth century also saw further development of the Russian-American scientific contacts which had originated in the last decades of the eighteenth century with the close participation of Benjamin Franklin. "The great Franklin, and the learned Society of Sciences in Philadelphia, whose founder he was, have perhaps as many admirers in Europe as in America, and I count myself among their number," B. F. J. Hermann, "Academicus Ordinarius und Professor der Mineralogie bey der Akademie der Wissenschaften in St. Petersburg," wrote to the Philosophical Society.[98] He stated that in the course of twenty years he had conducted a successful investigation of Siberia and had amassed an extensive collection of minerals. Along with his letter he forwarded to Philadelphia his two most recent books and a number of samples of Russian minerals.[99]

Hermann's personal initiative was not encouraged. The Philosophical Society ignored his request for membership, limiting itself to a formal expression of gratitude, although Hermann's formation on Russia and, even more, on Siberia could not but be of considerable interest. Nevertheless, official contacts between the St. Petersburg Academy of Sciences and the American Philosophical Society continued to develop successfully. A letter of January 10/22, 1803, written by the permanent secretary of the St. Petersburg Academy of Sciences, Nicholas Fuss, stated that the Academy had received the first five volumes of the *Transactions of the American Philosophical Society,* and in turn, had sent to Philadelphia the eleventh volume of its publication *Nova Acta.*[100] At an earlier date, Euler, Fuss's predecessor as permanent secretary, had sent the Philosophical Society the ninth and tenth volumes of this publication.

Levett Harris, the American consul-general in St. Petersburg, and, later, John Quincy Adams, the American minister, frequently served as contacts with the American Philosophical Society. In 1807 Fuss forwarded to Harris the fifteenth volume of the Academy's Transactions and the consul sent it to the Philosophical Society.[101] Later Harris sent the library of the Philosophical Society, at the request of John Vaughan, two dictionaries and two grammars, as well as the latest volume of the Transactions of the St. Petersburg Academy of Sciences.[102] Following the request of a well-known philologist, Professor Friedrich Adelung, he sent to the Philosophical Society Adelung's work on the similarities between the Russian language and Sanscrit—which at the time was erroneously considered to be a general ancestor of Indo-European languages.[103]

The St. Petersburg Academy of Sciences was the most important but not the only scientific center in Russia at that time. As early as 1755 Mikhail Lomonosov founded Moscow University, destined to play an outstanding role in the development of Russian science and education. There also existed a German University in Derpt and a Polish one in Vil'no. On 8/20 September 1802, Alexander I signed a manifesto on the establishment of ministries, among which was specified a Ministry of Public Education.[104] In the beginning of 1803 the Tsar established the "preliminary rules of public education," the basis for which was laid by the project prepared beforehand by A. Czartoryski. Educational districts headed by trustees were formed, and several new universities founded, among them those in Kharkov and Kazan! The statutes established by Alexander I were rather liberal: all the affairs of the university were to be managed by a professorial council, and the rector and his assistants were to be chosen through an election. Universities enjoyed considerable autonomy. They controlled the educational institutions responsible to them, and exercised the right of censorship, appointment of high school (gymnasium) teachers, and so on.[105] At first, the censorship rules of 1804 were interpreted in the spirit of liberalism; however, even in those years these rules could not stop the suppression of publication of works unfavorable to the tsarist government. Nevertheless, on the whole governmental measures in the field of education were perhaps the most radical among the few and limited reforms marking "the beautiful beginning of Alexandrian days" (Pushkin).

Detailed information on reforms in Russian education was brought to scientific circles in America by two outstanding Poles, J. Niemcewicz and J. Stroynowski. A prominent writer, historian, and political figure, participant in the Kosciuszko uprising, Julian Ursyn Niemcewicz moved to America in 1797.[106] Before long he was elected to membership in the Philosophical Society, and it was through him that the Society established its contact with Stroynowski, rector of the University of Vil'no, as well as with Czartoryski, who had long been a trustee of the Vil'no district. Stroynowski's letter to the American Philosophical Society about the reforms brought about by the Russian government in the field of education is especially interesting. It enclosed some documents concerning the University of Vil'no which had recently been signed by the Tsar. Stroynowski, a strong supporter of international scientific connections, remarked that "there is no doubt that the scientists and writers of all countries form among themselves a single association."[107]

New and much more important contacts between Russia and the United States occurred in the first decades of the nineteenth century on the highest level. The correspondence of Alexander I and Thomas Jefferson played a prominent role both in the political and cultural rapprochement between the two countries. Alexander I, "the actor on the throne," knew when necessary how to assume the pose of a liberal, and even of a republican, although essentially he had always been an autocrat and believer in the system of serfdom (at least in Russia). In order to establish contact with Jefferson, the Tsar decided to utilize a Swiss, Frédéric LaHarpe, who had been his tutor during the years from 1783 to 1794. La Harpe visited Russia from August 1801 to May 1802 and had an opportunity to become acquainted with some of the projects which were discussed by the Tsar and his "young friends" in the Secret Committee. "A weak and cunning autocrat" did not in the least object to talking to his former tutor about liberal reforms, political freedom, and even a constitution. In these discussions, according to La Harpe, the young Tsar never used the word "subjects," and referred to the Russians only as "my countrymen" and even "concitoyens." This in no way improved the lot of the Tsar's "concitoyens." Even the moderate liberal M. M. Speransky bitterly noted in 1802: "I find two estates in Russia: slaves of the Tsar and slaves of the landlords . . . . There are no truly free people in Russia except beggars and philosophers."[108]

On his return from St. Petersburg to Paris in the summer of 1802, La Harpe was full of optimism. Paraphrasing him, the English bookseller John Hurford Stone wrote to his friend, the famous scholar and philosopher Joseph Priestly, who had moved to America at the end of the eighteenth century: "Among the rulers of the day, your President enjoys the greatest respect and benevolence of the Emperor. . . . I am sure that he would be most grateful for information on the internal government of the United States. By this I mean the very mechanism of the government, i.e. the order of relations between the President and his ministers and their offices, between the ministries and the lower organs of the administration."[109]

News of Alexander I's interest in the civil government of the United States and in its President, reported in detail by John Hurford Stone as related by La Harpe, came to Jefferson both from Priestley and, somewhat earlier, from Priestley's close friend, Thomas Cooper. In his reply to Priestley of November 29, 1802, Jefferson recommended a number of works for the purpose of acquainting the Tsar with the state system and the constitution of the United States: Thomas Cooper's *Propositions Respecting the Foundations of Civil Government,* Chipman's *Sketches on the Principles of Government,* Priestley's own piece on *First Principles of Government,* as well as the famous *Federalist* papers by Hamilton, Madison, and Jay. Characteristically, Jefferson, by no means an advocate of decisive and hasty reforms, recommended some preliminary work as being necessary for preparing the nation for self-government. "Who could have thought the French nation incapable of it?" asked Jefferson, and added: "Alexander will doubtless begin at the right end by taking means for diffusing instruction and a sense of their natural rights through the mass of his people, and for relieving them in the meantime from actual oppression."[110]

Although Jefferson felt that it would be of great interest to engage Alexander I in foreign private correspondence,[111] in practice he had not undertaken any steps to establish direct contact with the Russian emperor. About a year later, in October 1803, La Harpe again approached Stone with a request that he act as intermediary for the rapprochement between the President of the United States and the Russian Tsar, which would be in his opinion "infinitely advantageous for both, and for the well-being of men." According to La Harpe, Alexander I admired the *Discourse* of President Jefferson and esteemed "cet eminent citoyen" greatly.[112]

This time, in order to establish contact with Jefferson, Stone decided to utilize Joel Barlow, an American poet and statesman living in France at the time. In forwarding La Harpe's letter to Jefferson, Barlow deemed it permissible to offer the American President lengthy considerations on the Russian Tsar and the possible ways of influencing him. He wrote that Alexander "is well acquainted with the English literature and language, with our revolution and history, with your character, principles and administration. He has mentioned you with particular respect in several of his letters. And the paragraph here extracted from one of his letters, La Harpe assures me, is sincerely intended by the Emperor as an invitation or an overture to a correspondence direct with you." Among the topics which could produce a useful exchange of opinion between Jefferson and Alexander I, Barlow mentioned liberty of the press and the education of people in general, freedom of the seas, and especially the principle of federalism, which in his opinion was little understood in Europe even in theory. An example for Russia could be set, in his opinion, by American transportation, bridges and canals, encouragement of agriculture and manufactures, as well as workhouses combined with confinement for criminals, and finally, "general reform and amelioration in criminal jurisprudence."[113]

Although Jefferson did not choose to avail himself of the wordy advice of his correspondent, Barlow's letter was instrumental in the establishment of a direct correspondence between the American President and the Russian Tsar. A suitable occasion for the establishment of a direct contact between them presented itself in the same year, 1804, when news reached Washington of Russian assistance in the freeing of an American frigate crew stranded on the shores of Tripoli.

> I avail myself of this occasion of expressing the exalted pleasure I have felt in observing the various acts of your administration, during the short time you have yet been on the throne of your country, and seeing in them manifestations of the virtue and wisdom from which they flow. What has not your country to hope from a career which had begun from such auspicious developments: Sound principles, pursued with a steady step, dealing out good progressively as your people are prepared to receive and to hold it fast, cannot fail to carry them and yourself far in the improvement of their condition, during the course of your life.[114]

These lofty words, written, one assumes, with the best intentions, were—to put it mildly—ill-suited for the characterization of Alexander I. Unfortunately, Thomas Jefferson was not alone in his illusions. Immoderate praise and noisy raptures in behalf of the young Tsar have reverberated for a long time in Russia and abroad.

In his reply of November 7/19, 1804, to Jefferson, Alexander I stated that in offering his assistance in the affair of the American frigate, he was especially glad that, while showing his respect for the worthy nation, he was able to please the President personally.

> I desire that this unmistakable token of my favorable disposition should serve to further the trade relations now being established between the two nations; it should be a pledge to your citizens of the hospitality, protection, and privileges which they will always enjoy in my country. I have always felt a great esteem for your nation which knew how to make noble use of its independence by creating a free and wise Constitution assuring the well-being of each and all.[115]

Today the Tsar's words about the free and wise constitution provoke only an ironical smile; they quite obviously were meant "for export." Alexander I enjoyed posing as a liberal when it was advantageous for him to do so, and Jefferson apparently accepted his words at their face value. Knowing through Priestley that Alexander wanted to gain detailed knowledge of the American government, Jefferson selected "the two best works" on the subject and requested Levett Harris to pass them on to the Tsar as his personal gifts. The four volumes of *Life of Washington* and a copy of the Constitution of the United States were forwarded by Harris on 4/16 August 1806 for Alexander's library through the intermediary of the minister for foreign affairs, A. Ia. Budberg.[116] Alexander I received the books the same time as Jefferson's second letter, dated 19 April 1806, which, along with new compliments about the Tsar, contained some important comments of mutual interest about the neutral rights of northern European nations, with Russia at their head. With Napoleon and Alexander in mind, Jefferson wrote: "Two personages in Europe, of which your Majesty is one, have it in their power, at the approaching pacification, to render imminent service to nations in general, by incorporating into the act of pacification, a correct definition of the rights of the neutrals on the high seas."[117]

Thanking the American president for the interesting works on the Constitution of the United States and for the flattering opinions he expressed, Alexander I wrote on 10/22 August 1806 that, if his intentions were crowned with success, Jefferson's approval would serve as a reward,

> because the nation led by you will participate equally in the benefits produced by them. I have no illusions about the greatness of the obstacles lying in the way of a return to the order of things conforming to the common interests of all civilized nations and firmly resisting the actions prompted by avarice and ambition. But this goal is too beautiful and too dear to my heart for me to give it up because of the difficulties on the way. That you should find justice in my views gives me great encouragement. So I value your letters all the more, and I cannot express the pleasure of receiving them in any better way than to ask for their continuation.[118]

Jefferson was interested in Russian books, and especially in "a work of Mr. Pallas, entitled *Vocabulaires comparés des langues de tout la Terre.*" In a covering letter accompanying Alexander's reply, Levett Harris noted that he had been unable to get Pallas' vocabulary and, instead was sending books by Rumiantsev (*Tableau du commerce de la Russie, 1802-1804*) and I. Pototcki (*L'Histoire ancienne des provinces de l'Empire de Russie*).[119] Still earlier, through Harris' mediation, Alexander's bust had been sent to Jefferson.

From what one can judge on the basis of published sources and available archival materials, direct personal correspondence between Jefferson and Alexander ceased in 1806. However, Russian connections with the President and the government of the United States became much more regularized as a result of the establishment of diplomatic relations and an exchange of envoys in 1808-9. This will be discussed in detail later; for the moment we need only note that Jefferson and Alexander did not forget their correspondence and utilized new avenues opened by the exchange of diplomatic missions for its continuation. Having appointed his secretary William Short minister to St. Petersburg in August 1808, Jefferson provided him with a personal letter to Alexander I. It is typical that he wrote it in his own hand. Unfortunately, Short had no occasion to use this introduction, since the Senate did not approve his candidacy, as he regretfully informed N. P. Rumiantsev on 1 May 1809.[120]

In turn, when Alexander I appointed A. Ia. Dashkov consul-general in Philadelphia and chargé d'affaires for the United States, he gave him a letter to be handed to the President of the United States.[121] Dashkov's appointment proved more successful; in point of fact, it did not demand any confirmation in Russia. He arrived in Washington the summer of 1809 to find as president James Madison, to whom, as new head of the government, on July 14, 1809, he handed Alexander's letter.[122] This letter opens the official correspondence of Russian diplomatic representatives in the United States with the American government.[123]

At the same time, Dashkov considered it necessary to attest his special respect to the retired president, Thomas Jefferson. He wrote Rumiantsev in the summer of 1809:

> Having known from Your Excellency of the respect with which His Majesty honors Mr. Jefferson, and being obligated by my instructions to present to him the assurances of His Majesty's friendship, I could not but assure him of that respect which he enjoys in the great Northern power. Since at the time of my arrival Mr. Jefferson had left the office of President, I have not presumed to inform him of anything official in the name of our August Ruler, but I thought that I shall deserve the approval of Your Excellency if I gave him to understand that I had hoped to arrive in the United States before he decided to leave the government, and mentioned that I have the happiness to bear the holograph of His Majesty for the President of the United States.[124]

An epilogue to the direct contacts between Alexander I and Thomas Jefferson was a visit to Monticello of F. D. Pahlen, Russian Minister to the United States. Upon his arrival in the United States in 1810, Pahlen wrote Jefferson, as instructed by Alexander I, that the Tsar continued to hold him in great respect. During his visit to Jefferson's estate in Virginia in the spring of 1811, the Minister repeated in person to the former president everything that he was instructed to convey. It is interesting to note that the minister saw the bust of Alexander I in Jefferson's study. Pahlen was greatly pleased with his trip to Monticello, and wrote to Rumiantsev enthusiastically: "Mr. Jefferson combines the rare qualities of statesman, scholar, and likable man. His active mind embraces everything that is useful or interesting; he hastens the progress of agriculture by inventing a new plow, while he rectifies the position of his country by astronomical observation. . . . He always speaks of his attachment for His Majesty the Emperor with the greatest warmth; he knows how to appreciate properly the rare qualities of the philanthropic sovereign whose bust is found in his study."[125]

Jefferson came to understand the true character of the "liberal" Tsar only many years later. "I am afraid," he wrote to Levett Harris in 1821, "our quondam favorite Alexander has swerved from the true faith. His becoming an accomplice of the soi-disant Holy Alliance, the anti-national principles he has separately avowed, and his becoming the very leader of a combination to chain mankind down eternally to oppressions of the most barbarous ages, are clouds on his character not easily to be cleared away. But these are problems for younger heads than mine. You will see their solution and tell me of it in another world."[126]

It hardly seems necessary to point out that the plan of converting the Russian Tsar to the new bourgeois-democratic faith was a foolhardy undertaking from the very beginning. Of course Alexander I could familiarize himself with the Constitution of the United States, peruse Washington's biography, and even make laudable comments on the content of his reading—but this had no effect whatsoever on his political actions.

One should not fail to observe an important aspect, that often eludes—or is consciously ignored by—Western scholars, in particular George Vernadsky. In an article about French and American influence on the reforms of Alexander I's epoch, written with Vernadsky's usual literary flair, a distinct tendency to blur the difference between the projects of the avant-garde revolutionary wing of the Russian society and the reformist activity of the government can be detected. It is, therefore, not accidental that he deduces that there was a remarkable similarity between the projects of the Russian government and of the Decembrists. "What is particularly striking about these plans to the point of view of the present study," wrote Vernadsky, "is their similarity to the projects of the government. Certain constitutional plans of the Decembrists, like those of the government, followed the principles of the French plan, others followed the American plan. The similarity is explained in part by the common sources from which the Decembrists and the Emperor's councilors drew their materials."[127]

In my research I am constantly dealing with the American influence on Russian society, and the last thing I want to do is to minimize it. On the contrary, since my subject calls for constant inquiry into the most diverse contacts with America, the reader might form an exaggerated notion of the degree of American influence, which generally was immeasurably smaller than French, German, or English influences. Nor do I have the least desire to belittle Russian interest in America; in fact I hope in some measure to prove the existence of such interest among the most diverse circles, from Radishchev to Alexander I and his entourage. But one must not fail to see the difference in the projects of the government and the revolutionary wing of the Russian society, because the basic goal of the former consisted in protecting and preserving precisely that which the latter intended in one way or another to eliminate. It is possible to prove a certain similarity between the plans of the Decembrists and the earlier projects of the Tsar, his "young friends" from the Secret Committee, and M. M. Speransky. But one should not forget that Speransky, who was considered practically a Jacobin by some tsarist dignitaries and was sent into exile by his ruler, was the same man who later was in charge of the trial of the Decembrists.

The history of the establishment of Russian-American scientific, cultural, and socio-political contacts is most instructive in another respect. The first contacts were formed in spite of enormous geographical distances, religious prejudices, and political barriers. The international scientific spirit which so brilliantly solved the secrets of the atom, found its eighteenth-century expression in the development of the theory of electricity. It affords me special pleasure to point out that at the origin of the first contacts between Russia and America shine in an undying light two great names—Lomonosov and Franklin—throwing light on the best traditions of the past and serving as a symbol for the future.

VI

RUSSIAN COLONIZATION OF THE NORTHWEST

In 1725, on the occasion of the launching of the famous Vitus Bering expedition, Peter I had sent personally written instructions in which he broached the question of "discovery of the joining point between Asia and America." Peter's idea was for the expedition, after its ships were built in Kamchatka, to sail north along the coast and "search where the land joined with America."[1]

Russian explorers answered Peter's question negatively: Asia was not "joined with America," and today the strait dividing the two continents bears Bering's name.[2] Justice, however, demands mention of the fact that as early as 1648, that is, eighty years before Bering's expedition, an Iakut cossack, Semen Dezhnev, and his daring companions crossed the famous Arian strait; it is to them that the honor of this remarkable geographical discovery belongs. Dezhnev rounded the northeastern part of Asia, so to speak, from the opposite side. He set out from the mouth of the Kolyma River and docked south of the mouth of the Anadyr River. Bering, who set out from the Kamchatka River toward the strait dividing Asia from America, actually covered only part of the route traversed long before by Dezhnev and his companions. Neither Dezhnev nor Bering saw the continent of North America. As the leading authority in this field, L. S. Berg, has demonstrated, the first person to discover the strait between Russia and America, strictly speaking, was I. Fedorov (1732), who not only saw Gvozdev's Islands and the shores of Asia and America but was the first person to put them on the map.[3]

The second expedition of Vitus Bering and A. Chirikov was of great importance in the early explorations of the northwestern American shoreline. The achievement of A. Chirikov was especially important, for he not only reached the northwestern shores of America but made a long voyage along its coastline. His map of the sea voyage of 1741 is the first map in the world to show North America on the basis of concrete data—not as a "Great Land" or a "Great Island" but actually as North America.[4]

It is easy to write of these matters now. Russian and Soviet scholars have performed an enormous task of studying the monumental literature, reading through poorly legible manuscript materials of the seventeenth and eighteenth centuries, and scrupulously investigating ancient maps. Owing to the labors of A. V. Efimov, L. S. Berg, A. I. Andreyev, S. B. Okun', and others, we take many deductions for granted. But not so very long ago the matters were very different. For example, F. A. Golder, an American scholar, doubted the verisimilitude of Dezhnev's voyage and considered the report of the Iakut cossack almost pure invention.[5]

On the basis of careful analysis of the available information (Dezhnev's reports and petitions to the Iakut voivode in 1655), Berg has proved that Dezhnev indeed made his voyage around northeast Asia.[6] Further research has shown that Dezhnev's expedition was not the accidental success of a daring seaman but an integral part of a broad colonizing movement across Siberia to the shores of the Pacific and the American Northwest.[7] Soviet historians have shown that the way for Dezhnev's voyage was prepared by earlier forays along the shore of the Arctic Ocean, and that was the starting point for new, and even more significant, later achievements.[8] It has been proved that Russia's discovery of America was not merely the result of governmental policy but the consequence of popular efforts. Among the many who deserve credit the names of S. Dezhnev, Peter I, P. Nagibin, A. Myl'nikov, A. Chirikov, and V. Bering stand out.[9]

Russian seamen and travelers opened the northeastern coast of Asia, discovered the strait dividing the Chukot Peninsula from Alaska, and were the first to explore the Great Land (of the northwest coast of America). The geographical problem of whether Russia and America were joined, was solved clearly, definitively, and negatively. This is by no means the most important result of Russian geographical explorations. Much more significant from the point of view of the commercial, political, and historical development was the establishment of contact between Asia and America. In this sense one is fully justified in saying that, as the result of Russian expeditions in the eighteenth century, Asia was "joined with America" through the establishment of more or less systematic and firm contacts. Russia became not just a European and Asiatic, but, to some extent, an American power. The term "Russian America" appeared and was used widely in literature and documents. From the middle of the eighteenth century on, Russian connections with America were firmly secured by the activity in the Pacific Northwest of numerous companies of Siberian merchants and manufacturers. After Bering's companions returned in 1742 from the island carrying his name, with a rich cargo of beaver furs, various enterprising Siberian merchants and fur hunters, led by thirst for acquisition, began equipping systematic expeditions to the Aleutian Islands. According to the data collected by V. Berkh, which is far from complete, between 1745 and 1798 there were more than eighty private expeditions. Besides their profitable commercial operations, they produced a substantial survey of Aleutian Islands. The appendix of Berkh's book shows that the total known value of furs exported by private companies for this period was 6,958,178 rubles, and in the case of many expeditions the value of the cargo remained unknown.[10]

The activity of Grigori Shelikhov, organizer of a series of voyages to the Pacific islands and founder of the first Russian settlements near the shores of North America, deserves special mention. The bulk of furs exported by the company of Shelikhov and Golikov was evaluated at nearly one and a half million rubles.[11] Although this figure alone shows the scale on which the company operated, the significance of Shelikhov's activity lies beyond this: it was not for nothing that Derzhavin referred to him as the "Russian Columbus."[12]

From the very beginning the colonization of northeast Asia, the Aleutian Islands, and Alaska was directly connected with the problem of Russian relations with the new republic created on the Atlantic coast of North America. Although when the Russian government learned about the rebellion of the English colonies in America it had carefully avoided any direct diplomatic relations with the "rebels," in the fall of 1779 it took the initiative in connection with events in the far Pacific North which at first glance might seem of little importance.

In the fall of 1779 a report was received in St. Petersburg from Irkutsk Governor-General Klichka about the appearance in the region of "Chukotski Cape" of "unrecognized" foreign vessels. This news so disturbed the tsarist government that it instructed the Russian minister in Paris, I. S. Bariatinsky, to get in touch with the "chargé d'affaires of the American settlements," Benjamin Franklin. Informing Bariatinsky about "the vessels approaching those shores," the head of the College of Foreign Affairs, N. I. Panin, wrote that Catherine,

> presuming those vessels to be American and from Canada, deigned to instruct me to inform Your Excellency of it, with the following imperial command: that you, having informed the chargé d'affaires of the

American settlements, Franklin, of the approach of those vessels to the abovementioned shores, ask him in your own name, whether he would not investigate if these vessels were actually American and if so, from which parts; and when he ascertains that they were indeed American, whether they could not procure and pass on to you the description and the map of their voyage, so that by studying them one could see whether it would be convenient or possible to establish direct navigation between the local regions and America by a direct and short route. In conclusion, I should like to tell you for your information, that Her Imperial Majesty deigned to command that, in case some unknown foreign vessels arrived in those parts, coats of arms should be made and sent to the Chukot people, to be hung on the trees on the shores of their habitations, to show the people disembarking from the vessels that these parts belong to the Empire of Her Majesty.[13]

A number of considerations make the document quoted of considerable interest for the study of Russian-American relations. It was the first official document issued directly by Catherine and Panin to the Russian representative abroad to communicate with "chargé d'affaires Franklin." Panin's letter shows that the Russian government already evidenced an interest in establishing "direct navigation between the local regions and America by a direct and short route." Finally, the document is another illustration of the constant anxieties of tsarist Russia in respect to the safety of its possessions in the Pacific North, and its striving to protect them from the foreign competitors.

Why did news of the appearance of "unrecognized" foreign vessels near faraway "Chukotski Cape" in the 1770's disturb the tsarist government to such an extent that it considered it possible to forget diplomatic formalities, strictly observed heretofore, and communicate directly with the representative of the "rebellious" American settlements, Benjamin Franklin? The reasons for this anxiety become clearer if one remembers the famous "mutiny" organized in 1771 in Bolsheretsk by M. Benyowski, who promised to return to Kamchatka's shores with foreign vessels.[14]

Benyowski (1746-1786) was a man with an unusual and complex biography. Descendant of Polish aristocracy, he was born in Hungary, took part in the rebellion of Polish confederates against Russia and later in the conspiracy of the adherents of the heir of the Russian throne Paul I, and was finally exiled by the government of Catherine II to faraway Bolsheretsk. In his fate, the events in Poland and Kamchatka are whimsically intertwined with daring voyages and adventures, contacts with Benjamin Franklin, two visits to the United States, and the history of the island of Madagascar where, for a time, Benyowski was "emperor."

Having organized a successful plot in Bolsheretsk, Benyowski and seventy accomplices captured the ship *St. Peter* and set out on a difficult and dangerous voyage round the world.[15] En route to Europe, the daring fugitives stopped in Japan, Formosa, and so on. About thirty people perished in the course of the voyage. When, at the request of the French government, Benyowski undertook an expedition to Madagascar, only eleven people followed him. Several of his companions remained in France, but most of them walked five hundred and fifty versts to Paris where they approached the Russian chargé d'affaires, N. K. Khotinsky, requesting him to arrange for their return to Russia.[16] Khotinsky's intercession on their behalf was successful, and he obtained the necessary means for sending the fugitives back to Russia, where they were promised imperial "forgiveness" and "quiet residence" in any place of their choice, with the exception of the two capitals.[17] Khotinsky was assisted by Denis Ivanovich Fonvizin, who worked in the College for Foreign Affairs at that period. "Since receiving your friendly letter," Fonvizin wrote him, "I have kept trying to arrange to remit to you the sum needed for repatriation of certain people, and at present I am sending you by a special delivery, with a ministerial letter of the Count Nikolai Ivanovich [Panin], credit for eight thousand livres."[18]

Benyowski's threat "to come back to Kamchatka with a hostile aim" made "not a little trouble not only for the Siberian officials but also for the higher government."[19] A new "chief commander," M. Bem, was sent to Kamchatka with wide powers granted by the empress for restoring order and surveying the "military command." The new commander was ordered in particular to send all soldiers and officers unsuited for service to Okhotsk—so that they "would not eat bread for nothing." The tsarist government carefully watched Benyowski's movements in France and, not being precisely aware of his intentions, was much disturbed by preparations for the Madagascar expedition. In the spring of 1773 Viazemsky wrote to Bem in a confidential letter from St. Petersburg that "the actual intention of his expedition is concealed," and expressed apprehension whether Benyowski, "acquainted with a free passage to Kamchatka and possessing information of its shores and inhabitants, might not attempt to encroach upon it in some way."[20]

Benyowski's venturesomeness might have posed many difficult questions for the tsarist government and aroused various doubts. Having returned to Paris in 1777, Benyowski, through the intermediary of his relative, Casimir Pulaski, proposed to the Continental Congress of the United States a project for turning the island of Madagascar into an American base in the struggle against England. He attempted to approach Benjamin

Franklin, and in August 1779 arrived in America. It is not necessary to dwell here on the details of his two sojourns there, neither very successful, since they are well documented.[21] Let us note only that in December 1781 Benyowski sent Franklin the manuscript of the first part of his memoirs and the "Journal of his voyage to Kamchatka,"[22] containing a detailed description of Siberia as well as some summaries of the Russian expeditions in the Pacific North gleaned from the unpublished documents.

One cannot doubt that the events which followed Benyowski's "mutiny" and the memory of his threat to return to Kamchatka with foreign support contributed to the already oversensitive suspiciousness of tsarist authorities. Moreover, the American side of Benyowski's activity—his contacts with Pulaski and Franklin as well as his departure for the United States in 1779—might have contributed to the idea of the "American" origin of the unrecognized vessels which appeared off the "Chukotski Cape." Although there is no documentary confirmation of this supposition (apart from the simple chronological coincidence), one must take such a probability into account. Also, Bariatinsky kept St. Petersburg informed in detail about the events in America, and his dispatches from Paris in 1779 systematically commented on the course of the War of Independence. Finally, in the summer of 1779 the Russian government was concerned with the international situation that had arisen in connection with the war in America, a preoccupation reflected in the secret report of the College of Foreign Affairs to Catherine II on July 31/August 11, 1779.

Circumstances indicate that the government's order to I. S. Bariatinsky in October 1779 to treat with Franklin on the subject of "unrecognized" foreign vessels could not have been accidental or ill-thought-out. In December 1779 Bariatinsky reported to Panin from Paris:

According to the order of Your Excellency of October 11 with regard to the report of Irkutsk Governor Klichka concerning the two ships presumed to be from Canada which appeared near the Chukot coast, I have had a private conversation with Franklin and inquired whether he has any information about those ships and whether he possesses a map of those seas and the presumed route from Canada to Kamchatka. Franklin replied that, so far as he knows, up to this time this route has not been found, consequently of course there could not be any maps of it. He knows only that, according to an old Spanish writer whose name he does not recall, some vessels set out from a strait called Hudson, which lies above Canada, in the land called Labrador, and reached Japan; but he thinks that this route, even if found, would be very difficult, not to say impossible; as to the abovementioned ships, he thinks that they are either Japanese or the English Captain Cook's who set out three years ago from England on a round-the-world voyage.[23]

Franklin's supposition that the ships approaching the Russian possessions were in reality Cook's third expedition (1776-1780) appears to be substantiated. Cook's ships *Resolution* and *Discovery* first appeared at those shores in 1778. The English explorer had failed to find the Northwest passage and the Asiatic shores presented the unpleasant possibility of an encounter with the hostile tribes of Chukchi. Cook turned south, and in October 1778 reached the island of Unalaska, one of the largest of the Aleutian Islands, with a good natural harbor. An American, John Ledyard, who was sent ashore, learned that the island had been discovered long ago by the Russians, and that Russian traders had a settlement there. It was here that Ledyard's first acquaintance with Russians took place. Gerasim Izmailov, who was on the island of Unalaska at the time, went aboard Cook's ship accompanied by a large group of Russians and natives, carried in twenty canoes. An excellent seafarer and cartographer, Izmailov succeeded in finding a common language with the English sailors and was extremely helpful to the expedition. As Cook himself testified, the Russian seaman was well informed about the geographical discoveries made in that region and pointed out mistakes in the maps shown to him.[24] While traveling in the northern regions of the Pacific, Captain Cook knew, as Vancouver did later, about many of the most important geographical discoveries made by Russian seafarers in this region, and used the works of G. Miller and Ya. Shtelin. Vancouver also valued Russian discoveries highly and used maps given to him by Russian traders.[25]

English ships made a second appearance off the shores of the Russian possessions in the spring of 1779, after the death of Captain Cook in the Hawaiian Islands. When, on 18/29 April, two foreign ships entered the Petropavlovsk harbor, they occasioned panic at Kamchatka: everybody was sure that the foreign vessels had hostile intentions. It was soon discovered however, that the ships had no interest whatsoever in Benyowski and that their voyage was for scientific purposes. Accordingly, the expedition was given a warm reception. The English received great help with provisions, which they badly needed ("22 fat oxen, and 250 poods of rye flour"), and they were enabled to send home news of Captain Cook's death.[26] After leaving the hospitable Petropavlovsk harbor, the expedition sailed north, "along the Asiatic coast," and again attempted to find "a Northern passage to Europe." Again the English seafarers were thwarted because of the ice, and on July 19, 1779, they turned back, returning to Kamchatka in early autumn.

The "unrecognized" foreign vessels seen approaching the Chukot shores, news of which was received in St. Petersburg in the autumn of

1779, were undoubtedly Cook's ships. Klichka himself had earlier informed his superiors of their arrival in Petropavlovsk harbor, and had received in August 1779 instructions from St. Petersburg to credit the provisions for the expedition to the government exchequer; also, since the route to Kamchatka "has become known to foreigners, it should be made ready to defend itself."[27] This last order "gave no end of trouble to fussy Klichka," who dispatched special messengers "all over the place."[28] The overcautiousness of the Irkutsk Governor made trouble for his St. Petersburg superiors too, since they had to search their brains for the origin of the "unrecognized" vessels. But this concern had one positive result: the decision to address "chargé d'affaires of the American settlements," Benjamin Franklin.

Once the results of Cook's third expedition became known, interest in the Pacific North rose considerably. During 1787-1789 the northwest shores of America were visited by Captains Meares on the ship *Nootka,* Dixon on the *Queen Charlotte,* and Portlock on the *King George.* In the autumn of 1787, the French expedition of LaPérouse put in at Petropavlovsk, and received a friendly reception. French Vice-Consul Lesseps was granted permission, as requested by LaPérouse, to travel across Siberia to St. Petersburg in order to deliver his dispatches to the Marquis de Castries, the French naval minister. In 1788 Unalaska was also visited by the Spanish ship *San Carlos.*[29]

The Russian monopoly on geographical discoveries in this region was coming to an end. At this time a new competitor was added to the old colonial rivals: the United States of America, which had but recently won independence. The voyage of John Ledyard, called the "American Marco Polo" by some excessively enthusiastic American biographers, served the purpose of a preliminary reconnoitering of the enormous expanse of Siberia, the Aleutian Islands, Alaska, and western regions of the continent of North America.

Ledyard had originally proposed sending a trading expedition to the northern regions of the Pacific. At the time this project seemed "wild and visionary" to his practical compatriots. Ledyard then went to Europe where, in 1785, he succeeded in interesting Thomas Jefferson in his plans.[30] The future initiator of the Lewis and Clark Expedition suggested to Ledyard the undertaking of a journey across Siberia to Kamchatka, thence on Russian vessels to the northwest shores of America and then on across the continent to the United States.[31] Naturally such an undertaking was unthinkable without special permission from the Russian authorities. Ledyard appealed to the Russian minister in Paris, I. M. Simolin, and to

Baron Grimm, through the intermediary of Marquis de Lafayette and Thomas Jefferson, for intercession in getting such permission from Catherine II.[32]

The tsarist government was always extremely wary of foreign competitors in the Pacific North, and at the time there were a number of additional reasons for concern about the safety of the Far Eastern possessions. The note of Catherine II's secretary, P. A. Soimonov, "On commerce and fur trade in Eastern Sea" (1786), and the report of A. R. Vorontsov and A. A. Bezborodko called special attention to methods of removing foreign competition in this region. Near the end of 1786 the government of Catherine II decided, on the basis of these reports, to build a port in the Okhotsk Sea and

> to announce officially our discoveries near the northwest shores of America, thus confirming the right to possession of the discovered lands . . . . But since such an announcement would hardly prove sufficient without material reinforcement, and might even in some way be detrimental to the dignity of the court, there could be installed in that sea a few military vessels which would defend this veto in the event that such a need arose . . . since there is no doubt that if not military, then some merchant vessels will continue their attempts of encroachment, as they did so recently.[33]

In the course of 1787 active preparation for a round-the-world expedition under the command of G. I. Mulovsky was begun, but it had to be postponed because of the aggravated international situation and the approaching war with Sweden. At approximately the same time another governmental expedition under the command of Joseph Billings (a member of Cook's crew) was sent to the northwest regions of Siberia and to the Pacific Islands. The duration of this expedition was approximately ten years (1785-1794).[34] Like many eighteenth-century Russian expeditions it was secret, and Catherine II did not wish to allow foreign observers to participate in it. In this connection, the Empress wrote to Baron Grimm in the summer of 1786 that Ledyard would do well to choose some other route besides Kamchatka.[35] Grimm did not succeed in persuading Catherine II to reconsider this decision,[36] and in mid-August informed Jefferson of her refusal to grant Ledyard permission for a journey across Siberia. "I saw Baron de Grimm yesterday at Versailles," Jefferson wrote Ledyard, "and he told me he had received an answer from the Empress, who declines the proposition made on your account. She thinks it chimaerical. I am in hopes your execution of it from our side of the continent will prove the contrary. I thought it necessary to give you this information that you might suffer no suspense from expectations from that quarter."[37]

The news of Catherine II's refusal and Jefferson's sensible advice that he undertake the journey from the American side of the continent did not alter Ledyard's plans. He decided to go to Russia without permission, departed from London in December 1786, and in March 1787 was in the "Aurora Borealis of a city," St. Petersburg.[38] The time of his arrival proved propitious, since Catherine II was absent from the capital on her famous trip to the Crimea with Potemkin and a great entourage of her retinue and foreign diplomats.

In the Russian capital Ledyard succeeded in getting in touch with the well-known naturalist, P. S. Pallas, and obtained his cooperation in getting the permission for traveling across Siberia. Referring to Jefferson and Lafayette, Ledyard appealed for help first at the English and then at the French embassies.[39] For some months the American had no success whatsoever. However, in May 1787 he received unexpected help from a new acquaintance, an officer from the entourage of the heir to the throne, Paul. It was through him that the necessary papers were finally procured.[40] These documents could not have passed severe scrutiny; nevertheless they gave Ledyard a chance to attempt the execution of his scheme. Provided with a passport from the provincial administrative board in St. Petersburg, issued on 20/31 May 1787, and travel orders from the post-office in which he was described as an "American nobleman," Ledyard set out for Moscow, and then via Ekaterinburg for Siberia.[41]

During his Siberian journey Ledyard stopped at Barnaul, Irkutsk, and Iakutsk, encountering great hospitality everywhere. "In Russia I am treated as an American with politeness and respect," he wrote to the Secretary of the American Mission in London, William Stephens Smith, "and on my account the healths of Dr. Franklin and General Washington have been drunk at the table of two Governors; and at Irkutsk the name of Adams has found its way." Ledyard also wrote that in Irkutsk he found himself "in a circle as gay, rich, polite and scientific as if at Petersburg." He was flattered to drink French and Spanish wines and conduct "philosophic walks" in the company of disciples of Linnaeus, the famous Swedish naturalist. (These prominent Russian scholars, members of the St. Petersburg Academy of Sciences, were Alexander Karamyshev and Eric Laksman.)[42]

Ledyard's observations, diary entries, and letters written during his Siberian journey, quoted abundantly by his biographer, Sparks, and printed in full by Watrous, are of great interest. Naturally, the traveler was not able to figure everything out correctly; some of his comments are superficial and naive, others are too sharp and even unjust, but they make all the more convincing his reiterated emotional accounts of the great hospitality and kindness of the Russian people. In particular, Ledyard recalled that he was rarely able to persuade his hosts to accept recompense for his dinner or favors offered to him. It is noteworthy that he made this long journey from St. Petersburg to Iakutsk practically without any money—at the expense of the "treasury" and with the cooperation of his new friends. In the course of his travels Ledyard called attention to another characteristic, quite unusual for the Western observer but typical of the Russian people: compassion and kindness to the exiles, on whose living conditions in Siberia he also made a number of interesting remarks.

I must say a few words about the scientific endeavors of the American traveler, as the result of which he became convinced that North America was populated from the Asian side, and that Tartars and American Indians were the same people.[43] He wrote about his deductions to Thomas Jefferson:

> I am certain that the difference in the colour of Men is the effect of the natural causes . . . . I am certain that all the people you call red people on the continent of America and on the continents of Europe and Asia as far south as the southern parts of China are all one people by whatever names distinguished and that the best general one would be *Tartar*. I suspect that *all* red people are of the same family. I am satisfied myself that America was peopled from Asia and had some if not all its animals from thence.[44]

Perhaps these deductions may not have been especially original, nevertheless they testified to the advanced and democratic views of Ledyard, who had not yet been influenced by theories about the inferiority of "colored" people which were then being disseminated among some of his contemporaries.

While in Russia, Ledyard was naturally interested in other things besides anthropological researches. His main object was to gain information about Russian discoveries in eastern Siberia and northwest America, and he questioned the well-known Russian merchants Shelikhov and Popov, Irkutsk Governor-General Jacoby, and many others about them. "Notes on conversations" with Ledyard, made by Georgi Shelikhov, "for the usefulness of the State," are of great interest in this connection.[45] "With warm curiosity," Shelikhov writes, "he asked me where and in which parts have I been, how far the trading settlements extend along the Northeast Ocean and on actual American land, in which places and under which degree of northern latitude do we have our establishments and governmental signs."

His interest in Russian possessions in the Pacific North did not stop with this. According to Shelikhov, Ledyard "was curious to learn whether there were many Russian vessels engaged in the trading industry nowadays," was interested in the number of Russian settlements, and, "above all, questioned me about those settlements which I have left on the actual American land." Although posing questions to Shelikhov, Ledyard was not particularly frank about the details of his sailing with Cook's expedition, preferring to respond to the counter-questioning of his inter-locutor by "dark decoys." Having little confidence in each other, both men limited themselves to generalities, Shelikhov trying as best he could to underline the extent and the long standing of the Russian possessions, and Ledyard defending the rights of the "English Crown."

Ledyard continued energetically collecting information about Russian discoveries and possessions in Iakutsk, the northeast extreme of his Siberian journey. In the late autumn of 1787, when he arrived in Iakutsk, many merchants and traders who had returned from the remotest regions were in town. Ledyard referred to them as "very interesting, hardy men." He noted in his journal that "some of them had been at the mouth of river Yenesey, others the Lena and others the Kolyma. Among them all there was hardly any place in the North or East where they had not been." A "rich intelligent merchant, Popoff," gave him an account of his travels "to the eastward on the American coast and also among the Kuril Islands."[46]

In Iakutsk, Ledyard met with unexpected success. In November 1787, Joseph Billings, head of the Russian governmental expedition, arrived in town. An account of their meeting was given by Billings' secretary, Martin Sauer: "In Iakutsk we found, to our great surprise, Mr. Ledyard, an old companion of Captain Billings in Cook's voyage round the world; he then served in the capacity of a corporal, but now called himself an American colonel, and wished to cross over to the American Continent with our Expedition." As former members of Cook's expedition, Billings and Ledyard soon became friends. The American moved to the house where Billings was staying and lived as "one of his family and his friend."[47]

It would seem that now, finally, nobody could interfere with the execution of his grandiose plan to travel from Siberia and reach North America. However, when in February 1788 Ledyard returned to Irkutsk, together with Billings, he was deported from within the Russian boundaries on the ukase of Catherine II, not in an easterly direction toward America, but west, to Moscow, and thence beyond the Russian border.

Literature provides several versions of the reasons for Ledyard's depor-tation from Irkutsk, as well as a multitude of guesses and suppositions.

Sauer's version, which assumes that Ledyard was deported as a "French spy" is well known.[48] Another witness of the event and a member of the Billings expedition, G. A. Sarychev, wrote that Ledyard was deported as a "troublesome person" and referred to the quarrel of the "impudent Englishman" with the Iakutsk commandant Marklovsky.[49] It is also frequently pointed out that capricious Catherine II had unexpectedly changed her attitude toward the American traveler and canceled the permission for the journey that she had granted earlier.[50] Later researchers expended a good deal of effort over the "riddle" of Ledyard, but even the most informed among them, such as his biographer, Sparks, in the nineteenth century and E. Dvoichenko-Markova in our own day, have been unable to clarify definitively the tangled story, although they did express well-founded doubts on a number of mistaken versions.[51]

I have succeeded, on the basis of documentary materials preserved in the central Moscow and Leningrad archives, in recreating the true circumstances of the affair, and in clarifying some additional details of Ledyard's Siberian journey. Of special interest is an extensive report from the Irkutsk Governor, Lieutenant-General I. V. Jacoby, to A. A. Bezborodko, 7/18 November 1787, the whole of which is dedicated to the "American nobleman John Ledyard," who arrived in Irkutsk in "mid-August of this year."[52]

"His being called a nobleman," wrote Jacoby, "aroused in me a great curiosity to inquire most cautiously about his intentions in such a remote region. Through the assistance of information offered by the Kolyvan governor, Lieutenant-General Meller, briefly touching on his stay only in Barnaul, I considered it not amiss to inquire what brought him to these parts." Ledyard showed his documents—the "passport" from the provincial administrative board in St. Petersburg and the travel orders from the post office—and announced that his main intention was "to learn all he can about local regions, while traveling here, and thus to acquire the information concerning natural history." The American also volunteered the information that he counted on the cooperation in his journey of "a certain Northeastern secret expedition," headed by Captain Billings.

The documents and explanations presented by Ledyard did not satisfy the cautious Governor-General, who, having offered "appropriate amenities," proceeded at the same time "to investigate personally about his journey." Ledyard himself informed Jacoby that the regions of the North Eastern Ocean," that is, various islands, are somewhat familiar to him, since he had traveled in those parts with Cook's expedition. "He was extremely curious," Jacoby continued, "about the islands in the

North Ocean," "In his elaborate questioning," Ledyard was eager "to learn the date of occupation by the Russian state, the number of local people engaged in the fur trade there, and the enterprises established in the islands."

When Jacoby explained that "Russia had gained possession of those parts a long time ago, through labors undertaken by her," and was receiving tribute from the local people, the American changed the conversation and asserted that "the shores lying to the north of California, up to 50 degrees toward the Cape of Saint Elias, had long been occupied by the English Crown, and that about ten thousand people of various European nationalities were dwelling there." (Ledyard obviously did not suffer from lack of imagination.) "The expedition led by Mr. Cook traveled to the 73rd degree of latitude; some of the people living near Chukot were made English subjects, as a token of which a tribute of beavers was collected from them." Both discussants apparently assumed that the "rights" for this or that land depended mainly on who managed to plunder the local population first and collect the tribute or *yasak*.

One cannot fail to observe that the excerpts from Jacoby's report quoted here agree in a number of details with Shelikhov's "Notes" on his conversations with the "voyager of English nationality." The order of questioning and the system of argumentation also coincide in their general features. One can thus safely assume that Shelikhov's "Notes" were known to Jacoby and served as a basis for his letter to Bezborodko. The assumption that these "Notes" directly influenced Jacoby accords with some other facts. In the course of 1787 Shelikhov maintained continuous contact with the Irkutsk governor-general, who was very favorably disposed toward the plan of enlarging Shelikhov and Golikov's company and granting it exclusive rights in the northeast America.[53]

In refuting Ledyard's statements, Jacoby wrote (taking a lead from Shelikhov):

> Besides, it is known to Your Excellency that not only the Cape of Saint Elias but even the lands toward California lying between Unalaska and the Hermogen Cape of Kodiak in a triangle south at 40 degrees and north at 65 degrees of latitude were found by the expeditions from our side. I take the liberty of assuring you that our companions there have even now continuous fur trading, while in the Chukot land, so far as I know, at 73 degrees of latitude, there just is no fur trading such as this American relates, with Mr. Cook presumably taking tribute in sea otters from the people there.

In conclusion, Jacoby wrote that Ledyard "suddenly came up with questions connected with finding out about the Kurile Islands and the Russian enterprises there; as he did not manage to obtain the information on these, he finally stated that those who are stronger will surely have the first right to occupy those islands."[54] To Jacoby, "inconsistencies in the traveler's words and thinking" served as "strong grounds for doubts about him, especially since he does not have a proper passport, except for the travel orders, even for this area." "It is quite possible," Jacoby deduced, "that he is sent here by the English Crown for reconnaissance of the local situation." In that period such a conclusion was natural. Both Shelikhov and Jacoby were extremely apprehensive of English competition in the Pacific North, and considered it most probable that Ledyard had been sent to reconnoiter not by France (and not by the United States), but by Great Britain.

Because of these doubts Jacoby decided to send Ledyard to Iakutsk "where there are fewer opportunities for the fulfillment of his intentions"; and also dispatched there "secret instructions to the commandant, Marklovsky, that, while giving a hospitable reception to Ledyard, he should not fail to note even the least of his shifty enterprises." The commandant was also instructed to "persuade Ledyard to remain in Iakutsk by stressing the difficulties of the passage to Okhotsk, detaining him inconspicuously until I look into his situation more closely." Marklovsky executed his orders precisely and reported to the Irkutsk Governor-General that the American's "mind is set at rest."[55]

Before leaving for Iakutsk, Ledyard had left "a letter to Professor Pallas in Petersburg, with a copy to be sent to England. It is now in my possession," Jacoby informed Bezborodko, "under the secret and special letter of the Councilor Karamyshev." Not daring to open the American's mail himself, the prudent Governor-General proposed that the mighty Bezborodko attend to it. "I beg you, dear Sir, to deem my remarks worthy of your attention, in case through the perusal of this letter the intentions of this man, hitherto concealed, might be easily revealed."

We do not know whether or not Bezborodko followed the "advice" and examined this correspondence. (We do know that Ledyard's Siberian letters reached England safely and have been preserved to our day.) But Bezborodko undoubtedly read Jacoby's own report. What is more, he informed Catherine II of it, and there is a notation on the original copy of his report: "On this, instructions were given to Jacoby, Eropkin and Passek, on December 21, 1787."[56] I would like to quote one of them, to P. B. Passek. According to this, Catherine wrote as follows:

Petr Bogdanovich. Since we received the information from the Lieutenant-General, Governor of Irkutsk and Kolyvan, Jacoby, that the American John Ledyard, after his request for permission to travel via Irkutsk and Okhotsk to America was denied, has arrived in those parts, we have instructed the abovementioned Lieutenant-General Jacoby to deport him with the appropriate supervision, without causing him any distress, to Moscow, to our commandant-in-chief there, General Eropkin, who is under instructions by us to dispatch this American in the same way via Smolensk to Polotsk; and you are instructed to expel him, upon arrival, across the border, with the admonition not to dare appear ever again anywhere within the limits of our Empire. We continue to hold you in our favor. [57]

Later, explaining the reasons for Ledyard's deportation to French Ambassador Ségur, Catherine referred to humane motives: she did not wish to be a party to his inevitable peril during his solitary journey across Siberia to America. However, Ségur had supposed that in reality the Empress did not wish the American to familiarize himself with the Russian possessions in America. [58] Undoubtedly the French diplomat was correct in this assumption.

Ledyard's deportation is sometimes regarded as evidence of ill-will on the part of the Russian government toward the United States. As I see it, there is no proof of ill-will. I have quoted Shelikhov's and Jacoby's most unfavorable testimony about Ledyard. It contains no mention of the United States whatsoever. At that time both Shelikhov and Jacoby feared English competition above all, and wondered whether Ledyard had been sent for "reconnaissance" by the "English Crown." Shelikhov referred to him as a "voyager of the English nation." And, taking into account that Catherine had earlier refused Ledyard permission to travel across Siberia, one could not realistically expect, after Jacoby's report, any other decision but the order for deportation.

One should not fail to note the curious wording of Catherine II's ukase: the American was to be dispatched beyond the borders of the Empire, "without causing him any distress." Jacoby received Catherine's ukase in February 1788. By that time Ledyard had already returned to Irkutsk, together with the "head of the geographical expedition, Billings." "In consequence of the ukase of Your Majesty," Jacoby dutifully informed Catherine on 1/12 February 1788, "today [he] has been deported from here to Moscow, under supervision, without causing him any insult, with an accompanying letter from me to the commander-in-chief, General

Eropkin. I have not omitted to instruct the police officers assigned to him what kind of treatment he should get while on the road."[59]

And so the Siberian journey of the "American Marco Polo" came to an end through the direct interference of Shelikhov and Jacoby. Both were strong advocates of the firm establishment of Russian influence in the Pacific North and were extremely wary of foreign competitors in this region. It was in these years that they advanced the project of forming a strong monopolistic company for the colonization of the northwest shores of America. This project was preceded by the practical activities of Russian merchants and fur traders of many years' standing in the Aleutian Islands and the Alaskan coast.

Shelikhov himself played an important role.[60] Having built three ships—the *Three Saints, Simon and Anna, St. Michael*—in Okhotsk, he "set out to sea on August 16, 1783, from the mouth of the river Urak . . . with 192 working people."[61] Thus began the voyage that became an important milestone in the assimilation of the northwest shores of America.

In evaluating Shelikhov's activity, Hubert Bancroft called him "the father and founder of Russian colonies in America."[62] Granted that by founding in the 1780's the first permanent Russian settlements on the islands of Kodiak and Afignak, Shelikhov laid a firm foundation for Russian America, his achievements go beyond mere practical activity. He was not only a successful merchant-organizer of large trading industries, but also a politician. He was aware of the results of his activity and possessed enviable political insight.

When he returned to Irkutsk from his "American voyage," in April 1787, Shelikhov presented Governor-General Jacoby with a series of notes and reports and various documentary materials resulting from his voyage of 1783-1786. "I considered it necessary," he informed Jacoby, "to survey suitable spots and fix my own private dwellings for whatever was needed. Above all, I endeavored to assert that our establishments were the first ones there, by penetrating as far as possible due south in America toward the coast of California, by establishing Russian dwellings and leaving our signs so as to discourage those who might have pretensions on those parts, and to stop the encroachment of other nations."[63] Calling attention to the recently increased competition of other powers, Shelikhov wrote that "other nations try to appropriate great gains in the Pacific North, while possessing neither the adjoining land nor the least right for that sea."[64]

In a special note concerned with the privileges of his company Shelikhov petitioned the tsarist government for "assistance," requesting in particular a twenty-year loan of 500,000 rubles (paragraph 8). He asked that his company be provided with about a hundred people "from military services and well-disciplined" (paragraph 2), and sought permission to hire people "with overdue passports" and "insolvent debtors" (paragraph 3). Anxious to be rid of "interference" from local authorities, and, "even more, of the governments set up in the Okhotsk region and in Kamchatka," Shelikhov proposed to put the company under the sole supervision of the Irkutsk governor-general (paragraph 1), with direct appeal to St. Petersburg in some important cases (paragraph 5). (This last was apparently a precaution to protect the company in the future from the possible arbitrariness of the Irkutsk authorities.) He further requested that his company be granted rights to "undertake commerce with Japan, China, India, the Philippines and other islands, and in America with Spaniards and Americans" (paragraph 6).[65]

Irkutsk Governor-General Jacoby not only firmly supported these proposals but also, in his report to the Empress of November 30/December 11, 1787, put a word in for granting the exclusive monopolistic rights to fur-trading in the "above-reported areas" to Shelikhov and his company.[66] (The cautious merchant kept silent in the beginning on the subject of this his most fervent wish.) In conclusion, the Governor-General stated that, since "Shelikhov might perchance be needed for some clarifications," he was dispatching him along with the report.[67]

Upon their arrival in St. Petersburg, in February 1788, Grigori Shelikhov and his companion Ivan Golikov took a new petition to Catherine II in which, along with restating former points, they requested monopolistic rights for their company. At the same time they considerably reduced the amount of the loan they asked for (from 500,000 to 200,000 rubles), which was indispensable, since "our income does not correspond to our zealous wish."[68]

In the spring of 1788, it seemed that Shelikhov's plans were approaching realization. The Commission for Commerce, in its report to Catherine II, signed by such influential persons as A. Vorontsov, Kh. Minikh, and P. Soimonov, recommended the acceptance of his proposals.[69] On April 6/17, the Permanent Council agreed with their opinion, suggesting in addition that, "when Her Majesty will graciously consent to grant these merchants 200,000 rubles without percentage, it would be most convenient to borrow this sum from the Tobolsk treasury."[70] Catherine was thus helpfully prompted not only as to the actual decision of the problem but even to the source from which the requested "assistance" could come.

Then, most unexpectedly, things took a very different turn. The Empress literally poked fun at the proposals presented by the Commission for Commerce report on the navigation and trade in the Pacific. "Such a loan," she wrote ironically, "reminds one of the proposal by a person who wanted to teach an elephant to speak in thirty years time, and being asked why such a long period was needed, replied: 'either the elephant will die, or I, or the person who lent me the money to teach the elephant.' "[71] In declining Shelikhov and Golikov's request, Catherine II observed that "this petition is a real monopoly. . .which is against my principles." The Tsarina obviously wished to appear a fundamental foe of any monopoly and an impartial defender of her subjects' rights. "Since Shelikhov and Golikov are worthy people, they want to be granted the exclusive trade rights, forgetting that there are other worthy people besides them." Because some traders were evil, "to deprive all of trade rights would be unjust," the Empress observed, further calling the monopoly a "hundred-headed monster."

What were the reasons for the failure of Shelikhov's projects? Was the Tsarina's openly expressed distaste for monopoly the main cause for refusal? How can such an unexpected collapse of a project that seemed all but accepted be explained? S.B. Okun' and A.I. Andreyev have argued that Catherine's refusal probably resulted not so much from her being a *fundamental* foe of monopoly as from the international situation of Russia already at war with Turkey and Sweden.[72] Essentially this is a correct, though perhaps overly generalized supposition.

Naturally, it can be questioned whether Catherine was the only one evaluating the international situation, with her advisers, members of the Permanent Council and the Commission for Commerce, unaware of the problem. Would it not be more correct to presume the existence of a dis-agreement on questions of foreign policy within the Russian government, and assume that Catherine's declining of the Shelikhov and Golikov petition for "assistance" reflected a struggle within the ruling circle? A remark made by Catherine II on 27 March/7 April 1788 is quite indicative in this respect: "Royal assistance is now directed toward the southern ac-tions, for the sake of which the savage American northern peoples and the trade with them are left alone."[73]

There is direct evidence connecting the refusal of assistance to Shelikhov and Golikov with the southern actions, that is, with the war with Turkey, initiated and conducted by the almighty Potemkin. Although at the time the Tsarina's favorite was near Ochakov, his sha-dow was invisibly present at St. Petersburg. Clearly, the influence of the Commission for Commerce, which was supporting Shelikhov's petition, could not be compared with that of the mighty favorite; besides it is a known fact that Catherine did not care for Vorontsov.[74] Would not that explain why the Tsarina's remarks on the report of the Commission for Commerce were so caustic?

Important reasons for the refusal are revealed also through analysis of the text of Catherine's remarks. She obviously did not trust these unknown Siberian merchants and their notes on North America. "It is they alone who talk about how well they manage; nobody out there has confirmed their assurances." Especially interesting is the connection of projects for colonization of America with the experience of the War for Independence of the United States. "The examples of American settlements," Catherine underlined, "are not flattering, and moreover not advantageous for the mother land." One can see the the Tsarina had not forgotten the successful War of Independence and did not want a possible future Russian version. Neither did she wish for military-political complications with other powers. "Spreading over into the Pacific will not bring firm advantages. It is one thing to trade, and quite another thing to capture."[75]

The only thing with which Catherine II graciously agreed, was the rewarding of Shelikhov and Golikov with silver swords and gold medals, "to be worn," as A. A. Bezborodko wrote, "on the neck, with the portrait of Her Majesty."[76] In point of fact, the royal reward bordered on sheer mockery: instead of the real help for which they asked, Shelikhov and Golikov were allowed to wear medals with the image of Catherine II who was responsible for turning down their projects. However, there was no other way out for the merchants except to thank their "wise possessor" for her remarkable "favor."

Putting aside for the time being their petition for a loan, and falling back, "with God's help, on their own resources,"[77] Shelikhov and Golikov—armed with swords and medals—persisted in their energetic activity, one in St. Petersburg, the other on the eastern periphery of the country. In order to avoid being accused of conniving to establish a monopoly, and at the same time to enlarge their scope of activity, Shelikhov began to create new "independent" companies. In 1790, alongside the main Northeastern American Company, there was formed the Predtechensky Company, so named after the trading ship. Somewhat later the Unalaska Company was formed, named after the island where Shelikhov had decided to establish a permanent trading settlement.[78] That same year a new manager of the Northeastern American Company, a Cargopol merchant, A. A. Baranov, was assigned to the island of Kodiak.

The whole subsequent history of Russian America is connected with his name; he was the main ruler of Russian colonies in America for twenty-eight years.[79]

In striving to earn the favor of Catherine II, Shelikhov and Golikov were enflamed by the religious zeal for "proselytizing God's word in America." The merchants requested St. Petersburg to send to America, at their expense, a parish priest "for professing the Gospels," and to allow them to establish a church on Kodiak Island. This time the Tsarina proved remarkably generous (the more so since the company undertook to defray expenses). Shelikhov's "loyalty" "was rewarded by the special will of the Empress Catherine II who ordered that a large clerical mission be sent, rather than one parish priest." In fulfillment of the royal will, Archimandrite Ioasaf with seven clerics were assigned to America.[80] "I have a good reason for congratulating you on the arrival of the guests," Shelikhov wrote Baranov in August 1794, when he was sending two new boats to Kodiak Island. "These guests are the holy Archimandrite Ioasaf with brethren, all of them assigned by the royal will of Her Majesty to preach God's word in America and for the enlightenment of peoples over there in the Christian faith. I am certain . . . that these guests will provide reliable support . . . for future welfare."[81]

Not counting too heavily on the "support of the holy Archimandrite Ioasaf with brethren," on the same boat Shelikhov sent to America "second guests": thirty-seven families of "unfortunates" for shipbuilding beyond the Cape of Saint Elias and for tilling the soil."

Striving to strengthen and enlarge his possessions, Shelikhov dreamed about establishing on the shores of the American mainland a new colonial center, Slavorossiia. In the same instructional letter to Baranov he wrote:

> Already during my stay in Kodiak it was known to me that the coast of American mainland, starting from the borders of Ugalakhnut habitations . . . has better air than Kodiak Island, since the winter there is very short and moderate . . . the summer is hot and long; the earth is soft, and there is enough space suitable for tillage; deciduous and other trees suitable for shipbuilding, as you yourself have been stating, are abundant. . . . Consequently, I find that it would be incomparably better for the permanent Russian habitation to be installed on the mainland rather than on the island, which could be invaded by foreigners any time, and from which—if need be—one could more easily seek refuge on the mainland. Moreover for reasons of policy known to you we should try to occupy the mainland rather than the islands.[82]

Shelikhov paid great attention to the external appearance of the new colonial center. He suggested that the settlement be laid out "as tastefully as possible," so that from the very beginning it could stand for a town rather than a village, and so that foreigners would not think that "even in America, Russians live in the same filthy way they do in Okhotsk, with stinking air and shortages of all necessities."[83]

On top of his energetic activity in northwest America, Shelikhov conceived some broad projects to develop commerce with Japan, China (via Canton), Batavia, and the Philippine Islands; he thought of creating a new port in the Okhotsk Sea and of colonizing the southern group of Kurile Islands (in 1795 a group of Russian settlers was actually sent to the islands of Urup and Iturup); finally, he developed an interesting plan for navigating the mouth of the Amur River. In this connection his report to Catherine II of 28 February/11 March 1794, on the development of commerce with Japan and the strengthening of Russian influence over the assimilated regions of North America, the Kurile, and the Aleutian Islands is particularly interesting.[84]

Shelikhov had no chance to realize these broad and daring projects: he died suddenly in Irkutsk in the summer of 1795. The following years were distinguished, on the one hand, by a sharp increase in factional struggle between different trading companies, sometimes resulting in armed encounters, and, on the other, by their tendency to unite, in the face of the threat of foreign competition, and to seek government protection to combat this threat.

In the summer of 1797 the "American Northeastern, North, and Kurile Islands Company" of Shelikhov and Golikov joined with a company of Irkutsk merchants headed by Myl'nikov to form the United American Company. On 3/14 August 1798 the companies were formally amalgamated in order "through common effort to multiply, disseminate, perfect, and affirm forever Russian commerce in the Northern, Northwestern, and Pacific Seas."[85] This unification of recent competitors did not change matters too much, since it only masked mutual contradictions without eliminating them. It is characteristic that the most acute struggle within the "United American Company" was accompanied by complaints and denunciations arriving in Irkutsk and in St. Petersburg in abundance.

Historians of the Russian-American Company, especially P. Tikhmenov and S. Okun', long ago investigated the complex circumstances preceding the formation of the company in 1799, so there is no need to discuss them in detail. The general policy of the tsarist government during these years has been clearly defined. It was no longer a matter of granting monopoly privileges to any private company, however powerful, but a matter of creating a mighty monopolistic concern for a successful counteraction against foreign expansion and for a firm mastery of the northwest of America, under direct government control.[86] This program was spelled out in the note of the College of Commerce of 5/16 August 1797, "On the harm of having many companies in America and on the advantages of uniting them," which was approved by Paul I. Developing the decision of August 1797, the College of Commerce, after lengthy preparation, presented to the Tsar in January 1799 a detailed outline on the "establishment of the North American Trade Company."[87]

In spite of the desperate resistance of the recalcitrant Irkutsk merchants and the complex intrigues at the court, the proposals of the College of Commerce received the Tsar's approval, and the appropriate ukase to the governing Senate was issued on 8/19 July 1799. On the same day, on the basis of projects presented by the College of Commerce, Paul I confirmed the final version of the "rules and privileges" of the company "for the next twenty years."[88]

The original copies of these documents, preserved in the archives, bear interesting penciled remarks and corrections.[89] All these corrections are scrupulously preserved in the final version. The identity of the final editor of the documents about the company's formation is unclear. Penciled corrections on texts of projects presented to the Tsar often were made by the Tsar himself, but it is doubtful in this case that he had made them, since many are long and some are of an editorial nature. What is obvious is the character of the views of the final editor and the trend of his corrections, which were of an extremely monarchist and flatteringly loyal style. It is sufficient to point out that in the original project the company was called simply "Russian-American." Such a title seemed inadequate to the final editor, who added: "Under the royal protection of His Majesty."[90] The loyal hand of the final editor, although powerful enough to alter a text signed by many influential tsarist dignitaries, proved powerless before common sense. Although this hand never forgot to enter the clumsy insertion throughout the constituent documents, in the future the company remained known as "Russian-American."

The sphere of the company's activity was defined in the first paragraph: "Owing to the discovery by the Russian seafarers in bygone times of the shores of northwest America, beginning with 55° northern latitude, and of the range of islands situated north of Kamchatka toward America and south of Kamchatka toward Japan, and by the right of possession of the same by Russia, the company is to use all industries and establishments which are found at the present time on the northeast shore of America from the above-described 55° up to the Bering Strait and beyond it, and also on the Aleutian Islands, Kuril Islands, and others, situated in the Northeast Ocean." At the same time the company was granted the right to make "new discoveries" on lands south of 55°, "if they were not occupied by any other nations[91] and have not become their dependencies," and to "conduct commerce with all surrounding states" (5). The tenth paragraph proclaimed the company's "exclusive right for all kinds of acquisitions, industries, commerce, establishments, and discovery of new lands."

The original "joint" capital of the company consisted of 724 thousand rubles divided into 724 shares. In accordance with the new "rules" another thousand shares was added to the then existing ones. Shelikhov's heirs, who were the principal shareholders, proposed that voting be established according to number of shares, with the right to vote determined by ownership of at least 25 shares. But St. Petersburg changed this procedure, and, according to paragraph 18 of the new rules, the right to vote was given to shareholders possessing not less than 10 shares, while votes were counted, not according to the number of shares owned but by the number of participants present at the meeting.[92] It is quite obvious that in making these changes the government responded to the interests of the new shareholders, "well-born nobility."[93]

The company was to be managed by the "Main Office," consisting of the principal director, M. M. Buldakov, and three more directors, I. Shelikhov, Myl'nikov, and Startsev. Grigori Shelikhov's son-in-law, N. P. Rezanov, influential in St. Petersburg court circles, held the position of "correspondent," performing to some degree a function of protecting and "soliciting" on behalf of the company in St. Petersburg.

In spite of the insistent "suggestions" of their Petersburg "correspondent" to the new directors to stop their endless "litigations and slanders" and care for "the usefulness for the state, if we are to keep a firm hold on matters," the obstinate Irkutsk merchants were not inclined to stop their struggle. Again, however, Shelikhov's heirs managed to conquer their competitors: the company's Main Office was transferred by tsarist ukase from Irkutsk to St. Petersburg. This facilitated the government's control and direction over its activities. The close ties of the company to the government were sealed in the spring of 1802 when "royal personages," including Emperor Alexander I, Dowager Empress Maria Fedorovna, and others, became shareholders. Such well-known statesmen as N. P. Rumiantsev, N. S. Mordvinov, and I. A. Vedemeier were also among the shareholders.[94]

The subordination of the Russian-American Company to the direct control of the government was not an accidental or in any way exceptional phenomenon. In his study of the East India Company, Karl Marx noted that when it "began to widen the net of its factories up to the scale of the empire, and when its competition with private Dutch and French merchants began to assume the character of rivalry between nations," the government of Great Britain began to interfere in its affairs.[95] Precisely at this time, in 1783-84, the Indian question in England was regarded as a governmental problem.[96] Marx's reflections on the subject of the East India Company apply to some extent to the Russian-American Company. In the beginning the Siberian merchants and traders acted more or less independently, although in encounters with foreigners they could usually count on the government's support. Direct interference by St. Petersburg in the affairs of private merchants and traders began when competition with private English and, as we shall see, American, merchants "began to assume the character of rivalry between nations." It was in this sense that the problem of colonization of northwest America became a "government problem" for Russia at the end of the eighteenth century. Recalling Marx's idea, one can conclude that as the British government sought the "rounding of its borders" and mastery over India under the cover of its East India Company,[97] the tsarist government used the Russian-American Company as a cover for the colonization of northwest America.

In the final stages of the formation of the Russian-American Company in 1799 it was decided that an official representation should be made to the British cabinet on the question of "infringements of British traders" on the shores of northwest North America belonging to Russia. On 7/18 March 1799, the Tsar sent the Russian minister plenipotentiary in London, S. R. Vorontsov, a special rescript about English merchants' interference with the United American Company in Russia's North American possessions.[98] Along with the rescript Vorontsov was sent Baranov's report and a similar one by the Irkutsk governor Alexei Tolstoy to the general procurator of the Senate, P. V. Lopukhin.[99]

Thus, defense of the interests of the "private" company was elevated to the level of government policy. In its efforts to defend existing Russian settlements from foreign claims and competition, the Russian-American Company, relying on the support of the tsarist government, attempted to broaden its sphere of influence as far as possible—including territory along the North American coast south of the 55th parallel. These trends were developed in the abovementioned secret "instruction" of company directors M. Buldakov, E. Delarov, and I. Shelikhov to A. A. Baranov on 18/30 April 1802, which had government approval.[100]

In respect to English claims on the territories we manage, you inquire up to which point should you affirm our possessions? The Main Office entrusts you to try to affirm Russia's right not only up to the 55° but also further, justifying it by the sea voyages of Captains Bering, Chirikov, and others, and referring as well to the voyages and trapping industries undertaken annually since those days by private parties. Try to show even some claim to the very Nootka Sound, so that, should the English Crown demand it, one could define the borders in some way up to the 50th°, or at least halfway to the 55th°, if it is impossible to go any further, since that part has not yet been occupied by them; consequently, up to this time Russia has priority there, so you should try your very best to accomplish this, and make haste to settle regular strongholds at the 55th°, since you will now have sufficient number of people arriving there.[101]

It was easier to announce broad colonization plans and monopolistic pretensions for the Pacific North than to carry them out. It was simple enough to grant the new company "exclusive rights for all kinds of acquisitions, trade, commerce, establishments, and discovery of new lands" by the Tsar's ukase. Similarly, one could make appropriate proposals to foreign Crowns. Finally, it was not difficult to draw up secret instruction to A. A. Baranov. But this did not make it easy to get rid of the rivalry of foreign powers, to strengthen and broaden the company's possessions, and to create exceptionally favorable conditions for its activity, isolating it from foreign competition.

Foreign merchants and seafarers had already appeared in the region that the company claimed, and with time their number increased rather than decreased. From 1792 on, enterprising merchants from the United States had become more and more active on the northwest coast of America in spite of numerous complaints by the Russian-American Company.[102] "From that time on," the main office of the company noted in the summer of 1808, "flotillas of five, ten, and sometimes even fifteen boats began arriving there, most frequently from the American republic. Right under the Russian eyes, they bring for exchange with savages woolens, heavy linen, ready-made clothes, footgear, guns, swords, pistols, cannons, gunpowder, and other small articles and trinkets, receiving from the savages at a great profit the furs of sea otters and other sea and land animals."[103] "Citizens of the United States of North America," the corporation complained on another occasion, "trade to the local inhabitants all sorts of firearms and cold weapons, gunpowder and lead, showing them also how to use the latter to harm our trappers."[104]

The most serious damage was inflicted on the Russian-American Company in the summer of 1802 by the demolition of the fortress which had been established on the island of Sitka several years before. Well-armed koloshes[105] suddenly attacked the Russian settlement with a "great force," burned the fortress, and destroyed a newly built boat in the harbor. These koloshes massacred about twenty Russians, including V. Medvednikov, and one hundred and thirty Aleutians; only a few inhabitants managed to escape. One of the trappers, A. Plotnikov, later told that he escaped through the window "and hid in a hollow treetrunk."[106] The evidence collected showed that the attack on the fortress was not accomplished without the participation of foreign competitors of the company—English and Bostonians.

Informing Baranov about the encounter between his party of trappers and the local inhabitants, and about the destruction of the fortress on the island of Sitka, I. Kuskov mentioned in particular that an American boat was wintering over at the "Hutsnov inlet," and that "native koloshes" were persuaded to destroy the Russian fortress.[107] Baranov later affirmed, on the basis of accounts from the "savages themselves," that

> the cause of the disaster and of assistance to it were the skippers of Boston boats, Crocker and Cunningham, with their crews, since they not only enticed the islanders to do this deed, but also traded them the gunpowder and weapons. Later, after the massacre of the Russians, they seized from the savages all the skins trapped by the Russians, consisting of 3,700 sea otters and other beasts, worth more than 300,000 rubles, and burned the company's boat, committing cruelties against the savages.[108]

The activity of the English ship *Unicorn,* under the command of Captain Barber, which was stationed near the island of Sitka at the moment of the attack, was also suspicious. After the destruction of the Russian settlement, the English took aboard the escaped trappers and then rescued some of those held captive by the Tlingits. Having delivered about twenty-six people into Pavlovsk Harbor on the island of Kodiak, Barber demanded, under threat of force, reparation for his "losses" to the extent of 50,000 rubles. Baranov finally agreed to pay him a ransom of sea otters valued at 10,000 rubles.[109]

Several years later, in 1805, the natives "possessing firearms gotten from the Bostonians, and being inclined toward fighting and cruelty," suddenly attacked the village of Slavorossiia on the mainland in the Iakutat Bay, "killing everyone and burning the village."[110] The company's situation was becoming more and more difficult. "The foreigners observing us with envious eyes," Rezanov informed St. Petersburg, give the natives "ideas about the weakness of our establishments, and I should not be surprised if a hundred riflemen with several thousand koloshes would attack Kodiak and destroy everything down to the foundations. They have English rifles, while we have the Okhotsk ones which have never been used since they were delivered here because they are good for nothing."[111]

It was only with great difficulty that Baranov succeeded in repossessing the island of Sitka in 1804. The wooden fortress, "provided with cannons and other small arms bought from the Bostonians," was taken by assault only thanks to the support of the ship *Neva*, under the command of Lisiansky, which had come from "round the world." A colonial center of Russian America, the fortress of Novo-Arkhangel'sk, was established on the island.[112]

Although trading with them for gunpowder and firearms, the koloshes were not unwilling to use these weapons against the Bostonians themselves. "In the Bay of Nootka," Khlebnikov wrote, "on March 23, 1803, they massacred the crew of the ship *Boston*, plundered it of goods, and burned the ship." Only two sailors succeeded in escaping, one of whom published his memoirs in 1815.[113] Another incident took place in the "Bay of Mill-Beik-Sound" in 1805. "When Skipper Porter, who had obtained 6,000 sea otters from the savages, let them come aboard his ship with more fur skins, he was shot instantly, along with several of his crew—by pistols which he himself had sold to the savages—and thrown overboard. Were it not for the daring resoluteness of the navigator, Adams, and the approach of another Boston ship under the command of Skipper Gill, which stopped this massacre, the whole of Porter's ship would have fallen to the savages."[114] Finally, the Bostonians themselves told Rezanov that, since the onset of their trade at the northwest coast of America, they had lost six vessels. Nevertheless, Rezanov added, "they are driven by the love of profit every year."[115]

The active trade of Yankee shipowners not only threatened the safety of Russian settlements but also gravely damaged their economic interests. Obtaining "soft junk" (fur) from the natives, the Americans carried it to Canton, and then returned home, having made great profits.[116] The Russian-American Company could not hold out against this foreign competition either in trade with the natives or in the fur sales on the Chinese markets. Meanwhile, the volume of the trading operations of American merchants was becoming quite considerable. "Not counting various fur pieces," the Main Office of the Russian-American Company noted in 1808, "each skipper receives in trade from the savages between a thousand and two and a half thousand pelts of beavers alone. All in all, they trade and take to the Canton market annually about 15,000 sea otters and 5,000 river beavers."[117]

The corporation considered the profits received by foreigners in Canton almost a direct theft from their own pockets. "These tradesmen greatly damage the Company, which alone has the right to trade with the savage islanders, who are Russian subjects, many of them baptized; and by doing so they deprive us of almost a million rubles worth of fur goods."[118] In explaining why the Russian-American Company could not compete with New England shipowners, the corporation noted: "The company employs many people, about ten ships, and more than fifteen fortresses and redoubts; from Okhotsk to Kiakhta it uses land transport, partly with pack horses, paying about eight rubles per pood for transportation costs, all of which adds up to 300,000 rubles. On the contrary, the abovementioned smugglers do not have such expenses and can trade to the Chinese for much less than we do."[119]

The commercial activity of New Englanders in northwest America was basically intermediary in character and purely for profit. Showing its inner "mechanism," Rezanov wrote in his secret letter to the directors of the company on 15/27 February 1806:

> Nowadays Bostonians conduct on the American coast trade in woolens, guns, gunpowder, steel and iron goods, ravenduck, and other goods which they buy from the English since they do not manufacture their own. . . . Depending on their success in exchanging their cargoes, after remaining here a year or two they proceed to Canton, where after trading the exchanged cargo for kitaika [cotton cloth], tea, and other goods needed by the United States, they return to Boston. They cannot set out to China directly from their own country because it would be impossible for them to dispose of these goods with the same profit as the English do; because of that . . . they are forced to resort to such difficult means.[120]

The exporting of fur goods directly to China by English and Americans made the Company's trade on the Russian-Chinese border in Kiakhta extremely difficult. This fact was well understood in St. Petersburg, and it was precisely in this connection that in the beginning of 1803 the minister of commerce, N. P. Rumiantsev, raised the question of Russia's vital need for a "Canton trade." "No matter how much the Company, enlarging operations, might try to keep up the price of furs, the English and Americans transporting their furs from Nootka Sound and the Charlotte Islands directly to Canton, will always have an advantage; this will continue until the Russians themselves find their way to Canton."[121]

The enormous difficulties encountered by the Russian-American Company during its first years were caused, not only (and not primarily) by external reasons such as the trading activities of Boston merchants but also by serious internal factors and the ugly bureaucratic organization of the company itself. The general condition of the colonies, in spite of government support, left much room for improvement. Archimandrite Ioasaf complained to Shelikhov that "French license" ruled in the colonies. (Naturally, the Archimandrite attributed his own special meaning to these words.) Rezanov defined the situation somewhat more precisely when he wrote that he found a "drunk republic" in the colonies. Finally, Soviet researchers have condemned "predatory exploitation of the colonies, disorganization, and misuses." On the whole, the various aspects of the Russian-American Company's economic activity are well known, and there is no need to touch upon them further in this book.[122]

The grievous condition of the colonies, the tyranny of local authorities, and all sorts of abuses and disorganization were the natural result of the retrograde serfdom regime of tsarist Russia. This reactionary regime, with its police-bureaucratic methods of governing, delayed the development of Russian industries in Alaska, which was discovered and assimilated through the efforts of glorious Russian seafarers and settlers. Serfdom, with its dependence of peasant on landlord, deprived Russian America of its greatest need: manpower. The acute shortage of manpower in the colonies resulted in surprising methods of increasing the numbers of Russian settlers. For example, after surveying Russian settlements in America in 1805, Rezanov proposed to the corporation: (1) "to beg from the throne" for permission to send to America annually at least one to two hundred exiles, chosen by the company; (2) "to direct here drunkards, healthy, skilled, and suited for work," on conditions mutually agreeable to the company and the landlords; (3) to send for a settlement in America "all purposely bankrupted merchants . . . with their creditors receiving from the company the moneys obtained from their earnings." Moscow alone, Rezanov commented, "after having supplied this region with people, would not lose a half of her idlers."[123]

Rezanov's proposals could not change the situation in the colonies in any essential way, and his faith in "idlers" was dubious indeed. Much more important was the fact that among the highest Russian dignitaries some individual statesmen (N. P. Rumiantsev, first of all) thought it feasible, from a consideration of general state interests and of the value of establishing permanent settlements in America, to permit "free people, such as merchants, townsmen, state and economic peasants, retired soldiers, and others, to migrate and settle in the establishments of the Russian-American Company," and who supported, at least in part, the company's wish to free those living in its settlements from the taxes imposed on them "by their former dwelling places." This proposal, however, proved unacceptable to the State Council, which in its meeting of 3/15 August 1808 declined Rumiantsev's proposal and decreed that "people engaged in the industries of the Russian-American Company may remain in its establishments on the same basis as before: that is, according to their obligations and contracts, without being exempt forever from general duties and conscriptions."[124]

It is not surprising, therefore, that the population of Russian America grew very slowly, and that in 1805 the number of Russian colonists was only about 470. In addition, a considerable number of Indians depended on the company. Thus, according to the census undertaken on Rezanov's order, there were more than 5,200 people in the jurisdiction of the Unalaska office and on the island of Kodiak.[125] Already in the beginning of the nineteenth century the company had a considerable number of *osedlost*, small settlements and forts. Describing these "fortifications" according to their condition in 1803, Tikhmenev numbers the following: on Kodiak, established by Shelikhov in the Harbor of Three Saints and in Pavlovsk Harbor, on the island of Afognak, Alexandrovskoe on the Kenaisky Cape, three in Kenaisky Bay (Georgievskoe, Pavlovskoe, and Nikolaevskoe); two in Chugatsky Bay, in the Harbor of Constantine and Elena, in Delarov Harbor (later found destroyed), Simeonovskoe at the Cape of Saint Elias, two in the Yakutat Bay (one of them, Slavorossiia, destroyed by natives in 1805), and on the island of Sitka (Novo-Arkhangel'sk).[126] To this list one should add the settlement of Dobroe Soglasie on the island of Unalaska.

One of the most acute problems concerning Russian settlers in America was that of supplying them with necessary provisions: food, clothes, firearms, sea gear, and so on. Transportation across roadless and sparsely populated Siberia, Okhotsk, and Kamchatka was exceptionally difficult, requiring enormous expense and subjecting the whole Iakutsk region, "through transporting the state's burdens," to enormous exhaustion. It was impossible to deliver very heavy weights. Ships' anchors had to be cut apart and smelted back together in Okhotsk; and in spite of this great expense one could not expect from them the required strength. Because of this the main office planned its first round-the-world expedition, "to be sent from the Baltic to America," enlisting the support of Rumiantsev.[127] In sending this expedition, the Russian government contemplated "for the good of the state, to look over American acquisitions and describe them, to open up trade with Canton, and to survey the possibilities of trade with Japan and other Asiatic regions."[128]

The first expedition to circumnavigate the globe was launched from

Kronstadt in the summer of 1803, under the command of I. F. Kruzen-
stern and Yu. F. Lisiansky. It lasted until 1806, and besides supplying
goods to Russian America, performed important scientific, political, and
commercial tasks.[129] A new round-the-world sailing was undertaken in
October 1806 on the sloop *Neva,* commanded by L. A. Hagemeister.[130]
After delivering goods to Russian colonies, the *Neva* spent the next few
years sailing between the northwest coast of America and Kamchatka.

Round-the-world expeditions, although of enormous scientific and
political importance, could not solve the problem of regularly supplying
necessary goods and provisions. Such expeditions were undertaken infrequently, involved enormous expenses, and were riddled with difficulties. The tense international situation during the epoch of the Napoleonic
Wars was also far from favorable for the launching of regular expeditions.

It is natural then that Russian settlers in America had to rely on their
own devices and seek more permanent, nearby, and reliable sources to
supply their colonies with provisions and other staples. As a result, commercial contacts with California (and other regions of so-called Spanish
America) and regular contacts with United States traders were established, and attempts were made to create a provisional base ("Ross"
settlement). The initiator of the direct contacts with California was N. P.
Rezanov, who embarked from Novo-Arkhangel'sk on the ship *Iunona*
(Juno) on February 25/March 9, 1806, under the command of N. A.
Khvostov, and reached San Francisco Bay a month later.[131]

Having assumed the role of "the commander-in-chief" of the Russian
colonies in America, Rezanov entered into negotiations with local Spanish
authorities. The governor of Upper California, José Arrilaga, came to San
Francisco in April 1806 in order to meet him.[132] "I shall tell you sincerely," Rezanov said to the Governor, "that we need bread, which we can
get from Canton; but since California is closer and has a surplus, which
she cannot dispose of elsewhere, I came here to talk to you, as the chief of
these regions, assuring you that we can establish some preliminary measures and forward them for favorable perusal and confirmation by our
authorities."

The problem faced by Rezanov was exceptionally complex. The
fanatical Madrid court scrupulously defended its colonial possessions
from all external connections and had forbidden any contacts with foreigners. Local authorities in the Spanish colonies did not dare ignore this
injunction, even though they suffered great inconveniences because of it.
In the course of a six weeks' stay in California, Rezanov demonstrated his
outstanding diplomatic gifts and earned the good will of the local authori-

ties. The Russian court official and the proud Spaniards soon found common language. Rezanov listened sympathetically to their complaints about "the impudence of Bostonians," whose vessels "constantly smuggle along the shores," "conduct illicit trade," and "with great effrontery look for means of installing themselves in the Spanish possessions."[133] For his part, the California governor listened with great pleasure to the discourse of his interlocutor on the development of mutual trade between the American regions of both states, as a result of which "the colonies will flourish," and "our shores, constituting a common link, would be always defended equally by both Crowns, with nobody able to intrude among them."

Rezanov's stay in California and his negotiations with the Spanish authorities resulted in one of the most romantic stories of the period. Being warmly welcomed into the home of the commandant, José Darío Argüello, Rezanov became intimate with his daughter, the beautiful María de la Concepción, considered the "beauty of California." "Beautiful Concepción," Rezanov wrote later to the Minister of Commerce in a "confession of his private adventures," increased her attentions to me from day to day, and her various favors, meaning so much to one in my situation, and her sincerity to which I had been indifferent for a long time, gradually began imperceptibly to fill the emptiness of my heart." (Rezanov's wife, Anna Grigor'evna Shelikhova, had died in 1802). "Courting the Spanish beauty daily," the forty-year-old Rezanov soon captured the imagination of the young Spanish girl and she agreed to marry him. At first, this was a "bolt out of the blue" for Concepción's parents, "brought up in the fanaticism" of the Catholic church. They repeatedly took the poor girl to church, to confession, and tried to persuade her to refuse, "but resoluteness on both sides finally appeased everyone." The incredible happened: the "holy fathers" gave in to the insistence of the fifteen-year-old Concepción. Her engagement to Rezanov and the signing of a betrothal agreement took place; final resolution was postponed until the Pope granted the permission for marriage.[134]

The epilogue of this romance is sad. When leaving hospitable California, Rezanov assured his youthful bride-to-be that he would return in two years. Later he instructed Baranov to confirm again, when he had an occasion to do so, that he would "stick to his word." But "high Providence" did not give him a chance to carry out this promise. On his way to St. Petersburg via Siberia, Rezanov "contracted a cruel fever" and died suddenly in Krasnoiarsk on 1/13 March 1807. Meanwhile, the beautiful Concepción remained touchingly faithful to her childhood sweetheart and, refusing to believe the tragic news, patiently awaited the return of her beloved to the shores of California. She spent her last years in a convent, where she died in 1857.[135]

Her true love brought much sorrow and little joy to poor Concepción, but it did help Russian America to survive one of the most difficult periods of its history. After Rezanov's engagement, various provisions, bread above all, poured into the hold of *Iunona* in such abundance that he had to ask for the "delivery to be discontinued," since the vessel could not take on more than 4,300 poods. Thus, "the initial experiment of commerce with California" proved very successful. As Rezanov pointed out, this commerce could amount annually to at the very least a million dollars. "Our American territory will not suffer any shortages; Kamchatka and Okhotsk will be supplied with bread and other provisions; Iakuts, burdened at present by the transport of bread, will be left in peace; the government will decrease the expenses allotted to the provisions for the military; there will be relief on bread prices in Irkutsk . . . customs will give new income to the Crown, Russia's internal industry will be noticeably encouraged."[136]

Before his departure from San Francisco, Rezanov addressed a special letter to the viceroy of the New Spain, José Iturrigaray, in which he cited in detail the mutual advantages from the development of the trade:

> New California, which produces various grains and cattle in abundance, can market her products in our settlements; she will be readily assisted in filling all needs through trade with our regions; the best means for achieving the well-being of her missions and for bringing the country to prosperity is exchange of surplus production for goods which do not have to be paid for in cash and the import of which is not beset with difficulties. . . . In the same measure the proximity of the transport will alleviate the existence in our settlements in the North, which at present have to bring from afar everything that the severity of the climate denies them.

In Rezanov's opinion these contacts, "predestined by nature itself," were evoked "to preserve forever the friendship between the two states possessing such extensive territories."[137]

In spite of Rezanov's death the Main Office of the Russian-American Company and the tsarist government in St. Petersburg tried to do everything they could to insure commercial ties with California and, if possible, the whole of Spanish America. Early in 1808 the chief director of the Russian-American Company, M. M. Buldakov, requested Alexander I "to solicit . . . the agreement of the Spanish Crown" to the opening of the company's trade with the Spanish possessions in America and permission "to send every year not more than two of their ships into the California ports of San Francisco, Monterey, and San Diego."[138]

Basing his argument on papers and journals left by Rezanov, Buldakov expounded in detail the advantages of this commerce. "California has an abundance of bread, and not possessing the means to dispose of it, annually lets 300,000 poods rot; American settlements, on the contrary, must get their bread transported across Siberia by land for more than 3,000 versts, costing the company about 15 rubles a pood." Noting further that California has an "overabundance of horned domestic cattle and horses," Buldakov wrote that the "Okhotsk and Kamchatka regions have the greatest need of such cattle, since they frequently suffer general famine." California had a "great shortage of all sorts of linens and iron," while Russia had "an overabundance not only of this metal and linens, but can supply other countries with these products without depriving herself." Referring to Rezanov's negotiations with the California governor, Buldakov emphasized that the Spaniards themselves were extremely interested in developing trade relations "with the Russians as their closest neighbors in America." "If the Madrid court were aware of the need of the local region," the California governor said, "it would surely establish commercial ties with Russia, by means of which mutual good would be attained, and Bostonians then would not corrupt the wild natives, especially if both states ordered a frigate or warship to cruise along the shores."[139]

The proposal of the Russian-American Company was not ignored. On April 20/May 2, 1808, the minister for foreign affairs and commerce, N. P. Rumiantsev, instructed the Russian minister in Madrid, G. A. Stroganov, to try to obtain permission from the Spanish government for the dispatching of two (or more) Russian ships annually to California ports, if necessary by concluding an appropriate convention to that end. For its part the tsarist government was prepared to permit "Spanish American ships to enter not only Russian American ports, but even Kamchatka, thus permitting mutually advantageous trade relations."[140]

Stormy events in Spain prevented Stroganov from executing Rumiantsev's instructions, as his dispatch from Madrid of May 28/June 9, 1808 indicates.[141] Other attempts to establish permanent trade connections between Russia and Spanish America were not realized either, although various projects to that end were proposed repeatedly.[142]

Rezanov's hopes that trade relations with California would make "illustrious giant steps" remained only a dream. It proved impossible to establish permanent commercial connections between Russian America and the rich, neighboring California. Russian settlers, with A. A. Baranov in the lead, had to content themselves with their own meager resources and establishing, without government sanction, business contacts with their rivals, the Boston shippers. I have already discussed the dangers of foreign competition in the Pacific North, and the fact that Bostonians were supplying the local population with firearms, undercutting the interests of the Russian-American Company, and so on. Too often historians have limited themselves to noting this negative side of the problem. However, the appearance of foreign traders in the Russian possessions in America had some positive results, connected in particular with the establishment and development of direct commercial contacts between Baranov and American shippers.

In the early nineteenth century American vessels regularly began visiting Russian America, particularly the islands of Kodiak and Unalaska, thus establishing the first business contacts with the company. According to Baranov's testimony, the first American vessel arrived at Kodiak in 1800, "on February 15, and in the end of same and in March two more from there."[143] In the spring of 1801 a merchant ship *Enterprise* arrived from New York, under the command of Captain Ezekiel Hubbel. Baranov, who was experiencing an extreme shortage of most goods at the time, considered it possible to ignore earlier injunctions and opened commercial contacts with the foreigners.[144] In the fall of 1803 he bartered for various goods to the sum of 10,000 rubles from Captain Joseph O'Cain, who was visiting Kodiak for a second time, having been there earlier as skipper of the *Enterprise*.[145] A Captain Gibitz traded in the Russian colonies that same year.[146] O'Cain's contacts with Baranov were not limited to trade. Twenty kayaks were put at the American's disposal, manned by Aleutians under Shvetsov's command, for a joint trapping expedition all the way down to California. When he returned to Kodiak in the spring of 1804, O'Cain brought back 1,100 sea otter skins.[147] In the course of that year Baranov bartered various goods to the sum of 37,000 rubles from American vessels docking in Kodiak. At this time the Americans offered to establish permanent trade connections, and Baranov gave them a list of staples needed by Russian colonies.[148]

Among American vessels docking in Novo-Arkhangel'sk in 1805, Rezanov mentions two three-masted schooners: the *Maria* (Captain Tresket) and the *Iunona* (Captain D'Wolf). The arrival of such ships not only enabled Rezanov and Baranov to buy extremely needed staples; it also allowed them to buy his ship from Captain D'Wolf for 68,000 Spanish piastres (part of the sum was paid in furs, the rest in promissory notes to the main office in St. Petersburg). Both sides were pleased by the results of the transaction. Five American sailors entered the service of the company. D'Wolf himself set out via Okhotsk to St. Petersburg to present his promissory notes for payment to the corporation of the Russian-American Company; his net profit was $100,000.[149]

In May 1806 a vessel belonging to an American, Jonathan Winship, arrived. Baranov made an agreement with him for a joint trapping venture at New Albion. The American ship was supposed to give cover to the trapping party of fifty kayaks under the guidance of Slobodchikov and two of his aides. At the expedition's end Slobodchikov, after an altercation with Winship, bought a small vessel in California and returned in August 1807, to the Russian possessions with the cargo of pelts worth 100,000 rubles, after a difficult voyage via Hawaii. Winship followed in September 1807. The joint catch consisted of 4,820 beavers of various kinds which were divided equally.[150]

Baranov made an important agreement on the island of Sitka on 6/18 September 1806 with his old acquaintance, Captain O'Cain of the *Eclipse*. It dealt with the question of opening up trade with Japan, in Nagasaki, with Canton, and with Batavia. The pelts sent with O'Cain included 1,800 sea otters, 105,000 seals, 2,500 beavers, and other goods, with a total value of 310,000 rubles. The American captain was given Baranov's letter to the governor of Nagasaki proposing the establishment of trade relations. However, this agreement did not bring the expected profits to the company. In Canton, O'Cain excluded the Russian commissioner from participation in the trade and sold the pelts at a great loss. He did not succeed in arranging for trade contacts with Japan, and, to top it all, on the way back from Kamchatka to Russian America he suffered a shipwreck.[151]

According to the company's records, by 1808 it had sold "to foreign hands" furs to the sum of 459,102 rubles, including beavers worth 153,640 rubles and seals worth 226,669 rubles.[152] These figures, even though they seem deliberately minimized, indicate that in the beginning the volume of foreign trade in Russian America was not great. Nevertheless, the establishment of direct trade contacts with foreigners (citizens of the United States primarily, and English in individual instances) as well as the first experiments in joint beaver trapping with Boston skippers proved profitable for both sides.

American skippers called on Baranov more and more often, and pressed insistently for joint beaver trapping. Some, such as Winship and O'Cain, came to Russian America more than once. In 1807 the *Derby* arrived in Kodiak from Canton. Selling Chinese goods, its skipper, B. Swift, made it an indispensable condition that Baranov agree to a joint trapping expedition similar to Winship's; he was furnished with "twenty-five kayaks with fifty natives under the command of two trappers." Baranov also collaborated with Captain Oliver Kimball of the ship *Peacock*, who received twelve kayaks manned by Aleutians under the command of V. P. Tarakanov, for his trapping needs. Tarakanov's experience and knowledge contributed greatly to the success of the expedition, and in August 1807 Kimball returned to Sitka with 1,231 beaver skins.[153] In May 1808 an agreement was made with Captain Ayres of the *Mercury*; he received twenty-five kayaks with Aleutians under the command of Shvetsov. The contract specified that, in case of the death of any of the Aleutians, Ayres was obligated to pay 250 dollars to the bereaved family.[154]

On the whole Baranov was satisfied with the results of his transactions, as he repeatedly mentioned them in his correspondence with I. A. Kuskov in 1806-1808.[155] Although the profits of joint trapping ventures had to be shared with foreigners, there were advantages since the major part of the expeditions took place outside the Russian colonies—where the number of sea otters was already much diminished as a result of ruthless extermination—spreading to more southern regions of the American Pacific coast down to California.

In undertaking business ventures with Yankee traders, Baranov and Rezanov counted first of all on securing a more or less permanent source for supplying the colonies with provisions. In this connection Rezanov proposed to organize the main "storage of goods" in Novo-Arkhangel'sk, "where the Bostonians would willingly come for their purchases." In exchange for staples of their own manufacture, such as flour, grain, butter, suet, and vinegar, Americans could, in his opinion, get wanted pelts without subjecting themselves to danger from Indians. "Boston Captain Swift," Rezanov wrote, "has already promised to make the first experiment of this trade, and this very spring Mr. Baranov is expecting a vessel from him."[156]

In this way, during these years the general policy toward Yankee traders in northwest America was influenced by two basic factors. On one hand, the commercial activity of American skippers in Russian possessions was greatly detrimental to the company. "North American republicans" sold local inhabitants "all sorts of firearms and weapons, gunpowder and lead," showed them "the manner of using the latter," and stirred them up against the Russians.[157] By taking pelt goods directly to Canton the

Americans and English were seriously undercutting the interests of the Russian-American Company and impeding its trade in Kiakhta. On the other hand, business contacts with American skippers, Baranov's purchase of necessary staples (mainly provisions, but also ships), and the organization of joint trapping expeditions made it possible for the Russian colonies to satisfy a considerable portion of their needs independently and even to look toward getting a certain income as a result of these transactions.

Originally, the Russian-American Company endeavored to arrange matters with the Yankee traders unofficially. "The committee appointed by the American Company in 1804 with imperial permission" decided to advise Baranov "to try by gentle means to restrain the Bostonians, if possible, from the sale of firearms," while in the meantime it made an attempt in St. Petersburg to negotiate with the United States. But Baranov's "gentle means" and repeated "reprimands" were of little avail. "The Americans, as free people," responded to his "reprimands" with laughter or explained that they were merchants and free to seek a profit. "They have not heard either from their own or our government about any prohibition of their trade with the savages."

The main office of the Russian-American Company had no recourse but to request support from their protectors in St. Petersburg. On April 21/May 3, 1808, Buldakov and Kramer addressed Rumiantsev with the petition already mentioned, "On the damage inflicted on the company by Bostonians." The corporation requested the "gracious assistance of the highest authority in forbidding foreigners, especially North American republicans, to trade with the savages, such being the custom in other European colonies in both Indies, and induce them to trade only with the company and nowhere else but on Kodiak as the main local Russian trading post." The corporation proposed "to conclude arrangements with those republicans who were willing, and which would be mutually agreeable and profitable."[158]

Minister of Commerce Rumiantsev, who by this time had became also Minister for Foreign Affairs, considered the company's solicitations just and supported them in full. He made a report to Alexander I in May 1808,[159] "On the presentation of the American Company about the Bostonians," in which he emphasized two basic points. First, "citizens of the North American United States, trading outside the company," barter "from the savages a considerable number of sea otters" and sell them in Canton much more profitably than the company could do in Kiakhta. And, second, traveling over the areas occupied by the company, "Bostonians impress on the local inhabitants views prejudicial to it, "prevailing upon them not to respect the Russians, and to support this corruption, they barter to them all sorts of firearms."

Supporting the petition of the Russian-American Company that it be granted assistance from the government, Rumiantsev asked the "highest will" for permission to "address the consul of the United States who resides here and impress him with the need to take appropriate measures, so that the government over there would forbid the North American republics to trade with the savages, would establish commercial relations with the company alone, and not in any other place but Kodiak as the main local Russian trading post; for which purpose the company would be certain to establish mutually agreeable and profitable arrangements, taking as an example those existing in other European colonies in both Indies."[160]

"The highest will" was granted, and Rumiantsev noted on the margins of his report: "To discuss the possibility of such resolution with the Consul of the United American States." On 17/29 May 1808 this question was for the first time put officially to the United States in a special note of Rumiantsev to the consul-general in St. Petersburg, Levett Harris.[161] The note called attention to the fact that citizens of the United States engaged in illegal trade with local inhabitants in the Russian possessions in America; and it proposed to conclude a special convention specifying that the commerce of these American citizens should take place only on Kodiak and only with the representative of the Russian-American Company. In his return letter to Rumiantsev of 19/31 May 1808, Levett Harris expressed "sincere satisfaction" with the proposal for the conclusion of the agreement which will put an end to the "irrégularités" and protect the commerce of both countries in that area. He promised to inform his government of the contents of this interesting note at the very first opportunity, and assured that it would receive all the attention it deserved.[162] One can see from the report sent by Harris to Secretary of State Madison on 1/13 June 1808 that, in addition to his official statement, Rumiantsev "attached" the private wish of the Emperor that the difficulties might be removed by means of the agreement he was proposing.[163] Utilizing his personal connections in the Main Office, Harris at the same time sent Washington detailed information on the Russian-American Company, and the translation of the note expressing complaints of the illegal activity of the United States' citizens.

By the spring of 1808 the question of trade with "North-American republics" in Russian possessions in America had reached the level of a government problem. To solve it, a proposal was made to the government of the United States that a special agreement be concluded. This agreement was designed, on the one hand, to protect Russian possessions from the undercutting of dangerous competitors by prohibiting the supply of firearms to the natives, and, on the other hand, to insure the development of regular commercial contacts between Russian America and Boston merchants. The activity of the Russian-American Company was becoming more and more important in defining Russia's general policy toward the United States; in particular, it made the tsarist government realize the necessity of establishing direct contacts with Washington.

Part Three

Russian-American Rapprochement, 1808-1812

The establishment of diplomatic relations between Russia and the United States between 1808 and 1812 and the consequent rapprochement between the two countries resulted from a series of international and internal developments. From the time of the War of Independence and Russia's Declaration of Armed Neutrality in 1780, the common interest of both nations to protect the rights of neutral navigation laid a firm foundation for rapprochement. It is not accidental, therefore, that in his well-known letter to Alexander I of April 19, 1806, Thomas Jefferson emphasized the concurrence of the interests of the United States with those of the countries of northern Europe, led by Russia, in the establishment of peace and the development of the maritime commerce of neutral nations. The President of the United States expressed the hope that the Russian Emperor would undertake the defense of these interests and would incorporate into the future act of pacification a correct definition of the rights of neutrals on the high seas.[1]

Mutually advantageous trade contacts played an essential role in Russian-American rapprochement. Although the initial volume of trade between the two countries was not great, gradually contacts with the American market began to assume a definite practical weight. As already stated, in the early years of the nineteenth century Russian exports to the United States totaled more than one and a half million dollars, and between seventy and eighty, or more, American ships docked annually in Russian ports.[2]

Striving to minimize the dependence of the Russian economy on Great Britain, the tsarist government and Minister of Commerce Rumiantsev tried their utmost to broaden the sphere of Russian commerce, and particularly encouraged the development of "direct trade" with the United States. As Rumiantsev pointed out in his report on the activity of the ministry of commerce for 1805,

> The political situation of the European powers and the diminution of commerce in Holland, Spain, and France herself led one to observe without fail that England alone remained abundantly in the field of our commerce, and in this position could become the mistress of purchasing prices for our products. Intending to preclude such a disadvantage, I turned my attention toward the United States, to try to engage the Americans in a rivalry with the English, and to try, because of the abundance of their articles needed by us, to establish direct connection between our commerce and the American.[3]

From the beginning of the nineteenth century, the interests of the Russian-American Company began to play a significant role in defining Russia's policy toward the United States. On the one hand, as noted, the illegal trade of Bostonians in the Russian possessions in America caused serious damage to the company; on the other hand, mutually advantageous business contacts between Boston shipowners and Russian colonists gradually developed. In both cases the establishment of direct diplomatic ties with the United States could open additional possibilities for the stabilizing of the company's relations with Americans.

Cultural and socio-political contacts contributed a great deal to rapprochement with the United States. The personal correspondence between Alexander I and Thomas Jefferson, discussed earlier, had special significance in laying the groundwork for direct diplomatic connections between Russia and the United States. The establishment of a top-level contact, so to speak, and the mutual exchange of friendly letters facilitated the official procedure connected with the exchange of diplomatic missions.

The most important reasons that defined the necessity of the Russian-American rapprochement are found in the international situation of the period, which should be discussed in somewhat greater detail. It seemed at that time that there could be no further barrier to Napoleon's military genius. It had taken only a few weeks for his utter defeat of Prussia. The devotion of the Prussian military to physical discipline, drill, and pedantry led that country to the unparalleled ignominy of Jena and Auerstädt. Both battles took place on the same day, October 14, 1806, and ended in the catastrophic defeat of the Prussian troops. On October 27 Napoleon entered Berlin. Friedrich-Wilhelm III, who, as Engels put it, "knew only two feelings: fear and corporal's arrogance,"[4] fled like a coward first to Koenigsberg, and then to Memel.

On November 21, 1806, the Berlin decree of the Continental Blockade, forbidding any trade with England and her colonies to all countries dependent on France, was signed in the Potsdam palace.[5] From then on unrelenting adherence to the harsh dictates of the Continental Blockade became the center of the whole diplomatic activity of the French government, signifying a new and decisive stage in Napoleon's struggle to dominate Europe. At the end of 1806 and the beginning of 1807 Russia, who continued amid difficult conditions her military actions against Napoleon's troops, remained France's only serious adversary.

In the bloody battle of Preussisch Eylau on January 27/February 8, 1807, Napoleon did not succeed in winning. In spite of the external glitter and might of Napoleon's France, the country was not yet ready to conduct a prolonged war on the limitless expanses of Russia. Napoleon was inclining toward a conclusion of peace and even a coalition with Russia.[6]

Various proposals for ending the hopeless war were advanced in the ruling circles of Russia as well. A numerous and influential "party of peace," whose membership included Grand Duke Constantin, A. A. Czartoryski, N. N. Novosiltsov, and A. B. Kurakin, opposed those who advocated a continuation of the war until final victory, who were led by the minister of foreign affairs, A. Ia. Budberg, and supported by Emperor Alexander I. The defeat of Russian troops under the command of L. Bennigsen near Friedland on June 2/14, 1807, decided the outcome of the campaign in favor of Napoleon and quickened the conclusion of the armistice. In the course of negotiations at Tilsit, Napoleon agreed to keep Prussia and preserve Russian borders on condition that Russia enter into the coalition against England and participate in the Continental Blockade. On June 25/July 7, 1807, Talleyrand, Kurakin, and D. I. Lobanov-Rostovsky signed a treaty of peace and friendship, and a treaty of defensive and offensive alliance between Russia and France.[7] In case England refused to conclude the armistice by December 1, 1807, "admitting that the flags of all nations must enjoy equal independence on the high seas, and to return all land seized by conquest from France and her allies since 1805," Russia was to take upon herself an obligation "to act as one with France," that is, to declare war and join the Continental Blockade. On August 30/September 11, 1807, Budberg resigned "because of ill health,"[8] and Rumiantsev became chief of staff of the Ministry for Foreign Affairs, being officially confirmed as minister in February 1808.

International relations during the Napoleonic era as a whole, and the history of Tilsit and the Continental Blockade, have been studied in detail both in Russian and Western literature. The works of the French historians Albert Sorel and Albert Vandal as well as the brilliant research on the Continental Blockade of E. V. Tarle, first published in 1913, are well known.[9] Various aspects of American foreign policy during this period, above all, relations with Great Britain and France, have been studied assiduously. But, as usual, the question of Russian-American relations remained outside the scholar's field of vision. Nevertheless, the post-Tilsit rapprochement between Russia and the United States represents a distinctive and significant phenomenon in the international relations of the period and merits special attention.

The unrelenting logic of international events made this rapprochement necessary and even inevitable. On October 26/November 7, 1807, a declaration concerning the break with England was published; two days later an embargo was imposed on English vessels and goods.[10] The role of Great Britain in Russia's foreign trade is well known. In 1802-1805 Russia's annual exports to England averaged 73 percent of all exported hemp, 91 percent of flax, 77 percent of lard, 71 percent of iron, 80 percent of bristle, 42 percent of wheat, and 43 percent of linen.[11] Deprived of the British market and in need of colonial goods and English industrial products, Russian landlords and merchants sought a solution in the encouragement of neutral, and particularly American, trade. Hence prospects for Russian-American commercial relations appeared favorable. Through the United States and from American ships Russia could obtain not only cotton, tobacco, and colonial goods, but in some cases the products of English industry, import of which directly from England was strictly forbidden.

The tsarist government viewed the United States, not without reason, as both the rival of Great Britain and the substitute for her (albeit far from an equal one) in respect to commerce. Naturally the Tilsit agreements did not eliminate French-Russian opposition, nor did they halt the struggle of the Russian government against Napoleon. Essentially these agreements signified only an admission by the tsarist government of the impossibility of destroying France by military means, and a desire to find other ways to counteract Napoleonic expansion while at the same time realizing Russia's own expansionist aims. The new Russian ally, with her enormous military might, seemed dangerous indeed. On the other hand, one could no longer count on the traditional partners, Austria and Prussia. It is natural, therefore, that rapprochement with the United States—even granted that country's relative weakness at the time—could assume a certain significance for the tsarist government.

The United States was interested in rapprochement with Russia to an even greater degree. Relations with both England and France were strained to the utmost and seemed close to the breaking point. From 1803 through 1812 the English captured 917, and the French 858 American vessels.[12] Stubbornly insisting on its "right" to remove English deserters from the American vessels forcibly, the British Navy before the War of 1812 captured about nine thousand American seamen, most of them natives of the United States.[13] This marauding practice, "a monstrous breach of any international law," as Marx put it,[14] in 1807 brought both countries to the brink of war. On June 22, 1807, the British warship *Leopard* fired upon the American warship *Chesapeake.* The American ship capitulated, and after a search the British captured four seamen, one of whom was adjudged a deserter and hanged immediately on the verdict of a war tribunal.[15]

As a reprisal measure against Napoleon's declaration of the Continental Blockade, England declared the so-called Orders-in-Council of January 7, November 11 and 15, and December 18, 1807, and March 30, 1808.[16] The first ukase of Charles Grey, Lord Howick, on January 7, 1807, was more or less moderate: American merchants could still sail to France, but their ships were forbidden to continue in search for new markets from one European port to another. After the approval in the royal council of the famous ukase of Spencer Perceval on November 11, however, all American ships with any kind of cargo, bound to any European port from which English merchants were excluded, were subject to capture. United States trade with the enemies of Great Britain could be conducted only through British ports and only with the license of British authorities. "By publishing her orders-in-council," Marx noted, "England admitted openly that she infringed upon the rights of neutral nations in general and the United States in particular."[17]

In justification of their illicit actions the government of Great Britain referred to Napoleon's Berlin decree. Obviously there was no doubt about the anti-French tendency of the rulings of the British cabinet. However, as a recent French study demonstrates, the Continental Blockade was not the only or the most important cause of the November ukases. In the author's opinion, they resulted primarily from the English trade policy, serious difficulties of the British economy, and acute commercial rivalry with the United States.[18]

News about the order of the British Royal Council of November 11, 1807, reached Washington on December 17. That very day Thomas Jefferson called an emergency meeting of the cabinet at which a decision to introduce a general embargo was unanimously agreed upon.[19] Albert

Gallatin alone had some doubts about the question, foreseeing not unjustifiably the harsh consequences to the United States of a permanent embargo. "From every point of view—privations, sufferings, revenue, effect on the enemy, politics at home, etc.—I prefer war to a permanent embargo," the Secretary of the Treasury wrote to the President the next day, arguing for the introduction of an embargo for a limited time.[20] A new meeting of the cabinet was called immediately, but the decision remained the same. On the same day, December 18, 1807, in a closed meeting of the Senate, the Vice-President read a message composed by James Madison, and after a short discussion the government's proposal to introduce a general embargo was approved by twenty-two votes, with six against it. Three days later, this decision was approved by the House of Representatives (eighty-two for, and forty-four against).[21] On December 22, 1807, the Embargo Act was signed by the President and became law. The administration and the Congress were, as we can see, exceptionally effective.[22]

The complex international situation of the United States, the increase of friction with France, and the threat of open conflict with Great Britain forced the American government to seek Russia's support. Of great interest in this respect is a notation concerning a talk between Consul-General Harris and Chief of the Ministry for Foreign Affairs Czartoryski, on 14/26 March 1806, which is preserved in the Archive for Foreign Policy (AVPR). Its contents show that Harris confidentially and at length informed the Russian government of the most important aspects of United States foreign policy and its dealings with England, France, and Spain.

In particular, the consul told Czartoryski about the war preparations taking place in the United States at the time, and about the rigging of forty frigates and a corresponding number of light vessels. "Mr. Harris further informed me that Congress is debating the question of enlarging the numbers of the land army up to 100,000 men." Depending on the circumstances, these armed forces, according to him, were intended for action against Spain, France, or England. Most serious, according to Harris, were the claims against England. "Congress decided not to permit the impressment of American sailors. . . . The government of the United States decided to make new representations at the London court and demand the return of 2,000 sailors impressed by the British."

Bearing on this question, the American consul expressed a desire that Russia offer "her kind services in London with the aim of inducing the British ministry to return to the principles of justice." This request for "kind services" was advanced in a cautious and unofficial form. Levett Harris made the point "that this idea was his, and that he was not authorized by his government to ask for the interference of the imperial court in the given circumstances." There is no doubt that Russia's interference—taking into account the state of Anglo-Russian relations at the time—would definitely be useful to the United States. At the same time, the absence of diplomatic relations between the two countries created a formal obstacle for rendering such kind services. This was the very circumstance that Prince Czartoryski pointed out in his answer: "no matter how strong was His Imperial Majesty's desire to remove all reasons for misunderstanding between the United States and Great Britain, it would be, in all probability, difficult for him to take part in this problem, considering the complete absence of pretext for it, since relations between Russia and the United States up to this time have not been even secured by the appointment of appropriate ministers."[23]

Although Harris made it clear that he had no authorization to request Russia's interference, the very fact of his appeal is significant in understanding the character of Russian-American relations and their general development.

Historians often quote Jefferson's letter of July 20, 1807, to William Duane, editor of the Philadelphia *Aurora*, in which the President of the United States wrote of Russia as most cordially friendly to the United States, the concurrence of Russian-American interests in respect to the rights of neutral navigation, and so forth.[24] In a sense Jefferson's evaluation suffers from some exaggeration, but on the whole it correctly reflected the existing situation: at that time Russia was the only great power objectively favorable toward the United States; and her support could turn out to be essential. In view of this, the desire of the government of the United States to establish direct diplomatic relations with St. Petersburg is understandable. "In the present complicated and critical state of the world, it is deemed of importance to cultivate the friendship of a Sovereign so influential as that of Russia may be, and who has authorized in several ways a belief that the just interests of the United States are not indifferent to him."[25]

VII

THE ESTABLISHMENT OF DIPLOMATIC RELATIONS

Materials in the Central Soviet Archives in Moscow and Leningrad and in the National Archive of the United States make it possible to trace fully and precisely the beginning of diplomatic relations between Russia and the United States.[1]

In principle, the question of a diplomatic exchange was agreed upon in London in the autumn of 1807, with the Americans taking the initiative. In his conversation with M. M. Alopeus[2] in August 1807, the American ambassador to England, James Monroe, pointed to the substantial expansion of trade relations between Russia and the United States and to the favorable prospects for their further development. "Following that, he expressed a wish for these two powers to make a decision about the mutual appointment of persons of an official character, thus establishing a mutually advantageous diplomatic connection." Informing St. Petersburg of the proposal, Alopeus expressed an opinion that at the present moment, with the French cabinet attempting to limit Russia's political influence in Europe, it would be expedient to broaden this influence in the direction of America.[3]

Following this "preliminary reconnaissance," Monroe officially informed Alopeus of President Jefferson's proposition to establish direct diplomatic relations between the two countries. "The minister of the United States of America, Mr. Monroe," Alopeus reported from London, "following the instruction of his government, asked me for a rendezvous, which took place without delay. The President of the States instructed him to express through my intermediary assurances of deep respect for the Emperor and the wish that His Imperial Majesty might take a favorable view of the establishment of direct and unentailed relations between

Russia and the United States, by appointing a minister to represent him in the United States. He added that, as the favorable response of His Imperial Majesty becomes manifest, the President would immediately address himself to the appointment of an American minister at the Russian Court."[4]

Alopeus' reports, as notations on the originals indicate, were received in St. Petersburg correspondingly on 3/15 September and 5/17 October 1807.[5] On the very next day, 6/18 October, Rumiantsev, the new chief of the Ministry for Foreign Affairs, reported the theoretical agreement of the Russian government to the exchange of diplomatic representatives. Rumiantsev noted that Alexander I had long since mentally selected a candidate for the post of his diplomatic representative in America, and at the same time expressed a wish that Levett Harris would be appointed to St. Petersburg from the American side. "I do not intend to conceal from you, Dear Sir," Rumiantsev continued, "that Mr. Levett Harris, who for some years has been occupying the post of American consul-general in St. Petersburg, has won the confidence of the imperial ministry by his behavior, as wise as it is tactful, therefore it would probably be found very satisfactory here if the choice of the American government for its diplomatic agent at the St. Petersburg Court were to fall on Mr. Harris." At the same time Rumiantsev made it clear that the Emperor "does not have the least intention of influencing the decision which the government of the United States would wish to make in the given circumstances, and no matter whom they appoint to the post in Russia, that person can be assured of the most courteous and friendly reception."[6]

Having received this dispatch, Alopeus informed the new American ambassador in London, William Pinckney, about the readiness of the Russian government to exchange diplomatic missions with the United States.[7]

Although theoretically the problem was resolved during the fall of 1807, practical preparations for the exchange of diplomatic representatives did not begin to take place both in Russia and in the United States until the next summer. On 8/20 May 1808 Rumiantsev, in a report to the Tsar, renewed his "solicitations" about "establishing in Philadelphia and in Boston two consul-generals, the need for whom is apparent in view of our emerging connections with the United States, and who would be extremely useful in such circumstances." As one can see from the notation on the margin, "His Majesty the Emperor deigned to sanction this report."[8]

Exactly a month later, on 8/20 June 1808, an imperial ukase was issued to the College of Foreign Affairs. "In view of our extended relations with the American United States," Alexander I saw it "useful to establish consulates in those parts," and to this end ordered that appropriate means be "extracted from the general state incomes, in addition to the sums allotted to maintaining the consular and ministerial posts." "To the post of consul-general in Philadelphia," it was noted, "we order sent an official in the department of the Minister of Commerce, the College Assessor Andrey Dashkov, entrusting him, also for the time being with the post of our chargé d'affaires at Congress, and appointing for him a secretary or an office clerk, according to the choice of the College."[9]

Several days later Rumiantsev informed Harris officially about the appointment of Dashkov and of the Emperor's desire to strengthen friendly connections between Russia and the United States;[10] and the new consul-general and chargé d'affaires was introduced to Alexander I.[11]

After being appointed consul-general in Philadelphia with the instruction to perform "for the time being" the duties of chargé d'affaires, Dashkov soon added to his initial modest title of College Assessor that of "correspondent of the Russian-American Company." In a letter of 21 July/2 August 1808 the Main Office asked Dashkov to accept this title and to render the company "help, protection, solicitation, and every favor" and honor it with special care and guidance in those affairs "which it has in its settlements in the northwest part of America, concerning commerce with the citizens of the abovementioned North American states."[12]

Before accepting this proposal, the cautious official decided, for safety's sake, to beg permission from Rumiantsev "both to accept the title of correspondent of the Russian-American Company, to solicit on its behalf in American United States . . . and to communicate directly with the Main Office of the said company and with the territories in its jurisdiction."[13] In order to dispel the College Assessor's doubts, Rumiantsev wrote that, in his "role as Minister of Commerce," he actually demands that Dashkov pay especial attention to "all that would bear on the advantages for the commerce of this company."[14]

Thus, on his departure for the United States, Dashkov had three titles simultaneously: that of chargé d'affaires at the United States Congress, consul-general in Philadelphia, and special representative, or "correspondent," of the Russian-American Company. Three special lengthy instructions were prepared for him before his departure: from the College of Foreign Affairs, the College of Commerce, and the Main Office of the Russian-American Company. These instructions served as a basis for all his consequent activity in the United States.

Of special interest are the detailed instructions to Dashkov from the College of Foreign Affairs, confirmed by the Tsar on 17/29, and signed on 18/30 August 1808.[15] The first thing that catches one's attention is the formal aspect: Dashkov was appointed to a country with a republican government, and he was strictly proscribed "to act in concurrence with the order established for the whole diplomatic corps by the decision of Congress" (paragraph 1). Apparently not relying too much on the effectiveness of general instructions, the College of Foreign Affairs pointed specifically to the need "to become acclimated to the traditions and customs of the country (paragraph 2), study its constitution, and desist from any interference in the internal affairs of the United States.

> In the course of your stay in the United States [paragraph 7 announced] you will have to adhere constantly to two rules: first, never discuss the government's actions; second, do not take the side of any party. You must observe the established order . . . not allowing yourself any deviations which might contradict the customs of the country. Taking into account that the executive power in the United States is limited by the Constitution, you will have to pay special attention to the preliminary acquaintance with it so as not to create difficulties for the government and to avoid probable refusals of your requests if you deviate from the principles established by the Constitution. This behavior, which is loyal and restrained, wholly directed toward the achievement of one aim only—to encourage active and direct trade between the two countries and to develop relations mutually advantageous for both—will not fail to make you agreeable to the American government and will enable you to fulfill the aims of your mission.

Upon his arrival in Washington, Dashkov was expected to assure President Jefferson personally of the Emperor's special friendship and to indicate "the lively interest which His Imperial Majesty indefatigably takes in the prosperity of the United States" (paragraph 3). "Your mission," the text of his instructions stressed, "has a commercial rather than a diplomatic purpose, and your behavior must conform with this understanding. In the course of your conversations with the President of the United States, members of the Congress, and the Secretary of State, you will try to convince them of the mutual advantages that both our nations will obtain by giving their trade all the range it is capable of" (paragraph 4). With an eye toward the successful fulfillment of consular affairs, Dashkov was permitted "to appoint agents in the main ports of the United States . . . from among American or foreign merchants enjoying universal respect" (paragraph 10). He was also put in charge of the activity of the Russian consul in Boston, about whose behavior he was instructed "to send from time to time a dispassionate and just account to the Imperial Ministry" (paragraph 8).

The parts of the instruction concerning the Russian-American Company and Latin America are of special interest. In the case of the former, Dashkov was to encourage the company's commercial contacts and to consider its memorandum a supplement to official instructions. "This privileged institution," it was pointed out in paragraph 11, "has a special right to the protection of the government and . . . since its offices in our possessions in northwest America maintain relations with the United States which are both active and interesting for us, you in your position can be quite useful to it." In particular Dashkov was instructed in paragraph 12 to call the attention of the President of the United States to the contents of the well-known note of Rumiantsev to Levett Harris of 17/29 May 1808 on the subject of the illicit trade of Bostonians in Russian possessions in northwest America and

> to try, by use of the arguments based on the principles of international law and the friendship existing between the two nations, to convince him to conclude the proposed convention, while veiling the significance it may have for the commercial interests of the Russian-American Company by that rather convincing consideration, that the safety of the subjects of His Imperial Majesty may be threatened and that such a convention might put an end to the further protests by removing this serious problem.

Concerning Latin America, in the existing circumstances Dashkov was especially instructed to inform the Russian government as regularly as possible "about the situation on the Leeward and Windward Islands, in Mexico, on Terra Firma, and in Peru."[16]

In conclusion, the hope was expressed that all Dashkov's actions, "in his role as a public person, would create for the Americans the most favorable opinion of the nation to which you belong."

As distinct from the instructions of the College of Foreign Affairs, which dealt with matters of principle connected with Dashkov's mission, the "admonition" of the College of Commerce was of a basically formal character. From the very beginning, the preparation of this admonition went through the usual office channels; as a result birth was given to an impersonal document compiled in conformity with the well-tried bureaucratic pattern. On 7/19 July 1808, at a meeting of the College of Commerce,[17] Rumiantsev made a proposal "to furnish A. Ia. Dashkov with all the information and regulations concerning the title of Consul, related to the commercial affairs," and a decision was made to "prepare an admonition corresponding to the instruction guiding Consul-General Fonton in Ragusa and in Dalmatia."[18] The usual clerical activity followed. The text of the admonition was confirmed at the meeting of the College of Commerce on 10/22 July,[19] signed on 28 July/9 August, and passed on to Dashkov on 7/19 September 1808. In compliance with its order, the new consul-general received, along with the admonition, a series of official reference publications: "The Active General Tariff" of 1797, "An Extract from the Rules and Regulations published in supplement or change of the same," "Maritime Customs Regulations," and "The Charter of Merchant Shipping."

The admonition of the College of Commerce, consisting of thirteen paragraphs, regulated Dashkov's consular functions in some detail. In particular, he was supposed to furnish Russian subjects with the "appropriate instructions which would serve toward the extension of their trade and toward averting the enterprises of the people of other nations which might be harmful to Russian commerce." He was also supposed to compile a detailed description of the state of commerce in his country of residence "and other areas connected with it" (paragraph 1). "In respect to Russian commerce" it was pointed out that "the College of Commerce is anxious to have your observations about its condition, whatever means you might find to bring it to prosperity" (paragraph 2). "You are especially advised," it was noted in paragraph 9, "to observe the honor of the Russian nation, to be of all possible help to the subjects of the same, to protect them in all just occurrences that might come up, and above all to remonstrate with them to preserve assiduously foreign confidence[20] in their goods and themselves and to see that all their actions be based on decency and honesty." The College of Commerce did not seem to rely too much on the decency and honesty of the consul himself, and specified, to avoid abuses on his part, that he should not demand any income for himself from the goods brought by Russian subjects, "but be content only with the annual salary accorded to your rank" (paragraph 5).

In addition to the official instructions, Dashkov also received a detailed memorandum of 20 August/1 September 1808 from the Main Office of the Russian-American Company.[21] Its compilers not only clarified carefully and thoroughly the general situation of the Russian colonies in America and the history of their relations with the United States, but also defined a number of concrete tasks connected with Dashkov's mission. Touching upon the question of the borders of Russian possessions, the corporation noted that "the farthest possession of the Company in America is at 57° 15' northern latitude and 146° longitude by Greenwich meridian. On this line the island Baranov (or Sitka) is situated," where there was established a "fortress, a settlement, and a port" of Novo-Arkhangel'sk. The company had not extended its possessions farther south because of "lack of time, chance, and, especially, of a sufficient number of Russian fur traders." "As soon as the times and chance will allow," the corporation indicated, "the company's industrial activity will advance to the Charlotte Islands, and further to the Columbia [River]." It was pointed out that the tsarist government had not yet had any "dealings or treaties" on the subject of borders and "future occupations" with other powers, and considered "belonging to it all that is at present occupied by the company and that will be occupied in the future by the right of first discovery and the independence of those territories." The expeditions of Bering, Chirikov, and Billings "began this by their discoveries, and the merchants' activity laid the foundation by their settlements."

With respect to the borders of Russian possessions, the Main Office called Dashkov's attention to "some rivalry" of the company with the United States "with regard to discoveries"; it was especially interested in the basin of the Columbia River. "The government of the North American States, which can be called neighboring to us because of its settlements on the shores opposite us on the same American continent," it was stated, "is thinking about appropriating the regions lying near the mouth of the Columbia River. It equipped an expedition on the upper Mississippi River to test the proximity of the Columbia River,[22] to find a close transportation to our side, and to establish a colony on the Columbia . . . Since the Russian-American Company also endeavors to occupy the mouth of that same Columbia River, having a real need for favorable and moderate climate and fertile lands, the company would like to have accurate knowledge of what successes their government had in discovering the Columbia River or other places near it." The Russian-American Company also counted on receiving "observations" from Dashkov on "how to view this republic in its industrial prospects and its influence on the territories in America occupied by the Russians."

The illicit trade of Yankees in Russian possessions in America was a cause of a special anxiety to the Main Office. Although objecting to "unlimited, unwarranted, and above all harmful trade of the American republicans with the savages," at the same time it did not reject ties with United States citizens; it even found them useful to some extent, "if only their trade were with the company directly and not with the savages," and "if they did not antagonize the savages against us and did not arm them with deadly weapons." Baranov's earliest business contacts with Bostonians had demonstrated to the corporation the importance of continuing permanent trade with the republicans; in this context Dashkov was told of the desirability "to acquaint the citizens of the United States with the company and to inspire in them trust and sympathy for it."

The Russian consul was also instructed to discover the origin of the most important goods that the Americans sold in the Russian possessions, "to engage the seafaring citizens of the said States" in business contacts, and to offer all possible assistance to the ship *Nadezhda* (Hope). "The administration of the company," it was noted, "entrusts to your utmost protection the ship *Nadezhda*, launched from here at present by the citizen of the said States, Joshua Martin, all the crew being Russian and the cargo consisting of Russian products. This ship, according to the calculations of the owner of the cargo, must put in at Boston and return here, making the voyage, circumstances permitting, in nine months."

To conclude the analysis of the documents connected with the appointment of Dashkov, one should mention a letter in Alexander I's own hand, "to his great and worthy friend, the President of the United States of America," dated 31 August/12 September 1808. "With a view of strengthening more and more the ties of friendship and mutual understanding existing between the Russian empire and the United States, and desiring above all to offer a manifest proof of my feeling toward yourself, Sir, and toward a nation so deserving of the high esteem in which I hold it, I have decided to name as my Consul-General and Chargé d'Affaires in your country the Counsellor Mr. André de Daschkoff, who will present this letter to you. Knowing his zeal and intelligence, I am hopeful that he will win your respect and good will by the wisdom of his conduct."[23] At the same time Dashkov was appointed a consul in Philadelphia, A. G. Evstaf'ev was appointed a consul in Boston. He occupied this post until 1826, playing a prominent part in the development of Russian-American commercial and cultural connections.[24] Upon instuctions from the College of Foreign Affairs, the College of Commerce decreed on 10/22 July 1808, "to prepare for the actuary Alexei Evstaf'ev, appointed as a consul to the city of Boston in the United American States, instructions similar to those prepared for Consul-General Dashkov," and to furnish him with the same official documents.[25]

Again the Muse of clerical inspiration prompted the officials of the College of Commerce to the simplest possible decision. Rather than burdening themselves with superfluous creative work, they simply copied the text of the "admonition" prepared for Dashkov several days before. On 20 July/1 August this document was formally confirmed on the meeting of the College of Commerce, and two months later (19 September/1 October 1808) it was handed to Evstaf'ev together with other official materials.[26]

At the same time that the clerical apparatus of the tsarist government in St. Petersburg was preparing materials for Dashkov's and Evstaf'ev's guidance, preparation was taking place on the other side of the ocean, in Washington, for the diplomatic mission to Russia. The question of the American minister to St. Petersburg was first raised in Washington in June 1808. Given a situation when the United States ministers to Paris and London might be called back to Washington momentarily, the expediency of establishing diplomatic representation in St. Petersburg was obvious. Even before he had information about Dashkov's mission in July 1808, President Jefferson had decided to send as minister plenipotentiary to St. Petersburg his old friend, William Short, who had previously occupied a number of diplomatic posts in Western Europe. It was assumed that the mission would be special, and that the Senate would be informed about it at the very last moment.[27] Secretary of State Madison signed the text of the official instructions to Short on September 8.[28] Along with his instructions, the minister received Jefferson's handwritten letter of August 29, 1808 to Alexander I. In sending Short to St. Petersburg, Jefferson hoped first of all to obtain Russia's support of the protection of the rights of neutral navigation against the encroachment of France and England, in case a general peace treaty were concluded.[29] The same idea was developed in the instructions of the State Department, "It being impossible to know what the future conduct of the belligerent powers may be toward neutrals, or to foresee what particular policy in relation to this continent may find its way into a general pacification, it cannot be unimportant to have in a party so powerful and influential as Russia a good will and wakeful attention to just rights and interests of the United States, as these may be involved in the course of events," Madison pointed out. The securing of "this advantage" was considered the primary object of the mission.[30]

The minister was also instructed to assist in the creation of more favorable conditions for American commerce, and with this aim to call upon Levett Harris, who had succeeded in winning the good will of the Russian government in the course of his stay in St. Petersburg. He was expected to make it clear to the Russian government that the existing laws which put Russia in a most-favored-nation position should offer a reciprocal opportunity to United States citizens in their trade with Russia. Concerning the embargo, Short was supposed to present it to the Emperor in a satisfactory light, pointing out that it resulted from the dangerous edicts of Great Britain and France. The embargo's effectiveness would be nullified if exceptions favoring "more just and friendly nations" were made; consequently, no exceptions could be allowed—even in regard to American trade with Russia.[31] President Jefferson was anxious that Short's mission not be delayed. On October 1, 1808, the envoy left Philadelphia, and on November 15 he arrived in Paris.

Rumiantsev was staying in the French capital that fall, and the envoy of the United States in France, General Armstrong, was able to give the head of the Russian Foreign Ministry some preliminary information on Short's mission. Rumiantsev expressed his complete satisfaction and assured Armstrong that, on the Russian side, "there will immediately be appointed a minister of equal rank." He further assured the American that he had tried to bring this about ever since his appointment as Minister for Foreign Affairs, because "having broken our trade relations with Great Britain, it became imperative to find another power to take her place."[32] On December 9, 1808, through Armstrong, Short requested a meeting with Rumiantsev.[33] In making an appointment for the next day, the Russian minister added that he was very pleased to learn about the appointment of the United States minister to Russia because he knew how highly the Emperor valued the cementing of amicable relations between the Russian Empire and the United States.[34]

Everything seemed to be working out exceptionally well. Short had friendly discussions with Rumiantsev in Paris and even hoped to come to an agreement about the rights of neutrals after his arrival in St. Petersburg. But instead of the expected instructions, in the spring of 1809 Short received from Washington news of quite another sort: the Senate had rejected his nomination and had generally expressed itself opposed to a special diplomatic mission to St. Petersburg.

It was in his last official message to Congress, on February 24, 1809, about ten days before leaving the presidency, that Jefferson had informed the Senate about his sending of a minister plenipotentiary to Russia.[35] Pointing out the importance for the United States of having Russia's support in case of general pacification negotiations, the President stated that he had commissioned Short to the post of minister plenipotentiary at the St. Petersburg Court in August 1808, and that the latter had already departed for his destination. The motives which led the Senate to reject the nomination are still not altogether clear. An opinion has been expressed that the negative decision can be explained not by the character of the mission but by Short's personality and the fact that he was disliked in the Senate.[36] It is also known that Senator Bradley of Vermont offered a resolution that any intercourse with Russia might "be carried with equal facility and effect by other public agents of the United States without the expense of a permanent minister plenipotentiary," and that Short's appointment was inexpedient and unnecessary. After a closed debate, Senator Bradley withdrew his motion on February 27, but then the Senate unanimously rejected Short's nomination.

Not only was the Senate's decision unexpected and quite unjustified from the point of view of elementary logic; it constituted a direct insult to the retiring President. Even Henry Adams, who was decidedly hostile to Jefferson, admitted its amazing absurdity. The accusation that the administration was inclined to excessive wastefulness and was obsessed by the persistent idea of sending American envoys hither and thither "to any of the courts of Europe" looked utterly incongruous when every senator knew that the United States had only one diplomatic representative on the continent of Europe—and even he could be recalled any minute. The eminent historian considered that "dislike of diplomacy was a relic of the old colonial status when America had been dependent on Europe—a prejudice rising chiefly from an uneasy sense of social disadvantage." "That the Senate should object," Adams pointed out further, "could have been no surprise to Jefferson; but that it should without even a private explanation reject abruptly and unanimously the last personal favor asked by a President for whom every Republican senator professed friendship, and from whom most had received innumerable favors, seemed an unpardonable insult."[37]

In any case, there was nothing for the retiring President to do but accept the situation. It is true that his successor, James Madison, attempted to set things right again just two days after assuming office. On March 6, 1809, without any warning, the post of minister plenipotentiary to St. Petersburg was offered to John Quincy Adams. In doing so, Madison referred to the significance of commercial connections between the two countries and to the importance of securing Russia's support as a kind of guarantee against England and France. The President said that he would present the list of new appointees for approval in half an hour; with no time for reflection, Adams agreed immediately.[38] But again the ill-starred mission was not confirmed: On March 7, 1809, the Senate voted seventeen to fifteen that appointing a minister to the Russian Court was inexpedient at the present. The thrifty congressmen considered the mission too expensive and unnecessary. (This did not prevent them, at the same time, from sending a minister to Rio de Janeiro.)[39]

Of course American legislators could better judge whether Russia or Portugal could bring greater advantage to the United States. At the end of 1807, following Portugal's occupation by French and Spanish troops, Prince-Regent João and his court had fled to Brazil; from that time on Rio de Janeiro had been the residence of the Portuguese Court. However, the stubbornness of the legislators placed the administration in a difficult position. Jefferson wrote Short on March 8, 1809, about the Senate's refusal to back the nomination with unconcealed bitterness: "We took for granted, if any hesitation should arise, that the Senate would take time, and that our friends in that body would make inquiries of us and give us the opportunity of explaining and removing objections. But to our great surprise and with an unexampled precipitancy they rejected it at once. This reception of the last of my official communications to them could not be unfelt."[40]

With "inexpressible regret" Short had to make unpleasant explanations to Rumiantsev, referring to the peculiarities of the American constitution. In a lengthy letter to the Russian minister he wrote that he could not express the extent to which the President was mortified and afflicted, and that the President was most anxious to have this aspect of the Constitution, which must be exceptionally difficult to grasp outside the boundaries of the United States, clarified and explained. Touching upon the motives of the Senate's decision and attempting to tone down the abruptness of the refusal, Short cited Jefferson's letter:

> all other motives were superseded by an unwillingness to extend our diplomatic connections . . . All were sensible of the great virtues, the high character, the powerful influence, and the valuable friendship of the emperor. But riveted to the system of unentanglement with Europe, they declined the proposition . . . . I pray you to place me *rectus in curia* in this business with the emperor, and to assure him that I carry into my retirement the highest veneration for his virtues.

Finally, in accordance with the instructions of the American government, Short wrote to Rumiantsev that the new President Madison will continue to do all he can to assure that in the future the United States will have a minister at the St. Petersburg court; that he will seize the first chance to bring the Senate to this view, and hoped for success before long, since the Congress was expected to meet in an extraordinary session that month.[41]

Before the Senate's decision became known, a minister to the United States was appointed in St. Petersburg. "Reciprocating the appointment to our Court of the Minister of Second Rank from the Congress of the United States," the Tsar's ukase of 1/12 April 1809 to the College of Foreign Affairs announced, "we order to direct there, as an envoy extraordinary and a minister plenipotentiary of Our Court, acting chamberlain Count Feodor von der Pahlen."[42] The staff of the mission to be established in Philadelphia, comprised of the minister, the counselor to the Embassy, and the secretary, was confirmed the same day.[43]

The Tsar's power in the Russian Empire, "through God's mercy," was not limited by any constitution, and Alexander I's ukase was not subject to additional confirmation. Consequently, Rumiantsev could inform Harris immediately, without apprehensions, of Pahlen's appointment and immediate departure for his point of destination.[44] The other staff positions were filled later; as counselor to the Embassy, Alexander I appointed College Counselor Petr Poletika, and as secretary, Court Counselor Fedor Ivanov.[45]

This time the formalities connected with an appointment of a new minister were executed quite swiftly, and in the summer of 1809 Pahlen departed;[46] early in August he informed Rumiantsev of his arrival in Paris.[47] By this time news of Short's ill-fated appointment had reached St. Petersburg. The Russian ministry could do nothing but express its regrets, and Rumiantsev was not inclined to cancel the diplomatic mission to the United States. In the draft of a dispatch to Pahlen, prepared on 2/14 July 1809, it was pointed out that the Emperor

> continues to wish you to leave for America as His minister, if the government of the United States does not foresee in the present circumstances any obstacles to your reception. That is why His Majesty orders you to depart for Paris, and there await a reply which will be conveyed to you either by Mr. Short or General Armstrong. His Majesty does not in the least insist that the American government at this exact moment appoint on the basis of reciprocity a minister of a rank similar to yours. His Majesty desires only that the warm amicable relations existing between His Empire and the United States be strengthened and extended.

Pahlen was also instructed to hint that Russia would be pleased if as chargé d'affaires were to be appointed Levett Harris, who in the course of his stay in St. Petersburg "was able to become most agreeable to His Majesty because of his qualities and his general behavior."[48]

Although dated 2/14 July, apparently this dispatch was not delivered immediately. Pahlen had already left Russia by that time, and the inscription on the final copy reads: "Sent to Paris 28 December 1809." In the meanwhile the Russian minister to the United States remained in France whence he regularly informed Rumiantsev of his observations of the general situation in Europe and America. His interesting memorandum, enclosed in a report of 14/26 November 1809, is of special value: "C'est de nos jours que commencera à dater l'époque fatale de la décadence de l'Europe et une ère plus propice pour l'Amérique qui sort de sa lethargie pour s'élever sur nos ruines." The Minister had in mind not only the United States, but America as a whole, surmising that in the future Spain's enormous possessions in the New World would assume "la place que la nature leur a indiquée." With enviable perspicacity, Pahlen foresaw the separation of Spanish America at the moment when there would be no hope of saving Spain, and the "ancienne maitresse du Nouveau Monde" would fall under the yoke of France. Then, he continued, would the seed of liberty manifest itself more openly in various provinces of Spanish America and in Mexico first of all. With regard to important future changes in international relations the Minister foresaw that it would be England, of all the European powers, who would derive enormous advantage from the serious changes in international relations, since the countries of the New World offered a huge market for her products.[49] So, the Russian minister's enforced delay in the French capital was not wasted, and the government received a sufficiently circumstantial and on the whole remarkably precise political prognosis, especially considering the time of the preparation of the memorandum: the eve of the Spanish American struggle for independence.

Short's nonappointment delayed Pahlen's departure for America somewhat, but it had no effect on the arrival in Philadelphia of Dashkov and Evstaf'ev.[50] The former arrived in Philadelphia safely on July 1, 1809;[51] Evstaf'ev reached Boston on August 24.[52]

Upon his arrival Dashkov sent Secretary of State Robert Smith in Washington an official request to be introduced to the President.[53] At first he was told that the session of Congress had been postponed until November and that President Madison and the Secretary of State had left Washington. This proved to be not quite correct. "Several days later I learned," Dashkov reported to St. Petersburg, "that the news of the arrival of our ship reached the President before he left Washington. He delayed his departure in order to wait for the mail and to receive me. Without awaiting a reply from the Secretary of State, which I could not have expected before several days, I left by post-horses and arrived in Washington on July 12."[54]

The details of Dashkov's sojourn in the American capital are known from a circumstantial memorandum with the description of his conversations with Secretary of State Robert Smith and President Madison.[55] On July 14, at the appointed hour, Dashkov, in full dress, presented himself to the State Department and was immediately conducted to Smith's office. "After the first general compliments," the Russian reported, "I handed my packet to the Secretary of State with the expression of my urgent desire to be introduced to Mr. President on the same day and with the request that he inform me of the behavior which foreign ministers are wont to observe when being introduced to His Excellency. Mr. Smith replied that no special ceremony exists beyond the usual politeness on both sides, and that I shall be received in the same manner as the ministers from France and England."

Nevertheless, some formal complications arose. Dashkov was most anxious, in accordance with his instructions, to deliver a speech, prepared in advance and addressed to the President and Congress, and later to make it generally known. Although the content of the speech presented no problem, the Secretary of State asked Dashkov, for reasons of formality, not to deliver it, promising "to find means to make its contents as public as I might wish."[56]

After half-hour talk, Mr. Smith conducted me to the President. Since Mr. Madison's house is separated from the Department only by a little garden, he proposed that we walk. We reached the visitors' parlor without any ceremony. Mr. President was informed of our arrival, and he came out to us immediately. The Secretary of State approached him to introduce me. The President shook my hand and received me warmly and simply. I handed him the letter of His Imperial Majesty, assuring him of the friendship of our great monarch and of the lively interest which His Imperial Majesty takes in the prosperity of the United States.

Having read the letter with great attention, the President began to talk of the gratitude of the United States for the kindness of His Imperial Majesty, and assured me that he personally feels most flattered. . . Here again, as in the course of my morning talk in the office of the Secretary of State, I tried to convince them of the mutual benefit for both nations to be derived from allowing trade between the two countries the full range of which it might be capable, and, following my instructions, I spoke to Mr. President of the lively interest, indefatigably manifested by His Imperial Majesty in the prosperity of the United States and of the constant readiness its government will always find of the Emperor to assist directly or indirectly in anything that might be advantageous for the American nation.

At parting, Madison invited the new chargé d'affaires to dine with him the next day, and Smith handed the President a copy of the abovementioned speech with the words: "This concerns you too, Mr. Madison." Dashkov clearly was having poor luck with the document to which he attached so much importance. "The President put the paper in his pocket," he wrote regretfully, "without even opening it."

The next day, July 15, the Russian diplomat called on the ministers, and then proceeded to dine with the President. Since the company consisted only of the leaders of the government and Madison's family, he deduced that "the dinner was given especially for the chargé d'affaires of His Imperial Majesty." After dinner another rather prolonged conversation between Dashkov and the President took place, in the course of which the President repeated his assurances that the United States respected the intentions of the Russian government toward the rights of neutrals and that they were grateful for the Emperor's attitude. "When the talk touched upon contacts between nations, he began by saying that the United States was always friendly toward those governments which wished to maintain sincere and honest relations with it. Since it seemed to me that he repeatedly returned to the word 'sincerity,' I dwelled in detail, to ensure that my mission might not create suspicions on the part of any party, on the respect of our government for the rights of neutral states, on the proofs of it offered the Americans in a number of cases, and finally on the high moral principles of our government with respect to political and commercial connections and its desire to establish such connections with the United States on the principles of mutual benefit."

President Madison immediately informed Dashkov that Short's appointment had been rejected by the Senate, "from fear lest, in the course of his stay in France, he assimilate the prejudices of that nation, contradicting the spirit of the American nation." Dashkov himself was inclined to believe that the reason for the Senate's rejection lay in the fact that Jefferson was too sure of success and did not undertake the usual preliminary consultations with the senators. The senators' desire to see a man loyal to them in the post of minister and Jefferson's impending departure from the presidency were in a large part conducive to the failure.[57]

Since the President and his family were leaving for the country on July 16, Dashkov considered it his duty to pay him a farewell call. The President begged him to return to Washington in November, when Congress would be in session and when all the foreign representatives customarily were in town. Before his departure from Washington, Dashkov also received confirmation for the performance of his consular functions.[58]

Dashkov supplemented his report on the talks with Madison and Smith with a lengthy memorandum of July 24, 1809, concerning general conditions in the United States, the policies of the government, the basic parties of the country, and so on .[59] While paying great attention to describing the two basic parties (Federalists, and Anti-Federalists or Democrats), the Tsar's diplomat encountered considerable difficulty in defining their principles, which changed depending on circumstances. In the end he accepted the traditional definition: Federalists as the adherents of strong central power and enlargement of the permanent army and navy; democrats as zealous defenders of freedom—the rights of states, opposition to a permanent army, and so on. At the same time he called special attention to the longstanding adherence of the Federalists to England and of the Democrats to France.

Evaluating the attitude in the United States toward the establishment of the Russian mission, Dashkov wrote:

> It appears to me that on the whole the Americans are unusually flattered by the arrival of the chargé d'affaires of His Imperial Majesty and hope for greater advantages from the closer relations between the two countries. In respect to Mr. Madison and the officials of the government, it seems to me that it is rather their vanity that is satisfied, while their conscience is not altogether convinced of the advantages the United States might derive from commercial relations with Russia. . . . I set myself a task of convincing them of the importance of our commerce for their country and of making them feel the value of mutual understanding with such a great power as Russia, for any state.

The story of the first steps undertaken by the Russian chargé d'affaires in the United States would be incomplete without mentioning his friendly correspondence with Jefferson. On July 5, 1809, while forwarding two letters intended for the eminent American statesman, Dashkov took advantage of the occasion to inform him of the great respect in which he is held by the "great northern power," favorably disposed toward the United States, and at the same time to assure him of his own deep esteem. In his reply Jefferson hailed the Russian diplomat as "the first harbinger" of friendly relations between Russia and the United States. "Both nations being in character and practice essentially pacific," he wrote, "a common interest in the rights of peaceable nations, gives us a common cause in their maintenance." In return, Dashkov expressed deep respect for "the great man" on behalf of the Russian government and himself.[60]

Shortly before Dashkov's arrival, the government of the United States finally succeeded in appointing a minister to Petersburg. On June 26, 1809, the President of the United States again put before the Senate the question of establishing a diplomatic mission in St. Petersburg and appointing John Quincy Adams to the post of minister.[61] This time the Senate made a positive decision. On June 27, 1809, the appointment of John Quincy Adams was confirmed by nineteen yeas against seven nays. Informing Dashkov of this, the President expressed the hope that the Russian government would appreciate the efforts of the United States, especially considering that the appointment of Mr. Adams took place before the arrival of the Russian chargé d'affaires.[62]

The selection of John Quincy Adams as minister to St. Petersburg was extremely apt. Young John Quincy had his first acquaintance with Russia in 1781-82, when he lived in St. Petersburg as a personal secretary to Francis Dana. Later he acquired extensive independent political experience, in particular while occupying the post of American minister in Holland and Prussia.[63] It is interesting to note that in March 1801, in Berlin, he had pointed out the expediency of establishing direct diplomatic contacts with Russia. Noting "the use and advantage" for the United States from having an official representative in the north of Europe, John Quincy Adams called special attention to the trade interests, which at that time appeared to him not unimportant.[64] He also considered that treaties of commerce with Russia and the Sublime Porte were by no means "such a useless waste of public money, nor such a proof of absurd policy" as they appeared to some cautious minds in America.[65]

Originally, as was traditional in his family, John Quincy Adams was a Federalist. Having left diplomatic activity after the retirement from the presidency of his father, John Adams, in the spring of 1801, young Adams was later elected to the Senate from his home state of Massachusetts. In 1806 he became a professor at Harvard University. To the great indignation of former Federalist friends, young Adams was inclined more and more to support the administration on questions of international relations, and in December 1807 he voted for the introduction of an embargo. Even though his personal prestige and influence remained considerable, his further presence in Congress became impossible after his break with the Federalists, and in the summer of 1808 he resigned before the expiration of his term.[66] In his letter to the Secretary of State he expressed an "ardent desire" to aid the administration, whose object was "the welfare of the whole Union."[67]

At first John Quincy Adams supposed that he could not leave for Russia before August 15, but he discovered that navigation in the Baltic closed very early. William Gray of Boston, who had systematic trade connections with Baltic ports, offered the new minister accommodations on his vessel at any time until the end of this month, after which time, navigation would become too hazardous to attempt.[68] At the same time Adams informed the Secretary of State that he planned to take to St. Petersburg his nephew, William Steuben Smith, as his private secretary. He was also taking three other young Americans: John Spear Smith, nephew of the Secretary of

State; Alexander Hill Everett, who later became a well-known diplomat; and Francis Calley Gray, son of William Gray.[69] These young men, who expected to acquire through this experience knowledge that might be necessary in the future, were willing to perform secretarial duties without pay. Adams embarked for St. Petersburg on Gray's ship *Horace,* on August 5, 1809, accompanied by his wife, his infant son Charles Francis, his wife's sister Catherine Johnson, and two servants.[70]

Adams was not given any new instructions before his departure for Russia. The main aims of his mission were still considered to be the best possible development of amicable relations and mutual understanding with Russia, attention to the rights and interests of the United States, and the securing of favorable conditions for the commerce of American citizens. The minister was also supposed to devote special attention to securing the rights of neutral navigation, since the United States counted on the support of the Russian government in this respect. As guidance, Adams was given the instructions previously prepared for Short and Armstrong.[71]

The voyage across the ocean safely over, John Quincy Adams arrived at Kronstadt on October 22, 1809.[72] From the very beginning his reception in the Russian capital was most cordial. On October 13/25 Levett Harris officially informed Rumiantsev of Adams' arrival[73] and asked the Chancellor to appoint a convenient time for his reception. The Chancellor replied immediately, and the visit of the American minister took place the same day at seven o'clock in the evening.[74] Several days later Adams was present at a diplomatic dinner, "in the style of the highest splendor," at the same house where he had dined in 1781 when it was occupied by Marquis de Vérac, then French minister. The magnificence and luxury of its appointments made a great impression on the American minister, although he was no novice at such affairs. He had been present at formal dinners in the largest Western capitals (Paris, London, The Hague, and Berlin), and ever since habitually had given a disproportionate amount of attention to detailed descriptions of ceremonial dinners and receptions of various sorts.[75] He was also much impressed by the external appearance of St. Petersburg, which he called the "city of princes" and "the most magnificent city of Europe or of the world."[76]

The official procedure connected with the arrival of the American minister was concluded on November 5, 1809, by the handing over of letters of credence and prolonged private conversations of John Quincy Adams and Alexander I, in the course of which the Tsar condemned England's policy on the high seas and expressed a firm intention of giving "the greatest

extension and facility" to Russian-American trade. "He said that as between Russia and the United States," Adams paraphrased, "there could
be no interference of interests and no causes for disunion but by means of
commerce the two states might be greatly useful to each other." The Tsar
also said approvingly "that with regard to the political relations of
Europe, and those unhappy disturbances which agitated its different
states, the system of the United States was wise and just."

The Tsar's remarks greatly satisfied John Quincy Adams. In turn, he
remarked that the United States, "being at once a great commercial and a
pacific nation, they were greatly interested in the establishment of a
system which should give security to the fair commerce of nations in time
of war." He assured that "the United States, by all the means in their
power, consistent with their peace and their separation from the political
system of Europe, would contribute to the support of the liberal principles
to which his Majesty had expressed so strong and so just an attachment."[77]

This avowed republican and scrupulous puritan soon enough found the
common ground with the Russian autocrat and familiarized himself with
the splendor of the Court. From the very first days of his stay in Russia,
Adams established a complete mutual understanding with both the Tsar
and Rumiantsev, which was greatly conducive to the mission's success.

The arrival of the American minister removed the last obstacle to the
conclusion of all formalities connected with the exchange of diplomatic
missions between the two countries. On November 15/27 Pahlen was given
a directive from St. Petersburg to proceed to his post.[78] On December 27
(old style), Alexander I signed extensive instructions to guide the activities
of the Russian minister in Washington.[79] "Through the wisdom of their
government and the virtues of the persons to whom they entrusted the
reins of power," the Emperor wrote in the beginning of his instructions,
"the United States of America have attained deserved respect in Europe.
No monarch on the continent has more respect for them than myself, since
I bestow constant attention to the wise actions of the persons whom they
invariably put at the head of their government."

Developing this idea, the Tsar instructed Pahlen to inform the American government of his sincere and deep interest in the United States and
his esteem for President Madison. At the same time he asked him to convey
to Jefferson how highly he honored his talents and integrity. Such great
attention and pointed courtesy of Alexander I to the United States and its
leaders represented more than the usual formal diplomatic politeness
(especially considering that it was intended for a republican government),

and attested to the desire of the Russian government for rapprochement with the overseas republic. Naturally, this desire can be explained, not by the Tsar's special sympathies for the United States and its leaders, described in such exalted terms in the instructions, but by the objective circumstances and realistic interests, already discussed.

These objective considerations were stressed in the text of the instruction. "The political interests of my empire combine in this regard," Alexander I pointed out (expressing Rumiantsev's ideas). "I see in the United States a kind of rival of England. I believe that its own interests will make it strive, to a greater degree than other powers of the European continent, to limit—if not put an end to—the perilous despotism of Great Britain on the high seas."[80] This idea is of paramount importance for understanding both the reasons for the Russian-American rapprochement in the period under discussion and the whole history of the relations between the United States and Russia. Russia saw the United States as a rival of England and a certain counterbalance for the proud mistress of the seas. Russia's contacts with America derived from the system of European politics and from Russian-English relations. It is not accidental, therefore, that Pahlen's instructions contained a survey of the international situation in connection with the Peace of Tilsit and a detailed account of Russia's relations with European countries.

With regard to direct relations with the United States, the instructions developed this basic position as follows:

> when the subject of the continental system comes up, make it clear that I have accepted and support it as the most effective means of forcing England, through an understanding of ideas of peace and humanity, to give up her despotic domination of the seas, the subject of much complaint on the part of the United States also. It is in the interests of my empire, and of all the other powers too, to create a universal maritime code, which will, once and for all, put an end to the fatal disputes about the rights of neutrals and warring powers. Russia laid the foundation for it by the maritime convention of 1780 with Denmark, joined in succession by Sweden, Prussia, Holland, Austria, Portugal, Naples, and, in fact, France and Spain. I am pleased to see that in their commercial treaties with continental powers and even with barbarian states, the United States has accepted our principle of neutral nations, and the only reason it was not included in the pact with Great Britain is the absence of any final agreement between them.

"No other nation," the Tsar continued,

> could work out this humane code and assure its success, better than that which you will serve as a representative. Its form of government, its

215

commercial life, the interests of the government and private persons must contribute equally to the manifold discussion of this important question; this will undoubtedly create a weapon capable of destroying the sophistry of the lawyers in the pay of the British cabinet. With these aims in view, I should like you to utilize the information of the Americans, to consult them on various aspects of it, and to forward to me their opinions and the intentions of their government in this beneficial cause. I should be most pleased to have this question solved once and for all, by general rules accepted and supported by all nations.

In a number of instances Pahlen's instructions repeated, with some changes, the points made in the instructions to Dashkov. Among the minister's duties was that of rendering all possible support and assistance to the Russian-American Company and of supplying the government with regular information about events in Spanish America. This seems to reflect Pahlen's memorandum on the prospects of the liberational movement in America. It is not accidental that in the instructions an opinion was directly expressed that, "if the war in Spain goes on, the vast and rich lands which she possesses in America . . . will form one or several states. It is difficult to calculate all the changes which might result in such event in the political and commercial contacts of Europe, but it is easy to foresee that these changes will be enormous."

With this in mind, the minister had to observe the prevailing mood in these countries and report on it to Petersburg at frequent intervals. In respect to the question of contraband commerce in the Russian possessions, Pahlen was instructed to call most urgently the attention of the American government to the "perilous consequences of such a trade," and to request it "prevent the repetition of such violations."

The Tsar's instructions were sent to Paris as soon as they were signed, and on 16/28 January, Pahlen informed Rumiantsev that he had received them along with other materials relating to his mission.[81] Some time later Pahlen was finally able to depart for his post, and after a voyage of fifty days he arrived in Philadelphia on May 29/June 10.[82] The formal procedure of establishing diplomatic relations was concluded on 14/26 June 1810, when the Tsar's minister officially handed his letters of accreditation to the President of the United States in Washington.[83] As can be seen from Pahlen's reports to St. Petersburg, his initial discussions with American government leaders were exceptionally friendly. "If my stay here continues to be as auspicious as its beginning, I shall be utterly delighted," he wrote Rumiantsev.[84]

Thus, toward the middle of 1810, all the formalities having to do with the exchange of diplomatic missions finally had been surmounted. The establishment of diplomatic relations proved to be involved and lengthy, and it took almost three years from the time of the original decision in the autumn of 1807 until the conclusion of official procedures in June 1810. From our present point of view this seems an unusually long time. To a large degree, it can be explained by the great distances and by the primitive means of communication. A certain delay took place in connection with Short's appointment; it did not, however, affect the development of relations between the two countries in any basic way. Flattering courtiers, inclined to exalt Alexander I's virtues on any pretext, suitable or unsuitable, did not hesitate to assign an exceptional role to the personality of the Russian emperor. Full of loyal adulation, Pahlen wrote Alexander I from Washington in June 1811 that he would remain known to future generations for having set an exceptional example of a mighty monarch seeking friendship with a republic, with an aim only of improving human welfare.[85]

The dispassionate court of history has long since reached a verdict, judging the "services" of Alexander I, as well as the whole Romanov dynasty, according to their merit. Concerning "human welfare," there was always a great deal of talk about it, even when realistic aims had nothing in common with this welfare. Naturally, both Russia and the United States were not guided in their mutual relations by abstract concern for "human welfare" but by thoroughly realistic interests. The tsarist government, in its own words, sought in the United States "a sort of a rival of England," and counted on rapprochement with America to alleviate the severe consequences of the Continental Blockade and to regulate the relations of the Russian-American Company with the Bostonians.

For its part, the United States, with relations with England and France deteriorating sharply, finding itself isolated diplomatically, was extremely interested in rapprochement with Russia, the only great power objectively favorably disposed toward it. The government of the United States counted on Russia's support, especially in securing the rights of neutral navigation, and hoped to derive profits from the development of the trade connections with the extensive Russian market.

All in all, the reasons for the rapprochement with the United States were objective. They resulted from the general international situation of the post-Tilsit period, and to a large degree were defined by the previous development of the Russian-American political, commercial, and cultural contacts.

VIII

THE EXPANSION OF TRADE CONTACTS

The assumption of the United States in introducing the embargo in December 1807 was that if all commerce were stopped and the warring powers deprived of the services of the American Navy, the governments of England and France would be forced to respect the American flag. The embargo, however, inflicted the greatest harm on the interests of the United States themselves. By introducing it the United States became, so to speak, isolated from the outside world and lost the advantages of a neutral position.

The indignation of American merchants and shipowners was beyond all limits. They had no desire to forego their enormous profits even if, for the sake of them, they had to sacrifice national prestige and reconcile themselves to insults and repressions by England and France. Thus, it is not surprising that from the very beginning the embargo policy was doomed to failure; from the autumn of 1808 on, its repeal was only a question of time and form. The so-called Non-intercourse Act was proposed in place of the embargo, and the United States was forced to give in without securing any guarantees from the British cabinet. Historians have called this a national humiliation for America. As a matter of fact, nobody in Congress came specifically to the defense of the new law; nevertheless, on 27 February 1809, the House of Representatives voted its acceptance (81 for and 40 against). As one congressman remarked, the passage of this bill "would be a novelty in legislation, for he believed it had not a friend in the house."[1]

Formally the new law prohibited commerce with the British possessions and with the countries under Napoleon's control; at the same time it allowed the President to renew contacts with powers that would stop violating the neutral rights of the United States. Of course nobody seriously expected that England and France, having resisted the embargo, would become more compliant after its repeal. It was also common knowledge that, as soon as an American vessel was at sea, nobody could control where, when, and with whom it chose to conduct its commerce. The embargo touched primarily upon British interests because most American trade was with England. Officially the new law put England and France on an equal footing; actually, because of the dominating position of the British fleet, the basic advantages were to be gained by the English.[2]

One way or another, the hateful embargo was ended, and in the spring of 1809 American ships put out at sea again. In July 1809 Levett Harris, consul-general of the United States in St. Petersburg, officially notified Rumiantsev that as of March the embargo was repealed and American vessels permitted to trade in all European ports except those of England and France and their dependencies.[3]

A period of unusually lively trade between Russia and the United States began at this time, influenced by a series of objective circumstances. The Russian economy was experiencing great difficulties because of the Continental Blockade and the severance of its traditional contacts with England. Russia's exports had declined catastrophically; the ruble's value had fallen 50 percent. By encouraging American commerce, though relatively small it was, the tsarist government intended to cushion to some extent the dire consequences of the Continental Blockade. For the United States, too, contact with the Russian market had considerable significance in those years, since a great part of its usual customers in Western Europe had been lost. It is not surprising, therefore, that informed observers have noted an unusual expansion of Russian-American trade contacts at that time. Of great interest in this connection is the detailed information on the conditions and prospects of Russian exports to the United States gathered by Pavel Svin'in in his original work *Vzqliad na respubliku Soedinennykh Amerikanskikh oblastei* (A View of the Republic of the United American Regions).[4]

In calling attention to the steady increase in trade with the United States since 1783, the author specifically singled out the following basic items of the Russian export:[5]

1. Sailcloth. "In 1811 its export from Kronstadt amounted to 66,700 pieces." According to Svin'in, sailcloth from the factories of Batashev, Khlebnikov, Temeriazev, and Bilibin was "much appreciated and in great demand."

2. "Ravensduck and fine linen. The use of these two articles in America is exceptionally great. In 1810, 74,000 pieces of ravensduck and 38,000

pieces of Flemish linen were exported from Kronstadt to America. Americans prefer goods from the factories of Uglevannikov, Ashostin, Gorbunov, and Solodovnikov; other factories, such as Vodovozov and Vishniakov do not fare as well . . . Flemish linen, exceptionally white and fine, is in great demand in America, and if the width of it were to be 60 arshin and 45 vershok, it would completely replace linen imports from Ireland."

3. Sacking. "Ordinary Russian sacking is too narrow for American use, and therefore they re-export it to Spain," Svin'in writes, recommending that the width be increased to 36 vershok.

4. Table linens. Svin'in notes that Americans began to use table napkins only recently, therefore one can hope that "this article will be in greater demand. In 1810 there was exported from St. Petersburg to America 930,000 arshin of this linen. Our napkins are preferred to the English ones because of their beauty and cheapness."

5. Hemp. "This article is most necessary for America, and Russia alone can supply it in needed quantities, that is why Americans imported it from Baltic Russian ports alone to the amount of 500,000 poods annually, and also a great deal from Archangel."

6. Iron. Americans imported iron mainly from Sweden and Russia, preferring Swedish because of its reliability. However, Svin'in notes, "a great quantity of iron bought from us can serve as a proof that our prices are preferable to them. In an average year they imported from Russia between 250,000 and 300,000 poods, and American merchants maintain that the import would double if the bars were better made. They would prefer that in 100 tons of iron there were 70 tons of flat bars of various sizes, 10 tons of squares, and 20 round ones. It would be desirable for our factories to accept this rule: they would gain by it, and we would completely win over the market from the Swedes."

7. Candles. Noting that in the United States there is a greater demand for yellow than for white candles, the author states that in 1810, 50,000 poods were exported to America from Kronstadt alone.

8. Bristle. Since "bristle factories" were introduced in America only recently, these goods will always be in great demand. "Ukranian bristle is preferred to any other."

In conclusion, Svin'in pointed out that Russia supplied and would continue to supply America with a multitude of other domestic produce: down, tallow, wax, leather, and so forth. "It would be very profitable to export our manufactured articles, such as hats, boots, mirrors, and morocco leather . . . These articles could sell in the United American

Regions for twice as much or more: for example, in America a pair of boots of the latest workmanship costs forty rubles of our money, a hat fifty rubles, and so forth."

Svin'in's prognosis proved overoptimistic, since it was based on the experience of the years 1810-1812, when prospects for Russian-American trade had been especially favorable. But even though he could be quite wrong in evaluating the prospects of further development of commerce between Russia and the United States, his data for the period under scrutiny, especially for 1810-11, can be considered reliable (bearing in mind the relative accuracy of statistics of the period). Svin'in's factual information and recommendations were based on his practical experience and are fully confirmed by some other materials, including the archival ones.

Analogous data can be found in the "notes" of the consul-general in Philadelphia, N. Ia. Kozlov, "on the goods imported into the United States, consisting of Russian produce and manufacture," which became the object of a special study in the Department of Foreign Trade, and later in the Department of Salt and Mining of the Russian Ministry of Finance. Naturally enough, special attention was paid to Kozlov's "notes" on iron. His information that the export of iron to the United States averaged between 250,000 and 300,000 poods a year, and that there was a possibility of doubling it, could not fail to raise the interest of the Department of Foreign Trade, which found "such a description deserving of respect" and sent an extract of Kozlov's report to the Department of Salt and Mining.[6] The contents of the extract coincide almost word for word with the extract from Svin'in's work, which is easily explained by the fact that Svin'in had been a secretary of the Russian consulate in Philadelphia until the summer of 1813, and naturally took part in the preparation of reports to St. Petersburg. Kozlov's report was much more detailed than Svin'in's on the subject of concrete technical demands on the Russian iron for the American market. There was a detailed description of the grading of iron, the width and circumference of round, square, and flat bars, and so on. "It is extremely desirable," it was pointed out, "for our blacksmiths to accept this new grading, for the profits which they will gain from this will reward their labors amply."

The fate of these proposals can be traced through materials of the Department of Salt and Mining. "Having studied the memorandum," the department "concluded that preparation of iron according to Kozlov's recommendation can bring sizable profit," and instructed the manager of the Zlatoust factories to make "samples for distribution to other state factories."[7] After this instruction was carried out, the department ordered that several samples more be made for distribution among private factories to see if some could utilize them.

Along with iron, hemp had an important place in Russian exports to the United States. According to American data, the import of Russian hemp in 1802-1804 averaged 88,830 cwt., valued at $779,473; in 1807 it increased to 135,775; and in 1811 to 205,853 cwt. In 1811 the import of cordage, tarred and untarred, was correspondingly 589,946 and 34,806 pounds, and the import of cables was 108,685 pounds.[8]

Analysis of Russian-American trade data shows a considerable growth in volume in the beginning of the second decade of the nineteenth century. While the average value of Russian import goods paying ad valorem duties (including iron and goods made of hemps and flax) in the years 1802-1804 was $1,302,217, in 1810, 1811, and 1812, it increased to $1,587,384, $3,043,033, and $2,163,460.[9]

The export of American goods to Russia increased even more in the course of these years, as these figures (in dollars) show.[10]

Year	Total exports	American goods	Foreign goods
1805	71,372	12,044	59,328
1806	12,407	3,580	8,827
1807	445,717	78,850	366,367
1808	embargo	embargo	embargo
1809	884,261	146,462	737,799
1810	3,975,696	1,048,760	2,926,936
1811	6,137,657	1,630,499	4,507,158

Although in 1805-6 American exports to Russia were for all practical purposes insignificant (even in 1807, the period of the greatest prosperity for the American trade, they reached only a half-million dollars), in a very few years this trade amounted to several million dollars, with 1811 as a record year. Of course $6,137,657 is not too impressive a sum, and seems insignificant in the light of present-day figures. In order to understand it correctly and to weigh its significance objectively, one has to take into account the whole complex of idiosyncratic conditions produced by the Continental Blockade. Besides, the figure of 6.1 million dollars is not that small a figure, judged by the scale of the period. Suffice it to say that in 1811 the whole American export amounted to 61 million dollars;[11] consequently, Russia's share was 10 percent of it.

It would be interesting to compare general data on the volume of trade between Russia and the United States with the number of American ships entering Russian ports in the beginning of the second decade of the nineteenth century. Unfortunately, the annual "views" of Russia's state commerce, published on Rumiantsev's initiative, were discontinued in 1808, and therefore we do not possess precise official information on this subject. However, even incomplete, the data at our disposal permit the deduction that the number of American ships bound for Russia increased sharply beginning in 1809. While in the late eighteenth and early nineteenth centuries American ships in Russia numbered in the dozens,[12] in 1810-1812 we must talk in terms of at least several hundreds. Proof of this can be found not only in the periodical publications—in particular, the regular information in *St. Peterburgskie vedomosti*—but also in some other documentary sources. In 1810, 120 American ships entered St. Petersburg alone, of which 30 were from Boston, 22 from New York, 15 from Salem, 8 from Philadelphia, and 6 from Baltimore.[13] According to Dashkov's information, in 1810 the number of vessels announcing Russian ports as their destination was 250. Apparently not all of these succeeded in entering Russian ports that year, but by August 20/September 1, 209 American ships had arrived. The next year, according to Dashkov's information, their number decreased, and only 151 Russian permits were issued. "American trade," Dashkov wrote to A. B. Kurakin, the Russian ambassador in Paris, "was less active in our ports in 1811 than it was in 1810 because of the increased attacks to which the United States flag was subject in the Baltic Sea on the part of French, Danish, and English corsairs."[14]

Dashkov was quite correct in calling the ambassador's attention to the difficulties encountered by American ships in the Baltic. However, one cannot agree with him that the volume of Russian-American trade had decreased in 1811 as compared with 1810. All other documentary materials, including official American statistics, definitely demonstrate that 1811 saw the greatest flourishing of United States commerce with Russia. There is no reason to doubt Dashkov's information about issuing only 151 entry permits to American vessels, but he himself remarks that "many American vessels, bound for our ports without a cargo, could not be registered by our consulates in America, since they arrived from other neutral countries and not from the United States." Taking into account the great volume of intermediary commerce of the United States (particularly the importing of various colonial goods and the products of British industry) and the fact that many American ships arrived in Russia without cargoes, one can assume with justification that in 1811 at least 200-250 American ships entered Russia's ports.

In any case, in July 1811, at the height of the navigation season, John Quincy Adams informed Secretary of State James Monroe that about 200 American ships with valuable goods had already arrived in Russia.[15] According to him, the Russian market was oversupplied by colonial products to such an extent that it was impossible to sell the cargoes brought in, while at the same time increased demand for Russian goods was causing their prices to skyrocket. Basing his calculations on the dispatches of American consuls Harris and Samuel Hazard, Crosby supposes that in 1811 about 225 ships flying the American flag arrived in Russia, including 138 to Kronstadt, 65 to Archangel, and about 30 to Riga, Revel, and other Baltic ports.[16]

Most American ships came to Russia from New England ports. According to Svin'in, in 1810 more than a hundred ships set out for Russia from Massachusetts alone. Dashkov called attention to this, too, pointing out that "two-thirds of the whole American commerce with Russia is conducted by the Eastern states, and that the two ports of Boston and Salem send approximately as many vessels as all the other states south of Connecticut." On the other hand, the goods brought to the Russian market were largely the produce of Southern states and the countries of Latin America (Brazil, the West Indies, and so on).

Before the second decade of the nineteenth century American ships arrived almost routinely at Baltic ports, above all, St. Petersburg. Official Russian statistics registered only infrequent arrivals of American ships in ports of the White Sea (Archangel). By 1810-11 Americans had substantially increased the sphere of their navigations. At its beginning, in 1810, Rumiantsev informed John Quincy Adams about the arrival of the first American ship sailing from Baltimore directly to Odessa, and expressed his satisfaction with the expansion of commercial contacts with the United States.[17] This event, in Rumiantsev's words, was to constitute an epoch in the commerce of the Black Sea, all the more remarkable since the American flag appeared there for the first time. Commenting on the "extraordinary numbers" of American vessels arriving in Russia in 1810, Adams named the two ports St. Petersburg and Archangel. Adams considered that among the causes for this increase was the fact that navigation was much safer in this region than in the Baltic.[18]

The following table, compiled from official statistical materials collected by Timothy Pitkin, gives a general idea of the growth of American exports.[19]

Product	1805	1807	1809	1810	1811
Cotton, Sea-Island (pounds)	–	–	67,188	–	113,435
Cotton other than Sea-Island (pounds)	–	–	557,924	3,769,137	9,255,404
Brown sugar (pounds)	–	52,852	1,271,180	6,139,529	4,408,289
White sugar (pounds)	44,476	297,844	922,077	5,257,366	10,200,139
Coffee (pounds)	129,577	149,271	1,283,100	4,048,909	5,113,891
Tobacco (hogsheads)	–	–	131	1,462	1,241
Whale oil (gallons)	24,072	–	22,535	6,797	–
Rice (tierces)	–	459	776	5,270	1,205
Beef (barrels)	10	–	12	437	197
Pork (barrels)	5	–	8	30	61

Admittedly, this table is far from perfect. Compiled from official material, it includes data on a number of export items of secondary significance, such as whale oil, beef, and pork, but does not contain information about some of the more important goods. Data on many colonial goods is missing in Pitkin's tables, although other sources indicate that such goods were delivered to Russia from America. For example, Svin'in in his enumeration of the most important items of American export to Russia named sugar, coffee, pepper, cotton, indigo, spices, wines, raisins, tobacco, and "all sorts of tree bark used for dyes."[20]

Consequently, although the table is not complete, it can be used to evaluate a number of the most important American exports, primarily cotton, the import of which to Russia grew swiftly: in 1809, 625,112 pounds; in 1810, 3,769,137; and in 1811, 9,368,839.

In 1811 no other country in Europe received such a great quantity of American cotton (Prussia's cotton import was 231,679 pounds; Spain's, 218,880 pounds; and the Hanseatic Cities (by means of licenses), 1,836,288 pounds). On the basis of these data, E. V. Tarle deduced that in 1811 Russia became the main supplier of cotton for the European spinning mills. "In 1811 colonial goods burst upon Russia in a wide wave," he wrote in his monograph on the Continental Blockade, "and from Russia, across its Western border to Prussia, and thence to the other countries of Europe. The Trianon tariff, which raised such enormous obstacles for the trade of colonial goods in Napoleon's dependencies, actually put Russia into a privileged position." A pood of Georgia and Louisiana cotton, which in 1810 cost in St. Petersburg 45-48 rubles, in a year fell to 25 rubles. "These were," Tarle noted, "prices of quite unheard-of cheapness . . . and comparing them, Napoleon could perceive clearly that some springs were being pressed in order to give colonial raw goods a wide access to the Russian empire."[21]

Before the Continental Blockade, in 1802-1806, Russia's import of cotton, according to Nebolsin's data, was quite small, averaging eight thousand poods. With the exception of the state-owned Alexandrian manufactory, there were no cotton spinning enterprises in the country, and the Russian cotton industry used mainly English yarn, the import of which reached impressive proportions (in 1805-6 it exceeded one hundred thousand poods a year). At this period the Alexandrian manufactory was still assimilating the methods of yarn production, and the owners of textile enterprises were reluctant to buy its produce. In 1806, for example, only 2,485 pounds of yarn were sold, in spite of the increased demand, while the amount of manufactured yarn was 41,930 pounds.[22]

The situation changed substantially when Russia joined the Continental Blockade. Yarn imports dropped sharply to 46,000 pounds in 1807, 36,000 in 1808, 53,000 in 1809, and 57,000 in 1810. Thus deprived, Russian textile mills began experiencing an acute shortage of raw materials. On the other hand, in the years of the Continental Blockade, conditions for the young cotton spinning industry, especially the Alexandrian factory, were most favorable.[23] Yarn prices went up considerably, even taking into consideration the deflation of currency, and from 1807 on, the Alexandrian manufactory made regular profits. As a result of the great demand for yarn, in 1807-8 all supplies, previously unrealized, were sold, technical reconstruction of production was accomplished, and the quality of the product substantially improved. The success of manufacture, the increase in its saleability, and especially the increases in the price of yarn led to enormous increases in the profits of the Alexandrian factory (from 36,000 rubles in 1807 to 667,000 in 1811).[24]

The prosperity of the manufactory in 1809-1811 was greatly furthered by the sharp increase in the import of American cotton, which became the basic raw material for the young cotton-spinning industry. As I have already said, originally cotton was brought to Russia in very small quantities; in spite of limited demand, apparently a shortage of raw cotton existed. Therefore it was not fortuitous that in March 1806 the administration of the Alexandrian factory advanced a project for sending its ship *Maria* to America with a cargo of hemp, linen, and iron for the first-hand purchase of raw cotton.[25] The enterprise seemed tempting, and soon it was decided to send two ships. Upon Rumiantsev's intervention, the Tsar ordered these ships to be exempt from the payment of duties, later affirming this decision even if the cargo were delivered in a neutral vessel.[26]

Taking advantage of this privilege, in 1806 the administration of the Alexandrian manufactory sent to Philadelphia two ships, the *Maria* and the *Ekaterina*. Apprehensive lest the ships be detained by the French military vessels cruising the American seas, the administration "instructed their correspondents to sell the ships," and ship the goods on two American vessels. Meanwhile the *Ekaterina* was shipwrecked en route to America, and the *Maria* "took advantage of the opportunity that presented itself" to detour to the island of Santo Domingo from where she brought to Philadelphia "twenty-four Russian sailors captured by the French and set ashore by them at the abovementioned island." The letter from the mill administration to Rumiantsev states that part of the goods from Philadelphia had already been delivered on an American ship, and the rest of the cargo was being prepared for shipping.[27]

The embargo introduced in the United States in 1807 affected the delivery of cotton to Russia. In 1808 the import of cotton was only seven and a half thousand poods, and the country experienced an acute shortage of raw materials for cotton-spinning. In its efforts to overcome this shortage, the Alexandrian mill bought cotton in the most diverse regions: in Odessa (so-called Macedonian or Smyrna cotton), in Astrakhan (Persian cotton), and in Orenburg (Bukhara cotton). The shortage continued until August 1809, when a big lot of high-quality American cotton was purchased.[28]

Further enormous expansion of American cotton imports in 1810 and 1811 not only satisfied the limited market in Russia, but, as mentioned earlier, created a surplus for supplying the cotton-spinning industries of European countries with raw material.

At first the question of United States exports to Russia, particularly American cotton, in the years of the Continental Blockade may seem insignificant. Careful study of it, however, would allow us to delineate a number of important problems connected with Russia's joining the Continental Blockade and with the history of the origin of the War of 1812. Although the history of these years has been studied in detail, there is no general agreement, especially about the influence of the Continental Blockade on the development of Russia's trade and industry. It is natural to assume that the break with England and the discontinuation of the import of British industrial products must have stimulated the development of Russian manufacture.

Such an opinion had been expressed already by the French ambassador in St. Petersburg, Caulaincourt,[29] and later by such well-known scholars as M. I. Tugan-Baranovsky, and M. N. Pokrovsky. To some extent it is shared by modern authors like S. A. Pokrovsky and M. K. Rozhkova.

None of them, however, studied the question in detail, and all utilized comparatively limited documentary source material.

On the other hand, in 1931 A. V. Predtechensky came out with an interesting work, proving on the basis of archival and published sources that the Continental Blockade had a negative influence on the whole Russian economy, including industry. As the author noted, the Continental Blockade interrupted foreign trade, created a series of unfavorable effects in the financial-economic sphere, and had a negligible influence on Russia's industrial development. The prohibitive tariff of 1810 had much more influence on the growth of industry, but even that could not compensate for the losses the Blockade inflicted on the country's entire economy.[30]

This opinion has also been expressed by V. K. Iatzunsky. The materials he used seem to testify to the flourishing of cotton-spinning in Russia. Both M. I. Tugan-Baranovsky and M. N. Pokrovsky pointed to the number of new cotton-spinning mills that sprung up as a result of the shortage of imported yarn, as a confirmation of their opinion. Such mills were indeed being established. Besides the Alexandrian manufactory in St. Petersburg, which was in existence earlier, Moscow's first cotton-spinning mill was established in 1808. By 1810 there were six cotton-spinning enterprises, four in Moscow and two in St. Petersburg. In 1811 there were eleven in Moscow alone, and in January 1812, according to a list prepared by the manager of the Alexandrian factory, there were sixteen "mechanical cotton-spinning mills," including nine in Moscow, two in St. Petersburg, and one each in Suzdal', Orlovskaia and Novgorodskaia provinces, Novinka, and Kupavna.[31]

The crux of the matter lies in the fact that the production of these enterprises, which were utilizing primarily American cotton, could not fulfill the demands of the textile factories. Therefore, on the whole, Russia's cotton industry, deprived of English yarn and receiving American cotton instead, was experiencing severe difficulties. As the United States could not take the place of England in the Russian market, American cotton, though contributing to the prosperity of the Alexandrian mill, could not fill the cotton textile industry's need for English yarn. It is characteristic that although originally, as a result of the Continental Blockade, yarn imports had fallen off sharply, in 1811 they rose to 122,000 poods, exceeding the average of 1805-6. But favorable conditions for the Russian cotton-spinning industry proved short-lived, and in March 1812 concerned Moscow factory-owners complained to Minister of Internal Affairs Kozodavlev about the extraordinary and quite unexpected import of "foreign cotton yarn, reputed to be American, but quite like the English one."[32]

As Predtechensky's study showed, the number of cotton textile factories (in Moscow province) during the Continental Blockade remained the same. Nor was there appreciable growth in most other branches of industry; in fact in some (the silk industry, for example) there was a notable tendency toward curtailment.[33] One cannot discover any real flourishing of industry. This stands to reason since all branches of an economy are closely interrelated. The Continental Blockade interrupted traditional commercial connections, had a sharply negative effect on the foreign trade turnover, brought about a passive trade balance and a drop in the ruble, and greatly curtailed the flow of free capital into Russia, thus undermining the very foundation of successful industrial development.

Expansion of trade with the United States only partially replaced the losses caused by the break with England; therefore one should not exaggerate the overall economic significance of Russian-American commerce in 1809-1811. What proved to be much more serious was the foreign policy aspect of this commerce, primarily its influence on the development of French-Russian contradictions.

When the American minister, John Quincy Adams, arrived in St. Petersburg in the autumn of 1809, he could not anticipate great success for his mission: he was supposed to defend the rights of a weak and faraway republic from the encroachments of the mightiest power—Napoleonic France—at the court of her official ally—tsarist Russia. Nevertheless, completely unexpectedly for everyone, including Adams himself, his stay in St. Petersburg from the very beginning was characterized by a remarkable and brilliant success.

To begin with, while en route to Russia, Adams learned about the many American vessels detained by Danish authorities. In Christiansand (Norway) alone there were upward of four hundred American seamen and 36 vessels seized by privateers under Danish colors, and 16 vessels were detained in the ports of Jutland. The overall value of the sequestered property amounted to five million dollars.[34] The owners and captains of captured vessels turned to Adams with a request for help. Although the minister had no instructions about the matter, he thought it possible to discuss it with the Danish Minister for Foreign Affairs, Count Bernstorff. On October 1, 1809, he made a trip to Bernstorff's country residence, but not finding him home was compelled to leave without getting any results.[35]

In the first talk he had with Rumiantsev, on 25 October 1809, soon after his arrival in St. Petersburg, the American minister called the Chancellor's attention to the illegal actions of Danish privateers. Although the Chancellor expressed his disapproval of their actions, he gave his interlocutor to understand that, given the conditions of the Continental Blockade so far, it was difficult to count on a more liberal system.[36] Indeed, soon Adams received another letter from Denmark informing him about the unexpected detention, on the orders of the Danish government, of American citizens' property in the ports of Holstein. Without much hope of success, and without any instructions from Washington, Adams decided to use his own initiative in appealing for help from the tsarist government. At the American Minister's request, a meeting between the envoy and Rumiantsev took place on 26 December 1809.[37] Adams asked for the "interposition of the good services" of the Russian government to induce Denmark to restore American property as speedily as possible. As Bemis noted, "John Quincy Adams was not one of those timid career diplomats whose rule for sure promotion in the course of time is to avoid any mistake by never assuming any initiative." In his talk with Rumiantsev, the American minister stated frankly that, since the subject of his request was not a part of his usual functions, he did not consider it expedient to send an official note. At the same time he expressed the hope that Alexander I would not disregard this request and would find a way to put appropriate pressure on Denmark.

In spite of his sympathy for the United States, Rumiantsev did not offer Adams any hope that such a difficult and delicate matter might succeed. The Chancellor stated that Denmark's action "was far from agreeable to him," and through the dispatches of the minister in Copenhagen, Lizakevich (or Lizakewitz) it was known to him that the "measure had given great dissatisfaction to Danes themselves. There was no occasion to disguise the fact that it was not a voluntary act on the part of the Danish government. It had been exacted by France, whose force at their gates was such as Denmark had no means of resisting."[38] Without much expectation that his request would be fulfilled, Adams nevertheless insistently argued the justice of his position. In the end, Rumiantsev agreed to transmit Adams' request to the Emperor. However, since Denmark's action had resulted from Napoleon's personal order, the Chancellor "was apprehensive there existed no influence in the world of sufficient efficacy to shake his determination."[39]

Adams understood quite well the dangers inherent in resisting Napoleon's will, especially on such a subject as violation of the Continental Blockade, not only for Denmark but also for Russia. After his conversation with Rumiantsev, he had little doubt that the outcome of his application would be negative. His general impression was that "the Count himself was fully persuaded of the truth of my representation, and that he really disapproved of the measures, but that Russia would not interfere in the case."[40]

Adams' surprise was great indeed when three days later he learned that the Emperor thought it possible to grant his request fully. On 29 December 1809 Rumiantsev informed the American minister that he had relayed his application to Alexander I. The Chancellor indicated that the Emperor's decision differed from his own recommendations, and that it was unusually favorable for the United States. Alexander I ordered "immediately to represent to the Danish government his wish that the examination might be expedited, and the American property restored as soon as possible." Rumiantsev had already discussed the matter that morning with the Danish minister, Baron de Blome, stressing that "His Majesty was greatly interested" in granting his wish.[41]

"The frank and candid manner" in which Rumiantsev treated the matter made an enormous impression on the American minister, and he told the Chancellor that while originally he had entertained little or no hope of success, he was now all the more delighted to find that his countrymen "would have the benefit of His Majesty's powerful intercession."[42]

Adams' countrymen benefited from the "powerful intercession" very soon: their property sequestered in the Holstein ports was released. In February 1810 Baron de Blome informed Rumiantsev that the Danish government would pay "the most particular attention to the interest which the Emperor had taken upon this occasion," and that Denmark's own intentions coincided with the wishes of the Emperor. As a result, on 27 February 1810, in his conversation with the American minister, Rumiantsev could express his satisfaction at the success of the transaction of the Russian government.[43]

Russia's "good offices" proved important: the value of the released American property was many times greater than the modest cost of maintaining the diplomatic mission in St. Petersburg, once considered useless by some thrifty congressmen.

What was attained so easily as a result of the intercession of the Russian government eventually became the subject of complex and lengthy negotiations. In March 1811 George Erving was sent to Denmark with a special mission to release the American vessels seized by Danish military ships, but he did not attain any marked success.[44] In the course of the Continental Blockade, the Danish navy seized 160 American ships, of which 42 were subsequently sequestered. Eventually the United States demanded that Denmark recompense it for losses amounting to $2,262,280.365. Although the loss was calculated precisely to the half-cent, the Americans obviously overstated their demands. Erving himself estimated the loss at $1,750,000, which was apparently closer to the truth. After years of litigation, Denmark agreed, in 1830, to a compensation of only $650,000.[45]

The United States was cognizant of the value of the Russian intercession, and Secretary of State Robert Smith instructed his Minister at St. Petersburg, on behalf of President Madison to convey to Alexander I, in the most appropriate form, his warmest appreciation.[46] A document written in Adams' characteristically small, clear handwriting has been preserved in the Archives. As directed, the minister expressed the appreciation of the United States Government for the good services rendered in December 1811, "on behalf of the American citizens whose property was sequestered in the ports of Holstein."[47]

The significance of the Russian government's actions on behalf of American commerce can be estimated correctly only by keeping in mind the general international situation. The fact is that, in his active and successful defense of the rights of neutral navigation, John Quincy Adams touched on a very sore spot of France's policy in Europe. Without suspecting it, or more precisely without wishing it, the minister stepped on Napoleon's painful corn. One cannot help agreeing with the remark of the well-known American historian Henry Adams that "if Adams had consciously intrigued for a rupture between France and Russia, he could have invented no means so effective as to cause the Czar's interference with Napoleon's control of Denmark."[48]

In Paris the Russian government's encouragement of neutral American trade continually called forth the almighty dictator's fits of wrath. Napoleon did not burden himself by defining which cargo is of English and which of American origin. It seemed to him much simpler to consider all ships and all cargoes as English, and to end the complex and tiresome bickering on this subject once and for all. In the spring of 1808 the sovereign of Continental Europe had simply decreed, because of the embargo introduced by the United States, that all vessels arriving in France, Italy, the Hanseatic towns, and Holland under the American flag are to be deemed English, and their papers false.[49] And, although in practice the French government had to relax this rigid rule in one way or another, the Empire's relations with the United States at times were in a state of semi-rupture.[50]

In an effort to strengthen the Continental Blockade still further, on

August 5, 1810, Napoleon signed a new law (the Trianon tariff) sanctioning enormous increases of the custom duties on the imports of colonial goods into France: sugar, cotton, coffee, tea, and so on.[51] On October 19, 1810, there followed a decree on confiscation of all British goods imported into France and her possessions.[52] "Caesar raged." On the European continent the bonfires of English cotton, woolens, coffee, and sugar were burning.

As the official declaration in the *Moniteur* of 10 July 1810 indicates, in France they stopped trusting even the certificates of their own consuls in the United States, who "depuis quelque temps" were forbidden to issue any documents on the origin of the cargoes. The French government insisted that England allows Americans to engage in commerce only to the extent that they transport British goods, hence all certificates of French consuls in the United States and all other papers the ships might present were deemed forgeries. "There was not a single ship arriving in Russian ports with so-called American papers which in reality had not come from England."[53]

Napoleon's annoyance over American trade in the Baltic was so great that he attempted to interfere directly in Russia's internal affairs—something he had never done before—by suggesting to the tsarist government that it stop importing colonial goods and accept the French tariff as a model. In his own letter to the Tsar of 23 October 1810, Napoleon informed him of six hundred English trade vessels which had been denied entrance to the ports of Mecklenburg and Prussia and headed for the Russian possessions. No matter what papers they have, under which names they hide, whether French, German, Spanish, Danish, Russian, Swedish, "Votre Majesté peut être sûre que ce sont des anglais." The almighty sovereign of the European continent insisted on no less than the confiscation of all colonial goods entering Russia and the introduction of a complete ban on their further import.[54]

Under such conditions, the defense of the rights of neutral navigation seemed exceptionally complex, if not hopeless. However, this question from its very inception was the center of attention of both Levett Harris and John Quincy Adams. Ever since his arrival in St. Petersburg, Adams had systematically raised the question in his conversations with the ministers of the tsarist government. His diary and his dispatches to Washington for 1810-11 contain detailed and systematic resumés of numerous conversations with Rumiantsev, Minister of Finance D. A. Gur'ev, and State Treasurer B. B. Campenhausen, who was entrusted with managing commercial matters. Adams' representation to the tsarist government in

August 1810 on the subject of American vessels detained in Archangel is characteristic.[55] These vessels arrived from Portugal, commerce with which country had been prohibited as of May 22, 1810. Adams insisted on their release on the grounds that at the time of their departure from Lisbon the ordinance was not yet known there.

In a conversation with Gur'ev of 10 September 1810, concerning his representations to Rumiantsev and similar applications by Harris, Adams expressed "infinite pleasure that the Emperor, in every one of the cases, had decided in our favor," as well as his obligation to Baron Campenhausen for immediately communicating to him these decisions.[56]

It was not always possible to determine the precise origin of a ship and its cargo, and Harris' and Adams' representations were the subject of long-drawn-out investigations in various governmental stages, up to the Committee of Ministers.[57] Nevertheless, the general attitude toward representations on behalf of the interests of American merchants and shipowners remained favorable. Rumiantsev repeatedly assured the American minister that the Russian government would be "glad to give every possible facility to the *direct* commerce between the United States and this country, and that he would cheerfully agree to any proper measure to promote its future extension."[58] A phrase of Rumiantsev, dropped in his conversation with Adams on 9 October 1810, became well known: "Our attachment to the United States is *obstinate—more obstinate than you are aware of.*"[59]

The American minister prized Russia's favorable attitude toward the United States and he hastened to assure Rumiantsev that the United States Government was well aware of it. He remarked that "indeed a comparison between the measures not only of France but of all the neighbors of Russia, in the North of Europe, Denmark, Prussia, Sweden, with regard to the commerce of the United States, with those of Russia, during the present year, would of itself be a strong indication to the Government and to the people of the United States of a disposition in Russia very different from that which they have experienced elsewhere, and it was impossible they could be insensible to it."[60]

Although Adams referred to Russia's position in the most complimentary way, even he could not foresee that the tsarist government would risk open conflict with her powerful ally, Napoleonic France, over the question of trade with the United States. It was only in Russia that the crowned despot met an unexpected and sharp resistance to his insistence on complete discontinuance of the importing of colonial goods into European countries. Alexander I had categorically declined Napoleon's demand on 7 December 1810 in his conversation with French ambassador Caulaincourt.[61] Some time later, on 19/31 December 1810, the famous Statement on Neutral Trade for 1811 was issued, with a list of goods accepted for export and import, consequent to the proposals of Minister of Finance Gur'ev; this received the approval of the majority of the State Council's members.[62]

Formally, the new tariff did not challenge the principles of the Continental Blockade in any way; one of its paragraphs prohibited the import of "enemy," that is, English, goods. However, by permitting the importing of any colonial goods and making concessions to neutral countries (meaning primarily the United States), the Statement represented in essence a concealed challenge to Napoleon. In its content, the tariff was protective, and its aim was to encourage the national industry. The Statement could not fail to call forth extreme irritation in Paris. The French had expected new concessions for their trade, but received instead a considerable rise in duties on a number of important export items: expensive wines, velvet, and, especially, Lyons silk, the import of which into Russia was virtually eliminated. No wonder that the new tariff ruined relations between Russia and Napoleon's empire; beginning at this time, the prospect of a military conflict between the two countries began to emerge.[63] In early 1811 Napoleon, irritated by the new tariff and by Russia's protest against French occupation of the Oldenburg duchy, seized upon the rumors of a forthcoming invasion by Russian troops of the Warsaw duchy as a pretext to undertake active military preparations, and in April even compiled a plan of operations against Russia.[64] From Paris, A. I. Chernyshev, A. B. Kurakin, and especially K. V. Nesselrode, using secret information received from Talleyrand, reported more and more frequently and insistently on the subject of Napoleon's preparations for war and the inevitability of a conflict between Russia and France.[65]

There was no lack of pretexts for a military conflict, but the Continental Blockade was undoubtedly one of the main ones. France did not conceal her irritation with Russia's persistent encouragement of American trade and continued importing of colonial goods. Although officially the rules of the Continental Blockade were strictly observed, it was well known in Paris that the arrival of sugar, coffee, and dyes on the Russian market not only did not decrease but actually, because of American mediation, were on the increase. This was the circumstance Napoleon had in mind when, in a conversation with A. I. Chernyshev, he pointed out that in the course of the summer of 1810 American ships brought to England "infinite profits" and "almost completely destroyed the meaning of the continental system by inundating the whole of Europe with colonial goods."[66]

The disobedient economy obviously mocked the mighty dictator to whom nothing seemed impossible. Napoleon could by one stroke of the pen destroy a whole duchy for violating the rules of the Continental Blockade—as he did in 1810 with Holland by simply decreeing its annexation to the French empire. He could demand for a wife the youthful daughter of the Austrian emperor without bothering to look at her even on their wedding day, yet still have the union considered a great honor for the most ancient and haughty dynasty. But he could not force Europe to deny itself coffee or sugar. Everybody preferred sweet tea, and cotton cloth could not be produced without raw cotton.

Following his instructions from Paris, Caulaincourt, the French ambassador in St. Petersburg, strongly protested against the new tariff, and in particular against the tsarist government's refusal to stop trading with the United States. The Duke de Vicence insisted that there was no theoretical difference between English and American commerce, since United States vessels transported British goods. But what could be forced upon Napoleonic dependencies proved impossible in the case of Russia, even for a brilliant French ambassador who enjoyed the favor of both Rumiantsev and the Tsar himself.

On the question of trade with the United States the Russian Chancellor showed extraordinary firmness, flatly contradicting Caulaincourt's reasoning. Rumiantsev stated that, on the contrary, the development of trade with both Americas would weaken England's position on the world market. "He reminded me," Caulaincourt reported, "that he had told me many times that while still a Minister of Commerce he did everything possible to establish trade connections with the Americans, whom he views as natural rivals of the English. It would be a political shortsightedness, he said, to allow relations with the Americans to deteriorate at the moment when they are so openly opposed to the English."[67]

One of the main international contradictions of the period arising during these years concerned trade with the United States. Fouché mockingly remarked that the simple people originally assumed that the War of 1812 started because of sugar and coffee.[68] Of course the acrimonious Minister of Police was right to correct this exaggeration. Nevertheless, in spite of its naiveté, it reflected the irreconcilability of Russia's economic interests with the Continental Blockade, the observance of which was doggedly forced upon her by Napoleon. Objective laws of political development which could be changed neither by Napoleon, nor Alexander I came into play here. As Engels pointed out, "economics proved stronger than diplomacy and the Tsar put together; trade relations with England were quietly resumed; the conditions of the Tilsit treaty were violated, and the War of 1812 broke out."[69]

The modest American minister, with his seemingly innocent complaints and appeals on the subject of detained ships and their cargoes, unsuspectingly was helping to intensify an enormous conflict. Throughout the winter of 1810-11 he kept up his persistent intercessions before the tsarist government on behalf of ships detained in Riga, Revel, and Libau—and also in Archangel and Kronstadt.[70] Many of the cases proved complicated and tangled, and the opposition of the French ambassador coupled with the bureaucratic procedure established by the Continental Blockade were serious impediments. Nevertheless, eventually Adams succeeded in his efforts: about 23 American ships were released in time for the spring 1811 navigation.[71] It is interesting that the first news of this was received by the American minister at a diplomatic dinner at the French ambassador's on 18 March 1811. As soon as he entered, he was approached by the State Treasurer, Baron Campenhausen, who informed him of the decision made by the Emperor Alexander the day before. As Adams recorded in his diary,

> the cases of all the American vessels (excepting that of the *Eliza* at Archangel) were definitively decided; that the cargoes and parts of cargoes which had not the necessary certificates should be admitted on the engagement of the persons interested in them to produce the certificates hereafter; that as to all the other small parcels which were under other circumstances of irregularity, the Emperor had also ordered that they also should be admitted, and that thus everything recognized as American should be cleared.[72]

The success which invariably accompanied Adams' appeals greatly puzzled the minister himself. It seemed improbable to him that the tsarist government would so persistently and systematically defend the rights of neutral navigation in the face of the terrible threat of an open military conflict with Napoleon, while the United States had patiently suffered humiliating insults to their flag by both England and France. For some reason, not clear to Adams, the Russian Tsar was more of an American than the American leaders themselves. The intercession on behalf of the United States before the Danish government, the greatest possible encouragement of American commerce, the systematic release of detained vessels, and finally the acceptance of a new tariff—all seemed an amazing dream, were it not an objective reality easily explained by the acute internal contradictions eating away at the ruins of the French-Russian alliance and the continental system. The unequal struggle of the brilliant French duke with the modest minister of the distant, overseas republic ended with the complete triumph of the American. Caulaincourt was finally compelled to admit failure. But, he said, "it seems you are great favorites here. You have found powerful protection, for most of your vessels have been admitted."[73]

The victory sustained by Adams in St. Petersburg in 1810-11 is referred to by American historians as "the most brilliant success of his diplomatic career."[74] It is hard to agree entirely with this opinion. In his declining years Adams called the treaty of 22 February 1819, with Spain annexing Florida and extending her border to the shores of the Pacific, "the most important moment" in his life and the result of the most successful negotiations ever conducted by the government of the United States.[75] On the whole there were quite a few brilliant successes in Adams' long political career. (Consider, for example, his outstanding role in the preparation of the Monroe Doctrine.) Apropos of his Russian mission, granted the merits of the American minister as a skillful and experienced diplomat, its success resulted not so much from Adams' actions as the powerful hidden currents of European politics which made a French-Russian breach inevitable. And, although in 1811 this breach was only a question of time, both sides still strove to observe certain amenities. The tsarist government was reluctant to provoke Napoleon and especially to be the first to start the war. On his part, the French Emperor was not yet ready to invade Russia and sought to gain time. It is indicative on the one hand that in a conversation with Chernyshev on 13/25 February 1811, Napoleon announced that (to paraphrase) one should not trouble himself to make war without a better reason than sugar and such goods. And yet that very evening he confirmed instructions to the French ambassador in St. Petersburg, General Lauriston, stating openly that he [Napoleon] did not trust any further negotiations, "unless the 450,000 men that His Majesty [i.e. Napoleon] mobilized, together with their vast equipment, caused serious reflection in the St. Petersburg cabinet, restoring the Tilsit system and returning Russia to the condition of inferiority in which she then was."[76]

In the meantime, events relentlessly approached the crash of the Tilsit system. In a farewell talk with Caulaincourt in May 1811, Alexander stated: "If Emperor Napoleon declares war, it is possible, even probable, that he will defeat us if we accept combat, but that will not bring him peace. The Spaniards have often been defeated and are neither conquered nor subjugated. However, they are not as distant as we are from Paris, and they do not have our climate or our resources. We will not compromise. We have space and we shall keep a well-organized army in being . . . If the issue of arms goes against me, I shall retreat to Kamchatka rather than yield provinces and sign treaties in my capital that will merely be truces. The French are brave, but long privations and a bad climate would weary and discourage them. Our climate, our winter, will make war for us. Wonders are brought about for you only where the Emperor is present, and he cannot be everywhere when his armies are far from Paris.''[77]

While the world watched with bated breath the approaching conflict between the two greatest empires, Napoleonic France and tsarist Russia, energetic and practical American merchants and shipowners hastened to seize the favorable opportunities for profitable operations. For a period of time, even though of short duration, the atmosphere for the development of Russian-American trade was exceptionally favorable. Adams was well aware of this. From private talks with Rumiantsev he carried away the firm conviction that the Chancellor was most favorably disposed toward the United States and was willing to offer all possible encouragement to Russian-American trade connections. Rumiantsev reminded him more than once that, while still the Minister of Commerce, he had been extremely anxious to offer every encouragement and facility to trade between the two countries. Now Minister for Foreign Affairs, he retained the same "ardent desire." The Chancellor stressed that he would gladly agree to any suitable measure for increasing direct trade with the United States, and was interested in particular in the possibility of encouraging American vessels to bring "money for the cargoes which they should take in return."[78]

Aware of this favorable atmosphere, Adams felt it expedient to raise the question of a special commercial treaty and strongly recommended this measure to his government. Adams' proposal attracted the attention of President Madison, and in February 1811 the Minister was instructed to open negotiations with the Russian government on the subject.[79] At the same time the headings of the future treaty, asserting "peace, friendship, and mutual understanding" between Russia and the United States, were sent to St. Petersburg.[80]

Having received his government's official sanction, Adams put the question to Rumiantsev in a conversation with the Chancellor on 4 July 1811. The American stated that

> from the idea which since [his] residence here [he] formed of the importance and mutual benefit of the commercial relations between the

239

United States and Russia, from the signal manner in which Russia had distinguished herself from all the other belligerent powers of Europe, in her treatment of the fair commerce and neutral rights of America, and from a wish to increase and render still more advantageous the commerce between the two countries, the idea and desire had occurred to [him] of cementing still further their amity by a treaty of commerce.

He then mentioned that he had suggested this idea to the American government and was now authorized to conduct negotiations. "I had thought it most advisable," Adams noted in his diary, "to make to him at first this verbal communication, instead of sending him an official note upon the subject. I requested him to consider it as confidential, so that at least it should be made known only when he thought it advisable."[81]

On his part, Rumiantsev again asserted "his great and long-settled attachment to the United States, and stressed that the encouragement of American commerce is not only the result of personal sympathy, but it had been with him long a maxim of policy. . . . It was the interest of Russia to encourage and strengthen and multiply commercial powers which might be the rivals of England, to form a balance to her overbearing power." Since he had often expressed these sentiments to the Emperor, who always "received them well and appeared impressed with the justice of them," Rumiantsev was confident that Adams' proposal would encounter no obstacles. The only difficulty he could foresee was that, "in the violent and convulsed state of commerce and of the world at this time, he hardly conceived it possible to agree upon anything, if he might be allowed the expression, that had common sense in it."[82]

Besides the international complications Rumiantsev had in mind, the state of Adams' personal affairs exercised a certain influence on the prospects of the agreement. Soon after his arrival in St. Petersburg, he had discovered that his modest salary did not correspond at all to the enormous expenses of "representation." An American minister abroad was entitled to an annual remuneration of nine thousand dollars (around forty thousand rubles), and approximately the same sum was allowed to cover the expenses of moving, house furnishing, postal expenses, and so on. If anything, this sum seemed excessive to the thrifty congressmen. This is not hard to understand: the President of the United States received a stipend of twenty-five thousand dollars a year (the Vice-President, only five thousand). On the other hand, comparison of Adams' salary with the expenses of the Duke de Vicence, which exceeded a million rubles a year, makes it clear why the American minister thought his salary insufficient.[83] The unusually high cost of living in the tsarist capital became a main source of complaint in letters to the United States and in diary notations of the economical and meticulous Puritan.[84] Abigail Adams, the minister's mother, was sufficiently alarmed by this situation to address the President directly with a request that he recall her son. As a consequence, Madison granted the minister permission to leave his post whenever he deemed it necessary to do so—at the same time asking him to prolong his stay in St. Petersburg as long as possible because of the importance of the mission.[85]

In a conversation with Rumiantsev on 8 January 1811 Adams informed him that he had received permission from his government to return to the United States, but did not expect to take his leave until the approach of summer. Both Rumiantsev and the Tsar expressed deep regret at the prospect of his departure and hopes that his stay might be prolonged.[86] Somewhat later, in February 1811, President Madison, with the concurrence of the Senate, appointed Adams an associate justice of the Supreme Court of the United States, and Robert Smith sent official notification of this to Pahlen and to Adams.[87] For many reasons, primarily because of family circumstances (his wife, Louisa, was expecting a child), Adams did not accept the new appointment and remained in St. Petersburg.[88]

Not knowing the decision of his government with regard to his mission, Adams did not propose officially that the treaty be concluded, referring in his conversation with Rumiantsev to "uncertainty both in the state of public affairs, and of his own situation here." The Chancellor remarked that, "from this uncertainty in the state of everything, it seemed really impossible to enter upon any discussion relative to commerce." Consequently, official negotiations were not undertaken at that time.[89]

In the course of their lengthy and informal conversations, Adams and Rumiantsev discussed a variety of political problems. They not only touched Russian-American relations as such, but discussed in detail many of the most important aspects of foreign policy: the relations of the United States with England and France, the problems of international trade and the Continental Blockade, the changes in the makeup of the British cabinet, and the peculiarities of Napoleon's political system. In Rumiantsev's opinion, the policy of the French government with respect to commerce was extremely contradictory and inconsistent and Napoleon was unreliable in this respect. "Every resolution, every act was the result of the impulse of the moment, the effect of an occasional impression." According to Rumiantsev, Napoleon "never considered that commerce was an interest in which all mankind was concerned; he saw in it nothing but the trade of a certain class of individuals." "But in truth," the Count said, "commerce is the concern of us all. The merchants are, indeed, only a class of individuals, bearing a small proportion to the mass of people, but commerce is the exchange of mutual superfluities for mutual wants—is the very chain of human association; it is the foundation of all the useful and pacific intercourse between nations; it is a primary necessity to all classes of people."[90]

Inviting Adams "to free conversation," the Russian minister used to say that they talked as "one private gentleman to another." Rumiantsev wanted Adams to consider him not as Chancellor of a mighty empire, but as a private individual in need of advice. Adams accepted this peculiar manner of consultation as a form of civility as well as personal sympathy.[91]

The stormy events of incipient revolution in Latin America provided a continuous subject of discussion for Adams and Rumiantsev. According to Adams, the Russian always had manifested an interest in South America.[92] He was concerned about the latest information on the situation in the Spanish colonies, the position of the European powers and the United States on this question, the general influence of the revolution in the New World on world commerce and international relations. Both men believed in the importance of expanding trade connections with the new states, and both accepted the inevitability of a break between Spain's colonies and the mother country.

While Adams judged correctly the prospect for revolution in Spanish America, he (like Rumiantsev) was wrong in estimating its consequences for Great Britain. Adams considered it self-evident that "the death-blow to the old colonial system of Europe" opposed the interests of England above all, since it undermined the very foundations of her power. He assumed that the Spanish and Portuguese colonies in America, having won their independence and the right to free trade with all countries, would force England to drop the monopoly system in her relations with her colonial possessions (he had in mind the British West Indies first of all).[93] Neither of the interlocutors took into account the fact that Great Britain, the world's greatest industrial and commercial power, had most to gain from the establishment of regular connections with the new extensive market in South America.

A distant political prognosis is too complex and dangerous a matter for us to accuse Adams or Rumiantsev of making an error in judging the results of secession from the mother country. What is much more to the point is the similarity of their views on the question of the advantages to be derived from the establishment of direct commercial ties with new states and their firm belief in the inevitability of the complete breakdown of the old colonial system in America.

In a very short time the Spanish American question outgrew the narrow framework of private consultations of the Russian Chancellor with the American minister; by the fall of 1811 it had become the subject of official discussion in the highest governmental spheres of tsarist Russia. Without touching upon all aspects of Russia's position in Spanish America's war for independence, I shall limit my discussion to matters connected with Russian-American relations, in particular the activities of John Quincy Adams and Levett Harris.[94]

In August 1811 Harris informed Rumiantsev of the arrival from New York of his countryman Courtland L. Parker, who for several years prior had lived in Caracas, and had authorization from the government of that country to treat with the Russian government. Harris informed the Chancellor that "the provinces of Caracas, Venezuela, and the vice-kingdom of Santa Fe" had seceded from Spain and established temporary governments, one of whose first acts was to open their ports to the commerce of all friendly countries. Having declared independence, the inhabitants of South America wanted to establish direct trade connections with Russia.

There followed two talks between Rumiantsev and Parker.[95] The American informed the Chancellor of the situation in South America and said that the new states would like to receive from Russia flax products, canvas, textiles, iron, and other goods. In a special note Parker also gave detailed information on trade and industry in the new states, especially Venezuela, which had proclaimed independence on 19 April 1810. In particular, he supplied a list of prices for goods produced in Caracas for the period 1800-1810.[96] Parker assured the Chancellor that, "no matter what was the outcome of the war with Spain, the fate of that country would not have any influence on the lot of her colonies in America, since they decided to rid themselves of the yoke of her dominion forever; that although they are at present governed under the name of Ferdinand, this name is used only as a symbol of power for the people, but power deprived of all influence and all means of action." Without disputing this information, Rumiantsev remarked that the main difficulty in the proposed relations consists in observing the rules of the Continental Blockade, which Russia is obliged to adhere to strictly. Nevertheless, the Chancellor did not consider this obstacle unsurmountable, as he stressed in a note to the State Council of 16/28 September 1811: "There can be no doubt in the usefulness for our commerce of this new expansion of independent relations with a country possessing in abundance various produce, even the most precious metals, but needing our surplus."[97]

Rumiantsev supposed that the establishment of direct commercial connections with the new states of Spanish America would not conflict with Russia's political connections, since Napoleon's Minister for Internal Affairs, Count Montolivet, had announced in the French Assembly that if Spain were deprived of her colonies, it would be by her own volition, and that the Emperor would never oppose the independence of countries on the American continent.[98] With this in mind, Rumiantsev believed "not only that will there be no difficulty in opening trade relations with these colonies, but that this trade should be permitted, provided that the permission was based precisely on the general rules of the Continental System."

Conforming with the instructions of Alexander I, on 16/28 September Rumiantsev sent Secretary of State M. M. Speransky his note and a project of a ukase for the Minister of Finance, D. A. Gur'ev, about the opening of Russian ports to Latin American ships, with the expectation that the matter would be discussed in the meeting of the State Council.[99] "Taking into consideration," it was pointed out in the project, "that since the changes that took place in the commercial system of the colonies of South America in consequence of the new political regime in that part of the world, opened their ports for all trading nations, we hold that, whatever mode of government be established there, it would not create an obstacle to commercial connections between their inhabitants and our subjects, so long as our enemies have no influence there."[100] In accordance with the rules of the Continental System, ships arriving from South America were obliged to present certificates from Russian consuls-general in the United States or in Rio de Janeiro.

A general meeting of the State Council to consider Rumiantsev's proposal, took place on 9/21 October 1811, and four members of the Council spoke in favor of it. The majority (twenty-one members) voted to postpone consideration of the measures, "until the government of the three provinces soliciting commercial relations with us is firmly established and officially recognized by us."[101]

Commenting on this decision, Adams wrote Secretary of State Monroe that the opposition resulted from fear that the acceptance of Rumiantsev's propositions would lead inevitably to recognition of the independence of Spanish America. Adams thought that this was exactly what the Chancellor had in mind. "The Russian policy as contemplated by him is to favor the independence of the provinces of South America which belonged to Spain. . . . It might be the wish of Count Romanzoff that Russia should be the first or among the first to recognize this new power."[102]

Explaining the rejection of Rumiantsev's proposals by the State Council, Adams pointed first to Great Britain and "a lurking English influence working at bottom."[103] He saw this influence as the real cause of the failure of the project, but actually the problem was much more complex. When one talks of foreign influence, mention must be made first of all of Spain, with whom in the autumn of 1811 secret negotiations were being renewed for the conclusion of a treaty of alliance.[104]

Even greater significance should be attributed to the acute internal disagreements existing in the ruling circles of tsarist Russia at that time. The reactionary majority of the State Council, reflecting the mood of the upper layers of Russian nobility, clearly did not share the "American sympathies" of Rumiantsev who, at about this time, began to lose his former influence. They linked his name with the hateful Tilsit peace and rapprochement with France. And, although the Chancellor avoided Speransky's fate and continued, formally at least, to head the Ministry for Foreign Affairs, he had many political adversaries and personal enemies in the State Council. These were the men who in all kinds of ways prevented the execution of Rumiantsev's plans especially since, in the eyes of the highest tsarist dignitaries, they appeared "Jacobin."

Significant in this respect are the letters State Council member Ober-Hofmeister R. A. Koshelev, apparently influenced by the representative of Spain's Council of Regents, Franciscu de Zea Bermúdez, wrote the Tsar in September-October 1811.[105] At that time Koshelev enjoyed the special confidence of Alexander I. He was entrusted to conduct secret negotiations with Zea Bermúdez, who returned to St. Petersburg in the fall of 1811. Anxious to avoid accepting the measures proposed by Rumiantsev, this extreme reactionary and mystic referred to the example of Catherine II, and called the rebelling colonies "victimes de souffle satanique."[106] Somewhat later, 11/23 October 1811, the Ober-Hofmeister complained bitterly to Alexander I that the infamous affair of the rebels was "being discussed in the Council officially, while the agent of a lawful government for more than four weeks cannot succeed in getting a vague official answer."[107]

On the same day, in another letter to the Tsar, Koshelev, without hesitating to slander, directly accused the "unworthy minister, envious of the glory of his sovereign," of permitting himself to put up "the dishonorable matter of Caracas" for scrutiny in the Council's Plenum, "without conforming to the established procedures," and of reading a ukase deliberately flaunting the monarch's will.[108]

Formally, Alexander reprimanded the overzealous Ober-Hofmeister, confirming the fact that the matter of Caracas was presented to the Council "in accordance with his instructions." The Tsar also stated that he would not suffer interference from an ambassador of any power, and that another person who assumed such "arrogance," would regret it.[109] However, on 27 October/8 November 1811, Alexander I penned a customary resolution on the decision of the State Council: "So be it according to the majority of voices," thus refusing to support Rumiantsev at a decisive moment.[110]

These actions reveal the duplicity of Alexander I. At that time the Tsar had not yet dropped the liberal pose which he used so skillfully during the first years of his rule. But at the same time, Alexander, who in the near future (March 1812) would send Speransky into exile in order to cement ties with Russian reactionaries, was anxious not to give the least cause for discontent to the majority of the State Council by his resolute interference. Submitting to the results of the voting and rejecting a really progressive measure, the Tsar actually acted at one with R. A. Koshelev and A. A. Arakcheyev.

The denouement of these events occurred the next year, 1812. Luís López Mendez, deputy of the newly declared independent provinces of South America, residing in London, on 12 January requested Levett Harris to offer his cooperation for getting the sanction of the St. Petersburg court "for the act of independence proclaimed by the people of Venezuela." Complying with this request, the American consul some time later presented Mendez's letter to Rumiantsev and had a private discussion with the Count on this subject. In the course of it Harris informed the Chancellor that, along with "all liberal and enlightened men," he was concerned with the "success of the just and great cause which our brethren of the New World had embraced" and that he was especially pleased to act as an intermediary, since, in the course of his long acquaintance with Rumiantsev, he had the honor "to know his sentiments about such subjects." According to Harris, "the Chancellor received this communication with a great deal of satisfaction," assured him as to the correct interpretation of his views, and stated that "he would bring the subject to the attention of the Emperor immediately."[111]

The same question was discussed by Rumiantsev and Adams on 4 February 1812. The Chancellor inquired about the position of the United States Government with regard to the Spanish American provinces, and, in particular, asked if they had representatives in Washington. Adams answered that he knew of Venezuelan representatives in the United States, and that the American government took a favorable view of the changes taking place in those provinces, considering them to be "generally advantageous to the interests of mankind." The envoy informed the Chancellor of this all the more readily since "from former conversations" and "other circumstances" he knew that Rumiantsev's views on the subject coincided with those of the United States Government.[112]

Having stated again that such concurrence indeed existed, Rumiantsev nevertheless expressed a doubt which throws additional light on the reasons for the State Council's rejection of his project in October 1811. "The people of those provinces had been kept in such a state of grievous oppression that he was afraid they would in accomplishing their emancipation exhibit examples of that sort of violence and those scenes of cruelty which experience had proved to be too common in such revolutions."

Although ready to accept a revolution of the "American type," Rumiantsev obviously did not want events to follow the course of the great French Revolution of 1789-1794, and expressed hope that in Spanish provinces it might be otherwise. Describing to the Imperial Council his project of opening free commerce with the new states, which would have implied recognition of their existence, Rumiantsev remarked: "Mais en cela j'ai echoué. The apprehension of those discords to which I have alluded prevented my success. On pourra cependant revenir par cet objet."[113]

Apparently Rumiantsev did not succeed in returning to this question. It is true that in a letter of 1/3 May 1812 to Monroe, Levett Harris mentioned that "the Council was occupied at several settings with the measure recommended by the Emperor, but finally, by a majority of two or three voices, rejected it. The present political state of Europe, and especially that of Spain to which the Emperor's attention was particularly invited, was the cause of the disagreement of the Council with the sentiments of the Sovereign."[114] Although Harris wrote about several sessions, his information seems to refer to discussion of Rumiantsev's project in the fall of 1811. The plenums of the Imperial Council convened very rarely, and study of archival material shows that there was no other general meeting on the question of relations with Latin America besides the one on 9/21 October 1811.

In response to a new proposal put forth by López Mendez in January 1812, Rumiantsev especially requested Harris to explain that

> He still retains the same sentiments as those he expressed to Mr. Parker, who initiated the subject of this correspondence; and that a deep interest is felt by His Imperial Majesty in the progress toward self-

government which South America is making; but that at present he cannot obtain the official recognition of Emperor Alexander of the independence of those provinces, whose political changes have become known here.

To cherish sentiments of amity favorable to the Spanish Americans and to afford countenance and protection to all commercial operations directed by them to the ports of His Empire will ever meet the feelings of the Russian Monarch and after the freedom and Sovereignty of the Provinces of South America have been recognized by Great Britain, He will not hesitate to follow so worthy an example. The political state of Europe at this moment prevents His doing more.[115]

Although no official recognition of the rebelling Spanish colonies in America was granted at that time (or, for that matter, later), in practice the Russian government encouraged rather than prevented contacts with South American markets.

A general expansion of the scope of Russia's foreign policy, a considerable increase in trade with the United States—and, through their mediation, with the countries of Latin America—led in 1811-12 to a certain reorganization of Russian diplomatic and consular representation in America. In the summer of 1811 Pahlen was appointed to the post of ambassador in Rio de Janeiro. According to the ukase of 16/28 July 1811, the embassy adviser, P. Poletika, and the secretary, F. Ivanov, were to accompany him.[116] Count Pahlen's exotic destination resulted from the fact that in 1807, in the aftermath of the French invasion, the Portuguese Court had fled to Brazil. Informing Adams of the transfer, Rumiantsev laughingly added "that it seemed to be a kind of destiny for Count Pahlen to visit all the sovereigns of America, and if another such place should arise in that hemisphere, he did not know but that they should charge him with commencing the diplomatic relations of Russia with it."[117] In connection with the Portuguese Prince-Regent's moving to Rio de Janeiro there arose a necessity for changes in the old Russian-Portuguese treaty of commerce of 1798, since now it had to be concerned not with goods produced in Portugal proper, but in her colonies, Brazil above all.[118]

This was clearly indicated in the instructions of 22 August/3 September 1811 given the new minister in Rio de Janeiro, signed by Alexander I and countersigned by Rumiantsev.

Since the transfer of the seat of the Portuguese government to Brazil, there is but one subject that might actually interest Russia in relation to this power, and that is commerce, the advantages of which are beyond doubt. All the merchants agree on this, and the last treaty with Great

Britain to be signed in Rio de Janeiro demonstrates its importance. Sharing this trade with the English will certainly prove profitable for Russia, and Brazil will also find it very expedient.

Although officially Pahlen's appointment to Rio de Janeiro was not connected with the war of independence in the Spanish colonies, naturally his position provided new opportunities for gathering information about the situation in that part of the world, for the development of commercial connections and perhaps even for the establishment of the preliminary diplomatic contacts with the new states. In this context, a passage in Pahlen's instructions, directly concerning Russia's attitude toward new states in Spanish America, is especially interesting:

> It is not improbable that some instigators of independence will approach you, in order to establish contacts with Russia. I am led to believe that this is the case by the fact that the new governments in Caracas, Santa Fe, and Venezuela have already thought of this. If they make any proposals of this nature to you, you will not refuse to hear them out, but you will limit yourself to the general assurances of protection offered by my State to all lawful commerce, avoiding any commitments that might prove premature. While waiting for circumstances to guide us as to what position to take with regard to them, one must flatter their vanity with an artfully presented prospect of the ease with which they will probably obtain recognition of their political existence, and above all, of those authorities they can later count on as favoring commerce with them, no matter what government is in power.[119]

The frank and somewhat cynical tone of the Tsar's instructions allows us to assume that, while the Russian government was interested in developing trade connections with South America, it avoided any firm commitment regarding legal recognition of the revolted colonies. In this sense Pahlen's mission filled the role of a preliminary reconnoitering; thus it is not surprising that Adams, in a conversation with Rumiantsev in February 1812, pointed out the advantageous situation of the minister in Rio de Janeiro "for observation not only in regard to that country itself, but to the scenes which were passing in the other parts of South America, particularly the Spanish provinces."[120]

At the time of Pahlen's transfer to Brazil, A. Ia. Dashkov was appointed to fill the post of minister to Washington vacated by the ukase of 16/28 July 1811, signed by Alexander I and Rumiantsev. A college assessor, Sverchkov, was appointed adviser to the mission.[121] On 20 July/1 August the Tsar signed Dashkov's accreditation papers, which were handed by the minister to President Madison, following the usual official procedure, on 3/15 November 1811.[122] Pahlen had been granted a farewell audience the day before,[123] but he did not leave for his destination until the following year, 1812. Not long before his departure he completed the writing of his extensive *Memoir* in which he summarized his American observations.[124]

The series of transfers among the staff of Russian representatives in America was completed by the appointment of N. Ia. Kozlov to the post of consul-general in Philadelphia on 5/17 August 1811.[125] At the same time Pavel Svin'in was appointed to the post of secretary to the consul-general in Philadelphia. On August 12/24, 1811, Rumiantsev signed detailed instructions for the new consul on behalf of the College for Foreign Affairs.[126] Kozlov was instructed to follow previously defined lines in his activities and to continue Russia's policy toward the United States, which "consisted especially in securing and furthering as much as possible direct trade connections between the two countries" (2).

The instructions obviously indicated Russia's desire to establish commercial contacts with those new states of South America which opened their ports for foreign trade. It was Kozlov's duty not to neglect any means in his power "to make Russia avail herself of any advantages this event [the political change in South America] might offer." With this in view, he was instructed to establish liaison with any inhabitants of the new states who might come to Philadelphia on business, informing them of the advantages of commerce with Russia, the protection they would encounter there, and the political interest of friendship with a power "of such great might" (3). Kozlov was specifically instructed to collect precise and detailed information on the new states of South America, and to try to procure their regulations for foreign and domestic trade published "since their detachment from the mother country" (4).

Besides the usual consular functions, Rumiantsev instructed the consul to observe "the state and progress of science and of letters, of arts and of industry . . . . All such products noted for unusual merit and usefulness fall into the category of things about which you are expected to give an account to the imperial ministry. You will also transmit all written works on these matters published by the reputable press" (10). This paragraph, somewhat unusual for instructions from the College for Foreign Affairs, attested to the fact that Kozlov was supposed to perform functions of a scientific and cultural representative.

The appointment of consular agents in the principal ports of North America in 1810-11 was meant to facilitate the expansion of commerce with the United States (and, through them, with the countries of Latin America). Already in the summer of 1808, in connection with his first appointment, Dashkov had been given the right to appoint as agents in the principal ports of the United States, "some persons from among the American or foreign merchants commanding general respect" (10).[127] Consequently, in the spring of 1810, he appointed the Baltimore merchant John Hoskins as his consular agent in the state of Maryland.[128] On 9/21 September 1810 Rumiantsev informed Dashkov that the Emperor granted his request to accord the title of vice-consul to the agents Dashkov appointed in American ports.[129] Under conditions of considerable expansion of Russian-American commerce in 1810-11 and necessity to observe strictly the formalities imposed by the Continental Blockade, it seemed expedient to establish a consular network in the United States. This measure was recommended by the adviser of the Washington mission, P. Poletika, in his well-known *Memorandum* on Russian-American relations.[130]

The number of Russian consular agents in the United States grew rapidly during 1811. In accordance with Pahlen's request of 8 May, the government of the United States officially admitted, on 12 June, John Bogart as Russian vice-consul in New York. By the summer of 1812, there were Russian consular agents in such cities as Norfolk, Providence, Portland, Salem, Charleston, and New Orleans.[131]

Of special interest are documents concerning the appointment of the first Russian consular agent to the island of Cuba in February 1813. An active adherent of "directorial connection with the Hispanic colonies," Kozlov sent St. Petersburg on 20 February 1813, a special dispatch recommending the completion of relations with the Hispanic colonies.[132] The consul-general informed Rumiantsev in great detail about the practical steps he had undertaken, and in particular about his conversations with the Spanish minister, Luis Onís. "According to this minister and to all the inquiries I have been able to make," Kozlov wrote, "it appears that the best place for our commerce in the colonies is Havana on the island of Cuba," since "it is here that the repository is found of all the produce of other Hispanic possessions, with which at present direct exchange is not yet possible."

Kozlov further stated that "for various considerations" he deemed it necessary to appoint an agent to Havana and had selected a "native subject, merchant Antonio Lynch," who understood English, French, and Spanish and was very knowledgable in commercial affairs, and whom he provided "with a patent naming him *Russian commercial agent in the island of Cuba.''* He had also provided the consular agent with special instructions, consisting of eleven articles regulating his functions in detail.[133]

Kozlov assumed that when the appointment of a Russian commercial agent became known in Cuba, it would call the attention "of the local merchants to the advantages of direct relations with us. According to Mr. Lynch, the Havanians themselves will hasten to send their ships to us, and I am inclined to believe this since this agent proposes to apply his own capital toward this end.'' Touching upon the general prospects of commercial connections with Latin America, the Russian consul wrote:

> Our goods are already known in the Hispanic colonies. Up to this time they were supplied by the Americans, who continue to do so even now through Havana by means of neutral vessels. Our export trade with the island of Cuba will consist of the same articles that we used to sell to the Americans. Their prices for all sorts of ironware, cables, ropes, duck, lard, glassware, mirrors, are very advantageous; we shall derive the most profit from the sales of rough and fine linens. In return we should receive sugar, coffee, indigo, cochineal, dyes, quinine, sassafras, and all the other products of South America.

Judging by the documents studied, Kozlov's hope to establish regular trade relations with Spanish America was not fulfilled, and the appointment of the commercial agent to Cuba did not bring the expected result. Apparently Lynch considered it more expedient not to risk his capital in establishing connections with the distant Russian market but to pursue more customary and, most important, more reliable commerce with Great Britain. A year and a half later, on 10 November 1814, Kozlov wrote to St. Petersburg: "Antonio Lynch whom I have appointed as our agent in Havana informs me that, being compelled by his business to depart for England, he will be unable to continue rendering his services. I shall try to find another agent to take his place."[134]

Further research in the archives may uncover new details connected with the appointment and activity of the first Russian consular agent in Havana, but even those documents known at present are of great interest regarding the early connections between Russia and Latin America, Cuba in particular.

Concerning Russia's relations with the United States, this chapter demonstrates that they were developing quite favorably. St. Petersburg's reaction to the news of the reception accorded Dashkov and Pahlen in Washington was one of complete satisfaction. In a letter to Pahlen of 7/19 December 1810, Rumiantsev noted that the Emperor was quite satisfied by the beginning of their activity in Washington and hoped that the minister would continue to expend his efforts toward developing amicable relations with the United States.[135]

In the beginning of 1811, surveying Russia's international situation, the Tsar wrote:

> The United States of America, having given me ample proof of its great desire to cultivate good relations with Russia and to establish continuing contacts with her, last year sent a Minister Plenipotentiary to reside at my court.... These relations can with time be of great use to Russia in extending her commerce.[136]

The American government held approximately analogous views of its relations with Russia. These were expressed laconically on 5 November 1811 in the text of President Madison's annual message to Congress. Touching upon relations with Russia, the President observed briefly that they were developing "on the best footing of friendship."[137] Some time later, Secretary of State Monroe specifically asked John Quincy Adams to convey to the Emperor that it gave President Madison great satisfaction to express his appreciation of the amicable position of the Russian government toward the United States, and that he had a firm intention to further the development of such a connection between the two countries.[138]

Naturally, the Russian minister in Washington wanted United States official documents to give flattering appraisals of Russia's role in the international politics more often and in greater detail, but even he could not conceal his satisfaction when he read the text of the President's message to Congress of 4 November 1812. He wrote to Rumiantsev on 23 October/4 November that he was pleasantly surprised by the President's favorable mention of Russia, and suggested that some credit for this should be attributed to his perseverence in showing the same degree of interest in the prosperity of the United States.[139]

Such friendly assurances were expressed systematically in the course of regular diplomatic contacts in both St. Petersburg and Washington, especially during the course of encounters between Rumiantsev and Adams. But the word "friendship," used so often in that period to describe relations between Russia and the United States can hardly be considered absolutely accurate. Russian-American "friendship" was mainly a "union of convenience," and one cannot talk about any real sincerity in the relations of tsarist Russia and republican America.

However, this does not affect the importance of the rapprochement between the two countries which took place during those years. In the complex conditions on the eve of the Anglo-American War of 1812 and the strained relations with the Western European countries caused by the introduction of the Continental Blockade, Russia was probably the only power that offered quite extraordinary protection to American commerce and on whom Americans could count for support. While staying in St. Petersburg, Adams to some extent fulfilled the function of an American representative to the European continent at large, and from March to November of 1811, during one of the most crucial periods, he was the only minister plenipotentiary of the United States in Europe.

IX

RELATIONS IN THE NORTHWEST AND THE
AGREEMENT OF 20 APRIL 1812

One of the most important tasks awaiting Dashkov and Pahlen in the United States was laying the groundwork for a treaty regulating Russian-American relations in northwest America. It was assumed in St. Petersburg that once diplomatic relations had been established, it would not be too difficult to persuade the Washington cabinet to conclude a treaty which would forbid the illegal sales of weapons to the natives in Russian-American Company's possessions and would permit United States citizens to trade exclusively with the company.

Having arrived in Washington in the summer of 1809, Dashkov decided that before sending an official notification to the Department of State, he would make preliminary inquiries into all "adjacent circumstances" such as: "the general circumstances and commerce of our Russian-American settlements; the government's attitude toward the kind of trade Americans engage in, in that territory; their rights with respect to foreign trade, and the rights of executive authorities over that trade; the conditions under which customs release ships."[1]

As one can see from the dispatches to Rumiantsev of 11 August and 15 November 1809,[2] Dashkov soon discovered that the task he had set for himself did not offer an easy solution. American merchants considered the sales of firearms to the local inhabitants a thoroughly legal enterprise and did not have the least desire to accept any restrictions. "The freedom of commerce of the United States," the consul-general informed St. Petersburg, "is almost unlimited . . . . The Americans load their ships with forbidden military goods, just as if they were any other kind, and announce their destination as they wish." The more Dashkov became

255

acquainted with the "adjacent circumstances," the more apparent were the difficulties of fulfilling his delicate mission. "It is very doubtful," he wrote in the same dispatch to Rumiantsev in November 1809, "that the government here would agree to make Americans deal with our trading station only."

The complexity of Dashkov's task was increased by the vagueness of his instructions on the subject of the borders of Russian possessions in America and on the character of the company's relations with local inhabitants. In his dispatch of 11 August 1809, Dashkov had already expressed an opinion that "the best way to prevent the Americans from trading in military contraband with the savages on the northwest shores of America would be to provide an article in the first convention with the United States, according to which both parties would forbid their subjects to sell or deliver the illegal military goods to the enemy of one of them"—and then to state that "Russian-American settlements are at war against the savage peoples surrounding them." Later, upon reflection, and "with some political examples in mind," Dashkov decided that in his negotiations with the government of the United States he would refer to all local inhabitants "near" Russian settlements, "dwelling on the northwest shores of America and on the islands, as being *under the power of Russian Empire*, and to their attacks . . . as *rebellious*."

Keeping these considerations in mind, the cautious consul finally ventured, on January 4, 1810, to send his first official note to Secretary of State Robert Smith, together with copies of letters exchanged by Rumiantsev and Harris in May 1808.[3] At the end of the note Dashkov wrote that, if the President found the idea of an agreement proposed by the Russian government a suitable means "for removing all further obstacles and strengthening the chains of friendship and mutual understanding existing between the two nations," he could officially inform the Government of the United States that he had been given the "necessary authority for opening these negotiations."[4]

It soon became clear that Dashkov's "authority" was insufficient. In the course of negotiations, the American side immediately pointed out the necessity of defining precisely the southern border of Russian possessions. But this was just the question Dashkov was obliged to take pains to avoid, according to the instructions given to him by the main office of the Russian-American Company. The Americans, too, proved not overly frank. It was not by chance that as soon as Dashkov "turned the conversation to Captain Lewis' expedition on the Columbia River," President Madison immediately became "exceptionally reserved."[5] Trying to persuade the government of the United States to be more flexible, Dashkov emphasized Russia's friendly attitude toward the United States. He repeatedly developed this idea in letters to the Secretary of State and in his talks with American congressmen. "I considered it my duty to impress on them," he wrote Rumiantsev on 25 March 1810, "that Russia is the only sincere supporter the United States would be able to find on the old continent in its early existence."[6]

As one can see from notations of conversations between Dashkov and Smith attached to the dispatch, these arguments did not produce the hoped-for impression on the Secretary of State. Smith continued to refer to the fact that the export of military contraband was permitted in the United States in the same way as the export of any other goods; and, even were it forbidden, it would be difficult to force American citizens to observe the restriction. The Secretary of State also expressed serious doubts that the Senate would approve such a measure, even if proposed by the executive branch.[7] "Having learned that I am not authorized to define the southern border of our possessions to serve as a demarcation line for the American vessels trading there," Dashkov wrote, "Mr. President finds it difficult to introduce a definite law forbidding the contraband trade."[8]

In its final version, the position of the United States Government on this question was expressed by Robert Smith in an official letter of 5 May 1810. Pointing out that "the President will have great satisfaction in any equitable arrangement," Smith at the same time stressed that, since Dashkov was not authorized "to fix a precise line of demarcation, no definitive adjustment could therefore be possibly made." In case this obstacle were removed, new complications of a delicate nature would arise. "If the Indians be under the Russian jurisdiction, the United States are only bound to leave their citizens to the penalties operating within the territorial limits. If the Indians are to be considered as Independent Tribes inhabiting an independent territory, Russia cannot of right prohibit other nations from trading with them, unless it be in contraband of war during a state of war, in which case she may enforce the prohibition on the high seas. If the Indians should fall under the character of rebels or insurgents against Russian authority the same rule may be applicable." According to Smith, the agreement was further complicated by the fact that the United States did not recognize similar pretensions of Spain in regard to the territories south of the Russian possessions. In summing up the Secretary of State pointed out that "such a measure is not within the authority of the Executive and could not well be formally proposed to the Legislature without the usual basis of mutual stipulations."[9]

On the same day official instructions for prospective negotiations were sent to Adams in St. Petersburg, with a special mention that it was necessary to establish the Russian border in such a way that "the limit should be as little advanced southwardly as may be."[10]

The unwillingness of Madison's government to conclude the agreement proposed by Dashkov can be understood in the light of the general position of the United States with respect to the American Northwest and the interests of American merchants there. Toward the beginning of the second decade of the nineteenth century, it became evident that the United States was becoming a new and dangerous competitor of the old colonial rivals in northwest America: Spain, Russia, and England. At first, the rights of the United States on the northwestern seaboard did not appear impressive: early information about the territory's wealth were based on the testimony of Ledyard, a member of Cook's expedition; on Captain Robert Gray's discovery, in May 1792, of the mouth of the Columbia River, so named after Gray's ship *Columbia*; and on the ensuing sailings of Boston shipowners engaged in commercial activities on the shores of Russian and Spanish possessions.

According to its initiators, with Thomas Jefferson first among them, the Lewis and Clark Expedition, undertaken in 1804-1806 with scientific and commercial aims, was supposed to supply the United States with some new, albeit rather belated, arguments for justifying their pretensions to the Columbia River Basin. At that time the need of the United States to possess an outlet on the Pacific coast seemed vital for the development of trade contacts with Asiatic countries. As trade with Asia expanded, "the road to India" over the continent was seen as one of the main arguments for obtaining an outlet on the shores of the "Southern Sea" (as the Pacific at that time was called in the United States).[11]

Northwest America had already begun to attract the attention of the big merchants and fur traders from such cities as Boston and New York. Foremost among them was John Jacob Astor, founder of that dynasty of millionaires, who became, as one of his biographers put it, "an apostle of the Empire." Commerce in tea and furs became one of the main sources of his enormous fortune. On 6 April 1808, the creation of the American Fur Company, with capital of one million dollars, belonging completely to John Jacob Astor, was announced in New York. On 22 June 1810, Astor organized its first West coast branch, the "Pacific Fur Company" with capital of $200,000, half of which was in his hands.[12] As Astor conceived it, the company's sphere of activity had to embrace the gigantic area of the American continent along the Great Lakes and the Mississippi River up to

St. Louis, west along the Missouri River toward the Rockies, and, finally, down the Columbia River all the way to the Pacific coast. In 1811 a fort and a trading station were built at the mouth of the Columbia River, and named Astoria in his honor.[13]

Extensive plans were connected with the establishment of this fort. It is interesting to note that Thomas Jefferson saw Astoria as "the germ of a great, free, and independent empire on the other side of the American continent." In Astor's more practical view, the fort was to serve as a place to store goods, and would provide an opportunity for the development of cross-continental trade to the basin of the Columbia River, and further to Canton and back.[14]

In discussing the complete ineffectiveness of official representations on the subject of the illegal arms trade by American citizens on the northwest seaboard, Pahlen noted that since "many influential persons in the Eastern states," not well-disposed toward the present administration, are involved in these operations, the government is reluctant to irritate them. "The information I have received on this subject," the minister informed Rumiantsev in July 1810, "convinces me more and more that the Government of the United States has neither the desire nor the power to put an end to this illegal trade."[15]

In Pahlen's opinion, this contraband trade in firearms was enhanced by the conditions under which expeditions to the Northwest were undertaken. The ships' captain and crew did not receive any salary, but were allotted a certain percentage of the profits. Therefore, it was to their interest to sell any goods, including war contraband, which might increase their incomes.[16] Taking these circumstances into consideration, both Pahlen and Dashkov thought their "desired aim" could be reached more effectively "without appealing for the good offices of the United States." "Some time ago," Pahlen wrote, "an American Fur Company received a patent from the local government to establish its enterprise at the mouth of the Columbia River; although its operations have not yet started, this company proposed to implement effectively the aims of our Court, without interference from the United States government."[17]

The initial contacts with the American Fur Company were established by Dashkov, who wrote to Rumiantsev on 15 November 1809 that he had begun negotiations "between the main office of the Russian-American settlements and a certain merchant from New York who is already familiar with this trade." "By such means," the consul concluded, "I am in hopes of reaching the desired object . . . rather than by the orders of the government here, even though these orders might be favorable to us."[18]

Indeed, even though the negotiations with the American government from January to May 1810 did not bring any practical results, the contacts with Astor's company were developing rather successfully. Astor himself was extremely interested in establishing firm business connections with the Russian-American Company and hoped in this way to weaken the position of his competitors, the Northwest Company and the Hudson Bay Company of Canada. With this in mind, he offered Pahlen an extensive "project of agreement between the Russian-American Company and American Fur Company for the purpose of excluding all outsiders from commerce and preventing the import of firearms for the local population." This project was sent to St. Petersburg as a supplement to the dispatch of 9/21 July 1810.[19]

Astor's project stipulated a series of measures on both the American and the Russian sides, in particular the establishment of a trading station on the Columbia River, which would function in the area between 44° and 55° North without interfering with Russian trade or crossing Russia's borders. Both companies were to be bound not to supply firearms to the local population in their respective regions. Russian settlements were to buy necessary goods only from the American Fur Company and were not to deal with individual private traders. The American company also offered its services for the sales of furs in Canton. Astor proposed a special stipulation for importing to Russia free of duty, "up to two thousand skins of black bear, badger, and polecat" annually. Both sides were to offer each other all possible mutual aid and, above all, cooperation in the matter of "removing outsiders from the commercial operations." In Astor's opinion the agreement would result in a dual achievement: "to engage in profitable trade and to deprive the local population of means to acquire firearms and military equipment."[20] In two or three years, private traders, having suffered losses, would be forced "to leave the northwest coast of America which would cease to offer profits for their speculations."[21]

After forwarding Astor's project to St. Petersburg, Pahlen undertook a trip to New York, whence he sent to Rumiantsev on 1/13 August 1810 a detailed dispatch describing the activity of the Northwest Company in Canada and citing the advantages of cooperation with the American Fur Company.

Certain differences in the activity of the English and the Americans in the Northwest should be noted. While American merchants operated primarily from the sea, the commerce of the British took place largely from the land. According to Pahlen's data, the number of employees of the mighty Northwest Company reached three thousand and its sphere of influence extended to the north from Lake Superior.[22] The "Canadian Northwest Company," the minister noted, "already has a station on the northernmost tributary of the Columbia River, and hopes to reach the coast." The agreement with Astor's company, in Pahlen's opinion, could prevent the appearance of "these undesirable neighbors" near Russian settlements. The American Fur Company, operating from the sea, had certain advantages, since its competitors had to traverse around six thousand miles overland (sailing over the Pacific Ocean was forbidden because of the privileges awarded the East Indies Company). "The combined efforts of the Russians and the Americans," Pahlen wrote, "would unconditionally remove from the seaboard the Northwest Company, as well as the American adventurers about whom there are so many complaints in our settlements."[23]

Astor threw himself into the activity with characteristic energy and range. A maritime expedition set out for the mouth of the Columbia River on the ship *Touquin* on 8 September 1810. An overland expedition headed by Wilson P. Hunt and Donald MacKenzie was equipped at almost the same time. Both of Astor's groups employed quite a few Englishmen, who previously had worked for the Northwest Company.[24]

Astor appointed A. B. Bentzon as a representative for the negotiations with the Russian-American Company.[25] This former adviser to the Danish king and to the governor of the island of Santa Cruz in the West Indies, who married Astor's daughter Magdalena in 1807, was considered a suitable choice for worldly St. Petersburg. On 18/30 September, Pahlen supplied him with a special passport and informed Rumiantsev of his mission in an appropriate procedure.[26]

Meanwhile, in St. Petersburg, the question of illegal trade in northwest America had been the subject of discussion between Adams and Rumiantsev ever since the late summer of 1810. As an additional argument for the conclusion of an agreement, the Russian Chancellor pointed to the advantages for the Americans of the intermediary trade between the Russian-American Company and Canton. However, this question did not greatly interest Adams, and the Minister tried to clarify through Rumiantsev how far south on the continent of America the Russian possessions extended. But this was a question to which Rumiantsev could not provide a satisfactory answer. In the course of further discussion, the Chancellor promised to report Adams' observations to the Emperor, adding "that it was an object concerning which they had no great solicitude." In Rumiantsev's opinion it was advisable to defer the discussion of boundaries to some future time.[27]

The position of the United States was stated differently in February 1811 in instructions given to Adams by Robert Smith on the occasion of the negotiating of a general commercial treaty with Russia. In particular, in the ninth article of the Headings of the proposed treaty provision was made that the United States would have most-favored-nation treatment in trade with the natives within the boundaries of Russian possessions (they were referred to as the Indians "who may be under the control of the Russian government"). With regard to independent tribes which might engage in war with Russia, it was forbidden to sell them firearms and military equipment. In general, until the final demarcation of the borders of America's northwest seaboard, commerce was expected to be conducted on a "mutually liberal footing."[28]

In spite of the friendly relations between Rumiantsev and Adams, the question of concluding either a special agreement about Northwest America or a general trade agreement between the two countries never was seriously discussed. After having exchanged preliminary ideas in the summer of 1811, both sides agreed that because of the tense international situation—particularly the threat of an Anglo-American war—it was not expedient to engage in commercial negotiations.

Neither Rumiantsev nor Adams wanted to jeopardize relations by discussing territorial boundaries in the American Northwest, and each hoped to be able to reach a more advantageous solution in the future. One cannot help but comment that the plans of the modest Puritan respecting future territorial borders of the United States would have amazed even the most zealous expansionist. For example, in a letter to his mother on 30 June 1811, the minister spoke of the United States as of "a nation coextensive with the North American continent, destined by God and nature to be the most populous and most powerful people ever combined under one social compact."[29] No less frankly in a letter to his father two months later he formulated the idea of United States sovereignty over the whole American continent. "The whole continent of North America appears to be destined by Divine Providence to be peopled by one *nation*, speaking one language, professing one general system of religious and political principles, and accustomed to one general tenor of social usages and customs."[30]

Naturally, Adams did not express such ideas in conversations with the Russian Chancellor, for his overall views of the "great future" predestined for the United States would hardly have been conducive to ironing out conflicts in Northwest America. It was more expedient to leave the delicate subject of natural rights and the designs of Divine Providence for the future.

Negotiations between the directors of the Russian-American Company and Astor's representative were more successful. Upon his arrival in St. Petersburg late in the summer of 1811, Bentzon immediately submitted the project for an agreement for perusal by the headquarters of the Russian-American Company, together with a note in which he argued that the conditions proposed by Astor would be advantageous for the Russians.

M. M. Buldakov, chief director of the Russian-American Company, made a series of comments on the margin of the American project, marked 26 August/7 September 1811.[31] In the main his objections concerned two questions: territorial demarcation on the Northwest and requests by Astor's company to permit the import of American furs to Russia. For the sake of avoiding an argument, Buldakov proposed to refrain from discussing the question of boundaries on the grounds that this question fell within the competence of the two governments and that the American Fur Company was not invested with the appropriate authority. The chief director obviously was unwilling to accept Astor's proposal that the Russian-American Company's sphere of activity be limited in the south by the 55th parallel. He proposed that the southern border of Russia's possessions, temporarily at least, be located south of the islands of Kodiak and Sitka, citing for this purpose the exploration of the mouth of the Columbia River undertaken on the initiative of Baranov, and the project of establishing a new Russian settlement in California. In respect to the territory between 44° and 55°, which, according to Astor's project, was to belong to the Americans, Buldakov proposed joint fur trapping by both companies. Regarding Astor's proposal that he act as an intermediary for the sales of Russian furs to the Chinese market in Canton, Buldakov repeated the company's early request, "soliciting permission for the Russians to travel to Canton." He also asked that a Russian military ship be sent to insure the safety of the company's settlements.

The main office of the Russian-American Company expressed its ideas on the subject of the agreement with Astor in a letter to Rumiantsev of 26 September/8 October 1811.[32] While approving in principle the idea of an agreement between the two companies, the corporation presented Rumiantsev with detailed objections to the territorial demarcation in Northwest America and the granting to the United States of the right to import furs to Russia. The corporation underlined that "the precise definition of borders in the northwest part of America is indeed the business not of both companies, but of both governments."

The Russian-American Company agreed not to trespass in "those places where the abovementioned fur company has established, or will establish, settlements permitted by those native inhabitants to whom the territory belongs." In turn it insisted that "the same right" should be observed by the American side, "in respect to the areas already occupied by the Russian-American Company, described by it, or explored by it, or about to be occupied by it; by this last to be understood that situation when there is no previous European settlement, or no pact binding it to some nation, or, if there is a pact by some nation yielding the territory to us, or, if it were given to us by the native inhabitants themselves." It was further pointed out that "in equal measure the permission to bring furs to Russia does not depend on the will and regulations of the Russian-American Company but is a matter for the government, to be judged in conjunction with the usefulness and profit for the national industry." Headquarters noted at the same time that Astor's company "can bring furs into one local port only and give them on commission to the Russian-American Company exclusively or hand them over to the company in America proper."

In regard to the other articles of the American project of agreement the corporation assumed in principle that there would be no obstacles to accepting them, though it stipulated some reservations. Business transactions with the Americans were to be based primarily on the concept of mutual profit. The Main Office considered it especially advantageous to obtain a pledge that firearms and military weapons would not be sold to the local inhabitants, "since Russians generally do not sell to American savages anywhere firearms or other weapons, gunpowder, or lead, but all these lethal articles are brought by citizens of the North American states."

After Rumiantsev relayed these remarks to Alexander I, the Main Office received "imperial consent" to start negotiations with Bentzon and conclude a "special mutual pact," corresponding with the company's own interests but with a proviso that its conditions were to be submitted to the government beforehand. "The following articles should be excluded from these negotiations," Rumiantsev wrote in October 1811, "article 1, on the definition of the borders between the American Fur Company and the Russian-American Company, as a matter pertaining to the governments of both countries, and any article regarding permission to bring furs into Russia by the American company, this permission also being a matter for the governmental decision."[33] In the course of further negotiations all the basic conditions of the agreement were quite easily resolved, with the exception of the question of the duty-free import of furs by Astor's company. On October 15/27, 1811, the Main Office of the Russian-American Company presented the plan of an agreement for Rumiantsev's perusal.

Since it made no mention of permission to import furs by American citizens, Bentzon categorically refused to sign this version. John Jacob Astor considered permission to import furs to Russia as one of the basic means for realizing his whole plan of cooperation with the Russian-American Company. Informing Rumiantsev on 14/26 October 1811, that agreement had been reached on all points except that of the fur imports, Bentzon resolutely insisted on obtaining permission for the American Fur Company to bring its furs to Russia; he argued that it would be advantageous not only for the Americans but for the Russians themselves.[34]

The Main Office of the Russian-American Company took another view of the matter. On 19/31 October it presented Rumiantsev with "a proposal of a reply to Mr. Bentzon's letter," signed by Buldakov.[35] It noted that the main purpose of Bentzon's visit to St. Petersburg "consists not in concluding an agreement . . . of mutual connections between the two companies," but in arranging for a duty-free import of bear and raccoon and other furs, as the only advantage for which that fur company is ready to offer its services." The corporation estimated that the Americans wanted to sell to Russia, "to her disadvantage," two thousand bearskins costing about 100,000 rubles, and also raccoons and other furs worth approximately the same amount. But "our Siberia," Buldakov pointed out, "is wealthy in furs, and Russian fur trappers should receive a legal profit from them." He found the compensation promised by Bentzon in the sum of 30,000 piasters in silver "quite incommensurate with the abovementioned fur imports, so that balance on the Russian side will be lost."

The further apprehension was expressed that a sizable amount of furs might be brought to Russia by Americans clandestinely. In Buldakov's opinion, the Canadians might follow this example. "It also looks suspicious," he wrote, "that this company does not wish to entrust its imported fur goods to the commission of our company, while it undertakes to take our goods on commission for sale in Canton."

Not counting on the possibility or advantageousness of any agreement reached with Bentzon, the corporation again complained about the actions of "seamen of the North American states" in a dispatch to Alexander I on 18/30 December 1811.[36] In the opinion of the company's directors, it was impossible to prevent contraband sales of firearms, "except by complete intimidation of North American seamen, who do not listen to the reprimands repeatedly made by Baranov, because of the freedom of their constitution and their right to sail and trade wherever they wish and are able to."

The dispatch again emphasized that the main purpose of the "fur company at the Columbia River, newly established by the New York merchants," and its representative, A. Bentzon, "consists only in obtaining permission to bring here fur goods acquired by them, which purpose is not without harm for Russian commerce and fur trade, since our vast and abundant Siberia and our fur-trapping in America can supply our needs quite sufficiently." In conclusion, the Main Office expressed the hope that the Tsar would not permit "further hampering of Russian industry by private American traders and the abovementioned company, which, having settled along the Columbia River and continuing, together with its other unrestrained cocitizens, to barter firearms with the natives, would destroy all chance of further fur trapping and completely upset the peacefulness of the Russian colonies."

The differences of opinion which arose in the course of negotiations between Bentzon and the directors of the Russian-American Company became a subject of a prolonged examination in the highest circles of the tsarist government. Rumiantsev found the corporation's arguments well founded, and two days later he repeated the basic contents of Buldakov's note in his report to Alexander I, "On the negotiations of the Directors of Russian-American Company with Mr. Bentzon."[37] However, the final decision was not taken right away. The Tsar wanted first to find out the opinion of the Minister of Finance, D. A. Gur'ev, on the possible consequences of granting Bentzon's requests. "His Majesty wished to instruct me," Rumiantsev wrote to Gur'ev, "that I inform your honor of all these circumstances . . . so that you would kindly let me know, for the purpose of reporting to His Majesty, what advantages or disadvantages might ensue from the granting of Mr. Bentzon's solicitation."[38] In its turn the dispatch of the corporation of 18/30 December 1811 became a subject of examination by the Minister of Internal Affairs, O. P. Kozodavlev.

Both high officials pointed out considerations which differed basically from the aims of the Russian-American Company. Gur'ev noted that the whole sum realized from the sales of American furs, 200,000 rubles, "is not significant enough to cause a disadvantageous effect in our trade balance, especially since Mr. Bentzon guarantees to buy and export Russian produce to the same sum, and on top of that to bring in 30,000 piasters." The Minister of Finance thought that "all these proposals, because of their very insignificance, do not constitute a sufficient reason to make exceptions to the general rules which forbid the import of said furs to Russia." To summarize, he wrote to Rumiantsev that, "if it was considered expedient to break the general rules in favor of the American Fur Company, then, in order to prevent larger imports than are now stipulated, the imports should be limited to a single port and it should be demanded that they be furnished with certificates from the Russian consul stating the quantity of fur."[39]

Kozodavlev also made some interesting remarks on the subject of the Russian-American Company's hopes that the tsarist government would defend the company's interests, basing his views on general considerations of governmental policies.[40] "I think," the Minister of Internal Affairs wrote, "that any means of discouraging North American encroachments utilizing force or arms, even though insured of success, are out of place precisely because of the conviction that it would be unjustifiable to change the state's regulations for one private company." Consequently, Kozodavlev proposed "that it would be best to make an effort through our representative in the United States to eliminate the American enterprises; and if all our solicitations and arguments proved ineffectual to persuade them of this, then Bentzon's proposal, especially with some limitations, would be the most plausible means."

It is difficult to deny the reasonableness of this letter: it would indeed have been unwarranted to quarrel with the United States just to defend the interests of the Russian-American Company. In the given circumstances, the agreement with Astor's company seemed the most logical way to eliminate the conflict which emerged in Northwest America. At the same time the author of the note obviously underestimated the unique situation of the "private" Russian-American Company in both domestic and foreign politics. In his opinion, the acceptance of Bentzon's proposals would result in "attaining a balance in the fur trade and preventing a monopoly if the Russian-American Company had in mind to establish one."

Such "naiveté" concerning the Russian-American Company is amazing. The company not only intended to establish a monopoly for the sale of American fur, but was striving to do so in all permissible and impermissible ways, even when it was an eighteenth-century private enterprise. Ever since 1799, when it was granted certain "privileges" by Paul I, the acceptance of this monopoly became a kind of government policy, a fact that Kozodavlev allowed himself to "forget" but one well-remembered by Rumiantsev. In itself, the question of the importing of American furs to Russia undoubtedly seemed petty and insignificant from the viewpoint of general state interests, but it touched on the company's rights and so undermined the principle on which its whole activity was based. This is why company directors resisted Bentzon's proposals so bitterly and finally achieved victory.

Neither Rumiantsev nor Alexander I had any intention of quarreling with the United States. Nor did they have ready means to prevent contraband trade on the northwest shores of America. Therefore, in his return letter to Bentzon, approved by the Tsar on 7/19 February 1812, Rumiantsev reiterated Alexander's complete satisfaction with Bentzon's role as mediator between the Columbia River Company and Russian-American Company, "on the subject of establishing business and amicable connections."[41] However, in regard to Bentzon's request that the American Company be allowed to export duty-free furs to Russia, the Chancellor displayed unexpected firmness on the grounds that such a measure would constitute a violation of the tariff "which His Majesty made it a rule not to change." Thus, Gur'ev's opinion was utilized in a rather peculiar way: the only thing borrowed from it was the apt reference to the famous tariff of 1810. Indeed, in the "Statement on Neutral Trade for 1811," the importing into Russia of all furs, with the exception of beaver, otter, and unborn animals subject to high duties, was forbidden.[42] Mention of the tariff was a natural pretext for denying Bentzon's request. "I can only suggest," Rumiantsev wrote in the conclusion of his letter, "that you negotiate with the Russian Company if it suits your mutual interests. Government interference is by no means necessary for this purpose."

Thus, the Russian-American Company succeeded in securing full support from the tsarist government. Rumiantsev did not agree with the opinion of his colleagues and definitively declined Bentzon's request that the American Fur Company be permitted to bring furs into Russia. The American representative was forced to capitulate and eventually to accept the agreement proposed to him back in October 1811.

On 20 April/2 May 1812, Bentzon appeared before the directors of the Russian-American Company and, showing his authorization of 21 January 1811, signed the agreement, adding a proviso that it had to be ratified by the American Fur Company in New York.[43] At the time, he noted that his signature did not obligate the Main Office in New York to ratify the agreement. The Russian signatories were Mikhail Buldakov, Venedikt Kramer, and Andrey Severin.

The Main Office forwarded the agreement to Rumiantsev on 30 April/12 May 1812. A copy was handed to Bentzon for ratification by the corporation of the American Fur Company, and another copy was sent to Baranov for his guidance after confirmation of the agreement by the

Americans.[44] On 20 December 1812, in New York, the president of the American Fur Company, John Jacob Astor, signed the text of the agreement; from that moment on, it was officially in effect.[45]

In accordance with the terms of the agreement, both companies were pledged not to trap either sea or land animals, and not to engage in any trade in areas where one of the parties had already established such activity (article 1). Both agreed not to sell the indigenous Indians any weapons or gunpowder, lead, bullets, or the like in any of the areas occupied by either company or to be occupied by either in the future (article 2). Astor's company was to transport to the Russian colonies in the company's vessels all provisions and staples ordered by the governor of the colonies, at prices agreed upon by him and the American Fur Company. In turn, the Russian-American Company agreed to purchase all such goods exclusively from the American Fur Company (article 3). Astor took upon himself the obligation to transport Russian fur goods to Canton in his vessels, remuneration for such services to be individually determined by the agreement with the governor of the colonies (article 5). Both companies were pledged to act as one whenever outsiders ventured to take advantage of the territories occupied at present or to be occupied in the future by either of the companies, so as to remove them, and in general agreed to extend mutual aid when needed (article 4). The duration of the agreement was to be four years, subject to renewal for the same length of time at the expiration of the term unless unforeseen circumstances required change.

The ratification of this 1812 agreement coincided with the years of the greatest flourishing of the business contacts of Russian settlements in America with the traders from the United States, particularly with Astor's company. Astor's first ship, the *Enterprise*, sailed from New York in November 1809, under the command of John Ebbets, with a cargo of produce for the Russian colonies in America.[46] In his letter to Baranov, Dashkov recommended Astor as the most active New York merchant, who "wishes to enter into an agreement with you, of at least three years' duration, to be a supplier of the staples needed by our colony," and "proposes the use of his vessels for transporting your goods to Canton." The Russian consul-general also informed Baranov that Astor intended to form "a colony on the northern shores of the Columbia River, near its mouth."[47] Astor himself stated in a letter to Baranov that he was giving Ebbets authority to negotiate the furnishing of Russian America with goods to the extent of one, two, or three cargoes of ships from 250 to 350 tons each."[48]

Although the cost of the goods brought in the *Enterprise* in the summer of 1810 exceeded local prices by almost 50 percent, Baranov as a start bought from Ebbets 54,000 rubles (27,000 piasters) worth of goods, which he paid for in furs. The governor of Russian America was too cautious to rush into a long-term agreement with Astor's company, "but made a list of staples at certain prices at which the cargoes of one or two ships would be acceptable."[49]

At the same time a contract was signed with Ebbets for the sale of a large supply of Russian furs in Canton and the purchase of Chinese goods needed by the colonies, trusting to the honesty of the American captain, "through the special respect of and confidence in the esteemed Mr. Astor." The goods shipped with Ebbets included about 3,000 sea beavers, 6,220 seals, furs of otters, foxes, polar foxes, and sables, and over 100 poods of whale whiskers and 17 poods of walrus tusks, with a total value of 145,611 rubles. According to the agreement, Ebbets was supposed to receive a 5 percent commission for goods bought and sold, and 36,000 rubles for transporting them.[50]

The goods received from Baranov were sold in Canton for 148,043 rubles, in other words, profitably: beaver skins went for 43 rubles (21.5 piasters), seals for 2 rubles, otters for 8, and so on. Ebbets returned to Sitka in May 1811 with a rich cargo of Chinese goods, including "100 boxes (?) of sugar candy, 1,000 pikol (1 pikol equaled 148 Russian pounds) of millet, 8,000 pieces of denim, 520 boxes of tea, 100 boxes of tea ware and 14 boxes of tableware, 1,200 pieces of various silk materials, and a goodly number of various small items, all in all to the sum of 64,000 piasters" or 150,000 rubles in local currency. Baranov was "quite pleased" with the transaction and in addition bought from Ebbets 35,000 piasters (70,000 rubles) worth of English goods; he paid for them in furs, with which the American set out again for Canton.[51]

In the autumn of 1811, after learning about Ebbets' successful transactions and receiving a list of goods needed by the Russian colonists, Astor sent to the Northwest another ship, the *Beaver,* under the command of Cornelius Soule. (This ship first brought equipment and people to Fort Astoria, and afterward, having taken Wilson Hunt on board in August 1812, proceeded to the island of Sitka.) The *Beaver* carried a sizable cargo of various goods, but, because prices compared unfavorably with those stipulated beforehand, Baranov bought only a part of it for 124,000 rubles, payment being made in furs.[52]

Some significant commercial contracts were concluded with other American merchants. In the 1/13 February 1812 report of the Main Office of the Russian-American Company to the general assembly of shareholders it was stated that, since 1808 Baranov had exchanged furs with

Boston merchants for "staples of livelihood and various needs of the company" to the sum of 142,859 rubles.[53] From other sources we know that Baranov's commerce on Sitka amounted to 1,170,000 rubles, including the purchase of five ships: *Iunona* (Juno), *Myrtle* (Kodiak), *Lydia* (Ilmen'), *Atahualpa* (Bering), and *Amethyst*. In payment the Americans received the: "sea beavers of various sorts, 4,884; beaver tails, 43,845; river beavers, 9,694; seals, 362,730; otters, 864; and foxes, 235." Besides that, 94,587.5 piasters were remitted to the Main Office in St. Petersburg. Since Baranov valued a piaster as two rubles, "the company suffered considerable losses as a result of this remittance" because of the devaluation of the paper ruble in Russia.[54]

As well as buying ships from the Americans, Baranov began to build his own in Novo-Archangel. Under the guidance of an American named Lincoln in 1807-1809 three new ships of high quality were built: *Sitka, Otkrytie* (Discovery), and *Chirikov*. In addition, *Alexander I* and *Iunona* (Juno) were rebuilt on Sitka.[55]

As the result of successful commercial contacts with American merchants, not only did the shortage of "staples of livelihood" in Russian America disappear but considerable stocks were put away. According to the report of 25 April/7 May 1811, "the governor of the colonies, Baranov, had stored various staples of livelihood, bartered from Boston seamen and delivered via Okhotsk, in such abundance that they will be sufficient for all settlements for three or four years."[56]

At the same time, the joint trapping industry of Russians and Americans on the shores of California was developing successfully. Boston shippers systematically concluded contracts with Baranov, received considerable numbers of kayaks (fifty or sixty) manned by Aleuts under the direction of Russian trappers, and set out to trap sea otters, on expeditions usually lasting from ten to fourteen months. K. Khlebnikov and an American researcher, Adele Ogden, supply some interesting information about these expeditions.[57] The extent of joint trappings can be judged from this table, adapted from their material.[58]

Year	Ship	Captain	Number of kayaks	Number of sea otter skins received by the company
1809	*O'Cain*	Jonathan Winship	50	2,728
1810	*Albatross*	Nathan Winship	68	560
	Isabella	William Davis	48	2,488
1811	*Amethyst*	Thomas Meek	52	721
	Katherine	William Blanchard	50	758
1812	*Charon*	Isaac Whittemore	—	896

In the course of only a few years joint trappings brought the company's share of sea otters to 8,151 (Khlebnikov erroneously estimates the figure once as 6,149 and another time as 7,140), persuading both parties that such a venture was profitable.[59] One should keep in mind, however, that the data used by Khlebnikov does not appear comprehensive. The table I compiled does not mention the Boston ship *Mercury* under the command of George Washington Eayrs, but the manuscript section of the Lenin Library preserves contracts of this captain with Baranov, dated 25 May/6 June 1808, and 10/22 September 1809.[60] According to Ogden, Eayrs was one of the most enterprising and daring American merchants to engage in commercial activities on the west coast of North America.[61] The same book informs us that in late 1810 four Boston ships were engaged in trapping near the California coast under contracts with Baranov (*O'Cain, Isabella, Mercury,* and *Albatross*).[62]

Tikhmenev notes that joint trapping expeditions operating off the California coast in 1811, 1812, and 1813, under skippers Whittemore, Blanchard, and Meek, brought to the company 270,000 paper rubles.[63] Although the profits of these expeditions "were shared with foreigners," the advantage of joint ventures consisted in the fact that they took place outside of Russian colonies, where the number of sea otters was already greatly diminished because of predatory extermination. At the same time, American traders, who gained substantial profits from business contacts with the Russians, valued Baranov's favors and spoke of him with gratitude and praise. Long ago Samuel Eliot Morison pointed out that the "old Northwest fur trade" was "Boston's high-school of commerce"; a recent investigator rightly added that "Baranov was the head schoolmaster."[64]

The Anglo-American War of 1812 damaged business contacts between the Russian-American Company and United States traders. In spite of the efforts of Dashkov and Astor, direct voyages of American vessels to Russian possessions almost stopped, and the conditions of the agreement of 1812 essentially remained unfulfilled. It is true that in September 1813 Dashkov sent word from New York about the departure of the *Enterprise,* under the Russian flag, with a cargo of goods for the Russian colonies in America.[65] But it has not been possible to uncover any details of this expedition.

At the same time Astor's company lost several ships (one was shipwrecked near the Sandwich Islands, another was destroyed by natives in the Bay of Nootka), and after the arrival of the British warship *Raccoon* in November 1813, the English took possession of Fort Astoria, renaming it Fort George. (Shortly before this the fort was sold to the Canadian Northwest Company.)[66]

The Russian-American Company was anxious to limit insofar as possible Baranov's contacts with foreign traders; therefore it was not too interested in the practical implementation of the agreement with Astor. In the fall of 1815, when the Main Office of the Russian-American Company informed Dashkov of a proposed round-the-globe expedition from St. Petersburg with goods for Russian America, it pointed out that, since these goods together with those delivered earlier on the ship *Suvorov* would suffice for several years, "we do not need Mr. Astor sending goods for us here"—all the more so, since the 1812 agreement was about to expire.[67]

The Russian-American Company's complaints about the commercial activities of foreign competitors in the Russian possessions—especially Bostonians trading in firearms with the local population—became more frequent. In the Main Office's report to the general assembly of shareholders, 1/13 February 1812, it was pointed out that

> Mr. Baranov complains strongly about the increasing number of seamen, citizens of the North-American United States, who bring their own and other colonial goods here and barter them to the Indians for furskins which they then take to Canton . . . Above all he complains that those seamen barter to the Indians firearms and other weapons, gunpowder, bullets, and lead, and that the Indians, having learned the use of these weapons, prevent the free and safe trading of Russian trappers.[68]

In particular, the Russian-American Company was much displeased by the activity of Wilson Hunt, Astor's attorney, who came up with "most cunning and base harassments" in the course of joint trading ventures with Baranov in 1812. After Fort Astoria passed to the English, Hunt arrived at Sitka on the ship *Pedler* in 1814, "with unknown intentions." The purpose of his visit, in the opinion of the Russian-American Company, was "smuggling trade with the islanders." "Like his fellow countrymen," Hunt engaged in selling firearms to the natives; in 1816 he had an open conflict with Baranov.[69]

In headquarters' view, "harmful competition" also took place as the result of Baranov's payment for American goods in furs, especially sealskins. "Skipper Bennett," Tikhmenev noted, "took the furs he received as payment for his cargo of staples to sell in Okhotsk; in order to keep these furs from falling into the hands of outsiders, the company's office there was compelled to buy them up at prices vastly exceeding those Baranov got for them in Novo-Arkhangel."[70] Having learned about this loss, the corporation instructed Baranov to limit joint ventures with foreigners and to save the sealskins for trade with the Chinese in Kiakhta. This limited contact with foreigners still further, and although in 1816 as many as fifteen foreign ships docked, Baranov bought only a small quantity of provisions, refusing to have any commercial dealings with the majority of the skippers, especially since they would not accept the promisory notes of the corporation, and demanded payment in Spanish piasters at the old disadvantageous rate of exchange.[71]

In order to reduce the dependence of Russian settlements on the Bostonians, the Russian-American Company spent much time seeking new ways of getting "livelihood staples"; it was especially anxious to establish permanent trade connections with California. The advantages of trading with this region had been recognized ever since 1806, when Rezanov first came to California. Participants in joint Russian-American trapping expeditions also had reported on the riches of the region.

In 1808-9 the ships *Nikolai* and *Myrtle* were dispatched to survey the coast and engage in independent sea otter trapping. Sending the expedition that fall "to the American shores of New Albion in the company's vessels, the *Myrtle,* and the *Nikolai,*" Baranov instructed I. A. Kuskov "to survey and describe the whole coast from Defuk Strait to California and set it on the map."[72] On the whole, the Kuskov expedition was successful. Although the schooner *Nikolai* was shipwrecked, the second ship, under Kuskov's command, returned to Sitka in October 1809 with a rich cargo of sea beavers (2,350 skins). In the course of his expedition, Kuskov found some areas suitable for settlement in Rumiantsev Bay (Maly Bodego), but because of the shortage of building materials and the defection of several members of his crew, the building of a fort was postponed.[73]

A new expedition to the coast of California to obtain a "most detailed survey" of the region, undertaken by Kuskov in 1810 on the *Juno*, ended in failure. Well-armed Indians attacked the ship near the Queen Charlotte Islands, and the expedition was forced to return to Novo-Archangel.[74]

Concerning the preliminary survey of the region for a proposed settlement, the directors of the Russian-American Company wrote

that Baranov sent an expedition to the coast of New Albion in search of a better spot for settlement than Kodiak or Sitka, and this expedition, headed by adviser-in-commerce Kuskov, did find one, near the California port of San Francisco in the Bodego Bay. However, settlement is being postponed until future time and orders; our traders, passing from Bodego to the California port of San Francisco, have surreptitiously surveyed the local situation, and have been directly across from the Spanish fortress, but have not seen any military or trade vessels, and while doing secret trapping of sea animals in the very bay, encountered complete peace everywhere . . . they also encountered local savage people who wanted to attack our people, taking them for the Spaniards, but learning that they were not Spanish, let them travel freely, from which we conclude that they are not pleased with their possessors.[75]

In its search to find "the most convenient and advantageous place" for the new colony, the Russian-American Company hoped to acquire new "help in the trapping industry" and to surmount "the obstacles to supplying our present settlements with staples of livelihood."[76] That the Main Office had for some time tried to get the government's cooperation in establishing regular commercial contacts with Spanish possessions in America, and establishing a Russian colony in California. On 20 December 1809/1 January 1810 Buldakov, "on behalf of the whole Russian-American Company," made a second representation concerning trade with California.[77]

Although the Main Office failed to win either Madrid's official sanction or concrete help from the Russian government, it was clear from the Tsar's reply conveyed through Rumiantsev, that St. Petersburg would not object to the organizing of a Russian settlement in California by the company itself. "While His Majesty refuses, in this case, to establish an official settlement in Albion," Rumiantsev wrote on 1/13 December 1809, "he offers the Corporation freedom to form such on their own, and in any case will encourage them by imperial protection."[78]

Inspired by this vague promise of imperial protection, Baranov sent a new California expedition on the schooner *Chirikov,* departing 22 January/3 February 1811. In his instructions to Kuskov, the head of the expedition, the governor of the colonies called attention to the actions of Astor's company, as well as of individual American merchants and fur traders (Winship, Brown, and Eayrs), who were exploring the Columbia River region. Armed with Alexander I's permission, Baranov instructed Kuskov to found a redoubt in California, dig a moat around it, find the places for docking of the vessels, and so on. He was also supposed to clarify the attitude of Spanish authorities to the founding of a Russian settlement, to investigate the reasons for the attack on earlier expeditions (in 1808-9 and 1810), and to enter into negotiations with the commandant of San Francisco for receiving provisions. Besides building a fortress, Kuskov was instructed to lay the ground for agriculture and cattle-breeding, to study local customs, and to prepare a dictionary of the Indian language. Baranov pointed out the necessity of "getting acquainted with the people as well as possible, and befriending them as much as they could through a most peaceful and friendly appearance and manner, avoiding the least unpleasantness, . . . and above all, not permitting any rudeness . . . on the part of our employees."[79]

Originally the expedition engaged only in surveying the coast and trapping sea otters. Upon his return to Sitka in the summer of 1811, Kuskov brought back 1,160 beavers and oil from cachalots.[80] In November 1811 the *Chirikov* again set out for California, and this time Kuskov succeeded in settling in the area selected by him at 38°30' north, 123°15' west, not far from Bodego Bay and about fifty miles from San Francisco. During the winter of 1811/12 he became acquainted with local Indian chiefs, presented them with gifts, and negotiated the ceding of the territory necessary for Russian settlement. Having obtained the necessary materials and working force, in May 1812 Kuskov laid the foundation for a settlement to be called Fort Ross, on a height well protected from possible attacks.[81] "The construction of the house for the governor, the barracks, the storehouse, and storage buildings, the kitchens, shops, the bath house, the leatherworks, the windmill, the cattleyard, and other services was accomplished in 1814."[82]

While the company had little trouble in negotiating with the local Indians, playing on their hatred of the Spanish oppressors, establishing relations with the Spanish authorities proved much more difficult. Since the Spanish government had forbidden trade with foreigners, "because of the fanaticism of the clergy," given the new conditions resulting from the rebellion "throughout Mexico" and the "establishment of a republican order," the Main Office hoped to entice the inhabitants of California to establish commercial connections and to get from them "various grains," "live and slaughtered cattle," "lard, silk, and cotton cloth and other necessities for our colonies."[83] "Because of circumstances in Europe and Spain herself, it seems to us," the Russian-American Company's proclamation of 15/27 March 1810 pointed out, "that you are exempt from any restrictions to your having commercial connections with Russians, especially since they are mutually advantageous."[84]

This "proclamation" was handed to the commandant of San Vicente Fort, Manuel Ruis, early in 1812 by Bakadarov, Baranov's attorney on Eayrs' ship *Mercury*. In reply, the Spanish commandant wrote in the spring of 1812 that California inhabitants "are pleased to consider the Russians as friends," but that the viceroy in Mexico "does not wish to permit such free trade"; he recommended again that Baranov address himself to Madrid through the Russian tsar.[85]

Nothing resulted either from a new "proclamation" sent from St. Petersburg by the corporation on the ship *Suvorov* in the fall of 1812,[86] or from the appeal of the company's directors to Rumiantsev and the Spanish consul, Zea Bermúdez, in the spring of 1814.[87]

Kuskov's efforts proved more successful. In the beginning of 1813 he received verbal permission from the governor of Upper California, José Joaquin de Arrillago, to engage in mutual trade, providing the company's vessels did not enter the port of San Francisco before the receipt of the official consent of the Spanish government.[88] For some time trade with California was conducted without obstacles, on the basis of this preliminary agreement. During the summer of 1815 Kuskov, who visited San Francisco on the schooner *Chirikov*, realized some profitable deals, as did the commissioner of the company, John Eliott de Castro, who sailed on the brig *Il'men'*. Produce such as wheat, lard, and flour was exchanged with the Spaniards for various manufactured objects such as fabrics, ironware, and candles.[89] In August 1815 the *Suvorov,* under the command of Lieutenant Lazarev, arrived in California. A member of the crew, S. Ia Uukovsky, noted that in California "we supplemented our provisions with the usual provisions . . . we bought several bulls, each between eighteen and twenty poods in weight, for not more than two Spanish thalers each, and put up excellent provisions of corned beef; the wheat which we also bought from the monks was quite cheap too."[90]

New complications ensued, however, after the arrival in California of Governor Pablo Vicente de Solá. In fall 1815 the company commissioners were detained in San Francisco, and the Aleuts engaged in fur trapping were taken into captivity.[91] The Spanish authorities renewed their demands for the removal of the settlement of Ross. A prolonged, and in general fruitless, diplomatic correspondence ensued.

The company's intent in founding the fortress and town of Ross was to "forestall the Americans" and to become firmly established on the shores of wealthy California. In the end this attempt failed, and the Russian colony in California was abandoned in the early 1840's.[92] Questions dealing with territorial borderlines with the United States and with the contraband sales of firearms in the Russian possessions in America also remained unresolved. Their further history is directly related to the genesis of the Monroe Doctrine and the conclusion of the Russian-American convention of 5/17 April 1824.[93]

At the same time, the systematic business contacts with Boston merchants operating in Russian America resulted in an extensive positive experience of mutually advantageous trade connections and the organization of joint Russian-American trapping expeditions. Although the agreement concluded on 20 April/2 May 1812 did not result in practical advantages—because the Anglo-American War of 1812 was about to begin—it testified to the possibility that contradictions and suspicions could be overcome through direct negotiations between the interested parties.

Part Four

The War of 1812 and Tsarist Russia

The year 1812 brought many changes into the life of European nations and into world history as a whole. At the start of that year the Napoleonic Empire seemed at the peak of its power, and the idea that disaster was awaiting it could hardly occur to anyone.

For fifteen years, with utter disregard for the national interests of European states, Napoleon had carved and recarved the political map of Europe as he pleased, with a victorious bayonet and a clever diplomatic pen. Actually, after Austerlitz, Jena, and Wagram this did not require special skill: a simple order sufficed. On the eve of the War of 1812 Napoleon was ruler of a hundred and thirty French departments, and sovereign of seven vassal-kingdoms and thirty monarchs. "From the Pyrenees to the Oder, from the Sund to Messina Strait—all is France," Russian ambassador Kurakin reported from Paris.[1] Long past was the time when wars conducted by France had a just, national, and revolutionary character. "When Napoleon created the French Empire by enslaving a number of old, large, vital, national states of Europe, the nationalist French wars turned out to be imperialist ones, giving birth *in their turn*, to the nationalist-liberational wars *against* Napoleon's imperialism."[2] The young but greedy French bourgeoisie had complete dominion over Western Europe and aspired to spread its influence over the entire world.

Engaged in a mortal struggle with his long-time rival, England, Napoleon strove to bend to his will the last independent stronghold on the European continent, Russia. The crowned ruler of the continent of Europe said to his aide-de-camp, Count Narbonne: "Aujourd'hui, c'est d'une extrémité de l'Europe qu'il faut reprendre à revers l'Asie, pour atteindre l'Angleterre."[3] Napoleon thought that after the complete defeat of Russia and the capture of Moscow, one touch of the French sword would suffice "pour faire tomber dans toute l'Inde cet échafaudage de grandeur mercantile."

The first units of Napoleon's troops crossed to the right bank of the Neman the night of 11/23 June 1812, and the bulk of 640,000 troops of the Grande Armée followed. Nor surprisingly, Russian headquarters did not expect an invasion at that particular time, since reconnaissance had disclosed nothing suspicious. Alexander I received the news of the crossing on June 12/24 at a ball for the Lithuanian aristocracy held at the estate of L. L. Benningsen.

On the eve of the invasion Count Lauriston, the French ambassador in St. Petersburg, handed Russia's acting Minister of Foreign Affairs, A. N. Saltykov, an official note, which informed that amazed dignitary that "His Imperial and Royal Majesty [Napoleon was Emperor of France and King of Italy] considers himself to have been in a state of war with Russia" since the moment of Prince Kurakin's request for passports, that is, from the end of April or beginning of May 1812.[4] It is easy to understand Saltykov's confusion: the Tsar and almost all of Russia's responsible military and political leaders were absent from St. Petersburg at the time. Although Lauriston's note was immediately dispatched to Vilno by special courier, the Tsar did not receive it until June 13—when the invasion of the Grande Armée had already begun. Having learned that war had begun, Alexander I made a last attempt at pacification: he sent Napoleon via Minister of Police A. D. Balashov a personal letter proposing to consider all that had occurred as a simple misunderstanding.[5] It is unlikely that by that time he had any serious hopes of success. The war had become a fact.

Almost simultaneously, the conflict between the United States and England broke out on the other side of the Atlantic. In June 1812, the President of the United States, James Madison, sent a message to Congress, recommending an immediate declaration of war against Great Britain.[6] The President cited unceasing insults to the flag of the United States and impressment of American sailors, violation by British military ships of the tranquility of the coast and safety of commerce of the United States, the declaration of the pretended blockade, and orders-in-council which crassly violated the rights of neutral navigation.

Declaring war proved a rather simple, and even relatively swift, matter (considering the usual practice of the American Congress). In three days (on 4 June 1812), without any special discussion, the House of Representatives approved the declaration of the war, 79 to 49. The debate in the Senate took somewhat longer, and the resolution was accepted with a number of changes only on 17 June, by a vote of 19 to 13.[7] It was returned to the House of Representatives, and approved on 18 June. At three o'clock in the afternoon of the same day President Madison signed the act declaring war against England; simultaneously, Secretary of State James Monroe announced it to the British minister in Washington, Augustus J. Foster.[8]

X

THE WAR OF 1812 AND ITS EVALUATIONS BY RUSSIAN DIPLOMATS

The War of 1812 between England and the United States has been treated in dozens of long and short books, special articles, surveys, and notes; yet there still is no unanimous opinion, in either bourgeois or Marxist literature, on a number of cardinal points concerning the origin and character of the conflict. To use the expression of a Canadian Marxist critic, Stanley B. Ryerson, the War of 1812 proved a "tangled skein," not easy to untangle.[1]

The English bourgeoisie, which could not reconcile itself to the loss of its colonies in North America, pursued a stubborn policy of hostility toward the United States, striving to undermine that country's commerce and economics. President Madison's Message to Congress on 1 June 1812 rightly accused Great Britain of "a series of acts hostile to the United States as an independent and neutral country."

In condemning England's actions on the high seas, Karl Marx noted that she "continued to violate the maritime rights of America, which she herself admitted. This continued since 1806 and was stopped on 23 June 1812, after the United States declared war on England on 18 June 1812. Thus, for six years England refused not only to make amends for her open violation of the law: she refused to stop this violation."[2]

In this sense the War of 1812 was to a great degree the continuation of the revolutionary struggle of the United States for independence. But it by no means signifies that the two wars were the same. Although the term "second War of Independence" has been used in Western historiography, it never received wide acceptance, even in the United States, and the best-informed and authoritative authors did not use it at all. Nor was this term used by Karl Marx, who mentioned this war only in passing and did not discuss its basic character.[3] With a very rare exception,[4] the term is not encountered in Soviet literature either, lest it create a one-sided or even false idea of the origin and character of the events of 1812.

During the thirty to thirty-five years following the War of Independence of 1775-1783 great changes took place in international politics and in the internal affairs of the United States. If one seeks the causes of the conflict only in the policies of England, and particularly in her actions on the high seas, it would be impossible to understand why mercantile New England so resolutely opposed the war. Conversely, why were representatives of the South and West, little concerned with violations of maritime rights, the most belligerent of all? It is impossible to answer these questions without taking into account the expansionist plans of powerful groups in the United States. Touching upon the problem, William Z. Foster writes: "The Americans, who were already distinctly expansionist, saw in this war a golden opportunity to carry through one of the major projects they had in mind, namely the absorption of Canada."[5]

The most ardent champions of the break with England were the so-called "War Hawks": Clay, Calhoun, Porter, Johnson, Harper, Grundy, and others. This group, consisting primarily of Southerners and Western-ers, had been active in Congress since 1810, and was in full control on the eve of the War of 1812.[6] Henry Clay was elected Speaker of the House of Representatives; John C. Calhoun took the leading position in the Committee on Foreign Relations in the House of Representatives. The records of the United States Congress, and the personal papers of Clay, Calhoun, and others contain much evidence testifying to the expansionist plans of the War Hawks.[7] As early as 1810, in a speech in the Senate, Henry Clay argued at length the necessity of war with England and the ease with which Canada could be conquered.[8] Somewhat later the ardent congress-man declared his hope of seeing, "ere long, the *new* United States . . . embracing not only the old thirteen States, but the entire country east of the Mississippi, including East Florida, and some of the territories to the north of us also."[9]

The appetite of the War Hawks grew fast, and in the sessions of the Twelfth Congress, which opened in November 1811, more belligerent voices sounded out. "I shall never die contented," announced Richard M. Johnson, "until I see [Great Britain's] expulsion from North America, and her territories incorporated with the United States."[10] "To me sir, it ap-pears," confidently announced another bellicose member of the House of Representatives, Robert G. Harper, "that the Author of Nature has marked our limits in the south, by the Gulf of Mexico; and on the north, by the regions of eternal frost."[11]

In their insistence on the annexation of English Canada and Spanish Florida, enthusiastic representatives from the West and the South paid little attention to elementary logic. Richard Stanford, a schoolteacher from North Carolina, remarked in this connection: "But how, Mr. Speaker, are we going to protect commerce? By taking Canada? . . . How will the capture of Canada protect our commerce? It will be like a man who, for the purpose of securing a rice field, should go fence his neighbor's corn field."[12] To be precise, it should have been said that the United States intended to "fence" two fields at the same time: one in the north, the other in the south. Such "fencing" seemed to balance Southern and Northern interests and satisfied both major sections of the union. It resulted in a single block of Northern and Southern expansionists, who sought the so-called "Canada-Florida Deal"—a concept that some contemporary authors resolutely reject.[13] Naturally, this "deal" was never formulated officially, but circumstances placed Southern and Northern expansionists in the same camp.

The idea of preserving equilibrium by the simultaneous annexation of Florida and Canada was formulated frankly and expressively by Felix Grundy of Tennessee in a speech in the House of Representatives on 9 December 1811.[14] It is in this sense that his speech was interpreted, not only by later historians (Henry Adams and Julius Pratt) but by his audience in Congress, particularly the famous Southern orator, John Randolph.[15]

Randolph was extremely critical of the War Hawks and bitterly mocked his colleagues' intentions. Speaking in the House on 16 December 1811, the eloquent spokesman for Southern interests announced: "Sir, if you go to war it will not be for the protection of, or defence of your maritime rights . . . Agrarian cupidity, not maritime right urges the war . . . Ever since the report of the Committee on Foreign Relations came into the House, we have heard but one word—like the whippoorwill, but one eternal monotonous tone—Canada! Canada! Canada!"[16]

John Randolph was right in mocking the hypocrisy and dishonesty of War-Hawks' Arguments, but one should not forget the important role of conflicting commercial and shipping interests. Actually, the content of these contradictions in the years immediately preceding the War of 1812 began to change. "It is not the carrying trade, properly so called, about which this nation and Great Britain are at present contending," Grundy stated. "The true question in controversy is of a very different character; it involves the interest of the whole nation: it is the right of exporting the productions of our own soil and industry to foreign markets."[17] Grundy's statement is significant, because it demonstrates the desire of the United States in the period of serious economic difficulties to increase the export of its goods.

Mindful of the frontier mood, General Andrew Jackson in the spring of 1812 saw the conquest of British possessions in North America as a vindication of the United States right to free trade, especially the right to a market "for the productions of our soil, now perishing on our hands because the *mistress of the ocean* has forbid us to carry them to any foreign nation."[18] "Our cotton is reduced to seven cents, and our tobacco is nothing," Robert Wright of Maryland stated in Congress, connecting this state of affairs with the policies of England and France, which had almost entirely arrested the flow of American goods to European markets.[19]

Speaker of the House Clay formulated the question in its essence: "We were but yesterday contending for the indirect trade—the right to export to Europe the coffee and sugar of the West Indies. Today we are asserting our claim to the direct trade—the right to export our cotton, tobacco, and other domestic produce to market."[20]

As I see it, the War of 1812 resulted from two main causes. First was England's avid policy—her striving to undermine the commerce and economy of the United States, despotic actions on the high seas and violation of the elementary rights of neutral navigation. The second cause was expansionism of the ruling circles in the United States, with their desire to annex Canada and Florida and to push back the Indian tribes. The untangling of these various factors, differing in content and character, which brought about the War of 1812 does not yet constitute a complete understanding of the problem. It is necessary to define which of these two basic tendencies predominated in a given period. The explanation can be reached only after a thorough examination of the domestic and international situation of the United States and Great Britain, as well events of the war years.

It has already been stated that 1812 was the crucial year of Napoleon's wars in Europe. England, completely isolated for all practical purposes, was experiencing one of the most difficult periods of her history. In this sense one cannot help but agree with James Madison when, defending the actions of his government many years later, he stressed that the moment for declaring war was well chosen.[21] Obviously 1812 was an unsuitable moment for the realization of Great Britain's aggressive intents toward the United States. With no desire whatsoever to cease her tyrannical behavior on the seas, in one way or another England had to confront the realism of international events.

The Marquis of Wellesley, and after him Viscount Castlereagh (who became Great Britain's Minister for Foreign Affairs in February 1812 and kept this post until his death in 1822) repeated again and again hackneyed arguments justifying the despotic actions of the British navy by blaming Napoleon's policy and decrees.[22] The British cabinet insisted that the orders-in-council would be repealed only after France officially and unconditionally repealed her decrees with respect not only to the United States but also to all nations. Britain's position was stated in detail in Castlereagh's well-known instructions of April 10, 1812, to Foster, the British minister in Washington.[23] The implacable and aggressive attitude of England on this occasion has often been commented on in historical literature; yet, it should be noted that this position, on the eve of the War of 1812, was no harsher than in preceding years. On the contrary, it was marked by a certain leaning toward reconciliation: one of the instructions of April 10 even contained some basic concessions relative to the system of licenses.[24]

Special attention should be paid to Castlereagh's "private" letter to Foster on the same day. The Minister for Foreign Affairs instructed the minister to behave "with the utmost conciliation towards America," and not to provoke a rupture. "You will firmly adhere to the principles, on which this Government considers itself bound to act," Castlereagh instructed, "but you are to avoid pressing them upon America, in such a manner as might expose the negotiation to an abrupt termination." Striving to delay a break as long as possible, the British minister noted that with time "it will become more and more difficult for the American Government to embark that Country in a War with Great Britain."[25] Naturally, this was not a question of the British government's love of peace, but a calculated, tactical maneuver, resulting from awareness of the undesirability of embarking on a war in the summer of 1812.

Foster was unable to fulfill the complex mission entrusted to him, and he did not succeed in preventing the breakdown of British diplomacy. Besides, in May and early June of 1812 an unexpected event disturbed the activity of the British cabinet. The afternoon of May 11 a certain Bellingham entered the lobby of the House of Commons. An embittered maniac, armed with a pistol, he considered himself entitled to compensation for some losses suffered in Russia. For this reason he apparently intended to kill Lord Gower, former English ambassador in St. Petersburg. Chance kept Gower away, and Bellingham discharged his pistol into British Prime Minister Spencer Perceval, killing him.[26] A new government was formed by Lord Liverpool.

The irony of history was that just as Congress in Washington declared war on Great Britain, the hated orders-in-council were repealed in London. On June 16, 1812, two days before the official declaration of war, Lord Castlereagh officially announced in Parliament the intention of the British cabinet to cancel the orders-in-council relating to the United States, and at once sent Foster instructions to that effect.[27] By the time the British ambassador was paying his farewell call at the White House, on 23 June 1812, the ill-fated orders-in-council of 7 January 1807 and 26 April 1809,[28] limiting the entry of foreign mercantile vessels into the ports of France and her dependencies, had already been revoked. By this order of 23 June 1812 the British Royal Council permitted American ships to enter these ports after 1 August, on condition that the American government repeal its limitations relating to British commerce.[29]

There was no transatlantic cable in those days, and the decision of the British government did not reach the United States for a long time. (Foster did not receive the text of the instructions of June 17 until July 22, in Halifax, en route to England; instructions did not reach Washington until August 5.) There is no point in trying to guess what might have happened had modern means of communication been in existence at that time. But the war did not stop even after the news that the orders-in-council were repealed reached the United States.

The day after war was declared, Foster proposed that military actions be postponed until London learned about it. He offered to go to England himself with any proposal the American government might wish to make. Washington declined this offer. During his farewell visit, the minister again urged the suspension of hostilities "until further intelligence should be received from Great Britain," and inquired whether the repeal of orders-in-council would bring a cessation of hostilities. He was told that there was no such prospect, and that the repeal of the orders-in-council would have to be accompanied by a promise to begin negotiations on impressments.[30]

The disappointed minister was compelled to leave Washington without achieving any results. Nor did positive results ensue from negotiations between Castlereagh and the American chargé d'affaires, Jonathan Russell. The stumbling block was the American demand that the impressment of seamen be discontinued and that those already impressed be freed, which was rejected by the British.[31] On 30 September 1812, Admiral John Borlase Warren, acting on instructions of the British government, sent Secretary of State Monroe an official communication concerning the repeal of the orders-in-council and proposed the immediate cessation of hostilities between the two countries.[32] The United States declined this proposal, pointing to its demand for the discontinuance of impressments. While insisting on conditions which would secure a firm and lasting peace,[33] the United States actually did not want at that time to make any concessions for restoring peace with England, hoping for military successes and further favorable changes in the international situation. "Had the French Emperor not been broken down as he was, to a degree at variance with all human probability, and which no human sagacity could anticipate, can it be doubted that Great Britain would have been constrained by her own situation and the demands of her allies, to listen to our reasonable terms of reconciliation?" asked James Madison many years later.[34]

It is hardly necessary to point out that England's actions and unexpected "conciliation" were not dictated by any sincere desire for peace and cessation of piracy on the high seas. (The British stubbornly refused to halt impressment.) They were a tactical move, a diplomatic maneuver. The true character of the "peace-loving" British cabinet soon became obvious. Napoleon's defeat in Russia and the initial successes of British troops in America definitively dispersed all illusions in this regard.

Without minimizing the importance of international problems and the great military epic taking place in Europe in 1812, it must be stated that the decisive influence on the character of the Anglo-American War of 1812 was domestic politics. In his speech before the Senate in 1810, Henry Clay boasted "that the militia of Kentucky are alone competent to place Montreal and upper Canada" at the feet of the conquerors.[35] On 6 May 1812, John Calhoun declared that the conquest of "the whole of upper and part of lower Canada would take only four weeks."[36] Of course the eloquent speaker of the House of Representatives and his colleague from the Foreign Affairs Committee were not military experts, which could not be said about General Andrew Jackson. But the latter too painted rosy prospects for the American people, when, on 7 March 1812, he called for volunteers to war against "the eternal enemies of American prosperity," and spoke about the "conquest of all the British dominions upon the continent of North America" in order to "seek some indemnity for past injuries, some security against future aggressions."[37]

The expansionist plans of the United States' leaders did not excite any enthusiasm among the American population, however. Early in 1812 the bellicose Congress approved a measure providing for the enlargement of the regular army of 10,000 by an additional 25,000. A measure permitting the President to call up 50,000 volunteers for a year was approved on February 6. In April, Congress authorized the calling up of 100,000 men.[38] But these important decisions remained mostly on paper. It did not prove possible either to raise sufficient numbers of volunteers or to enlarge the regular army to any significant degree.

These and other circumstances were systematically reported upon by the Russian minister, Dashkov, who doubted that the United States government would succeed in popularizing the war,[39] and by the new consul-general in Philadelphia, N. Ia. Kozlov.[40] "Statements by the members of Congress and the newspaper dispatches printed under their influence," Kozlov wrote to Rumiantsev in March, "filled all the states with rumors of the inevitability of war with England. However, these threats had no effect, and the government considered it necessary to take firmer steps. Therefore, the President is authorized to call 25,000 regular troops, 50,000 volunteers, to increase the navy, to rebuild the fortresses; there is talk about levying extraordinary taxes for the duration of the war, and on top of that it is proposed that a loan be arranged . . . Although so far neither the money nor the navy or army is in existence, there are arguments in the sessions of Congress as to the best measures for the conquest of Canada and Quebec. On the other hand, the government proposes to annex both Floridas. Parts of these are already occupied by the states, and the English Court has protested against this violation."[41]

Because of the scarcity of money in the United States and "the difficulty of raising the proposed number of troops for the conquest of empty and impassable Canada," Kozlov was not inclined to believe that the "altercations" with England would lead to actual war. "Except for the members of the government," he informed Rumiantsev, "I do not find anyone here who believes that such an event will occur. The British Minister, who frequently entertains members of Congress, joked with them about the bloodshed threatening the inhabitants of Canada, and local merchants who have already started sending their ships to Europe in disregard of these military auguries, make one think all the more that the United States will find some means of prolonging the strife with England without entering upon a war."[42]

About two months later Kozlov wrote to St. Petersburg: "The bill to raise 25,000 regular troops, 50,000 volunteers, and 100,000 militia encounters insurmountable difficulties in execution. Up to now the states' army has not been extended over 7,000."[43] Although the prognosis of the Russian consul in respect to the probability of armed conflict with England proved erroneous, he was unquestionably right when he mentioned "general revulsion against the war, and the slowness with which the decisions of Congress were carried out."[44]

Immediately after the declaration of war the numerical power of the army was given on paper as 36,700, but in reality not more than 10,000 men remained under arms.[45] Russian minister Dashkov cited the last figure as the most trustworthy, adding that American troops "are badly armed and still worse trained."[46] In general, both historians and contemporary witnesses call attention to the complete absence of military enthusiasm among the population.

By the end of 1812 the size of the army was claimed to be 58,000, but in spite of all the efforts of the government, it never attained even half of that figure.[47] The situation was still worse with volunteers and militia, who not only refused to annex Canada, but would not even participate in any military operations outside their own state.[48] Henry Adams is quite justified in remarking that, in proportion to the population, the war efforts of 1814 were ten times less than those of 1864, during the Civil War.[49]

The cabinet in Washington encountered enormous difficulties in the area of finance as well. From 1812 to 1815 the government's expenses exceeded its usual income by $68,800,000, and the war had to be financed principally by loans. Between 14 March 1812 and 3 March 1815 Congress issued six loans to the sum of more than $80,000,000. Actually, until 1815 it succeeded in getting only $41,000,000, of which by far the largest part (87 percent) came from New York, Philadelphia, Baltimore, and the District of Columbia. The richest part of the country, New England, provided only 7 percent, and the bellicose South and West even less: 6 percent.[50]

The difficult position of Madison's government was further aggravated by the Federalist states, particularly by the open discontent in Massachusetts, Connecticut, and others. New England, with an important strategic position on the Canadian border, had the greatest concentration of population and material means. Its refusal to offer its militia to the central government and to support financial measures could not but undermine the country's war effort.

The summer of 1812 a well-known Boston lawyer, John Lowell, published, under the pseudonym of A New England Farmer, a series of caustic antigovernment pamphlets entitled: *Mr. Madison's War.*[51] The Federalists obviously sinned against truth when they accused President Madison of being practically the only person responsible for the war, which was allegedly being conducted entirely in the interests of France. Nevertheless, the widely used term "Mr. Madison's war" reflected discontent with the war and the government's policies. Nor was the opposition of the Federalist states limited to propaganda. By continuing the commerce with Canada and offering loans to the English, the Federalists actually entered the road of open treason. It is interesting that Prevost, commander-in-chief of the British troops, stated on 27 August 1814 that "two thirds of the army in Canada are at this moment eating beef provided by American contractors, drawn principally from the states of Vermont and New York."[52]

On the strength of all these facts, it can be definitely stated that the war started by the United States in the summer of 1812 was basically different in its character and causes from the truly liberating and revolutionary struggle of 1775-1783. The young capitalist state at this stage not only defended its lawful rights, but sought to take advantage of favorable circumstances for the fulfillment of its own expansionist plans on the continent of North America. The young predator, having cut its second teeth, was attempting to test their strength on its former oppressor.

The observant Dashkov repeatedly emphasized in dispatches to St. Petersburg the striving of the United States for all possible expansion of its borders. "Their invasion of Canada, the conquest of which is more of an actual reason for the war than their intention to make England respect their neutral rights; their behavior toward the Indians, whose lands they long for and strive to possess by any means; finally, their attack on east Florida, their participation in the revolution in the northern provinces of Mexico, and the recent occupation of the Spanish Fort Mobile," in his words, presented "sufficiently convincing proof that a very premature taste for conquest had already been inculcated into the American government."[53]

At first it might seem improbable that the United States, with its badly trained army, small navy, and half-empty treasury, could go to war against the greatest power of the day. The population of Great Britain was almost 20,000,000, and the country had at its disposal enormous financial means, excellent industry, a strong army, and an invincible navy, glorying in the fame of Lord Nelson. The British navy counted more than 1,000 ships, of which, in June 1812, 700 were at sea, including 260 frigates and ships of the line. The United States navy had only 17 units, including 8 frigates, of which 3 were unseaworthy; it also had a twenty-gun ship, the John Adams, and eight small guard ships and brigs; there were no ships of the line whatsoever.[54]

If, from a strategical point of view, war with England seemed senseless, the practical correlation of powers in the American war theater was quite different. England, engaged in a mortal struggle against Napoleon's France, had no military forces to spare. Her best troops, under the command of Wellington, were engaged in the Pyrenees; her economy was exhausted by the Continental Blockade; and numerous coalitions against Napoleon required colossal financial expenditures. In Canada there were only about 5,000 soldiers stationed in scattered garrisons over an enormous territory.[55] The population of this province was no more than 500,000—while the United States already numbered almost 8,000,000. Besides, a considerable proportion of Canada's inhabitants were of French origin and hostile to the British.

Therefore, although in practice the United States could not conquer England at sea, the conquest of Canada could appear as a relatively simple and quite feasible matter. It is also evident that the very declaration of war by the United States would be incongruous if they had not counted on annexing the British possessions in North America.

As so often happens, reality soon upset all preliminary calculations and prognoses. A bitter disappointment awaited the War Hawks right at the start of the war. Not only was General Hull unable to conquer Canada, but he suffered an ignominious defeat in Detroit (16 August 1812).[56] Considering the numerous and detailed descriptions of the war, there is no need to recreate the tangled picture of its military actions. In general, the Americans could not boast of any serious land successes, with the exception of the capture in the spring of 1813 of defenseless York (Toronto). In this operation, they distinguished themselves mainly by burning the Parliament buildings and by looting private homes, the public library, and a church.[57]

In spite of numerous failures and defeats (contributed to in no small measure by the mediocrity and helplessness of Generals Hull, Dearborn, Wilkinson, and others), until the summer of 1814 the balance of power remained on the side of the United States, which managed on the whole to maintain the initiative. The successful action on the Great Lakes, particularly the victory on Lake Erie (September 1813), secured control over the important internal waterways. Kozlov, carefully following the development of military actions, reported in the spring of 1814 that the cabinet in Washington "does not cease to take all possible measures for insuring that the present campaign would be more successful than the former ones. All attention is concentrated on the conquest of Canada . . . The army of the States, which last February consisted of 18,000 foot soldiers and 12,412 officers, is much increased at present, and the recruitments continue."[58] Somewhat later he wrote that the United States intended first of all to "clear the Lakes of enemy flotillas," then "to attack Montreal, which is the main object of local desires."[59]

However, objectives which could not be reached in 1812 could hardly be realized in 1814. As Napoleon suffered defeats in Europe, the attitude of the British government vis-à-vis the United States was becoming harsher;

there was no trace left of "peace-loving." On the contrary, from the spring of 1813 on, the United States began to seek ways of restoring peace. Toward the summer of 1814, alarming news of the occupation of Paris by the allied troops, of the fall of Napoleon, and of large military units being sent to Canada began to reach the United States. "This news," Kozlov reported, "much alarmed the Washington cabinet, which had never thought such an event possible. The anxiety is further increased by the rumors which are being spread to the effect that England is sending here from Bordeaux a large part of the army previously under the command of Wellington."[60]

England's military forces in North America were rapidly increasing, and in August 1814, according to Kozlov, there were 40,000 English troops.[61] Commenting on the war's further prospects, the Russian noted with enviable farsightedness:

> Everybody is sure that the government will finally have to give up its pretensions, but there is an apprehension that England might make demands that might block the road to a speedy armistice. Such demands might relate to forbidding Americans to fish at the Ternevskaia [Grand?] Banks and the Labrador coast, or to commerce with the West and East Indies, or to the return to the Spaniards of Florida and Louisiana and to conceding to England lands on the Canadian side. If England indeed has such intentions, then the fishing and the trade with the Indies would become a stumbling block for any rapprochement, and it would seem quite improbable that the London Court would ever be able to deprive the Americans of those advantages which constitute the well-being of all the northeast states. Up to now they have taken hardly any part in the war, but there is no doubt that no matter how displeased they are with the government, at the first news of such demands on the part of England, they will not fail to reconcile themselves with the President and to supply him with the means for a successful continuation of the war, and would themselves furnish the army sufficient to repulse the British attack and capture Canada from them. If the London Court indeed decided to support its demands by utilizing between 50,000 and 60,000 troops, even such force would be insufficient to bend the Americans to their will. Such troops might ravage several cities, but will not be able to conquer the land whose inhabitants are so scattered that they need not fear great harm from the enemy.[62]

The War of 1812 brought not a few surprises for both sides, but the greatest were probably the naval operations. While the superior land forces of the Americans did not achieve any significant success on the Canadian border, in spite of repeated attempts, the small navy of the United States proved a worthy opponent for the mistress of the seas.[63] In spite of losses, by 1813 the United States navy had grown considerably. As

Svin'in noted, the United States had at its disposal 23 warships, including 10 frigates, plus 180 gunboats; and 10 more frigates were being built. In the course of military operations the Americans had "proved their superiority over all the nations in the naval art."[64] Encounters of American warships with British ones almost invariably concluded in the United States' favor. True, the significance of these victories was more symbolic than practical, since they could not inflict any serious harm on the British navy, but this did not prevent the Americans from taking unusual delight in the success of their warships.

The actions of American privateers, who inflicted a painful blow on British merchant shipping, was much more effective. Small, light, and quick ships of the United States (occasionally their number reached 500) gave the English a great deal of trouble. The *America*, "king" of New England's privateers, captured twenty-six British vessels worth more than a million dollars. All in all, in the course of the war the Americans captured or destroyed about two thousand English ships.[65]

In explaining the unexpected naval successes of the United States one should take into account the important moral factor so often neglected by military specialists, who are mainly concerned with the simple count of military units, quality of equipment, number of troops, and so on. The conquest of Canada did not, and could not, arouse the enthusiasm of the people. American soldiers and militia refused to fight to further the predatory plans of the War Hawks. On the other hand, from the very beginning the war at sea was a just struggle to secure the lawful rights of the United States as an independent and neutral state. This circumstance to a large degree explains the surprise which the Americans presented to the British navy. The proud mistress of the seas was forced to take seriously this unexpected rival who dared challenge her maritime monopoly. In a circular dated 26 December 1812, Lord Castlereagh announced the blockade of Delaware and the Chesapeake Bay.[66] Although at first the blockade had little effect, the English continued to enlarge and strengthen it. On 26 May 1813, Admiral Warren issued an order for the blockade of New York, Charleston, Port Royal, Savannah, and the Mississippi River. (Actually only the New England ports remained outside the blockade.) This was followed by even more severe proclamations (16 November 1813) by Admiral Warren, and, on 25 April 1814, by Admiral Alexander Cochrane: the whole coast of the United States was declared to be in a state of "strict and rigorous blockade."[67]

By 1814 the American navy was almost annihilated; the English had also succeeded in sweeping almost all American privateers off the ocean. About 450 vessels had been captured and taken to Halifax, Nova Scotia.[68]

Released from European operations, the British navy in the early summer of 1814 held full control over the maritime approaches to the United States. This aided the actions of English troops on land and afforded the chance of dealing unexpected blows.

On 18 August 1814, Admiral Cochrane informed the government of the United States that, as a "measure of retaliation" for the destruction committed by the Americans in Upper Canada, he had issued an order "to destroy and lay waste such towns and districts upon the coast as may be found assailable."[69] The first victim was the capital, Washington. On August 19, 4,000 British soldiers under the command of General Ross disembarked in the Chesapeake Bay; supported by ships under the command of Admiral George Cockburn, they moved on Washington, encountering practically no resistence.

Panic ensued in the American capital. There was no shortage of "commanders," but not a single military officer with a modicum of common sense. About 1,500 soldiers and 5,000 militia were hurriedly assembled from surrounding towns, paticularly Baltimore, an artillery battery was built, and so on.[70] The command was entrusted to mediocre General Winder, who finally decided to engage the enemy at a place called Bladensburg, near Washington, on August 24.[71] Although the Americans had at their disposal not less than 7,000 men, these forces could not have possibly been called an army.[72] Utter confusion resulted in the inability to rebuff a small detachment of English professionals. "The men from Baltimore dispersed, the artillery galloped away, and the militia fled," Dashkov reported not without irony.[73] The American government fled the capital. Occupying Washington, 24-25 August 1814, the English burned the Capitol, the White House, and other government buildings, then, wasting no time, returned to their ships. Nobody thought of pursuing them, and President Madison himself was hiding in the Virginia woods.[74]

"In spite of all the abovestated circumstances, humiliating as they are for the American government and people," Dashkov noted in his dispatch to St. Petersburg, "I should be cautious not to conclude before your Excellency that this nation is lacking in the means of defence and repelling enemy attack: the inner strength and resources of this people are not negligible."[75] In conclusion, from a strategic point of view the occupation of the American capital was not important, but it symbolized the seriousness of the situation at the beginning of autumn 1814.

The Ghent peace negotiations, which opened on August 8, 1814, soon reached an impasse because of England's exorbitant demands, and on August 19 the American negotiators wrote to James Monroe that at present they had no hope for peace whatsoever.[76] Among other conditions, the English delegates insisted on territorial concessions, including a part of the territory of the future state of Maine, in order to build a road from Halifax to Quebec; on forbidding the United States to maintain a navy and build fortifications on the Great Lakes; on the simultaneous conclusion of peace with those Indian tribes which had fought on the side of England, and on the creation of a buffer Indian state; and on discontinuing fishing in North Atlantic waters (off the shores of the British possessions).

The arrival in Canada of fresh English reinforcements constituted a realistic threat to the territorial integrity of the United States, and the occupation of Washington showed that even the deep rear was vulnerable. The situation was further complicated by the position of the Federalist leaders and threats of secession by the Northeastern states. Thus, during the actual course of the war, its character began to change substantially, and in its final stage, because of the development of the patriotic movement, its character became more and more one of a struggle to secure the independence and territorial integrity of the United States.[77] This is the sense in which William Z. Foster's remark about the War of 1812 should be taken: "had England won this war—and for a time the issue was in doubt—that country would undoubtedly have tried to re-establish her old colonial regime on the wreckage of the United States. For the Americans, therefore, the War of 1812 was a just and defensive war."[78]

Of great interest in this connection is the letter of a member of the American delegation to the Ghent peace negotiations, James A. Bayard, to one of the Federalist leaders, Robert Harper, written in the most critical days of August 1814, when the harsh position and the exorbitant demands of the British cabinet became known. Bayard was a Federalist, and it is hard to suspect him of any special patriotism or sympathy for the Republican government, and this is what makes his testimony especially valuable. "If the war continues," he wrote, "it is no longer the war of our administration. It will be in its character as well as in its operations a defensive war. The views of the British Cabinet are undoubtedly altered by the great changes which have taken place on this Continent." Speaking of Great Britain, Bayard continued: "She is jealous of the increasing resources of our country, of the aptitude of our people for commerce and navigation and prowess in naval enterprise. She sees at the present moment a state of things which may never occur again in which she is left without an apprehension of the interference of any European power to exert her whole strength against us. The effort will be made to crush us altogether and if that be impracticable to inflict such wounds as would put a stop to our growth or at least retard it."[79]

Bayard finished his letter on 20 August, after the so-called ultimatum—the note of the British delegates of 19 August—had been received. "Their terms were those of a Conqueror to a conquered People," the Senator wrote indignantly. "I trust in God that when the character of the war is so totally changed and when we are not simply contending for the honor of the nation but driven to fight for its existence—the Federalists will prove themselves, what I have always believed them to be, the true and faithful friends of their country. As to the origin of the war we are all agreed. But when peace is refused upon just and moderate terms and the most extravagant pretensions are advanced, what is left for us but to fight manfully or submit to disgrace and ruin."[80]

Similar views were expressed by other members of the American delegation in Ghent, particularly John Quincy Adams, who wrote on 29 August 1814: "Great Britain has opened to us the alternative of a long, expensive, sanguinary war, or of submission to disgraceful conditions and sacrifices little short of independence itself. It is the crisis which must try the temper of our country."[81]

Although in the early days of the war Americans as a rule had tried to avoid joining the army and had refused to participate in the military action against Canada, signs of a patriotic desire to repel the enemy later appeared. "In Baltimore, New York, and even in Philadelphia," Kozlov wrote in August 1814, "the inhabitants are extremely disturbed. The first of these cities is indeed in danger, but New York is already put into a defensive condition. And in regard to Philadelphia, it is improbable that the English would dare to make any attempts at it."[82] "Nevertheless," the consul reported a little later, "all possible preparations have been undertaken here for such a possibility. The town is full of militia. The drums beat all over the place, drill is everywhere . . . Enormous batteries are built on the shores of Schuylkill and Delaware, and only cannons are lacking for the city to be brought to a state of complete security."[83]

In New York, in the course of several days 25,000 men took to arms, determined to defend the city. Among them there were the workers of the New York Manufacturing Company, the members of the city's Typographical Society, and others.[84] The British had to forgo their plan to occupy New York, but they attempted to repeat the "Washington experiment" in respect to Baltimore. Between 3,000 and 5,000 troops disembarked and approached within five miles of the city. However, the Baltimore citizens had prepared their defenses: they constructed entrenchments and erected batteries manned by sailors. The overall number of the city's defenders was 16,800 men, under the command of a U.S. Senator, Major-General Samuel Smith. The English met strong resistance on the distant approaches to Baltimore, and the fire from the light British ships on September 13 did not seriously harm the American batteries. Seeing that the "surroundings of the city" are occupied by "numerous militia consisting in large part of the Baltimore inhabitants themselves," Colonel Brooke, commanding the English forces (General Ross had been wounded), decided "to leave his undertaking" and hurriedly returned to the ships.[85] The composition of the national anthem of the United States, "The Star-Spangled Banner," resulted from this event.

The invasion of an 11,000-strong British army under the command of General Prevost, the Governor of Canada, undertaken in the beginning of September 1814, also ended in complete failure. Prevost was unable to conquer Plattsburg (an American base on Lake Champlain), and the British flotilla was defeated on 11 September 1814 by weaker American forces. Commenting on these events, Kozlov remarked: "The British encroachment of Plattsburg on Lake Champlain had even worse consequences. After a stubborn attack on the fort defending this town, their troops had to retreat with losses. At the same time their flotilla was broken and taken by the Americans."[86]

This unexpected defeat demonstrated that, even for a strong professional army, action on the American territory was far from being the easy matter it was originally thought. On the other hand, the United States' position remained very difficult. "The latest events in Europe," Kozlov wrote in November 1814, "the appearance on these shores of new British squadrons with landing forces, the shortage of means for repelling the enemy felt everywhere here, and above all the complete exhaustion of the treasury, a consequence of the discontinuation of American trade, compelled the President to call Congress before the appointed time."[87]

One of the most important issues of the Congressional session which opened on 20 September 1814 was the examination of the financial situation and the search for measures to cope with the ever-growing war expenditures.[88]

The harsh terms proposed by the British cabinet to the negotiators in Ghent became known in October 1814. "Congress found England's conditions excessive," Kozlov reported to Rumiantsev on November 8.

> The people who had expected a speedy conclusion of the peace, are extremely embittered by them, and the Democrats are trying to excite them still further. The government looks at all this with pleasure, hoping that the Federalists, convinced by now of the necessity to continue the war, would act at one with it. However, so far this hope has not been justified in any way. People generally are fed up with this war; but

nowhere do they curse it and its perpetrators more than they do in the region of Massachusetts, whose whole well-being depended on trade and fishery. Its inhabitants, deprived of their industry on one hand and paying high taxes on the other, had hoped that the government would use at least a part of their taxes to provide them with the means of defence. But on the contrary, all the money was spent for the conquest of Canada; not a single cannon was sent to Massachusetts; and the enemy was permitted to occupy the whole of the Maine region without any resistance . . . The Boston administration, basing their complaint on the enemy's invasion of Maine and using this as a proof of the inability of the Washington cabinet to conduct the war properly, decided to take upon themselves the defense of the province, and instructed the governor to raise 10,000 troops, borrow one million thalers for war expenditures, and invite neighboring regions to form a confederation with them."[89]

Federalist leaders Pickering, Strong, Otis, Lloyd, and others continued their separatist activity, taking advantage of the difficult position of Madison's government and speculating on the discontent of the population. On 17 October 1814, the Massachusetts legislature issued an invitation to the other New England states to take part in a conference,[90] and on December 15 the famous Federalist convention took place in Hartford.[91] Upon its adjournment, in January 1815, the commissioners were sent to Washington with a demand that the Constitution be amended, states be granted the right to raise their own armed forces, the population of New England be exempted from taxes and conscription, and so on. If these demands were not met, the Federalist leaders threatened to conclude a separate peace with England and secede from the Union.[92]

Considering the acute domestic antagonisms, serious financial crisis, chronic shortages of armed forces, and wide discontent with the government's inept conduct of the war, at first the possibility of concluding peace at Ghent on 24 December 1814 may seem a lucky opportunity for the United States. However, this was not a question of good will on the part of England or an accidental error of the British cabinet. The situation was such that the British armed forces could not inflict a serious defeat on the Americans, and the number of failures suffered by the British troops in the fall of 1814 showed that it would be no easy matter to conquer the United States. In his sharp—and, one must admit, not always just—comments on Madison's administration, Dashkov invariably added "however, the nation contains strength and force sufficient to repel the external enemy . . . Judging by the successful defeats of the enemy by various state militias, there is reason to conclude that, if the nation were more unanimous with the government in continuing the war, the English would have been rebuffed everywhere in their efforts to intrude upon these borders."[93]

The American troops under the command of General Jackson, unaware of the conclusion of peace in Ghent, not only resisted the assault of the strong British expedition at New Orleans, but on January 8 won a complete victory over General Sir Edward Pakenham's troops.[94] This was the greatest American success of the war, and it brought enormous popularity to General Jackson. Commenting on this victory, Kozlov reported on 13 February 1815: "Compared with the number of troops used by the English for this expedition, the means that Americans had at their disposal for repealing this assault were so negligible that both the public and the government were ready to consider New Orleans lost. However, the errors of the British authorities, their impulsiveness, and especially the haughtiness with which they judge the Americans not only saved the city but also did much damage to the idea of England's power, which has prevailed here until now." The English, "relying in equal measure on bravery and on the numbers of their choice troops," were expecting to take by attack "the earth entrenchments" constructed by the Americans, but suffered defeat. "They renewed the attack in a few days, but were completely defeated and lost many generals, a considerable number of officers, and up to four thousand regulars. After this lesson, the English were forced to return to their ships in such a hurry that they had no time to take with them either their wounded or their artillery."

"The saving of New Orleans," Kozlov continued, "naturally is a lucky event for this country in general and for the western regions especially. Every nation is apt to delight in victories over an enemy, but Americans, who are infected with vanity from their infancy, let this circumstance go to their heads. Nowadays they consider themselves superior to the English both on sea and on land. The editor of the official newspaper, at a loss as to which famous commander General Jackson could be likened, ended up calling him the American Bonaparte."[95]

Although Kozlov's (or Dashkov's) description of the battle of New Orleans was not very precise, and his remarks on the character of the American people somewhat simplistic, he must be given credit in one respect: he managed to evaluate quite objectively the real situation in the United States and understand much of what at that time, and even later, seemed surprising and incomprehensible to well-informed specialists. "Considering the present conditions of these states," Kozlov wrote,

the internal discord, the overall distrust or disobedience of the government, and the extreme shortage of money, it would seem that

Americans would soon be compelled to agree to the exorbitant demands of the London court. However, experience proves that the internal situation of the republic is not in the least conducive to such an expectation on the part of England. So far the shortage of money has not prevented the government from maintaining the army or building ships and frigates with remarkable speed. Disrespect for the federal government did not prevent the repelling of the enemy at Plattsburg, the destruction of his fleet on Lake Champlain, or the uniting of the citizens of Baltimore in defense of their property. Concerning the people's complaint about taxes, they are considered heavy only because local inhabitants have never paid taxes of this sort before.

"No matter how far the internal discord reaches," the consul continued,

and until there is a severance of the Northern states, which one need not yet fear, Americans will not cease to pursue the war. The size of their regular army is large enough to repulse any attempt on the part of Canada, and every region has made its own arrangements for defending its coastal cities. The example of New Orleans proves that the defensive situation of this republic is commensurate at least with those forces which England could use up to this time against the United States.[96]

Dashkov's general conclusions about the War of 1812 are also of considerable interest. "The recent war," he noted in a dispatch to St. Petersburg, "seems to confirm three following important opinions: (1) that the building of ships, the military equipment, and the quality of personnel, as well as the innate enterprise of the Americans and frequently their unreasoning valor give them a decided edge over the English in those encounters when the forces are equal; (2) that Americans have all those qualities which form the best soldiers; (3) that each war makes this country less and less dependent on English manufactures."[97]

One cannot discuss the War of 1812 without commenting on its effect on the unification of the United States. It is not only a question of Americans managing to protect their national independence and territorial integrity, of the disintegration of the Federalist party as the result of the war, and the end of New England separatism. It is essential to note the internal consolidation of the American people as an independent nation. In September 1815 a writer for *Niles' Weekly Register* noted that "the people begin to assume, more and more, a *national character*"; these words were published in the newspaper's first issue printed on beautiful new type—of American manufacture.

In studying the emergence of the American nation, Western historians[98] usually call attention to the external forms and attributes of an independent state, such as a national coat of arms, a flag, an anthem; they analyze the Declaration of Independence and the Constitution; but they often overlook the most important factor: the development of capitalism, the emergence of a domestic market, the formation of an economic community. Yet these processes were essential for the emergence of the American nation, and in this sense the War of 1812 was very important.

The United States went to war with England to secure its rights on the sea and to conquer Canada. After two and a half years of hard struggle neither of these objectives was achieved. Instead, however, an important result of the war was economic: the laying of a firm foundation for national industry. In this sense, whatever the subjective intentions and goals of the governments of either the United States or England might have been, the War of 1812 proved to be the continuation of the revolutionary War of Independence.

The editors of a ten-volume economic history of the United States (Henry David, Harold Faulkner, Louis Hacker, Curtis Nettels, and Fred Shannon) point out that, in the course of the forty years following 1775, the American people brought forth, not only a new nation, but also a new national economy. However, Curtis Nettels, author of the volume on *Emergence of a National Economy: 1775-1815* emphasize that during this period there were no basic changes in the economic life of the United States. It is true that the cotton gin, the river steamboat, and the machines of the factory system made their appearance, but the country was still on the verge of decisive changes.[99] The industrial revolution had just begun, and only in the advanced Northeast. Many years would pass before the United States became a completely independent and developed industrial power.

XI

RUSSIA'S ATTEMPTED PEACE MEDIATION

Russian diplomacy during the Anglo-American War of 1812 was the subject of my article published in 1961.[1] Written mainly on the basis of archival documents, it outlines the diplomatic mediation undertaken by Russia in the interests of peace between England and the United States. There is no reason to re-examine its basic deductions, but further study of the richest materials of the Russian archives, and acquaintance with documents of the National Archives and a number of valuable publications from the United States, such as the papers of John Quincy Adams and Albert Gallatin, made it possible to extend and supplement this work.

First, we can outline more surely the motives which led the Russian government to offer to mediate, and we can isolate the significance of commercial interests. I have already discussed Russian-American rapprochement and the expansion of commercial relations in the beginning of the second decade of the nineteenth century. The approaching war between England and the United States threatened to suspend the commercial ties between Russia and America which were progressing so successfully in 1810-11, and Russia's ruling circles were fully cognizant of this fact.

"The extent of American commerce with Russia this year depends entirely on the outcome of the discord between this republic and England," Dashkov wrote to Kurakin in the very beginning of 1812.

I visualize quite clearly all the consequences, unfavorable for our commerce, of the break between the United States and England. I hope, however, that this last blow to continental trade will not be dealt. I base my predictions both on the military weakness and unpreparedness of

304

this country and on the sober evaluation by the English of their own political interests, but without taking into consideration the erroneous politics and passions which might overthrow all reasonable deductions.[2]

Consequent events dashed hopes for a peaceful termination to the conflict; "the passions which might overthrow all reasonable deductions" were definitely gaining the upper hand. In response to unceasing violations by the British navy, the Congress of the United States passed the ninety-day embargo, signed by President Madison on 4 April 1812.[3] As a result of this act, trade with Russia was in danger of complete cessation. Dashkov and Kozlov urgently sought some indirect means to preserve the most rudimentary Russian-American commercial relations.

In a dispatch to Rumiantsev that spring, Kozlov noted that, in connection with the embargo, he thought it necessary to "impress upon American merchants through our agents in the Southern states and in Boston new ways of continuing commerce in colonial products with us by operating through the Spanish possessions and various other neutral ports."[4] In a circular letter to Russian consular agents in Boston, Charleston, New Orleans, and Savannah, he pointed out that the captains of ships sailing to Latin American ports (Caracas, Vera Cruz, and others), "with the intention of picking up colonial goods for export to Russia," are entitled to receive all the documents necessary for the bringing of their goods to Russian ports, after receiving "at the point of embarkation, appropriate certificates from local authorities."[5] (This document has importance as a sort of recognition of the new governments set up in the rebelling Spanish colonies in America.) The consul-general also informed Rumiantsev that "several American vessels, which departed this year for Havana and Cádiz to fetch cargoes destined for our ports, arrived at American shores after the introduction of the embargo, and, therefore, dropped anchor without entering the port, sending a request to Consul Evstaf'ev for the papers necessary for admittance. I instructed him not to put the slightest obstacle before such vessels and to supply them with certificates without any hindrance."[6]

Shortly after the United States declared war on Great Britain, Dashkov thought of offering the services of the Russian flag to American ships.[7] He reported to St. Petersburg on 20 July/1August 1812 that merchants who wished to take advantage of this flag were given a pass on condition that they go to Russia and there go through the formality of securing a document stating that the vessel was the property of a Russian subject. The Minister also described measures he had undertaken to encourage the sending to Russia of neutral ships sailing from South America.[8]

Naturally, all the efforts of Dashkov and Kozlov could not compensate for the cessation of direct commercial relations which followed the embargo and open warfare between the United States and England. A cursory look at the reports of the arrivals of foreign ships in Kronstadt, regularly appearing in the Russian press (*St. Peterburgskie vedomosti* and *Severnaia Pochta*), shows that trade relations between Russia and America were almost completely discontinued after the onset of the Anglo-American War. On 23 July/4 August 1812 the *St. Peterburgskie vedomosti* reported the arrival in Kronstadt, between 27 May/8 June and 10/22 July, of 82 foreign ships, of which 16 were American, 17 were Swedish, and so on.[9] By August the number of American ships had fallen sharply, though English ships were registering in ever-growing numbers.[10] Between 12/24 August and 28 August/9 September 1812, 82 ships arrived—5 American, with cargo, and 6 were English.[11] Of 57 merchant ships which arrived between 26 August/7 September and 10/22 September, 30 were English ships, and only 1 was American.[12] The English merchants who had lost their monopoly on the Russian market during the period of the Continental Blockade very soon regained their former position, almost entirely displacing their American competitors.

Commenting on the trade relations between Russia and the United States in 1812, Kozlov wrote:

> The war and the two months of embargo preceding it hindered all communications with Russia from here. The commerce of the Americans with our ports has been declining because of these circumstances, and in all probability will cease altogether for a long time unless our merchants or neutral nations take some part in it.
>
> During the last navigation only 65 ships left for Russia from American ports, 30 to St. Petersburg, 14 to Archangel, 2 to Riga, and 19 to various foreign ports and to Russia afterward. The majority of these ships sailed from New York or from Massachusetts ports.
>
> Having taken beforehand some measures for prolonging as far as possible commercial ties with America, I found a way during the embargo for several ships to depart for our ports with cargoes of Spanish colonial goods; but since the declaration of the war, the sailing of ships to the Baltic and generally to the northern countries of Europe has been completely cut off . . . .
>
> This complete interruption of the American commerce and the disappearing hope for the speedy restoration of peace, of necessity created an increase in the prices of all foreign goods. Our products are becoming scarcer day by day. Many ships coming from Russia left their cargoes in England; others were captured by enemy corsairs. Our linens, duck, ropes, etc. must become more expensive in proportion to Congress' dreams of putting American naval forces into a respectable state.[13]

In discussing the role of commercial ties in the formation of the tsarist government's policy toward the United States, I am calling attention only to one—and far from the most important—reason for Russia's interest in regulating the Anglo-American conflict. There is no doubt that the main reason was Russia's desire to unify all forces in the struggle against Napoleon and to prevent the diverting of England's attention to the American theater of military action. As we shall see, a significant part was also played by Russia's long-standing interest in protecting the rights of neutral navigation.

All researchers (including Henry Adams and Hildt) begin the history of the Russian attempt to terminate the war between the United States and England in September 1812, when the first conversation between Rumiantsev and John Quincy Adams took place. However, documents show that the Russian government had already undertaken the first important diplomatic step in April 1812, through representatives in Sweden.[14] Of exceptional interest is a proposal made by P. K. Suchtelen, who was sent to Sweden in the spring of 1812 with a special commission and actually performed the duties of a Russian minister there. A special instruction in Rumiantsev's own hand, approved by Alexander I, directed Suchtelen to undertake to establish a contact through Swedish Crown Prince Bernadotte and the English diplomat Edward Thornton with the aim of achieving Great Britain's speedy abolition of her orders-in-council, thus avoiding war with the United States. "Having studied the state of relations between Great Britain and America," the Russian Chancellor wrote, "His Majesty the Emperor came to the conviction that it is impossible for Great Britain not to do everything in her power in order to avoid war with the United States; and she cannot avoid this war if she does not revoke the so-called orders-in-council. Apparently the majority of Parliament considers their repeal advantageous, and the nation, it seems, also wishes it."

The tsarist government was well informed of the state of affairs and gave its future ally sensible and opportune advice. "His Majesty presumes," Rumiantsev continued,

> that it is in the interests of Great Britain not to wait until the revocation of her orders becomes a forced consequence of the peace treaty with the United States, but to proclaim it (and that would be both more advantageous and proper) as a principle in the interest of nations, which in their turn will repeal the rules constricting them as a result of Milan and Berlin decrees.
>
> How many political problems would be solved by such wise proclamation! How many difficulties it would create for the Emperor Napoleon![15]

When Rumiantsev authorized Suchtelen to undertake through Bernadotte and Thornton these proceedings, "with the aim of achieving such
important results," he had in mind the need to rally quickly all forces for
the forthcoming combat with Napoleon. At this time Sweden became the
scene of the most important diplomatic negotiations, and Suchtelen and
Russian chargé d'affaires P. A. Nikolai were given special instructions on
the conducting of these negotiations.

Stressing the significance of the forthcoming struggle, Rumiantsev
wrote in one of these instructions:

> England cannot fail to understand that the forthcoming war against
> the formidable might of France, her eternal enemy, will be the last
> one . . . The question which the armies will decide is whether all the
> monarchies will preserve their independence . . . It is a kind of crusade
> to which every one is called upon to contribute with all the means en-
> trusted by Providence and determined by his position and local circum-
> stances. Thus, England's role at present is clearly defined. She must
> contribute to the common cause her naval forces, munitions, and vict-
> uals, and serve as a treasurer for the belligerent nations; she must be
> ready to furnish them the monetary means necessary for the utilization
> of all military forces in the war against the natural and permanent
> enemy of the British Empire, and make it possible for them to conduct
> the war, if necessary, for a long time.[16]

Suchtelen's dispatch of 27 April/9 May 1812 shows that he followed his
instructions and discussed with Thornton the repeal of the orders-in-
council and the desirability of avoiding a conflict between England and
the United States.[17] It was not difficult to achieve this, since the English
diplomat regularly visited Suchtelen, who swiftly won his confidence.
Thornton assured Suchtelen that the British government had already
resolved to repeal the old decrees limiting the trade of the United States,
and showed him a corresponding printed document. The British diplomat
felt that England's decision to revoke the orders-in-council at the moment
Napoleon revoked the Milan and Berlin decrees, "would deprive him of all
hope for the war between Great Britain and America."[18]

It is difficult to evaluate Russia's April maneuver without studying
British documents, primarily materials in the London archives, but there
is no doubt that Thornton relayed the content of his talks with Suchtelen
along to the British cabinet. Eventually, whether or not influenced by the
Russian *démarche,* the British revoked the orders-in-council, albeit belatedly, on 23 June 1812, without however, succeeding in preventing the
conflict with the United States.

The beginning of the Anglo-American armed conflict placed the Russians in an ambiguous position. In declaring war on Great Britain, the

United States was anxious to stress that it did not consider itself the ally of France, and that it especially hoped to preserve amicable relations with Russia. As early as 1 July 1812 Monroe had stressed in a letter to John Quincy Adams that there was no reason, "why the war between the United States and Great Britain should affect in the slightest degree, the very friendly relations which now exist between the United States and Russia. It is the sincere desire of this Government to preserve to their utmost extent, those relations, with that power."[19]

The opening of diplomatic relations with the United States and Russian-American rapprochement, as has been pointed out, were brought about by a common desire to protect neutral navigation and by the struggle against England's maritime despotism. Russia could not but sympathize with the United States' defense of the rights of neutral powers, which constituted the official motive for declaring the war on England. Until the beginning of 1814, Chancellor Rumiantsev, a confirmed adversary of England's maritime despotism, was in charge of Russian foreign policy. In 1813 and in 1814 the British cabinet constantly feared that in one way or another Russia would propose for discussion the question of the rights of neutral commerce—either in a European Congress for settling peace conditions with France or during negotiations to settle the Anglo-American conflict.

On the other hand, the struggle with France constantly demanded close rapprochement of Russian and English forces. Suchtelen, Nicolai, and Thornton signed a Russian-English peace treaty on 6/18 July 1812 in Örebro, Sweden;[20] according to Article 3, both sides were obligated to defend each other. A similar Anglo-Swedish treaty was signed at the same time,[21] thus creating a union of these three countries against Napoleon. Alexander I and K. V. Nesselrode, his confidential agent and a virtual leader of foreign policy, who was staying in the General Headquarters with the Emperor, could not disregard the interests of their principal ally. Russian-English ties were becoming closer as the war against Napoleon expanded. The dependence of the members of the coalition on English subsidies was also becoming greater. This made the question of Russia's attitude toward the United States and toward the Anglo-American War of 1812 a complex and delicate matter. It also explains a certain inconsistency in Russian diplomacy and contradictions within the tsarist government itself.

However, there can be no doubt that from the very beginning of the Anglo-American war, Russia was anxious to facilitate its speedy conclusion. Dashkov did not give up hope for a peaceful settlement when he wrote in an official note to the Secretary of State:

Even though the United States found themselves involved in the war in spite of all their efforts to avoid it, they are the only truly neutral country. The continuation of this policy is the object of Russia's sincere hopes with regard to America. The government of His Imperial Majesty will be always pleased to help maintain due respect for the rights of neutrals. At the same time, it cannot but wish that the quarrel of the United States could be settled promptly and honorably, and that the consequences of the started hostilities would not become so grave as to prevent the desirable reconciliation.[22]

As soon as news of the Anglo-American war reached St. Petersburg, in September 1812, Russia offered the belligerents its mediation for peaceful settlement. Undoubtedly, the Russian government took this mission very seriously, for it made the offer at a time when, it seemed, Russia could take little interest in events in far-off America: the battle of Borodino occurred on September 7, and in the middle of that month Napoleon entered Moscow.

On 21 September 1812 Rumiantsev informed Adams of Russia's intention to act as a mediator and inquired whether the minister "was aware of any difficulties or obstacle on the part of the Government of the United States" in regard to such an offer. Although Adams had no special instructions, he answered that he was "very sure that whatever determination they might form upon the proposal of the Emperor's mediation, they would receive, and consider it as a new evidence of his Majesty's regard and friendship for the United States," and that he "was not aware of any obstacle or difficulty which could occasion them to decline accepting it."[23] Rumiantsev also informed him that he had already discussed the matter with the English ambassador, Lord Cathcart, who had dispatched an account of this discussion to his court.

On 30 September/12 October Dashkov was authorized to make an official offer of mediation to the United States government.[24] Earlier, on 6/18 September, similar instructions had been given to P. A. Nikolai, who was at the same time appointed to the post of chargé d'affaires in London. Rumiantsev wrote in his instructions to Nikolai: "Peace between Russia and England seemed to be of enormous benefit to the commerce of almost all maritime nations by relieving them of that continuous annoyance and anxiety to which they have been exposed almost constantly during the last few years . . . However, since the onset of the war between America and England, this result has been jeopardized." The Chancellor pointed out that, anxious to prevent the difficulties which might result from direct negotiations, the Emperor had offered Great Britain and the United States his mediation, and that, if accepted, the "negotiations for such advantageous rapprochement could begin in St. Petersburg under the direct auspices of His Majesty."[25]

While it was natural for the Russian government to express anxiety over the discontinuance of commercial relations with the United States, which had such a successful start, England could only rejoice on this score. Immediately after the official renewal of commercial connections with Russia, in August 1812, Great Britain began actively regaining her former position and even seeking what was essentially a monopolistic role in the Russian market, worrying a certain group of Russian landowners and merchants. The blockade of American ports and gross violations by the British navy of the neutral navigation upset relations between Russia and England. In March 1813 the Russian ambassador in London, Count Christopher Lieven, was compelled, upon request from the Russian merchants in London, to protest sharply to the British ministry, expressing the "regret which his Court was experiencing" on account of the blockade of the American coast, "a measure so ruinous to Russian commerce."[26]

When the offers of mediation were being made, it was clearly understood in St. Petersburg (and this was decisive at that moment) that war in America could not but deflect a considerable part of the English land and naval forces, and, especially, monetary means so necessary for the struggle with Napoleon.[27] In December 1812 Lieven frankly announced to English Minister for Foreign Affairs Castlereagh that Alexander could not remain indifferent to the disintegration of forces "because of a war as remote and foreign to the great goal of humanity as is the American war."[28]

What, then, was the attitude of the governments of the United States and England to Russia's peace initiative?

The first news of Russia's offer of mediation reached Washington on 24 February 1813. John Quincy Adams' dispatches and Rumiantsev's letter to Dashkov of 30 September/12 October 1812 were delivered to the United States by J. L. Harris, nephew of the American consul-general in St. Petersburg.[29] On 15/27 February, Dashkov orally conveyed the contents of Rumiantsev's letter to Secretary of State Monroe. Monroe accepted it *ad referendum* and promised to reply soon.[30]

Ten days later, on March 8, Monroe invited Dashkov for a talk and informed him that President Madison agreed with pleasure to the mediation of His Majesty, and the decision was made to exchange official notes.[31] Dashkov's note was sent the same day, and on March 11 Monroe sent his answer informing Dashkov that the President of the United States "willingly accepts," Russia's mediation.[32]

On March 9 the Washington *National Intelligencer* printed a report of the mediation offer made by the Russian minister; this was soon reprinted in other American newspapers, including the *Weekly Register*. The communiqué made it clear that the Government of the United States viewed the offer positively, "which having peace solely and simply for its object, may be beneficial, and cannot be injurious to the United States."[33] As time went on the American press continued to pay a great deal of attention to Russian mediation.[34]

It is not hard to understand the readiness with which the United States accepted Russia's offer of mediation: there were telling reasons. Most important was the news of Napoleon's rout and his flight from Russia. The retreat of the French army from Moscow began on 18 October 1812; its pitiable remnants crossed the Berezina, 26-28 November, and the Neman in December 1812.

At the same time, the war with England was taking an unfavorable turn for the United States. Hope for a speedy conquest of Canada had not been realized. Financial difficulties, internal differences, and popular unrest were becoming increasingly acute. Such a specialist as Henry Adams evaluated matters in the spring of 1813 as follows: "With the overthrow of Napoleon's authority and the close alliance between Great Britain and Russia, the last chance of forcing concessions from England vanished. A long war, with no prospect of success, lay before the United States."[35] The possibility of being left without a friend in the world while carrying on a hopeless war gave to Russia's friendship, Adams remarked, "a value altogether new."[36]

Given these conditions, negotiations with England through Russia's mediation were the best chance for the United States. Neither President Madison nor Secretary of State Monroe doubted that Russia's attitude was favorable and that acceptance of her mediation would be advantageous. "We are at present occupied with the Mediation of Russia." Madison wrote 2 April 1813,

> That is the only power in Europe which can command respect from both France and England; and at this moment it is in its Zenith. We shall endeavor to turn this mediation to the best account, in promoting a just peace. We are encouraged in this policy by the known friendship of the Emperor Alexander to this country; and by the probability that the greater affinity between the Baltic and American ideas of maritime law . . . will render interposition as favorable as will be consistent with the character assumed by him.[37]

Later, discussing the expediency of accepting mediation, Monroe noted that "the influence of Russia would never be exerted against a just code of neutral rights."[38]

The composition of the American delegation to St. Petersburg testifies to the importance the United States attached to the negotiations. As Monroe wrote John Adams, "the occasion was thought of that high importance to require according to the usage of our country a special mission of three."[39] It was composed of Minister John Quincy Adams, already in St. Petersburg; Senator James Bayard, representative of the Federalists; and Secretary of the Treasury Albert Gallatin, one of the best-known American statesmen of that day.

Mindful of the advantages of Russia's mediation, Monroe wrote in the confidential part of the instructions to members of the mission: "There is not a single interest which you have to arrange in which Russia and the other Baltic powers may not be considered as having a common interest with the United States. It is not to be presumed that the Emperor of Russia will wish the United States to make concessions which are to operate to his own disadvantage" (confidential paragraph 4). And further: "A good intelligence between the United States and Russia respecting neutral rights may have an important influence in securing them from violation, in any future war, and may even tend to prevent wars, to the advantage of all nations" (confidential paragraph 5).[40]

The United States also counted on signing a commercial treaty in St. Petersburg. This question was touched upon in a preliminary manner by Monroe in his conversation with Dashkov on 11/23 March 1813. Dashkov reported to Rumiantsev that Monroe "stressed his conviction that the peace negotiations in St. Petersburg would be advantageous for the belligerents, and added that this circumstance could even serve to bring a treaty with Russia which could be taken as an example for other powers and would open favorable prospects for the expansion of commerce between Russia and America after the conclusion of peace." Dashkov answered that, as a personal opinion, he did not exclude the possibility that, "if such a transaction is advantageous to the United States and if it establishes principles favorable for commerce, the imperial government will not refuse to give proof of Friendship, provided there is no unforeseen objection."[41] Encouraged by this reply, the Government of the United States, on 23 April 1813, provided Adams, Gallatin, and Bayard with appropriate credentials.[42]

Several days later American delegates were given detailed instructions. "The President presuming that the mediation of the Emperor of Russia may afford a favorable opportunity for improving our relations with Russia herself, is disposed to avail himself of it, so far as it may be done, to the mutual advantage of both countries," wrote the Secretary of State. "With this view, he has thought it proper to authorize you to enter into a Treaty of Amity and Commerce with that power." The basis for this treaty, in the opinion of the United States Government, had to be the most-favored-nation principle. "A good intelligence between the United States and Russia respecting neutral rights" was also considered an "object of highest importance."[43]

Before his May departure for St. Petersburg it was necessary for Gallatin to complete pressing business in the Treasury Department. Most important was the loan of $16,000,000, subscription for which was begun on 16 March. At the time the treasury was virtually empty. According to Gallatin, there was "hardly money enough to last till the end of the month."[44] Originally it seemed that the new loan would be a failure, but once financial circles became aware that Russia's mediation might bring peace, the situation changed sharply. "Since then," according to the report of Kozlov, Russian consul-general in Philadelphia, "all obstacles to the loan have been overcome, and the Treasury received all the $16,000,000 at no more than 7 1/2 percent."[45] Indeed, with the support of the three biggest financiers, John Jacob Astor, Stephen Girard, and David Parish, who provided $10,000,000 by 7 April 1813, Gallatin succeeded in collecting an even greater sum. In the Federalist circles a conviction prevailed that Girard and Parish made Gallatin's appointment as a delegate to the peace talks a condition for supporting the loan.[46]

Russia's minister in Washington, Dashkov, developed an active mediatory activity in the spring of 1813. His solicitation and the special visit of Russian mission adviser Sverchkov to British Admiral Warren were responsible for securing the passports for Gallatin's and Bayard's voyage to St. Petersburg.[47] More than that, Dashkov decided to take advantage of the favorable situation and attempt to secure an armistice on his own initiative; to this end he gave appropriate instructions to Sverchkov. Warren agreed to the Russian minister's proposal, and informed him of preliminary conditions for negotiations.[48] However, when Dashkov cautiously, so as not to "compromise the good will" demonstrated by Warren, made inquiries of the American government, it was brought out that the discussion of impressments was entrusted to the United States' representatives sent to St. Petersburg.[49]

Although the Russian proposal of mediation met a favorable reception in the United States, the reaction of the British cabinet was altogether different. Early English military successes had made the war quite popular among the ruling circles; twice, in the end of 1812 and in the fall of 1813, the English parliament had unanimously, without vote, approved welcoming addresses to the Prince-Regent and the Ministry on the subject of the war. In late 1812 and in 1813 the British government had no desire what-soever to seek peace with the United States—and especially not through negotiations with Russia's mediation, considering the common interests of Russia and the United States in questions of commerce and maritime law. Nevertheless, not wishing to irritate her principal ally unnecessarily, the British cabinet abstained from giving a final and categorical refusal of mediation, under the pretext that Admiral Warren, commander-in-chief of the British armed forces in America, had already been authorized to seek a peace settlement with the United States.

Reporting on his first talk with the Prime Minister Lord Liverpool in October 1812, Russian chargé d'affaires Nikolai wrote: "The Prime Minister expressed his appreciation of such a friendly act on the part of His Imperial Majesty . . . and informed me that Admiral Warren is en-trusted with the authority for restoring peace between belligerents," and that, consequently, "it would perhaps be wiser not to undertake anything new" until information has been received on the results of these negotia-tions which are expected in a month.[50] Lord Castlereagh, in a conversation with Nikolai on November 12, expressed himself in the same way. The British minister noted that he valued infinitely the Russian Emperor's offer of mediation, but "in view of the authority with which Admiral Warren is entrusted, and, on the other hand, in view of the striving of the American government to continue the war at all cost, there is nothing left to do, apparently, until the population over there begins to groan under the burden of war taxes."[51]

On December 10 Adams spoke with Rumiantsev about the initial reac-tion of the British government to the proposed mediation. Rumiantsev said that "they had neither accepted nor rejected it, but had hinted that it would not be acceptable in America; that they thought the time was not yet come. But it appears they had sent out Admiral Warren with powers to negotiate."[52] On his part Adams assured the Chancellor, in reviewing the Secretary of State's instructions, of the United States' desire to continue amicable relations with Russia, and stressed that the American govern-ment did not wish to enter into any intimate contact with France.

After Rumiantsev verified the position of the United States with John Quincy Adams, he relayed it to the British government.[53] In this matter Adams acted upon his own discretion, and some historians feel that he erred: that in dispelling England's apprehensions, he strengthened her unyielding position.[54] However, this could hardly have had any important influence on the position of the British cabinet. On 18 November 1812 Lord Castlereagh handed a note to Nikolai in which he let it be clearly understood that England was not anxious to accept Russian mediation. "His Royal Highness," it was stated, "admits regretfully that because of the nature of demands on which the United States has lately been considering it necessary to justify the continuation of the war, the interference of a friendly power will not facilitate the restoration of the peace."[55]

On his arrival in London in December 1812, Russian ambassador Lieven seized the first opportunity to resume discussion of mediation. In his conversation with Castlereagh he had fully presented Russia's position toward the Anglo-American war, expressed concern on the subject of the distraction of English forces away from the struggle against Napoleon for the sake of continuing the American war, and stressed that Russia's own interests compelled her to seek the speediest termination of the armed conflict between England and the United States. In resuming the offer of mediation, or as he put it more mildly, "good services," Lieven noted that, "after the great sacrifices recently sustained by Russia, she needs more than ever to protect her commerce; her commerce with America is not the least part of it, and this American war creates many obstacles for it."[56] Castlereagh's response was to repeat almost verbatim everything that he had already told Nikolai. "England, as everybody knows," Castlereagh stated, "believed she could prevent the war by revoking the orders-in-council, but the American Government, obviously bent on the war, kept insisting on one point, that of impressments, and neither the English nation nor the English ministry would ever concede this point." The British minister further pointed out that the whole behavior of the United States government proves "that they are set on the war, and that it is France who pushes them into it, since it is much to her interest to see the English in a combat with the Americans; that, consequently, until the latter decided to act independently, there could not be any negotiation that could bring the happy result, which is even more in England's interest than in Russia's."

In other words, Castlereagh, unwilling to accept Russia's mediation, was anxious to obscure the real reasons for England's harsh position and to stress by all means the aggressive and unyielding attitude of the United States. Apparently he did not find it difficult to convince the tsarist envoy with whom he immediately found a common language. (It is not surprising that Lieven suited the London Court quite well and stayed in his post over thirty years!) Lieven quoted Lord Castlereagh's remark that the British ministry, "naturally timid and in the habit of consulting the voice of the nation, did all it could to preserve the peace with the United States, and it depends entirely on the latter to restore it."

However, the British government did not succeed in putting the blame for the continuation of the war and refusal of Russian mediation on the

United States. In May 1813, news of Dashkov's Washington activity and American consent for Russian mediation was received in London. Lord Castlereagh was finally forced to state directly and categorically that England refused any Russian mediation. In his talk with Lieven, Castlereagh announced that "the character of dispute between England and America" does not permit the interference of a third party.[57] This announcement was made at the moment when Russia was already firmly involved in the European war and was to some extent dependent on the actions of all members of the coalition and on British subsidies.

Having refused the mediation, the British government did not dare to ignore the Russian move completely. In the same conversation with Lieven, Castlereagh hinted for the first time that the British government would agree to negotiations with American delegates if these negotiations took place in London and without any intermediary. "Castlereagh told me," Lieven wrote, "that this question touches too closely on the special interests, and even on the national feelings of the English, for it to be discussed anywhere else."[58]

Thus, of two evils—direct negotiations and negotiations through an intermediary—the British government chose the lesser: direct negotiations. This move was to a certain degree a direct result of Russia's peace initiative. In confirming his refusal of mediation in the beginning of July 1813, Castlereagh explained England's consent to negotiate with the United States as a desire "to offer His Imperial Majesty a chance to realize his amicable intentions and at the same time to give him a proof of England's desire to put an end to this struggle in which nobody is a winner." The British Minister assured that the British Court was ready to appoint representatives to negotiate with the American plenipotentiaries, but that, however, these negotiations could not take place anywhere except London.[59]

In evaluating England's consent to direct negotiations, Henry Adams wrote that "this advantage was gained by the Russian offer of mediation, and was intended not to pacify America but to silence Alexander and Roumanzoff."[60] Compelled to consent to negotiations with the United States, England was anxious to create advantageous conditions for conducting them, and of course to protect them most decisively from interference by Russia. Discussing this question in detail, Castlereagh wrote to the English ambassador in St. Petersburg on 14 July 1813: "It is of great importance to strip any negotiation between America and us even of the *appearance* of foreign intervention."[61] Instructing Cathcart to insist on London or, if the worst came to the worst, on Gothenburg as a place for negotiation, Lord Castlereagh noted that yielding on this point "would

317

give to our refusal of the mediation the air of a shabby pretense." He argued that the Emperor, "if he knows anything of England, must be convinced that no Government dare surrender the right of search for enemy's property, or British subjects." It was considered impossible even to discuss the question of maritime rights; the exclusion of all such questions was a necessary condition for England's participation in general negotiations in Europe. "Great Britain may be driven out of Congress, but not out of her maritime rights, and, if the Continental powers know their own interests, they will not hazard this."[62]

Since a convenient opportunity availed itself, Castlereagh informed the American plenipotentiaries of the English position through an indirect channel. While Gallatin was passing through Gothenburg, he asked his bankers, Baring Brothers and Company, to inform the British government of his mission. Alexander Baring's long answer, written on 22 July 1813, apparently after consultation with Castlereagh, detailed England's desire to conduct the negotiations separately, and directly with the American plenipotentiaries, without Russian mediation, either in London or Gothenburg, since the war between England and the United States was "a sort of family quarrel, where foreign interference can only do harm and irritate at any time, but more especially at the present state of Europe, when attempts would be made to make a tool of America" in a manner which he was sure Americans would not sanction. Baring also pointed out quite directly that, if the American plenipotentiaries have instructions to adhere pertinaciously to their demands on the question of impressments, their coming to Europe and negotiating anywhere would be "useless for any good purpose."[63]

All these events took place against the background of the tense situation in Europe. In May 1813 Napoleon fought the victorious battles at Lützen and Bautzen. In June a temporary armistice was concluded with Metternich's mediation. Complex negotiations on the expansion of the coalition against Napoleon and on the English subsidies were taking place. And precisely at this time it became known that England had refused the mediation offer and that the United States had sent a mission to St. Petersburg.

After Rumiantsev heard from Lieven, on June 22, he informed Adams of the English refusal, on the grounds that the character of their differences with the United States was such that the British cabinet did not think it "suitable to be settled by mediation."[64] However, Rumiantsev did not consider, or did not wish to consider, the English government's reply as definitive and thought that it might be expedient to resume the offer of mediation. The Chancellor did not want to accept the possibility that

Russia might be left out of negotiations in which he saw the means "definitively to change the principle of England's policy, so despotic and so destructive for the well-being of neutral powers."[65] Because of that in his letters he tried to convince the Tsar that the interest and dignity of the empire demanded that he not give up the idea of mediation nor leave the American mission in St. Petersburg unattended.[66]

Pressured by England and influenced by his new advisers, the Tsar hesitated. His first impulse was to insist that England accept Russian mediation. On 6/18 July he sent Rumiantsev a short note; "I thoroughly approve your view on the question of mediation and authorize you to act accordingly."[67] However, soon his opinion began to change. Late in July after he had received Lieven's abovementioned dispatch of 4/16 July informing him of England's consent to negotiate directly with the American plenipotentiaries, Alexander instructed Nesselrode to relay the following reply to the English government:

> Desire to see the end of the quarrel, extremely perilous for both sides, led His Imperial Majesty to offer his mediation to Great Britain and the United States; as soon as the British government thought it appropriate to decline this offer we considered it nonexistent. While this correspondence was taking place, Congress apparently decided to send its plenipotentiaries; His Majesty does not know, up to now, where they have undertaken to announce their powers; however, if it so happens that they would wish to begin any sort of negotiation, Your Excellency can give assurances that it will be proposed to them to go to London."[68]

Approximately the same answer was given by Alexander to Lord Cathcart, as he wrote to Castlereagh from Reichenbach on 5 August 1813.[69]

Alexander withdrew his offer of mediation at a time when it was unclear whether or not England would ratify a recently signed convention on subsidies[70] and would agree to the increase of payments for which the Russian government was pressing insistently. Taking advantage of Russia's financial difficulties, the British cabinet put barely concealed pressure on Alexander's government, asking for concessions in matters of trade, Russia's promise not to discuss questions of maritime law during peace negotiations with France, and the withdrawal of mediation in Anglo-American affairs.[71] The announcement of the withdrawal of mediation and the formal oral concession on the question of neutral rights contained in the instructions to Lieven of 28 July/9 August apparently were supposed to constitute a payment for British "generosity."

Meanwhile, 21 July 1813, Gallatin and Bayard arrived in St. Petersburg, and on July 24 John Quincy Adams presented them to Rumiantsev. The American plenipotentiaries acquainted the Chancellor with copies of their powers and credential letter signed by Madison, and some time later both sides exchanged official notes.[72] 22 July/3 August 1813, Adams, Gallatin, and Bayard sent Rumiantsev a note offering to effect a commercial treaty between Russia and the United States.[73] Although Rumiantsev was an active adherent of expanding commercial ties with the United States, he did not feel it was expedient to start new negotiations because of the current situation and Alexander I's absence from the capital.[74] Besides, the Americans did not press their offer, since their main task was to conclude peace with England. This question absorbed all the consequent attention of both Rumiantsev and the American plenipotentiaries.

Rumiantsev was aware of the American desire for peace negotiations through Russia's mediation; his communique from Alexander I authorized him to act "according to his judgment." Knowing nothing about the decision which the Emperor had recently arrived at, he came up with a plan whose goal was to keep "the mediation in such an important matter" in Russia's hands, and attempted to realize it in spite of the refusal of the British government.[75]

On 19/31 August 1813 Rumiantsev officially informed the American plenipotentiaries that, upon learning of their appointment, Alexander I had instructed him to renew the offer of mediation. Accordingly, the Chancellor authorized Russian Ambassador Lieven in London to pass on to Lord Castlereagh an appropriate note, the copy of which was simultaneously sent to the American plenipotentiaries.[76]

Still earlier, while preparing his instructions to renew the mediation offer, Rumiantsev acted in close accord with the American delegation. In a conversation on 19 August 1813 he inquired what Adams' reaction would be if England proposed to transfer negotiations to London. Adams' reaction was as follows: If the negotiations, though at London, were still under Russian mediation, he did not foresee any special obstacles. If, however, the negotiations were to be direct, the American delegation could not take part in them, since, as could be seen from their statement of powers, they were authorized to conduct negotiations only with Russian mediation.[77] At the same time American delegates announced that they were willing to wait patiently as long as there was the least reason to hope that England would agree to mediation.[78]

The American plenipotentiaries' reaction to the offer of direct negotiations conveyed in a letter of Alexander Baring, received in St. Petersburg on 17 August, is also significant. After a conversation of about two hours with Gallatin and Bayard on the subject of the letter, Adams made the following notation in his diary: "The wish to draw us to London is very freely avowed, but nothing, other than vague and general expressions, to encourage a hope that we should have any prospect of success there."[79]

In a dispatch of 16/28 August 1813, Rumiantsev instructed Lieven to hand Castlereagh an enclosed note renewing the offer of mediation.[80] Rumiantsev considered it possible to "satisfy the desire of the British to transfer negotiations to London," with Lieven conducting them.[81] All the materials being sent to Lieven were shown to the members of the American delegation beforehand, and Rumiantsev made some alterations in the text requested by Gallatin.[82]

On September 7 the American plenipotentiaries acquainted Rumiantsev with the content of Baring's letter of July 22 and their answer to it.[83] "Mr. Gallatin," Rumiantsev wrote to Alexander,

> read me several passages from his answer: he wrote Mr. Baring that he sees absolutely no obstacles to the negotiations taking place, with Your Majesty's consent, in a place other than Petersburg, but that the full-powers with which they are furnished completely exclude the possibility for their conducting the peace negotiations without Your Majesty's participation; that to make them write for different full-powers would, besides many difficulties, delay the cause of the armistice . . . Mr. Gallatin does not have any doubt, Sire, that Mr. Baring's letter was dictated to him by the Ministry.[84]

Hoping for Russia's direct mediation, the American plenipotentiaries valued highly her support in negotiations. Gallatin repeatedly expressed a typical belief that "Russia is the only power who is a true friend of America" (*La Russie est la seule puissance vraiment amie de l'Amérique*),[85] and showered lavish praise on the Tsar—this, however, was done by almost all statesmen of the period.

At the time Rumiantsev conferred with the American mission in St. Petersburg and was laying the groundwork for the renewal of the mediation offer in London, English plenipotentiaries at the Emperor's military headquarters were preparing their official refusal of Russian mediation. As the new English ambassador to Russia, Lord Walpole, later stated, he himself "had written Lord Cathcart's note to Nesselrode of 1st September; that he thinks it was written in Prague 23 or 24 of August, but not presented until they came to Töplitz."[86] It is easy to understand the delay, since the armistice with Napoleon had expired on August 10 and the decisive stage of the 1813 campaign had begun. Napoleon had his last great victory in the battle before Dresden, and the allies had retreated to Bohemia. Returning to Töplitz, Alexander found himself facing, on top of numerous matters connected with the struggle against Napoleon, the complex problem of mediation in the Anglo-American war.

In a note of 1 September 1813, Lord Cathcart categorically declined the offer of mediation and requested the good offices of Russia for conveying to the American plenipotentiaries an offer to come to London or Gothenburg for direct negotiations with English representatives.[87] Alexander delayed answering Cathcart for about a month. However, when Nesselrode finally presented an answer to the British diplomat on 22 September/4 October, it was quite specific. "His Majesty," Nesselrode wrote, "without any hesitation informed the American plenipotentiaries of the offer by the British ministry to conduct direct negotiations with it either in London or Gothenburg. Milord Cathcart can be sure that as soon as their reply reaches the main headquarters, the undersigned will not delay informing him of it."[88]

Under normal conditions it is difficult to suppose that Nesselrode would not convey the content of the Cathcart note to the Americans. But the note was never even delivered to Rumiantsev, who remained in St. Petersburg in a most ambiguous position. Correspondence with the Chancellor was conducted personally by Alexander. When he received Rumiantsev's detailed information on the instructions sent Lieven for renewing the offer of mediation, instead of informing the Chancellor of the latest note from the British ambassador, with what was essentially its definitive and final refusal, Alexander wrote Rumiantsev three personal notes in a row, approving the instructions given Lieven and ordering that the credential letters of the American plenipotentiaries be accepted.[89]

It is hard to say whether the Tsar understood the position he was placing his Chancellor in. Perhaps he hoped that in spite of its refusal the English government would eventually decide to make some concessions. He really may not have seen—or wish to see—any contradictions in his position. However, Count Lieven in London could not fail to see them; consequently, he refused to present Rumiantsev's note to Castlereagh, and wrote to Nesselrode on 16/28 September:

> In connection with the announcement I made to the English ministry, according to the instruction given me in His Majesty's name, to the effect that the American plenipotentiaries will be allowed by our Court to address their proposals to London, it seemed to me that the presentation of the abovementioned note would constitute acting against the imperial will, and consequently I considered it necessary to delay the execution of the orders contained in the dispatches of the Chancellor until I had received instructions.[90]

Count Lieven overestimated his own mental abilities in presuming to see contradictions in matters where the Tsar did not wish to do so. In November 1813 Nesselrode sent him strict orders to follow the Chancellor's instructions and present the note to the English government, adding that

> His Majesty does not in the least consider that the sense of this note contradicts the instructions which he sent you directly through me. In my dispatch of 28 July/9 August I informed you that the Emperor would propose to the American plenipotentiaries that they go to London. This proposal was made to them. They agreed to transfer the place of the negotiations to London, but noted at the same time that they would be able to conduct the negotiations only with Your Excellency's mediation, because of the limitations in their full-powers. Since the changes in the wording of these full-powers could be made only after a considerable loss of time, His Majesty did not consider himself justified in refusing to pass on to the English government the proposals of the American plenipotentiaries contained in the project of a note sent to Your Excellency by the Count Rumiantsev.[91]

As a result of these events, Rumiantsev found himself in a most difficult situation. The actual leadership obviously had been slipping from his hands. With every passing day the American plenipotentiaries were becoming more and more impatient and inquired more often about England's answer. The Chancellor did all he could to make the stay of the American mission in St. Petersburg as interesting as possible: he arranged formal dinners, presented the members of the delegation to the Emperor's family, and so on. In accordance with Alexander's intention to give the plenipotentiaries a special token of distinction, Rumiantsev even offered to defray the expenses of the legation or to present them with some production of Russian manufacture, if this was "compatible with forms and usages" of America.[92] The Americans declined this extraordinary attention, stating that their Constitution forbid public officers to accept presents or personal donations of any kind from foreign sovereigns. The application of John Quincy Adams on behalf of Marquis de Tracy,[93] a prisoner of war in Russia, was not ignored; Alexander permitted him to come to St. Petersburg and stay in the home of the American minister.[94]

The day after Rumiantsev received Alexander's letters from Töplitz approving his actions, he acquainted Adams with their contents.[95] In particular, the Chancellor pointed out a note of 8/20 September 1813, in which the Tsar wrote: "J'approuve complètement, Monsieur le Comte, votre lettre au Comte de Lieven, sur les affaires d'Amérique, et je vous prie de poursuivre cette affaire de même."[96] At the same time, Rumiantsev sent the American delegates an official note informing them that the Emperor authorized him to accept their credential letter and to apologize for his delay in answering which resulted from the circumstances of the military campaign.[97] The official ceremony at which the credential letter was presented by Gallatin, Adams, and Bayard took place immediately after, on October 12.[98]

Meanwhile, time was passing, and Rumiantsev still was not able to fulfill the main thing: to communicate to the Americans the English government's answer to the offer of mediation, and Cathcart's note of 1 September 1813 (which he had never received from the Emperor's headquarters). The only thing the Chancellor was able to tell Gallatin on 3 November 1813 was that Count Lieven had not presented Rumiantsev's note with the offer of mediation. According to Gallatin, the Count was "greatly mortified" at this conduct of Count Lieven's, and he felt it "peculiarly as affecting himself." He said he had forwarded Lieven's dispatch to the Emperor without comment but with a request that he read it in full and "give him orders what to do upon it." The wounded Rumiantsev also remarked that the offer of mediation was originally the Emperor's own idea, and that the latter had insisted on it himself.[99]

British diplomats did not fail to take advantage of the ensuing situation. The new ambassador in St. Petersburg, Lord Walpole, was eager to destroy Rumiantsev's influence and to force a wedge into relations between Russia and the United States. In a conversation with Harris, the secretary of the American mission, on 3 November 1813 Walpole insisted that before his departure from England he had had a conversation with Lord Castlereagh on the subject of mediation. Castlereagh had told him that he first heard of it through a notice of a passport given by Admiral Warren for a vessel carrying the American envoys in the spring of 1813, after which the British cabinet immediately determined to decline the mediation, but manifested willingness to conduct direct negotiations with the United States either in London or in Gothenburg. After Lord Cathcart brought this to the Emperor's knowledge, the latter replied that he could do no more in this business and instructed the Chancellor to express his regret to the American plenipotentiaries and to inform them that he could not undertake any further measures. Lord Walpole expressed regret that the American delegates had been detained in St. Petersburg so long, stating the view that "the disposition to peace was on both sides so strong, that he believed if they could but get to treat, they would easily come to terms." Harris explained, however, that the American delegates had no authorization to treat other than by mediation. Walpole responded that if negotiations were undertaken, the British government would accept their authority, "such as it is, without hesitation."[100]

Walpole spread his version of the Russian mediation as widely as possible. On 20 November 1813, at a reception at court, the ambassador talked loudly in the presence of a large circle of guests, saying that his government never had a hint of Russia's mediation until the communication from Admiral Warren.[101] Much later, on 2 April 1814, he told Adams directly that knowledge of Cathcart's note had been withheld from the Americans purposely, and that "Romanzoff had got into his head some wild and absurd project of a congress, and a maritime law, and he (Walpole) was as sure as he was of his own existence, and he believed he could prove it, that Romanzoff had been *cheating us all.*"[102]

The prolonged stay of the American plenipotentiaries in St. Petersburg and the vague state of the question about Russian mediation created an atmosphere conducive to all kinds of suppositions, false versions, and press insinuations. Back in May 1813 the *Weekly Register* had noted that British newspapers were not writing a thing about Russian mediation; therefore, they made a deduction in Boston that there had been no such offer.[103] In September a report appeared (disclaimed in the *National Intelligencer*) that the offer of mediation had been made by Dashkov without any authorization from St. Petersburg.[104]

Walpole's version not only provoked anxiety among the American plenipotentiaries but also influenced later historians. Even such an informed author as Hildt did not escape its influence, for he affirmed that the English first learned about the mediation through news of Warren's issuing of a passport for the vessel carrying the American envoys.[105] This dubious "news" was presented almost as an important scientific discovery, for Hildt noted in the conclusion of his monograph that the offer of mediation was not made, as the Russian government asserted, simultaneously to England and the United States.[106] Actually, the documents examined—the London correspondence above all—demonstrate indisputably that Russia's proposal of meditation was made to England even somewhat earlier than to the United States, in September 1812. In fall 1812 Liverpool and Castlereagh discussed the proposal with Russian representatives in London, first with Nikolai, then with Lieven. However, although Walpole obviously distorted the facts with regard to Russia, and especially with regard to Rumiantsev, he was absolutely correct on one point: England was decidedly opposed to Russia's mediation and was willing to agree only to direct negotiations. As Lieven reported in December 1813, "the opinion of the whole nation on this problem is so definite that not a single ministry would venture not to share it."[107]

To decide once and for all the question of Russian mediation, the British cabinet initiated a direct correspondence with the Government of the United States. On 4 November 1813 Castlereagh sent a letter to Secretary of State Monroe proposing that direct negotiations for peace be opened; Cathcart's note to Nesselrode of 1 September 1813, was enclosed. He wrote that, according to Cathcart, the American plenipotentiaries in St. Petersburg had made it clear in response to Cathcart's note that they had no objections to negotiations in London and had no more desire than England did for involvement in the European affairs, but that their grant of full powers limited them to negotiations with Russia's mediation. Therefore Castlereagh suggested that the President send the plenipotentiaries new instructions so as to avoid further delays.[108]

British diplomacy could well feel triumphant: it had succeeded in isolating the United States. Russia was plunged even deeper into the tangled web of European affairs. On 16-18 October 1813, in the "battle of the nations" near Leipzig, Napoleon suffered a defeat from which he could not recover. The forces were too unequal. New nations kept joining the struggle against France. The retreat of Napoleon's forces beyond the Rhine had begun.

The fate of Chancellor Rumiantsev was also decided. True, Alexander had not yet officially retired the Minister for Foreign Affairs, in spite of his repeated requests, but the whole political system connected with the name of Rumiantsev had long since been buried. In a conversation with Gallatin, the Chancellor admitted frankly that he had delayed resigning his office only on account of the American mission and that he could no longer transact the Emperor's business: the Emperor had forbidden any other person to write to Rumiantsev, and himself sent only short notes "which were all kindness and condescension, but answered nothing upon matters of business."[109]

In January 1814 the American plenipotentiaries again inquired officially about the state of affairs, but the Chancellor, in spite of his sympathy for them, could tell them nothing new except that Lieven refused to present to Castlereagh the note with the repeated offer of mediation.[110] Under the circumstances, further sojourn in St. Petersburg was unnecessary, and Gallatin and Bayard informed Rumiantsev that they were leaving on 25 January 1814.[111]

On February 1 Rumiantsev invited John Quincy Adams to his home and showed him Lieven's dispatch of 26 November/8 December 1813, which had just come from the Emperor's headquarters. The Ambassador gave a detailed account of the steps which Castlereagh had undertaken to initiate direct negotiations with the United States and of the British minister's direct message to Washington. At Adams' request, the Chancellor later reviewed the contents of this dispatch in an official note addressed to the American minister.[112]

Along with official business on February 1 the Chancellor told Adams a number of interesting details concerning himself personally. Adams noted in his diary the contents of this conversation, quite unusual in diplomatic practice, and then sent the information to Washington in a confidential dispatch, specifying that it was intended for information only and should not be publicized under any circumstances.[113] Rumiantsev had talked to Adams, as was his habit, in a most friendly and frank manner. He told him that, "from the commencement of the new year he had removed from the hotel of the Department of Foreign Affairs to his own house, and was there quietly waiting for his discharge," for which he repeatedly asked the Emperor. "My feelings are entirely American (Je puis dire que j'ai les entrailles Américaines); and were it not for my age and infirmities, I would go now to that country."[114] The wounded statesman mentioned the idea of going to America several times, once in particular in a conversation with Gallatin and Bayard in January 1814. It is hard to say how firm was the Russian Chancellor's intention, but there is no doubt of his sincerity.

I have touched several times on various aspects of Rumiantsev's activity and views, in the light of the war of opinions inside the tsarist government and the general tendencies of Russia's foreign policy. The documents cited make it difficult to agree with the biased, one-sided evaluation of him that is widely accepted. Rumiantsev's name is too often associated with the humiliating Tilsit peace and the so-called "pro-French" orientation of foreign policy. In justice, it must be said that Rumiantsev had nothing to do with the Tilsit peace. The active role in its conclusion was played by A. B. Kurakin, D. I. Lobanov-Rostovsky, and others. Back in 1806 Rumiantsev stated in a meeting of the State Council about the subject of the attitude toward France after Austerlitz that "abrupt groveling for peace" is beneath Russia's dignity.[115]

But this is not what is most important. The role Rumiantsev played in establishing relations with the United States, as well as his most interesting project of establishing commercial ties with the new nations of Latin America in the fall of 1811 has already been discussed. It was far from an accidental paradox that the Chancellor of the Russian Empire was a devoted adherent of rapprochement with the United States, and even tried to establish direct contacts with the rebellious Spanish colonies. It was the result of completely objective factors, and part of a policy whose roots went back to the Armed Neutrality of 1780. All possible encouragement of Russian merchants, the defense of neutral navigation, the desire to protect foreign trade from excessive dependence on England, rapprochement with the United States, and the encouragement of the direct contacts with the

American market—these are different branches of a single system of foreign policy, whose active champion Rumiantsev had been ever since the beginning of the nineteenth century.

Extreme reactionaries in the Tsar's entourage hated Rumiantsev, considering him, along with Speransky, almost a Jacobin. Although I am far from ascribing leftist tendencies to Rumiantsev (who at best was a moderate liberal), it is obvious that he was not in the same camp with Arakcheev, Koshelev, and Nesselrode. It is an error to saddle him with "pro-French" or "pro-American" orientation. Rumiantsev always acted with the interests of Russian landowners and merchants in mind or, more precisely, with the interest of that segment of them which feared excessive English influence in the Russian market.

In spite of the failure of Russia's mediation attempt, the American plenipotentiaries had a unanimous high opinion of Rumiantsev's activity. Adams called the Chancellor a "sincere and genuine Russian patriot," asserting that of the statesmen with whom it had been his fortune to have political relations, he never knew one who carried into public life more of the principles and sentiments of spotless private honor. He blamed a "powerful and implacable English influence," that had incessantly worked against him, for the demise of Rumiantsev's influence.[116]

Having received permission from the United States government to open direct negotiations with England, Adams, in an official note of 26 March/ 7 April 1814, informed the Russian government of his impending departure. At the same time he denied that the American plenipotentiaries had replied to Cathcart's note of 1 September 1813, since they did not even know anything about it.[117]

Adams repeated these arguments in the course of his farewell conversation with Rumiantsev on 23 April 1814. The Chancellor confirmed that he had never received Cathcart's note, expressing the supposition that "Lord Walpole had written to Lord Cathcart reports of the conversations, loose and unofficial, from which these assertions might have arisen." The Chancellor thought that "all this proceeded from the double mode of transacting business—here through one channel, and at the headquarters through another. But he (the Count) had always been frank and explicit with us." Adams then reported Rumiantsev's words in his Diary, "Another might have shuffled and equivocated," and, as "was customary both in England and France, left our notes three or four months unanswered. That was not his way of doing business; he had told us at once and immediately that he had received nothing from the Emperor on the subject, and the Emperor had forbidden Count Nesselrode to write him anything, except merely to transmit official documents to him. If we had ever answered as Lord Castlereagh pretended, let them produce our answer. It must be in writing, for nothing but a written document could be such an answer."[118]

In a letter to Monroe dated 15 April 1814, Adams noted that "it was apparently the object of the British Cabinet, in rejecting the Russian mediation, to withhold, if possible, from the public eye all evidence, not only of that rejection and of the motives upon which it was founded, but even that the offer had been made."[119]

The government of the United States opened direct negotiations with England most reluctantly. In his answer to Lord Castlereagh of 5 January 1814, Monroe expressed on behalf of the President regret that England declined Russian mediation, thus creating a new obstacle to the opening of negotiations for peace.[120] The United States was aware of the reasons for England's refusal of Russian mediation and of England's aims. "Why has Great Britain rejected the Russian mediation?" Monroe wrote in a special note on the subject.

> Because she dreaded it. Why has she offered to treat directly with us? because she wished to prevent a concert between the United States and the northern powers, to prevent our affairs, as she says, being mixed with those of the continent. . . . She now invites us to treat by ourselves, to separate us from the continent, that is, from our friends. . . . Her object is to treat with us apart from the continent, and get us to make a treaty disadvantageous to us without the aid which we might get by a concert and friendly communication with the northern powers.[121]

Although accepting Castlereagh's offer of direct negotiations, the United States government was anxious to avoid any deterioration of relations with Russia, and asserted most decisively its desire to preserve mutual understanding between the two countries. When, on 7 January 1814, Monroe informed Dashkov that the President had consented to the opening of direct peace negotiations with England, he commented that these negotiations had originated through Russia's friendly intercession.[122]

According to the instructions from Washington of 8 January 1814, the American plenipotentiaries were to inform the Russian government of "the sensibility of the President to the friendly disposition of the Emperor, manifested by the offer of his mediation, the regret felt at its rejection by the British Government, and a desire that, in the future, the greatest confidence and cordiality and the best understanding may prevail between the two governments."[123] Early in February 1814, the Secretary of State wrote to Adams in similar terms. The offer of mediation, according to him, constituted an interesting era in relations between the United States and Russia, and he expected that the development and strengthening of the amicable character of these relations would become the President's goal in the future.[124]

The Peace Commission the United States government sent abroad was exceptionally strong and able.[125] In addition to the former delegates, it included Henry Clay, a well-known leader of the War Hawks and a man with his eye on the future presidency, and Jonathan Russell, a young diplomat who had served as chargé d'affaires in Paris and London on the eve of the War of 1812. Although Adams was its official head, the most prominent figure of the delegation was Albert Gallatin, whose opinion carried the most weight.

On the contrary, the British cabinet did not consider it necessary to send to Ghent diplomats of any prominence, even though such men as Castlereagh, Canning, Wellesley, and Grenville were available. It was thought quite proper to send Lord Gambier, Henry Goulborn, and William Adams. Although the American plenipotentiaries had no worthy opponents at the conference table, their position, objectively speaking, was not easy. Because of this, both on the eve of negotiations and in the course of them, the American delegates repeatedly turned to Russia, as the only power on whose support they could count, with requests to influence the British cabinet and make its position more flexible. In the spring of 1814 Gallatin was especially active in this way—even attempting unsuccessfully to utilize the American minister in Paris, William Crawford, to arrange a meeting with Alexander I.[126] (It is interesting that Gallatin and Crawford utilized Poletika as a reliable messenger for secret correspondence.) Somewhat more successful was the activity of the Marquis de Lafayette, who in late May 1814 succeeded in having an exchange with Alexander I on the question of mediation. In answer to the Marquis' insistent request that he make a third attempt to bring about peace, the Tsar replied that his forthcoming journey to London would "afford opportunities" and that he would do all he could.[127]

Finally, on June 17, during Alexander's visit to England, Gallatin and Harris succeeded in obtaining an audience with the Tsar. The American plenipotentiaries and Lafayette, as well as American government leaders (particularly Madison and Monroe), referred to Alexander, in both official and private letters, most favorably, even flatteringly, as "the sincere friend of the cause of liberty," "liberator and pacifier of Europe," and "friend of the United States." The "noble" Alexander I knew how to charm visitors and at that time continued to play "the role of the hero of liberalism."[128] It is not surprising therefore, that both Gallatin and Lafayette spoke enthusiastically of their encounters with the Russian autocrat, who, as a result of heroic efforts on the part of the Russian people, was revered as Napoleon's conqueror. The "merciful Tsar" was not too en- couraging to the American plenipotentiaries, although he assured them that his friendship for the United States was unimpaired: "England will not admit a third party to interfere in her disputes with you." Alexander I said at a meeting with Gallatin and Harris, "This is on account of your former relations to her (the colonial state), which is not yet forgotten."[129]

On the second day after this meeting, Gallatin, as agreed, addressed an official note to the Tsar, expressing the hope that, as a result of Russian cooperation, the United States would finally incline the British cabinet to- ward peace, "although the powerful armament, particularly of land forces, sent by England to America on the eve of opening the negotiations for peace may create a suspicion that she will not make it but on inadmis- sible terms." In conclusion, he expressed in his elegant French[130] the heartfelt assurance that America would always preserve a warm recollec- tion of this and several other proofs of the Emperor's friendly regard.[131]

The American plenipotentiaries did not abandon hope for Russia's support, even after official talks began in Ghent on 1 August 1814. Ac- cording to Vedemeier, in September 1814 chargé d'affaires Harris "spoke with some anxiety about the unsatisfactory state of their affairs in the Ghent Congress, "and asked the Russian government to make "new soli- citations" on their behalf.[132]

Throughout the entire period the position of British diplomacy re- mained harsh and unyielding. The very choice of a provincial Belgian town as the seat for negotiations testified to the British desire to isolate them from foreign interference. "I am not surprised that the Emperor should inquire pourquoi *Gand*? et pourquoi Gothenburg? but these ques- tions can be answered only by the British government," wrote Adams. "We should much have preferred treating in St. Petersburg."[133]

Even at a distance, Russia gave the English ministers cause for concern. Therefore it was not accidental that the English tried in all sorts of ways to create an impression of moderation and love of peace. Prime Minister Liverpool wrote Castlereagh in Vienna on 27 September 1814: "I fear the Emperor of Russia is half an American and it would be very desirable to do away with any prejudices which may exist in his mind, or in that of Count Nesselrode, on this subject."[134]

Although the Russian government did not interfere directly, the course of the Vienna Congress and acute antagonisms between the recent allies could not help but influence negotiations in Ghent. In order to confront Russia and Prussia in Vienna, England had to end the Ghent negotiations as speedily as possible and terminate the prolonged war in America. When, at the concluding stage of negotiations, the English government decided to abandon its territorial claims, one of the reasons it gave for the decision was the unsatisfactory state of negotiations in Vienna.[135]

After long and complex negotiations, the Ghent peace treaty was signed on 24 December 1814. The treaty passed over in silence, rather than resolved, the points which had brought about the War of 1812: the questions of borders, freedom of the seas, the rights of the neutral powers, and so forth. The treaty stipulated, in particular, the mutual abandonment of captured territory (article 1); the return of prisoners (article 3); the cessation of military actions against the Indians (article 9); and the obligation to take decisive measures to abolish traffic in slaves (article 10). Mixed commissions were formed to define the borders.[136] In other words, the basic content of the treaty was reduced to a simple stopping of military actions and the restoration of old borders.

When the ruling circle of the United States started the War of 1812 they had no doubt that they would be able to capture Canada without much effort and bring about fundamental changes in Britian's despotic policy on the high seas. By the fall of 1814 they were satisfied with a settlement without territorial losses. The American people managed to preserve their independence, but they had to give up all attempts to change Great Britain's position on the question of neutral navigation and commerce.

Commenting on the conclusion of the treaty, Harris wrote in a secret communication to Vedemeier on 8/20 January 1815:

> The conditions of the peace treaty between the United States and England, signed on 24 December 1814, are based on the principle of *status quo ante bellum*. By mutual agreement, all the questions of maritime rights are left aside . . . . Neither side made any territorial concessions, but certain points of the former border will be examined by the plenipotentiaries appointed by both powers, and in case they do not come to an agreement, the controversial points will be brought for the decision by a friendly monarch.

In conclusion, Harris thanked the Russian government on behalf of the United States for its offer of mediation which, in spite of the completely different attitudes of the belligerents "undoubtedly, was conducive to success."[137]

The cooperation of Russian diplomacy proved to be necessary for the United States at later stages also. In the summer of 1815, the American chargé d'affaires addressed Vedemeier with a request that he help the American plenipotentiaries through Italinsky, Russia's minister in Constantinople, to conclude peace with the Algerians.[138]

The Ghent treaty was followed by the conclusion of the commercial Convention of 1815, an 1817 agreement to demilitarize the Great Lakes, the agreement of 1818 on the North Atlantic fisheries, establishment of borders in the north, and the so-called "joint possession" of Oregon. The question of the interpretation of the first article of the Ghent treaty, relating to the evacuation of British troops, remained open for a long time. Since the two sides could not arrive at an agreement, in the beginning of 1820 it was decided—as proposed by the American minister in London, Richard Rush, and agreed to by the British government—to transfer this dispute to the arbitration of Alexander I (in accordance with article 5 of the 1818 Convention).

This appeal to Alexander I may have appeared "whimsical," as John Quincy Adams put it, since two English-speaking powers asked the Russian Tsar's help to interpret the precise meaning of a text which they themselves had written. As a result of the grammatical analysis of the text of the first article of the Ghent treaty, the Russian government judged the point of view of the United States to be more correct. The Convention was signed in St. Petersburg on 30 June/12 July 1822, with Russian mediation, in conformity with Alexander's decision as to the actual meaning of the first article.

In the last analysis, Russia's position during the Anglo-American War of 1812 facilitated the armistice and played a role vis-à-vis the United States. Although declining her offer of mediation, England, recognizing Russia's clearly expressed desire to see the Anglo-American war ended, agreed to direct negotiations. Later on, Russia's position was a substantial factor which influenced the 1814 negotiations in Ghent and the 1822 resolution of the dispute over the first article of the Ghent treaty.

XII

CULTURAL CONTACTS AND AMERICAN ATTITUDES
TOWARD THE RUSSIAN WAR OF 1812

During the early years of the nineteenth century Russian-American rapprochement extended beyond the sphere of diplomatic and commercial relations. A considerable expansion of scientific and cultural contacts took place. John Quincy Adams and Levett Harris in Russia, and Dashkov, Pahlen, Kozlov, and especially Evstaf'ev, Poletika, and Svin'in, in America, performed more than narrow diplomatic and consular functions. In a sense they were ambassadors of culture, who encouraged the development of scientific, literary, and socio-political ties between the Russian and American peoples.

Russian representatives in the United States, in their careful study of that country, manifested an interest in agriculture and industry as well as in the most important technical inventions. In January 1811 Dashkov provided Rumiantsev with detailed information on agricultural crops indigenous to America and sent to Russia seeds of grapes and various plants.[1] Later, he succeeded in obtaining a cotton gin, which, in his words, had brought success to United States commerce, and "could produce similar results in the south of Russia."[2]

Dashkov and Svin'in even more actively championed the steamboat, and official negotiations for the utilization of Fulton's invention in Russia began in October 1812. They resulted in signing of a ukase in December 1813, authorizing Fulton to build steamboats in Russia on condition that he adhere to certain obligations, including technical documentation.[3] Dashkov, Evstaf'ev, and Svin'in continually persisted in bringing various American inventions to Russian attention.[4]

The activities of Adams and Harris were of great importance to the developing of contacts between American scientific centers—the Philosophical Society in Philadelphia, the Academy of Arts and Sciences in Boston, and Harvard University—and St. Petersburg Academy of Sciences, the Medico-Surgical Academy, and the Moscow Society of Natural Sciences. According to his diary, Adams maintained personal contact with St. Petersburg Academy of Sciences members Tilesius, Fuss, Hermann, and Schubert; with the prominent Russian explorer Krusenstern, Count Laval; and with the director of the Engineering Institute, Betancourt. He exchanged publications and visited museums and scientific establishments. While remaining a scientific dilettante, he used his personal initiative in this area just as he did in diplomacy. For example, having learned from his reading that Professor Schubert had made observations on the comet of 1807, Adams paid him a call and presented him with a volume of *Memoirs* of the American Academy of Arts and Sciences containing Bowditch's observations on the comet.[5] During visits to the Naval Academy and other educational institutions, Adams was much impressed by the high level of mathematical education. According to his observations, "the study of mathematics was given much more attention than in America"—girls even received more instruction in it than he deemed sensible.[6]

On his departure from Boston, Adams had received from Judge John Davis a collection of North American minerals; he passed this on to the Society of Amateurs of the Natural Sciences at Moscow University. On 30 April/12 May 1810, John Adams, "President of the American Academy in Boston," and Joseph Willard, Vice-President of the American Academy and the "Président de l'Université à Boston" were elected honorary members of this learned society, and John Davis, "secretary of the Academy," became a regular member of it. Somewhat earlier, on 3/15 February 1810, the Director of the Society, Gotthelf Fischer, informed John Quincy Adams that he had been elected to membership in the Society, and proposed that they engage in a regular correspondence.[7] Early in 1811 Karl Etter asked the American minister to forward to the United States his collection of Russian minerals. On Adams' recommendation, this collection, consisting of sixty-four pieces, was sent to the American Academy of Arts and Sciences in Boston. In turn, Etter received samples of American minerals from the United States.[8] In November 1812, contacts between the Boston Academy and Russia were strengthened by the election of Fisher, Fuss, and Schubert; Etter had become a member even earlier, on 19 August 1812.[9]

Of considerable interest are the first direct contacts between American physicians and the Russian Medico-Surgical Academy in St. Petersburg, founded in 1798. In December 1810, Benjamin Rush, a well-known American scientist, sent Alexander I, through John Quincy Adams, a report on his medical work; the Tsar responded by sending him a valuable ring. In February 1812 Rush was elected to membership in the Medico-Surgical Academy. In a letter dated 13 November 1812, Rush asked J. Q. Adams to pass on to the Academy, through its President, Ia. V. Villie (James Wylie), a copy of his medical observations and inquiries, acknowledging that he had learned of his election to the Academy.[10] Also in 1812 Ricketson, a lesser known American physician, sent to Russia a number of medical books, including his own work, *Means of Preserving Health and Preventing Diseases.*[11]

The letters of John Quincy Adams and Levett Harris to the Philosophical Society in Philadelphia and the Academy of Arts and Sciences in Boston indicate that a fairly regular and fruitful exchange of scientific publications took place in the course of those years. Adams was especially anxious to enlarge the library of Harvard College, where he had once taught. On 11 April 1810, he paid a special visit to Tilesius to request his aid in procuring all volumes of the *Transactions* of the Academy of Sciences at St. Petersburg necessary to complete Harvard's collection.[12] With the help of Harris, Tilesius established in October 1813 direct scientific correspondence with Casparo Wistor, anatomy professor at Philadelphia; several years later (on April 16, 1819), he became a member of the American Philosophical Society.[13]

While in St. Petersburg, Adams acquired about three hundred books, including Krusenstern's *Reise um die Welt in den Jahren 1803, 1804, 1805, und 1806* in German,[14] personally presented to him by the author, and Pallas' well-known work, *Flora Rossica,* which Adams procured for Harvard with great difficulty and for a considerable sum.[15] However, both Adams and Harris mostly sent to the United States dictionaries, grammars, and special works on the Russian language.[16]

Adams' role in the development of scientific and cultural contacts between the United States and Russia was indeed important, but it is regrettable that neither he nor the secretary of the mission, A. H. Everett (later a well-known journalist and editor), had persistence and patience enough to master the Russian language. Adams certainly had ample time for this task: he was in Russia as a minister for more than four and a half years, not to mention his 1781-82 stay in St. Petersburg. During those years he took down detailed notes on the weather, made lists of correspondents and expenditures, and constructed endless tables of different weights and measures used in Russia. (The results of this last-named hobby proved useful in 1821 when Adams demonstrated his remarkable knowledge of this subject in preparing a report on weights and measures for the United States Congress.)[17]

It is interesting to speculate on the important consequences that might have ensued if Adams, Everett, Gallatin, or any of the outstanding American leaders who spent time in Russia had devoted some of their energy to studying the achievements of Russian literature and to acquainting the American public with them. At the time Russian literature was represented by such figures as Lomonosov, Karamzin, Zhukovsky, and Derzhavin—and after 1814 the brilliance of Pushkin began to sparkle. Adams and Everett were not devoid of literary interests. Adams read Latin and Greek and was especially fond of fables. During his stay in St. Petersburg he bought five collections of fables in French, but apparently he never heard of Krylov, although Krylov's first book of fables, which came out in 1809, was enjoying an overwhelming success.[18] As a result, the American minister, who succeeded so quickly in winning the favor of the Tsar and establishing a friendship with the Chancellor, was completely isolated from the Russian public and from the avant-garde literary milieu.

The role of Adams' counterparts in America was quite different in this respect. Until recently, little was known about the attitude of the United States toward Russia. Research on the subject was considered impossible because of the unavailability in Russian libraries of American periodicals of the first half of the nineteenth century and other documentary materials. But further investigation of the archives and libraries of Moscow and Leningrad brought to light a number of valuable sources which could be used to explore the attitude of various groups in America toward Russia and the Russian-French war of 1812, and to illuminate the extensive and useful activities of Evstaf'ev, Russian consul-general in Boston, Svin'in, secretary of the consulate in Philadelphia, and embassy adviser Poletika.[19]

Little was known about Russia in the beginning of the nineteenth century in the main European countries, let alone the United States. Incredible tales and fables prevailed in the West as a result of poor information and biased insinuations. Foreigners who spent a little time in Russia and later published superficial and unobjective observations were considered authorities. The work of E. D. Clark, widely circulated both in Europe and America, is a characteristic example.[20]

This absence of objective information on Russia was a serious handicap not only to the formation of public opinion in the United States but to the development of Russian-American relations in general. In his dispatches to St. Petersburg, Dashkov complained that the government in Washington was indifferent to the development of relations with Russia. He blamed this on national prejudices and ignorance of Russia's resources and the advantages of commercial relations between the two countries.[21]

The small "Russian colony" that developed after the establishment of diplomatic and consular relations between Russia and the United States had an enormous task to inform the American public about the Russian empire and her resources, customs, and culture. Reporting on early steps in this direction, Dashkov called attention to the publication in the United States of some special items on Russia. The first was a tragedy by A. G. Evstaf'ev, a supplement to which, *Collection of Anecdotes* (about Peter the Great), came out later as a separate publication.[22] An influential Philadelphia newspaper printed, as a supplement, a portrait of Alexander I—by a well-known American painter, advised by Svin'in—as well as an article on the Russian government, which, according to Dashkov, produced a great interest on the part of the readers and an increase in the number of subscribers. The last work mentioned by Dashkov was written by Poletika and circulated as an offprint from a journal popular in Federalist circles. The author subjected Clark's inaccurate book to detailed critical analysis, thus providing a more objective idea of Russia.[23]

Early in 1812 Poletika presented the American Philosophical Society with a rare copy of *Russkaia Pravda,* the earliest (eleventh century) of the Russian law codes.[24] Another valuable gift, Karamzin's *Pantheon of Russian Writers,* was presented to the American Philosophical Society by Svin'in, who made a special translation into English of an essay on Lomonosov.[25] Svin'in's book, published in Philadelphia in 1813, was a detailed account of living conditions in Russia, the customs and traditions of the people, and descriptions of Moscow and St. Petersburg. Citing the example of Clark's book, Svin'in advised his readers to distrust the superficial testimony of foreigners who publish suppositions for the sake of entertaining the public. According to him, such "witnesses" laughed at the "stupidity" of the Russians, when they saw bonfires in the streets, imagining that the Russians were trying to warm the air. The author actively championed Russian-American rapprochement.[26] Also of great interest to foreign readers were the colorful descriptions of Moscow and St. Petersburg, comments on daily life in Russia, cossacks, Caucasus, and so on.

The literary and social activity of A. G. Evstaf'ev, Russian consul in

Boston, deserves special attention. He has attracted little attention, and only a few fragmentary, sometimes contradictory, biographical details are available. Nevertheless, Evstaf'ev, like Poletika, Svin'in, and Karzhavin, deserves to occupy an honored place in the history of early Russian-American cultural and socio-political connections. [27] Evstaf'ev's interesting book on Russia's resources in case of war with France was popular in both Western Europe and America. Based on a careful analysis of statistical materials and the history of earlier wars, he concluded that Russians could successfully repulse an assault by the enemy's army. This book, reprinted many times both in the United States and in England, was heatedly discussed in the periodical press. [28] In response to his opponents, Evstaf'ev published in Boston a booklet in which he mocked "the extraordinary ignorance of Dr. Clark and Edinburg reviewers concerning Russian affairs."[29] Naturally one cannot always agree with Evstaf'ev and Svin'in. Their descriptions of living conditions in Russia are often idealized; but on the whole they are more reliable than the "scholarly works" of Clark and his colleagues.

The exploits of the Russian people in their 1812 war showed the world the enormous potential force of Russia which had evaded earlier, superficial glances of Western "travelers," and confirmed the prognosis given in Evstaf'ev's book.

Events of 1812 in Russia concerned more than the fate of that country. The fate of Europe, and in the last analysis, of the entire world, depended in many ways upon the outcome of battles in Russian fields. The great victory of the Russian people dealt a shattering blow to Napoleon's adventurist pretensions toward world dominion. In many countries people were expressing joy at the defeat of Napoleon's army. [30] The successes of Russian arms activated the struggle of oppressed European nations against French domination; each new report of successes strengthened their faith in eventual liberation. [31]

It is not surprising, therefore, that the heroic struggle of the Russian people attracted attention throughout Europe—and not only Europe. In far-off America too, events in Russia were closely watched. In order to understand the attitude of the American public toward the war in Russia it is necessary to take into account the influence of a number of complex factors. First of all, since 18 June 1812 the United States had been at war with England, Russia's main ally in the struggle against Napoleon. Far from being interrupted, however, Russian-American relations continued on their favorable course, and it was Russia from whom the United States expected to receive some support at the peace negotiations.

THE WAR OF 1812 AND TSARIST RUSSIA

Hostile propaganda and erroneous notions, long present in Western literature, have hindered the formation of correct ideas about Russia and the Russian people. Since no distinction was formerly made between tsarist autocracy and the Russian people, such hostile evaluations of Russia have even emerged from usually progressive circles. Finally, any analysis of American public opinion must take into account the struggle of political parties and class positions within the United States. It is understandable, therefore, that from the very beginning, there were basic differences in the American attitude toward events of the Russian war of 1812.

The earliest American responses to the news of the Borodino battle are indicative. As usual, the Philadelphia *Aurora* with its pro-French position, was unable to evaluate circumstances objectively. On 10 November 1812, its editor, William Duane, published a lengthy article speculating on the possibility of Russian defeat and the conclusion of peace. If Moscow was captured, the author considered it inevitable that "the Russian nation must assume a new character, and will undergo *partition*." He also predicted that the conquest of Russia might result in the "transporting from the Volga to the shores of the British Channel, legions as barbarous as those of sanguinary ferocity under Suwarrow—*friends of peace and religion.*"[32]

Later, in December, the semiofficial *National Intelligencer* reprinted a tendentious article by Cobbett, which noted maliciously: "Napoleon approaches Moscow. Perhaps he is now there; and yet we are told of the bravery and patriotism of the Russians." Without any comprehension of the peculiar tactics of the Russian army, Cobbett admired Napoleon: "The greatest of conquerors of whom history speaks have not in their whole lives performed half what he has performed since he left Paris last time . . . There is not, in my opinion, the smallest chance of anything being done to obstruct him in the North."[33]

The attacks of Duane and Cobbett did not remain unanswered. Protesting letters appeared in newspapers, and on December 3 the *Boston Gazette* printed "Cobbett and Duane versus Russia," an article which rebuffed the attempts of the *Aurora,* to slander Russia.[34] Some American newspapers, especially those in New England (the *Boston Gazette, Weekly Messenger,* and others) regularly published commentaries which were objective and favorable to Russia. On 20 November 1812, James Cutler's *Weekly Messenger,* following a short dispatch on the battle of Borodino, printed a long article entitled "The State of War in Russia," in which it was suggested that French dispatches should not be trusted.

They [the Russians] may retreat and Napoleon may get to Moscow; but have they not retreated before? Had their armies been broken in the retreat? It is these armies, and not Moscow that he must conquer, ere he can hope for the successful accomplishments of his daring views.[35]

A detailed account of the Borodino battle was printed in the *Boston Gazette,* which called the battle of 7 September 1812, "the most bloody battle that has ever been fought in modern Europe." Although the official French bulletin admitted the loss of only ten thousand people, the author of the article compared this figure with obviously underestimated earlier data and concluded that Napoleon's losses in dead and wounded must have been at least fifty thousand.[36] As we know, he was not far from the truth.

The autumn of 1812 brought the United States a number of confusing dispatches from faraway Russia: the retreat of the Russian army; the bloody battle at Borodino; the abandoning of Moscow; and, finally, the enormous fire in the ancient capital. The lies of boasting French bulletins, the insinuations of Duane, and the mockery of Cobbett made it difficult to assess correctly the character and significance of these events. Nevertheless, even under these conditions some individuals in the United States could evaluate them correctly and firmly believed in the unconquerability of the heroic Russian people. One such testimony must be quoted. Moving even now, one hundred and fifty years after it was written, it is a letter from Joseph Hopkinson of Philadelphia to the Russian minister in the United States:

Moscow is taken, yet the nation is undismayed. The people who could with their own hands, fire an ancient and splendid city, as dear to their hearts as Jerusalem ever was to the idolatry of the Jews; who could put the burning brand to the palaces of their princes and the temples of their God; who could strip and abandon the dwellings of their ancestors and the houses of their nativity, such a people must be invincible. What unparalleled magnanimity! How little is all greatness of Napoleon compared with this single deed . . . What a sublime sacrifice! Moscow in her splendour was the *pride* of Russia, but in her flames she is her *glory* . . .

"Russia has gained more true, unperishable greatness in that single hour, than France by all her victories and conquests," wrote Hopkinson; in conclusion he expressed his full confidence in the final victory of the Russian people over Napoleon.[37]

The reports of the Russian army's brilliant victories over Napoleon, and his expulsion from Russia, which arrived in the United States early in

1813, made an enormous impression on the Americans. Consul-General Kozlov in Philadelphia described the initial reaction to them:

> This news made the greatest impression on minds here. . . . The local papers printed the news under the title *Des nouvelles glorieuses,* which was not given to the Americans' own successes over the English. . . . The treacherous insinuations of our enemies, which were quite impressive up to now . . . are now turned to shaming the French party, contributing to the stronger assertion of the idea of our actual might, and makes people marvel at the firmness of spirit with which we made the greatest sacrifices in order to repulse the enemy. The burning of Moscow amazed local inhabitants. They thought here that after the French entered the capital we would have accepted all their proposals.[38]

"The effect of this news upon the Americans," Dashkov wrote from Washington two weeks later, "is almost incredible. . . . All the statements of the French insinuators and scribblers of all sorts hired by their editors to slander Russia disappeared like fog after sunrise . . . I have letters from Boston, New York, and Philadelphia, informing me joyfully that people congratulate each other on Russian victories, as if they were their own! The American people," the Russian consul-general continued, "instead of seeing Russia conquered, see her triumphant; instead of inexperienced generals and newly conscripted troops, they see the art, the manliness, and sufficient organization for upsetting the designs of French military leaders and destroying their army of whose success previously they had not even dared to have doubts."[39]

Russian victories were widely commented on in American newspapers. The *Boston Gazette,* for example, printed a detailed description of Russian victories in an article entitled "American Liberty defended by the Cossacks of the Don."[40] Many of the articles and notes on the Russian war published in the American press came from a pen of A. G. Evstaf'ev. This includes the observations of "a highly esteemed and enlightened correspondent," printed in the *Boston Gazette* along with the Cossack article, and probably also the abovementioned article about Duane and Cobbett. We can only marvel at how precisely and circumstantially the Boston consul reported on the campaign in Russia, while being far away from his country and often having none but French bulletins for information. He gave detailed and amazingly exact evaluations of the battle of Borodino, of its actual significance for the outcome of the war, of the idea and tactics of Kutuzov's strategy, of the character of the war against Napoleon.[41] However, it should be noted that, although Evstaf'ev justly condemned Napoleon's aggression, he tended to overemphasize the liberational significance of the campaign of 1813. He overlooked the self-seeking aims of the tsarist government, and lavished immoderate praise on "Europe's deliverer": Alexander I. That, however, can be attributed in part to his position as a Russian official.

American responses to the Russian war of 1812 were not limited to newspaper articles, statements by individuals, or letters to the Russian mission. In the spring of 1813 special celebrations took place in a number of towns, in the presence of many prominent representatives of the American public, members of Congress, well-known lawyers, and others. According to Dashkov, the most striking was Boston's celebration of the Russian victory. A church service in the Stone Chapel on 25 March was followed by an oration and a banquet. "The whole city expressed its enthusiasm."[42] An account of this celebration published in leading American papers including *Niles' Weekly Register*,[43] reprinted the text of speeches by the well-known Federalist leader Harrison Gray Otis and Evstaf'ev. The main orator, Otis, ended his speech by saying: "Let us hail these glorious events as a prelude to better times for our country, as well as the immediate cause of happiness and liberty to others."[44] A detailed account of this celebration was published in a booklet in 1813. Young Alexander Everett, recently returned from St. Petersburg, who was present at the festival, composed an ode about the children of Russia, who have flown "from their castles and huts" to fight "for the freedom of Russia, and rights of mankind." This ode was written to the tune of "Anacreon in Heaven" which served, a year and a half later, as a basis for the American anthem, "The Star-Spangled Banner."[45]

Another great celebration of Russian victories over Napoleon took place on 5 June 1813, in Georgetown in the District of Columbia. About three hundred people were present, including many prominent Federalist leaders, Senators, members of the House of Representatives, Russian Minister Dashkov, and foreign consuls.[46] In opening the meeting, the presiding officer, George Custis, called upon his audience to express their sympathy for solidarity with Russia. He said that in the flames of Moscow, the aggressor found "a funeral pyre for his ambition."[47] He urged Russia to go forward with its task of liberating Europe from Napoleon's domination. He also acclaimed that Kutuzov's name, along with Washington's, should be included in the list of noble heroes, deliverers of their country, and benefactors of humanity.[48]

The main speech was delivered by Robert Harper.[49] The brilliance of delivery, convincing argumentation, style, and content—even if one discounts the excessive praises of "Alexander the Deliverer" typical of that time—combined to make the speech a great success for the famous lawyer. Talking of the "memorable battle of Borodino," Harper stated: "In this

343

shock of two mighty empires, where one struggled for universal domination and the other for national independence. . . . the hitherto triumphant progress of the invader was at length arrested. He was repulsed and beaten, though not discomforted. But he there received his death wound." "It was then," the orator continued, "that the superior genius of Koutousoff conceived that profound plan of future operations, which in its development and execution has produced such wonderful results." Carefully analyzing the causes of Napoleon's defeat, Harper stressed: "It was not therefore the premature winter, nor the severity of the climate, but the skill and prowess of his enemies, by which he was destroyed." Harper rated Russian victory as of the highest importance to mankind.

Another exceptionally high evaluation of the victory's significance was given by J. Allen Smith, who visited Russia in the early nineteenth century and remained on friendly terms with the Vorontsov family. In June 1813, in a letter to Vorontsov from Philadelphia, Smith wrote that the annals of world history had nothing comparable to Russia's victory, and mentioned that he was congratulated by everybody in America for his correct evaluation of Russian soldiers.[50] He considered Russian victories as victories for all of humanity and thought that Russia had put up "a barrier against a torrent which threatened to overwhelm the whole world."[51]

One should not assume, however, that all American responses to the Russian war were positive. Then, as at any other time, there was no shortage in the United States of political and social activists of the most varied views; there were a great many newspapers, and various political parties and groups in existence.[52] It is not surprising, therefore, that celebrations of Russian victories encountered many protests from various segments of the American public, whose mood was expressed by a well-known journalist and literary man, Robert Walsh. His objections to the celebration of Russia's victories over Napoleonic France, expressed in letters to Robert Harper, were later brought out as a separate publication.[53]

Walsh held a most negative opinion of Russia and the Russian people. This "enlightened" author saw fit to state that "there is no government, or peoples, on record, whose history is more atrocious, in almost every stage!"[54] Stressing in the extreme the characteristic "barbarism" of the Russians, Eastern despotism, and the absence of civilization, Walsh expressed apprehensions of Russia's boundless schemes of conquest.[55]

Some Western researchers have crowned Walsh with the dubious laurels of the first discoverer of the Russian menace. According to Professor J. Shulim, he was the first American who gave "the clearest warning during the Napoleonic era of a Russian menace to the world."[56] I do not intend to dispute Walsh's priority in this question, but, to put it mildly, such "laurels" could hardly be considered honorable. The tendentiousness of Walsh's observations about the "Russian menace" seem obvious, and one cannot but agree with Harper's objections. While agreeing that France's complete subjugation to Russia's domination would have been just as dangerous as the conquest of the Russian empire by Napoleon, Harper stressed that he never considered such a possibility. He assumed that the end result of Napoleon's defeat in Russia would have been the expulsion of the French from Germany, Holland, and Italy, a confining of them within the Rhine, the Alps, and the Pyrenees.[57]

In 1813 Evstaf'ev subjected *Correspondence respecting Russia* to detailed critical analysis. On the basis of much factual material he proved the flimsiness of Walsh's insulting fabrications and stressed again that the Russian struggle against Napoleon had a just and liberational character.[58]

In considering the position of American society in respect to the Russian War of 1812, one must remember that Republicans (or Democrats) as a rule were negatively inclined toward Russia—England's ally in her struggle with Napoleon. On the other hand, the Federalists, inclined toward agreement with England and representing the industrial Northeast, took a favorable position. This fact, acknowledged by modern historians, was pointed out at the time by Dashkov and Kozlov in dispatches to Rumiantsev.[59] Russian victories were acclaimed warmly in New England; and celebrations were not infrequently open criticisms of a Democratic administration which had dragged the country into a war with England. On April 24, 1813, the *National Intelligencer* reminded American readers that Russia was Britain's main ally and that the celebration of tsarist victories "believed the success of Russia to be auspicious to the cause of our enemy." The paper pointed out that instead of "Russian victories" Bostonians should celebrate "Russian Mediation."[60] Duane, French minister Sérurier, and others made a great effort to arouse the displeasure of the United States government on this subject, and in a certain sense they succeeded. Monroe complained to Dashkov about Evstaf'ev's behavior during the Boston celebrations of Russian victories, although he agreed not to take further action.[61]

One could hardly expect the government of the United States, itself in the throes of an Anglo-American war, to express joy over the shattering defeat in Russia of the Napoleonic empire, England's main enemy. On the other hand, it would be a serious mistake to consider for this reason that the attitude toward Russia and Russian victories of the (Democratic) Republican Party and the government of the United States was hostile in principle. It is worth recalling Thomas Jefferson's letter to Duane of 20 July 1807, in which the founder of the Republican Party, trying to cool the anti-Russian ardor of the *Aurora*'s editor, wrote of Russia as the power "most cordially friendly" to the United States, mentioning the similarity of American and Russian interests and sentiments regarding the question of the rights of neutral navigation, and so on.[62] Jefferson also made exceptionally sharp references to Napoleon.

A high opinion of the heroic efforts of the Russian people in the struggle with Napoleon was also held by John Quincy Adams. Living in St. Petersburg, the American minister had a good opportunity to observe conditions within Russia and to receive regular information on the course of various military operations. In spite of the retreat of Russian troops, Adams was inclined toward optimism, and was not ready, as were some of his Western colleagues, to bury the Russian army prematurely. As early as July 1812, he noted that "the Russians have been retreating to unite their forces."[63] Commenting on the successful results of the general strategy of the Russian command, he wrote: "The Fabian system, which succeeded in our revolutionary war, which Lord Wellington has with equal success adopted in Spain and Portugal; and which even in this country had triumphed a century before over Charles the Twelfth of Sweden, has again been signally triumphant over the *Hero* of the present age."[64]

In giving a general evaluation of events of 1812 in a dispatch to the Secretary of State in February 1813, this skeptical and usually restrained puritan did not conceal his admiration for the patriotic behavior of all classes of Russian society during the Napoleonic invasion. "The spirit of patriotism has burst with the purest and most vivid flame in every class of the community. The exertions of the nations have been almost unparalleled, the greatest sacrifices have been made cheerfully and spontaneously . . . . In the most trying extremity they have been calm and collected, deeply anxious, but uniformly confident and sanguine in their hopes of the result."[65]

In summarizing the attitude of the American public toward Russia and the Russian war of 1812, it should be noted that the significance of the events was not grasped immediately or by large numbers of people. Not everybody understood the war's character or the unusual situation within Russia. Conflicting comments were also made in the press about the ensuing struggle to liberate Europe from Napoleonic domination and about the role of the Russian army in these events.[66] But the very fact of these sharp discussions, disputes, and differing viewpoints shows that Russia had ceased to be an unknown and mysterious country, some vague geographical entity, and had begun to acquire concrete and realistic features in American eyes. In these years the United States discovered the enormous potentialities of the heroic Russian people, and learned about conditions of life and customs in Russia, her state system, and her resources.

No less significant was a careful study by the Russian representatives of the situation in the United States, its political and economic development, and the activity of the American government and Congress. In February 1812, shortly before his departure from Philadelphia, Pahlen sent to St. Petersburg a detailed memorandum in which he collected and systematized valuable information about economic and political conditions in the United States.[67] In the course of his ten-year stay, Dashkov collected an enormous amount of material on various aspects of American life. Among his papers there are valuable surveys of the development of Russian-American commerce, numerous extracts from literary sources, and his own observations on the socio-economic and political development of the United States, translations of official documents and treaties, descriptions of organization of schools, orphanages, and hospitals, diary notes, and so on.[68] Unfortunately, this valuable documentary material was never definitively organized by Dashkov and the Russian public remained unacquainted with it.

The activity of Svin'in and Poletika was much more successful in this respect. Soon after his return to Russia, Svin'in published his American observations in the pages of a popular journal *Syn otechestva* (The Son of the Fatherland). This interesting essay attracted immediate attention, and was reprinted in 1815 and 1818 in expanded form, with the author's illustrations.[69] Svin'in's book contains a number of subtle and interesting observations on American industry and commerce, the national characteristics of Americans, their living conditions, and so on. One can only marvel at the author's acumen in collecting this information. Of course, it is not always possible to agree with all his views, especially when he stresses his negative attitude to the stormy revolutionary events in France and on the island of Santo Domingo, then juxtaposes to them the revolution in North America. Occasionally there are factual inaccuracies and unjust evaluations (for example, in respect to the Indians), but on the whole Svin'in's work should be considered a landmark in Russian literature.

Of still greater interest is P. I. Poletika's book. Although it came out only in the 1820's, it included his observations during his first sojourn in the United States in the early years of the second decade.[70] The author's progressive views become obvious as one reads the book, for Poletika did not conceal his liberal sympathies. He analyzes the administering of justice in

America in great detail and refers admiringly to *habeas corpus* and court juries. He sympathizes with the oppressed Indians and condemns slavery. As a rule, Poletika's observations are very precise. He utilized the 1810 and 1820 censuses, and was able to avoid the oversimplification and errors which characterize many contemporaneous works. When the book was translated into English in 1826, its publisher praised the author's erudition, pointing out his familiarity with conditions in the United States and the objectivity of his remarks.[71]

Poletika analyzed with great acumen the unique historical development of the United States, particularly the role of the frontier. By continually extending the borders, Poletika observed, American settlers deprived the Indians of lands that belonged to them either by force or under the guise of formal contracts. As a result of swift territorial expansion and the colonization of new land, the customs and culture of the colonists, along with their way of life, were subjected to basic change. As it moved west, "civilization" grew fainter; traveling across the country, Poletika said, "you can ascend and descend the scale of civilization."[72]

Not surprisingly, this remarkable work has never been printed in Russia in its entirety. In the reactionary atmosphere which characterized the country after 1820 it would have been difficult to account for the publication of a work which openly defended a constitutional form of government and characterized slavery as absolute evil.[73] Even abroad, Poletika published his work anonymously, especially since he continued to occupy an official post.

The varied and valuable information collected by Russian diplomats greatly facilitated the dissemination of information about the United States, not only to the tsarist government but also to the wide circles of the reading public. Poletika and Svin'in produced works valuable to both the Russian and the foreign public. If originally a side product of Russian-American rapprochement in the field of foreign policy, these observations, made during the authors' stay in America in a diplomatic capacity, were a factor in strengthening and developing friendly connections between the Russian and American people.

Conclusion

This book was undertaken with the aim of investigating relations between Russia and America in their early stages, and detailing their diplomatic contacts, as well as early scientific, cultural, socio-political, and commercial connections between the two countries.

After studying the heterogeneous and rich files of the basic Soviet archives, receiving some manuscripts (microfilm) and printed materials from the United States, and utilizing numerous Russian, American, and Western European publications, the correspondence and works of statesmen, scientists, and public figures, memoirs and reference books, newspapers, and statistical materials, it was possible to recreate a documented picture of the formation of Russian-American relations and follow their development chronologically for a considerable period: 1775-1815.

My main general deduction, on the theoretical plane, is the documentary refutation of the "age-long" and "natural" enmity between Russia and America, a tendentious assertion widely used for propaganda purposes during the "cold war" years by reactionary Western politicians and historians. Many other important problems of both general and specialized nature were also solved in the course of investigation. Study of Russian diplomacy, through archival documents of the period of the War of Independence, established that, although no formal recognition of the United States as an independent nation took place at that time, there are grounds for asserting that Russia recognized the new state de facto. Whatever the subjective sympathies and motives of the tsarist government, in general during the difficult years of the United States struggle for freedom Russia played a positive role in the improvement of the international situation of the revolted colonies and the diplomatic isolation of England and, as a result, in the victory of the United States. The Declaration of Armed Neutrality, officially approved by the Continental Congress of the United States in October 1780, had enormous international significance.

Of considerable interest in this connection was the uncovering of documents, heretofore unknown, establishing the existence of Russian-American trade contacts and the first sailing of Russian ships from Bordeaux to the shores of the far-off transoceanic republic. More or less regular direct commercial contacts between America and Russia and systematic registries of the American flag in Kronstadt had been established by 1783. By the end of the eighteenth century several dozen American ships were arriving at St. Petersburg's port annually; although on the whole the volume of the first commercial connections was small, the very fact that Russia was trading with republican America while there were hostilities against revolutionary France attests to an important difference between the French and American policies of tsarist Russia.

Theoretically, the American War of Independence of 1775-1783 and the French Revolution of 1789-1794, as similar phenomena produced a sharply negative reaction on the part of the ruling classes, in Russia as in other feudal-absolutist states. But this was only in theory. In practice the international situation was quite favorable toward America (as distinct from France) because of concrete reasons which have been discussed in detail in this book. Events in America affected primarily the interests of Great Britain, a fact which could not but please her European rivals. Besides, such events took place far away, beyond the ocean, and seemingly did not present any threat to the existing regime—while the great revolutionary storm of 1789-1794 broke out in the very center of Europe and created a real prospect of the collapse of the old order and the whole feudal-absolutist regime.

The growth of a conservative trend in the United States after the War of Independence, as shown by the suppression of Shays' Rebellion (1786-1787) and the Federalists' coming to power during the presidencies of George Washington, 1789-1797, and John Adams, 1797-1801, should also be taken into account. It is significant that in the spring of 1799 unofficial negotiations between Vorontsov and King, the Russian and American ministers in London, led to a preliminary agreement on the question of a treaty of commerce and diplomatic relations, and St. Petersburg even agreed officially to exchange appropriate missions. A natural result of the development of commercial connections between the two countries was the recognition, in the fall of 1803, as American consul-general in St. Petersburg of Levett Harris, who also performed some diplomatic functions.

CONCLUSION

The materials examined showed that the events and ideas of the American Revolution were warmly received by the avant-garde members of Russian society. Acute class conflicts, the cruel oppression of serfdom combined with new bourgeois forms of exploitation brought about by capitalism, which started its growth in the depths of feudalism; the mighty wave of the peasant movement, which did not subside even after the suppression of Pugachev's rebellion—all these helped create an atmosphere favorable for the dissemination of revolutionary, democratic, and liberational ideas throughout Russia.

Given the conditions of tsarist autocracy, it was impossible to speak openly of the rights of the Russian people to revolution, to democratic freedoms, and to political change, but a number of factors made it possible to write more or less objectively about the American people's right to freedom and independence and the successful revolutionary war against England. At the same time publication in the serf-regime of enormous factual material about the United States War of Independence acquired special meaning because of its content. Reports of the successful military actions of the colonists against royal troops, the victorious conclusion of the war for independence, and the establishment of a republican state in America made the Russian reader look critically at the reality around him, compare republican America with serf-regime Russia, and opened to him the possibility of successful struggle against tsarist autocracy.

Most important from this point of view was the cultural activity of N. I. Novikov, who published on the pages of *Moskovskie vedomosti* and in journals and books he edited, extensive material on America and the American Revolution. The Russian people can also be justly proud of Radishchev, who glorified the American Revolution in his immortal "Liberty," and gave a profound and detailed analysis of the situation in America in his *Voyage from St. Petersburg to Moscow*. Radishchev and Novikov valued highly the revolutionary achievements of the American people, but wrathfully condemned Negro slavery and the annihilation of the Indians.

A great deal of attention in this work is paid to the question of the first Americans in Russia and to eighteenth-century travels in the United States of Russian subjects. On the basis of previously unknown documents it was possible to clarify a number of tangled circumstances connected with the presence in Russia of John Paul Jones and John Ledyard. The American voyage of F. V. Karzhavin and his social and political views were subjected to careful, detailed analysis on the basis of the archival and printed materials.

The formation of scientific, cultural, and socio-political connections between Russia and America in the second half of the eighteenth and the early nineteenth centuries is of considerable interest. Lomonosov, Richman, and Epinus in Russia were well acquainted with the scientific work of Franklin and valued it highly; their own important contribution to the study of electricity was known in America. Franklin had a high opinion of the achievements of his Russian colleagues and maintained contacts with the St. Petersburg Academy of Sciences.

Official contacts between the American Philosophical Society in Philadelphia and the Academy of Sciences in St. Petersburg were established in the 1770's, and in 1789 Franklin was made a foreign member of the Russian Academy. Leonard Eyler was made a member of the Academy of Arts and Sciences in Boston in 1781. Ties between American scientific bodies and the St. Petersburg Academy of Sciences were further strengthened by the election to membership of such prominent St. Petersburg academicians as Pallas, Fuss, and Fischer.

In the late 1780's, on Catherine II's request, contacts "on the highest level" were established through the mediation of the Marquis de Lafayette. Valuable material on the tongues of the American Indians was sent to Russia through the direct intercession of Washington and Franklin for the comparative dictionary being prepared. Personal correspondence between Alexander I and Thomas Jefferson in the early nineteenth century constituted an important basis for the exchange of diplomatic missions.

In the early nineteenth century Russians watched closely the successes of the young republic and studied the possibility of utilizing the American experience to encourage national industry. With this in mind Minister of Finance Gur'ev arranged for Russian publication of a well-known paper of Alexander Hamilton. "The similarity of American United Provinces with Russia," wrote V. Malinovsky, an important Russian of the Enlightenment, in the introduction to his translation of the book, "appears both in the expanse of the land, climate and natural conditions, in the size of population disproportionate to the space, and in the general youthfulness of various generally useful institutions; therefore all the rules, remarks and means proposed here are suitable for our country."[1]

Relations with the United States in northwest America, as an aspect of the general problem of Russian colonization of Alaska in the eighteenth and early nineteenth centuries, were analyzed. Study of documentary sources confirmed that the commercial activity of "Bostonians" inflicted grave harm on the Russian-American Company. The citizens of the United States sold local inhabitants firearms, gunpowder, and bullets, and aroused them against the Russians. The Americans undermined the company's interests by carrying furs directly from Russian America to Canton, therefore damaging Russian-Chinese trade in Kiakta. I was able to ascertain that the appearance of American traders in Russian America also had important positive results, especially the establishment of direct commercial contacts with the United States. Baranov's business contacts with "Boston shipowners," the purchase of necessary goods (provisions and vessels, above all), and the organization of joint fur-trapping expeditions made it possible for Russian colonies in the first fifteen years of the nineteenth century to take care of a large portion of their needs, without help from the Russian government, as well as obtain a large number of sea-otters through trade with Americans.

In the spring of 1808 the problem of illegal American trade in Russia's possessions in America was put before the United States officially. The tsarist government proposed a special treaty, whose aim would be twofold; to protect Russian possessions from the undermining activity of dangerous competitors by forbidding them to supply the local population with weapons; and to develop regular commercial ties between Russian America and the United States. Although the official negotiations which followed, first in Washington and then in St. Petersburg, were not successful, an agreement between the Main Office of the Russian-American Company and the American Fur Company of John Jacob Astor was signed on 20 April/2 May 1812.

The figure of the Russian minister for Foreign Affairs, Chancellor Rumiantsev, is presented in a new light, illuminating his prominent role in rapprochement with the United States and his 1811 plan to open up trade channels with the new states of Latin America.

While recording the differences and clash of opinions in St. Petersburg and Washington, I show that the causes of Russian-American rapprochement and the establishment of diplomatic relations in 1808-9 were quite objective. They were the outgrowth of the general post-Tilsit international situation, and were largely defined by the development of Russian-American commercial, cultural, and socio-political connections. Both Russia and the United States were influenced in their relations, not by the abstract notions about the "welfare of mankind," but by realistic considerations.

Alexander I and Rumiantsev saw in the United States, "a sort of rival of England," and expected that the expansion of American commerce might alleviate the harsh consequences of the Continental Blockade and stabilize the relations of the Russian-American Company with the "Bostonians." For their part, the United States, whose relations with England and France were in a state of crisis, was interested in breaking through the diplomatic isolation and developing friendly relations with Russia, at that time the only great power favorably disposed toward it. The American government was especially anxious to gain Russia's support in the matter of neutral navigation, and hoped for profits from the expansion of trade with the extensive Russian market.

The friendly reception of Dashkov and Pahlen in the United States, the brilliant success of Adams' mission in St. Petersburg, the swift expansion of Russian-American trade in 1810-11, the offer of Russian mediation in the Anglo-American War of 1812, and other seemingly paradoxical facts resulted from objective causes and concrete circumstances, not from any "American sympathies" of the tsarist government or "amicable feelings" toward Russia of the Washington cabinet.

Russian-American friendship was a union of convenience, accordingly there is no need to talk about sincerity in the relations between tsarist Russia and republican America, even in the period of closest rapprochement. The fragility of this "friendship" was evident in every sharp change in the international situation. For example, the development of antagonisms in Northwest America, and especially the beginning of the Anglo-American War, made it impossible for Astor's agreement of 20 April/2 May 1812 with the Russian-American Company to be realized. The coalition with Great Britain against Napoleon and Russia's increasing dependence on English subsidies forced the tsarist government to accept Britain's refusal of its offer to mediate in the Anglo-American War. At the same time, differences between Rumiantsev, on the one hand, and Alexander I and his new leader of foreign policy Nesselrode, on the other, became apparent, resulting in removal of the Chancellor from political activity and his consequent resignation in 1814.

The attitude toward Russia in the United States during this entire period varied a good deal. On the whole, very little was known in America about eighteenth-century Russia, although her position in the War of Independence was highly appreciated, especially her call for Armed Neutrality. As a rule, Federalist leaders were inclined to be favorably disposed toward Russia, while the Democrats (Republicans, they were usually called) were negative. However, neither group distinguished between the Russian government and the Russian people. The pro-French *Aurora* of Philadelphia and *Weekly Register* of Baltimore and the semi-official *National Intelligencer* of Washington frequently printed biased reports, made sharp comments on Russia and Russian people, and wrote about the "savage country," "legions of barbarians," and so on. The Federalist press, especially New England papers like the *Boston Gazette* and *Weekly Messenger*, took a favorable position toward Russia.

Disagreements concerning the evaluation of Russia became clearly apparent for the first time in 1812-1814, when Napoleon's defeat by the Russian army was widely commented on in the United States. Russia, until then an almost unknown and enigmatic country, began to assume in American eyes definite, realistic dimensions. It was at this time that they learned something about her resources and the enormous potentialities of the heroic Russian people, who succeeded under the harshest conditions of feudal oppression in halting the previously unconquerable aggressor and liberating Europe from Napoleon's dominion. One must note especially the high praise given Russia by such prominent Americans as Franklin, Washington, Jefferson and J. Q. Adams, and the special events in Georgetown and Boston celebrating the Russian victory over Napoleon.

Consequently, in discussing the favorable development of Russian-American relations, and pointing to the existence of friendly traditions between the Russian and American peoples, and the mutual usefulness of long-standing scientific, cultural and socio-political, commercial and diplomatic contacts, I do not intend to present an idealized picture and create an impression that no disagreement or antagonism existed between Russia and America.

In the course of the past two centuries, including the period under discussion, 1775-1815, one can find a number of moot points, contradictions, and even conflicts, whose solution was complicated by the differing socio-political systems of the two countries. To ignore class contradictions, to write about "sincere" and "forgotten" friendships of Tsars and Presidents, as some authors with monarchist sympathies do, is just as inaccurate as to spread propaganda about "age-long hostility." The lesson of Russian-American relations consists not in the absence of differences and conflicts, but in the fact that history testifies to the possibility of overcoming them—not with the help of weapons, but peacefully, by means of negotiation. It was so in the past, and one wants to believe that it will be so in the future.

Appendix

Writings and Sources on Early Russian-American Relations

At this time relations between the Soviet Union and the United States of America are attracting universal attention. All of us talk, think, and argue a great deal about the present and the future course of these relations; yet we know surprisingly little about their past. What was the origin of diplomatic, commercial, and socio-political connections between Russia and the United States, and how did ties develop? How did the first scientific and cultural contacts between the countries come to be established? Finally, what are the main lessons to be learned from Russian-American relations, and how can study of them prove useful for modern times?

The differences between our epoch and the second half of the eighteenth century are enormous; I do not intend to force simplified analogies upon the reader. Not do I wish to exaggerate the significance of historical traditions or apply the same measurement to events which differ totally in their class and social nature. The lessons of history derived from an analysis of relations between the Russia of feudal serfdom and the bourgeois United States of the eighteenth and nineteenth centuries cannot be transferred mechanistically to our times. Nevertheless, it is important to know and interpret them correctly. To date, however, the origin of Russian-American relations in this period has not received detailed investigation in either Russian or Western literature, nor has much serious documented work been done even with respect to specific problems. Moreover, the worst years of the Cold War saw an attempt in the West to utilize the history of Russian-American relations to foster the idea that something like a "natural" and "age-long" hostility between Russia and the United States existed.

This idea was advanced by such a political figure and ideologist of

357

"power politics" as John Foster Dulles. Reactionary historians and journalists dug up facts to prove that a "Russian menace" had existed in the past and continued in the present. They pointed to the traditional conflict of interests between Russia and America and propagated hostility and distrust between the two nations. As a result, in the late forties and early fifties a great many books and articles in Western Europe and in the United States presented a one-sided, and in some cases actually falsified, conception of the history of Russian-American relations.

A book by a well-known historian of American foreign policy, Thomas A. Bailey's *America Faces Russia*, published in 1950, is a sad example of this sort of investigation. After breaking down, in the initial chapter, "the legend of the Cordial Catherine," he proceeds to decry as "myths" and "legends" the old notion of the benevolent attitude of Russia during the periods of the War of Independence in North America in 1775-1783, the Anglo-American War of 1812-1815, and the Civil War in 1861-1865. According to Bailey, from the day of its emergence until our day, Russia has taken an extremely hostile position toward the United States. He discerns a "muscovite menace" to the Western hemisphere as early as the first quarter of the nineteenth century.[1]

Bailey's weighty volume, unfortunately, is by no means an isolated example of this approach to the history of Russian-American relations. The same tendencies are evident in the scientifically worthless book by an American specialist on Russian affairs, Clarence Manning; to a degree in the monograph of the West German historian Erwin Hölzle; in a popular book by Victor Alexandrov, published in Paris in 1958; and in others.[2]

In reviewing historical events in the light of contemporary conflicts, Manning rehashes the hackneyed thesis of the Western propaganda that contemporary Kremlin authorities no less than the Tsars have always striven for conquest, and that the interests of Russia and the United States in the past as well as the present have invariably clashed.[3]

The methodological position taken by Hölzle is approximately analogous although his source documentation is more impressive. He views Russian colonization primarily as an attempt to extend Russian domination from the Arctic to California, and the United States appears as the defender of freedom and democracy on the American continent. Following the traditions of the German geopolitics, Hölzle devotes much of his monograph to an account of the struggle of the two world powers in the field of "ideology and space," juxtaposing American democracy and the "autocracy" of the Russian Tsars.[4]

The influence of the Cold War is also felt in the collection of articles

America and Russia: A Century and a Half of Dramatic Encounters, edited by Oliver Jensen and published in New York in 1962. The authors, among them Bertram Wolf, William Hale, E. M. Halliday, and Marshall Davidson, see their book not so much as a survey of the consecutive history of the relations between the two countries as an attempt to select from this history "certain key moments and events that shaped the past into the present."[5] The general picture of Russian-American relations seen in the light of their interpretation proved rather tendentious. Examining the past (including the early nineteenth century) from the point of view of the present, the authors see these relations as the history of "dramatic encounters"; they overstate the anti-Russian aspect of the Monroe Doctrine, and exaggerate Russia's expansionist intentions in California.[6]

Contemporary advocates of the "natural hostility" between Russia and the United States are by no means original. As early as 1905, Oscar Strauss, a well-known lawyer and member of the permanent court at The Hague, published an article sharply criticizing Russia's policy toward the United States. Selecting facts and documents in an arbitrary and biased way, Strauss set out to prove that ever since the War of Independence, Russia's position had been hostile and that the American people have nothing to thank her for.[7] As for the "Russian menace" to Western civilization, this concept was advanced for the first time in American literature more than a hundred years ago by Robert Walsh who published his polemical *Correspondence Respecting Russia*[8] in 1813.

Relying on arbitrarily chosen examples, adherents of the concept of "natural hostility" have created a one-sided and occasionally even falsified picture of Russian-American relations. The objective lessons of the past in the final accounting are hard to harmonize with the thesis of "age-long hostility." The indisputable fact is that Russia and the United States never fought each other except for American intervention at the time of the Russian Civil War; on the contrary, they have been allies in the most critical years of contemporary history, the First and Second World Wars. In periods that were difficult and complicated for the American people, such as the Revolutionary War, the War of 1812, and the Civil War, Russia's position toward the United States was objectively favorable.

This does not mean of course that there have been no contradictions, disputes, and even conflicts between the United States and Russia, with solutions complicated by the differences in their socio-political systems. To ignore class contradictions and write about the sincere and "forgotten friendship" of the tsars and the presidents would be just as wrong as to advocate a thesis of "natural hostility."

A book by Alexander Tarsaidze, published in New York in 1958, is a characteristic example of this. The author set himself the task of reminding both countries of their "extremely amicable past," arguing that until 1917 not only were there no wars, but there were no serious diplomatic conflicts between tsarist Russia and the United States.[9] There is only one Russia within Tarsaidze's field of vision—that of the tsars, ministers, and diplomats—while the United States is represented by presidents, secretaries, and envoys. The other Russia—represented by progressive social circles, revolutionary-democrats, and the people—was beyond the limits of his attention. It is also significant that Tarsaidze carried his study only to 1917. As a result the reader gets the impression that the friendly relations existing between Russia and the United States ceased after the overthrow of the Romanovs' dynasty (an event Tarsaidze obviously regrets). This thesis about the "extremely amicable past" of relations between tsarist Russia and the United States is erroneous. There never was and never could be any "sincere" friendship between the tsars and the presidents. Russian-American relations developed along favorable lines because of specific objective reasons, not as a result of pro-American "sympathies" on the part of Catherine II, Alexander I, N. P. Rumiantsev, A. M. Gorchakov, or any other Russian Tsar or minister.

Fundamental methodological faults, such as narrow diplomatic approach, absence of class analysis, disregard of the socio-economic factors, and the role of the masses, are found to some degree not only in the above-mentioned works of contemporary Western authors but also in a number of other works written from the point of view of bourgeois objectivism.

John Hildt's monograph, of great interest for our purposes, was published in 1906 as one of the Johns Hopkins University studies. This small book—the first dealing with early Russian-American diplomatic negotiations—remains to this day the most detailed and objective investigation of early relations between the United States and Russia, from the War of Independence to the end of the first quarter of the nineteenth century.[10] Hildt relies on a comparatively limited supply of exclusively American sources, and summarizes the history of the first diplomatic contacts somewhat superficially and with a number of factual errors. His research, nonetheless, was a significant attempt to obtain a chronological perspective on relations between Russia and the United States.

Among the many works on American history and the specialized textbooks in American foreign policy, one deserves special mention: the old nine-volume work by Henry Adams, devoted to the administrations of Thomas Jefferson and James Madison.[11] The venerable historian is partial in his judgment, and particularly unfair to Thomas Jefferson, but his understanding of the international and domestic American situation and his knowledge of English and American sources, including archives, cannot be denied. It is not surprising that, although Adams' study was first published at the end of the nineteenth century, its scholarly value continues into our times. Moreover, it was Henry Adams who gave perhaps the most thorough and documented account of Russia's position on the eve of the War of 1812, insofar as this was possible, given the absence of Russian materials at his disposal and the limited framework of his study.

I single out the merits of old studies by Adams and Hildt because, in view of the paucity of serious research in the history of Russian-American relations, they stand out. With the exception of some general surveys and a few hopelessly outdated specialized books dealing with individual issues, there is nothing in American historiography concerning the problems of the formation and development of early Russian-American relations.[12] Even such key problems of diplomatic history as Russia's position in the struggle of the North American colonies for independence from England, the establishment of Russian-American diplomatic relations, and the question of mediation in the War of 1812 have not received detailed treatment.

The state of research into the establishment of early cultural, scientific, and socio-political ties is even more deplorable. It is true that in the wake of the Second World War interest in these aspects of Russian-American relations increased somewhat. A number of specialized articles—even books—appeared; however, the general picture changed very little. Characteristic of this situation is a monograph by Max Laserson of Columbia University entitled *The American Impact on Russia, 1784-1917*, published in New York in 1950 and 1962. Among his teachers the author names such well-known scholars as M. Kovalevsky, M. Tugan-Baranovsky, and M. Ostrogorsky; he refers to Russian sources in a number of instances and offers some interesting comparisons, but on the whole his book resembles a popular survey rather than a serious piece of research.

The starting date for Laserson's monograph, 1784, when, the author states, "Benjamin Franklin was elected an honorary member of the Imperial Russian Academy of Sciences in St. Petersburg," constitutes a surprising and almost comical mistake.[13] This event took place five years later; hence the book's very title is incongruous.[14] The work contains many other factual errors, plus too few well-grounded deductions—all of which indicate a lack of familiarity with documentary material.

Almost the only American work in which serious attention is paid to Russian writings and sources from the sixteenth to eighteenth centuries is a small bibliographical survey by Avrahm Yarmolinsky. Especially valuable is the material relating to the earliest information about America to appear in Russian sources since the sixteenth century. At the same time, however, an important question—the attitude of the Russian press during the War of Independence—is treated cursorily and with an obvious bias. In noting, for instance, that the events of the American Revolution were allotted considerable space on the pages of the Russian press, Yarmolinsky maintains that they were presented "entirely from the British point of view." Even reports which, the author points out, originated in New York, Boston, Philadelphia, or Rhode Island, seemed to reflect an exclusively loyalist position.[15]

A useful general survey of American visitors to Russia from the end of the eighteenth century onward was compiled by Anna Babey.[16] Her information, however, is far from exhaustive. Although she mentions Francis Dana, John Quincy Adams, John Paul Jones, John Ledyard, and Levett Harris (the last two with factual errors),[17] she fails to refer to J. Allen Smith, Joel Poinsett, Adrian Benson, and many other Americans who visited Russia at the beginning of the nineteenth century. As a rule Mrs. Babey limits herself to short remarks based solely on printed American sources. Her biased generalizations about American travelers' observations are highly questionable. The book's main value lies in its extensive and carefully compiled bibliography of rare non-Russian publications, primarily documentary materials published by Americans who have been to Russia.[18]

In view of the inadequate study of Russian-American relations in Western literature and the existence of numerous false notions and biased accounts, which received especially wide circulation during the Cold War years, the need for a comprehensive and objective Marxist study is evident. Unfortunately, to date very little has been accomplished in this field in Soviet historical literature. Nineteenth-century Russian historiographers devoted their chief efforts to the study of relations with the European system—primarily France, but also England, Austria, Prussia, and other nations. This tradition has continued to some extent, with the result that we have many works, both general and specialized, which deal with European nations, in particular France and England. To this day, however, we have no monograph encompassing any single significant period of time in Russian-American relations (with the exception of the well-known book of M. M. Malkin, *Grazhdanskaia voina v Ssha i tsarskaia Rossiia* [The Civil War in the United States and Tsarist Russia], which appeared in 1939).

The shortcomings of the scholarship in the field of Russian-American relations have been repeatedly pointed out in Soviet historical writings, such as the historiographical review of Soviet publications on United States history, whose authors have specifically pointed to the "unfortunate gap in the investigation of Russian-American relations."[19] This situation has also been noted repeatedly by the prominent Soviet scholar and corresponding member of the Soviet Academy of Sciences, A. V. Efimov, who has made valuable contributions both to the basic evaluation of the problem as a whole and to some specific aspects of it. His survey of the earliest period of United States history, and his chapters on the history of American foreign policy in volume I of *Istoriia diplomatii* (The History of Diplomacy) are well known.[20]

Attention is paid to Russian-American relations in both of these works and in a number of cases new archival material is uncovered. Efimov's original research into the history of the great Russian geographical discoveries of the seventeenth and eighteenth centuries, based on study of hitherto unknown documents, maps, and rare printed sources, is also of interest. I have, on repeated occasions, referred to these works in later chapters. Here it is enough to point out one original and fruitful idea developed by the author in his work on the history of the great Russian geographical discoveries. In dealing with the problem posed by the periodization of Russian-American relations, Efimov notes: "America was included within the sphere of Russian foreign policy not in 1809, when formal diplomatic relations with the United States were first established, and not in the period of the War of Independence, but considerably earlier, after Peter I shattered Sweden's might, and Russia, having become one of the great powers, entered the field of world politics of the time."[21]

In reality, the exchange of diplomatic representatives in 1809 signified, as was shown in this study, not the initial, but the concluding stage in the establishment of relations between Russia and the United States. The way was paved for this act of foreign policy not only in the first decade of the nineteenth century, when widely known diplomatic contacts occurred leading to the formal decision to exchange diplomatic missions. To a great extent it was prepared throughout the entire eighteenth century, when the groundwork was laid for the future Russian-American rapprochement, and the first economic, cultural, socio-political, and scientific contacts between the two nations were established.[22]

As Efimov has noted, America was already included within the sphere of Russian foreign policy in the first half of the eighteenth century, mainly as a result of brilliant Russian geographical discoveries in the North Pacific. It should also be mentioned that in the spring of 1698 a meeting between Peter I and William Penn took place during the Russian Tsar's stay in England.[23] At approximately the same time (1699-1700) a significant amount of American tobacco entered the Russian market through England, and thereafter more or less regular, although indirect (through the mother country), trade connections were established between Russia and North America. Written accounts of various kinds calling attention—often in generalized but still sufficiently definite form—to various aspects of commercial contacts with distant America also began appearing at that period. On the other side of the Atlantic the image of Peter the Great, as Tsar-reformer was firmly implanted in the minds of American readers by the colonial weekly newspapers at the beginning of the eighteenth century.[24]

In the final analysis, however, the most important and decisive landmark in the history of Russian-American relations was the war for independence of 1775-1783. It was not just a matter of the commencement of direct diplomatic and trade contacts between the two countries at the time of the War of Independence. The American Revolution introduced qualitatively new features into the nature of the relations between Russia and the United States. These considerations led to the selection of 1775 as the starting point for the present study. Although the official date of independence, July 4, 1776, was declared somewhat later, in a sense this was but a formality. From April 1775 on, the Americans defended their independence by deed, with guns in their hands, and this was what mattered. But while selecting 1775 as the starting point, it is necessary in a number of instances to direct attention to an earlier period and to review the history of geographical discoveries starting with the first half of the eighteenth century, the activity of Russian hunting and fishing expeditions on the northwestern shores of America, and the establishment of the first scientific, social, and political contact, starting in the middle of the eighteenth century.

As regards the concluding date of this book, the decision was taken to halt at 1815, a year representing an important landmark in American as well as European history. In January 1815 the armed conflict between the

United States and Great Britain was terminated, while in Europe the grandiose epic of the Napoleonic wars came to its conclusion. In the history of Russian-American relations the year may serve as a fully justifiable and logical termination point for the entire stage of the establishment of diplomatic, commercial, and socio-political ties, and opens a new period of their further development.[25]

Although historians can claim only a small achievement in the study of early Russian-American cultural and socio-political ties, literary and cultural historians have attained considerably greater success. Among them one cannot fail to notice the names of A. I. Startsev and E. Dvoichenko-Markova. As long ago as the early forties Startsev published in *Internazionalnaia Literatura* (International Literature) a series of articles on Alexander Radishchev, Benjamin Franklin, and eighteenth century Russian society.[26] Although V. P. Semennikov earlier had indicated the similarity of some motifs in Radishchev's celebrated "Liberty" to American themes and to the writings of Abbé Raynal, Startsev studied this problem thoroughly, using a wide array of published sources as well as some archival materials.

Startsev's published works constitute the basis for his doctoral dissertation entitled The American Revolution, Radishchev, and Russian Society of the Eighteenth Century.[27] He relates his research to the "Radishchev cycle" and points out that A. N. Radishchev is central to his subject.[28] But Startsev's works are of considerable interest not only for their research into the great Russian revolutionary of the eighteenth century. His account of the general historical background is expert and thorough, and he is the first to analyze the problem of the attitude of the Russian public opinion to the United States. There are, to be sure, some gaps in his work, and even errors: there is too little treatment of Novikov's decade with *Moskovskie Vedomosti* (Moscow Record) (1779-1789), and a failure to demonstrate the fundamental differences in the positions of this newspaper and the official *Sankt-Peterburgskie Vedomosti* (St. Petersburg Gazette).[29] But this in no measure detracts from the overall value of Startsev's researches which have obvious importance for the historian as well as the student of literary and cultural affairs.

The articles and research notes of E. Dvoichenko-Markova, who has earned a niche of her own by the originality of her themes, merit special attention. She is a specialist of a somewhat unusual type and of varied interests. An expert in the life and works of A. S. Pushkin, Dvoichenko-Markova has written on Rumanian literature, and worked in France, Rumania, the United States, and the Soviet Union. During her stay in the

United States she published a whole series of articles and research notes on the history of early Russian-American cultural relations.[30]

The theme of Franklin and Lomonosov was suggested as early as the end of the eighteenth century by Alexander Radishchev in his celebrated book *Puteshestvie iz St. Peterburg a v Moskvu* (A Journey from St. Petersburg to Moscow). The lives and activities of these geniuses have long been studied in America as well as Russia. It was believed, however, that there had been no direct contacts between Franklin and Lomonosov, and in the most authoritative publications it was stated with absolute certainty that Russian academicians had not corresponded with the famous American.[31] However, in 1947 Dvoichenko-Markova proposed an interesting hypothesis of the possibility of a direct communication from Franklin to Lomonosov in 1765, presenting proof of the existence of communication between the American and his colleagues in Russia.[32] Although the possibility of such direct communication seems unlikely,[33] the familiarity of American scientists with Lomonosov and their interest in him is undeniable. The author also deserves credit for her thorough study of long-standing contacts between the American Philosophical Society and the Academy of Sciences in St. Petersburg.[34]

The reliability of Dvoichenko-Markova's information (with rare exception a check failed to disclose any substantial inaccuracies), and the inclusion in her works of appendixes consisting of documentary material from the archives of the American Philosophical Society, make it possible to use her works as a valuable source. However, the unusually varied and scattered nature of the subjects dealt with constitute shortcomings. Dvoichenko-Markova studies in detail specific individual questions (Ledyard's journey, the activities of navigator G. Izmailov), but does not attempt to formulate an overall picture, to analyze the events she examines from the point of view of Russian-American relations, and to evaluate the facts cited. Her lack of familiarity with Russian archives also makes itself felt.

Among Soviet investigators, besides A. I. Startsev, in a field adjacent to that of E. Dvoichenko-Markova, was M. I. Radovsky, who published a small book on Franklin's contacts with Russia. This work provides a useful summary of material, and points out that a considerable interest in Franklin existed in Russia from the middle of the eighteenth century down to the celebration of his anniversary in 1956.[35]

Along with the history of early Russian-American cultural and sociopolitical relations I have concentrated on the history of the Russian colonization of Northwest America and the contacts with the United States thus established. When touching on the general history of the colonization of the Northwest, I must stress two highly significant specialized studies of the Russian-American Company, published by P. Tikhmenev and the prominent Soviet historian S. B. Okun'.

Tikhmenev's two-volume work, with its valuable appendix, is not only a detailed study of the company's activities, but also, to a certain extent, can serve as a primary source. Tikhmenev's work was published in 1861-63, more than a hundred years ago, and was, so to speak, a "departmental" history. Its aim was to glorify the activities of the Russian-American Company, which allegedly concerned itself with the spread of "enlightenment," the bridling of the passions of "the primitive savages," and the introduction into the colonies of "the general organization of public services and amenities."[36] After having sketched such an idyllic picture, the author himself apparently had cause to doubt its authenticity and diffidently noted that the period under scrutiny was marked "with unavoidable necessity" by "cruelty, willfulness, and general disorder of every sort." But on the whole, the modern researcher, with a critical approach to the author's general conceptions, will find in Tikhmenev's work, despite its clearly biased nature, invaluable material on the history of the Russian-American Company, especially in view of the fact that he made use of documents from the central administration which have since disappeared.

The well-known work of Professor Okun', based upon extensive use of various archival materials, has many merits. Its principal concern is the expansion of tsarist Russia into the northern basin of the Pacific Ocean, conducted under the cover of the company.[37] Okun' details conditions prevailing among Russian fur traders, as well as indigenous populations in the territories under the company's management. Although certain aspects of this work require some re-evaluation and correction, on the whole it preserves its great value up to the present day.

The availability of the abovementioned works makes it unnecessary to detail the history of the assimilation of Russian America. Accordingly, I shall concentrate on the study of the activity of the Russian-American Company only to the extent that it is involved in relations with the United States. This aspect of the history of Russian America has not been investigated, and therefore should receive much attention.

The review of Western and Soviet historiography on the beginnings of relations between Russia and the United States of America enables me to outline in general the basic intention of this book and to present the most important problems it deals with.

Despite the rather significant range of works by Soviet and Western authors just mentioned, the history of Russian-American relations still has not received full, well-documented treatment. The present monograph attempted a detailed and comprehensive investigation, on the basis of primary sources (archival materials and published documents), of the early period of relations between Russia and the United States, that is, their establishment in 1775-1815. Along with a detailed analysis of diplomatic relations between the two countries, I have investigated the development of the first Russian-American trade contacts, as well as scientific, cultural, and socio-political ties in the eighteenth and early nineteenth centuries. A great deal of attention has been devoted to explaining attitudes of Russian society as a whole, and its progressive circles especially, toward the United States and toward the American Revolution. Finally, one of the most important objectives of this book was the study of relations between Russia and the United States in Northwest America, whose development led to the signing of a special agreement between the Russian-American Company and John Jacob Astor's American Fur Company in the spring of 1812.

Although a number of valuable studies of individual problems in the establishment of Russian-American relations (such as the history of cultural and socio-politico ties in the eighteenth century) exist, it was necessary to begin with primary data, and then, on the basis of such sources, to recreate a more or less connected narrative of events.

The works of Karl Marx, Friedrich Engels, and V. I. Lenin served as the theoretical and methodological base of the study. First to be mentioned must be the articles and letters of Marx and Engels devoted to various problems of the history of the United States and Russia at the end of the eighteenth and first half of the nineteenth centuries, the basic work by Lenin entitled *Razvitie Kapitalizma v Rossii* (The Development of Capitalism in Russia), and others. Russian-American relations derived from and depended upon the general European system in many respects, and in others on Russia's Far-Eastern policies. A comprehensive study and proper understanding of them is therefore possible only by taking into account the state of Russia's relations with England and the nations of the European continent, and the activities of the Russian-American Company. But, since along with diplomatic history, trade, socio-political, and cultural ties between Russia and the United States were also examined in detail in this work, the difficulties in studying and drawing conclusions from an unusually wide and varied range of documentary sources have been readily apparent.

Of the major official publications of tsarist Russia one must first mention *Sbornik Russkogo istoricheskogo obshchestva* (Collection of the Russian Historical Society), almost half of whose 147 volumes are devoted to foreign policy in the eighteenth and first half of the nineteenth centuries; the *Polnoe sobranie zakonov Rossiiskoi imperii* (The Complete Collection of Laws of the Russian Empire), with volumes XIX-XXXIII dealing with the period 1775-1815; F. Martens' *Sobranie traktatov* (Collection of Treaties); and *Arkhiv Gosudarstvennogo soveta* (The Archive of the State Council). Although one must bear in mind the official character of these publications, as well as many other shortcomings typical of their period of publication (including technical defects, the lack of full indexes, and so on), they retain to this day great scholarly significance, thanks to the colossal amount of documentary material included in them. Unfortunately, not all important aspects of Russian policy were given thorough enough treatment, even in the comparatively popular field of diplomatic history. The *Sbornik Russkogo istoricheskogo obshchestva* devoted an inordinate amount of attention to the diplomatic correspondence of foreign representatives in St. Petersburg (French, English, Austrian, and Prussian envoys), to the detriment of the Russian documentation itself. Relations with individual countries were covered equally, with prime attention paid to Europe, Far Eastern problems were poorly covered, and the American theme in effect completely omitted.

In their time the multivolume publications dealing with Russian-French relations, published by A. Trachevsky, S. Goriainov, N. M. Romanov, A. A. Polovtsov, N. M. Shilder, and others, which covered the diplomatic struggle in the period of the Napoleonic wars received wide international recognition.[38] But relations with England (as with the other European nations) were not well documented although they are of greatest interest for this work. Among the most important shortcomings of Russian publications on foreign policy is the very method of compiling selected documents. Prime attention was paid to diplomatic dispatches, while far less often are general reports, plans, communiques by high officials in the tsarist government, and instructions from the Ministry of Foreign Affairs to Russian diplomats abroad found. Only in part may this shortcoming be compensated for by the study of published materials from personal archives. I have made wide use in particular of the rich collection of papers of the Vorontsov family,[39] *Arkhiv grafov Mordvinovykh* (The Archive of the Counts Mordvinov), the memoirs of Adam Czartoryski, P. Stroganov, the published political correspondence of Catherine II, documents of Alexander I, the letters and papers of K. Nesselrode, and others.

The new definitive publication of materials from the Russian Ministry of Foreign Affairs, undertaken by the Commission for the Publication of Diplomatic Documents of the Soviet Ministry of Foreign Affairs, will provide a comprehensive presentation of Russia's foreign policy and its role in international relations. Volumes I-IV and VI of the first series have already appeared, covering the period from March 1801 to March 1809, and 1811 to 1812.[40]

There is no need to dwell upon the merits of this publication, which has received critical acclaim in the Soviet and Western press. I should merely like to mention that on its pages Russian relations, not only with Europe, but with nations of Asia, the Far East, and America, have been elucidated for the first time. Thus, the foundation has been laid for comprehensive documentary study of Russian foreign policy and diplomacy. Simultaneously a number of selections of documents and research articles based on materials from the Soviet archives, relating to problems touched upon in *Vneshniaia politika Rossii* (The Foreign Policy of Russia) and including relations with the United States, have been published in the historical journals.

Despite the significance of published Russian documents, especially *Vneshniaia politika Rossii*, the basic sources of my work have been materials in the central Soviet archives in Moscow and Leningrad, the first of which to be discussed must be the rich funds of the *Arkhiv vneshnei politiki Rossii* (Archive of Russian Foreign Policy, abbreviated AVPR).

Actually, diplomatic correspondence with the United States in the early years is comparatively sparse. There are only a few small files (*delo*) dealing with Dana's stay at St. Petersburg,[41] and only in 1804 did systematic correspondence begin with the American consul Harris, then with minister John Quincy Adams; this has been examined up to 1815.[42] A few letters exchanged between Thomas Jefferson and Alexander I from 1804 through 1806 have also been preserved.[43] The primary correspondence was carried on by the Russian Department of Foreign Affairs with its diplomatic and consular representatives in the United States after the establishment of relations in 1809.[44] The materials of the tsarist legation in Washington, which include important documents pertaining to the practical affairs of the Russian mission in the United States together with originals of the instructions received from St. Petersburg by the representatives, are of great value.[45] Registers of outgoing dispatches permit a determination of the full composition of the Russian minister's correspondence.[46]

Research into the problem of the establishment of Russian-American ties is complicated by great difficulties in the search for documentary materials which have been deposited in the most diverse locations (refer-red to as *fonds*). The student of relations with the United States must peruse the extensive correspondence with practially every major European capital: London, Paris, The Hague, Madrid, and at times Stockholm, Rio de Janeiro, and Constantinople. Moreover, in many cases these materials serve not as some sort of peripheral or supplemental means to broaden the documentary base, but as the chief source of information concerning the Russian diplomatic position vis-à-vis the United States. This is particular-ly true with regard to the attitude of Russian diplomacy toward the War of Independence in North America. In order to determine the government's position, it was necessary to investigate first of all the state of Russian-English, and also of Russian-French, relations for the entire duration of the war (1775-1783), and in certain instances to examine diplomatic corre-spondence starting back in 1763. Only on the basis of a detailed familiar-ity with the correspondence with London, Paris, The Hague, Vienna and occasionally Madrid and other European capitals,[47] was it possible to re-create the general system of Russia's European policy as well as her position regarding the rebellion in the English colonies in America.

It also was necessary to become acquainted with the European corre-spondence of the Russian Department of Foreign Affairs for later periods, as a result of which important documents concerning the attitude of the tsarist government to such questions as the recognition of the United States[48] and the conclusion of a trade treaty between Russia and the United States[49] came to light. Materials from the European diplomatic correspondence for the first decade and a half of the nineteenth century have been extensively utilized. The most interesting material for this period was dispatched from London and Paris,[50] but documents from other capitals have also been used.[51]

For the history of relations with the United States in Northwest Ameri-ca, documents in the *Glavnyi arkhiv* (Main Archive) and from the com-paratively recently created special *Sobranie dokumentalnykh materialov po istorii Russko-Amerikanskoi kompanii i russkikh vladenii v Severnoi Amerike* (Collection of Documentary Materials on the History of the Russian-American Company and Russian Possessions in North America) are of primary importance.[52] Documents in the Russian-American Com-pany files have found their way into AVPR from the most varied central and local archives; at present they comprise the most significant and valu-able collection of materials for this company.

Along with the documents in AVPR, files from the following central ar-chives in Moscow and Leningrad have been included in the present work:

TsGADA (Central State Archive of Ancient Acts); TsGAOR (Central State Archive of the October Revolution); TsGIA (Central State Historical Archive); TsGAVMF (Central State Archive of the Navy); the valuable manuscript collections of the Institut Russkoi Literary, Pushkinskii Dom (Institute of Russian Literature, Pushkin House); the Leningrad branch of the Institute of History of the USSR Academy of Sciences; and the manuscript divisions of the Lenin State Library in Moscow (GBL); the M. E. Saltykov-Shchedrin Public Library in Leningrad (GPB); the Archives of the USSR Academy of Sciences.

The papers in the personal archive of A. Ia. Dashkov, Russian minister to the United States, housed in TsGAOR and consisting of extensive official and personal correspondence, surveys of Russian-American commercial ties, diary notes, excerpts from various foreign books on the United States, and so forth, are of value.[53] A great many highly interesting documents were uncovered in TsGIA among the materials of the Ministry of Finances, the State Council, the College of Commerce, and others for the first decade and a half of the nineteenth century, and in TsGADA for the earlier period (the end of the eighteenth century). Materials directly related to the establishment of the first consular and diplomatic relations between the United States and Russia were found in these archives.[54] Together with the documents in AVPR, and the personal files of Dashkov and P. Svin'in (GPB, fond 679), use of these materials permitted a determination of the exact development of early ties between Russia and the United States and the subsequent official exchange of diplomatic missions.

Examination of documents relating to the visits of John Paul Jones and John Ledyard to Russia[55] and to the first trade connections between Russia and America,[56] was of great importance, as were the journals of the Committee of ministers and protocols of the general meeting of the State Council.[57] Of value for historians as well as philologists are documents dealing with F. V. Karzhavin, stored in the manuscript division of Pushkin House,[58] and in the archives of the Leningrad Branch of the Institute of History of the Soviet Academy of Sciences.[59] The last-mentioned archive also contains a rich collection of Vorontsov family papers; this, and the Vorontsov collection in TsGADA (fond 1261), sheds light on early first trade contacts with America.[60] A good supplement to the Russian-American Company fond in AVPR is found in A. A. Baranov's correspondence with I. A. Kuskov; other materials on the attempt to open trade relations with California are located in the Manuscripts Division of the Lenin State Library.[61]

A study of the materials of the higher state institutions, above all, of the

Department of Foreign Affairs, uncovers the deep inner mainsprings of the direction of foreign policy, the penetration of the secrets of tsarist diplomacy, and the tracing of its "bureaucratic mechanism."Lenin noted perceptively that "the nation's bureaucracy" in fact directs the "Russian state."[62] In giving a detailed picture of the system of government taking shape in the nation, Lenin wrote: "There is no elected government in Russia, and it is not only the rich and noble who govern, but the worst of them. Those govern who are most efficient at informing, who ruin other people more skillfully, who lie and slander to the Tsar, flatter and fawn. They govern in secret; the people do not know, and cannot know, what laws are prepared, what wars are set to be waged, what new taxes are to be introduced, which bureaucrats are rewarded and for what, which are removed. In no other country is there such a great number of bureaucrats as in Russia." "The tsarist autocracy," Lenin concluded, "is the autocracy of bureaucrats."[63]

As a rule, the most important decisions on questions of foreign policy were subject to the final approval of the Tsar; but this approval was in most cases strictly a formality. In sprawling handwriting the Tsar of all the Russias habitually wrote "Byt' po semu" (so be it) on the various "humble opinions" and notes, drafts of instructions to diplomatic representatives abroad, and numerous important, sometimes quite essential, and often completely insignificant, official documents. "The Tsar simply confirms the will of several dozen important and very notable bureaucrats," wrote Lenin, further stating that "the Tsar does not govern the country—the autocracy of a single person is just talk! A clique of the richest and noblest bureaucrats govern Russia."[64]

It is possible to trace back the most important decisions on questions of foreign policy first and foremost through so-called internal correspondence—the reports of the directors of the Department of Foreign Affairs to the Tsar, records of meetings of high state officials (particularly sessions of the State Council), special notes of various sorts, plans, "secret opinions," and so forth. A secret report of the College of Foreign Affairs to Catherine II of July 31 (August 11), 1779 serves as a characteristic example.[65] In this important document the key aspects of the nation's foreign policy vis-à-vis England's war in Europe and America are noted and Russia's position with regard to the rebellious colonies is defined. Subsequent actions of Russian diplomacy corresponded in general to the ideas sketched out in the report.

The internal mechanism of tsarist Russia's policy was kept strictly hidden from foreign observers, and to the outsider it appeared that there were no serious disagreements and contradictions within the ruling clique. But familiarity with the archival funds of tsarist Russia's higher state institutions permits us to re-create the conditions preceding the making of any particular decision, to trace the struggle of opinions within the ruling camp, and to determine the actual role of the people standing at the head of the tsarist government (including the Tsar himself). Of particular significance is the revelation of the motives behind the unexpected refusal by Catherine II in 1788 of a project by G. Shelikov and I. Golikov to establish a monopoly company for the colonization of Northwest America, despite the fact they were supported by the Commerce Commission and the State Council. The nature of the corrections made by the final editor in the constituent documents for the creation of the Russian-American Company in 1799 (see Chapter VI) is also interesting. Even more significant is an analysis of the materials from a discussion in the autumn of 1811 by a plenum of the State Council of Chancellor N. P. Rumiantsev's memoir concerning the inauguration of direct trade relations with the rebellious Spanish colonies in America, and also an analysis of subsequent disagreements and waverings within the tsarist government in connection with the question of mediation between the United States and England in 1812-1814.[66]

Documents discovered in TsGADA and AVPR permitted me to obtain more information and, in a number of cases, to revise old ideas concerning N. P. Rumiantsev—in particular to show his prominent role in the development of Russian-American relations. Although Alexander I sharply rebuked his trusted satrap, Ober-Hofmeister R. A. Koshelev, for his malicious political denunciation of Rumiantsev in the autumn of 1811, in the decisive moment the Tsar failed to support his Minister of Foreign Affairs. Alexander's evasive and wavering position in American affairs finally compelled Rumiantsev to leave government affairs and hand in his resignation, which was accepted in August 1814. Actually, however, K. V. Nesselrode, constantly at the Tsar's side and carrying on all important diplomatic correspondence, had been de facto Minister of Foreign Affairs since 1813.

Frank A. Golder was the only American researcher familiar with Russian archival materials. In 1914 he visited Russia and made a short inventory of archival documents relating to American history.[67] Golder's guide maintains its usefulness to this day for all investigators working in the history of Russian-American relations. One must, however, approach this work critically, realizing that it is far from exhaustive. For instance, Golder's inventory contains absolutely no mention of the valuable documents from the Russian diplomatic materials originating in the United States, known as the materials of the "mission" or legation in Washington, although they are of the utmost significance. The war of England's North American colonies for independence is only cursorily covered in Golder's works; there are only a few entries of little significance in the guide.[68] Nor does the note by Golder in *The American Historical Review* give anything like a full presentation of Russia's position during the American War of Independence.[69] Even the most important documentary materials found in the correspondence with the major European capitals during these years remained outside the field of vision of the American investigator, who included in his guide only a few specific documents.

Along with Russian materials, in the course of my work I made extensive use of documents from the National Archives in Washington, including instructions from the State Department to American diplomats abroad,[70] and reports of ministers at St. Petersburg.[71] Important additions and more precise judgments resulted from studying the correspondence of the Russian diplomatic mission to the United States[72] and also the dispatches of the American consul in St. Petersburg, Levett Harris.[73] Finally, on the basis of documents in the National Archives in Washington I was able to explain the puzzle of the "theft" by Irkutsk Governor-General I. A. Piel of Shelikhov's account of his travels along the northwestern coast of America, which so perplexed A. I. Andreev and S. B. Okun. The trouble, by the way, simply resulted from a mistake by the American historian Hubert H. Bancroft in the translation of a Russian document:[74] the journal of Shelikhov's wanderings was stolen not *by* Piel, but "from the chancellery of Mr. Piel" which of course is not the same thing.[75]

I have tried to compensate for an inadequate use of American archival documents by using a broad range of published materials: important official publications, proceedings of Congress, papers of government figures, various special editions of diplomatic correspondence, thematic collections of documents and memoirs. Among the most important official publications on American history I should mention the *American State Papers,* encompassing the period from the end of the eighth decade of the eighteenth century to the beginning of the third decade of the nineteenth (1832), and also the well-known proceedings of Congress, published originally as the *Debates and Proceedings in the Congress (Annals of Congress).*[76] Together with official documents, the proceedings of Congress provide extensive and valuable material about the foreign as well as internal policy of the United States, and in a number of cases (for instance, in the study of the activities of the War Hawks on the eve of the War of 1812) serve as a basic source. However, it must be stated that the proceedings of the end of the eighteenth and the first decades of the nineteenth centuries differed considerably from contemporary proceedings. Material for the *Annals of Congress* was taken basically from newspaper reports and was subjected to revision and condensation; the actual publication of the *Annals* took place many years later.

The extensive materials in the *American State Papers* are divided into ten series, including foreign relations, finances, commerce and navigation, and military affairs. The documents which dealt with questions of foreign policy were of greatest interest for my work, naturally,[77] although I devoted attention to other series. Despite the shortcomings of this publication, issued more than one hundred years ago, it encompasses all aspects of the activities of the American government for a comparatively extended period of time, and is unique in this regard. Unfortunately, publication was discontinued, and up to our time documents are being published which relate only to special fields of United States government activity—foreign policy, for example.[78]

The earlier, rather than more recent years were important for my documentation work for the period of the American Revolution. In this regard the proceedings of the Continental Congress, encompassing the period from 1774 to 1789,[79] the diplomatic correspondence of the United States of America from 1783 to 1789,[80] and especially Francis Wharton's *The Revolutionary Diplomatic Correspondence of the United States,*[81] deserve mention. Of utmost interest are the concluding volumes of this edition (particularly volume VI), in which materials relating to Francis Dana's mission to St. Petersburg are published.

The collection of presidential messages edited by James Daniel Richardson, the basic publication of American treaties by David Hunter Miller, and the numerous general and specialized documentary publications on American history edited by Henry Steele Commager, Albert Bushnell Hart, and John Bassett Moore were also of great value. In a number of instances official documentation from the archives of Western European nations proved a helpful supplement to American collections, for example, the well-known British publication, *British and Foreign State Papers,* the proceedings of the English Parliament (*The Parliamentary Debates*), and G. F. von Martens' famous collection of treaties (*Recueil des principaux traités, Supplement au Recueil, Nouveau Recueil des traités*).

To an even greater degree than official documentation, I made use of the correspondence, diaries, and memoirs of the leading governmental figures of the time. Deserving of special mention are the multivolume collections of papers of Benjamin Franklin, George Washington, John Adams, Thomas Jefferson, John Quincy Adams, James Monroe, James Madison, Albert Gallatin, Andrew Jackson, John Paul Jones, Henry Clay, John Calhoun, and James Bayard, as well as the correspondence of Napoleon I, Lord Castlereagh, Prince Metternich, and James Harris (Lord Malmesbury) and the memoirs of General Caulaincourt, Count Goertz, von Dohm, and many others.

Of particular interest are the papers of the Adams family, and foremost of course those of John Quincy Adams, the first American minister to Russia (1809-1814), and later Secretary of State and President of the United States.[82] The Adams family manuscript materials, carefully preserved by descendants, were transferred to the control of the Massachusetts Historical Society in 1956. American specialists are unanimous in stressing the value of this extremely rich collection; its microfilming and subsequent publication has been acknowledged as one of the most important tasks underwritten by the National Historical Publications Commission.[83] L. H. Butterfield, editor in chief of the Adams Papers, estimates that the series will run to almost one hundred volumes;[84] this is not surprising for, according to Henry Adams, his grandfather "did nothing but write."[85]

An important segment (approximately half) of John Quincy Adams' huge diary was published by Charles Francis Adams over the period 1874-1877; this edition preserves its great scholarly value to the present.[86] On many problems John Quincy Adams' diary presents material which cannot be found in any other source. As minister to Russia, Adams noted in detail the gist of his conversations (including private and unofficial ones) with the leaders of the Russian government. He met especially frequently with Chancellor N. P. Rumiantsev, and their prolonged and frank discussions touched on the most varied international and domestic problems. The minister also conversed frequently with Alexander I, not only at official ceremonies but when meeting him regularly during his walks through St. Petersburg.

My experience has shown that, with regard to information of a factual nature, Adams' diary is, as a rule, reliable as a source. Repeated checks of his notes with other documentary materials, including archival sources, have failed to disclose any serious misrepresentations. Apparently Adams did not intend his observations for publication. This is reflected in the style and contents of the manuscript. For him a diary was necessary primarily as a record of facts needed in his practical affairs, and for self-control. It was also a convenient means for frank expression of ideas.

Along with the diary, the correspondence of John Quincy Adams, published in part by the prominent American editor of documents Worthington C. Ford, is of great value.[87] It is surprising that in 1917 this important publication was discontinued because it could not pay its own way.[88] Financial considerations were decisive, and since that time historians have had cause more than once to regret that Ford's publication did not find a successor. Happily, the earlier period of Adams' activities (to 1815) were covered in the first five volumes Ford managed to publish, and although they are not to be found in Soviet libraries, I finally succeeded in obtaining them from the United States. The significance of this edition is magnified still more because private American archives remained unavailable to me until 1968, and Adams' correspondence served as a basic source of information on his mission to St. Petersburg.

The papers of James A. Bayard and, more especially, Albert Gallatin's correspondence—also obtained from the United States—served as essential supplements to Adams' papers in dealing with the activities of the special American commission to St. Petersburg, 1813-1814.[89]

Among the other most important American publications utilized in the present work, I must not fail to mention the works and correspondence of Benjamin Franklin, found in successive editions by Jared Sparks, Albert H. Smyth, and Leonard Wood Labaree. The most authoritative edition of Franklin's papers up to now has been the Smyth edition (1907),[90] generously placed at my disposal by V. D. Kazakevich. At the same time I had to make extensive use of the older edition of the great American's works (1840),[91] and especially the new publication of Franklin's papers, which began appearing in 1959 under the editorship of Labaree;[92] which contains many important documents (in particular, letters bearing witness to Franklin's contacts with the Petersburg Academy of Sciences, his familiarity with the works of Lomonosov, and so on).

On the whole the number of documentary publications issued in the United States under the aegis of the National Historical Publications Commission has significantly increased since the 1950's. I found the first volumes of the papers of John C. Calhoun, Henry Clay, and especially Thomas Jefferson to be of great use. It is impossible not to go into more detail concerning the last of these. The fact is that the best old editions of

Jefferson's correspondence (under the editorship of Paul Ford, and the "memorial edition") until recently were not found in the U.S.S.R. On the other hand, the four-volume collection of this prominent American statesman and man of the Enlightenment found in our libraries fails completely to meet contemporary scholarly demands, and cannot be considered a serious source for the study of the immense Jeffersonian epistolary legacy. It is for this reason that the new publication, begun by Julian P. Boyd in 1950, is of such value.[93] This edition differs significantly from previous American documentary collections and to a certain extent establishes new criteria for publications of its sort.[94] Deserving of particular mention are the high technical level of the edition and especially the fact that letters addressed to Jefferson, as well as those from him, are included. The new edition contains variants and rough drafts of documents, which are accompanied by detailed and competent annotations. It is still too early to evaluate the new edition,[95] because it is far from complete, but there are grounds to assume that in the end researchers will obtain thorough familiarity with the abundant archives of Thomas Jefferson.

Thanks to extensive use of archival material and documentary publications, the author rarely had to resort to the press for factual information. The shortcomings of the press as a documentary source are well recognized. Deliberately false reports have found their way into even the most reliable of newspapers, such as the *Times* (London), *Moniteur* (Paris), *Weekly Register* (Baltimore), *National Intelligencer* (Washington), or *Sankt-Peterburgski vedomosti.* Conjectures and ungrounded interpretations of various sorts were reprinted by one newspaper from the other, complicating the elucidation of the historical truth, which could later on be established only by studying the appropriate archival documents. It was usually easier to locate information of a strictly factual nature in the appropriate documentary publication in more exact and systematized form.

This does not mean that I avoided the periodical press and refused to use it as a source. I made extensive use of *Sankt-Peterburgskie vedomosti* and other Russian newspapers and magazines, particularly in gathering information concerning the entry of American ships into Russian ports, ascertaining the nature and time of appearance of various sorts of official communications, and so on. The British *Annual Register,* which carried on its pages much official material, was also used as a source for documentary information.

APPENDIX

The major reason for examining the periodical press and published literature of the last quarter of the eighteenth and the beginning of the nineteenth centuries was to study the attitude of the public, primarily the Russian public, toward America, the American Revolution, and Russian relations with the United States.

The situation with regard to the availability in Soviet libraries of the American periodical press for the earlier years is not a happy one. It was once thought that there were no complete files of American newspapers and journals for the first half of the nineteenth century in the U.S.S.R. Nevertheless, I discovered complete files of the most famous and influential newspaper of the time—the Baltimore *Weekly Register,* published by Hezekian Niles starting in 1811—in the Library of the Academy of Sciences in Leningrad.[96] Individual issues and excerpts from American newspapers, sent to St. Petersburg by Russian diplomatic representatives in America, also proved highly valuable. Taken together with the published literature of the time, such material made it possible to trace the attitudes of various segments of American society toward Russia, and to describe conflicting opinions in the United States on this subject in the years 1812-1815.

I succeeded in investigating much more fully and systematically the attitudes of various segments of Russian society toward the United States, and particularly in juxtaposing the position of the semiofficial government organ *Sankt-Peterburgskie vedomosti* (St. Petersburg Gazette) with the newspaper issued in Moscow by Nikolai Novikov (*Moskovskie vedomosti,* Moscow Gazette, 1779-1789).

Among Russian journals devoting considerable attention to the subject of America, those deserving special mention are Novikov's publications (in particular his celebrated *Privablenie k "Moskovskim vedomostiam"* (Supplement to "Moscow Gazette"); the publications of N. M. Karamzin *Moskovski Zhurnal,* (Moscow Journal), and especially *Vestnik Evropy*, (Europe's Messenger); *Politicheskii zhurnal* (Political Journal), printed at Moscow University by P. A. Sokhatsky; *Akademicheskie ivestiia* (Academic News); and *Syn otechestva* (Son of the Fatherland).

The serious interest of the Russian press in America and the American Revolution was by no means accidental or casual. The revolutionary events taking place in the English colonies in North America were inseparably linked with the overall world historical process; they were tightly intertwined with the socio-political development of the European nations.

With regard to America and the American Revolution two basic political tendencies manifested themselves quite distinctly at the time: the progressive, republican-democratic, and the reactionary, feudal-serf-owning.

Russian society could not remain indifferent to the rebellion of the English colonies and the formation of the new nation. Those with a reactionary monarchical orientation did not hide their aversion to bourgeois principles and to the new republic across the ocean; however, progressive segments of Russian society welcomed the American Revolution, expressing sympathy and support for the struggle for independence.

To trace the struggle of opinions through the pages of the Russian press of the time is a complicated affair. The country was subjected to strict censorship. Moreover, Russian newspapers and journals as a rule printed nothing but translations from various foreign publications. Nevertheless, the very subject of the translated material, the general orientation of the selection, and specific editorial comments permit us to discern the positions of the publishers.

Works of notable Russian scholars, men of letters, public figures, navigators, and travelers which touched upon the American theme, were studied systematically, as were a significant number of translated books on America. I attempted to cover the widest and most varied range of materials, from Catherine II's correspondence with Baron Grimm, Princess E. R. Dashkova's memoirs and N. M. Karamzin's works, to *Protokoly zasedanii konferentsii imperatorskoi Akademii nauk* (Proceedings of Sessions of the Conference of the Imperial Academy of Sciences) and the scientific works of M. V. Lomonosov, G. V. Rikhman, F. U. Epinius, and others.

The works of Russia's most progressive personalities of the time—N. I. Novikov, D. I. Fonvizin, F. V. Karzhavin, and particularly A. N. Radishchev—proved to be of exceptional interest. Novikov's extensive publishing activities in the 1770's and 1780's were of major significance for the propagation of the progressive ideas of the Western Enlightenment and the American Revolution. With regard to the ode "(Liberty)" and *A Journey from St. Petersburg to Moscow,* I can state without exaggeration that in depth of analysis of the events and ideas of the American Revolution, in richness of content, and in mastery of exposition, they may be placed alongside the most distinguished works in world literature on the American Revolution.

A few words concerning specialized books by Russian authors which are devoted to the United States are in order. The first appeared in early 1783, that is, as the American War of Independence was concluding. A short work by D. M. Ladygin, of a handbook type, it offered the reader a general impression of the new state which was coming into existence in North America.[97]

Although Ladygin's brochure and several other works on America of that period were mainly of a compilative nature, entirely different evaluations must be given to books by P. P. Svin'in and P. I. Poletika, who spent several years in the United States and made thorough studies of the nation. Svin'in's essay was first published in Russia in 1814 in the journal *Syn otechestva* (Son of the Fatherland), and later appeared out in separate editions in 1815 and 1818.[98] The original work of P. I. Poletika was published abroad in the 1820's.[99] Despite certain shortcomings connected with the time of publication and the limitations of the author's point of view (this pertains chiefly to Svin'in), the research value of these books, richness of their factual content, and number of interesting generalizations and conclusions concerning the uniqueness of American historical development continues down to the present.

I have mentioned the most important documentary sources of a primarily general nature. In the course of work, however, I made extensive use of various sorts of specialized publications which played an important—at times decisive—role in the solution of certain concrete problems such as the colonization of Russian America, John Paul Jones's stay in Russia, F. V. Karzhavin's American journey, and early Russian-American trade relations.

Naturally I had to make extensive use of official statistical materials and collections (particularly the well-known works of G. Nebol'sin and Timothy Pitkin),[100] diverse reference works and guides, and numerous general and specialized works of Russian and American history. Taking into consideration the existence of detailed accounts of key problems of Russian and American history as well as of international relations in the period under review, I tried to limit general information to the barest minimum and did not attempt to undertake fresh research on the American War of Independence, international relations in the age of the Napoleonic wars, the international situation in Russia in the eighteenth and early nineteenth centuries, and so forth. The only possible exception was the War of 1812, a problem not yet sufficiently studied in Marxist historiography and on which many conflicting views had been advanced (see Chapter X). For the rest I limited myself to the shortest possible introductory observations, a few necessary explanations in the course of the exposition, and references to specialized literature.

Moving on to the basic study, I consider it my duty to note the cooperation and aid constantly rendered by employees of the Archive of Russian Foreign Policy. Of great benefit was a discussion of the author's monograph at a session of the Sector of American History at the Institute of History of the U.S.S.R. Academy of Sciences November 27, 1964, in the course of which valuable advice and suggestions were offered. As it was recommended that the manuscript be defended as a doctoral dissertation,[101] corresponding members of the Academy of Sciences A. A. Guber and A. V. Efimov,[102] Professor S. A. Gonionsky, and Doctor of Historical Sciences A. M. Stanislavskaia undertook the responsibility of familiarizing themselves thoroughly with the work and acting as official critics at a session of the Academic Council of the Institute of History.

I wish to express special gratitude to my teacher, corresponding member of the Academy of Sciences Aleksei Vladimirovich Efimov, whose constant attention, advice, and support rendered invaluable aid.

After the present work had gone to press in the U.S.S.R., microfilm of American archival material relating to the stay of John Quincy Adams in St. Petersburg in 1781-1782 and 1809-1814, from the Massachusetts Historical Society in Boston, was sent to Moscow in exchange for copies of documents from AVPR.[103] The manuscript diary kept by Adams during his stay in Russia and "official" and "private" letterbooks belonging to the American ambassador, revealed the full extent of his correspondence. Documents addressed to members of the Adams family from August 1809 through April 1814 were of particular value. Among them one finds numerous originals of letters which reflect not only Adams' official diplomatic activity but also his extensive scientific and cultural ties (particularly his correspondence with Robert Fulton, Benjamin Rush, and Gotthelf Fischer).[104] Although all the basic documents from this period had already been published or were known from materials in AVPR and the National Archives in Washington, study of the Adams Papers provided an additional checking point, and in individual cases helped to make more precise certain details relating to the activities of the first American minister to St. Petersburg.

The author has also been able to familiarize himself with a series of new works published by Soviet and foreign scholars since 1965 (for example, an article by the Danish researcher A. Rasch, a book by the American Alfred W. Crosby dealing with Russian-American trade in the late eighteenth and early nineteenth centuries and studies by S. G. Fedorova, Dieter Boden, Ekkehard Völki and David M. Griffiths),[105] a number of old publications formerly unobtainable in Soviet libraries. In this respect I am especially grateful to the Director of the Oregon Historical Society, Thomas Vaughan, for sending me in 1970 the "memorial edition" of the *Writings of Thomas Jefferson*, edited by Andrew A. Lipscomb and Albert E. Bergh, and originally published in 1903, which I have placed at the disposal of the Lenin Library in Moscow.

An examination of all these materials has enabled me to make a number of additions in the original text and to remove misprints and factual inaccuracies. The book's text and all the basic conclusions remain by and large unchanged.

NOTES

INDEX

ABBREVIATIONS

AN SSSR	Archive of Arkhiv Akademii Nauk SSSR (Archive of the USSR Academy of Sciences)
ASP FR	*American State Papers, Foreign Relations*, Washington, 1832-1859
AVPR	Arkhiv vneshnei politiki Rossii (Archive of Russia's Foreign Affairs)
GBL OR	Otdel rukopisei Biblioteki SSSR im. V. I. Lenina (Manuscript Division of V. I. Lenin State Library)
JCC	*Journals of the Continental Congress, 1774-1789*, Washington, 1904-1937
LGU	Leningradskii gosudarstvenyyi universitet (Leningrad State University)
LOII	Arkhiv Leningradskogo otdeleniia Instituta istorii AN SSSR (Archive of the Leningrad Division of the Institute of History of the USSR Academy of Sciences)
NA	National Archives, Washington, D.C.
PAPS	*Proceedings of the American Philosophical Society,* Philadelphia, Pennsylvania
PSZRI	*Polnoe sobranie Zakonov Rossiiskoi imperii s 1649 g.* (Complete Collection of the Laws of the Russian Empire since 1649), vols. XIX-XXXII (1775-1815), vols. XL, XLV. SPB., 1830
ROIRL	Rukopisnyi otdel Instituta russkoi literatury AN SSSR (Manuscript Division of the Institute of Russian Literature of the USSR Academy of Sciences)
SbRIO	*Sbornik Imperatorskogo Russkogo Istoricheskogo Obshchestva* (Collection of the Imperial Russian Historical Society)
TsGADA	Tsentral'nyi gosudarstvennyi arkhiv drevnikh aktov (Central State Archive of the Ancient Acts)
TsGAOR	Tsentral'nyi gosudarstvennyi arkhiv Oktiabr'skoi revoliutsii (Central State Archive of the October Revolution)
TsGAVMF	Tsentral'nyi gosudarstvennyi arkhiv voenno-morskogo flota SSSR (Central State Archive of the Navy)
TsGIA	Tsentral'nyi gosudarstvennyi istoricheskii arkhiv SSSR (Central State Historical Archive)
VPR	*Vneshniaia politika Rossii XIX i nachala XX veka* (Russia's Foreign Policy in the Nineteenth and Early Twentieth Centuries), Moscow, 1960-1965

Part One. Russia and the War of Independence in North America

1. Lenin, *Polnoe sobranie sochinenii,* 37: 48-49.
2. For an analysis of recent literature on the American Revolution see Richard B. Morris, *The American Revolution Reconsidered* (New York, 1967); Jack P. Greene, ed., *The Reinterpretation of the American Revolution 1763-1789* (New York, 1968); N. N. Bolkhovitinov, "Voina SShA za nezavisimost' i sovremennaia amerikanskaia istoriografiia" (The American War of Independence and Contemporary American Historiography), *Voprosy istorii* (Problems of History), 1969, no. 12, pp. 73-78.
3. H. Aptheker, *Istoriia amerikanskogo naroda,* vol. 2: *Amerikanskaia revoliutsiia 1763-1783* (tr. from English, Moscow, 1962). This book is largely historiographical and contains an analysis of the main points of view on the character of the War of Independence (see pp. 23-41 and *passim*).
4. A. V. Efimov, *Ocherki istorii SShA:* G. N. Sevost L'ianov et al., eds., *Ocherki novoi i noveishei istorii SShA* (Essays on the New and Contemporary History of the United States, Moscow, 1960), vol. 1; A. A. Fursenko, *Amerikanskaia burzhuaznaia revoliutsia XVIII v.* (The American Bourgeois Revolution of the Eighteenth Century, Moscow and Leningrad, 1960).
5. H. Doniol, *Histoire de la participation de la France à l'établissement des Etats-Unis d'Amérique* (5 vols., Paris, 1886-1892); E. S. Corwin, *French Policy and the American Alliance of 1778* (repr. Hamden, Conn., 1962).
6. M. L. Brown, transl. and ed., *The American Independence through Prussian Eyes: A Neutral View of the Peace Negotiations of 1782-1783: Selections from Prussian Diplomatic Correspondence* (Durham, N. C., 1959).
7. "Catherine II and the American Revolution," *AHR,* 21(1915):92-96.
8. F. P. Renaut, *Les relations diplomatiques entre la Russie et les Etats-Unis (1776-1825). Catherine II et les insurgés. La mission Dana (1776-1783)* (Paris, 1923); Cresson, *Francis Dana: A Puritan Diplomat at the Court of Catherine the Great* (New York, 1930).
9. Wharton, *Correspondence,* 2:447-448.
10. L. M. Sears, *A History of American Foreign Policy* (New York, 1938); J. H. Latane and D. W. Wainhouse, *A History of American Foreign Policy* (New York, 1941); J. Pratt, *A History of the United States Foreign Policy* (Englewood Cliffs, N. J., 1955); R. J. Bartlett, *Policy and Power: Two Centuries of American Foreign*

Relations (New York, 1963); T. A. Bailey, *A Diplomatic History of the American People* (7th ed., New York, 1964).

11. Bemis, *A Diplomatic History of the United States* (New York, 1955), pp. 38-45. Bemis' monograph, *The Diplomacy of the American Revolution,* remains to this day the most substantial investigation of the diplomatic history of the War of Independence. Bemis admits that the Armed Neutrality initiated by Russia was, in itself, a "powerful instrument in bringing about Great Britain's isolation." At the same time, the eminent historian obviously contradicts his own facts when he asserts that sympathetic interest in the American revolution was a "rare phenomenon" beyond the borders of France, and its manifestation had a "passive" and "purely theoretical character." It is only recently that a basic monograph has appeared which attempts to present a detailed account of Russia's position in the course of the complex diplomatic struggle preceding the conclusion of the Paris peace of 1783. The book utilizes an enormous documentation from practically all of the greater and lesser capitals of Europe from Madrid to Stockholm, not to mention the American materials. The only thing not found at the author's disposal were the documents in the Russian archives. Naturally, this absence is reflected in the pages of the book dealing with the position of the St. Petersburg court (Richard B. Morris, *The Peacemakers: The Great Powers and American Independence* [New York, 1965], pp. 158-190).

12. *Politicheskaia perepiska imp. Ekateriny II* (Political Correspondence of the Empress Catherine II, 9 vols., St. Petersburg, 1885-1914), in *SbRiO* as vols. 48, 51, 57, 67, 87, 97, 118, 135, 145.

13. Prince Obolensky, comp., *O vooruzhennom morskom neitralitete. Sostavleno . . . po dokumentam Moskovskogo glavnogo arkhiva ministerstva inostrannykh del* (On the Armed Naval Neutrality. Compiled . . . from the Documents of the Moscow Main Archives of the Ministry for Foreign Affairs, St. Petersburg, 1859); published in *Morskoi Sbornik* (Naval Review), vols. 43-44, Sept.-Dec. 1859, nos. 9-12.

Chapter 1.   Russian Diplomacy and the War of 1775-1783

1. A. S. Musin-Pushkin to Nikita I. Panin, 31 Oct./11 Nov. 1774, in AVPR, Snosheniia Rossii s Angliei, 1774 g., d. 261, l. 158.

2. *Ibid.,* ll. 158-159.

3. See Musin-Pushkin to Panin, 3/14 Feb. 1775, in *ibid.,* 1775 g., d. 266, ll. 18ff.

4. *Ibid.*

5. Musin-Pushkin to Panin, 10/21 Feb. 1775, *ibid.,* op. 35/6, d. 266, l. 28.

6. For draft instructions to Chernyshev see *ibid.,* 1768 g., op. 36/6, d. 202, l. 3. Concerning the significance of the instructions, see V. N. Aleksandrenko, *Russkie diplomaticheskie agenty v Londone v XVIII v.* (Russian Diplomatic Agents in London in the Eighteenth Century, 2 vols., Warsaw, 1897), 1:38.

7. *SbRIO,* 12:16ff.

8. F. Martens, *Sobranie traktatov* (Collection of Treaties), vol. 9(10): *Traktaty s Angliei 1710-1801 gg.* (Treaties with England, 1710-1801, St. Petersburg, 1892), pp. 242-259.

9. *Ibid.,* pp. 259-287.

10. George III to Catherine II, 1 Sept. 1775, in *SbRIo,* 19:478-479.

11. Suffolk to Gunning, 1 Sept. 1775, in *ibid.,* pp. 476-478; for the draft treaty see pp. 483-487.

12. Catherine II had in mind Caroline-Mathilde, wife of Danish King Christian VII, who died 10 May 1775.

13. Catherine II to Madame Bielke, 30 June/11 July 1775, in *SbRIO,* 27:44. The translation from the French is precise. See also Efimov, *Ocherki Istorii SShA* (Essays in the History of the United States, Moscow, 1955), pp. 112-113.

14. *SbRIO,* 27:44. Catherine thereafter maintained her conviction concerning the inevitability of the loss by England of her colonies in America: "Que dites-vous de ces colonies qui disent adieu à jamais à l'Angleterre?" she asked her correspondent one year later (see Catherine II to Madame Bielke, 5/16 Sept. 1776, *ibid.,* p. 119). And still later, in returning to an evaluation of George III, Catherine wrote: "En de mauvaises mains tout devient mauvais. Franklin, Deane, pour avoir dit les choses comme elles étaient, lorsqu'ils étaient en Angleterre, ne méritaient point d'être pendus: il fallait les écouter, et agir en anglais; il fallait ne point provoquir les Américains, pour faire pencher la balance du côté du roi." (see the draft of a letter from Catherine II to an unidentified woman, 7/18 June 1778, *ibid.,* p. 154).

15. Catherine II to George III, 23 Sept./4 Oct. 1775, *SbRIO,* 19:500-501.

16. See Gunning's report to Suffolk of 20 Sept./1 Oct., no. 60, and 26 Sept./7 Oct. 1775, nos. 62, 64, *ibid.,* pp. 489-499, 503-505.

17. V. G. Lizakevich, adviser to the Russian embassy in London, gave detailed information in this regard in a report to Panin, 29 Dec. 1775/9 Jan. 1776, in AVPR, Snosheniia Rossii s Angliei, 1775 g., d. 267, ll. 121-122.

18. Lizakevich to Panin, 9/20 Aug. 1776, *ibid.,* 1776 g., d. 274, ll. 152-153.

19. Panin to Catherine II, 10/21 Oct. 1776, *SbRIO,* 145:243-244.

20. Bariatinsky to Osterman, 4/15 Dec. 1776, in AVPR, Snosheniia Rossii s Frantsiei, 1776 g., d. 312, l. 245.

21. *Ibid.,* ll. 245-248.

22. Musin-Pushkin to Panin, 19/30 Dec. 1777, in AVPR, Snosheniia Rossii s Angliei, 1777 g., d. 282, ll. 27ff.

23. H. S. Commager, ed., *Documents of American History* (New York, 1958), 1:105-107; hereafter cited as Commager, *Documents.*

24. To I. A. Osterman, 26 Feb./9 March 1778, AVPR, Snosheniia Rossii s Frantsiei, 1778 g., d. 333, ll. 76-77.

25. To his sister Argamakova, 31 Dec. 1777/11 Jan. 1778, in *D. I. Fonvizin. Sochineniia, Pis'ma i izbrannye perevody* (D. I. Fonvizin: Works, Letters, and Selected Translations, St. Petersburg, 1866), p. 428.

26. 20/31 March 1778, *ibid.,* pp. 331-332.

27. To his sister Argamakova, Aug. 1778, *ibid.,* p. 445.

28. P. V. Viazemsky, *Polnoe sobranie sochinenii* (Complete Works, St. Petersburg, 1880), 5:91.

29. Although Catherine II personally and through A. Lanskoi, thanked her foreign correspondent for the dispatching of pamphlets of "l'illustre Franklin," and the notes of "Bonhomme Richard" were found to be "delicieux," the Empress a short time later, in pointing to a portrait of the great American, noted to her secretary A. V. Khrapovitsky: "I do not like him." See the letters to Grimm of 8/19 and 10/21 May 1781, *SbRIO,* 13:303, 310; *Dnevnik A. V. Khrapovitskogo* (The Diary of A. V. Khrapovitsky, Moscow, 1901), p. 1 (notation for 6/17 July 1782).

30. "Prince Bariatinsky, the Russian ambassador, was particularly civil to me this day at Court, apologised for what passed relating to the visit, expressed himself extremely sensible of my friendship in covering the affair, which might have occasioned him very disagreeable consequences, etc." Benjamin Franklin, *Autobiographical Writings*, ed. Carl Van Doren (New York, 1948), p. 553; see also Radovsky, *Veniamin Franklin i ego sviazi s Rossiei*, pp. 42-43; A. I. Startsev, "Veniamin Franklin i russkoe obshchestvo XVIII veka," *Internasional'naia literatura*, 1940, no. 3-4, p. 216.

31. *Polnoe sobranie sochinenii*, 37:56.

32. On the mission of James Harris see Madariaga's monograph *Britain, Russia* (my detailed review of this book was printed in *Istoriia SSSR*, 1964, no. 1, pp. 206-209). Documentary materials concerning Harris' negotiations are also found in J. H. Harris, ed., *Diaries and Correspondence of James Harris, First Earl of Malmesbury* (London, 1845), vol. 1; hereafter cited as Harris, *Diaries and Corr.*

33. James Harris to Panin, April 1778, in AVPR, Snosheniia Rossii s Angliei, 1778 g., d. 596, ll. 21-24.

34. *Ibid.*, d. 595, ll. 3-8.

35. Harris to Panin, 26 Nov. 1779, *ibid.*, 1779 g., d. 600, ll. lla-13.

36. To Harris, 5-7/16-18 Dec. 1779, *ibid.*, d. 599, ll. 15-16.

37. Catherine II to Simolin, 15/26 July 1779, in Aleksandrenko, *Russkie Diplomaticheskie agenty* 2:*Materialy*, pp. 195-199.

38. 8/10 March 1779, in *The Writings of George Washington: From the Original Manuscript Sources, 1745-1799*, ed. John C. Fitzpatrick (40 vols., Washington, 1931-1944) (hereafter, Washington, *Writings*), 14:220.

39. To George Clinton, 6 March 1779, *ibid.*, p. 196.

40. Secret report of the College of Foreign Affairs to Catherine II, 31 July/11 Aug. 1779. The original is preserved in AVPR, Sekretnye mneniia, 1725-1798 gg., d. 597, ll. 100-114; published in *Arkhiv kniazia Vorontsova*, 34:388-405.

41. According to Madariaga's calculations, England seized seventeen Russian ships in the course of the war (*Britain, Russia*, p. 374).

42. See, for example, Musin-Pushkin to Panin, 28 Nov./9 Dec. 1778, AVPR, Snosheniia Rossii s Angliei, 1778 g., d. 288, l. 241.

43. Catherine II to Simolin, 8/19 Nov. 1779, in AVPR, Londonskaia missiia, 1779-1781 gg., op. 36, d. 345, ll. 62, 66; published in part in Aleksandrenko, *Russkie diplomaticheskie agenty*, 2:200-202.

44. See *O vooruzhennom morskom neitralitete*, pp. 29ff.

45. Catherine II to Simolin, 27 Feb./9 March 1780, in AVPR, Londonskaya missiia, 1779-1781 gg., d. 345, ll. 2-6.

46. It was later reported that the fleet equipped at Kronstadt and divided into three squadrons was destined for the defense of neutral navigation in the Mediterranean Sea, at "Lisbon Hills," and in the North Sea (see Catherine II to Simolin, 7/18 June 1780, *ibid.*, ll. 10-11.

47. For the text of the declaration of 27 Feb./9 March 1780, see *O vooruzhennom morskom neitralitete*," pp. 64-66; F. Martens, *Sobranie traktatov*, 9(10):307-310.

48. Marx and Engels, *Sochineniia* (Works, 2nd ed., 39 vols., Moscow, 1954-1966), 22:25.

49. Carl Bergbohm, *Die bewaffnete Neutralität 1780-1783* (Berlin, 1884).

50. P. Fauchille, *La diplomatie française et la ligue des neutres de 1780* (Paris, 1893).

51. J. B. Scott, ed., *The Armed Neutralities of 1780 and 1800* (New York, 1918).

52. C. W. Dohm, *Denkwurdigkeiten meiner Zeit* (Hannover, 1814-1818), 2:100-150. Comte de Goertz, *Mémoire ou précis historique sur la neutralité armée et son origine, suivi de pièces justificatives* (Bâle, 1801).

53. Among the adherents to this point of view were such competent authorities as G. Martens, G. Garden, and the above-mentioned C. Bergbohm; see Bergbohm, *Die bewaffnete*, pp. 239-247.

54. Leshkov, *Istoricheskoe issledovanie nachal neitraliteta otnositel'no morskoi torgovli* (A Historical Investigation into the Origins of the Neutrality Concerning Naval Trade, Moscow, 1841), pp. 105-107; Danevsky, *Istoricheskii ocherk neitraliteta* (A Historical Essay on the Neutrality, Moscow, 1879), pp. 69-77.

55. *Ocherki istorii SSSR. Period feodalizma. Rossiia vo vtoroi polovine XVIII veka* (Essays in the History of the USSR: The Period of Feudalism: Russia in the Second Half of the Eighteenth Century, Moscow, 1956), pp. 128ff.

56. Bemis, *The Diplomacy of the American Revolution*, p. 151. See also O. Feldbaek, *Dansk neutralitets-politik under krigen 1778-1783* (Copenhagen, 1971), pp. 39, 77.

57. See Aptheker, *Istoriia amerikanskogo naroda*, 2:229-230, 235, 243.

58. To Ingersoll, 28 July 1814, in G. Hunt, ed., *Writings of James Madison* (9 vols., New York and London, 1900-1910), 8:282-286; hereafter cited as Madison, *Writings*.

59. To Catherine II, 5 Nov. 1779, in Harris, *Diaries and Corr.*, 1:265; *Istoriia diplomatii* (The History of Diplomacy, 2nd ed., Moscow, 1959), 1:394.

60. Harris to Stormont, 13/24 Dec. 1780. A record of the conversation of 7/18 Dec. is in Harris, *Diaries and Corr.*, 1:355.

61. F. Martens, *Sobranie traktatov*, 9(10):297. On the whole, Martens, although he offers an interesting and documented exposition of the history of the declaration of Armed Neutrality, is prone to overestimate the personal role played by Catherine, to whom he ascribes the chief, if not exclusive authorship. Madariaga also tends to overevaluate the Empress' role (*Britain, Russia*, pp. 173ff.).

62. See *Arkhiv kniazia Vorontsova*, 9:133; *Dnevnik A. V. Khrapovitskogo*, p. 485; also *Russkii Arkhiv* (Russian Archives), 1875, 2:123-124.

63. This refers also to such an informed investigator as Francis Renaut, who mistakenly suggests that Russian policy with regard to Holland was passive (*Les Provinces Unies et la Guerre d'Amérique* [3 vols., Paris, 1924-1932]).

64. The first person to draw my attention to the role played by D. A. Golitsyn was Iu. Ia. Moshkovskaia, to whom also belongs the distinction of having uncovered the extensive archival materials dealing with this question. Golitsyn's activities are also elucidated, although incompletely (by considering only Dutch sources), in Madariaga (*Britain, Russia*, pp. 151-154, 160, 168-169).

65. Concerning Golitsyn's views on the peasant question see V. I. Semevsky, *Krest'ianskii vopros v Rossii* (The Peasant Question in Russia, St. Petersburg, 1888), vol. 1.

66. For more detail see I. S. Bak, "Dmitrii Alekseevich Golitsyn (filosofskie, obshchestvenno-politicheskie i ekonomicheskie vozzreniia)" (Dmitrii Alekseevich Golitsyn [Philosophical, Socio-Political and Economic Views]), in *Istoricheskie zapiski* (Historical Notes, Moscow, 1948), 26:258-272.

67. A. A. Bezborodko to I. A. Osterman, 21 May/1 June 1782, AVPR, Vysochaishe aprobovannye doklady po snosheniiam s inostrannymi derzhavami, 1782 g., d. 8, l. 185. Reviewing Catherine's policy toward the United States, a member of the Russian Ministry later wrote with justification: "The Court of St.

Petersburg went so far in its rigidity that Prince Golitsyn received a very strong reprimand for having accepted and dispatched a packet from America to Mr. Dana, who was in St. Petersburg as a traveler possessing plenary powers recognizing him as minister of the United States of America" (TsGADA, f. 15, d. 214, ll. 1ff.).

68. In this regard I. A. Osterman wrote on 6/17 May 1782: "At the present time, when the Estates-General of Holland have officially recognized Mr. Adams as Minister Plenipotentiary of the United States of America, it has become necessary that I notify Your Excellency that Her Imperial Majesty does not wish that you on your part display in any manner her approval of this step. In this connection, Prince, you must decline a reception or a visit from Mr. Adams, as well as from any other person accredited by the colonies separating from Great Britain" (AVPR, Snosheniya Rossii s Gollandiei, 1782 g., d. 28, l. 10). In these measures, formally based on strict neutrality, class sympathies of the tsarist government, apart from diplomatic considerations, clearly told. Somewhat later this order was rescinded, a matter which will be discussed below.

69. 7/18 Feb. 1780, *ibid.*, 1780 g., d. 207, ll. 35-39. (A similar report was sent to Osterman at the same time; *ibid.*, ll. 41-46.)

70. 3/14 March 1780, *ibid.*, d. 206, ll. 3-6.

71. 5 June 1780, in Franklin, *Writings*, 8:82. A copy of Franklin's letter was evidently passed on by Dumas to Golitsyn, and was attached to the latter's report of 27 May/7 June 1780, in AVPR, Snosheniia Rossii s Gollandiei, 1780 g., d. 208, l. 36.

72. Washington, *Writings*, 20:122.

73. 26 April 1780, in Wharton, *Correspondence*, 3:632-633.

74. *JCC*, vol. 18:Sept. 7-Dec. 29, 1780 (Washington, 1910), p. 866.

75. These instructions were issued 27 Nov. 1780; see E. Albrecht, "Die Stellung der Vereinigten Staaten von Amerika zur bewaffneten Neutralität von 1780," *Zeitschrift für Völkerreht und Bundesstaatsrecht*, Bd. VI, Ht. 5 and 6, 1913, s. 443.

76. Resolution of the Continental Congress of 5 Oct. 1780, in *JCC*, 18:905-906. The approval by the United States of the Russian Declaration of Armed Neutrality was also reported in the Russian press; see *S.-Peterburgskie vedomosti* (St. Petersburg Record), 1781, no. 17.

77. 8 March, 1781, AVPR, Snosheniia Rossii s Gollandiei, 1781 g., d. 218, l. 24.

78. See, for example, Hölzle, *Russland und Amerika*, p. 36.

79. From the protocols of the Continental Congress for 1 Sept.-5 Oct. 1780, AVPR, Snosheniia Rossii s Gollandiei, 1781 g., d. 218, l. 26.

80. For more detail see Chapter VI.

81. *JCC*, 18:1155-1156.

82. *Ibid.*, p. 1166.

83. *Ibid.*, pp. 1166-1173.

84. See the instructions from Huntington to Dana, 19 Dec. 1780, *ibid.*, pp. 1168-1169; Wharton, *Correspondence*, 6:201.

85. Secret Report of the College of Foreign Affairs to Catherine II of 31 July/11 Aug. 1779, in AVPR, Sekretnye mneniia, 1725-1798 gg., d. 597, l. 114.

86. "Protocol Concerning the Armed Neutrality of 5 March 1780, written in the hand of A. A. Bezborodko," in "O vooruzhennom morskom neitralitete," p. 89.

87. 7/18 Feb. 1780. For the full text see AVPR, Snosheniia Rossii s Gollandiei, 1780 g., d. 207, ll. 35-39; Bezborodko to Rumiantsev, 26 Feb./8

March 1780, *Pis'ma A. A. Bezborodko k grafu P. A. Rumiantsevu 1775-1793 gg.* (Letters of A. A. Bezborodko to Count P. A. Rumiantsev, 1775-1793, St. Petersburg, 1900), p. 62.

88. Vérac to Vergennes, Sept. 1, Oct. 11, 1780, in Griffiths, "Nikita Panin, Russian Diplomacy and the American Revolution," pp. 13-14; Morris, *The Peacemakers,* pp. 169-170; Catherine II to I. M. Simolin, 27 Oct./7 Nov. 1780, in AVPR, Londonskaia missiia, 1779-1781 gg., op. 36, d. 345, ll. 15-17.

89. See Catherine II to Simolin, 30 Jan./10 Feb. 1781, in *ibid.*, ll. 90-92.

90. Decree assigning Golitsyn and Morkov as mediators, 18/29 April 1782, in TsGOAR, f. 728, op. 1, ch. 1, d. 174. For credentials of the same date see *ibid.*, d. 284, ll. 1-2.

91. See the secret report of the College of Foreign Affairs to Catherine II, 9/20 April 1781, in AVPR, Sekretnye mneniia, 1742-1799 gg., d. 593, ll. 163-176 and 177-186.

92. Golitsyn to Osterman, 7/18 April 1780, in AVPR, Snosheniia Rossii s Gollandiei, 1780 g., d. 207, ll. 68ff.

93. In this regard see Madariaga, *Britain, Russia,* pp. 223-227; Harris to Stormont, 13/24 Dec. 1780, in Harris, *Diary and Corr.,* 1:357; V. T., "Iz diplomaticheskoi perepiski Dzhemsa Garrisa—1777-1782" (Excerpts from the Diplomatic Correspondence of James Harris, 1777-1782), *Russkaia Starina* (Russian Antiquity), 35:457-458 (Sept. 1908).

94. Bezborodko to Osterman, 14/25 Feb. 1782, in AVPR, Vysochaishe aprobovannye doklady po snosheniiam s inostrannymi derzhavami, 1782 g., d. 8, ll. 43-44. The Vice-Chancellor, of course, carried out this order, and the corresponding instructions were sent to Morkov; see Osterman to Morkov, 21 Feb./4 March 1782, in AVPR. Snosheniia Rossi s Gollandiei, 1782 g., d. 236, ll. 1-2.

95. See, for example, Simolin to Panin, 12/23 March 1781, in AVPR Snosheniia Rossii s Angliei, 1781 g., d. 320, ll. 157-158.

96. Simolin to Osterman, 7/18 June 1782. For the full text see *ibid.*, 1782 g., d. 332, ll. 7-10.

97. Commager, *Documents,* 1:117-119.

98. See John Adams to Robert Livingston, 9, 12, and 16 July 1783, in Wharton, *Correspondence,* 6:529, 539, 551-552.

99. Bariatinsky to Osterman, 13/24 Aug. 1783, in AVPR, Snosheniia Rossii s Frantsiei, 1783 g., d. 397, ll. 43-44.

100. John Adams to the President of the Continental Congress, 5 Sept. 1783, in Wharton, *Correspondence,* 6:674-676.

101. See Simolin to Panin, 26 March/6 April 1781, in AVPR, Snosheniia Rossii s Angliei, 1781 g., d. 320, ll. 188-189.

102. Harris to Lord Grantham, 28 Feb./11 March 1783, Harris, *Diary and Corr.,* 2:36-38; J. Hildt, *Early Diplomatic Negotiations,* p. 23.

103. In letters to his father and mother, John Quincy Adams described his journey to Russia and the impressions of his arrival in St. Petersburg, sometimes childishly naïve, and sometimes surprisingly mature. Russia appeared to the young diplomat a mysterious country "of princes and slaves." Enraptured by the splendor and luxury of the capital's palaces, he at the same time sharply criticized the existing order. "No body I believe will assert that a people can possibly be happy who are subjected to personal slavery," wrote young John Quincy in a short essay written on his return from Russia and based upon personal observations and published information. In this same essay he decisively condemned a system whereby the people were for all practical purposes denied the right to go abroad, and at the same time he noted the great desire of the serfs to receive their freedom.

"I have seen a man who gave to his landlord for his liberty and for that of his descendants 450,000 roubles," wrote Adams, and justly perceived in this fact proof that the Russian people prize their personal freedom highly; see *Writings*, 1:4-13; and Mainwaring, *John Quincy Adams and Russia*, p. 6.

104. Because of the necessity of continuing his education, J. Q. Adams left St. Petersburg, 30 Oct. 1782; see *Writings*, 1:7.

105. Dana to Osterman, 24 Feb./7 March 1783, and 10/21 April 1783, in Wharton, *Correspondence,* 6:275, 390.

106. The record of Dana's meeting with Osterman, 12/23 April 1783, in AVPR, Snosheniia Rossii s SShA, 1783 g., d. 1, ll. 1-4. Commenting on the position of the tsarist government on the question of recognition of the American representative, Bezborodko wrote: "The minister of the American Free States, Mr. Dana, has been living here for some time and had announced himself formally. His recognition and the granting of an audience to him have been suspended until the conclusion of the definitive treaty; after that, a minister will be sent from here to America also." See Bezborodko to Rumiantsev, 28 Feb./11 March 1783, *Pis'ma Bezborodko k Rumiantsevu,* pp. 103-104.

107. Dana to Osterman, 27 April/8 May 1783, in Wharton, *Correspondence,* 6:411-415.

108. Osterman to Dana, 3/14 June 1783, in AVPR, Snosheniia Rossii s SShA, 1783 g., d. 3, ll. 1-2. "Draft of a verbal response to the American Dana concerning his recognition here in a public capacity from the American United States" was presented by Bezborodko to the Empress and received her approval, 29 May/9 June 1783 (AVPR, Vysochaishe aprobovannye doklady po snosheniiam s inostrannymi derzhavami, 1783 g., d. 9, l. 91). Osterman's "verbal note" is translated and published in Wharton, *Correspondence,* 6:494-495.

109. The record of Osterman's meeting with Dana, 3/14 June 1783, in AVPR, Snosheniia Rossii s SShA, 1783 g., d. 1, ll. 5-6.

110. Dana to Osterman, 5/16 June 1783, in Wharton, *Correspondence,* 6:495.

111. Robert Livingston to the President of Congress, 26 Feb. 1783, *ibid.,* pp. 264-265.

112. J. Hildt, *Early Diplomatic Negotiations,* p. 26. In passing on this resolution of Congress, Robert Livingston noted that Dana's powers permitted him to conduct negotiations for a commercial agreement but not to sign it (see Livingston to Dana, 1 May 1783, in Warton *Correspondence,* 6:403-404.

113. *Ibid.,* p. 482. For America's relationship to the Armed Neutrality, see also Albrecht, "Die Stellung der Vereinigten Staaten," S. 436-449; W. S. Carpenter, "The United States and the League of Neutrals of 1780," *American Journal of International Law,* 15 (1921): 511-522.

114. Dana to Osterman, 3/14 Aug. 1783, in Wharton, *Correspondence,* 6:656.

115. Concerning this, see the correspondence of Vérac with Dana, Vergennes, and La Luzerne, in Renaut, *Les relations diplomatiques,* pp. 119-120, 177-178, 182-183, 326ff.

116. Huntington's instructions to Dana, 19 Dec. 1780, in *JCC,* 18:1168-1169; Wharton, *Correspondence,* 6:201.

117. Bariatinsky to Catherine II, 29 June/10 July 1783, in AVPR, Snosheniia Rossii s Frantsiei, 1783 g., d. 393, l. 204. A curious incident in this regard was "the Constitution of the Thirteen United American Provinces" (The Articles of Confederation?) and the medal minted in honor of their independence sent by Benjamin Franklin in Sept. 1783 to Bariatinsky for transmission to Catherine II, a mission immediately carried out by the Russian minister; see Bariatinskii to Catherine II, 30 Aug./10 Sept. 1783, in *ibid.,* d. 394, l. 10.

118. Kolychev to Osterman, 7/18 June 1784, in AVPR, Snosheniia Rossii s Gollandiei, 1784 g., d. 271, ll. 9-10.

119. Osterman to Kolychev, 23 Aug./3 Sept. 1784, *ibid.,* d. 268, l. 7. At first glance my conclusion concerning the actual recognition of the United States by the government of Catherine II might appear to be a "modernization"; however, the documents cited speak for themselves in a sufficiently clear manner. As for the "modernization," it is necessary to turn one's attention to the short review of Catherine's policies vis-à-vis the United States compiled from materials of the College of Foreign Affairs by one of its members approximately 170 years ago, in which the author essentially comes to an analogous conclusion; see the Review of Russian Relations with the United States during the Reign of Catherine II, n.d., in TsGADA, f. 15, d. 214, ll. 1-18. (By internal evidence the date of this review can be no earlier than 1796 and no later than the early 1800's.)

120. Griffiths, "Nikita Panin, Russian Diplomacy and the American Revolution," p. 15.

Chapter 2.   The Attitude of Russian Society to the American Revolution

1. On the attitude of the Russian society to the events of the French revolution, see M. M. Shtrange, *Russkoe obshchestvo i frantsuzskaia revoliutsiia 1789-1794 gg* (The Russian Society and the French Revolution of 1789-1794, Moscow, 1956).

2. See *SbRIO,* vol 23: *Pis'ma imp. Ekateriny II baronu Mel'khioru Grimmu* (Letters of the Empress Catherine II to Baron Melchior Grimm, St. Petersburg, 1878); vol 33: *Pis'ma barona Mel'khiora Grimma k imp. Ekaterine II* (Letters of Baron Melchior Grimm to the Empress Catherine II, St. Petersburg, 1881).

3. N. D. Chechulin, ed., *Zapiski kniagini Dashkovoi* (Memoirs of the Princess Dashkov, St. Petersburg, 1907), p. 137.

4. Pushkin, *Polnoe sobranie sochinenii* (Complete Works, Moscow and Leningrad, 1949), 8:125.

5. M. V. Nechkina, "Vol'ter i russkoe obshchestvo" (Voltaire and the Russian Society), in V. P. Volgin, ed., *Vol'ter: Stat'i i materialy* (Voltaire: Essays and Materials, Moscow, 1948), p. 69.

6. *Trudoliubivaia pchela* (An Industrious Bee, St. Petersburg, Nov. 1759), p. 704. See also A. P. Sumarokov, *Polnoe sobranie sochinenii* (Complete Works), ed. N. I. Novikov (Moscow, 1787), 9:156-157.

7. "Dissertatsiia o veroiatneishem sposobe, kakim obrazom v Severnoi Amerike pervye zhiteli poiavilis'. S latinskogo na rossiiskii perevedennaia grafom Artemiem Vorontsovym" (A Dissertation on the Most Probable Way in Which the First Inhabitants Appeared in America: Translated from the Latin language into Russian by Count Artemii Vorontsov), *Sobranie luchshikh sochinenii* (Collection of Best Works, 1762), 4:173.

8. *Opisanie zemel' Severnoi Ameriki i tamoshnikh prirodnykh zhitelei* (Description of the Lands of North America and Their Native Inhabitants, tr. from German by A. R., St. Petersburg, 1765).

9. *Akademicheskie Izvestiia* (Academic News), 1779. 3:267, 391; 1780, 4:19, 185.

10. *Ibid.*, 1779, 3:267.

11. W. Robertson, *Istoriia o Amerike* (St. Petersburg, 1784), books 1-2. In his preface Robertson wrote of his successful travels in Russia and collecting materials on the geographical discoveries in the American Northwest, which enabled him to

make "a detailed description of the progress and extent of Russian discoveries" (see pp. viii-ix).

12. D. M. Ladygin, *Izvestie v Amerike o seleniiakh aglitskikh.* It is characteristic that the author used the new name of the state which emerged in place of the old English colonies in North America—"United Provinces." He should also be credited with advocating the expediency of establishing and developing trade between Russia and the new state (see pp. 58-59).

13. J. B. Bossu, *Novye puteshestviia v Zapadnuiu Indiiu* (New Travels in West India, tr. from French, 2 vols., Moscow, 1783).

14. F. V. Taube, *Istoriia o aglinskoi torgovle, manufakturakh, seleniiakh i moreplavanii onye v drevnie, srednie i noveishie vremena do 1776 goda; s dostovernym pokazaniem spravedlivykh prichin nyneshnei voiny v Severnoi Amerike i prochikh tomu podobnykh veshchei do 1776 goda.* (History of English Trade, Manufactures, Settlements, and Navigation in Ancient, Middle, and Modern Times up to 1776; with Reliable Evidence of the Just Causes of the Present War in North America and Other Similar Matters up to 1776, tr. from German, Moscow, 1783).

15. *Ibid.*, p. 121n.

16. G. T. Raynal, *Histoire philosophique et politique des établissements et du commerce des Européens dans les deux Indes* (10 vols., Geneva, 1780-1781). The chapters on the American Revolution were also published as a separate edition; see G. T. Raynal, *Révolution de l'Amérique* (London and The Hague, 1781).

17. For more on Raynal's work in Russia see L. Lekhtblau, "Iz istorii prosvetitel'noi literatury v Rossii" (Toward a History of the Enlightenment in Russia), *Istorik-marksist* (Marxist Historian), 1939, no. 1(71), pp. 197-202.

18. 24 July/4 Aug. 1780, in *SbRIO*, 23:183.

19. To Grimm, 1-4/12-15 April 1782, *ibid.*, pp. 231, 235. Catherine was also acquainted with an earlier version of Raynal's work, and as early as the end of 1774 she instructed Count Munich to read and comment upon the section on Russia; see Catherine II to Grimm, 21 Dec. 1774/1 Jan. 1775, *ibid.*, p. 13.

20. P. I. Bogd[anovich], "O Amerike," *Akademicheskie Izvestiia,* 1781, 8:671-672.

21. Only many years later, in the beginning of the nineteenth century, was the incessant interest of the Russian public in Raynal's work taken into account, and an especially prepared experimental "translation" of his work was published "by imperial command"; see *Filosoficheskaia i politicheskaia istoriia o zavedeniiakh i kommertsii evropeitsev v obeikh Indiiakh, sochinennaia abbatom Reinalem*; tr. by [Grigorii Gorodchaninov], (6 parts, St. Petersburg, 1805-1811).

22. *S.-Peterburgskie vedomosti*, 22 June/3 July 1781, no. 50.

23. *Moskovskie vedomosti* (Moscow Gazette), 13/24 Nov. 1781, no. 91.

24. *S.-Peterburgskie vedomosti*, 13/24 Nov. 1781, no. 86.

25. M. V. Muratov and N. N. Nakoriakov, eds., *Knizhnaia torgovlia* (Book Trade, Moscow and Leningrad, 1925), p. 98. Tsarist authorities became especially uneasy about the rapid growth of the book trade in the 1790's, after the beginning of the revolution in France. Prince A. A. Prozorovsky had reason to complain to Catherine II in a letter of 20/31 May 1792, that "all of the books published in France can be bought here clandestinely" and asked her to limit the sales of foreign books. In her last official resolution, 16/27 Sept. 1796, Catherine II established strict supervision over literature from abroad, and toward the end of Paul I's reign, in April 1800, all import of foreign books into the Russian Empire was prohibited; see V. V. Sipovsky, "Iz proshlogo russkoi tsenzury" (From the Past of Russian Censorship), *Russkaia Starina*, 1899, 98:164-166, 451.

26. A more or less systematic description of the War of Independence appeared in Russian translation in 1790, in the form of a supplement to Cooper's book on English history: "Sokrashchennaia aglinskaia istoriia s drevneishikh do nynesh-nikh vremen, sochinennaia g. Kuperom, po rasporiazheniiu grafa Chesterfil'da s privosokupleniem v dopolnenie iz drugogo avtora opisaniia voiny Anglii s Soedi-nennymi Amerikanskimi Oblastiami," (An Abbreviated English History from Ancient Times to the Present, Written by Mr. Cooper by Order of Lord Chesterfield with a Supplement by Another Author on the War between England and the United American Provinces, St. Petersburg, 1790), pp. 171-238. As can be seen from the dedication to E. R. Dashkova, the translator was Ivan Livotov.

27. For a detailed description of the above-mentioned journals, see P. N. Berkov, *Istoriia russkoi zhurnalistiki XVIII veska* (A History of Russian Journalism in the Eighteenth Century, Moscow and Leningrad, 1952), pp. 320, 326, 348, 413.

28. See, in particular, "Vypiska iz pisem nekotorogo filadel'fiiskogo zhitelia k svoemu priiateliu Barbe di Burg v Parizhe" (An Excerpt from the Letters of a Philadelphian to His Friend Barbeu du Bourg in Paris), *Sobranie raznykh sochinenii i novostei* (Collection of Diverse Works and News, March, 1776), pp. 14-15.

29. *Akademicheskie Izvestiia*, 1781, 7:244-254.

30. P. Bogd[anovich], "O Amerike," *ibid.*, pp. 225, 363, 528; *ibid.*, 1781, 8:646, 784, 934. This work was devoted largely to the Spanish possessions in America, and only at the very end (8:934ff.) did Bogdanovich address himself to the state of the "English settlements." It is important, however, to note that the author condemned "destructive autocracy" and saw in it a reason for the dissemination of "precious liberty" in the English colonies "on the edge of the New World."

31. M. N. Shprygova, "Voina Ameriki za nezavisimost' v osveshchenii 'Moskovskikh vedomostei' N. Novikova" (The American War of Independence as Dealt with by N. I. Novikov's *Moskovskie Vedomosti*), *Nauchnye doklady vysshei shkoly. Ist. nauki* (University Papers: Division of History), 1961, no. 3, pp. 74-89; A. I. Startsev, *Amerika i russkoe obshchestvo* (America and Russian Society, Moscow, 1942); and "Amerikanskaia voina za nezavisimost' v russkoi pechati kontsa XVIII v." (The American War of Independence in the Russian Press of the Late Eighteenth Century), *Istoricheskaia Literatura* (Historical Literature), 1940, nos. 5-6. For additional information see the qualifying dissertation of M. N. Nikol'skaia (Shprygova), *Russkaia pechat' o voine Severnoi Ameriki za nezavisimost v XVIII veke* (The Russian Press on the War of Independence in North America in the Eighteenth Century, Moscow, 1968).

32. See *Russkii arkhiv*, 1911, no. 9, pp. 108-116.

33. *S.-Peterburgskie vedomosti*, 13/24 Feb. 1775, no. 13; *Moskovskie vedomosti*, 24 Feb./7 March 1775, no. 16.

34. Thomas Gage, royal governor of Massachusetts and commander in chief of British forces in America.

35. *S.-Peterburgskie vedomosti*, 16/27 June 1775, no. 48; *Moskovskie vedomosti*, 30 June/11 July 1775, no. 52.

36. *S.-Peterburgskie vedomosti*, 19/30 June 1775, no. 49; *Moskovskie vedomosti*, 3/14 July 1775, no. 53.

37. *S.-Peterburgskie vedomosti*, 30 June/11 July 1775, no. 52. This dispatch (absent from *Moskovskie vedomosti*) should be compared with the report of the Russian ambassador in London, A. S. Musin-Pushkin, to Panin, 1/12 June 1775 (AVPR., f. Snosheniia Rossii s Angliei, 1775 g., d. 266, ll. 92-93). Referring to the same official English materials, Musin-Pushkin wrote somewhat mildly about a conflict between the "royal and American provincial troops." He noted that in

contrast to "previously published details," the court newspaper attributed the beginning of military activities "to Americans who, from houses and hiding places, surreptitiously shot at the royal troops sent to destroy American war supplies."

38. *S.-Peterburgskie vedomosti*, 14/25 Oct. 1775, no. 83.

39. *Moskovskie vedomosti*, 14/25 July 1775, no. 56.

40. *S.-Peterburgskie vedomosti*, 7/18 July 1775, no. 54; *Moskovskie vedomosti*, 17/28 July 1775, no. 57.

41. *S.-Peterburgskie vedomosti*, 14/25 July 1775, no. 56; *Moskovskie vedomosti*, 28 July/8 Aug. 1775, no. 60.

42. For the reaction in the Russian press to Franklin's mission, see Startsev, "Veniamin Franklin i russkoe obshchestvo XVIII veka," *Internatsional'naia literatura*, 1940, nos. 3-4, p. 213ff.; Radovsky, *Veniamin Franklin*, pp. 24-33.

43. *S.-Peterburgskie vedomosti*, 29 Dec. 1777/9 Jan. 1778, no. 104.

44. For a detailed account of Novikov, see G. Makogonenko, *Nikolai Novikov i russkoe prosveshchenie XVIII veka* (Nikolai Novikov and the Russian Enlightenment of the Eighteenth Century, Moscow and Leningrad, 1951).

45. Cited from VI. Orlov, *Russkie prosvetiteli 1790-1800-kh godov* (Russian Philosophes of 1790-1800, Moscow, 1953), p. 35.

46. A. N. Neustroev, *Istoricheskoe rozyskanie o russkikh povremennykh izdaniiakh i sbornikakh za 1703-1802* (Historical Investigation into Russian Periodical Publications and Almanacs for 1703-1802, St. Petersburg, 1874), p. 69.

47. *Moskovskie vedomosti*, 3/14 Nov. 1781, no. 88; N. I. Novikov, *Isbrannye sochineniia* (Selected Works, Moscow and Leningrad, 1954), p. 565.

48. Such an authoritative bibliographer as A. N. Neustroev names the same figure for the period before 1779 (see *Istoricheskoe rozyskanie*, p. 69).

49. N. M. Karamzin, *Sochineniia* (Works, St. Petersburg, 1848), 3:545-546.

50. *Moskovskie vedomosti*, 8/19 Jan. 1780, no. 3.

51. For details see Shprygova, "Voina Ameriki za nezavisimost'," pp. 77-80. During these years even those who previously had supported it "with great heat" began to speak out for the termination of the perilous war (*Moskovskie vedomosti*, 16/27 May 1870, no. 10).

52. *Ibid.*, 1/12 Jan. 1780, no. 1.

53. *S.-Peterburgskie vedomosti*, 22 May/2 June 1780, no. 41.

54. *Ibid.*, 25 Aug./5 Sept. 1780, no. 68.

55. *Moskovskie vedomosti*, 25 March/5 April 1780, no. 25.

56. "Perechen' odnogo pis'ma iz Filadel'fii" (Summary of a Letter from Philadelphia), *ibid.*, 22 April/3 May 1780, no. 33.

57. *Ibid.*, 23 Oct./3 Nov. 1781, no. 85.

58. See *ibid.*, 1782, nos. 102-103; 1783, nos. 2-4, and many others.

59. *Ibid.*, 10/21 Sept. 1782, no. 73.

60. The elucidation of published materials and the printing of special comments were characteristic of the Russian press of that period. As a rule, these "comments" make it possible to form an idea of the editor's or translator's attitude to the published materials, and, in some cases, they have a definite, independent significance. This device was first used by Iakov Kozel'sky in the 1760's, and later by Radishchev whose translation of Mably's work, *Reflections on Greek History*, was published by Novikov in 1773. The translation was accompanied by Radishchev's commentaries, among which there was the famous comment "on autocracy"; see Makogonenko, *Nikolai Novikov*, pp. 396-397.

61. *Moskovskie vedomosti*, 2/13 Sept. 1783, no. 71.

62. *Moskovskoe ezhemesiachnoe izdanie* (Moscow Monthly Publication), 1781, 2:189-190, 193.

63. *S.-Peterburgskie vedomosti,* 17/28 Feb. 1783, no. 14.

64. *Ibid.,* 22 Sept./3 Oct. 1783, no. 77.

65. Novikov, *Izbrannye sochineniia,* p. 568.

66. *Ibid.,* pp. 507-561. This tract was published as an unsigned editorial in *Pribavlenie k Moskovskim Vedomostiam* (Supplement to the *Moscow Record*). Makogonenko assumes that the author of the tract was Novikov himself. Some investigators erroneously attribute the authorship to Raynal; see L. Lekhtblau, "Iz istorii prosvetitel'noi literatury v Rossii," p. 202. Nor could Raynal have been the author of the article "Poniatie o torge nevol'nikami" (The Concept of the Slave Trade), as will be discussed below.

67. Novikov, *Isbrannye sochineniia,* p. 529.

68. *Ibid.,* p. 538.

69. *Ibid.,* p. 534.

70. "Kratkoe opisanie zhizni i kharaktera gen. Vasgintona" (A Short Description of the Life and Character of Gen. Washington), *Pribavlenie k Moskovskim vedomostiam,* 1784, pp. 362, 369.

71. Novikov, *Izbrannye sochineniia,* p. 577. A systematic persecution of Novikov, including the curtailment of his social activities, began at this time and ended with his arrest and the complete destruction of his publishing business in 1792. See *ibid.,* pp. 577-672.

72. Among them one can name "O vliianii nezavisimosti Soedinennykh Oblastei Severoamerikanskikh v politicheskoe sostoianie Evropy" (The Influence of the Independence of the North American United Regions on the Political Situation of Europe), *Pribavlenie k Moskovskim vedomostiam,* 1784, pp. 306, 313, 321, 329, 337; "Razmyshleniia o predpriiatiiakh, kasaiushchikhsia do torgovli s Severnoi Amerikoi" (Reflections on the Enterprises Touching upon the Trade with North America), *ibid.,* 1783, pp. 302, 305, 309, 311; "Obraz pravleniia i grazhdanskie ustanovleniia v Amerike" (The Government and Civil Statutes in America), *ibid.,* 1783, p. 516; "Vseobshchee opisanie amerikanskikh nravov" (A General Description of American Mores), *ibid.,* 1784, pp. 489, 497, 505, 513, 521; "Izvestie o Pensil'vanii" (Information about Pennsylvania), *ibid.,* 1784, p. 137; "Torgovlia evropeitsev v Amerike" (The Commerce of Europeans in America), *ibid.,* 1783, p. 265, and others.

73. *Ibid.,* 1784, nos. 72-74, pp. 521-564. Without sufficient grounds, several authors, among them V. I. Rabinovich, have attributed this article and some other works on American subjects to F. V. Karzhavin. See Rabinovich, *Revoliutsionnyi prosvetitel' F. V. Karzhavin* (The Revolutionary Philosopher F. V. Karzhavin, Moscow, 1966), p. 44; *S gishpantsami v Novyi Iork i Gavanu* (With the Spaniards to New York and Havana, Moscow, 1967), p. 42.

74. Novikov, *Izbrannye sochineniia,* p. 562.

75. *Moskovskie vedomosti,* 24 April/5 May 1787, no. 33. See also *ibid.,* 3/14 Feb., 3/14 April 1787. In spite of the unfavorable tone of the dispatches concerning Shays' rebellion, an attentive reader could draw his own conclusions about the events when he found out, for example, that the rebels' leader Sher (whether called Sher or Shair, it is still the same Shays) "served during the last war with the American troops where he proved his fearlessness. All of those grumbling against the burden of taxes, of whom there are a great many, seem to be inclined to serve under his command" (*S.-Peterburgskie vedomosti,* 2/13 April 1787, no. 27).

76. For a more detailed account of Radishchev and his views, see G. P. Makogonenko, *Radishchev i ego vremia* (Radishchev and His Times, Moscow, 1956); Startsev, *Radishchev v gody "Puteshestviia"*; G. Shtorm, "Potaennyi Radishchev" (The Secret Side of Radishchev), *Novy Mir* (New World), 1964, no.

11, pp. 115-161. I deal only with Radishchev's attitude toward America and the American Revolution.

77. A. N. Radishchev, *Polnoe sobranie sochinenii* (Complete Works, 3 vols., Moscow and Leningrad, 1938-1952), 1:14.

78. V. P. Semennikov, *Radishchev: Ocherki i issledovaniia* (Radishchev: Essays and Investigations, Moscow and Petrograd, 1923).; A. I. Startsev, "O zapadnykh sviaziakh Radishcheva" (On Radishchev's Western Contacts), *Internatsional'naia literatura*, 1940, nos. 7-8, pp. 256-265.

79. Even V. I. Semevsky wrote about this (*Byloe* [The Past], 1906, no. 1, p. 26).

80. In both cases the very device of the address is similar, Radishchev invoking the "glorious," and Raynal the "heroic" land. Although the content of Radishchev's 46th strophe is quite different, being deeper and broader than the corresponding paragraph of Raynal's, there is significant coincidence in the ending of the text. Raynal expressed regret that a free and sacred country would not contain his ashes; Radishchev longed that this country would at least "receive his ashes." See Semennikov, *Radishchev*, with reference to *"Révolution de l'Amérique" Par l'abbé Raynal* (A Londres, 1781), p. 87. Startsev points out that the reference really should be to the *Philosophical History* of Raynal since the "Révolution de l'Amérique" is only an extract (comprising the last fifteen chapters of the eighteenth book) from a new, enlarged edition of the *Philosophical History* of 1780. See Startsev, "O zapadnykh sviaziakh Radishcheva."

81. In recent years, several scholars—D. P. Lang in England, K. Bitner in East Germany, and R. P. Thaler in the United States—have been engaged in intensive research on the "Western sources" in Radishchev's work; see Lang, *The First Russian Radical Alexander Radishchev, 1749-1802* (London, 1959). For a critical analysis of the book see E. G. Plimak, "Zlokliucheniia burzhuaznoi comparativistiki" (Misadventures of Bourgeois Comparativistics), *Istoriia SSSR,* 1963, no. 3, pp. 183-213.

82. Radishchev, *Polnoe sobranie sochinenii*, 1:15.

83. Semennikov, *Radishchev*, p. 7; Radishchev, *Polnoe sobranie sochinenii*, 1:444. A hypothesis that four strophes of the ode (including the above cited 46th and 47th) were written by Radishchev in his last years (probably in 1799) was advanced by Shtorm ("Potaennyi Radishchev," pp. 144-148, 156).

84. Radishchev, *Polnoe sobranie sochinenii*, 1:16-17.

85. *Puteshestvie* was first printed by Radishchev in his *Free Press* in 1790. In spite of repeated attempts to publish it legally, the work was forbidden by tsarist authorities for more than a hundred years. The first complete and scholarly edition of *Puteshestvie*, edited by N. P. Pavlo-Silivansky, came out in 1905 (see Radishchev, *Polnoe sobranie sochinenii,* 1:470ff.). In 1958 *Puteshestvie* was published in the United States; see A. N. Radishchev, *A Journey from St. Petersburg to Moscow*, ed. R. P. Thaler, transl. L. Wiener (Cambridge, Mass., 1958).

86. Radishchev, *Polnoe sobranie sochinenii*, 1:346-347; see also Laserson, *The American Impact on Russia, 1784-1917*, pp. 66-67. As Startsev has convincingly shown in his dissertation, American constitutional materials came to Radishchev's notice through the rare French edition: *Recueil des loix constitutives des colonies angloises, confédérées sous la dénomination d'Etats-Unis de l'Amérique Septentrionale—auquel on a joint les actes d'independance, de confédération et autre actes du Congrès général, traduit de l'anglois. Dedié à M. le Docteur Franklin. A Philadelphia et se vend à Paris 1778;* see A. I. Startsev-Kunin, "Amerikanskaia revoliutsiia, Radishchev i russkoe obshchestvo XVIII veka," pp. 226, 299-303.

87. Radishchev, *Polnoe sobranie sochinenii*, 1:334.
88. *Ibid.*, pp. 316-317.
89. Startsev, "O zapadnykh sviaziakh Radishcheva," p. 262.
90. Radishchev, *Polnoe sobranie sochinenii*, 1:324.

Chapter 3. Russians in the United States and Americans in Russia at the End of the Eighteenth Century

1. N. P. Durov, "Fedor Vasil'evich Karzhavin," *Russkaia Starina*, 1875, 12:272-297.

2. See M. P. Alekseev, "Filologicheskie nabliudenia F. V. Karzhavina (Iz istorii russkoi filologii v XVIII v.)" (F. V. Karzhavin's Philological Observations: Toward a History of Russian Philology in the Eighteenth Century), *Romanskaia filologiia* (Romance Philology, Leningrad, 1961), pp. 8-36; A. I. Startsev, "F. V. Karzhavin i ego amerikanskoe puteshestvie" (F. V. Karzhavin and His American Journey), *Istoriia SSSR*, 1960, no. 3, pp. 132-139; Dvoichenko-Markov, "A Russian Traveler to Eighteenth Century America," *PAPS*, 97:350-355 (Sept. 1953).

3. F. V. Karzhavin to V. N. Karzhavin and A. I. Karzhavina, 1 Sept. 1785, in Archive of LOII, f. 238, 1 (N. P. Likhachev's collection), karton 146 (F. V. Karzhavin) d. 3, l. 17.

4. F. V. Karzhavin to V. N. Karzhavin, Sept. 1773, *ibid* l.1; the reply of the "former father" to the "damned" and "ungrateful" son "Fed'ka" of 12/23 Nov. 1773, *ibid.*, ll. 3-5.

5. "Skazka pokazuiushchaia ukratse, v kakoe vremia i v kakikh mestakh ia nakhodilsia" (A Tale Indicating in Brief at What Time and in Which Places I Have Found Myself, 1788), in ROIRL, Materials on Karzhavin from P. Ia. Durov's collection, f. 93, op. 2, d. 100, ll. 7-10. One of the versions of "Skazka" was published by N. P. Durov in *Russkaia Starina*, 1875, 12:273-278.

6. F. V. Karzhavin to V. N. Karzhavin, 19 May 1775, in Archive of LOII, f. 238, k. 146, d. 3, l. 8.

7. See ROIRL, f. 93, op. 2, d. 100, corresponding ll. 273, 274, 276, ll. The last date, 15 April 1787, allows one to place the date of Karzhavin's departure from Virginia to Martinique, and then to Russia, at no earlier than the middle of April 1787.

8. Dvoichenko-Markov, "A Russian Traveler," p. 330.

9. See Startsev, "F. V. Karzhavin," p. 137.

10. See *Sem'ia vol'nodumtsev. Roman ekaterininskogo vremeni* (A Family of Free-thinkers: A Novel of the Days of Catherine the Great), in *Niva* (The Cornfield), 1872, nos. 1-19.

11. *Arkhiv kn. Vorontsova*, 3:308ff.

12. After his return from America *Sokrashchennyi Vitruvii ili Sovershennyi Arkhitektor. Perevod arkhitectury pomoshchnika Fedora Karzhavina* (The Abbreviated Vitruvius or the Perfect Architect, Translated by the Architectural Assistant Fedor Karzhavin, Moscow, 1789) was published in Novikov's University Press.

13. Archive of LOII, f. 238, k. 146, d. 20. l. 1.

14. F. V. Karzhavin, *Vozhak, pokazyvaiushchii put' k luchshemu vygovoru bukv i rechenii frantsuzskikh. Le guide français par Théodore Karjavine* (St. Petersburg, 1794), pp. 198-199, 211.

15. *Arkhiv kn. Vorontsova*, 3:312-322.

16. ROIRL, f. 93, op. 2, d. 100, 1. 7; *Russkaia Starina,* 1875, 12:274-275.
17. *Ibid.* The ROIRL text of "Skazka" differs somewhat from the version published in *Russkaia Starina.*
18. Cited from Dvoichenko-Markov, "A Russian Traveler," p. 351.
19. *Ibid.,* pp. 351-352.
20. ROIRL, f. 93, op. 2, s. 100, 1. 7. Karzhavin described his first journey to the United States in a letter to Bar from St. Pierre (Martinique), 15 April 1780 (see *ibid.,* 1. 201ff.).
21. *Russkaia Starina,* 1875, 12:289.
22. ROIRL, f. 93, op. 2, d. 100, 1. 8.
23. F. V. Karzhavin to V. N. Karzhavin and A. I. Karzhavina, 1 Sept. 1875, in Archive of LOII, f. 238, k. 146, 3, 1. 16 ob.
24. *Russkaia Starina,* 1875, 12:276. Karzhavin's information corresponds with other sources: Marquis de Vaudreuil was the captain of the ship *Le Fendant* which was stationed in York Harbor from 20 Nov. 1779 until 25 Jan. 1780; see Jefferson, *Papers,* 3:210-211, 247-248.
25. Startsev, "F. V. Karzhavin," p. 139. Naturally, all this remains only a working hypothesis which could not be confirmed by any direct documentary evidence. The perusal of the Jefferson papers for the corresponding period (vol. 3) did not yield positive results.
26. E. I. Karzhavin [and F. V. Karzhavin], *Remarques sur la langue russiènne et sur son alphabet. Publ., corr. et augm. par Théodore Karjavine* (St. Petersburg, 1791).
27. Ph. Karjavine, *Description du peau, vu au microscope. En français et en russe* (A Carouge, 1789), cited in Dvoichenko-Markov, "A Russian Traveler," pp. 353-354.
28. F. V. Karzhavin to K. P. Karzhavina, 27 April 1797, in ROIRL, f. 93, op. 2, d. 100, 1. 87.
29. Carlo Bellini to Karzhavin, 1 March 1788 (in Italian), *ibid.,* 1. 236. Bellini's friendly epistle was an answer to Karzhavin's letter of 6 Nov. 1787. Startsev was the first to call attention to this letter and to a number of other previously unknown documents (see *Istoriia SSSR,* 1960, no. 3, p. 138). Among Karzhavin's papers there is a letter from another American correspondent, Louis Bernard, of 1 May 1789, which reads in part: "After your departure for Russia I had no news of you, dear friend, and only through Mr. Bellini to whom you wrote from Paris did I learn of your safe arrival in this capital." It is thus evident that, having arrived in Paris early in 1788, Karzhavin wrote to Bellini (see Bernard to Karzhavin, 1 May 1789, in ROIRL, f. 93, op. 2, d. 100, 1l. 213-214).
30. F. V. Karzhavin to N. K. Khotinsky, 25 Nov. 1786, *ibid.,* 1l. 261-263.
31. *Ibid.,* 1. 265.
32. F. V. Karzhavin, *Frantsuzskie, rossiskie i nemetskie razgovory v pol'zu nachinatelei* (French, Russian, and German Conversations for the Use of Beginners, St. Petersburg, 1803), p. 64. On another occasion Karzhavin said that he "visited in Virginia Petersburg, saw Philadelphia and Boston . . . was taken as military prisoner by the English . . . traveled with the Spaniards by sea to New York, French Cape and Havana on the island of Cuba." See I. Karzhavin and [F. V. Karzhavin], *Remarques sur la langue russiènne et sur son alphabet.* A short bibliography of Karzhavin's works with interesting annotations was compiled by Durov in *Russkaia Starina,* 1875, 12:291-294.
33. [F. V. Karzhavin]. *Novoiavlennyi vedun, poveduiushchii gadanie dukhov* (The New Sorcerer Revealing the Fortune-Telling of the Spirits, St. Petersburg, 1795), p.iv.
34. *Ibid.,* p. 65.

35. *Ibid.*, p. 71.

36. [F. V. Karzhavin], *Kratkoe izvestie o dostopamiatnykh prikliucheniiakh kapitana d'Sivilia . . . Per. F[edora] K[arzhavina]* (A Short Report of the Memorable Adventures of Captain de Seville . . . Transl. by F[edor] K[arzhavin], Moscow, 1791), pp. 26-27.

37. ROIRL, f. 93, op. 2, d. 100, l. 12.

38. Alekseev, "Filologicheskie nabliudeniia F. V. Karzhavina," p. 36. Quite recently the personality of F. V. Karzhavin and his American journey again attracted the attention of several Soviet authors. See, for example, Rabinovich, "S gishpantsami v Novyi Iork; Gavanu" (To New York and Havana with Spaniards); Iu. Ia. Gerchuk, "Etnograficheskie nabliudeniia russkoyo puteshestvennika F. V. Karzhavina (konez XVII)" (Ethnographical Observations of a Russian Traveler, F. V. Karzhavin [End of the 18th Century]), *Sovetskaia etnografiia* (Soviet Ethnography), 1972, N1, pp. 143-153.

39. Gerald W. Johnson, *The First Captain: The Story of John Paul Jones* (New York, 1947), pp. 289, 290, 297ff.

40. The materials of the trial (witnesses' testimony, medical reports, etc.) are largely unfavorable to John Paul Jones; see TsGAVMF, f. 223, pp. 1, d. 63, ll. 71-73, 75, 76, and *passim*. Perhaps the only exception is the testimony of "titular counselor Pavel Dmitrievsky, who occupied the position of interpreter for Rear Admiral Chevalier Paul Jones," *ibid.*, l. 78. Not being a specialist in legal matters, I am unable to form any adequate conclusion on the subject. However, it seems evident that so long as there was no official court proceeding, the "guilt" of the accused remained unproven, even in a purely formal fashion. Moreover, if one takes into account the definite denials by Jones himself, there is no basis to consider him guilty. Unfortunately I was unable to locate in Moscow libraries an important publication of Jones's papers in Russian archives made by F. A. Golder in 1927; Golder, *John Paul Jones in Russia* (Garden City, 1927).

41. See, for example, Jones to Ryleev, 2/13 April 1789, in TsGAVMF, f. 72, op. 1, d. 349, 1. 489; to Grigorii Potemkin, 13/24 April 1789, *ibid.*, f. 223, op. 1, d. 63, l. 66, et al.

42. *Memoirs of Paul Jones, Late Rear-Admiral in the Russian Service* (London, 1843), 2:155-170 (hereafter cited as Jones, *Memoirs*); L. F. Segiur, *Zapiski grafa Segiura o prebyvanii ego v Rossii v tsarstvovanie Ekateriny II (1785-1789)* (Memoirs of Count Ségur of His Stay in Russia during the Reign of Catherine II [1785-1789], St. Petersburg, 1865), pp. 369-370.

43. Jones, *Memoirs*, 2:110-111, 143, 156ff.; Segiur, *Zapiski*, p. 367; Samuel Eliot Morison, *John Paul Jones: A Sailor's Biography* (Boston, 1959), p. 389.

44. See Jones, *Memoirs*, 1:307ff.

45. TsGAVMF, f. 227, op. 1, d. 51, l. 177.

46. Jones, *Memoirs*, 1:323-324.

47. TsGAVMF, f. 227, op. 1, d. 53, l. 148. The appointment of Jones to the rank of Rear-Admiral was later formalized by the appropriate "proposal" to the Black Sea Admiralty on 20/31 May 1788 (*ibid.*, f. 245, op. 1, d. 21, l. 19).

48. Jones to Lafayette, 15/26 June 1788. For the full text see Jefferson, *Papers*, 13:582-584.

49. Jones, *Memoirs*, 1:323-326.

50. TsGADA, f. 168, d. 166, l. 2; Jefferson, *Papers*, 13:583.

51. Jefferson, *Papers*, 13:583.

52. *Ibid.*, 13:45.

53. Jones to Potemkin, 30 May/10 June 1788, TsGAVMF, f. 223, op. 1, d. 63, ll. 1-2.

54. See the report of Brigadier Aleksiano, 29 May/9 June 1788, on the transfer

of command of the squadron in the Liman to Jones, in TsGAVMF, f. 197, op. 1, d. 67, l. 131.

55. A. V. Suvorov, *Dokumenty* (Documents, Moscow, 1951), 2:415, 418-420; *Istoriia russkoi armii i flota* (History of the Russian Army and Navy, Moscow, 1912), 8:96-98; *Boevaiia letopis' russkogo flota* (The Battle Chronicle of the Russian Navy, Moscow, 1948), pp. 111-112. See also the dispatches of Jones to Potemkin of 17-18/28-29 June 1788, in TsGAVMF, f. 223, op. 1, d. 63, ll. 14-16.

56. Jones, *Memoirs,* 2:3.

57. TsGAVMF, f. 245, op. 1, d. 17, ll. 9-10.

58. Jones, *Memoirs,* 2:93.

59. *Ibid.,* pp. 29, 42, 87. This circumstance is justly noted by more competent biographers of the Admiral. Morison observes that Jones' "devastating experiences had been with German and Greek adventurers, but he liked Russian sailors, both officers and enlisted men, and they respected him" (see *John Paul Jones,* p. 390).

60. In discussions of the victories in the Liman in June 1788, it is sometimes noted that they were achieved "due to the precise and resolute orders of Rear Admiral Nassau-Siegen." In connection with the Rochensalm battle, however, the specialists assert that Nassau-Siegen's "confusing orders" led to disorganization and were responsible for a senseless defeat. See, e.g., Suvorov, *Dokumenty,* 2:415n, 420n; *Boevaia letopis' russkogo flota,* pp. 111-112, 142-143; *Istoriia russkoi armii i flota,* 8:93, 96, 148.

61. Jones, *Memoirs,* 2:51, 66.

62. *Ibid.,* p. 41. The award was given for his participation in the battle of 7/18 June 1788, and at first Jones expressed to Potemkin his appreciation of this award (see Jones to Potemkin, 9/20 July 1788, in TsGAVMF, f. 223, op. 1, d. 63, l. 32).

63. Jones to Potemkin, 24 July 1790, in Jones, *Memoirs,* 2:226.

64. Suvorov, *Dokumenty,* 2:415.

65. Jones, *Memoirs,* 2:32-33.

66. Suvorov to Potemkin, 10/21 June 1788, in Suvorov, *Dokumenty,* 2:415-416.

67. Suvorov to Potemkin, 26 May/6 June 1788, *ibid.,* p. 411. It is also known that Suvorov had prophetically warned Jones that "wounds and death are not the only risks of war. Injustice is no less certain." See Phillips Russell, *John Paul Jones: Man of Action* (New York, 1927), p. 239.

68. Jones, *Memoirs,* 2:225.

69. Potemkin to Catherine II, 31 Oct./11 Nov. 1788, *ibid.,* p. 94.

70. Jones to Jefferson, 26 and 31 Jan. 1789, in Jefferson, *Papers,* 14:506, 515-516.

71. Jones, *Memoirs,* 2:97.

72. Jones to Osterman, 31 Jan./11 Feb. 1789, in TsGADA, f. 168, d. 166, ll. 2-3.

73. Jones, *Memoirs,* 2:172; Jefferson, *Papers,* 14:686-689.

74. See A. N. Petrov, *Vtoraia turetskaia voina v tsarstvovanie imperatritsy Ekateriny II, 1787-1791 gg.* (The Second Turkish War in the Reign of the Empress Catherine II, 1787-1791, St. Petersburg, 1880), vol. 1, Supplement, pp. 19-27.

75. A. M. Stanislavskaia, "Rossiia i Angliia v gody vtoroi turetskoi voiny 1787-1791 gg." (Russia and England during the Second Turkish War), *Voprosy istorii,* 1948, no. 11, pp. 26-49.

76. Jones, *Memoirs,* 2:97.

77. Vorontsov to Bezborodko, 1789, in *Arkhiv kn. Vorontsova,* 9:481.

78. Jones, *Memoirs,* 2:110-111.

79. *Ibid.*, p. 181.
80. *Ibid.*, pp. 176-177.
81. *Ibid.*, pp. 177-178.
82. *Ibid.*, p. 178.
83. Jones to Osterman, 31 Jan./11 Feb. 1789, in TsGADA, f. 168, d. 166, l. 2.
84. Jones to Catherine II, 25 Feb./8 March 1791, *ibid.*, ll. 4-5; Jones, *Memoirs*, 2:232, 234.
85. Jones to Grimm, 9 July 1791, in TsGADA, f. 168, d. 166, l. 6; Jones, *Memoirs*, 2:237.
86. *Ibid.*, p. 311.
87. Catherine II to Grimm, 15/26 Aug. 1792, in *SbRIO*, 23:575.
88. Jones, *Memoirs*, 2:71-72.
89. Littlepage to Jefferson, 12 Feb. 1789, in Jefferson, *Papers*, 14:544-545.
90. See Babey, *Americans in Russia, 1776-1917*.
91. TsGAVMF, f. 243, op. 1, d. 1224, l. 1. John Lloyd Stephens, *Incidents of Travel in Greece, Turkey, Russia and Poland* (2 vols., New York, 1838), I, 264.
92. Archive of LOII, f. 36, op. 2, d. 205, l. 10. I date Smith's letter from Sevastopol in the spring of 1804 since, judging by his correspondence, he was still in Cherkessk on 25 Feb. 1804, intending to go to the Crimea in March and then to proceed to Constantinople (*ibid.*, l. 3). On 16 April 1804 he wrote a farewell letter to Alexander I from Sevastopol, in which he thanked him for the hospitality shown him during his stay in Russia (AVPR, f. Kantseliariia, d. 3327, ll. 15-16).
93. Smith to Vorontsov, 25 June 1815, in Archive of LOII, f. 36, op. 2, d. 205, ll. 11-12.
94. Louis Adamic, *A Nation of Nations* (New York and London, 1945), p. 147. In Hector Saint John de Crèvecoeur's *Letters from an American Farmer* (London, 1782) (*Lettres d'un Cultivateur Américain,* Paris, 1787, pp. 154, 174) there is mention of a visit to the Pennsylvania botanist John Bartram from a "citoyen de . . . les bords du lac Lagoda," Iwan Alexiowitz. The authenticity of this fact is most doubtful, and many researchers have assumed that Crèvecoeur has described himself under the guise of a Russian traveler. See Dvoichenko-Markov, "The American Philosophical Society and Early Russian-American Relations," *PAPS*, 94 (1950):550.
95. *Neshchastnye prikliucheniia Vasiliia Baranshchikova, meshchanina Nizhnego Novgoroda, v trekh chastiiakh sveta: v Amerike, Azii i Evrope s 1780 po 1787 g.* (The Unfortunate Adventures of Vasilii Baranshchikov, Citizen [meshchanin] of Nizhni Novgorod, in Three Parts of the World: America, Asia, and Europe, from 1780 to 1787, St. Petersburg, 1787, 1788, 1793).
96. See "Nachrichten über die Familie Wetter nob. von Rosenthal in Ehstland," Central State Historical Archives of the Estonian Socialist Republic, f. 854 (Office of Estland nobility), op. 2, d. CII 128, l. 1, 15; d. CIV 54, l. 1, 20, *et al.*
97. Mark Mayo Boatner III, *Encyclopedia of the American Revolution* (New York, 1966), pp. 946-947, refers to F. B. Heitman, *Historical Register of Officers of the Continental Army* (Washington, 1914) and to an article by T. H. Anderson in *Ohio Archeological and Historical Society Publications,* 6(1898):1-34.
98. *Encyclopedia of the American Revolution,* p. 946.
99. Archive of LOII, f. 238, k. 146, d. 9, l. 4.
100. See, for example, T. Heyden, *Der Missioner Fürst Augustin Gallizin* (Hamburg, 1859); S. M. Brownson, *Life of Demetrius Augustin Gallitzin* (New York, 1873) (I have used the French edition, Paris, 1880). Some details of Golitsyn's life, his distressing financial situation, and a meeting with him were

described in 1809 by A. Ia. Dashkov, Russian Consul-General in Philadelphia. In the same memorandum Dashkov mentioned that in America he chanced upon two persons of Russian extraction not belonging to the gentry (TsGAOR, f. 907, op. 1, d. 57, l. 23).

Part Two. Russian-American Relations during the Late Eighteenth and Early Nineteenth Centuries

1. The problem of the formative stages of the capitalist structure and the decay of feudalism was the subject of a lengthy discussion among such well-known scholars as N. M. Druzhinin, M. V. Nechkina, and S. G. Strumilin. Some of the participants of this discussion (Strumilin, for example) placed the origin of capitalist relations in the beginning of the seventeenth or even sixteenth century; others placed it much later: in the forties, sixties, and seventies of the eighteenth century. The prevailing point of view at present puts the beginning of the transitional period in the 1760's. "This period shows the beginning of decay of the old formation and the development of a capitalist way of production, not in an accidental and rudimentary form, but as a process that may be delayed, but can no longer be suppressed, by the old formation"; see *Perekhod ot feodalizma k kapitalizmu v Rossii.* (Transition from Feudalism to Capitalism in Russia, Moscow, 1969), pp. 17-18; M. V. Nechkina, "K itogam diskussii o 'voskhodiashchei' i 'niskhodiashchei' stadiiakh feodalizma" (On the Results of the Discussion of 'Ascending' and 'Descending' Stages of Feudalism), *Voprosy Istorii,* 1963, no. 12, pp. 31-51.

2. *Ocherki istorii SSSR,* pp. 7, 127.

3. See, for example, TsGADA, f. 19, d. 433, l. 4.

4. *Ocherki istorii SSSR,* p. 126.

5. V. K. Iatsunsky, "Krupnaia promyshlennost' Rossii v 1790-1860 gg." (Russian Heavy Industry, 1790-1860), *Ocherki ekonomicheskoi istorii Rossii pervoi poloviny XIX veka* (Essays on the Economic History of Russia in the First Half of the Nineteenth Century, Moscow, 1959), p. 153.

6. E. V. Tarle, *Sochineniia,* 4:464.

7. *Ibid.,* p. 465.

8. B. B. Kafengauz and A. A. Preobrazhensky, "Problemy istorii Rossii XVII-XVIII vv. v. trudakh sovetskikh uchenykh" (The Problems of the History of Russia in the Seventeenth-Eighteenth Centuries in the Works of Soviet Scholars), *Sovetskaia istoricheskaia nauka ot XX k XXII s'ezdu KPSS* (Soviet Historical Science between the 20th and 22nd Congresses of CPSU, Moscow, 1962).

9. See especially, S. G. Strumilin, *Istoriia chernoi metallurgii v SSSR* (The History of the Ferrous Metal Industry in the USSR, Moscow, 1954), vol 1: *Feodal'nyi period (1500-1860)* (The Feudal Period [1500-1860]); B. B. Kafengauz, *Istoriia khoziaistva Demidovykh v XVIII-XIX vv.* (The History of Demidovs' in the Eighteenth-Nineteenth Centuries, Moscow and Leningrad, 1949), vol 1.

10. Lenin, *Polnoe sobranie sochinenii,* 3:471.

11. *Ibid.,* p. 485.

12. "Obstoiatel'naia vedomost' o sostoianii fabrik i zavodov za 1805 god" (A Detailed Memorandum on the State of the Factories and Mills for 1805), TsGADA, f. 19, d. 379b, l. 5. A detailed list of the metallurgical works in the eighteenth century is provided in N. I. Pavlenko, *Istoriia metallurgii v Rossii XVIII veka. Zavody i zavodovladel'tsy* (The History of Metallurgy in Russia of the Eighteenth Century: Factories and Factory Owners, Moscow, 1962).

13. See Lenin, *Polnoe sobranie sochinenii,* 3:485.

14. Nebolsin, *Statisticheskie zapiski,* 2:215.

15. *Ibid.,* p. 214.

16. A. M. Stanislavskaia, *Russko-angliiskie otnosheniia i problemy Sredizemnomor'ia* (Russian-English Relations and Problems of the Mediterranean, Moscow, 1962), pp. 65-67.

17. *Ocherki istorii SSSR,* p. 127. Especially famous were masts and other ship timbers from the port of Riga, which were exported to almost all of the European maritime powers; see Nebolsin, *Statisticheskie zapiski,* 2:216.

18. See V. G. Sarychev, "Russkie korablestroitel'nye materialy v ekonomike Anglii XVIII v." (Russian Shipbuilding Materials in the Economy of England in the Eighteenth Century), *Sbornik nauchnykh rabot Leningradskogo instituta sovetskoi torgovli* (A Collection of Scientific Papers of the Leningrad Institute of Soviet Trade), 1958, no. 14.

19. Tarle, *Sochineniia,* 4:451.

20. See Marx and Engels, *Sochineniia,* 23:462.

21. *S.-Peterburgskie vedomosti,* 11/22 Aug. 1783, no. 64. A later dispatch from Boston (20 Sept. 1783) stated that "a very big ship" carrying merchandise valued at 150 pounds sterling was being readied for a China voyage; *ibid.,* 28 Nov./9 Dec. 1783, no. 95.

22. See F. Lee Benns, "The American Struggle for the British West India Carrying Trade, 1815-1830," *Indiana University Studies,* 10:7 (March 1923).

23. Hunter Miller, ed., *Treaties and Other International Acts of the United States of America* (Washington, 1931), 2:245-274.

24. Emory R. Johnson, *et al., History of Domestic and Foreign Commerce of the United States* (Washington, 1922), 1:135-136.

25. Leonard D. White, *The Federalists: A Study in Administrative History* (New York, 1948).

26. *Historical Statistics of the United States,* p. 538.

27. Johnson *et al., History of Domestic and Foreign Commerce,* 2:6.

28. *Ibid.,* 1:130-131.

29. P. Svin'in, "Vzgliad na respubliku Soedinennykh Amerikanskikh Oblastei," *Syn otechestva,* 1814, pt. 18, pp. 5-6; and *Opyt zhivopisnogo puteshestviia po Severnoi Amerike,* p. 27.

30. Curtis P. Nettels, *The Emergence of a National Economy: 1775-1815* (New York, 1962), p. 263.

31. *Historical Statistics of the United States,* p. 445.

32. Pitkin, *A Statistical View,* p. 370.

33. Johnson *et al., History of Domestic and Foreign Commerce,* 2:14.

34. G. F. Martens, *Supplément* (Gottingue, 1876), 2:563-572.

35. *Historical Statistics of the United States,* p. 538.

36. Johnson *et al., History of Domestic and Foreign Commerce,* 2:18.

37. *Historical Statistics of the United States,* p. 302.

38. Pitkin, *A Statistical View,* p. 111.

39. *Historical Statistics of the United States,* p. 538.

40. Johnson, *et al., History of Domestic and Foreign Commerce,* 2:20.

41. Nettels, *The Emergence of a National Economy,* p. 324.

42. Pitkin, *A Statistical View,* p. 363.

43. Johnson, *et al., History of Domestic and Foreign Commerce,* 2:29.

44. See, correspondingly, G. F. Martens, *Supplément,* 2:399-405, 389-397; F. Martens, *Sobranie traktatov,* 6:286-294.

45. According to some data, fifteen vessels declaring their home ports to be in the British North American colonies passed through the Sound on their way to some port in the Baltic before 1776. It is possible that some of them were heading for the Russian ports. In any case, it is known that in 1764 one of the American ships returned to New York from St. Petersburg with a cargo of leather, cordage, linens, duck, and sailcloth. See William J. Fredrickson, "American Shipping in the Trade with Northern Europe, 1783-1860," *Scand. Econ. Hist. Rev.,* 4 (1956):110; Virginia D. Harrington, *The New York Merchant on the Eve of the Revolution* (Gloucester, Mass., 1964), p. 198. New evidence concerning successful voyages of American ships to Russia in the 1760's may be found in Norman E. Saul, "The Beginnings of American-Russian Trade, 1763-1766," *William and Mary Quarterly,* 3d ser. 26:596-600 (Oct. 1969).

46. Jacob Myron Price, *The Tobacco Adventure to Russia,* p. 72; L. A. Nikiforov, *Russko-angliiskie otnosheniia pri Petre I* (Russian-English Relations during the Reign of Peter I, Moscow, 1950), pp. 37-41.

47. For detailed tables of the export of American tobacco to Russia, 1698-1775, see Price, *The Tobacco Adventure to Russia,* pp. 101-102.

48. *Ibid.,* p. 95.

49. TsGADA, f. 19, d. 360, l. 2ff. ("Mémoire sur les avantages d'un commerce direct entre l'Empire de Russie et les Etats-Unis de l'Amérique Septentrionale").

50. "Mémoire sur les productions de l'Amérique Septentrionale analogues à celui de l'Empire de Russie," in TsGADA. f. 19, d. 360, l.7 ob. Judging by its contents, the "Mémoire" dates from the closing period of the War of Independence. In l. 6 there is a penciled notation: "de l'année 1781 à 1782."

51. Archive of LOII, f. 36, op. 1, d. 543, l. 66.

52. *Ibid.*

53. Guillaume Eton, "Sur le Chanvre de l'Amérique," *ibid.,* d. 563, l. 95. The Memorandum apparently dates from the early 1790's. In any case, it was not written before 1788, since Eton mentions his talks with John Paul Jones during the Ochakov siege.

54. The original is in AVPR, f. Sekretnye mneniia, 1725-1798, gg. d. 597, ll. 100-114.

55. D. M. Ladygin, *Izvestie v Amerike o seleniiakh aglitskikh,* pp. 58-59.

56. Von den Handlungsvortheilen, welche aus der Unabhöngigkeit der vereinigten Staten von Nord-Amerika für das russische Reich entspringen. Ein Versuch von M. Karl Philip Michael Snell, Rektor der Domschule zu Riga. Riga, bey Johann Friedrich Hartknoch, 1783. (Dr. P. Ia. Krupnikov [Riga] acquainted me with this rare publication, which I was unable to locate in the Moscow libraries.)

57. See a review of Snell's book in *Ezhenedel'nye izvestiia vol'nogo ekonomicheskogo obshchestva 1788 goda* (Weekly News of the Free Economic Society for 1788), 1:164-165.

Chapter 4. Trade Connections between Russia and the United States

1. Wharton, *Correspondence,* 6:502-503.

2. Crosby, *America, Russia, Hemp, and Napoleon,* pp. 40-44.

3. Morison, *The Maritime History of Massachussetts, 1783-1860* (Boston, 1921), p. 154; Phillips, "Salem Opens American Trade with Russia," *The New England Quarterly,* 14:685-689 (Dec. 1941).

4. G. A. Zamiatin, *Ksenofont Alekseevich Anfilatov, Ocherk ego zhizni i*

deiatel'nosti (Ksenofont Alekseevich Anfilatov: His Life and Activity, St. Petersburg, 1910), p. 76.; S. Okun', "K voprosu o russko-amerikanskikh otnosheniiakh v nachale XIX veka" (On the Question of Russian-American Relations in the Beginning of the Nineteenth Century), *Nauchnyi Biulleten' LGU* (Scientific Bulletin of the Leningrad University), 1946, no. 8, pp. 19-20; "Pervye russkie korabli v Amerike (1805-1955) (First Russian Ships in America [1805-1955]), *Rechnoi transport* (River Transport), 1956, no. 10, pp. 30-31.

5. For full text see AVPR, f. Sekretnye mneniia, 1742-1799, d. 593, ll. 187-196 (italics mine).

6. Nebolsin, *Statisticheskie zapiski,* 2:104.

7. From the Latin *consignatio.*

8. TsGADA, f. 276, op. 1, d. 668. The original of Wittfooth's report of 12 May 1788, ll. 2-3; translation, l. 1. One should keep in mind that Wittfooth did not know Russian, but the translations of his reports are preserved in the archives, and were utilized here after checking with the original.

9. TsGADA, f. 276, op. 1, d. 668, l. 4.

10. Radishchev, *Polnoe sobranie sochinenii,* 3:316.

11. To the College of Foreign Affairs, 26 Dec. 1778, AVPR, f. Snosheniia Rossii s Frantsiei, d. 684, ll. 20-22, 23-24.

12. To the College of Foreign Affairs, 1(?) Aug. 1780, *ibid.,* d. 688, ll. 3-6, 7-16.

13. In Archive of LOII, f. 36, op. 1, d. 544, l. 84.

14. Among the little-known (and still not fully confirmed) bits of information about indirect Russian-American contacts during the War of Independence, there is a curious episode in Archangel in 1781 involving the construction by a certain A. Bel (apparently one of the aliases of Stephen Sayre) "of a ship for the use of rebellious British colonies." Having learned of this fact from Bel's letter to Franklin, the Empress instructed Archangel Governor-General Mel'gunov to investigate this matter in detail and "in every proper manner to put obstacles in the way of ship construction for the Americans, not allowing anyone except known and reliable persons to engage in this activity." The ship was built and "set afloat," and Mel'gunov wondered if there were "any doubt about launching the ship." On 3/14 July 1781 Bezborodko informed the Governor-General that Catherine II considered that "Your Excellency had done very well in allowing the launching, and that in the future there should not be any obstacles for the launching of the ships except where there were clear signs that the Americans were building them at their own expense, in which case Her Majesty would expect Your Excellency to report this fact"; see *Russkii Arkhiv,* 1893, book 1, no. 3, p. 314. On Stephen Sayre's activities in Russia, see Griffiths, "American Commercial Diplomacy in Russia, 1780-1783," *William and Mary Quarterly,* 3rd ser., 27: 384-389 (July 1970).

15. Secret Journal of Foreign Affairs, 7 May 1784, *Diplomatic Correspondence of the United States, 1783-1789,* 7 vols. (Washington, 1834), 1:110-116.

16. Hildt, *Early Diplomatic Negotiations,* p. 30.

17. In AVPR, f. Snosheniia Rossii s Frantsiei, 1784, op. 93/6, d. 411, l. 201.

18. To Bariatinsky, 22 Sept. 1784, *ibid.,* l. 198.

19. Bariatinsky to Catherine II, 15/26 Sept. 1784, *ibid.,* ll. 196-197.

20. Cited from Hildt, *Early Diplomatic Negotiations,* p. 30, n. 91.

21. Phillips, "Salem Opens American Trade," p. 686.

22. *Ibid.,* p. 688.

23. TsGADA, f. 19, op. 1, d. 262 (On the arrival of foreign ships in the port of Kronstadt," 1743-1810, 14 parts).

24. TsGADA, f. 19, op. 1, d. 262, ch. XI (Kronstadt reports of 1781-1784). Meanwhile, notices of American vessels began to appear, albeit infrequently, in Russian newspapers and journals. Thus, among the 890 ships of diverse nationalities which arrived in St. Petersburg's port in 1784, 81 were Russian, 365 English, 10 Spanish, 10 French, and 5 American (*Neues St. Peterburgischen Journal vom Jahre 1784*, p. 372). News of foreign vessels was also published systematically in *S.-Peterburgskie vedomosti.*

25. TsGADA, f. 19, op. 1, d. 262, ch. XII, l. 93.

26. *Ibid.*, l. 94.

27. *Ocherki istorii SSSR*, p. 128.

28. TsGADA, f. 19, op. 1, d. 433 (A. K. Razumovsky's Papers), l. 83.

29. *Politicheskii Zhurnal* (Political Journal), 1791, 5:183-184.

30. TsGADA, f. 168, d. 166, l. 3.

31. John Jepson Oddy, *European commerce shewing new and secure channels of trade with the continent of Europe* (London, 1805), p. 126; Wilhelm Friebe, *Über Russlands Handel, landwirschaftliche Kultur, Industrie und Produkte; nebst einigen physischen und statistischen Bemerkungen* (Gotha and St. Petersburg, 1796), I (Supplements); TsGADA, f. 19, op. 1, d. 262, ch. XIII, l. 39.

32. See "Vzgliad na torgovye snosheniia mezhdu Rossiiskoiu imperieiu i Amerikanskimi Soedinennymi Statami" (A View of the Trade Relations between the Russian Empire and the American United States), 9/21 June 1808, in TsGAOR, f. 907 (A. Ia. Dashkov), op. 1, d. 107, ll. 55-100 (esp. 57).

33. *Gosudarstvennaia torgovlia v raznykh ee vidakh* (State Trade in Various Aspects), 6 books, 1802-1807 [St. Petersburg, 1803-1808?]).

34. *Gosudarstvennaia torgovlia 1807 g. v raznykh ee vidakh* (St. Petersburg, 1808?), Table 22.

35. The data are taken from Charles Evans, ed., *Exports, Domestic, from the United States to All Countries from 1789 to 1883, Inclusive* (Washington, 1884), p. 80. For data on the export of foreign goods for 1805-1807, see Pitkin, *A Statistical View*, p. 231. As Evans notes, before 1803 no distinction was made between the export of goods of American and of foreign origin; see *Exports, Domestic*, p. 12.

36. Hildt, *Early Diplomatic Negotiations*, p. 32.

37. Nebolsin, *Statisticheskie zapiski*, 1:29-30.

38. *Ibid.*, p. 29.

39. *Ibid.*, 2:230-231.

40. *Ibid.*, p. 235.

41. See Pitkin, *A Statistical View*, pp. 90-91, 122-123, 125-126, 128-129, 157, 159, 161.

42. See, in particular, TsGAOR, f. 907, op. 1, d. 107, l. 60-63.

43. See *Arkhiv Marksa i Engel'sa* (Marx and Engels Archives, Moscow, 1948), 10:313.

44. Nebolsin, *Statisticheskie zapiski*, 1:29.

45. TsGAOR, f. 907, op. 1, d. 107, l. 59.

46. To Alexander I, 4/16 May 1806, in *VPR*, vol. 3, no. 54, pp. 150-151.

47. To Alexander I, no later than 28 Dec. 1806/9 Jan. 1907, *ibid.*, no. 180, p. 459 (the date of the signing of the preliminary note).

48. Pitkin, *A Statistical View*, pp. 230, 257.

49. Oddy, *European Commerce*, p. 126 (summarized data).

50. TsGAOR, f. 907, op. 1, d. 107, ll. 69, 71.

51. *Ibid.*, l. 77.

52. Pitkin, *A Statistical View*, p. 232.

53. Aage Rash, "American Trade in the Baltic, 1783-1807," *Scand. Econ. Hist. Rev.,* 13(1965):50-54. A bolt (piece) was the equivalent of 31.4 meters.

54. Crosby, *America, Russia, Hemp, and Napoleon,* pp. 24, 14.

55. See Gouverneur Morris, *Diary of the French Revolution* (Boston, 1939), vol. 2.

56. 12/23 Jan. 1791, in *Arkhiv kn. Vorontsova,* 18:8.

57. S. R. Vorontsov to A. R. Vorontsov, July 1795, *ibid.,* 9:342. For the acquaintance of Morris with Vorontsov, see Morris, *Diary of the French Revolution,* 2:374ff.

58. Vorontsov to Paul I, 15/26 March 1799, in AVPR, f. Snosheniia Rossii s Angliei, 1799, op. 35/6, d. 509, l. 112. According to King's correspondence, the desirability of establishing closer relations between Russia and the United States was indicated by Vorontsov in November 1798. Pointing to the considerable trade of the Americans in the Baltic, Vorontsov raised the question of the expediency of a commercial treaty, and suggested contacting their respective governments in this connection; see King to Pickering, 10 Nov. 1798, in *The Life and Correspondence of Rufus King,* 2:463-464. (Cited from Hildt, *Early Diplomatic Negotiations,* pp. 31-32. Hildt erroneously places this conversation in Nov. 1799. This mistake is repeated by contemporary historians; see Laserson, *The American Impact on Russia,* p. 98.)

59. Vorontsov to Paul I, 15/26 March 1799, in AVPR, Snosheniia Rossii s Angliei, 1799, op. 35/6, d. 509, ll. 112-113. Indeed, on 6 Feb. 1799, soon after the news of the conversation between Vorontsov and King was received in the United States, President Adams appointed the American Minister Plenipotentiary at the Court of St. James's, Rufus King, to negotiate a treaty of amity and commerce between the United States and Russia; see James D. Richardson, ed., *A Compilation of the Messages and Papers of the Presidents 1789-1897* (Washington, 1896-1899), 1:282. Detailed instructions for the conclusion of the treaty were issued on 1 May 1799 (Hildt, *Early Diplomatic Negotiations,* pp. 32-33).

60. Paul I to Vorontsov, 23 April/4 May 1799, in AVPR, f. Sonsheniia Rossii s Angliei, 1799, op. 35/6, d. 507, l. 3.

61. Hildt, *Early Diplomatic Negotiations,* pp. 34-35.

62. Richardson, *Messages and Papers,* 1:173; NA, Consular Despatches:St. Petersburg, vol. 1 (John Russell's letter of 13 Dec. 1794 from Boston, and a duplicate of 17 Dec.).

63. J. Q. Adams, *Writings,* 2:518.

64. This ceased to be necessary because soon after the murder of Paul I relations with England were resumed and "ships and property of British subjects sequestered in Russia were returned to the owners." *VPR,* vol. 1, no. 9, p. 38.

65. J. Q. Adams, *Writings,* 2:513n.

66. Levett Harris to James Madison, 25 Oct. 1803, in NA, Consular Despatches:St. Petersburg, vol. 1 (pages are not numbered). Hildt mistakenly states that Harris was appointed as consul on 11 Nov. 1803 (*Early Diplomatic Negotiations,* p. 453); the documents in the archives show that by then he had already arrived in Russia and had started to perform his consular functions.

67. Levett Harris to James Madison, 27 Oct./17 Nov. 1803, in NA, Consular Despatches:St. Petersburg, vol. 1.

68. TsGADA, f. 276, op. 1-2, d. 3032, l. 399.

69. TsGIA, f. 796, op. 87, d. 268; TsGADA, f. 276, op. 2, d. 425, 467; also N. M. Gol'dberg, "Russko-amerikanskie otnosheniia v nachale XIX veka."

70. The frigate *Philadelphia* was part of the American squadron sent to the Mediterranean in 1801 to fight the Tripolitan corsairs interfering with American

trade. For the circumstances of the capture of the frigate by the corsairs see the letter of the Commander of the American squadron, E. Preble (AVPR, f. Kantseliariia, d. 3327, ll. 21ff.). On the American-Tripolitan war see N. A. Khalfin, *Nachalo amerikanskoi ekspansii* (The Beginning of American Expansion, Moscow, 1958), pp. 46-49; L. B. Wright and J. M. Macleod, *The First Americans in North Africa: William Eaton's Struggle for a Vigorous Policy against the Barbary Pirates* (Princeton, 1945).

71. Harris to Vorontsov, 20 Jan./1 Feb. 1804, in AVPR, f. Kantseliariia, d. 3327, ll. 6-7; also NA, Consular Despatches; St. Petersburg, vol 1.

72. Appropriate instructions were indeed sent to the Russian envoy in Contantinople, A. Ia. Italinsky, on 2/14 Feb. 1804; see AVPR, f. Kantseliariia, d. 111.

73. Vorontsov to Harris, 25 Jan./6 Feb. 1804, in *VPR,* vol. 1, no. 249, pp. 609-610. As can be seen from the letters of Squadron Commander Preble to Levett Harris of 7 June 1804, Preble was so impressed by the news of Russian mediation that he instantly freed a vessel under the Russian flag captured by his squadron during the blockade of the Tripoli shores. Preble also stated that his personal wish, and that of his government, was to utilize every opportunity for development of friendly relations between the two countries (for the corresponding letters of Harris and Preble, see AVPR, f. Kantseliariia, d. 3327, ll. 18-32). However, the American squadron in the Mediterranean eventually continued to "detain Russian merchant vessels under various pretexts," in connection with which the Russian Minister Plenipotentiary in Naples, D. P. Tatishchev, was authorized "to enter into a relationship with the commader of that squadron and to try by peaceful means to divert him from such impermissible exploits as would eventuate in great displeasure, often leading to actual rupture, which I would much prefer to avoid"; see Alexander I to Tatishchev, 18 Feb./2 March 1805, in *VPR*, vol. 2, no 108, p. 331.

74. The aged Vorontsov had practically removed himself from affairs since Jan. 1804, and the Ministry of Foreign Affairs was headed by the Assistant Minister, Prince Adam Czartoryski, one of Alexander I's young friends and a member of the Secret Committee. See also a new book of Patricia Kennedy Grimsted, *The Foreign Ministers of Alexander I: Political Attitudes and Conduct of Russian Diplomacy, 1801-1825* (Berkeley and Los Angeles, 1969), pp. 99-100 and ch. 4.

75. 16/28 Feb. 1804, in *VPR,* vol. 1, no. 254, p. 617.

76. Italinsky to Czartoryski, 16/28 March 1804, *ibid.,* no. 269, pp. 669-670.

77. To Czartoryski, 4/16 April 1804, *ibid.,* no. 276, pp. 684-685.

78. To Livingston, 1/13 April 1804, *ibid.,* no. 274, pp. 680-681.

79. 4/16 April 1804, *ibid.,* no. 277, p. 685.

80. Madison to Vorontsov, 10 June 1804, in AVPR, f. Kantseliariia, 3325, ll. 4-5.

81. For original of this letter see *ibid.,* 1. 6; in *Novaia i noveishaia istoriia,* 1959, no. 2, p. 154.

82. "Zapiska o delakh kuptsa Anfilatova dlia obshchestvennoi pol'zy" (A Memorandum on the Affairs of the Merchant Anfilatov for Public Use), in TsGIA, f. 560, op. 22, d. l, l. 133. For a detailed account see Zamiatin, *Ksenofont Alekseevich Anfilatov,* the biography written on the occasion of the centenary (1810-1910) of the Slobodsky Anfilatov Public Bank.

83. Dec. 1805, in TsGIA, f. 13, op. 2, d. 1128, l. 3; Zamiatin, *Ks. Al. Anfilatov,* pp. 75-76, Supplements, p. 227. The exact date is missing in the original. Zamiatin indicates that the letter was received on 28 Dec. 1805 (Old

style). However, this date seems doubtful since on 3/15 Dec. Rumiantsev presented an appropriate report to Alexander I.

84. It was received not only directly from America, but also from European countries. "Last year alone," Rumiantsev wrote, "the import of this commodity from Europe reached the value of almost a million and a half rubles." 3/15 Dec. 1805, in TsGIA, f. 13, op. 2, d. 1128, ll. 1-2 (a draft of a report).

85. *Ibid.*

86. Alexander I to Rumiantsev, 29 Dec. 1805/11 Jan. 1806, in *VPR*, vol. 3, no. 3, p. 23; Zamiatin (*Ks. Al. Anfilatov,* pp. 78-79) published this document with the wrong date: December 26, 1805.

87. 30 Dec. 1805/11 Jan. 1806, in TsGIA, f. 13, op. 2, d. 1128, l. 7; Zamiatin, *Ks. Al. Anfilatov,* Supplements, p. 228.

88. S. F. Ogorodnikov, *Ocherk istorii goroda Arkhangel'ska v torgovo-promyshlennom sostoianii* (An Essay on the History of the City of Archangel in Its Commercial and Industrial Aspects, St. Petersburg. 1890), p. 261; Zamiatin, *Ks. Al. Anfilatov,* p. 80. In the same fond of the Department of Customs Collection in TsGIA there is filed a rather similar case of appeal to Rumiantsev on 5/17 March 1806, by the management of the Alexandrian manufactory which was proposing to send the ship *Maria* to the United States with a cargo of hemp, linens, and iron, and to return with cotton (TsGIA, f. 13, op. 2, d. 1156).

89. TsGIA, f. 560, op. 22, d. 1, l. 135.

90. *S.-Peterburgskie kommercheskie vedomosti* (St. Petersburg Commercial Journal), 17/29 Oct. 1807, no. 42.

91. *Ibid.,* 12/24 Dec. 1807, no. 50. In 1809 Anfilatov sent a third vessel, *Ksenofont,* from Archangel to the United States. However, "it did not reach America, and has not returned to Russian ports." Anfilatov's loss was estimated at 450 thousand rubles. Although by 1812 Anfilatov's affairs were in complete disarray, he had not given up the idea of improving them by sending another ship to America. After the termination of the Napoleonic wars, in February 1816, he addressed Alexander I with a new petition, but this time without success; see TsGIA, f. 560, op. 22, d. 1, ll. 134-136.

92. See Zamiatin, *Ks. Al. Anfilatov,* Supplements, pp. 228-229; Rumiantsev's report to Alexander I, confirmed by the Tsar on 1/13 Nov. 1807, in TsGIA, f. 13, op. 2, d. 1128, ll. 18-19.

93. Zamiatin, *Ks. Al. Anfilatov,* pp. 89-90.

94. Pitkin, *A Statistical View,* p. 364. Information for later years shows some increase in the general tonnage of Russian vessels in American ports during their most difficult period of war with England, 1812-1815:

Year	Tonnage	Year	Tonnage
1810	230	1814	4431
1811	—	1815	940
1812	2671	1816	1890
1813	6363		

Compiled from Pitkin, *A Statistical View,* p. 365; P. P. Svin'in, "Torgovye snosheniia Rossii s Soedinennymi Amerikanskimi Oblastiami i vzgliad na general'nuiu torgovliu poslednikh" (Trade Connections between Russia and the United American Regions, and a View of the Latter's General Commerce), *Otechestvennye zapiski* (Fatherland Notes), 1820, pt. 4, p. 96.

95. Zamiatin, *Ks. Al. Anfilatov,* p. 76.

96. See the report of the Minister of Commerce, N. P. Rumiantsev, for 1805, in *VPR*, vol. 3, no. 180, p. 459.

97. "Zapiska po delu kuptsa Anfilatova" (A Memorandum on the Case of Merchant Anfilatov), in TsGIA, f. 560, op. 22, d. 1, ll. 129-132.

98. "Vzgliad na torgovye snosheniia mezhdu Rossiskoiu imperieiu i Amerikanskimi Soedinennymi Statami," 9/21 June 1808, in TsGAOR, f. 907, op. 1, d. 107, l. 87.

Chapter 5. The Development of Scientific, Cultural, and Socio-Political Connections

1. Radishchev, *Polnoe sobranie sochinenii,* 1:391.

2. *Experiments and Observations on Electricity, Made at Philadelphia in America by Mr. Benjamin Franklin and Communicated in Several Letters to Mr. P. Collinson, of London, F. R. S.* (London, 1751). A later edition of *Experiments* (London, 1769) was sent by Franklin to Russia with the inscription: "From the author." See also V. Franklin, *Opyty i nabliudeniia nad elektrichestvom* (Moscow and Leningrad, 1956).

3. Franklin's scientific activity was expertly depicted by P. L. Kapitsa in a lecture on 17 Jan. 1956, on the 250th anniversary of Franklin's birth; see *Vestnik AN SSSR* (Proceedings of AS USSR), 1956, no. 2, pp. 65-75, and Kapitsa, *Zhizn' dlia nauki: Lomonosov, Franklin, Rezerford, Lanzheven* (Life for Science: Lomonosov, Franklin, Rutherford, Langevin, Moscow, 1965), pp. 21-35.

4. Kapitsa, "Nauchnaia deiatel'nost' V. Franklina" (Benjamin Franklin's Scientific Activity), *Vestnik AN SSSR,* 1956, no. 2, p. 72.

5. *S.-Peterburgskie vedomosti,* 12/23 June, 1752, no. 47, pp. 371-372.

6. Lomonosov to P. P. Shuvalov, 26 July/6 Aug. 1753, in G. V. Richmann, *Trudy po fizike* (Works on Physics, Moscow, 1956), p. 545 (supplements). On the significance of Richmann's work see also T. P. Kravets and M. I. Radovsky, "K 200-letiiu so dnia smerti akademika G. V. Rikhmana" (On the 200th Anniversary of the Death of Academician G. W. Richmann), *Uspekhi fizicheskikh nauk* (Progress in the Physical Sciences), vol. 51, no. 2, 1953.

7. See, for example, the works of Richmann published for the first time in 1956 in *Trudy po fizike:* "Discussion of Recently Invented Means to Avert Lightning from Buildings," "Reflections, Proved by Experiments, on the Resemblance between the Artificial Electricity and the Natural Electricity Produced by Lightning, and on the Means of Averting the Lightning," "Observations on Electricity Produced by Thunderstorms," "Franklin's Experiments," and many others.

8. See M. V. Lomonosov, *Polnoe sobranie sochinenii* (Moscow and Leningrad, 1952), vol. 3: *Trudy po fizike* (Works on Physics), pp. 15-99.

9. *Ibid.,* pp. 121-123; 147-149.

10. *Ibid.,* p. 103.

11. *Ibid.,* p. 105.

12. F. U. T. Epinus, *Teoriia elektrichestva i magnetizma* (The Theory of Electricity and Magnetism, Leningrad, 1951). For numerous references to Franklin, see Index, p. 561.

13. *Ibid.,* pp. 10-11.

14. M. I. Radovsky, *Veniamin Franklin i ego sviazi s Rossiei,* p. 8.

15. "Acta Academiae Scientiarum Imperialis Petropolitanae pro anno MDCCLXXVII" (St. Petersburg, 1780), p. 26.

16. Dvoichenko-Markov, "Benjamin Franklin," *PAPS*, 91:252.

17. Franklin, *Papers*, 5:154-155. "Account of the Death of Georg Richmann (Extract of a Letter from Moscow, dated August 23)," *ibid.*, pp. 219-221.

18. Franklin to Heberden, June 7, 1759, in Franklin, *Writings*, 3:479-482.

19. Franklin, *Papers*, 10:265-266; *Letters and Papers of Ezra Stiles*, ed. Isabel M. Calder (New Haven, 1933), pp. 11-14; cited in G. M. Lester, "Znakomstvo uchenykh," *Voprosy istorii estestvoznaniia i tekhniki*, 1962, no. 12, p. 143.

20. John Winthrop to Ezra Stiles, 21 Feb. 1764; cited in Lester, "Znakomstvo uchenykh," p. 143.

21. Franklin, *Writings*, 6:23-26.

22. Dvoichenko-Markov, "Benjamin Franklin," pp. 250-251, 253; "The American Philosophical Society," *PAPS*, 94:549-610. The latter work is used here as a source in connection with the American Philosophical Society.

23. Franklin, *Papers*, 12:71-77.

24. The reference is to the expedition planned by Lomonosov, which actually took place only after his death.

25. For the full text of Stiles's letter see Lester, "Znakomstvo uchenykh," pp. 145-147. The Latin original of this letter is preserved in the American Philosophical Society; Papers of Dr. Franklin, 49:19.

26. The idea that the polar ocean is free of ice had been widely accepted ever since the sixteenth century and was maintained to the beginning of the twentieth century. Only the drift of the *Fram* (1895-96) and Peary's reaching the North Pole in 1909 proved that this view was mistaken. For more details see L. S. Berg, "Lomonosov i pervoe russkoe plavanie dlia otkrytiia severo-vostochnogo prokhoda" (Lomonosov and the First Russian expedition in Search for the Northeast Passage), *Izvestiia Geograficheskogo Obshchestva*, 1940, no. 6.

27. Dvoichenko-Markova, "K istorii russko-amerikanskikh nauchnykh sviazei vtoroi poloviny XVIII v" (Toward a History of Russian-American Scientific Contacts in the Second Half of the Eighteenth Century), *Sovetskoe Slavianovedenie* (Soviet Slavic Studies), 1966, no. 2, p. 44.

28. Franklin, *Papers*, 12:194-196. On Franklin's interest in Russian geographical discoveries and his acquaintance with the works of Miller, Shteller, Krashenchikov, and Shtelin, see *Papers*, 5:268, 10:90-92, 94; Dvoichenko-Markova, "K istorii russko-amerikanskikh nauchnykh sviazei," p. 46.

29. Franklin, *Papers*, 12:71-72, n. 8.

30. The Historical Society of Pennsylvania, William David Lewis, Miscellaneous Letters and Documents. The first publication of the letter was made by me in *Amerikanskii Ezhegodnik, 1971* (American Annual, 1971), Moscow, 1971, pp. 330-331.

31. *Transactions of the American Philosophical Society, Held at Philadelphia, for Promoting Useful Knowledge*, Vol. 1: *From January 1st 1769, To January 1st 1771* (Philadelphia, 1771).

32. Dvoichenko-Markov, "The American Philosophical Society," p. 549.

33. See *Protokoly zasedanii konferentsii imperatorskoi Akademii nauk s 1725 po 1803 g.* (Minutes of the Conference Meetings of the Imperial Academy of Sciences from 1725 to 1803, St. Petersburg, 1900), 3(1771-1785):144.

34. Dvoichenko-Markov, "The American Philosophical Society," p. 552.

35. *Akademicheskie Izvestiia*, 1779, 2:193, 205, and others.

36. Franklin, *Works*, 10:248.

37. Besides the abovementioned Colonel Josiah Harmar and General Richard Butler, they were Commissioner Benjamin Hawkins (later a member of Congress

from South Carolina), geographer Hutchins, and others. See Washington to Hutchins, 20 Aug. 1786, in Washington, *Writings,* 28:525; to Butler, 27 Nov. 1786, *ibid.,* 29:88-90ff.

38. Franklin, *Works,* 10:299.

39. Washington to Lafayette, 10 Jan. 1788, in Washington, *Writings,* 29:374.

40. *Ibid.,* pp. 374-75.

41. *Ibid.,* p. 375.

42. *Sravnitel'nyi slovar' vsekh iazykov i narechii po azbuchnomu poriadku raspolozhennyi* (Comparative Dictionary of All Languages and Dialects Arranged According to Alphabetical Order), 4 vols., St. Petersburg, 1790-1791. In the summer of 1812 this edition was presented to the American Philosophical Society by Dashkov. Later, in answer to a special request from America, Adelung sent to the Society the first edition of the *Dictionary* prepared by Pallas in 1787-1789 (*Linguarum totius orbis vocabularia comparativa; augustissimae cura collecta* [St. Petersburg, 1787-1789]; see Dvoichenko-Markov, "The American Philosophical Society," pp. 563, 583, 588). The first American minister to Russia, John Quincy Adams, was interested in Pallas' *Dictionary* and discussed it in April 1810 with Tilezus, a member of the Petersburg Academy (see J. Q. Adams, *Memoirs,* 2:115).

43. See Dvoichenko-Markov, "The American Philosophical Society," pp. 561-563, 584-589. As can be seen from the correspondence, Du Ponceau held a very high opinion of *Vocabularium Comparativum* and utilized the comparative method in his own investigations of American Indian languages.

44. Du Ponceau to Adelung, 16 Dec. 1817; the English version of this letter is preserved in the archive of AS USSR. f. 89, op. 2, d. 43, ll. 1-2; see also Dvoichenko-Markov, "The American Philosophical Society," p. 584.

45. See Dvoichenko-Markov, "Benjamin Franklin," p. 254; Franklin, *Writings,* 10:346.

46. Dvoichenko-Markov, "The American Philosophical Society," p. 555. An excerpt from these *Transactions* was published in 1792 in Russian translation under the title "Izvestiia o Severnoi Amerike" (News of North America). See *Novye ezhemesiachnye sochineniia* (New Monthly Publications), 1792, 67:10-24, 68:16-28.

47. Archive of AN USSR, f. 1, op. 2, 1791, d. 6, l. 8.

48. *Protokoly zasedanii* (St. Petersburg, 1911), 4(1786-1803):269-270.

49. The Papers of Princess E. R. Dashkov (née Countess Vorontsov), *Arkhiv kn. Vorontsova,* 21:286. Contact with America in those days was no easy matter. During the war with Sweden (1788-1790) one of the parcels addressed to Princess Dashkov with a letter from Franklin was intercepted by the Duke of Suedermanland, brother of the Swedish king. The Duke was punctilious enough to send the parcel through a truce envoy to Admiral Gregg in Kronstadt, with an accompanying letter to the Princess. "As a foreigner and a close friend" of the Princess, the Admiral immediately sent the parcel directly to the State Council, from where it was sent to the Princess in her country home, by order of the Empress, in complete safety, without being unsealed! The Princess' "post" worked perfectly and was not subjected to any censorship, either abroad or in Russia. Princess Dashkov had the highest opinion of Franklin, considering him "a superior man, who combined a profound erudition with a simplicity of manners and appearance, as well as natural modesty and a great deal of tolerance toward others." *Ibid.,* pp. 285-286; cf. Dvoichenko-Markov, "The American Philosophical Society," p. 556.

50. John Churchman was elected as a foreign member of the St. Petersburg

Academy of Sciences in January 1795, having been proposed by Princess Dashkov; see *ibid.*, pp. 557-558; *Protokoly zasedanii,* 4:409.

51. Princess Dashkov instructed the distinguished astronomer, Academician Theodor Schubert, to familiarize himself with Williams' work, and the former reported on it favorably. But the experiments made by the Russian Admiralty in the Baltic did not confirm Williams' observations. For a definitive solution of the problem as to what extent Williams' experiments on the influence of shoals and rocks on the temperature of the water (conducted in American waters) could be useful in averting shipwrecks, the scientists recommended conducting new experiments in wider sea basins. See *Protokoly zasedanii*, 4:328, 364: Radovsky, "Iz istorii russko-amerikanskikh nauchnykh sviazei," *Vestnik AN SSSR,* 1956, no. 11, pp. 94-95.

52. Anniversary Oration, Delivered May 21st, before the American Philosphical Society, Held in Philadelphia, For the Promotion of Useful Knowledge, for the Year 1782. By Doctor Thomas Bond, Vice-President of that Society. Philadelphia: Printed by John Dunlap [1782], pp. 31-32.

53. *Protokoly zasedanii,* 3:577.

54. *Rukopisnye materialy Leonarda Eilera v arkhive AN SSSR* (Manuscript Materials of Leonard Euler in the Archives of the Academy of Sciences of the USSR, Moscow, 1962), 1:226.

55. Dvoichenko-Markov, "The Russian Members of the American Academy of Arts and Sciences," *PAPS,* 109:53 (Feb. 1965). This article mentions 30 Jan. 1782 as the date of Euler's election. Judging, however, by the above-cited entry in the minutes of the conference, it must have occurred earlier. The minutes mention Joseph Willard's letter of 1 June 1781, and the notation itself refers to 28 Feb./11 March 1782, by which time news from Boston dated 30 Jan. could not yet have been received in St. Petersburg.

56. *Memoirs of the American Academy of Arts and Sciences to the End of the Year 1783* (Boston, 1785), vol. 1.

57. *Nova Acta Academiae Scientiarum Imperialis Petropolitanae,* 1788, p. 10; 1792, p. 6.

58. *Protokoly zasedanii,* 4:204. On Franklin's election see also *Nova Acta Academiae Scientiarum,* 1789, p. 8.

59. Franklin, *Works,* 10:405-406.

60. Euler to Franklin, Nov. 1789, Archives of the Academy of Sciences of USSR, f. 1, op. 3, d. 83, l. 2.

61. See also Startsev, "Veniamin Franklin i russkoe obshchestvo XVIIIv.," *Internatsional'naia literatura,* 1940, books 3-4.

62. *Uchenie dobrodushnogo Rikharda* (The Teaching of Good-natured Richard, St. Petersburg, 1784). Earlier still, on 4/15 June, 1778, in *St.-Petersburgskie ezhenedel'nye sochineniia* there appeared an extract translated from the French edition, *La Science du Bonhomme Richard.* From time to time other extracts from Franklin's work appeared in Russian periodicals. In Feb. 1778 G. L. Braiko's new journal, *S.-Peterburgskii vestnik,* published some excerpts from Franklin's letter to Miss Stevenson, under the title "Otsvetakh plat'ia (iz pis'ma gospodina Franklina)" (On the Colors of Garments: From Mr. Franklin's Letter) and in June 1780 the same journal printed Franklin's epitaph (see *S.-Peterburgskii vestnik,* 1780, pt. 6, p. 38). As early as March 1776 there was published "Vypiska iz pisem nekotorogo filadel'fiiskogo zhitelia k svoemu priiateliu Barbe de Burg v Parizhe" (Extract from the Letters of a Philadelphia Inhabitant to His Friend Barbeu Dubourg in Paris) praising the civil government in America in which "everything proceeds according to natural order." According

to the author, in the laws of Pennsylvania "there rules simplicity the like of which there had not been in history," etc. (See *Sobranie raznykh sochinenii i novostei,* March 1776, pp. 14-15). There is little doubt that a "Philadelphia inhabitant" was probably Franklin: French scholar Barbeu Dubourg was a great friend and translator of Franklin, and the contents of the extract correspond fully with Franklin's views.

63. Franklin, *Izbrannye proizvedeniia* (Selected Works, Moscow, 1956), p. 493.

64. *Kak blagopoluchno vek prozhit', nauka dobrogo cheloveka Rikharda* (How to Live Happily: The Science of Good Man Richard, Moscow, 1791).

65. *Mémoires de la vie privée de Benjamin Franklin, écrits par lui-même, et addressés à son fils,* 1791.

66. *Moskovskii zhurnal,* 1791, pt. 4, p. 355. Karamzin kept up his interest in Franklin. In 1798 he printed several moral-philosophical parables of Franklin in *Panteon inostrannoi slovesnosti* (Pantheon of Foreign Literature, book 3, pp. 221-225) which he edited. See also N. Karamzin, *Perevody* (Translations, St. Petersburg, 1835), 8:143, 145, 148.

67. "Otryvok is zapisok Franklina, pisannykh im samim," (An Excerpt from Franklin's Memoirs Written by Himself), *Priiatnoe i poleznoe prepprovozhdenie vremeni* (Pleasant and Useful Pastime, Moscow, 1798), 20:3-23.

68. See also "Otryvok iz Franklinovykh zapisok" (An Excerpt from Franklin's Memoirs), *Sobranie raznykh sochinenii Veniamina Franklina* (Collection of the Diverse Works of Benjamin Franklin, Moscow, 1803), pp. 165-191.

69. L. Feuchtwanger described Franklin's stay in Paris with characteristic literary mastery in *Lisy v vinogradnike* (Foxes in the Vineyard, Moscow, 1959).

70. Franklin, *Izbrannye proizvedeniia,* p. 418.

71. See Dvoichenko-Markov, "Benjamin Franklin and Leo Tolstoy," *PAPS,* 96:119-128 (April 1952).

72. *Otryvok iz zapisok Franklinovykh s prisovokupleniem kratkogo opisaniia ego zhizni i nekotorykh ego sochinenii* (An Excerpt from Franklin's Memoirs with the Addition of a Short Account of His Life and Some of His Works, Moscow, 1799); *Sobranie raznykh sochinenii Veniamina Franklina* (Collection of Different Works of Benjamin Franklin, Moscow, 1803).

73. "Moral' ot shakhmatnoi igry" (Morals of Chess), *ibid.,* pp. 22-30.

74. "Zamechaniia o voine" (Remarks on the War), *ibid.,* pp. 81-85.

75. "Zamechaniia o dikikh Severnoi Ameriki" (Remarks Concerning the Savages of North America), *ibid.,* pp. 86-102.

76. "Otvet ot Veniamina Franklina lordu Gove" (Benjamin Franklin's Answer to Lord Howe), *ibid.,* p. 116.

77. *Uedinennyi poshekhonets* (A Solitary Wise Man of Gotha), 2:552-557, (Sept. 1786).

78. See Franklin, *Works,* 2:177. On the circumstances of the composition of this work see *ibid.,* 8:473.

79. *Sobranie raznykh sochinenii,* pp. 33-35.

80. *Ibid.,* p. 36.

81. *Irtysh prevrashchaiushchiisia v Ipokrenu* (Irtysh Transformed into Hippocrene), pp. 56-57.

82. *Moskovskii zhurnal,* 1791, pt. 2, p. 218.

83. "Vasginton," *Muza. Ezhemesiachnoe izdanie na 1796 g.* (The Muse: A Monthly Publication for 1796), p. 31.

84. *Moskovskie vedomosti,* 1789, no. 84.

85. *Politicheskii zhurnal,* 1791, pt. 1, p. 34.

86. "Istoricheskie i statisticheskie dostopamiatnosti Severnoi Ameriki" (Historical and Statistical Memorabilia of North America), *Politicheskii zhurnal,* 1797, pt. 2, book 1, p. 11.

87. "Umnozhenie zhitelei i velikie uspekhi torgovli v Severnoi Amerike" (The Increase in Population and Great Strides in Commerce in North America), *Vestnik Evropy* (The Messenger of Europe), 1802, pt. 4, pp. 155-156.

88. "Obshchestva v Amerike (Perevod s manuscripta)" (Societies in America [Translated from a Manuscript]), *ibid.,* 1802, pt. 6, p. 315.

89. N. M. Karamzin, *Sochineniia* (Works, Petrograd, 1917), 1:104.

90. "Obshchestva v Amerike," p. 315.

91. *Vestnik Evropy,* 1802, pt. 1, pp. 75-76.

92. *Ibid.,* p. 88.

93. *Ibid.,* p. 89.

94. See V. Orlov, *Russkie prosvetiteli 1790-1800 godov* (Russian Men of the Enlightenment of 1790-1800, Moscow, 1953), p. 64.

95. *Ibid.,* p. 489, and others.

96. *Periodicheskoe izdanie* (Periodical Publication), 1804, pt. 1, pp. 43-47; *Talia, ili Sobranie raznykh novykh sochinenii v stikhakh i proze* (Thalia, or Collection of Various New Works in Verse or Prose, bk. I, St. Petersburg, 1807). Although originally the essay "The Negro" had a defensive subtitle "translated from the Spanish," it was undoubtedly Popugaev's original work; see Orlov, *Russkie prosvetiteli,* p. 297.

97. For details see *ibid.,* pp. 298ff.

98. For the full text see Dvoichenko-Markov, "The American Philosophical Society," p. 584.

99. *Naturgeschichte des Kupfers* and *Statistische Schilderung von Russland.* Hermann also promised to send to Philadelphia his forthcoming work, *Mineralogischen Reisen in Siberien.*

100. Dvoichenko-Markov, "The American Philosophical Society," p. 592.

101. Harris to American Philosophical Society, 3/15 July 1807, *ibid.,* p. 590.

102. Harris to Vaughan, 5/17 July 1811, *ibid.,* p. 591.

103. Harris to American Philosophical Society, 28 Aug./9 Sept. 1811, *ibid.,* p. 591; *Rapports entre la langue Sanscrit et la langue Russe* (St. Petersburg, 1811), reviewed in *Port Folio,* July 1812, p. 37.

104. *PSZRI,* 28:243-248.

105. See especially *ibid.,* vol. 28, nos. 21498-21500; and A. V. Predtechensky, *Ocherki obshchestvenno-politicheskoi istorii Rossii v pervoi chetverti XIX v.* (Essays on the Socio-Political History of Russia in the First Quarter of the Nineteenth Century, Moscow and Leningrad, 1957), pp. 179ff.

106. J. V. Niemcewicz collected his interesting observations on life in the United States in his book *Podróze po Ameryce 1797-1807* (Travels in America, 1797-1807, Wroclaw and Warsaw, 1959); English translation by J. E. Budka in *Collections of the New Jersey Historical Society,* XIV (1965), under the title *Under Their Vine and Fig Tree.*

107. Stroynowski to American Philosophical Society, 27 Sept./9 Oct. 1803, in Dvoichenko-Markov, "The American Philosophical Society," p. 589.

108. M. M. Speransky, "O korennykh zakonakh gosudarstva, 1802" (On the Basic Laws of the State), *Proekty i zapiski* (Projects and Reports), prepared for publication by A. I. Kopaev and M. V. Kukushkina, ed. S. N. Valka (Moscow and Leningrad, 1961), p. 43.

109. Stone to Priestley, n.d. Probably written in the summer of 1802, since on 29 Oct. 1802 Priestley forwarded it to Jefferson; see V. M. Kozlovsky, "Tsar'

Aleksandr I i Dzhefferson. Po arkhivnym dannym" (Tsar Alexander I and Jefferson: Based on Archival Data), *Russkaia Mysl'* (Russian Thought), 1910, no. 10, p. 82.

110. Jefferson to Priestley, 29 Nov. 1802, *ibid.,* p. 83. See also N. Hans, "Tsar Alexander and Jefferson: Unpublished Correspondence," *The Slavonic and East European Review,* 32:217 (Dec. 1953); hereafter cited as *SEER.* It is curious that Hans (who incidentally received a special grant from the United States Department of State) published "for the first time" practically the same documents as Kozlovsky. Reference to the fact that the necessary copy of *Russkaia Mysl'* was not preserved in the British Museum could hardly serve, either for Hans or for the editors of the journal, as sufficient basis to consider these documents as "unpublished." *(Ibid.,* p. 215.)

111. See Jefferson to Cooper, 29 Nov. 1802, *ibid.,* p. 217.

112. La Hazpe to Stone, 20 Oct. 1803, in *Russkaia Mysl',* 1910, no. 10, p. 84; Hans, "Tsar Alexander and Jefferson," p. 218.

113. Barlow to Jefferson, 11 Feb. 1804, *ibid.,* pp. 218-220; Kozlovsky, "Tsar' Aleksandr I i Dzhefferson," pp. 85-86.

114. Jefferson to Alexander I, 15 June 1804, *ibid.,* pp. 87-88; Hans, "Tsar Alexander and Jefferson," p. 221. Original in AVPR, f. Kantzeliariio, d. 3325, l. 6.

115. Alexander I to Jefferson. On the copy of the letter there is the Tsar's notation "So be it. November 3, 1804" and also following clerical inscription: "Signed and handed over to Consul-General Levett Harris at the conference on 20 December 1804." (See AVPR, f. Kantseliariia, d. 6033, ll. 3-4; published in *Novaia i noveishaia istoriia,* 1959, no. 2, pp. 154-155; *VPR,* vol. 2, no. 84, pp. 254-255.) On the same day Harris was also handed the reply of the Minister for Foreign Affairs, A. R. Vorontsov, to the official letter of 10 June 1804 from United States Secretary of State Madison (see AVPR, f. Kantseliariia, d. 3325, ll. 4-5; *VPR,* vol. 2, no. 85, p. 255).

When Kozlovsky was working in the American archives he could not find any answer from Alexander I to Jefferson's first letter. He observed, however, that in his letter to Alexander I of 19 April 1806 Jefferson referred to the Tsar's letter of 20 Aug. 1805. Kozlovsky expressed a well-founded doubt that Alexander could take such a long time in answering the first letter of the American President, and suggested that an earlier answer from the Tsar might exist (see *Russkaia mysl',* no. 10, pp. 88-89). In 1957, looking through the materials of AVPR, I found a draft of Alexander's answer to Jefferson approved by the Tsar on 3 Nov. 1804 (old style). On the other hand, Hans quoted a letter from Alexander I to Jefferson of 20 Aug. 1805 (received on 3 Dec. 1805) with a reference to the Library of Congress, Jefferson Papers, vol. 152, p. 26550 *(SEER,* 32:221-222). Comparison with the French text left no doubt that this is the same document. The matter is even further complicated by the fact that Laserson quotes an excerpt from the same letter in English translation, but with a new date—7 Nov. 1804—and with a footnote that the French original is preserved in the Pierpont Morgan Library in New York *(The American Impact on Russia,* pp. 82-83).

The microfilms of Harris' dispatches recently received from the United States have clarified this tangled sequence. First, it was established that on 20 Dec. 1804/1 Jan. 1805, Vice-Minister for Foreign Affairs A. A. Czartoryski actually handed to Harris the letters of Alexander I and A. R. Vorontsov (see Harris to Madison, 20 Dec. 1804/1 Jan. 1805, in NA, Consular Despatches; St. Petersburg, vol. 1), thus, the accuracy of early dating was confirmed. At the same time the later dating in Hans' publication was also explained. It transpired that several months later, at a festive masked ball in Petersburg on 28 July 1805, the Emperor Alexander I honored the American consul with "special attention" and in the course of conversation inquired about the delivery of his letter to the President of the United States. Since Harris could not give a definite answer, and did not exclude the possibility that the ship carrying the letters might have perished during the winter storms, Alexander I remarked: "I shall give you another one and shall ask you to inform the President at the same time that it is a duplicate." In the conclusion of his dispatch to Madison of 23 Aug./4 Sept. Harris wrote that Prince Czartoryski, during this meeting, passed on to him the enclosed letters, copies of which he forwarded to Madison in his letter of 1 Jan. (NA, Consular Despatches; St. Petersburg, vol. 1).

The incredible mix-up was resolved to the satisfaction of all. Everybody proved to be right, and for a while I have quite forgotten about Laserson. The private Morgan Library in New York was so far away that I could not even imagine working in it. However, as often happens, an occasion to visit it presented itself quite unexpectedly. In February 1968 I came to New York on the scholar exchange program. Naturally, I could not but visit the building on East 36th Street which houses the Pierpont Morgan Library. The Library administration proved very amiable, and in a few minutes I held in my hands the document from which an excerpt had been quoted by Laserson. There was no doubt about the authenticity of the letter. The French text was written in a beautiful hand on an ancient sheet of paper. At the bottom was the familiar sweeping signature: "Alexandre" and the date: "à St. Péterbourg ce 7 Novembre 1804." On the reverse of the second sheet there was a short notation: "Recd May 21." The tangled matter of dating the letter from Alexander I to Jefferson was resolved. To summarize: The project of the letter was approved by the Tsar on 3/15 and signed on 7/19 November 1804. The letter was officially passed by Czartoryski to Harris at the conference of 20 Dec. 1804/1 Jan. 1805, and received in America on May 21. Concerned that the letter might not have reached Jefferson, Alexander I signed a duplicate on 20 Aug./ 1 Sept. which duplicate was received by Jefferson on 3 Dec. 1805.

116. See Jefferson to Harris, 18 April 1806, and Harris to Budberg, 4/16 Aug. 1806, in *Russkaia mysl'*, 1910, no. 10, pp. 90-91.

117. *Ibid.*, pp. 89-90; *SEER*, 32:222-223.

118. *VPR*, vol. 3, no. 103, pp. 260-261.

119. Jefferson, *Writings*, 11:102; *Russkaia mysl'*, 1910, no. 10, p. 92.

120. Jefferson, *Writings*, 11:153-154; AVPR, f. Kantseliariia, d. 3337,ll. 2-4.

121. Alexander I to the President of the United States, 31 Aug./12 Sept. 1808, in *VPR*, vol. 4, no. 152, p. 336.

122. For a detailed account by Dashkov of his meeting with Madison and Smith, see AVPR, d. Kantseliariia, d. 9236, ll. 24-28.

123. See NA, Russia; notes, vol. 1, 31 Aug. 1808.

124. Dashkov to Rumiantsev, 28 July 1809, in AVPR, f. Kantseliariia, d. 9236, ll. 13-14.

125. Pahlen to Rumiantsev, 3/15 May 1811, in *VPR*, vol. 6, no. 40, pp. 109-110.

126. Jefferson to Harris, 12 Dec. 1821 in Jefferson, *Writings*, 19:227; *Russkaia mysl'*, 1910, no. 10, pp. 93-94.

127. George Vernadsky, "Reforms Under Czar Alexander: French and American Influences," *The Review of Politics*, 9:61 (Jan. 1947).

Chapter 6. Russian Colonization of the Northwest

1. Instruction of 5/16 Feb. 1725, in vol. VII, *PSZRI,* no. 4649, p. 413. Still earlier, on 2/13 Jan. 1719, Peter I personally inserted into the instructions for geodesists Evreinov and Luzhin a task to find out whether "America joined with Asia . . . and to put everything correctly on the map" (*ibid.,* vol. V, no. 3266, p. 607; A. B. Efimov, *Iz istorii velikikh russkikh geograficheskikh otkrytii,* p. 148. The question put by Peter I was not casual. Both in Russia (Saltykov's projects) and in Western Europe (Leibnitz' projects) there existed at that time an interest in the search for the Northeast passage—the way across the Antarctic into the Pacific, into China and India. Lomonosov was also concerned with this problem; see L. S. Berg, "Lomonosov i pervoe russkoe plavanie" (Lomonosov and the first Russian naval expedition), *Izvestiia Geograficheskogo Obshchestva,* 1940, no. 6, pp. 713-730.

2. V. Berkh, *Pervoe morskoe puteshestvie rossiian, predpriniatoe dlia resheniia geograficheskoi zadachi: soediniaetsia li Aziia s Amerikoiu? i sovershennoe v 1727, 28, 29 godakh pod nachal'stvom flota kapitana 1-go ranga Vitusa Beringa* (The First Sea Voyage of the Russians Undertaken for the Solution of the Geographical Problem: Whether Russia Joins with America: Conducted in 1727, 1728, and 1729 Under the Direction of the Captain of the First Rank Vitus Bering, St. Petersburg, 1823).

3. L. S. Berg, *Otkrytie Kamchatki i ekspeditsiia Beringa 1725-1742 gg.* (The Discovery of Kamchatka and Bering's Expedition of 1725-1742, Moscow and Leningrad, 1946), p. 103. The fact that I. Fedorov and M. Gvozdev reached North America was established by Efimov on the basis of studying original archival documents (*Iz istorii velikikh russkikh geograficheskikh otkrytii,* pp. 177-178). By the time of the first Bering expedition (1725-1729), it was known in Russia, as well as in Western Europe, that Asia "did not join with" America, and the data of Dezhnev's expedition became the property of geographical literature and cartography (see Berg, *Otkrytie Kamchatki,* p. 57).

4. Efimov, *Iz istorii velikikh russkikh geograficheskikh otkrytii,* p. 187.

5. F. A. Golder, *Russian Expansion on the Pacific 1641-1850* (Cleveland, 1914), pp. 67-95.

6. There were three editions of Berg's *Otkrytie Kamachatki:* 1924, 1935, and 1946. I have used the edition of 1946. On Dezhnev's voyage see *ibid.,* pp. 27-38.

7. In addition to the well-known books of M. I. Belov and V. I. Grekov, see also B. P. Polevoi, "O Tochnom tekste dvukh otpisok Semena Dezhneva 1655 goda" (On the Precise Text of Two Notes by Simeon Dezhnev in 1655), *Izvestiia AN SSSR, seriia geographicheskaia,* 1965, no. 2; R. V. Makarova, *Russkie na Tikhom okeane vo vtoroi polovine XVIIIv. "* (Russians on the Pacific in the Second Part of the Eighteenth Century, Moscow, 1968); S. G. Fedorova, *Russkoe naselenie Aliaski i Kalifornii. Konez XVIII veko-1867 g.* (The Russian Population of Alaska and California. Late 18th Century-1867, Moscow, 1971).

8. See N. S. Orlova, compiler, A. V. Efimov, ed., *Otkrytiia russkikh zemleprokhodtsev i poliarnykh morekhodov XVII veka na severo-vostoke Azii. Sb. dokumentov* (The Discoveries of Russian Land Travelers and Arctic Sea Voyagers of the Seventeenth Century in the North-east of Asia: A Collection of Documents, Moscow, 1951).

9. See A. V. Efimov, *Iz istorii russkikh ekspeditsii na Tikhom okeane* (*pervaia polovina XVIII v.*) (Toward a History of Russian Expeditions in the Pacific [First Half of the Eighteenth Century], Moscow, 1948), pp. 208-210; and *Iz istorii velikikh russkikh geograficheskikh otkrytii,* pp. 235-236.

10. V. Berkh, *Khronologicheskaia istoriia otkrytiia Aleutskikh ostrovov* (A Chronological History of the Discovery of the Aleutian Islands, St. Petersburg, 1823), p. 131, and table I: "Information on furs exported by private companies." For more complete information see the recent book of R. V. Makarova, *Russkie na Tikhom okeane,* pp. 182-187. An interesting summary table on the voyages of Russian merchants and traders before 1790 was found by Efimov among the papers of A. R. Vorontsov (see TsGADA, f. 1261, d. 874, in connection with the new listing of the Vorontsov papers). It was entitled "Historical Table on Russian Sea Companies Engaged in the Fur Trade through the Islands of the Northwest Sea and Further, Which Made Important Discoveries, with the Addition of Some Historical Information and Adventures." On Russian navigation see also the fundamental work of Bancroft, *History of Alaska,* pp. 99-156.

11. Berkh, *Khronologicheskaia istoriia,* table II.

12. At the present time, the navigation of Russian merchants and fur traders in the Pacific north, and, in particular, the activity of Shelikhov's company in the Aleutian Islands and in America, is known primarily through Andreev's valuable publications; see *Russkie otkrytiia v Tikhom okeane i Severnoi Amerike* (Russian Discoveries in the Pacific and North America), ed. and introduced by A. I. Andreev (Moscow, 1948). This collection mainly contains materials relating to the activity of Shelikhov's company for the years 1785-1794 (pp. 178-376).

See also the new edition of Shelikhov's "Wanderings" with detailed commentaries of B. P Polevoi. G. I. Shelikhov, *Rossiiskogo kuptsa Grigoriia Shelikhova stranstvovaniia iz Okhotska po Vostochnomu okeanu k amerikanskim beregam.* (Wanderings of a Russian Merchant, Grigorii Shelikhov, from Okhotok over the Eastern Ocean to the American Shores, Khabarovsk, 1971).

13. Panin to Bariatinsky, 11/22 Oct. 1779, in AVPR, f. Snosheniia Rossii s Frantsiei, 1779, d. 345, ll. 91-92.

14. The events of 1771 in Bol'sheretsk and their consequences are described in a considerable number of special works, among which one should single out the articles of V. Berkh: "Pobeg grafa Ben'evskogo iz Kamchatki vo Frantsiiu" (The Flight of Count Benyowski from Kamchatka to France), *Syn otechestva,* 1821, nos. 27-28; "Zapiski kantseliarista Riumina o prikliucheniiakh ego s Beniovskim" (The Memoirs of Clerk Riumin of His Adventures with Benyowski), *Severnyi arkhiv,* 1822, nos. 5-7; "Zapiska o bunte, proizvedennom Beniovskim v Bol'sheretskom ostroge i posledstviiakh onogo" (Memoir on the Benyowski Rebellion in the Bol'sheretsk Jail and the Consequences Thereof), *Russkii arkhiv,* 1865, no. 4, pp. 417-438. Also worth mentioning is the work of A. S. Sgibnev based on the materials of the secret investigation of the Benyowski rebellion in the papers of the Irkutsk Archive: "Bunt Ben'evskogo v Kamchatke v 1771 g." (Benyowski's Rebellion in Kamchatka in 1771), *Russkaia starina,* 1876, 15:525-547, 756-769. The *Memoirs* of Benyowski himself, published in two parts and translated into all the major European languages (*Voyages et mémoires de Maurice Auguste comte de Benyowski* [Paris, 1791]), are widely known.

15. For the list of the most prominent people mentioned in the judicial investigation of Benyowski's rebellion, see Sgibnev's article in *Russkaia starina,* pp. 540-541. Several people, in particular navigator-apprentices D. Bocharov and G. Izmailov, who later worked for Shelikhov, were carried away by Benyowski against their will.

16. *Russkii arkhiv,* 1865, no. 4, pp. 432-433.

17. Catherine II to Viazemsky, 2/13 Oct. 1773, *ibid.,* pp. 433-434.

18. 27 June/8 July 1773, in AVPR, f. Snosheniia Rossii s Frantsiei, 1773, d. 283, l. 1.

19. For additional details see *Russkaia starina*, 1876, 15:762-763.

20. 26 March/6 April 1773, *ibid.*, pp. 763-764.

21. See E. Dvoichenko-Markov, "Benjamin Franklin and Count M. A. Benyowski," *PAPS*, 99:405-417 (Dec. 1955).

22. Benyowski to Franklin, 24 Dec. 1781, *ibid.*, p. 414.

23. 15/26 Dec. 1779, in AVPR, f. Snosheniia Rossii s Frantsiei, 1779, d. 344 ll. 173-174.

24. See E. Dvoichenko-Markova, "Shturman Gerasim Izmailov" (Navigator Gerasim Izmailov), *Morskie Zapiski* (Naval Transactions, New York, 1955), vol. 13, no. 4; James Cook, *Voyage to the Pacific Ocean* (London, 1784), 2:497-500; *Poslednee puteshestvie okolo sveta kapitana Kuka* (St. Petersburg, 1788), pp. 85-87 and especially Ia. M. Svet, ed., *Tret'e plavanie Kapitana Kuka* (The Third Voyage of Captain Cook, Moscow, 1971), pp. 390-392, 395-396, 571-572, 616-617.

25. "From the enclosed maps and the voyage of Vancouver and Pujet," it was pointed out later in the secret "instruction" to the governor (glavnyi pravitel) of the Russian colonies in America, A. A. Baranov, "you will see that they themselves marked those territories as occupied by our activities, calling them Russian trading stations. Vancouver describes Russians' dealing with Americans with great praise, saying that they acquired mastery over wild peoples not by conquest but by searching out the ways to their hearts. Noting from the third volume of Vancouver's voyages that some of your traders gave to the English the maps of your navigations, the Main Office (Glavnoe Pravlenie) considers it its duty to reprove you about this." See M. M. Buldakov, E. I. Delarov, and I. Shelikhov to Baranov, 18/30 April 1802; NA, Records of the Russian-American Company, 1802-1867, 1:3-4.

26. *Russkaia starina*, 1876, 15:765-766; *Poslednee puteshestvie . . . kapitana kuka,* p. 124; Svet, *Tret'e plavanie Kapitana Kuka,* pp. 486-519.

27. *Russkaia starina*, 1876, 15:767.

28. *Ibid.*

29. See, in particular, La Pérouse's letter to Irkutsk Governor-General I. Jacoby, 28 Sept. 1787 (TsGADA, Gos. Arkhiv, f. XXIV, op. I, d. 62, 1783-1787, ch. III, ll. 343-343a), and "Relation d'un voyage fait en Californie par un batiment espagnoi" (AVPR, f. Snosheniia Rossii s Ispaniei, 1789, d. 455, ll. 59-60).

30. Jared Sparks, *Life of John Ledyard, the American Traveller* (Boston, 1864), pp. 201ff.

31. E. Dvoichenko-Markov, "John Ledyard and the Russians," *The Russian Review,* 11 (1952):213. The editor of a recent collection of pertinent documents (Stephen D. Watrous, ed., *John Ledyard's Journey through Russia and Siberia, 1787-1788: The Journal and Selected Documents* [Madison, 1966], pp. 37-38) points out that Ledyard may well have had such a plan in mind before consulting Jefferson and receiving his encouragement and aid.

32. See Sparks, *Life of John Ledyard,* pp. 214-215; Jefferson, *Papers,* 10:170-171.

33. *Russkie otkrytiia v Tikhom okeane,* pp. 65-66.

34. The valuable works of G. A. Sarychev and M. Sauer were published as early as the beginning of the nineteenth century. The basic documentation is preserved in TsGAVMF (f. Billings). For a detailed account of the sources and literature on this expedition see A. I. Andreev's circumstantial introduction to the collection of documents *Russkie otkrytiia v Tikhom okeane,* pp. 68-71.

35. "Pis'ma imp. Ekateriny II baronu Mel'khioru Grimmu," *SbRIO,* 23:378.

36. See *ibid.,* pp. 381, 424.

37. 16 Aug. 1786, Jefferson, *Papers,* 10:258.

38. Ledyard to Jefferson, 19 March 1787, *ibid.,* 11:217.

39. *Ibid.,* p. 218.

40. Sparks, *Life of John Ledyard,* p. 231.

41. TsGADA, Gos. Arkhiv, f. XXIV, op. 1, d. 62, 1783-1788, ch. II, l. 419.

42. See Dvoichenko-Markov, "John Ledyard," pp. 211, 216.

43. Watrous, *Ledyard's Journey,* p. 162.

44. Ledyard to Jefferson (received 3 July 1788), in Jefferson, *Papers,* 13:306.

45. "Notes on the conversations of the voyager of English nationality, Levdar, during his stay in Irkutsk, with the merchant Grigory Shelikhov . . . . " Here and below I cite a certified typescript copy of Shelikhov's "notes" sent to AVPR from the State Archives of the Krasnoiarsk Region (AVPR, f. Sobranie dok. materialov po ist. Rossiisko-Amerikanskoi kompanii i russkikh vladenii v Sev. Amerike [hereafter cited as RAK], d. 419, ll. 1-4. It is at present kept in TsGADA, f. 796, op. 1, d. 298, ll. 1-2.) It is possible that the almost illegible manuscript was not deciphered with the utmost accuracy. In any case, the general contents of the document allowed me to establish that this voyager was indeed Ledyard, in spite of being called "Levdar." There are references to the proposed route of Ledyard's voyage to the American continent, "thence to go alone across North America," a mention of his visiting Russian possessions with Cook's expedition, etc. The document is not dated, but Shelikhov's conversations can be placed in August 1787, during the period of Ledyard's stay in Irkutsk. (See also Waltrous, Ledyard's Journey, p. 158-159.) The original manuscript copy of this document (Report of conversation with an Englishman) is in Library of Congress, Yudin Collection, Russian-American Company Papers, box 2, N29.

46. Dvoichenko-Markov, "John Ledyard," p. 218.

47. M. Sauer, *An Account of a Geographical and Astronomical Expedition to the Northern Parts of Russia* (London, 1802), p. 99; Dvoichenko-Markov, "John Ledyard," p. 219.

48. Sauer, *An Account of a Geographical and Astronomical Expedition,* pp. 99-101.

49. G. A. Sarychev, *Puteshestvie po severo-vostochnoi chasti Sibiri, Ledovitomu moriu i Vostochnomu okeanu* (A Voyage across the Northeast Part of Siberia, the Arctic Sea, and the Eastern Ocean, Moscow, 1952), p. 92.

50. See, for example, Laserson, *The American Impact on Russia,* pp. 96-97.

51. See Sparks, *Life of John Ledyard,* pp. 363 ff.; Dvoichenko-Markov, "John Ledyard," p. 220. The leading contemporary American authority on this subject, Stephen D. Watrous, admitted in 1966 that the order for Ledyard's arrest remained a mystery. "Catherine, of course, gave the order for Ledyard's arrest; but it is as yet impossible to determine who advised her about his activities and whereabouts, or perhaps urged her to take this measure." Watrous, *Ledyard's Journey,* p. 46.

52. TsGADA, Gos. arkhiv, f. XXIV, op. 1, d. 62, 1783-1788, ch. II, ll. 419-422. Although the addressee is not named specifically in Jacoby's report, "Your Excellency the Count" is clearly A. A. Bezborodko, as can be deduced from the reference in the report to Catherine II of 1/11 Feb. 1788 (*ibid.,* ch. III, l. 82).

53. Jacoby to Catherine II, 30 Nov./11 Dec. 1787, in *Russkie otkrytiia v Tikhom okeane,* pp. 250-265.

54. Here and below I continue to cite Jacoby's report to Bezborodko of 7/18 Nov. 1787 (TsGADA, Gos. arkhiv, f. XXIV, op. 1, d. 62, 1783-1788, ch. II, ll. 420-422).

55. *Ibid.,* l. 421. This clarifies the reasons for the "excessive politeness of the

Iakutsk commandant" toward the American traveler, and the "touching" concern for his health, which Ledyard himself found annoying. According to Sarychev, Ledyard was treated warmly by everyone. "The Commandant invited him to his home and table, and when the cold weather arrived, he ordered some warm clothing to be made for him." The reasons for Ledyard's unexpected "arrogance" and daring to challenge Marklovsky to a duel can be seen more clearly, too; see Sarychev, *Puteshestvie,* p. 92.

56. TsGADA, Gos. arkhiv, f. XXIV, op. I, d. 62, 1783-1788, ch. II, l. 419; see also the notation of 16/27 Dec. 1787 in the diary of Catherine II's secretary, A. V. Khrapovitsky, *Dnevnik* (Diary, Moscow, 1901), p. 34.

57. To P. B. Passek, 21 Dec. 1787/1 Jan. 1788, with the notation: "Accepted 1 January, 1788, Petr Passek," in TsGIA, f. 1329, op. 3, 1787, d. 233, l. 306.

58. Ségur to Lafayette, Aug. 1823, in Sparks, *Life of John Ledyard,* p. 366.

59. TsGADA, Gos. arkhiv, f. XXIV, op. 1, d. 62, 1783-1788, ch. III, l. 82.

60. Shelikhov's first biography was published by K. T. Khlebnikov in *Russkii invalid* (Russian Invalid), 1838, nos. 77-84; *Syn otechestva,* vol. 2, pt. 3, pp. 66-83, Soviet historians and men of letters repeatedly turn to his biography (B. Iurkevich, S. N. Markov, and others). A recent biographical essay is B. P. Polevoi, *Grigory Shelikhov—"Kolomb rosskii"* (Gregory Shelikhov—"Russian Columbus", Magadan, 1960).

61. "Zapiska Shelikhova stranstvovaniiu ego v Vostochnom more" (The Memoirs of Shelikhov on His Travels in Eastern Sea), *Russkie otkrytiia v Tikhom okeane,* pp. 226-227. The original version of the memoir was prepared by Shelikhov soon after his return in the spring of 1787 to Irkutsk, and was published for the first time by A. I. Andreev in 1948. But a revised version, published in Russian in 1791 and supplemented in 1792 by the description of the travels of the experienced Russian seafarers who worked for Shelikhov, E. A. Izmailov and D. I. Bocharov, enjoyed great popularity. Since then, this report was re-issued several times in Russia and translated into foreign languages.

The origin and content of the book of Shelikhov's "wanderings" has been a subject of meticulous analysis both in the United States (H. H. Bancroft, A. Yarmolinsky) and in the Soviet Union (S. B. Okun', A. I Andreev); thus, there is no need to dwell on this problem in detail. I should like to mention just one point. Hubert Bancroft, the "king" of American historians, brought out in English an extract of the secret instruction of the Main Office of the Russian-American Company which he got from the Sitka archives. It seemingly demonstrated that after Jacoby's departure, his successor, Mr. Piel, stole Shelikhov's travel journal. "As a proof of this," we read in Bancroft's book, "may serve you the endorsed book of *Grigor Shelekov's Travels.* It is nothing but his journals transmitted to Governor-General Jacobi, on whose retirement it was stolen from the chancellery by Mr. Piel and printed against the will of the deceased" (see *The History of Alaska,* p. 223). Soviet researchers Okun' and Andreev got interested in this problem and called attention to the fact that Irkutsk Governor-General I. A. Pil' (Piel), suspected of the theft, was an active supporter of Shelikhov and would hardly have been willing to publish a document that might harm his protegé (see Okun', *Rossiisko-amerikanskaia kompaniia,* p. 24; Andreev, *Russkie otkrytiia,* p. 38).

The answer to the riddle lies simply in the incorrect translation of the Russian document, by which the eminent American historian confused both Okun' and Andreev. In the course of giving Baranov a strict order not to send any important information to Irkutsk, "where no secret can be kept," the directors of the Russian-American Company wrote: "The book of Grigory Ivanovich Shelikhov's travels may serve as a proof of this. It is nothing but his journal, transmitted by him to former Governor-General Jacoby, on whose transfer it was *stolen from the office of Mr. Pil'* [my italics] and printed in Moscow against the will of the deceased; ignorance had sacrificed even the state secret for the sake of the mean profit." (See secret "instruction" of M. M. Buldakov, E. I. Delarov, and I. Shelikhov to the "main administrator in America," A. A. Baranov, of 18/30 April 1802, in NA, Records of the Russian-American Company 1802-1867, vol. I (Roll I), p. 6. The English translation of this document was made for Bancroft by his assistant, Ivan Petrov. See Bancroft Library, Berkeley, Calif., HHB, P-K 67.) Thus, the mistaken use of the preposition "by" instead of " of " led to the maligning of Pil' who should be exonerated, even if the theft as such did take place.

62. Bancroft, *History of Alaska*, p. 222.

63. 19/30 April 1787, in *Russkie Otkrytiia*, p. 212.

64. *Ibid.*, p. 213.

65. Shelikhov's note on the privileges of his company, May-Nov. 1787, *ibid.*, pp. 223-226.

66. *Ibid.*, p. 259.

67. *Ibid.*, p. 265.

68. Golikov and Shelikhov to Catherine II, Feb. 1788, *ibid.*, p. 268.

69. Report of the Commission on Commerce to Catherine II, March 1788, *ibid.*, pp. 269-279.

70. Minutes of the Permanent Council of 6/17 April 1788, *ibid.*, p. 280.

71. Notations in Catherine II's own hand, on the report of the Commission on Commerce (1788), in AVPR, f. RAK, d. 36, ll. 1-2; *Russkie otkrytiia*, pp. 281-282.

72. Okun', *Rossiisko-amerikanskaia kompaniia*, pp. 29-30; *Russkie otkrytiia*, pp. 44-45. Professor Okun', in particular, noted that already in the 1760's Catherine II offered exceptional privileges to the companies of Iugov and Trapeznikov, and to A. Tolstykh, who, nevertheless, could not take advantage of their rights. At the same time, it is hard to agree with Okun's notion of the role that relations with England played in this matter. How can one talk about the preparation of a Russian-British rapprochement and even an alliance, about which Okun' is writing, when it is known that precisely at that time relations with England became extremely tense and generally seemed close to the breaking point. For more details see A. M. Stanislavskaia, "Rossiia i Angliia v gody vtoroi turetskoi voiny 1787-1791" (Russia and England during the Second Turkish War, 1787-1791), *Voprosy istorii*, 1948, no. 11, pp. 26-49.

73. A. F. Bychkov, ed., *Pis'ma i bumagi imp. Ekateriny II, khraniashchiesia v Publichnoi biblioteke* (Letters and Papers of the Empress Catherine II Kept in the Public Library, St. Petersburg, 1873), p. 65.

74. According to Catherine II's secretary, A. V. Khrapovitsky (diary notation of 27 April/18 May 1788), the Empress frankly announced that "in twenty-five years she has not seen a report similar to one made by the Commission for Commerce about Shelikhov: They are giving away the Pacific as a monopoly. Just give them a pretext. The president [Count A. R. Vorontsov] has a far-off view for his profits'." See "Pamiatnye zapiski A. V. Khrapovitskogo, stats-sekretaria imp. Ekateriny II. Izdanie polnoe, s. prim. G. N. Gennadi" (Memoirs of A. V. Khrapovitsky, State Secretary of the Empress Catherine II: Complete Edition, with Notes by G. N. Gennadi), *Chteniia v imperatorskom obshchestve istorii i drevnostei rossiiskikh pri Moskovskom universitete* (Papers of the Imperial Society of History and Russian Antiquities at Moscow University), 1862, April-June, bk. 2, Moscow, 1862, pt. 2, p. 59.

75. AVPR, f. RAK, d. 36, ll. 1-2.

76. To the Procurator-General of the Senate, Viazemsky, 4/15 Sept. 1788, in *Russkie otkrytiia*, p. 283.

77. Shelikhov to Pil', 11/22 Feb. 1790, *ibid.*, p. 295.

78. See Tikhmenev, *Istoricheskoe obozrenie*, pt. 1, pp. 31-32.

79. See K. Khlebnikov, *Zhizneopisanie Aleksandra Andreevicha Baranova, glavnogo pravitelia rossiiskikh kolonii v Amerike* (Biography of Alexander Andreevich Baranov, Governor of the Russian Colonies in America, St. Petersburg, 1883); H. Chevigny, *Lord of Alaska: Baranov and the Russian Adventure* (London, 1946).

80. *K istorii Rossiisko-amerikanskoi kompanii: Sbornik dokumental'nykh materialov* (Toward the History of the Russian-American Company: A Collection of Documentary Materials, Krasnoiarsk, 1957), p. 35.

81. 9/20 Aug. 1794, in *Russkie otkrytiia*, pp. 336-337.

82. *Ibid.*, pp. 337-338.

83. Shelikhov and Polevoi (Golikov's trustee) to Baranov, 9/20 Aug. 1794, in Tikhmenev, *Istoricheskoe obozrenie*, pt. 2, Supplements, p. 71; S. B. Okun', *Rossiisko-Amerikanskaia kompaniia*, p. 33.

84. AVPR, f. RAK, d. 105, ll. 1-15.

85. Tikhmenev, *Istoricheskoe obozrenie*, pt. 1, Supplements, p. 4.

86. Okun', *Rossiisko-amerikanskaia kompaniia*, p. 39.

87. College of Commerce to Paul I, Jan. 1799, in AVPR, f. RAK, d. 130, ll. 1-6. The original is signed by P. Soimonov and others.

88. *PSZRI*, 25:703-704.

89. AVPR, f. RAK, d. 130, ll. 7-13, 15-17. The importance of the organizational documents of the Russian-American Company indicates the need for their publication along with a precise account of the preparation of the final text.

90. AVPR, f. RAK, d. 130, l. 7.

91. In the original the word "occupied" is penciled in instead of "discovered." The final editor of the text obviously intended to facilitate further colonization of the Northwest all the way to California (*ibid.*, l. 15).

92. These changes had already entered the project presented to Paul I by the College of Commerce; see *ibid.*, l. 12.

93. Okun', *Rosssiisko-amerikanskaia kompaniia*, p. 45.

94. List of the shareholders, early nineteenth century, in TsGADA, f. 796, op. 1, d. 182, ll. 1-2.

95. Marx and Engels, *Sochineniia*, 9:185.

96. *Ibid.*, pp. 151, 154.

97. *Ibid.*, p. 155.

98. Paul I to Vorontsov, 7/18 March 1799, in AVPR, f. Snosheniia Rossii s Angliei, 1799, op. 35/6, d. 507, ll. 4-5.

99. See *ibid.*, ll. 13-16, 6-7. A map of the American coast discovered by the Russian seafarers was also enclosed (l. 21).

100. The last list of the instruction bears a notation: "Approved in the committee consisting of the honorable gentlemen the shareholders who were present at His Excellency Minister of Commerce Count Nikolai Rumiantsev', on April 8, 1802." (NA, Records of the Russian-American Company, 1:7).

101. Buldakov, Delarov, and Shelikhov to Baranov, 18/30 April 1802, *ibid.*, p. 2.

102. The issue of the illegal trade of the North Americans, or "Bostonians" as they were then called, in Russian possessions in America was treated in detail in a note by M. M. Buldakov and V. V. Kramer to Rumiantsev of 21 April/3 May

1808, "on the undercutting inflicted on the company by Bostonians" (*VPR,* vol. 4, no. 104, pp. 241-243); in the instruction of the corporation of the company to Dashkov of 20 Aug./1 Sept. 1808 (TsGAOR, f. 907, op. 1, d. 56, ll. 2-7; AVPR, f. Gl. arkh. II-3, 1805-1817, op. 34, d. 8, l. 18ff.); and in "A Note on the North Americans' trade in the Russian colonies in America, December 23, 1816" (AVPR, f. Kantselyariia, d. 12182, ll. 31-49).

103. Corporation of Russian-American Company to Dashkov, 20 Aug./1 Sept. 1808, in AVPR, f. Gl. arkh. II-3, 1805-1817, op. 34, d. 8, ll. 21-22.

104. AVPR, f. Kantseliariia, d. 12182, l. 31ff.

105. Koloshes was the name Russians used for the tribe of Tlingits populating the southeast part of Alaska and adjoining islands: Baranov, Admiralteistvo, Chichagov, and others. (See A. V. Efimov and S. A. Tokarev, eds., *Narody Ameriki* (Peoples of America, Moscow, 1959), 1:151ff.

106. See the testimony of A. Plotnikov and others who escaped from the Koloshes, in Tikhmenev, *Istoricheskoe obozrenie,* Vol. 2, Supplements, pp. 174-180.

107. 1/12 July 1802, in *K Istorii Rossiisko-amerikanskoi kompanii,* p. 119.

108. *VPR,* vol. 4, no. 104, p. 242.

109. Tikhmenev, *Istoricheskoe obozrenie,* 1:88-89.

110. *VPR,* vol. 4, no. 104, p. 242; no. 40, p. 106; also AVPR, f. Kantseliariia, d. 12182, l. 34.

111. To the Directors of the Russian-American Company, 6/8 Nov. 1805, in Tikhmenev, *Istoricheskoe obozrenie,* vol. 2, Supplements, p. 207.

112. See AVPR, f. Gl. arkh. I-13, d. 12, 1805-1808, ll. 4-5.

113. Khlebnikov, *Zhizneopisanie A. A. Baranova,* p. 124.

114. *VPR,* vol. 4, no. 104, p. 242.

115. To the Directors of the Russian-American Company, 6/18 Nov. 1805, in Tikhmenev, *Istoricheskoe obozrenie,* vol. 2, Supplements, p. 203.

116. AVPR, f. Kantseliariia, d. 12182, l. 33.

117. Main Office of the Russian-American Company to Dashkov, 20 Aug./1 Sept. 1808, in AVPR, f. Gl. arkh. II-3, 1805-1817, op. 34, d. 8, l. 22. After a visit to Canton with the ships *Nadezhda* and *Neva* at the end of 1805, a clerk of the Russian-American Company, F. I. Shemelin stated that "in 1804 there were three ships with sea-otters in Canton: Captain O'Cain had 3,100 sea otters, Swift, 3,000, and Brown, 2,100, to the sum of 8,200 sea otters; the first were sold for 24 piasters, and the last for 23 piasters. This time we found three ships with the same furs, which preceded us into this port from America. Captain Stargell has 5,202 sea-otters, Adams, 5,800, and Trasket, 2,800; all in all, 14,002 sea otters. *Neva* had 4,007, *Nadezhda,* 414, so that this year there were brought to Canton 18,423 sea otters." See *VPR,* vol. 3, no. 2, pp. 18-19; and Shemelin, *Zhurnal pervogo puteshestviia rossiian vokrug zemnogo shara* (Journal of the First Voyage of the Russians around the Globe, 2 vols., St. Petersburg, 1816-1818).

118. AVPR, f. Gl. arkh. II-3, 1805-1817, op. 34, d. 8, l. 22.

119. *Ibid.,* l. 23.

120. Tikhmenev, *Istoricheskoe obozrenie,* vol. 2, Supplements, p. 234.

121. Rumiantsev's report to Alexander I, "On the Canton Trade," 20 Feb./4 March 1803, in *VPR,* vol. 1, no. 157, p. 386. Rumiantsev's proposal received approval both from the Tsar and from "the Committee of the Ministers." On 23 Feb./7 March 1803, N. N. Novosil'tsov forwarded to Rumiantsev an extract from the journal of the Committee of the Ministers pointing out that the report on the trade with Japan and in Canton was "with the royal sanction, approved by the Committee." A close study of the archival material connected with the first Russian global

expedition in 1803-1806 and with Iu. a. Golovkin's ambassadorship in China in 1805-1806 shows that the Russian government continued in the course of these years to pay serious attention to the question of opening the Canton trade. See, particularly, Rumiantsev's report to Alexander I of 16/28 Jan. 1805, section I, "To open trade in Canton and in the Yellow Sea," in *VPR*, vol. 2, no. 95, pp. 297-298. On the failure of Golovkin's embassy, besides material published in the second and third volumes of *VPR*, see *Iz bumag grafa Iu. A. Golovkina* (From the Papers of Count Iu. A. Golovkin, St. Petersburg, 1904).

122. Besides the abovementioned works, attention should be called to an article by V. F. Shiroky, which describes the company's activity in the first decades of the nineteenth century; see "Iz istorii khoziaistvennoi deiatel'nosti Rossiisko-amerikanskoi kompanii" (From the History of the Economic Activity of the Russian-American Company), *Istoricheskie zapiski* (Moscow, 1942), 13:207-221.

123. To the Directors of the Russian-American Company, 6/18 Nov. 1805, Tikhmenev, *Istoricheskoe obozrenie*, vol. 2, Supplements, p. 206. On the subject of the acute shortages of people in the colonies and the methods of drafting manpower, see AVPR, f. RAK, d. 190, 186, and others.

124. *VPR*, vol. 4, no. 120, pp. 270-271, 617.

125. Tikhmenev, *Istoricheskoe obozrenie*, 1:139.

126. *Ibid.*, p. 117.

127. See the report of the Main Office of the Russian-American Company to Alexander I, 29 July/10 Aug. 1802, in *VPR*, vol. 1, no. 99, pp. 266-269, and Rumiantsev's report to Alexander I, 27 March/8 April 1803, *ibid.*, no. 166, pp. 403-405.

128. *Ibid.*, p. 405.

129. There is rich archival material and an enormous amount of specialized literature on this expedition. Of great value are the memoirs of the members of the expedition themselves: I. F. Kruzenshtern and Iu. F. Lisiansky as well as G. I. Langsdorf, G. T. Tilezus, F. I. Shemelin, and others. See Kruzenshtern, *Puteshestvie vokrug sveta v 1803, 4, 5 i 1806 godakh* (A Voyage around the Globe in 1803, 4, 5 and 1806, 3 vols., St. Petersburg, 1809-1812). A new but incomplete edition came out in 1950. See also Lisiansky, *Puteshestvie vokrug sveta v 1803, 4, 5 i 1806 godakh* (A Voyage around the Globe in 1803, 4, 5 and in 1806, 2 vols., St. Petersburg, 1812). The expedition itself was embittered by the acute conflict between Rezanov and Kruzenshtern. Judging by the material in AVPR, emanating basically from Rezanov, he had a definite legalistic basis for his pretensions to head the expedition. In the general instructions given him on 10/22 July 1803, it is stated directly that both vessels (*Nadezhda* and *Neva*) were entrusted to his command (paragraph 1) (*VPR*, vol. 1, no. 207, p. 492). However, this hardly agrees with either the instructions which had been given earlier to Kruzenshtern or with the opinion established in the modern literature; see V. V. Nevsky, *Pervoe puteshestvie rossiian vokrug sveta* (The First Voyage of the Russians around the Globe, Moscow, 1951), and other works on Kruzenshtern.

130. See AVPR, f. Gl. arkh. II-3, 1806-1810, op. 34, d. 4. In 1807-1811, the war sloop *Diana* under the command of V. M. Golovnin made a voyage around the world, visiting the Russian colonies in America in the summer of 1810. In 1813-1816, the ship *Suvorov*, under the command of M. P. Lazarev sailed from Kronstadt to Russian America and back. See Golovnin, *Sochineniia i perevody* (Works and Translations, 5 vols., St. Petersburg, 1864); V. M. Golovnin, *Puteshestvie na shliupe* Diana *iz Kronshtadta v Kamchatku, sovershennoye pod nachal'stvom flota leytenanta Golovnina v 1807-1811 godakh* (A Voyage on the Sloop *Diana* from Kronstadt to Kamchatka, Made under the Command of the

Navy Lieutenant Golovnin in 1807-1811, Moscow, 1961); N. Ivashintsev, *Russkie krugosvetnye puteshestviia s 1803 po 1849 god* (Russian Circumglobal Voyages from 1803 until 1849, St. Petersburg, 1872).

131. Rezanov's voyage to California was described in detail in his lengthy confidential dispatch to the Minister of Commerce, Rumiantsev, 17/29 June 1806. For the text of the dispatch, with considerable abbreviations, see Tikhmenev, *Istoricheskoe obozrenie,* vol. 2, Supplements, pp. 253-283. The original is in TsGIA, f. 13, op. 1, d. 687, ll. 1-21 (the ending of the dispatch is missing). See also Hector Chevigny, *Russian America: The Great Alaskan Venture, 1791-1867* (New York, 1965), pp. 105-129.

132. Rezanov called him "Don José de Arillaga, Governor of both Californias."

133. For a detailed account of the first Boston ships in California in 1796 and their conflicts with Spanish authorities, see A. Ogden, *The California Sea Otter Trade 1784-1848* (Berkeley and Los Angeles, 1941), pp. 32-44.

134. In a number of details the text of Rezanov's letter to Rumiantsev of 17/29 June 1806 (cited here as published by Tikhmenev), differs little from the cited version preserved in the archives. Cf. Tikhmenev, *Istoricheskoe Obozrenie,* vol. 2, Supplements, p. 264; TsGIA, f. 13, op. 1, d. 687, l. 15.

135. The opinion that Concepción did not learn the exact circumstances of Rezanov's death until 1842 (see Jensen, *America and Russia,* p. 49) apparently is mistaken since Baranov considered it his duty to inform her father of this tragic event in 1808; see GBL OR, f. 204, k. 32, d. 10.

136. TsGIA, f. 13, op. 1, d. 687, l. 13.

137. 5/17 May 1806, in *VPR,* vol. 3, p. 692.

138. 28 Jan./9 Feb. 1808, in *VPR,* vol. 4, no. 65, pp. 163-164.

139. Cited from the text of Buldakov's dispatch to Alexander I, 28 Jan./9 Feb. 1808, *ibid.*

140. *VPR,* vol. 4, no. 102, pp. 235-236.

141. Stroganov to Rumiantsev, 28 May/9 June 1808, in AVPR, f. Kantseliariia, d. 7513, l. 680. On the events of 1808 in Spain, see I. M. Maisky, "Napoleon i Ispaniia" (Napoleon and Spain), *Iz istorii obshchestvennykh dvizhenii i mezhdunarodnykh otnoshenii* (From the History of the Social Movements and International Relations, Moscow, 1957), p. 299-305; I. M. Maisky, *Ispaniia 1808-1917* (Spain, 1808-1917, Moscow, 1957), pp. 42-58.

142. An interesting note on the opening of trade with Spanish America (undated, on the kind of paper used in 1805) is preserved in GBL OR, f. 255, k. 15, d. 33. It contains a proposal to write to Madrid for permission to send three Russian ships to Havana, Puerto Rico, and Buenos Aires. In the opinion of the author of the note this could effect the conclusion of a treaty of commerce enabling Russia to send one or two ships with Russian products to New Spain. In TsGIA (f. 13, op. 2, d. 1417) are preserved some documents connected with the request of the merchant Ivan Kremer for permission to send to South America two ships under the Brazilian flag, laden with Russian cargo; see Kremer to Rumiantsev, 23 May/4 June 1808, in *VPR,* vol. 4, no. 122, pp. 272-273. For other material connected with the project of commercial connections with Spanish America, see N. N. Bolkhovitinov, comp., "Otnoshenie Rossii k nachalu voiny Latinskoi Ameriki za nezavisimost' " (Russia's Attitude to the Inception of Latin America's War of Independence), *Istoricheskii arkhiv,* 1962, no. 3.

143. Baranov to Larionov, 24 July/5 Aug. 1800, in Tikhmenev, *Istoricheskoe obozrenie,* vol. 2, Supplements, p. 145.

144. Khlebnikov, *Zhizneopisanie A. A. Baranova,* pp. 63-64; Tikhmenev, *Istoricheskoe obozrenie,* 1:86.

145. Ogden's monograph supplies a useful, albeit incomplete, list of the vessels which touched the northwest coast of America (see *The California Sea Otter Trade,* Appendix, pp. 155-182). See also the recent article by Mary E. Wheeler, "Empires in Conflict and Cooperation. The 'Bostonians' and the Russian-American Company," *Pacific Historical Review,* 40: 419-441 (Nov. 1941).

146. AVPR, f. Gl. arkh. II-3, 1805-1817, op. 34, d. 8, 1. 20. Here (as in other instances where I could not establish the precise English spelling of proper names), I am keeping the transcription of the Russian originals, although it might not correspond to modern rules.

147. Khlebnikov, *Zhizneopisanie A. A. Baranova,* pp. 75-77.

148. Tikhmenev, *Istoricheskoe obozrenie,* 1:93.

149. See *ibid.,* 1:144-145; vol. 2, Supplements, pp. 203-204. This voyage became the subject of the book published in the United States.

150. See Capt. John D'Wolf, *A Voyage to the North Pacific and a Journey through Siberia More Than Half a Century Ago* (Cambridge, 1861). For the evaluation of D'Wolf's book see Babey, *Americans in Russia,* p. 139.

151. Baranov to I. A. Kuskov, 24 March/5 April 1808, in GBL OR, f. 204, k. 32, d. 6, 1. 97 verso ff.; Khlebnikov, *Zhisneopisanie A. A. Baranova,* pp. 108-114; Tikhmenev, *Istoricheskoe obozrenie,* 1:169-171; *Materialy dlia istorii russkikh zaselenii po beregam Vostochnogo okeana"* (Materials for the History of Russian Settlements on the Shores of the Pacific, St. Petersburg, 1861), 3:14-15.

152. "Estimate of the fur goods sold into foreign hands in America from the time of the establishment of the Russian settlements until 1 January 1808," in AVPR, f. RAK, d. 183, 1. 1.

153. Baranov to Kuskov, 18/30 June 1807, in GBL OR, f. 204, k. 32, d. 6, 1. 86; Tikhmenev, *Istoricheskoe obozrenie,* 1:171; Ogden, *The California Sea Otter Trade,* p. 50.

154. Khlebnikov, *Zhizneopisanie A. A. Baranova,* p. 121; Ogden, *The California Sea Otter Trade,* pp. 52-53. For the text of the contract between Baranov and Eayrs of 19/31 May 1808, see GBL OR, f. 204, k. 32, d. 11.

155. See *ibid.,* d. 6.

156. To the Directors of the Russian-American Company, 15/27 Feb. 1806, in Tikhmenev, *Istoricheskoe obozrenie,* vol. 2, Supplements, p. 235.

157. The quotations here are from the "Note on the Commerce of North Americans in the Russian colonies in America" (AVPR, f. Kantseliariia, d. 12182, 1. 31-32) and from the instructions of the Russian-American Company to Dashkov of 20 Aug./1 Sept. 1808 (AVPR, f. Gl. arkh. II-3, 1805-1817, op. 34, d. 8, 1. 18ff.).

158. *VPR,* vol. 4, no. 104, pp. 241-243.

159. *Ibid.,* no. 106, pp. 246-247 (the date, in Rumiantsev's hand, is illegible); TsGIA, f. 13, d. 382, 1. 5.

160. *VPR,* vol. 4, no. 6, pp. 246, 247.

161. *Ibid.,* no. 117, pp. 267-268.

162. AVPR, f. Kantseliariia, d. 3335, 1. 5-6.

163. NA, Consular Despatches; St. Petersburg, vol. 1.

Part Three. Russian-American Rapprochement, 1808-1812

1. Jefferson, *Writings,* 11:103-106.

2. On the role of Russia in the Baltic trade of the United States see also the

recent studies of Rasch, "American Trade in the Baltic, 1783-1801," *Scand. Econ. Hist. Rev.,* 13(1965):31-64; and Crosby, *America, Russia, Hemp, and Napoleon.*

3. *VPR,* vol. 3, no. 180, p. 459.

4. Marx and Engels, *Sochineniia,* 2:567-568.

5. A. J. H. Clercq, *Recueil des traités de la France* (Paris, 1880), 2:194-196. Somewhat later, on 17 Dec. 1807, an even stricter decree was issued in Milan, according to which a vessel under any flag, which visited an English port or submitted to any demand of British ships, was held to be the enemy's property and was subject to confiscation upon entering a French port (*ibid.,* pp. 242-244).

6. Napoleon to Talleyrand, 14 March 1807, *Correspondance de Napoléon Ier* (32 vols., Paris, 1858-1870), 14:440.

7. See *VPR,* vol. 3, nos. 257-258, pp. 631-646.

8. N. K. Shil'der, *Imperator Aleksandr* (Emperor Alexander, St. Petersburg, 1904), 2:299.

9. Albert Sorel, *Evropa i frantsuzskaia revoliutsiia* (Europe and the French Revolution), transl. N. I. Kareev (8 vols., St. Petersburg, 1892-1908), vol. 7: *Kontinental'naia blokada—Velikaia imperiia 1806-1812* (Continental Blockade—The Great Empire, 1806-1812, St. Petersburg, 1908); A. Vandal', *Napoleon i Aleksandr I, Franko-russkii soiuz vo vremia Pervoi imperii* (Napoleon and Alexander I: The Franco-Russian Alliance during the First Empire, 3 vols., St. Petersburg, 1910-1913); E. V. Tarle, *Sochineniia,* vol. 3.

10. *VPR,* vol. 4, no. 37, pp. 98-101; *PSZRI,* 29:1316.

11. A. V. Predtechensky, "K voprosu o vliianii' Kontinental'noi blokady na sostoianie torgovli i promyshlennosti v Rossii." (On the Problem of the Influence of the Continental Blockade on the State of Commerce and Industry in Russia), *Izvestiia AN SSSR, Otd. Obshch. nauk,* 1931, no. 8, p. 894.

12. *American State Papers, Commerce and Navigation,* 2:635; *Ocherki novoi i noveishei istorii SShA* (Moscow, 1960), 1:139.

13. J. F. Zimmerman, *Impressment of American Seamen* (New York, 1925).

14. Marx and Engels, *Sochineniia* 15:454.

15. Henry Adams, *History,* 4:1-26.

16. See correspondingly, G. Martens, *Nouveau Recueil,* 1:31-33, 444-452; 3:8. On the history of the Orders in Council, see Henry Adams, *History,* 4:79-104.

17. Marx and Engels, *Sochineniia* 15:454.

18. F. Crouzet, "Groupes de pression et politique de blocus: remarques sur les origines des Ordres en Conseil de novembre 1807," *Revue Historique,* 228 (1962):72. For a critical survey of Crouzet's works see V. G. Sirotkin in *Novaia i noveishaia istoriia,* 1964, no. 3 and in *Voprosy Istorii,* 1963, no. 3.

19. Henry Adams, *History,* 4:167, 170.

20. Gallatin to Jefferson, 18 Dec. 1807, in Gallatin, *Writings,* 1:368.

21. Richardson, *Messages,* 1:433; *Annals of Congress,* 10th Congress, 1st Session, pp. 50-51, 1216-1228.

22. At the moment of decision in Washington the official text of the Order in Council of 11 Nov. 1807 had not yet been received, and it is not mentioned in the President's message of 18 Dec.

23. *VPR,* vol. 3, no. 31, pp. 93-95.

24. Jefferson, *Writings,* 11:292; F. R. Dulles, *The Road to Teheran* (Princeton, 1944), p. 17.

25. Madison to Armstrong, 9 Sept. 1808, in NA, Diplomatic Instructions: All Countries, 7:17 (in original, mistakenly dated 1809).

Chapter 7. The Establishment of Diplomatic Relations

1. A number of documents from AVPR were published by the author in 1959. See *Novaia i noveishaia Istoriia,* 1959, no. 2, pp. 151-162.

2. M. M. Alopeus was in London since Feb. 1807 on a specal assignment. For practical purposes he fulfilled the role of Russian minister.

3. Alopeus to A. Ia. Budberg, 9/21 Aug. 1807, in *Novaia i moveishaia istoriia,* 1959, no. 2, p. 155.

4. To Budberg, 13/25 Sept. 1807, *ibid.,* pp. 155-156. The prevailing opinion in the American literature (including recent publications) is that the establishment of diplomatic relations with Russia in 1808-1809 was the result of an overture to the United States made by the tsarist government, and by Emperor Alexander I in particular. (See Mainwaring, *John Quincy Adams and Russia,* p. 9). Present documentation establishes beyond doubt that the initiative came from the government of the United States and from President Jefferson personally.

5. AVPR, f. Kantseliariia, d. 6810, ll. 300, 370-371.

6. Rumiantsev to Alopeus, 6/18 Oct. 1807, in *Novaia i noveishaia istoriia,* 1959, no. 2, pp. 156-157.

7. Alopeus to Rumiantsev, 2/14 Dec. 1807, in AVPR, f. Kantseliariia, d. 6810, l. 550.

8. TsGIA, f. 13, op. 2, d. 1408, l. 1.

9. *Ibid.,* l. 4; TsGADA, f. 276, op. 1, d. 675, l. 2.

10. 13/25 June 1808, in AVPR, f. Kantseliariia, d. 3334, 1.4; *ASPFR,* 3:298; Harris to Madison, 7/19 June 1808, in NA, Consular Despatches: St. Petersburg, vol. 1.

11. TsGIA, f. 13, op. 2, d. 1408, l. 2. The official paper appointing A. Ia. Dashkov as a consul-general in Philadelphia was signed by Alexander I on 10/22 July 1808. The original is kept among Dashkov's personal papers in TsGAOR, f. 907, op. 1, d. 57.

12. Main Office of the Russian-American Company to Dashkov, 21 July/2 Aug. 1808, *ibid.,* d. 52, l. 1; TsGIA, f. 13, op. 2, d. 1408, l. 7.

13. Dashkov to Rumiantsev, 25 July/6 Aug. 1808, *ibid.,* l. 6.

14. To Dashkov, 30 July/11 Aug. 1808, in TsGAOR, f. 907, op. 1, d. 59, l. 1.

15. For the full text of the instruction see *Novaia i noveishaia istoriia,* 1959, no. 2, pp. 157-160. The date of the signing is established from the extract made for the Main Office of Russian-American Company (AVPR, f. G. arkh. II-3, 1805-1817, op. 34, d. 8) and from a reference in Dashkov's report to Rumiantsev, of 1 May 1810 (AVPR, f. Kantseliariia, d. 9238, l. 25).

16. In the original: "îles du Vent et Sous-le-Vent, de celui du Mexique, de la Terre Ferme et du Pérou."

17. Minutes of the meeting; see TsGADA, f. 276, op. 1, d. 675, l. 14.

18. K. K. Fonton occupied the post of Consul-General in Ragusa, Dalmatia, and Kotora, since 1801.

19. See Minutes of the Meeting of the College of Commerce of 10/22 July 1808, in *VPR,* vol. 4, no. 135, pp. 302-305; also TsGADA, f. 276, op. 1, d. 675, ll. 6-12; and TsGIA, f. 13, op. 2, d. 1408, ll. 9-14.

20. So in the document.

21. Buldakov, Kramer, and Zelensky to Dashkov, 20 Aug./1 Sept. 1808, in TsGAOR, f. 907, op. 1, d. 56, ll. 2-7; AVPR, f. Gl. arkh. II-3, 1805-1817, op. 34, d. 8, ll. 18-28.

22. The Lewis and Clark expedition (1804-1808) which was sent on Jefferson's initiative to the mouth of the Columbia River.

23. *VPR,* vol. 4, no. 152, p. 336.

24. For more details on Evstaf'ev's activity in the United States see Chapter 12 of the present work. Some interesting, although incomplete, information is cited by M. P. Alexeev in a short article, "A. G. Evstaf'ev-russko-amerikanskii pisatel' nachala XIX veka" (A. G. Evstaf'ev, Russian-American Writer of the Beginning of the Nineteenth Century), *Nauchnyi biulleten' LGU,* 1946, no. 8, pp. 22-27.

25. Minutes of the meeting of the College of Commerce, 14/26 July 1808, in TsGADA, f. 276, op. 1, d. 675, ll. 16-17.

26. Minutes of the meeting of the College of Commerce, 20 July/1 Aug. 1808, *ibid.,* ll. 18-21.

27. Jefferson, *Writings,* 12:156; Hildt, *Early Diplomatic Negotiations,* p. 39.

28. Madison to Short, 8 Sept. 1808, in NA, Diplomatic Instructions: All Countries, 7:11-14. The same instructions were given to John Quincy Adams when he was appointed instead of Short to St. Petersburg (J. Q. Adams, *Writings.* 3:322-328).

29. Jefferson to Alexander I and Jefferson to Short, 29 Aug. 1808 in Jefferson, *Writings,* 12:153-154; Hildt, *Early Diplomatic Negotiations,* p. 39.

30. To Short, 8 Sept. 1808, in NA, Diplomatic Instructions: All Countries, 7:12; see also Madison to Pinckney, 9 Sept. 1808, *ibid.,* p. 15.

31. Madison to Short, 8 Sept. 1808, *ibid.,* p. 12.

32. Armstrong to Madison, 24 Nov. 1808, *ASPFR,* 3:299.

33. Armstrong to Rumiantsev, 9 Dec. 1808, in AVPR, f. Kantseliariia, d. 3333, l. 3.

34. Rumiantsev to Armstrong, 9 Dec. 1808, *ibid.,* l. 2.

35. Richardson, *Messages,* 1:461.

36. John Quincy Adams to Louisa Catherine Adams, 9 March 1809, in Adams, *Writings,* 3:291; also Hildt, *Early Diplomatic Negotiations,* p. 41, with reference to a letter from Pickering to King of 2 Feb. 1810; and J. Q. Adams, *Memoirs,* 1:544.

37. Henry Adams, *History,* 4:467.

38. J. Q. Adams, *Memoirs,* 1:545.

39. See Henry Adams, *History,* 5:11; J. Q. Adams, *Writings,* 3:291.

40. Jefferson, *Writings,* 12:264; Henry Adams, *History,* 4:468.

41. Short to Rumiantsev, 1 May 1809, in AVPR, f. Kantseliariia, d. 3337, ll. 2-4.

42. TsGIA, f. 1329, op. 3, d. 301, l. 1.

43. *Ibid.,* l. 2.

44. Rumiantsev to Harris, 4/16 April 1809, in *Novaia i noveishaia istoriia,* 1959, no. 2, p. 160.

45. The Ukase to the College of Foreign Affairs, 20 April/1 May 1809, in TsGIA, f. 1329, op. 3, d. 301, l. 215.

46. See letter of F. P. Pahlen to Rumiantsev, 22 June/4 July 1809, in AVPR, f. Kantseliariia, d. 12161, ll. 4-5.

47. Pahlen to Rumiantsev, 25 July/6 Aug. 1809, *ibid.,* ll. 6-7.

48. Rumiantsev to Pahlen, 2/14 July 1809, *ibid.,* d. 12160, ll. 2-3.

49. For the full text of Pahlen's memorandum see *ibid.,* d. 12161, ll. 22-25.

50. Dashkov learned of the Senate's rejection of Short's nomination literally on the eve of his departure for the United States from Dunkirk in early May 1809; see Dashkov to Rumiantsev, 6 May 1809, in TsGAOR, f. 907, op. 1, d. 57, l. 8.

51. AVPR, f. Kantseliariia, d. 9236, l. 13.

52. TsGADA, f. 276, d. 675, l. 27. His voyage was not without adventure: The *Nadezhda,* on which he traveled, was shipwrecked, and most of the material he

had received from the College of Commerce perished. He managed to save only some papers, in particular the abovementioned "admonition," by tying them to his person (see Evstaf'ev to the College of Commerce, 23 Feb./3 March 1809, *ibid.*, l. 25). The College of Commerce was in no hurry to replace Evstaf'ev's papers, and he had to ask for them twice, from Boston (see Evstaf'ev's reports of 21 Sept. 1809 and 10 April 1810, *ibid.*, ll. 27, 29). For the dispatching of the appropriate material see *ibid.*, ll. 28, 33.

53. To Robert Smith, 2 July 1809, in NA, Russia: Notes, 1:5. Along with his letter Dashkov forwarded a number of Harris' reports.

54. To Rumiantsev, 22 July 1809, in AVPR, f. Kantseliariia, d. 9236, l. 13.

55. For the full text of Dashkov's note of 24 July 1809 (Supplement F), see *ibid.*, ll. 24-28. Strictly speaking, Dashkov, being only a chargé d'affaires, could not expect to be introduced to the President. The exception attested to the importance which the government of the United States attributed to its relations with Russia, and was explained by the fact that Dashkov had a letter from Alexander I (Hildt, *Early Diplomatic Negotiations,* pp. 42-43).

56. For the sake of fairness, one should note that the speech prepared by Dashkov was really worthy of attention, and even differed from the usual formal samples by a certain individuality. "Living among your fellow citizens I shall often feel I have not changed my residence. I shall always admire the native creations of genius, the rapid progress of civilization, and a wilderness once more yielding in every respect to enterprises of men who are protected by laws, guided by science, and successfully cultivating the arts."
(Supplement A; See AVPR, f. Kantseliariia, d. 9236, l. 15; and NA, Russia: Notes, 1:16.)

57. Dashkov related the circumstances bearing on the appointment of the American envoy to Russia in a special memorandum (Supplement D), AVPR, f. Kantseliariia, d. 9236, l. 21.

58. For the Act of recognition of Dashkov as Consul-General, signed by Madison and Robert Smith, 15 July 1809, see NA, Russia: Notes, vol. 1 (the number of the list is unclear).

59. Supplement "S"; see AVPR, f. Kantseliariia, d. 9236, ll. 17-20.

60. Jefferson to Dashkov, 12 Aug. 1809 and Dashkov to Jefferson, 2 Sept. 1809, in Jefferson, *Writings,* 12:303-304; TsGAOR, f. 907, op. 1, d. 57, ll. 11-12.

61. See Richardson, *Messages,* 1:471; *ASPFR,* 3:298.

62. AVPR, f. Kantseliariia, d. 9236, l. 28. One should note incidentally that Hildt is mistaken in dating Dashkov's arrival in the United States in June and assuming that Adams' appointment took place "several days later" (see *Early Diplomatic Negotiations,* pp. 42-43). In reality, it was just the opposite. Dashkov arrived in Philadelphia on 1 July, while the appointment of Adams was confirmed on 27 June, i.e., several days earlier. See also Robert Smith to J. Q. Adams, 29 June 1809, in NA, Diplomatic Instructions: All Countries, 7:45-46. Having learned of Adams' appointment, Dashkov exchanged friendly letters with him and forwarded to St. Petersburg his first reports from America through Adams (see Dashkov to Adams, 10, 22, 23 July 1809, in TsGAOR, f. 907, op. 1, d. 57, ll. 9, 10).

63. A letter to Skelton Jones of 17 April 1809 gives a brief idea of the preceding activity of John Quincy Adams (see Adams, *Writings,* 3:292-305).

64. To Abigail Adams, 10 March 1801, in Adams, *Writings,* 2:512.

65. *Ibid.,* p. 513.

66. See Bemis, *John Quincy Adams,* pp. 143-149.

67. To Robert Smith, 5 July 1809, in Adams, *Writings,* 3:328-330. (This document, like all of the other letters of John Quincy Adams to the Secretary of State, is kept in NA, Diplomatic Despatches: Russia, vol. 1.)

68. J. Q. Adams to Robert Smith, 7 July 1809, in Adams, *Writings,* 3:330.

69. *Ibid.,* p. 331. During his stay in St. Petersburg Adams continued regular correspondence with William Gray, looked after his son Francis, and counseled Gray on handling his business in Russia. (See AP, John Quincy Adams, Letterbooks, "Private," Reels 135, 139; Bemis, *John Quincy Adams,* p. 154.)

70. J. Q. Adams, *Memoirs,* 2:3. The frigate *Essex* was ordered by the President for Adams' voyage, but it arrived in Boston a day after the Minister had departed. (Bemis, *John Quincy Adams,* p. 154; Adams, *Writings,* 3:331.)

71. Smith to Adams, 20 July 1809, in NA, Diplomatic Instructions: All Countries, 7:47-48. For the text of the instructions of Madison to Short of 8 Sept. 1808, and to Armstrong of 14 March 1806, see J. Q. Adams, *Writings,* 3:322-328. On the basis of his conversations with the President in the middle of June 1809, Dashkov came to the conclusion that the Government of the United States apparently desired to form a treaty of commerce with Russia, and he thought that Adams was entrusted with this task. "If the time for such a treaty has come," Dashkov wrote further, "I shall do everything in my power to collect a number of facts for Your Honor's information, referring to the commerce and treaties of commerce of the United States with other powers, which could be in some measure useful for the greater advantage and stability of our settlements in America." See AVPR, f. Kantseliariia, d. 9236, 1. 28. Although at that time Adams had no official assignment to conclude a treaty of commerce, in general, such a possibility apparently was not excluded.

72. Adams, *Memoirs,* 2:45.

73. *Novaia i noveishaia istoriia,* 1959, no. 2, pp. 160-161.

74. Adams to Smith, 14/26 Oct. 1809, in Adams, *Writings,* 3:351-352; NA, Diplomatic Despatches: Russia, vol. 1.

75. See Adams, *Memoirs,* 2:48-49.

76. *Ibid.,* p. 53.

77. *Ibid.,* pp. 52-53; Adams to Smith, 6 Nov. 1809, in NA, Diplomatic Despatches: Russia, vol. 1.

78. AVPR, f. Kantseliariia, d. 12160, ll. 7-8.

79. Alexander I to Pahlen, 27 Dec. 1809/8 Jan. 1810, in AVPR, f. Pos-vo v Vashingtone, d. 2, ll. 32-42. This document was published in part in *Novaia i noveishaia istoriia,* 1959, no. 2, pp. 161-162. Even though the instructions were signed by Alexander I and, in accordance with the practice of those days, were presented in his name, the main part of their preparation belonged to Rumiantsev, whose signature also appears on the document. It is interesting to note that already on 15 Nov. 1809, in his conversation with John Quincy Adams, the Chancellor had very circumstantially outlined the general policy of Russia toward the United States and even proposed that in drawing the instructions for the Comte de Pahlen he would insert anything that Adams thought might be useful "to the great end of drawing closer the relations between the two countries." See Adams, *Memoirs,* 2:66.

80. It is characteristic that in the abovementioned conversation with Adams, Rumiantsev noted that "the English exclusive maritime pretensions, and views of usurpation upon the rights of other nations, made it essential to them, and especially to Russia, that some great commercial state should be supported as their rival; that the United States of America were such a state, and the highest in-

terest of Russia was to support and favor them, as by their relative situation the two powers could never be in any manner dangerous to each other; that he had been many years inculcating this doctrine at this Court; that the Emperor had always manifested a favorable opinion of it" (Adams, *Memoirs*, 2:65).

81. Pahlen to Rumiantsev, 16/28 Jan. 1810, in AVPR, f. Kantseliariia, d. 12163, l. 6. The dispatch of 15/27 Nov. was received by him not long before (see Pahlen to Rumiantsev, 8/20 Jan. 1810, *ibid.*, l. 2).

82. See Pahlen to Rumiantsev, 2/14 June 1810, *ibid.*, l. 20; Pahlen to Smith, 12 June 1810, in NA, Russia: Notes, 1:30-31.

83. Pahlen to Alexander I, 14/26 June 1810, in AVPR, f. Kantseliariia, d. 12163, ll. 21-24. For the text of the letter of credence of 10/22 May 1809, see NA, Russia: Notes 1:36-40.

84. Pahlen to Rumiantsev, 18/30 June 1810, in AVPR, f. Kantseliariia, d. 12163, l. 29.

85. Pahlen to Alexander I, 14/26 June 1810, *ibid.*, l. 23.

Chapter 8. The Expansion of Trade Contacts

1. *Annals of Congress*, 10th Congress, 2nd Session, p. 1539.

2. See Perkins, *Prologue to War*, pp. 223-260; Henry Adams, *History*, 4:432-453; Herbert Heaton, "Non-Importation, 1806-1812," *The Journal of Economic History*, 1(1941):179-198.

3. Harris to Rumiantsev, 14/26 July 1809, in AVPR, f. Kantseliariia, d. 3337, l. 6. In the margin there is a penciled note in Rumiantsev's (?) hand: "faire un extrait pour la Gazette de Commerce." See also Dashkov's dispatches from France for 18 March and 20, 27 April 1809, in TsGAOR, f. 907, op. 1, d. 57, ll. 4, 6, 7-8.

4. The author of this work is an interesting personality in the history of Russian culture. Pavel Petrovich Svin'in (1788-1839), a man of letters, an artist, and founder of the Journal *Otechestvennye Zapiski*, was connected with the Ministry for Foreign Affairs as secretary to the elderly Chancellor Vorontsov since March 1805. He was also a member of Seniavin's expedition to the Mediterranean; and on 5/17 Aug. 1811, he was appointed by Alexander I's ukase to the post of secretary to the Consul-General in Philadelphia. Having spent about two years in the United States, he became well acquainted in the course of his activity with the general situation in the country and especially with the state of Russian-American trade (see GPB, f. 679 (P. P. Svin'in), d. 9, and others). Upon his return to Russia he published a number of books and articles on the subject of his American obser-vations, such as the state of commerce between the United States and Russia, the invention of the steamship, General Moreau, and the visual arts in the United States, which have not lost their interest even today (see A. Yarmolinsky, *Picturesque United States of America 1811, 1812, 1813: Being a Memoir on Paul Svenin* [New York, 1930]; Dimitri Fedotoff-White, "A Russian Sketches Philadel-phia: 1811-1813," *The Pennsylvania Magazine of History and Biography*, 75:2-24 [Jan. 1951]; Dieter Boden, *Das Amerikabild in Russischen Schriftern bis zum Ende des 19. Jahrhunderts* [Hamburg, 1968], pp. 53-72). Later, during a difficult period of extreme reaction in Russia, in the 1820's and 1830's, Svin'in joined with those who celebrated nationalism, autocracy, and orthodoxy. Condemning this aspect of his activity and mocking his "patriotism," Pushkin remarked: "Pavlusha swore that there were in the home of his parents a cook's apprentice-astronomer, a post-boy-historian, and that the poultry-man Proshka wrote verses better than

Lomonosov." See A. S. Pushkin, *Polnoe sobranie sochinenii* (Moscow, 1949), 11:101.

5. I preserve Svin'in's order of subject matter, even though it does not correspond precisely to the importance of various articles of Russian-American commerce. Since all concrete data on the volume of Russian exports to the United States was omitted from Svin'in's book, *Opyt zhivopisnogo puteshestviia po Severnoi Amerike* (pp. 28-29), I reproduce them from the earlier magazine publication (see *Syn otechestva,* 1814, ch. 18, pp. 7-11).

6. TsGIA, f. 37, op. 3, d. 192, ll. 4-5.

7. Here and below I cite the dispatch of Section II of the Department of Mining and Salt Affairs of 31 March/12 April 1814, in TsGIA, f. 37, op. 3, d. 192, ll. 1-3.

8. Pitkin, *A Statistical View,* p. 232.

9. *Ibid.;* TsGAOR, f. 907, op. 1, d. 107, ll. 101-102.

10. Compiled from Pitkin, *A Statistical View,* p. 231; Evans, *Exports, Domestic,* p. 80.

11. *Historical Statistics of the United States,* p. 538.

12. In the period of the greatest activity in the American trade in 1807, about 90 ships entered Russian ports (see *Gosudarstvennaia torgovlia 1807 q. v raznykh ee vidakh,* Table XXII).

13. TsGAOR, f. 907, op. 1, d. 68, l. 1. For the sake of comparison it should be noted that the general number of all other foreign vessels entering the port of St. Petersburg was 389, including 65 from Sweden, 58 from Prussia, and so on.

14. 5/17 Jan. 1812, in *VPR,* vol. 6, no. 104, pp. 259-261; M. F. Zlotnikov, *Kontinental'naia blokada i Rossiia* (The Continental Blockade and Russia, Moscow and Leningrad, 1966), pp. 296-297.

15. 22 July 1811, in NA, Diplomatic Despatches: Russia, vol. 2.

16. Crosby, *America, Russia, Hemp, and Napoleon,* p. 224-225. Hazard was appointed to the post of American Consul in Archangel in July 1811, and regularly informed both the State Department and John Quincy Adams as to the state of American commerce in the White Sea. See Rumiantsev to Adams, 18/30 July 1811, and Hazard's numerous letters in AP, Letters Received and Other Loose Papers, Reels 412-415; NA, Despatches from the United States Consuls in Archangel, 1811-1869, vol. I (Microcopy No. 481).

17. Rumiantsev to Adams, 11/23 March 1810, in AVPR, f. Kantseliariia, d. 3338, l. 4. For Adams' reply of 14/26 March 1810, see *ibid.,* d. 3339, l. 5. See also Dashkov to Duc de Richelieu, 4 Oct. 1809, in TsGAOR, f. 907, op. 1, d. 57, ll. 12-13.

18. J. Q. Adams, *Memoirs,* 2:154. In 1810 and 1811, 56 and 65 American ships arrived at Archangel (Crosby, *America, Russia, Hemp, and Napoleon,* p. 191-192, 224). Even in 1812, in spite of a sharp reduction in the general volume of trade, 32 American ships visited this port (*Report of American Trade at Archangel in 1812* [data summarized]); AP, Letters Received and Other Loose Papers, Reel 414; Hazard to Monroe, 1/13 Jan. 1813, *ibid.,* Reel 415).

19. Pitkin, *A Statistical View,* pp. 90-91, 122-123, 125-126, 128-129, 131-132, 134-136, 157, 159, 161. There are no data for 1806, and the embargo was introduced in 1808.

20. Svin'in, "Vzgliad," p. 6.

21. See E. V. Tarle, *Sochineniia,* 3:364-365. Tarle's deductions were recently developed by Zlotnikov who noted in particular that in the years of the blockade "Russia supplied western European markets with considerable quantities of

cotton, sugar, dyes, metals, coffee, cocoa, spices, and other colonial products. This intermediary trade in 1812 brought 2,664,200 silver rubles in profits" (*Kontinental'naia blokada,* pp. 325-326.) See also A. L. Narochnitsky "Ob istoricheskom znachenii kontinental'noi blokady" (On the Historical Signifi-icance of the Continental Blockade), *Novaia i noveishaia istoriia,* 1965, no. 6, pp. 51-63.

22. See V. K. Iatsunsky, "O vliianii kontinental'noi blokady na russkuiu khlopchatobumazhnuiu promyshlennost' " (The Influence of the Continental Blockade on the Russian Cotton Industry), *Voprosy narodnogo khoziaistva SSSR. K 85-letiiu akd. S. G. Strumilina* (Moscow, 1962), pp. 300-310. This article is based on the study of the Alexandrov Manufactory's archives (TsGIA, f. 758, op. 24). Of great interest are the observations of John Quincy Adams, who visited the manufactory in April 1810. The American Minister left a circumstan-tial description of the hard conditions of life and labor at the Manufactory which employed about five hundred orphans from Moscow and St. Petersburg, aged 8-10 and 21-25. The strict regime of the establishment imposed barracks discipline and a 12-hour working day (not counting extra hours for which they were paid). See Adams, *Memoirs,* 2:111-115.

23. See *ibid.,* p. 114.

24. See Iatsunsky, "O vliianii kontinental'noi blokady," pp. 302-307.

25. The Board of Directors of the Alexandrov Manufactory to Rumiantsev, 5/17 March 1806, in TsGIA, f. 13, op. 2, d. 1156, l. 1.

26. Alexander I to Rumiantsev, 16/28 March 1806, *ibid.,* l. 5; 15/27 March 1807, *ibid.,* f. 1329, op. 3, 1807, d. 292, l. 611.

27. The Board of Directors of the Alexandrov Manufactory to Rumiantsev, 23 Nov./5 Dec. 1807, *ibid.,* f. 13, op. 2, d. 1156, ll. 23-24. (The contents and quantity of the cargo delivered to the Alexandrov Manufactory from Philadelphia have not been ascertained. The only known fact is that "the duty on it was up to 73 thousand rubles," *ibid.,* l. 28.)

28. See Iatsunsky, "O vliianii kontinental'noi blokady," p. 304.

29. See Caulaincourt to Napoleon, 5 Feb. 1810; to Champagny, 21 March 1811; [Romanov] Nikolai Mikhailouid, *Diplomaticheskie snosheniia Rossii i Frantsii . . . 1808-1812* (Diplomatic Relations between Russia and France . . . 1808-1812, 7 vols., St. Petersburg and Petrograd, 1905-1914), 4:271, 5:370, and others.

30. A. V. Predtechensky, "K voprosu o vliianii kontinental'noi blokady" (The Problem of the Influence of the Continental Blockade), *Izvestiia AN SSSR. Otd. Obshchestvennykh nauk,* 1931, no. 8, p. 898.

31. See *Sbornik svedenii i materialov po ministerstvu finansov* (Collection of Information and Materials on the Ministry of Finance, St. Petersburg, 1865), vol. 3, no. 9, p. 159; M. I. Tugan-Baranovsky, *Russkaia fabrika* (Russian Factory, Petrograd, 1922), p. 57; M. N. Pokrovsky, *Imperialisticheskaia voina* (The Imperialistic War, Moscow, 1934), p. 11; Iatsunsky, "O vliianii kontinental'noi blokady," pp. 308-309.

32. Quoted from A. V. Predtechensky, "k voprosu o vliianii kontinental'noi blokady," p. 898.

33. *Ibid.,* pp. 918-919.

34. See J. Q. Adams, *Memoirs,* 2:21ff.; Adams to R. Smith, 23 Sept. 1809, in *Writings,* 3:346-347; Henry Adams, *History,* 5:409; Bemis, *John Quincy Adams,* p. 170.

35. Adams, *Memoirs,* 2:36; *Writings,* 3:348; Adams to Smith, 4 Oct. 1809, in NA, Diplomatic Despatches: Russia, vol. 1.

36. Adams to Smith, 14/26 Oct. 1809, in NA, Diplomatic Dispatches: Russia, vol. I.

37. For a detailed account of the conversation, see Adams to Smith, 7 Jan. 1810, *ibid.;* Adams, *Writings,* 3:372ff.; *Memoirs,* 2:81ff. The contents of Adams' dispatch, as in other cases, coincide almost word for word with his Diary notations.

38. Adams, *Memoirs,* 2:83.

39. *Ibid.,* p. 87.

40. *Ibid.*

41. *Ibid.,* p. 88.

42. *Ibid.,* p. 89.

43. *Ibid.,* pp. 100-101; Adams to Smith, 24 March 1810, in NA, Diplomatic Despatches: Russia, vol. 1.

44. Commenting on the results of this mission, the Russian minister in Washington wrote on 3/15 Dec. 1811, that the Danish government had suspended judicial proceedings against those captured ships which had possessed documents of the origin of their goods before 13 Nov. 1811; that, however, it refused to revoke the verdicts which were accorded earlier, as well as that article of the royal instructions which declared the vessels under British escort as prize (Dashkov to Rumiantsev, 3/15 Dec. 1811, in AVPR, f. Kantseliariia, d. 9240, ll. 74-90).

45. See Bemis, *John Quincy Adams,* p. 171; also *ASPFR, 3:*327, 344, 523, 529-536; J. B. Moore, *Digest of International Arbitrations* (Washington, 1898), 5:4549ff.

46. Smith to Adams, 21 June 1810, in NA, Diplomatic Instructions: All Countries, 7:102-103.

47. To Rumiantsev, 9/21 Oct. 1810, in AVPR, f. Kantseliariia, d. 3339, l. 20. As was usually done, Rumiantsev reported the contents of the note to the Emperor, who then authorized the Chancellor to inform the Minister of his interest in the well-being and prosperity of the United States. See Rumiantsev to Adams, 27 Oct./8 Nov. 1810, *ibid.,* d. 3338, ll. 7-8.

48. Henry Adams, *History,* 5:411.

49. Napoleon to Gaudin, 17 April 1808, in *Correspondance de Napoléon,* 17:16.

50. See Tarle, *Sochineniia,* 3:331.

51. G. Martens, *Nouveau Recueil,* 1:513-514; Tarle, *Sochineniia,* 3:203.

52. Martens, *Nouveau Recueil,* 1:522-523.

53. Cadore to Kurakin, 2 Dec. 1810, in *Correspondance de Napoléon,* 21:297. This question was also discussed by Adams and Rumiantsev on 28 Aug. 1810 (Adams, *Memoirs,* 2:157; *Writings,* 3:498).

54. *Correspondance de Napoléon,* 21:233-234. Napoleon's correspondence with the Tsar for 1801-1812 was published separately; see S. Tatistheff, *Alexandre Ier et Napoléon d'après leur correspondance inédite* (Paris, 1891).

55. Adams, *Memoirs,* 2:143ff.

56. *Ibid.,* p. 160.

57. One such tangled affair concerning an American ship which brought to Russia a forbidden cargo of English lead was presented for the minutes of the Committee of Ministers in a note of 8/20 Sept. 1808 (see TsGIA, f. 1263, op. 1, 1808, d. 7, ll. 28-31). Undoubtedly, in a number of cases, American ships carried English goods; in this sense the protests of the French government were quite justified. A considerable number of ships came from England in ballast, a fact openly admitted by Adams in his conversation with the French ambassador in St. Petersburg (see Adams, *Memoirs,* 2:307-308). Moreover, Levett Harris utilized his

connections in court and the good will of the tsarist government to build a fortune for himself by acting as advocate in dubious cases for exorbitant fees. It took Adams a long time to see through this unprincipled greed and venality, although as early as 1810 a certain Donovan had placed a complaint against Harris, stating that he personally had paid the Consul three thousand rubles (see AP, J. Q. Adams, Diary, 19 Sept. 1810, Reel 31, p. 155). Harris' activities in this respect became known to the public only after the American merchant William David Lewis, upon his return home from Russia in 1819, initiated a lawsuit against him. Harris was accused of using his official position for mercenary motives. In the course of a notorious and lengthy trial, Harris' lawyer admitted that Harris had made a fortune but contended that he had acted not as a consul but as a merchant! See Bemis, *John Quincy Adams,* p. 169; J. B. Rhoads, "Harris, Lewis and the Hollow Tree," *American Archivist,* 25:295-314 (July 1962); Mainwaring, *John Quincy Adams and Russia,* pp. 14, 61-62.

58. Adams, *Memoirs,* 2:147.

59. *Ibid.,* p. 180; AP, J. Q. Adams, Diary, Reel 31, p. 164; Adams to Smith, 12 Oct. 1810, in NA, Diplomatic Despatches: Russia, vol. 1; Bemis, *John Quincy Adams,* p. 174; Hildt, *Early Diplomatic Negotiations,* p. 52; *ASPFR,* 5:443.

60. Adams, *Memoirs,* 2:180.

61. Caulaincourt to Napoleon, 8 Dec. 1810, in *Diplomaticheskie snosheniia Rossii i Frantsii,* 5:221-230.

62. *Arkhiv Gosudarstvennogo soveta* (Archive of the State Council, St. Petersburg, 1881), vol. 4, pt. 2, pp. 1138-1152 (Minutes of the meeting of 2/14 Dec. 1810); *PSZRI,* 31:486-492, 45:58-62 (The Book of Tariffs, 3rd Section).

63. E. V. Tarle, *Napoleon* (Moscow, 1957), p. 272; *VPR,* vol. 6, nos. 5, 32, 135, 136, 139, and the corresponding notes.

64. *Ibid.,* pp. 694-695, 730-731, and others.

65. For extensive documentary material see *VPR,* vol. 6; *SbRIO,* vol. 21; and especially Ch. R. V. Nesselrode, *Lettres et papiers du chancelier comte de Nesselrode* (Paris, 1905), vol. 3:1805-1811. One should note, in particular, A. I. Chernyshev's dispatches of 3/15 Jan. and 9/21 Feb. 1811 (in *SbRIO,* 21:49-66, 145-156); letters of Nesselrode to Speransky of 4/16 Feb. (in Nesselrode, *Lettres,* 3:317-323) and 9/21 Feb. 1811 (in *VPR,* vol. 6, no. 26, pp. 75-77). For an analysis of Nesselrode's letters see E. V. Tarle, *Talleyrand* (Moscow, 1957), pp. 107-112.

66. A. N. Popov, *Otechestvennaia voina* (Patriotic War, Moscow, 1905), 1:138.

67. To Champagny, 15 Jan. 1811, in *Diplomaticheskie snosheniia Rossii i Frantsii,* 5:263.

68. Cited from Tarle, *Sochineniia,* 3:367.

69. Marx and Engels, *Sochineniia,* 22:30.

70. See especially Adams, *Memoirs,* 2:191-192, 194-195, 233-236, and also the numerous notes to Rumiantsev enclosed in a copy among Adams' dispatches, in NA, Diplomatic Despatches: Russia, vol. 1.

71. Adams to Smith, 26 March 1811, *ibid.,* vol. 2; Bemis, *John Quincy Adams,* p. 171.

72. Adams, *Memoirs,* 2:246.

73. *Ibid.,* p. 226. Judging by the entry in Adams' diary of 10 March 1811, Caulaincourt was informed that no American ship among those with which Adams was concerned had been confiscated (AP, J. Q. Adams, Diary, Reel 31, p. 222).

74. Henry Adams, *History,* 5:420.

75. Adams, *Memoirs*, 12:78.

76. See *VPR*, vol. 6, no. 32, pp. 90-91, 693-694; Vandal, *Napoléon et Alexandre Ier*, (Paris, 1897), 3:311.

77. *VPR*, vol. 6, p. 701; Caulaincourt, *Mémoires du général de Caulaincourt*, ed. Jean Hanoteau (Paris, 1933), 1:292-293.

78. Adams, *Memoirs*, 2:147, 207.

79. Smith to Adams, 13 Feb. 1811, in NA, Diplomatic Instructions: All Countries, 7:149-151. The copy (otpusk) in NA is not dated; however, Adams, in his dispatch of 2 June 1811, refers to receiving the instruction of 13 Feb. 1811 with the power for negotiating the treaty of commerce. The original of this important document is preserved among Adams' papers (AP, Letters Received and Other Loose Papers, Reel 414).

80. Heads of a Treaty between the United States of America and the Emperor of All the Russias, *ibid.*, pp. 151-154.

81. Adams, *Memoirs*, 2:271.

82. *Ibid.*, pp. 271-272.

83. *Ibid.*, pp. 72, 132ff.

84. Adams kept a precise list of all of his expenses in St. Petersburg. In America, the annual budget of his family had been only $2,680, but in the Russian capital it rose to $10,680 (in 1813, according to his precise notations, it came to $11,741.52 or 50,678.02 rubles). See Mainwaring, *John Quincy Adams and Russia*, pp. 31-34.

85. See the private letter from Madison to Adams, 16 Oct. 1810, in Adams, *Writings*, 3:518-519.

86. Adams, *Memoirs*, 2:218.

87. See Pahlen to Rumiantsev, 11/23 Feb. 1811, in AVPR, f. Kantseliariia, d. 12165, l. 18; Smith to Adams, 26 Feb. 1811, in NA, Diplomatic Instructions: All Countries, 7:145-146; Adams, *Memoirs*, 2:275. Soon after, Secretary of State Smith retired and James Monroe was appointed in his place. It is interesting to note that as a "consolation," the President offered Smith the post of envoy in St. Petersburg; but after thinking it over, the latter refused. See Pahlen to Rumiantsev, 27 March/8 April 1811, in AVPR, f. Kantseliariia, d. 12165, l. 26.

88. See Adams to Monroe, 2 June 1811, in Adams, *Memoirs*, 2:275-276. Early in 1812 Adams informed Rumiantsev that the President had instructed him to remain at his post in Russia and had nominated another person in his place to the Supreme Court of the United States (*ibid.*, p. 335).

89. *Ibid.*, p. 289; AP, J.Q. Adams, Diary, 6 Aug. 1811, Reel 31, p. 275ff.

90. Adams, *Memoirs*, 2:336.

91. *Ibid.*, pp. 144, 159, 290ff.

92. *Ibid.*, pp. 102, 217ff.

93. *Ibid.*, pp. 182-184, 217, 339-340.

94. I discussed this question for the first time on the basis of new archival material in "Otnoshenie Rossii k nachalu voiny Latinskoi Ameriki za nezavisimost' " (Russia's Attitude toward the Beginning of Latin America's War of Independence), *Istoricheskii Arkhiv*, 1962, no. 3, pp. 120-131. A number of documents (nos. 65, 77, 85, and others) are also included in vol. 6 of *VPR*. Russia's general position in Latin America's War of Independence is the subject of a new monograph by L. Iu. Slezkin, *Rossiia i voina za nezavisimost' v Ispanskoi Amerike* (Russia and the War of Independence in Spanish America, Moscow, 1964). See also Ekkehard Völkl, *Russland und Lateinamerika, 1741-1841* (Wiesbaden, 1968), pp. 189-192.

95. See "Notation of two conversations of the Chancellor of the Russian Empire with Mr. Parker, citizen of New York and dwelling in Caracas," Aug. 1811, in AVPR, f. Administrativnye dela, II-3, 1811, d. 17, ll. 8-15.

96. *Ibid.*, ll. 1-4.

97. "Note on the Opening of trade relations with Spanish Colonies," 16/28 Sept. 1811, in *Istoricheskii Arkhiv*, 1962, no. 3, pp. 125-127.

98. TsGIA, f. 1148, op. 1, 1811, d. 2, ll. 12-13.

99. Rumiantsev to Speransky, 16/28 Sept. 1811, in *Istoricheskii Arkhiv*, 1962, no. 3, p. 125.

100. *Ibid.*, p. 127.

101. Minutes of the general meeting of the State Council, 9/21 Oct. 1811, *ibid.*, pp. 127-128. The original minutes are preserved in TsGIA, f. 1148, op. 9, 1811, d. 13, ll. 48-53. Although all of the signatures in the original were finally deciphered, it proved impossible to determine how the members voted, since neither the minutes nor the material connected with their preparation have any information on this subject.

102. 26 Oct. 1811, in Adams, *Writings*, 4:256; 29 Feb. 1812, *ibid.*, pp. 300; NA, Diplomatic Despatches: Russia, vol. 2.

103. 29 Feb. 1812, Adams, *Writings*, 4:300-301; NA, Diplomatic Despatches: Russia, vol. 2.

104. Zea Bermúdez to Koshelev, 16/28 Sept. 1811, in AVPR, f. Kantseliariia, d. 3279, ll. 17-20; and N. M. [Romanov], *Imperator Aleksandr I: Opyt istoricheskogo issledovaniia* (The Emperor Alexander I: An Experiment in Historical Investigation, St. Petersburg, 1912), vol. 2. See also I. Zvavich, "Ispaniia v diplomaticheskikh otnosheniiakh Rossii v 1812 g." (Spain in Russian Diplomatic Relations in 1812), *Istoricheskii Zhurnal*, 1943, books 3-4.

105. See especially Bermúdez's letter of 23 Sept./5 Oct. 1811, in which the Spanish diplomat complained to Koshelev about the chimerical projects of the emissaries of the revolted colonies, which contained "the seeds of discord" (AVPR, f. Kantseliariia, d. 3279, ll. 26-28).

106. Koshelev to Alexander I, 23 Sept./5 Oct. 1811, in N. M. [Romanov], *Imperator Aleksandr I*, vol. 2, Supplement, p. 48.

107. *Ibid.*, p. 51.

108. *Ibid.*

109. Alexander I to Koshelev, 11/23 Oct. *Ibid.*, p. 4.

110. *Istoricheskii Arkhiv*, 1962, no. 3, p. 129.

111. Harris to Monroe, 1/13 May 1812, *ibid.*, p. 130.

112. See Adams, *Memoirs*, 4:339-340; Adams to Monroe, 29 Feb. 1812, in Adams, *Writings*, 4:300; NA, Diplomatic Despatches: Russia, vol. 2.

113. As usual, the diary entry of 4 Feb. 1812 coincides almost word for word with the text of the consequent official dispatch to the Secretary of State.

114. Harris to Monroe, 1/13 May 1812, in *Istoricheskii Arkhiv*, 1962, no. 3, p. 130.

115. Harris to López Mendez, 19/31 March 1812, *ibid.*, p. 129.

116. See Rumiantsev to Pahlen, 28 July/9 Aug. 1811, in AVPR, f. Pos-vo v Vashingtone, d. 4, l. 3. Poletika preferred to decline the new appointment in a hot climate on his doctor's advice; see Poletika to Rumiantsev, 19/31 Oct. 1811, in AVPR, f. Kantseliariia, d. 12165, l. 100.

117. Adams, *Memoirs*, 2:280-281. The Russian Chancellor sent Adams official notification of Pahlen's new appointment on 18/30 July 1811 (AVPR, f. Kantseliariia, d. 3340, l. 4).

118. This question was discussed for the first time in the State Council on 7/19

Feb. 1810, at the initiative of Rumiantsev. Soon after, in March of the same year, a temporary agreement was reached following an exchange of letters with Portugal's chargé d'affaires, specifying the lowering of duties on goods brought from Brazil (see *Arkhiv Gosudarstvennogo soveta*, vol. 4, no. 2, p. 1137; *PSZRI*, 31:173). In the spring of 1811, Rumiantsev again presented to the Council the project of the declaration specifying lowering by half the duties on goods brought to Russia from Portuguese colonies (see *VPR*, vol. 6, no. 29, pp. 83-84, 692; *Arkhiv Gosudarstvennog soveta*, vol. 4, no. 2, pp. 1160-1162). The final agreement on extending the terms of the Russian-Portuguese treaty of 1798 on amity, commerce and navigation was concluded on 29 May/10 June 1811 (*VPR*, vol.6, no. 168, pp. 420-421).

119. To Pahlen, 22 Aug./3 Sept. 1811, *ibid.*, no. 58, pp. 156-159.

120. Adams, *Memoirs*, 2:339.

121. The ukase of the College for Foreign Affairs of 16/28 July 1811, in AVPR, f. Pos-vo v Vashingtone, d. 4, l. 18; Rumiantsev to Dashkov, 28 July/9 Aug. 1811, *ibid.*, l. 17; TsGAOR, f. 907, op. 1, d. 74, l. 1. In the spring of 1812, a translator for the College for Foreign Affairs, Divov, was appointed to the mission in Philadelphia; see Rumiantsev to Dashkov, 27 March/8 April 1812, in AVPR, f. Pos-vo v Vashingtone, d. 5, l. 22.

122. See *ibid.*, d. 4, ll. 22-23; Dashkov to Alexander I, 3/15 Nov. 1811, in AVPR, f. Kantseliariia, d. 9240, ll. 51-52; NA, Russia: Notes, 1:69.

123. Pahlen to Alexander I, 2/14 Nov. 1811, in AVPR, f. Kantseliariia, d. 12165, l. 108-110.

124. *Memuar o Soedinennykh Shtatakh Ameriki* (A Memoir on the United States of America), 11/23 Feb. 1812, *ibid.*, d. 12166, ll. 5-52.

125. TsGIA, f. 1329, op. 3, d. 310, l. 174.

126. For the full text of the instruction to Kozlov of 12/24 Aug. 1811, see *VPR*, vol. 6, no. 55, pp. 147-154.

127. The instruction to Dashkov of 18/30 Aug. 1808, in *Novaia i noveishaia istoriia*, 1959, no. 2, p. 159.

128. Dashkov to Rumiantsev, 1/13 May 1810, in AVPR, f. Kantseliariia, d. 9238, l. 25.

129. Rumiantsev to Dashkov, 9/21 Sept. 1810, in AVPR, f. Pos-vo v Vashingtone, 1810 d. 3, l. 82.

130. See Poletika's *Mémoire* on the relations between Russia and the United States, 30 May/11 June 1811, in AVPR, f. Kantseliariia, d. 7697, l. 2-17.

131. Pahlen to Monroe, 8 June 1811, NA, Russia: Notes, 1:57; Monroe to Pahlen, 12 June 1811, in AVPR, f. Pos-vo v Vashingtone, d. 4, l. 12. The United States government took a highly favorable attitude to further requests for establishing Russian consulates and vice-consulates in various American ports. See especially Dashkov's letter to Monroe of 8 July 1812, about the appointment of Beverly Chess as a Russian vice-consul in New Orleans, and the reply of the Secretary of State of 14 July 1812 (NA, Russia: Notes, 1:77; AVPR, f. Pos-vo v Vashingtone, d. 5, l. 67). Among Russian consular agents in the United States were also John Swift (Alexandria, Va., 3 Apr. 1810), Fortescue Whittle (Norfolk, Va., 31 Mar. 1810), Thomas Dees (Charleston, S.C., 4 Apr. 1811), John Prince (Salem, Mass., 13 Apr. 1812), Samuel Snoss (Providence, R.I., 10 Apr. 1812), Ebenezer Mayo (Portland, Me., 29 Apr. 1812); list of Russian consuls in the United States in AVPR, f. Pos-vo v Vashingtone, d. 16.

132. To Rumiantsev, 20 Feb. 1813, in AVPR, f. Kantseliariia, d. 2585, ll. 24-30.

133. *Ibid.* Instructions pour M. Antonio Lynch, agent commercial de Russie

dans l'ile de Cuba in *ibid.*, ll. 31-32.

134. To Rumiantsev, 10 Nov. 1814, *ibid.*, d. 9243, ll. 103-104. In a dispatch to Nesselrode, dated 9/21 Dec. 1816, Kozlov mentioned the appointment of the new commercial agent in Havana but gave no name.

135. AVPR, f. Pos-vo v Vashingtone, 1810, d. 3, ll. 80-81.

136. Alexander I to Mocenigo, 21 Jan./2 Feb. 1811, *VPR*, vol. 6, no. 10, pp. 22-23.

137. Richardson, *Messages*, 1:491. The first to suggest that the President in his Message to Congress take special notice of Russia's friendly attitude toward the United States was John Quincy Adams in his dispatch to the Secretary of State of 2 Aug. 1811 (NA, Diplomatic Despatches: Russia, vol. 2).

138. 23 Nov. 1811, in NA, Diplomatic Instructions: All Countries, 7:180.

139. *VPR*, vol. 6, pp. 595-596; *Annals of Congress*, 12th Congress, 2nd Session, pp. 11-16; AVPR, f. Kantseliariia, d. 9240, ll. 74-90; d. 12168, ll. 223, 243-248; f. Pos-vo v Vashingtone, d. 5, ll. 84-85.

Chapter 9. Relations in the Northwest and the Agreement of 20 April/2 May 1812

1. Dashkov to Rumiantsev, 15 Nov. 1809, in AVPR, f. Kantseliariia, d. 9236, l. 89.

2. See *ibid.*, ll. 76-77, 89-92.

3. American State Papers. Foreign Relations (ASP, FR), 5:438-439.

4. For the original of Dashkov's note to Smith of 4 Jan. 1810, see NA, Russia: Notes, pp. 14-15. A certified copy of this document was sent by the Consul-General to St. Petersburg along with the report of 6 Jan. 1810 (AVPR, f. Kantseliariia, d. 9238, ll. 5-6).

5. Dashkov to Rumiantsev, 25 March 1810, ASP, FR, 5:440-441.

6. *Ibid.*, l. 67.

7. *Ibid.*, ll. 47-65.

8. To Smith, 24 April 1810, *ibid.*, l. 96; NA, Russia: Notes, 1:25-26.

9. ASP, FR, 5:441-442, original in AVPR, f. Pos-vo v Vashingtone, d. 3, ll. 39-40; f. Kantseliariia, d. 9238, l. 98; see also Dashkov to Smith, 10 May 1810, in NA, Russia: Notes, 1:28-29.

10. Smith to Adams, 5 May 1810, in ASP, FR, 5:440.

11. For more detail see R. G. Cleland, "Asiatic Trade and the American Occupation of the Pacific Coast," *American Historical Association Annual Report 1914* (Washington, 1916), 1:283-289.

12. See A. D. H. Smith, *John Jacob Astor* (Philadelphia and London, 1929), pp. 134, 137.

13. See Thomas Clark, *Frontier America* (New York, 1959), pp. 448-451; R. Riegel, *America Moves West* (New York, 1956), pp. 153-154; M. Mattes, "Jackson Hole, Crossroads of the Western Fur Trade, 1807-1829," *Pacific Northwest Quarterly*, 37:93-97 (April 1946).

14. Jefferson to Astor, 9 Nov. 1813 in Jefferson, *Writings*, 13:432; Astor to J. Q. Adams, 4 Jan. 1823 in ASP, Misc., 2:1009.

15. 9/21 July 1810, in AVPR, f. Kantseliariia, d. 12163, l. 35.

16. *Ibid.*, ll. 35-36.

17. *Ibid.*, l. 37a.

18. *Ibid.*, d. 9236, l. 91. Later on, Dashkov was an invariably active adherent of

developing business contacts with John Jacob Astor; direct commercial contacts of the American Fur Company with Russian settlements in America were established through him. See the correspondence between Dashkov and Astor and Baranov for 1809-1815, in TsGAOR, f. 907, op. 1, d. 55.

19. For the full text of Astor's project, see AVPR, f. Kantseliariia, d. 12163, 1. 39ff. *VPR,* vol. 6, pp. 711-713. See also Pahlen to Rumiantsev, 14/26 Oct. 1810, AVPR, f. Kantseliariia, d. 12163, ll. 67-68. On l. 378 there is a notation to the effect that Astor's project was conveyed later to the "directors of the American Company with the letter of 24 September 1811."

20. In the original: "D'accaparer un commerce avantageux, et d'ôter aux indigènes les moyens de se procurer des armes et des munitions."

21. See AVPR, f. Kantseliariia, d. 12163, ll. 43-44 (summary).

22. Pahlen to Rumiantsev, 1/13 Aug. 1810, *ibid.,* l. 49.

23. *Ibid.,* l. 50.

24. A. D. H. Smith, *John Jacob Astor,* pp. 137ff. Washington Irving, *Astoria* (New York, 1895), 1:48-76, 170-183, *passim.*

25. Pahlen to Rumiantsev, 19/31 Aug. 1810, in AVPR, f. Kantseliariia, d. 12163, l. 54.

26. Pahlen to Rumiantsev, 14/26 Oct. 1810, *ibid.,* ll. 67-68; d. 12165, l. 117. Bentzon left for Russia in March 1811 (Smith, *John Jacob Astor,* p. 139).

27. Adams, *Memoirs,* 2:152-153, 179-180, and others; Adams to Smith, 5, 30 Sept./12 Oct. 1810, in NA, Diplomatic Despatches: Russia, vol. 1; ASP, FR, 5:442-443.

28. NA, Diplomatic Instructions: All Countries, 7:153.

29. Adams, *Writings,* 4:128.

30. To John Adams, 31 Aug. 1811, *ibid.,* p. 209.

31. AVPR, f. Gl. Arkh. II-3, 1805-1817, op. 34, d. 8, ll. 85-93.

32. See *VPR,* vol. 6, no. 70, pp. 180-181.

33. To Buldakov and Kramer, 4/16 Oct. 1811, *ibid.,* no. 75, p. 191.

34. TsGIA, f. 560, op. 4, d. 5, ll. 10-11.

35. *Ibid.,* ll. 12-13.

36. *VPR,* vol. 6, no. 99, pp. 249-251.

37. *Ibid.,* p. 722.

38. 26 Oct./7 Nov. 1811, in TsGIA, f. 560, op. 4, d. 5, l. 2.

39. 16/28 Jan. 1812, *ibid.,* ll. 14-16.

40. For the full text, see TsGIA, f. 18, op. 5, d. 1201, ll. 12-15. The letter is addressed to Rumiantsev, but there is no date and no signature. The author of the letter is supposed to be O. P. Kozodavlev (see Okun', *Rossiisko-Amerikanskaia kompaniia,* p. 74). Apparently the document was compiled no earlier than 16/28 Jan. 1812, perhaps on that same day.

41. 7/19 Feb. 1812, in *VPR,* vol. 6, no. 115, p. 285.

42. *PSZRI,* 31:489; 45(section III):60.

43. For the text of the agreement between the American Fur Company and the Russian-American Company of 20 April/2 May 1812, see *VPR,* vol. 6, no. 156, pp. 385-388.

44. *Ibid.,* p. 729.

45. An original text of the convention of 20 Dec. 1812, in French, signed by Astor, and stamped with the seal of the American Fur Company is preserved in the archives (AVPR, f. Pos-vo v Vashingtone, d. 5, ll. 41-42).

46. Astor to Dashkov, 4 Nov. 1809, in TsGAOR, f. 907, op. 1, d. 138, l. 1.

47. 7 Nov. 1809, *ibid.,* d. 55, ll. 3-10.

48. Nov. 1809, *ibid.,* d. 138, ll. 5-6.

49. Tikhmenev, *Istoricheskoe obozrenie,* 1:179-180; Khlebnikov, *Zapiski,* p. 137.

50. *Materialy dlia istorii russkikh zaselenii (Sources for the History of Russian Settlements),* no. 3, pp. 15-16; Khlebnikov, *Zapiski,* pp. 138-139; Tikhmenev, *Istoricheskoe obozrenie,* 1:180.

51. Khlebnikov, *Zapiski,* pp. 139-140; Tikhmenev, *Istoricheskoe obozrenie,* 1:180; *Materialy dlia istorii,* no. 3, pp. 15-18.

52. Tikhmenev, *Istoricheskoe obozrenie,* 1:180-181; D. O. Johansen and M. Gates, *Empire of the Columbia: A History of the Pacific Northwest* (New York, 1957), pp. 133-134. Concerning the *Beaver* and disagreements about prices, see also Astor to Baranov, 10 Oct., and Dashkov to Baranov, 1/12 Oct. 1811, in TsGAOR, f. 907, op. 1, d. 55, ll. 15-18.

53. *VPR,* vol. 6, no. 112, p. 278.

54. *Materialy dlia istorii,* no. 3, p. 13.

55. *Ibid.,* pp. 12-13.

56. Report of the Corporation of the Russian-American Company, 1/13 Feb. 1812, in *VPR,* vol. 6, no. 112, p. 279.

57. Ogden, *The California Sea Otter Trade,* pp. 45-47.

58. The table is adapted from Khlebnikov's materials (*Materialy dlia istorii,* no. 3, p. 10; Khlebnikov, *Zapiski,* p. 148, with additional checking against Ogen).

59. *Materialy dlia istorii,* no. 3, p. 9.

60. GBL OR, f. 204, k. 32, d. 11.

61. Ogden, *The California Sea Otter Trade,* p. 52ff.

62. *Ibid.,* pp. 53-54. Some additional information may be found in F. W. Howay, *A List of Trading Vessels in the Maritimes Fur Trade, 1785-1825* (Kingston, 1973), pp. 83-87, *passim.*

63. Tikhmenev, *Istoricheskoe obozrenie,* 1:172.

64. Khlebnikov, *Zapiski,* p. 149; Morison, *Maritime History of Massachusetts,* p. 261; Wheeler, "Empires in Conflict and Cooperation," p. 431.

65. To Monroe, 28 Sept. 1813, in NA, Russia: Notes, 1:116.

66. Main Office of the Russian-American Company to Dashkov, 16 Oct. 1814, in TsGAOR, f. 907, op. 1, d. 55, ll. 25-27; Tikhmenev, *Istoricheskoe obozrenie,* 1:182-183; Johansen and Gates, *Empire of the Columbia,* pp. 136-139.

67. Main Office of the Russian-American Company to Dashkov, 28 Aug./9 Sept. 1815, in TsGAOR, f. 907, op. 1, d. 154, ll. 1-2.

68. *VPR,* vol. 6, no. 112, p. 279.

69. This conflict is described in detail in *A Note on the Northamericans' commerce in the Russian colonies in America, 23 December, 1816,* signed by Buldakov, Kramer, Severin, and Zelensky, in AVPR, f. Kantseliariia, d. 12182, ll. 31-49. A quite different and more objective description of the events which led to the conflict was given by Captain M. P. Lazarev in his memorandum of 16/28 Jan. 1817; NA, Records of the Russian-American Company, 1:17-40; TsGAVMF, f. 212, d. 3735, d. 133-158.

70. Tikhmenev, *Istoricheskoe obozrenie,* 1:172. Somewhat later, similar furs were brought to Kamchatka by Captain Pigot. In spite of the fact that sales were strictly forbidden, Pigot managed to sell his goods to the Kamchatka commissioner, with the transfer of the money to the Main Office, at fifteen rubles (in currency) a skin (he had obtained them in Novo-Archangel at two rubles, 50 kopecks a skin) to the sum of 61,000 rubles. The Main Office refused to pay this bill, basing its decision on the assumption that colonial decrees were well-known to the buyer.

71. *Ibid.*, p. 173.

72. 14/26 Oct. 1808, in GBL OR, f. 204, k. 32, d. 34, l. 107ff. See also "Orders of Baranov to the company's employee, Tarakanov, 18/30 Sept. 1808 (*ibid.*, d. 7), to navigator Bulygin, 22 Sept./4 Oct. 1808 (*ibid.*, d. 8), to navigator Petrov, Oct. 1808 (*ibid.*, d. 9).

73. See Kuskov's report to Baranov, 5/17 Oct. 1809, in GBL OR, f. 204, k. 32, d. 15; *Materialy dlia istorii,* no. 3, pp. 10-11, 137; Tikhmenev, *Istoricheskoe obozrenie,* 1:207-208. On independent Russian expeditions to California, see also Ogden, *The California Sea Otter Trade,* pp. 57ff.

74. Tikhmenev, *Istoricheskoe obozrenie,* 1:208.

75. Main Office of the Russian-American Company to Rumiantsev, 16/28 May 1811, in *VPR,* vol. 6, no. 44, pp. 119-20.

76. Report of the Main Office of the Russian-American Company to the General Assembly of Shareholders, 1/13 Feb. 1812, *ibid.,* no. 112, p. 280.

77. "Recapitulation on resuming commerce with California," in TsGIA, f. 13, op. 2, d. 1414, l. 5; GBL OR, f. 255, k. 15, d. 34.

78. Note on the colony of the Russian-American Company named Ross, *Materialy dlia istorii,* no. 3, pp. 167, 172; Archives of Count Mordvinovs (St. Petersburg, 1902), 6:668.

79. See Baranov's instructions to Kuskov of 18/30 Jan. and 20 Jan./1 Feb. 1811, in GBL OR, f. 204, k. 32, d. 12; *VPR,* vol. 6, p. 272.

80. *Materialy dlia istorii,* no. 3, pp. 11, 137-138.

81. Tikhmenev, *Istoricheskoe obozrenie,* 1:208ff.; V. Potekhin, *Selenie Ross* (Settlement Ross, St. Petersburg, 1859), pp. 9-10; *Istoricheskaia zapiska o selenii Ross na beregakh Novogo Al'biona* (A Historical Note on the Settlement Ross on the Shores of New Albion), in AVPR, f. RAK, d. 363, ll. 7-11.

82. *Materialy dlia istorii,* no. 3, p. 138.

83. *VPR,* vol. 6, no. 112, p. 281.

84. For the full text of the "proclamation" signed by Buldakov and Kramer, see Potekhin, *Selenie Ross,* pp. 5-8; GBL OR, f. 255, k. 15, d. 34.

85. Potekhin, *Selenie Ross,* pp. 14-15; GBL OR, f. 255, k. 15, d. 34-35.

86. Potekhin, *Selenie Ross,* pp. 15-17. On the *Suvorov's* setting out on a circumglobal voyage from Kronstadt to Russian America in the fall of 1812, see *Zhurnaly komiteta ministrov* (Journals of the Committee of Ministers, St. Petersburg, 1881), 2:536; TsGIA, f. 1263; op. 1, 1812, d. 29, ll. 194-212.

87. See Buldakov, Kramer, and Severin to Rumiantsev, 15/27 May 1814, in GBL OR, f. 255, k. 15, d. 35; text of the note "On Russia's Commerce with California" presented to Zea Bermúdez, *ibid.,* d. 34.

88. Tikhmenev, *Istoricheskoe obozrenie,* 1:213.

89. *Materialy dlia istorii,* no. 3, pp. 146-147.

90. M. P. Lazarev, *Dokumenty* (Moscow, 1952), 1:44; Slezkin, *Rossiia i voina,* pp. 83-84.

91. See GBL OR, f. 204, k. 32, d. 25, 37.

92. In addition to the above-mentioned works, see also Okun', *Rossiisko-Amerikanskaia kompaniia,* pp. 112-144; E. O. Essig, "The Russian Settlement at Ross," *Quarterly of the California Historical Society,* 12 (1933): 191-209, with a fine bibliography; *ibid.,* pp. 210-216. For a review of Russian sources relating to the history of California, see an article of F. A. Shur in *Amerikanskii Ezhegodnik* (American Annual), 1971, 295-319.

93. See N. N. Bolkhovitinov, *Dokrina Monro* (Monroe Doctrine, Moscow, 1959), pp. 186-209, 287-294; idem, "Russia and the Declaration of the Non-Colonization Principle: New Archival Evidence," *Oregon Historical Quarterly,* 72:101-126 (June 1971).

Part Four. The War of 1812 and Tsarist Russia

1. Popov, *Otechestvennaia voina*, 1:3.
2. Lenin, *Polnoe sobranie sochinenii*, 30:5-6.
3. Albert Vandal, *Napoléon et Alexander Ier*, 3:344-345.
4. 10/22 June 1812, *VPR*, vol. 6, p. 756.
5. 13/25 June 1812, in S. Tatishchev, *Alexandre Ier et Napoléon*, pp. 587-588; *VPR*, vol. 6, no. 177, p. 442; for the text of Balashov's report on his visit to Napoleon, see *Zapiski Imperatorskoi Akademii nauk*, vol. 43, supplement 1, pp. 14-31.
6. Richardson, *Messages*, 1:499-505.
7. *Annals of Congress*, 12th Congress, 1st Session, pp. 1629-1637, 265-298.
8. See *British and Foreign State Papers* (London, 1841), vol. 1, pt. 2, p. 1322.

Chapter 10. The War of 1812 and Its Evaluation by Russian Diplomats

1. *The Marxist Quarterly*, no. 2 (Summer, 1962), pp. 16-23.
2. Marx and Engels, *Sochineniia*, 15:454-455.
3. *Ibid.*, pp. 399, 403, 511.
4. See *Novaia Istoriia* (Moscow, 1958), 2:200.
5. William Z. Foster, *The Negro People in American History* (New York, 1954), p. 72.
6. See J. Pratt, *Expansionists of 1812* (Gloucester, 1957; 1st ed., 1925), pp. 48-52; T. Clark, *Frontier America*, pp. 260-288.
7. See especially the new editions of *The Papers of Henry Clay*, ed. James F. Hopkins (Lexington, 1959), vol. 1, and of *The Papers of John C. Calhoun*, ed. R. Meriwether (Columbia, S. C., 1959), vol. 1.
8. *Annals of Congress*, 11th Congress, 1st Session, pp. 579-580.
9. *Ibid.*, 3rd Session, p. 63.
10. *Ibid.*, 12th Congress, 1st Session, pp. 457, 458.
11. *Ibid.*, p. 657.
12. *Ibid.*, p. 677.
13. This idea, which had been advanced by Pratt, was criticized by Burt, Brant, and others. See A. L. Burt, *The United States, Great Britain and British North America from the Revolution to the Establishment of Peace after the War of 1812* (New Haven, 1940), p. 305; Irving Brant, *James Madison: Commander in Chief* (Indianapolis, 1961), pp. 17-18. Pratt's point of view (1925) on the War of 1812 is undergoing revision in contemporary American historiography. Although Perkins in his fundamental monograph of 1961 was still somewhat cautious, Horsman in 1962 and, especially, Brown in 1964 completely ignored the expansionist tendency in the United States policy on the eve of the War of 1812. It is characteristic that Brown generally considers that there were no "War Hawks" as such in the Congress: "Federalist opponents of the war, men not privy to the views of Republicans, coined the term "war hawk." They relied on false appearances. No Republican ever really answered this description." Brown points out: "Republicans were willing to give their votes for war even without assurance that either Canada or Florida would ever be annexed. In the face of many obstacles it is doubtful that anyone voted for the war primarily on the basis of future annexation of these areas." See R. H. Brown, *The Republic in Peril: 1812* (New York and London, 1964), pp. 44, 130, and *passim*. For a short sketch of the historiography of this problem see N. N. Bolkhovitinov, "Proiskhozhdenie i kharakter anglo-amerikanskoi voiny 1812 g." (The Origin and Character of the Anglo-American War of

1812), *Ot Aliaski do Ognennoi Zemli,* ed. I. A. Grigulevich et al. (From Alaska to Fire Land, Moscow, 1967), pp. 142-154; idem, "Sovremennaia amerikanskaia istoriografiia: novye techeniia i problemy" (Contemporary American Historiography: New Trends and Problems), *Novaia i noveishaiia istoriia,* 1969, no. 6, p. 119.

14. *Annals of Congress,* 12th Congress, 1st Session, pp. 426-427.

15. *Ibid.,* pp. 441ff.; Henry Adams, *History,* 6:141; Pratt, *Expansionists of 1812,* pp. 140-141.

16. *Annals of Congress,* 12th Congress, 1st Session, p. 533.

17. *Ibid.,* p. 424.

18. J. Bassett, ed., *Correspondence of Andrew Jackson* (7 vols., Washington, 1926-1935), 1:221-222.

19. *Annals of Congress,* 12th Congress, 1st Session, pp. 470-471.

20. *Ibid.,* p. 601.

21. Madison to Wheaton, 26-27 Feb. 1827, in Madison, *Writings,* 9:274.

22. B. Mayo, ed., *Annual Report of the American Historical Association for the Year 1936,* vol. 3: *Instructions to the British Ministers to the United States, 1791-1812* (Washington, 1941); Perkins, *Prologue to War.*

23. Mayo, *Instructions,* pp. 353-363. The English minister conveyed their contents to the Secretary of State on 30 May (*ASPFR,* 3:454-457).

24. Mayo, *Instructions,* pp. 363-367.

25. *Ibid.,* p. 368.

26. Castlereagh to Foster, 11 May 1812, *ibid.,* p. 379; Henry Adams, *History,* 6:284-285; Lavis and Rambo, eds., *Istoriia XIX veka* (History of the Nineteenth Century, Moscow, 1938), 2:72.

27. Castlereagh to Foster, 17 June 1812, with the text of the memorandum enclosed, the contents of which were conveyed to both houses of the British Parliament. Mayo, *Instructions,* pp. 381-383.

28. G. Martens, *Nouveau Recueil,* 1:444-452, 483-484.

29. *Ibid.,* pp. 547-549; *ASPFR,* 3:433; Mayo, *Instructions,* p. 383.

30. Burt, *The United States, Great Britain and British North America,* p. 313; Brant, *Madison: Commander in Chief,* pp. 33-34.

31. *ASPFR,* 3:585, 594.

32. AVPR, f. Kantseliariia, d. 3344, l. 44. (An extensive official correspondence on this subject was sent to the Russian government by Gallatin in the summer of 1813; *ibid.,* ll. 20-66.)

33. Monroe to Warren, 27 Oct. 1812, *ibid.,* l. 46. See also *Annals of Congress,* 12th Congress, 2nd Session, pp. 1197-1198.

34. Madison to Wheaton, 26-27 Feb. 1827, in Madison, *Writings,* 9:274.

35. *Annals of Congress,* 11th Congress, 1st Session, pp. 579-580.

36. Calhoun, *Papers,* 1:104-105. It was, by the way, precisely this belligerent politician (eventually to become an extreme separatist and apologist of slavery), who was the author of the report of the Committee on Foreign Affairs of 3 June 1812 which argued the necessity of a rupture with England (*ibid.,* pp. 109-112, 122-123).

37. Bassett, *Corr. of Andrew Jackson,* 1:220-222. On the expansionist plans of the United States leaders with respect to Canada, see also S. B. Ryerson, *The Founding of Canada: Beginnings to 1815* (Toronto, 1960), pp. 293-315.

38. *Annals of Congress,* 12th Congress, 1st Session, pp. 33-37, 596-691 *passim*; Henry Adams, *History,* 6:294-295; Pratt, *Expansionists of 1812,* pp. 144-145.

39. See, for example, Dashkov to Kurakin, 5/17 Jan. 1812, in *VPR,* vol. 6, no. 104, pp. 259-260.

40. Their dispatches and the enclosed documentation represent valuable and so

far almost unused source materials for the War of 1812.

41. 7 March 1812 (Kozlov dated his dispatches in New Style), in AVPR, f. Kantseliariia, d. 9242, 1. 3.

42. *Ibid.,* 1. 4.

43. To Rumiantsev, 30 April 1812, *ibid.,* 1. 63. In the same dispatch the Consul called special attention to the fact that "particular letters from London confirm that England is not disposed to be the first to start the war with the Americans."

44. *Ibid.,* ll. 63-64.

45. Henry Adams, *History,* 6:295.

46. To Rumiantsev, 19 June/1 July 1812, in AVPR, f. Kantseliariia, d. 12168, 1. 134.

47. Burt, *The United States, Great Britain and British North America,* p. 323.

48. Pratt, *Expansionists of 1812,* pp. 160-161.

49. Henry Adams, *History,* 7:385.

50. Nettels, *The Emergence of a National Economy,* p. 332.

51. *Mr. Madison's War. A Dispassionate Inquiry into the Reasons Alleged by Mr. Madison for Declaring an Offensive and Ruinous War against Great Britain. By a New England Farmer* (Philadelphia, 1812).

52. Henry Adams, *History,* 7:146.

53. To Rumiantsev, 30 June/12 July 1813, in AVPR, f. Kantseliariia, d. 12170, 1. 261. For more details on the United States actions in respect to Spanish Florida and Mexico, see S. A. Gonionsky, "Territorial'naia ekspansiia SShA v nachale XIX v." (Territorial Expansion of the United States in the Beginning of the Nineteenth Century), *Novaiia i noveishaia istoriia,* 1958, no. 5, pp. 33-50; N. N. Bolkhovitinov, "Prisoedinenie Floridy Soedinennymi Shtatami" (Acquisition of Florida by the United States), *ibid.,* 1959, no. 5, pp. 110-119; M. S. Al'perovich, *Voina za nezavisimost' Meksiki (1810-1824)* (The War for Mexico's Independence, 1810-1824, Moscow, 1964), pp. 217-224.

54. Brant, *Madison: Commander in Chief,* p. 39.

55. Burt, *The United States, Great Britain and British North America,* p. 319.

56. Henry Adams, *History,* 6:289-295; A. R. Gilpin, *The War of 1812 in the Old Northwest* (East Lansing, Mich., 1958), pp. 109-125.

57. Burt, *The United States, Great Britain and British North America,* pp. 332-333. W. B. Kerr, "The Occupation of York (Toronto), 1813," *Canadian Historical Review,* 5:9-21.

58. To Rumiantsev, 7 April 1814, in AVPR, f. Kantseliariia, d. 9243, 1. 25.

59. To Rumiantsev, 27 May 1814, *ibid.,* 1. 53.

60. To Rumiantsev, 30 June 1814, *ibid.,* 1. 57.

61. To Rumiantsev, 27 Aug. 1814, *ibid.,* 1. 70.

62. To Rumiantsev, 30 June 1814, *ibid.,* ll. 60-61.

63. See, especially, H. M. Brackenbridge, *History of the Late War between the United States and Great Britain* (3rd ed., Baltimore, 1817), pp. 55-57.

64. Svin'in, *Opyt,* pp. 25-26.

65. Nettels, *The Emergence of a National Economy,* pp. 337-338.

66. *British and Foreign State Papers: 1812-1814* (London, 1841), vol. 1, pt. 2, pp. 1360-1361.

67. Henry Adams, *History,* 7:262ff.; AVPR, f. Kantseliariia, d. 3346, 1. 48ff. (Harris to Vedemeier, 30 Aug./11 Sept. 1814 and the copy of Cochrane's proclamation of 25 April).

68. Henry Adams, *History,* 8:128; Burt, *The United States, Great Britain and British North America,* p. 318; Nettels, *The Emergence of a National Economy,* pp. 335-336.

69. To Monroe, 18 Aug. 1814, in *ASPFR,* 3:693; AVPR, f. Kantseliariia, d. 9243, ll. 76-79.

70. *Ocherki novoi i noveishei istorii SShA* (Essays on the Modern and Recent History of the United States, Moscow, 1960 1:144.)

71. See Winder to Armstrong, 24 Aug. 1814, in *American State Papers: Military Affairs,* 1:548.

72. Henry Adams, *History,* 8:141.

73. To Rumiantsev, 1/13 Sept. 1814, in AVPR, f. Kantseliariia, d. 12172, 1. 136. On the capture of Washington, see also Kozlov to Rumiantsev, 27 Aug. 1814, *ibid.,* d. 9243, ll. 70-71.

74. Henry Adams, *History,* 8:146-148, 151ff. (There also is extensive material in *American State Papers: Military Affairs,* vol. 1.)

75. To Rumiantsev, 1/13 Sept. 1814, in AVPR, f. Kantseliariia, d. 12172, l. 40.

76. *Documents Relative to the Negotiations for Peace between the United States and Great Britain* (Philadelphia, 1814), p. 53. This compilation was published in the fall of 1814 with the aim of proving the unacceptability of the demands advanced during the negotiations in Ghent by the British Plenipotentiaries. See also *ASPFR,* 3:709.

77. I give only the most generalized, schematic account of events, and consequently cannot go into any detail, such as the operations of General Wilkinson and Jackson in Spanish Florida in 1813-14, or the unceasing, cruel struggle against the Indian tribes.

78. Foster, *The Negro People in American History,* p. 72. One also cannot help noticing an idiosyncratic "Canadian factor" which played a definite part in the outcome of the war and exerted an influence on the further development of Canada as an independent nation. According to Ryerson. Anglo-Canadian nationalism was engendered by the resistance to American expansion. Therefore, it is not accidental that in Canada the War of 1812 is known as a national, and sometimes even "Canadian War of Independence." Of course, to some extent the anti-American feeling of Canadians engendered by the War of 1812 also resulted from loyalty to England and strengthened their chains to her. At the same time this feeling was a manifestation, albeit in embryo, of the national consciousness of the Canadian people. Having defended their homes from the invasion of the United States, the Canadians proved to be much less tolerant of further colonial dependence on Great Britain (Ryerson, *Founding of Canada* [Russian transl., Moscow, 1963], pp. 322-323, On resistance to the United States see pp. 304-321).

79. 19-20 Aug. 1814, in Donnan, *Papers of James A. Bayard,* pp. 317-318.

80. *Ibid.,* p. 318.

81. To Crawford, 29 Aug. 1814, in Adams, *Writings,* 5:105.

82. To Rumiantsev, 27 Aug. 1814, in AVPR, f. Kantseliariia, d. 9243, l. 71.

83. To Rumiantsev, 17 Sept. 1814, *ibid.,* l. 75.

84. Philip S. Foner, *Istoriia rabochego dvizheniia v SShA* (History of the Labor Movement in the United States, Moscow, 1949), 1:114-115, and *History of the Labor Movement in the United States* (New York, 1947), 1:94.

85. Kozlov to Rumiantsev, 17 Sept. 1814, in AVPR, f. Kantseliariia, d. 9243, ll. 74-75; Dashkov to Rumiantsev, 18/30 Sept. 1814, *ibid.,* d. 12172, ll. 156-158; Henry Adams, *History,* 8:166-272.

86. To Rumiantsev, 17 Sept. 1814, in AVPR, f. Kantseliariia, d. 9243, 1. 75; Henry Adams, *History,* 8:102-112.

87. To Rumiantsev, 7 Nov. 1814, in AVPR, f. Kantseliariia, d. 9243, 1. 82.

88. *Ibid.,* ll. 82-87.

89. *Ibid.*, ll. 100-101.

90. *The Weekly Register,* 7:179.

91. Henry Adams, *History,* 8:287-310.

92. As later transpired, Governor Strong of Massachussetts sent an agent to Sherbrooke in Halifax to conclude for New England a separate peace and union with Great Britain (see J. S. Martell, "A Side Light on Federalist Strategy," *AHR,* 43:553-556; Burt, *The United States, Great Britain and British North America,* p. 344).

93. To Rumiantsev, 20 Dec. 1814/1 Jan. 1815, in AVPR, f. Kantseliariia, d. 12174, l. 4.

94. For more details see C. B. Brooks, *The Siege of New Orleans* (Seattle, 1961).

95. To Nesselrode, 13 Feb. 1815. For the full text see AVPR, f. Kantseliariia, d. 9244, ll. 2-5. Several days later Dashkov reported on this battle: "The English expedition consisted of 9,000 people, but no more than 6,000 were used in the disembarkation. The English attacked the entrenchments twice and were repelled, with the loss of their leader, Packenham, a multitude of officers, and more than 3,000 crack troops. The garrison which protected the entrenchments consisted of 1,500 regular troops and about 4,000 militia. The losses on this side are so small that it is almost unbelievable, but true nevertheless, that the number of killed does not extend to 400 people. "The English," Dashkov justly concluded, "have learned too late that European tactics do not suffice against the Americans." (To Rumiantsev, 8/20 Feb. 1815, *ibid.,* d. 12174, l. 11.)

96. To Nesselrode, 13 Feb. 1815, in AVPR, f. Kantseliariia, d. 9244, ll. 4-5.

97. To Rumiantsev, 8/20 Feb. 1815, *ibid.,* d. 12174, l. 11.

98. Marcus Cunliffe, *The Nation Takes Shape, 1789-1837* (Chicago, 1959), pp. 122ff.

99. Nettels, *The Emergence of a National Economy,* pp. vi, 1, 130. For more details see also N. N. Bolkhovitinov, "Nekotorye problemy genezisa amerikanskogo kapitalizma (XVII-pervaia polovina XIX v.)" (Certain Problems of the Genesis of American Capitalism, from the Seventeenth to the first half of the Nineteenth Century); in S. D. Skazkin et al., eds., *Problemy genezisa kapitalizma* (Problems of the Genesis of Capitalism, Moscow, 1970), pp. 128-199.

Chapter 11. Russia's Attempted Peace Mediation

1. N. N. Bolkhovitinov and S. I. Divil'kovsky. "Russkaia diplomatiia i anglo-amerikanskaia voina 1812-1814 godov" (Russian Diplomacy and the Anglo-American War of 1812-1814, *Novaia i noveishaiia istoriia,* 1961, no. 4, pp. 31-45.

2. 5/17 Jan. 1812, in *VPR,* vol. 6, no. 104, pp. 259-261. Dashkov repeatedly expressed similar views in his dispatches to St. Petersburg. In a letter to Rumiantsev, the Minister noted in particular that in the case of pacification of the Anglo-American conflict he foresaw great profits for Russia's commerce, and emphasized that preservation of good relations between Russia and the United States was in Russia's interest (23 Feb./6 March 1812, in AVPR, f. Pos-vo v Vashingtone, d. 3, ll. 35-41).

3. *Annals of Congress,* 12th Congress, 1st Session, pp. 2262-2264.

4. 30 April/12 May 1812, in AVPR, f. Kantseliariia, d. 9242, l. 64.

5. 14 April 1812, in *VPR,* vol. 6, no. 142, pp. 357-358.

6. 30 April/12 May 1812, in AVPR, f. Kantseliariia, d. 9242, ll. 64-65.

7. To Rumiantsev, 19 June/1 July 1812, *ibid.,* d. 12168, ll. 139-141.

8. To Rumiantsev, 20 July/1 Aug. 1812, *ibid.,* ll. 143-154.

9. *S.-Peterburgskie vedomosti,* 23 July/4 Aug. 1812, no. 59.

10. See Alexander I's ukase on resuming commercial relations with England, 4/16 Aug. 1812, in *VPR,* vol. 6, no. 228, p. 541.

11. *S.-Peterburgskie vedomosti,* 13/25 Sept. 1812, no. 74.

12. *Ibid.,* 24 Sept./6 Oct. 1812, no. 77.

13. To Rumiantsev, 21 Dec. 1812, in *VPR,* vol. 6, no. 283, pp. 650-652.

14. See, especially, AVPR, f. Kantseliariia, d. 10825, 10827.

15. 12/24 April 1812, in *VPR,* vol. 6, no. 149, p. 369.

16. *Ibid.,* no. 150, pp. 371, 373.

17. To Rumiantsev, 27 April/9 May 1812, in AVPR, f. Kantseliariia, d. 10825, l. 175.

18. Suchtelen to Rumiantsev, 28 April/10 May 1812, in *VPR,* vol. 6, no. 157, pp. 391, 392.

19. NA, Diplomatic Instructions: All Countries, 7:215; *ASPFR,* 3:625.

20. *VPR,* vol. 6, no. 199, pp. 491-492.

21. *British and Foreign State Papers,* vol. 1, pt. 1, 15-17.

22. To Monroe, 2 Aug. 1812, in *VPR,* vol. 6, no. 227, p. 541.

23. Adams, *Memoirs,* 2:401-404, 411-413, 415. See also Adams' dispatches to Monroe of 30 Sept. and 17 Oct. 1812, in NA, Diplomatic Despatches: Russia, vol. 2; Adams, *Writings,* 4:389, 401.

24. *VPR,* vol. 6, no. 247, pp. 582-583.

25. *Ibid.,* no. 236, pp. 558-559.

26. Lieven to Castlereagh, 31 March/12 April 1813, in AVPR, f. Kantseliariia, d. 6829, l. 32.

27. In some circles there existed apprehension (mistaken, as it later turned out) that the war between the United States and England would increase French influence in Washington. Stressing Russia's desire for a termination of the Anglo-American War, Nesselrode wrote about the necessity "to put an end to the success of the French intrigues in this part of the New World" (to Lieven, 28 July/9 Aug. 1813, in AVPR, f. Kantseliariia, d. 6835, l. 103).

28. Lieven to Rumiantsev, 24 Dec. 1812/5 Jan. 1813, *ibid.,* d. 6822, l. 62.

29. Brant, *Madison: Commander in Chief,* p. 155.

30. Dashkov to Rumiantsev, 1/13 March 1813, in AVPR, f. Kantseliariia, d. 12170, ll. 80-82.

31. Dashkov to Rumiantsev, 5/17 March 1813, *ibid.,* ll. 98-99. The reply was delayed because President Madison, in order not to give Great Britain an impression of capitulation, had first delivered the traditional Message to Congress on 4 March 1813, which was quite belligerent in tone; only after did he officially accept the offer of mediation (Brant, *Madison: Commander in Chief,* p. 156).

32. Dashkov to Monroe, 24 Feb./8 March 1813, in NA, Russia: Notes, 1:91-93; Monroe to Dashkov, 11 March 1813, in AVPR, f. Kantseliariia, d. 12170, ll. 72-73.

33. *The Weekly Register,* 13 March 1813, 4:32.

34. *Ibid.,* pp. 65, 81, 100, 159, 209, 377-379, 402.

35. Henry Adams, *History,* 7:33.

36. *Ibid.,* 7:30.

37. To Nicholas, 2 April 1813, in Madison, *Writings,* 8:243-244.

38. *The Writings of James Monroe,* ed. S. M. Hamilton (7 vols., New York, 1898-1903), 5:279.

39. 19 April 1813, *ibid.,* p. 251; also, Monroe to Jefferson, 7 June 1813, *ibid.,* pp. 267-268.

40. Monroe to Gallatin, Adams, and Bayard, 15 April 1813, in NA, Diplomatic Instructions: All Countries, 7:269-270; Monroe, *Writings*, 5:256 (open text of the Instructions, in *ASPFR*, 3:695-700).

41. 12/24 March 1813, in AVPR, f. Kantseliariia, d. 12170, ll. 111-112. Some time later, Dashkov forwarded to St. Petersburg "A project of various items for possible inclusion into the treaty or agreement which might be concluded between Russia and the United States," *ibid.*, ll. 174-219.

42. *Ibid.*, d. 3344, ll. 16, 19.

43. Monroe to Adams, Gallatin, and Bayard, 27 April 1813, in Donnen, *Papers of James A. Bayard*, pp. 215-216.

44. To Madison, 5 March 1813, in Gallatin, *Writings*, 1:532.

45. To Rumiantsev, 22 April 1813, in AVPR, f. Kantseliariia, d. 2585, l. 58.

46. Henry Adams, *History*, 7:44-45; Brant, *Madison: Commander in Chief*, p. 158.

47. Dashkov to Rumiantsev, 25 March/6 April 1813, in AVPR, f. Kantseliariia, d. 12170, ll. 138-140; Dashkov to Monroe, 15 April 1813, in NA, Russia: Notes, 1:97-98; *The Weekly Register*, 3 April and 8 May 1813, 4:81, 159.

48. AVPR, f. Pos-vo v Vashingtone, d. 6, ll. 70-73.

49. *Ibid.*, ll. 146, 154.

50. Nikolai to Rumiantsev, n. d. (received 4/16 Nov. 1814), in AVPR, f. Kantseliariia, d. 6820, ll. 4-5.

51. Nikolai to Rumiantsev, 1/13 Nov. 1812, in *VPR*, vol. 6, no. 256, pp. 598, 599.

52. Adams, *Memoirs*, 2:433.

53. *Ibid.*, pp. 427-428, 431-432; Adams to Monroe, 11 Dec. 1812, in NA, Diplomatic Despatches: Russia, vol. 2. In a dispatch to Lieven of 30 Nov./12 Dec. 1812, Rumiantsev instructed the new Russian ambassador in London to "utilize with the aim of rapprochement between England and the United States" Adams' assurance that the United States did not foresee anything that could bring them closer to France than they are at the present time (*VPR*, vol. 6, no. 7, p. 86).

54. Hildt, *Early Diplomatic Negotiations*, p. 62.

55. AVPR, f. Kantseliariia, d. 6820, l. 30.

56. Cited here and below is Lieven's dispatch to Rumiantsev of 24 Dec. 1812/5 Jan. 1813, in *VPR*, vol. 6, no. 290, pp. 664-666.

57. Lieven to Rumiantsev, 13/25 May 1813, in AVPR, f. Kantseliariia, d. 6829, ll. 293-294.

58. *Ibid.*

59. Lieven to Nesselrode, 4/16 July 1813, in AVPR, f. Kantseliariia, d. 6834, ll. 2-3.

60. Henry Adams, *History*, 7:343.

61. To Cathcart, 14 July 1813, in *Correspondence, Despatches and Other Papers of Viscount Castlereagh* (London, 1852), 9:35.

62. *Ibid.*, pp. 34-35.

63. Gallatin, *Writings*, 1:545-546.

64. Adams, *Memoirs*, 2:479; Adams to Monroe, 26 June 1813, in NA, Diplomatic Despatches: Russia, vol. 2.

65. Rumiantsev to Alexander I, 24 June/6 July 1813, in AVPR, f. Kantseliariia, d. 7942, ll. 200-201.

66. Rumiantsev to Alexander I, 14/26 July 1813, *ibid.*, d. 7942, l. 226.

67. *Ibid.*, d. 7944, l. 389.

68. Nesselrode to Lieven, 28 July/9 Aug. 1813, *ibid.*, d. 6835, ll. 102-103.

69. C. K. Webster, ed., *British Diplomacy, 1813-1815* (London, 1921), p. 16.

70. The convention on subsidies and union between Russia and England, concluded in Reichenbach on 3/15 June 1813 (F. Martens, *Sobranie traktatov,* 11:169-174).

71. See Lieven to Nesselrode, 4/16 July 1813, in AVPR, f. Kantseliariia, d. 6834, 1. 5.

72. Adams, *Memoirs,* 2:491ff.; Gallatin, Adams, and Bayard to Rumiantsev, 18/30 July 1813, in AVPR, f. Kantseliariia, d. 3344, ll. 2-3. For copies of credential letters and Madison's letters of 6 May 1813, see *ibid.,* ll. 4-5, 11. For Rumiantsev's reply to the American Plenipotentiaries, see *ibid.,* d. 3345, ll. 2-4.

73. *Ibid.,* d. 3344, 1. 9.

74. Rumiantsev to the American Plenipotentiaries, 24 July/5 Aug. 1813, *ibid.,* d. 3345, 1. 5. As was done with other official documents, Rumiantsev sent a copy of this note to Alexander I who returned it with a mark of approval. This was the way in which the Tsar approved other documents emanating from Rumiantsev.

75. Rumiantsev to Alexander I, 21 Aug./2 Sept. 1813, *ibid.,* d. 7942, 1. 321.

76. *Ibid.,* d. 3345, 1. 5 (copy with Alexander I's approbation).

77. Adams, *Memoirs,* 2:511.

78. Donnan, *Papers of James A. Bayard,* pp. 231-236.

79. Adams, *Memoirs,* 2:509.

80. AVPR, f. Kantseliariia, d. 6831, ll. 100-101.

81. Rumiantsev to Alexander I, 13/25 Aug. 1813, *ibid.,* d. 7942, 1. 282.

82. For more details see Adams, *Memoirs,* 2:516-518.

83. Gallatin to Baring, 27 Aug. 1813, in Gallatin, *Writings,* 1:564-567.

84. 27 Aug./8 Sept. 1813, in AVPR, f. Kantseliariia, d. 7942, ll. 331-332.

85. To Harris, 1/13 Sept. 1813, in Gallatin, *Writings,* 1:575; Gallatin to General Moreau, 2 Sept. 1813, *ibid.,* p. 579.

86. Adams, *Memoirs,* 2:593.

87. To Nesselrode, 1 Sept. 1813, in *ASPFR,* 3:622; AVPR, f. Kantseliariia, d. 1478, 1. 17.

88. *Ibid.,* d. 1478, 1. 17.

89. 6, 8, and 10 Sept. 1813 (Old Style), *ibid.,* d. 7944, ll. 398, 405, 410.

90. *Ibid.,* d. 6834, 1. 91.

91. 14/26 Nov. 1813, *ibid.,* d. 6835, 1. 196.

92. Adams, *Memoirs,* 2:504-505.

93. Son of Destutt de Tracy, author of the well-known *Commentaire sur l'esprit des lois de Montesquieu,* first published in the United States through Jefferson's intervention, and which subsequently influenced the Russian Decembrists, particularly P. I. Pestel (M. V. Nechkina. *Dvizhenie dekabristov* [Decembrist Movement, Moscow, 1955], 1:283; Dvoichenko-Markov, "Jefferson and the Russian Decembrists," *The American Slavic and East European Review,* 9:162-168 [Oct. 1950]).

94. Adams, *Memoirs,* 2:522.

95. *Ibid.,* pp. 529-532 (10 Oct. 1813).

96. *Ibid.,* p. 531.

97. 28 Sept./10 Oct. 1812, in AVPR, f. Kantseliariia, d. 3345, ll. 7-8.

98. Adams, *Memoirs,* 2:532-534. It soon became known that in July 1813, the United States Senate rejected by one vote Gallatin's appointment on the grounds that the functions of the Secretary of the Treasury and a minister plenipotentiary were incompatible (Monroe to Gallatin, 5 Aug. 1813, in NA, Diplomatic Instructions: All Countries, 7:305-306; *The Weekly Register,* 7 Aug. 1813, 4:377-379). Having learned about this from the newspapers, Gallatin accordingly informed

Rumiantsev on 3 Nov. 1813.

99. Adams, *Memoirs,* 2:541-542.

100. *Ibid.,* 2:542-543. In a dispatch of 22 Nov. 1813, Adams informed Monroe of the categorical refusal by the British cabinet of Russian mediation and of the offer to conduct direct negotiations (NA, Diplomatic Despatches: Russia, vol. 2).

101. Adams, *Memoirs,* 2:551-552.

102. *Ibid.,* p. 591.

103. *The Weekly Register,* 29 May 1813, 4:209.

104. *Ibid.,* 4 Sept. 1813, 5:5.

105. Hildt, *Early Diplomatic Negotiations,* pp. 68-69.

106. *Ibid.,* p. 193.

107. To Nesselrode, 15/27 Dec. 1813, in AVPR, f. Kantseliariia, d. 6834, ll. 309-310.

108. Castlereagh to Monroe, 4 Nov. 1813, in *ASPFR,* 3:621.

109. Adams, *Memoirs,* 2:553-554 (3 Jan. 1814).

110. Adams and Bayard to Rumiantsev, 31 Dec. 1813/12 Jan. 1814, in AVPR, f. Kantseliariia, d. 3346, ll. 4-5; Rumiantsev to the American Plenipotentiaries, 5/17 Jan. 1814, *ibid.,* d. 3347, ll. 3-4.

111. Adams and Bayard to Rumiantsev, 7/19 Jan. 1814, and Gallatin to Rumiantsev, 10/22 Jan. 1814, *ibid.,* d. 3346, ll. 6-7, 8ff.

112. Adams to Rumiantsev, 21 Jan./2 Feb. 1814; Rumiantsev to Adams, 23 Jan./4 Feb. 1814, *ibid.,* d. 3346, l. 18, and d. 3347, l. 9.

113. Adams to Monroe, 5 Feb. 1814, in Adams, *Writings,* 5:12-18; Adams, *Memoirs,* 2:568-573.

114. Adams, *Writings,* 5:13. The diary notation quotes in French (*Memoirs,* 2:571; AP, J. Q. Adams, Diary, Reel 32, p. 65).

115. *VPR,* vol. 3, p. 651.

116. To Monroe, 5 Feb. 1814, in Adams, *Writings,* 5:15-16.

117. To Vedemeier, 26 March/7 April 1814, in AVPR, f. Kantseliariia, d. 3336. ll. 23-24; Adams, *Writings,* 5:29-33.

118. Adams, *Memoirs,* 2:599-600.

119. Adams, *Writings,* 5:35.

120. AVPR, f. Kantseliariia, d. 12170, ll. 310-312.

121. Hamilton, *Writings of Monroe,* 5:280.

122. AVPR, f. Kantseliariia, d. 12170, ll. 305ff.

123. Monroe to Adams and Bayard, 8 Jan. 1814, in NA, Diplomatic Instructions: All Countries, 7:310.

124. Monroe to Adams, 3 Feb. 1814, in *ibid.,* p. 328.

125. See Bemis, *John Quincy Adams,* p. 189; Instructions to the American Plenipotentiaries of 28 Jan. 1814, in NA, Diplomatic Instructions: All Countries, 7:311-321. For the open part see *ASPFR,* 3:700-701; for the secret part, Donnan, *Papers of James A. Bayard,* pp. 263-265. In one of the secret paragraphs Monroe developed his ideas on the reasons for England's refusal of Russian mediation and on the advantages of this mediation for the United States (NA, Diplomatic Instructions: All Countries, 7:319). He also stressed the necessity of preserving mutual understanding with Russia and other Baltic powers, as if the negotiations were conducted with Russian mediation (*ibid.,* p. 320).

126. Gallatin to Crawford, 21 April 1814, in Gallatin, *Writings,* 1:602-605; Crawford to the American Plenipotentiaries, 13 and 24 May 1814, *ibid.,* pp. 614-617.

127. Lafayette to Crawford, 26 May 1814, *ibid.,* pp. 623-624.

128. Marx and Engels, *Sochineniia,* 14:511.

129. Gallatin to Monroe, 20 June 1814, in Gallatin, *Writings,* 1:633.

130. He was of Swiss origin and to the end of his days spoke English with an accent.

131. Gallatin to Alexander I, 19 June 1814, in Gallatin, *Writings,* 1:629-631 (English translation); for the French original, see AVPR, f. Kantseliariia, d. 1657, ll. 3-4.

132. Vedemeier to Nesselrode, 8/16 Sept. 1814, *ibid.,* d. 7953, l. 76.

133. To Harris, 9 July 1814, in Adams, *Writings,* 5:58.

134. A. T. Mahan, "The Negotiations at Ghent in 1814," *AHR,* 11:78 (Oct. 1905).

135. Liverpool to Castlereagh, 18 Nov. 1814, in Henry Adams, *History,* 9:42.

136. Miller, *Treaties,* 2:574-584.

137. AVPR, f. Kantseliariia, d. 3348, ll. 6-7.

138. See Harris' letters to Vedemeier and Italinsky of 27 July/8 Aug. 1815, *ibid.,* ll. 14, 16. On l. 15 there is a notation to the effect that Harris' address was sent to Italinsky in Constantinople with a letter of 2/14 Aug. A month later Italinsky wrote of the first steps undertaken by him in Constantinople in this connection (to Harris, 2/14 Sept. 1815, *ibid.,* d. 3349, l.3).

139. Adams, *Memoirs,* 5:160; F. Martens, *Sobranie traktatov,* 11:289-299.

Chapter 12. Cultural Contacts and American Attitudes toward the Russian War of 1812

1. To Rumiantsev, 6 Jan. 1811, in TsGAOR, f. 907, op. 1, d. 72, ll. 1-2; A List of North American Plants, *ibid.,* ll. 3-4. Still earlier, F. P. Pahlen sent cotton seeds to St. Petersburg (see Pahlen to Rumiantsev, 13/25 Dec. 1810, in AVPR, f. Kantseliariia, d. 12163, ll. 103-104).

2. See Dashkov's report to Nesselrode about the activity in the United States for ten years, in TsGAOR, f. 907, op. 1, d. 102, l. 3, and also a detailed description of a cotton gin, *ibid.,* d. 104, ll. 1-2. In the United States, on the other hand, there was considerable interest in the Russian experience, particularly in the method of production of high quality Russian hemp. In a special note to Adams in the summer of 1810, Secretary of State Smith described this as a matter of "great national importance" and asked for information not only on the methods of hemp culture in Russia, but also on the ways of preparing it for sale. See Smith to Adams, 5 June 1810, in AP, Letters Received and Other Loose Papers, Reel 409. In Nov. 1810, Adams sent to Washington all the information that he could gather on this subject, including extracts from books, drawings with explanations, etc. See Adams to Smith, 17/29 Nov. 1810, and the supplements "On the Culture and Preparation of Hemp in Russia," and "On the Culture of Hemp," in NA, Diplomatic Despatches: Russia, vol. 1.

3. Dashkov to Rumiantsev, 4 Jan. 1811, in AVPR, f. Kantseliariia, d. 9240, ll. 2-3; *PSZRI,* 32:698; Adams to Fulton, 29 Jan. 1814, in Adams, *Writings,* 5:12. In view of Fulton's inability to fulfill the conditions of the ukase and of his premature death on 13 Feb. 1815, the rights of his heirs for privileges in Russia were canceled. For more details, see V. S. Virginsky, *Robert Fulton, 1765-1815* (Moscow, 1965), pp. 214-251. A number of documents on this subject are pre-

served in the Adams Papers, including the originals of Letters from Fulton, Rumiantsev, and Kozodavlev. One can point, particularly, to the first letter of the inventor to J. Q. Adams of 6/18 Nov. 1812, Rumiantsev's letters of 6/18 Nov. and 8/20 Jan. 1814, Kozodavlev's letter of 29 Jan./10 Feb. 1814, and others: AP, Letters Received and Other Loose Papers, Reels 413-417.

4. See, especially, the minutes of the meeting of the Committee of Ministers, 6/18 Oct. 1817, on the subject of Evstaf'ev's note about the machines brought by him from America, and also the presentation of Dashkov to Nesselrode on 29 Aug./10 Sept. 1819 of a *fusil à dix coups* invented by Thomas Barry (TsGIA, f. 1263, op. 1, d. 128, ll. 136, 167-176; TsGAOR, f. 907, op. 1, d. 94, ll. 3, 7, and others).

5. Adams, *Memoirs*, 2:220.

6. Mainwaring, *John Quincy Adams and Russia*, p. 42.

7. See Davis to Adams, 1 Aug. 1809; and Fisher to Adams, 3/15 Feb. 1810, in AP, Letters Received and Other Loose Papers, Reels 408-409; Mainwaring, *John Quincy Adams and Russia*, p. 50. Upon his return from the United States, Dashkov became an honorary member of the Society of Amateurs of the Natural Sciences. See the Society's Diploma of 15/27 March 1824, signed by Fisher (TsGAOR, f. 907, op. 1, d. 96, l. 2).

8. Etter to Adams, May 1811, in AP, Letters Received and other Loose Papers, Reel 411; Adams to Josiah Quincy, 21 May 1811, in Boston Athenaeum—American Academy, Letters, 3:79; Mainwaring, *John Quincy Adams and Russia*, p. 49.

9. Dvoichenko-Markov, "The Russian Members," *PAPS*, 109:56; Boston Athenaeum —American Academy of Arts and Sciences, Records, 1:268,269.

10. Dvoichenko-Markov, "The American Philosophical Society," *ibid.*, 94:566; Rumiantsev to Adams, 27 Dec. 1810 (Old Style), in AP, Letters Received and Other Loose Papers, Reel 410; Rush to Adams, 15 Jan., 13 Nov. 1812, and others, *ibid.*, Reels 413-414.

11. Ricketson to Adams, 14 March 1812, *ibid.*, Reel 413.

12. Adams, *Memoirs*, 2:115.

13. Tilesius to Wister, Oct. 1, 1813, Oct. 1813, Jan. 27, 1814 (Old Style), in American Philosophical Society, B W 76, pp. 36, 37.

14. A. J. von Krusenstern, *Reise um die Welt in den Jahren 1803, 1804, 1805, und 1806* (St. Petersburg, 1810), Erster Teil.

15. Adams to Davis, 14 Sept. 1810, in AP, J. Q. Adams, Letter-book, "Private," Reel 135, pp. 224-225; Mainwaring, *John Quincy Adams and Russia,* pp. 42, 46.

16. It is interesting to note that in the list of books enclosed in one of Adams' letters to the President of Harvard University, Samuel Webber, there is, under No. 6, a work by Karzhavin (Adams to Webber, 8 June 1810 in AP, J. Adams' Letter-book "Private," Reel 135). It is a book of E. N. Karzhavin, printed by F. V. Karzhavin in St. Petersburg in 1789 and, again in 1791, in a corrected and augmented edition (*Remarques sur la langue russiènne et sur son alphabet,* Publ., corr. et augm. par Phéodore Karjavine).

17. Mainwaring, *John Quincy Adams and Russia*, pp. 50-51.

18. *Ibid.*, pp. 44ff.

19. One part of the present section is published in the journal *Novaia i noveishaiia istoriia,* 1962, no. 6, pp. 93-97.

20. See E. D. Clark, *Travels in Various Countries of Europe, Asia and Africa* (6 vols., London, 1810-1823). The first volume, devoted largely to Russia, was re-

issued several times and was translated into German and French. A most extensive collection of old foreign publications about Russia is kept in the State Public Library in Leningrad (Collection *Rossica*). See *Bibliothèque Impériale Publique de St. Pétersbourg Catalogue de la Sec. des Rossica ou Ecrits sur la Russie en Langues Etrangères* (2 vols. St. Petersburg, 1873).

21. Dashkov to Rumiantsev, 10/22 Dec. 1812, in AVPR, f. Kantseliariia, d. 12168, ll. 261-264.

22. A. Eustaphieve, *Reflections, Notes and Original Anecdotes Illustrating the Character of Peter the Great* (Boston, 1814).

23. Dashkov to Rumiantsev, 26 Feb./9 March 1812, in AVPR, d. 12168, l. 34.

24. For the text of the notation of 17 Jan. 1812, see Dvoichenko-Markov, "The American Philosophical Society," p. 570. Poletika was elected as a foreign member of the Society in 1822 (*ibid.*, p. 610).

25. Svin'in to the American Philosophical Society, *ibid.*, pp. 595-596.

26. P. Svin'in, *Sketches of Moscow and St. Petersburg* (Philadelphia, 1813), p. 2. The book is illustrated with "nine coloured engravings, taken from nature." Svin'in (Svenin) was a member of the Academy of Fine Arts in St. Petersburg (see GPB, f. 679, d. 10, l. 1). In America he established contact with the Academy of Arts in New York and apparently became an honorary member (this fact is mentioned on the title page of the book), thus establishing the first direct contact between the Academies of the two countries. While in the United States, Svin'in painted a great many water colors which were highly appreciated by specialists. See S. P. Feld, "Two Hundred Years of Water Color Painting in America," *Antiques*, Dec. 1966, p. 844. Fifty-two water colors are reproduced in A. Yarmolinsky, *Picturesque United States of America, 1811, 1812, 1813: Being a Memoir on Paul Svenin* (New York, 1930).

27. Among the very few investigators whose attention was drawn by Evstaf'ev's activity I must single out the names of such prominent scholars as M. P. Alekseev, to whose note I referred to in Chapter VII (note 24), and Leo Wiener (see Wiener, "The First Russian Consul at Boston," *The Russian Review*, 1:131-140 (April 1916).

28. I used the second Boston edition (1813) and examined earlier London editions (A. Eustaphieve, *The Resources of Russia in the Event of a War with France with a Short Description of the Cozaks* (2d ed., corrected and improved with an appendix, containing a sketch of the campaign in Russia, Boston, 1813; 3rd ed., London. 1813).

29. *Reply to the Edinburgh Reviewers, By the Author of The Resources of Russia, etc.* (Boston, 1813), p. 6. The booklet apparently was a reply to a lengthy review in *The Edinburgh Review or Critical Journal*, 21:219-252 (Feb. 1813).

30. See the publication of M. Radetsky and N. Gorokhova, "1812 god: mir privetstvoval velikuiu pobedu russkogo naroda" (The Year 1812: The World Greeted the Great Victory of the Russian People), *Mezhdunarodnaiia zhizn'* (International Life), 1962, no. 8, pp. 154-158; N. G. Gutkina, "Otkliki v Anglii na Otechestvennuiu voinu 1812 goda" (English Responses to the Patriotic War of 1812), *Novaia i noveishaia istoriia*, 1962, no. 5, pp. 84-91.

31. See materials of the session of the Committee of Historians of the USSR and East Germany dedicated to the 150th anniversary of the war of liberation of 1813 in Germany (papers by N. M. Druzhinin and A. L. Narochnitsky were published in *Voprosy istorii*, 1964, no. 4); A. G. Vlaskin's article is in *Novaia i noveishaia istoriia*, 1962, no. 5, pp. 72-83, and other works.

32. *Aurora*, 10 Nov. 1812.

33. *The National Intelligencer,* 8. Dec. 1812 (from Cobbett's Weekly Register *Northern Star).*

34. *The Boston Gazette,* 3 Dec. 1812.

35. *The Weekly Messenger,* 20 Nov. 1812.

36. *The Boston Gazette,* 3 Dec. 1812.

37. 11 Dec. 1812, in AVPR, f. Kantseliariia, d. 12168, ll. 271-272.

38. To Rumiantsev, 14 Jan. 1813, *ibid.,* d. 2585, l. 2ff.

39. To Rumiantsev, 16/28 Jan. 1813, *ibid.,* d. 12170, ll. 22-27, partially published by M. Radetsky and N. Gorokhova in *Mezhdunarodnaiia Zhizn',* 1962, no. 8, pp. 154-158.

40. *The Boston Gazette,* 21 Jan. 1813.

41. The exceptional precision of Evstaf'ev's "predictions" and the valuable factual material of his works led his Boston editors Monroe and Francis to propose to him a publication of excerpts from his works. This resulted in an interesting compilation in which are collected excerpts from his books, booklets, and pamphlets, and also passages from numerous articles in various American newspapers, usually published without a signature; see *Memorable Predictions of the Late Events in Europe, Extracted from the Writings of Alexis Eustaphieve, Esquire* (Boston, 1814). As most other rare, foreign editions, Evstaf'ev's books, with personal autographs, are kept in the Collection *Rossica.* See also N. M. Gol'dberg, *Russko-amerikanskie otnosheniia.* This collection has the largest number of foreign publications on the War of 1812 in the world (more than 1,100 books, pamphlets, and broadsides). See *Voprosy istorii,* 1962, no. 6, pp. 208-212.

42. To Rumiantsev, 19 June/1 July 1813, in AVPR, f. Kantseliariia, d. 12170, l. 254. See also, Kozlov to Rumiantsev, 1 May 1813, *ibid.,* d. 2585, ll. 72-74.

43. *The Weekly Register,* 10 April 1813, 4:89-91. Earlier, Niles' newspaper paid close attention to the Russian War of 1812, although it was far from objective in its judgments on Russia.

44. *Ibid.,* p. 90.

45. *Sketch of the Church Solemnities at the Stone Chapel and Festival at the Exchange, Thursday, March 25, 1813, in Honour of the Russian Achievements* (Boston, 1813); Mainwaring, *John Quincy Adams and Russia,* pp. 19-20; Wiener, "The First Russian Consul at Boston," pp. 136-137.

46. The Festival was reported in the newspapers with inaccuracies (see *Federal Republican and Commercial Gazette,* 7 and 9 June 1813). A separate pamphlet was published later: *The Celebration of the Russian Victories, In Georgetown, District of Columbia; on the 5th of June, 1813* (Georgetown, 1813).

47. *Ibid.,* p. 2.

48. *Ibid.,* p. 4. The Russian Minister expressed deep appreciation to Custis in a letter of 7 July 1813 and sent him a medal as a special token of respect. In his answer Custis wrote: "Russia hath warred in the very noblest cause for which a brave nation ever drew the sword, for the proudest, for the holiest right." ("The Right of Self-Government," *ibid.,* p. 39.)

49. For the full text of Harper's speech, see *ibid.,* pp. 10-27.

50. 24 July 1813, in Archive of LOII, f. 36, op. 2, d. 205, ll. 7-8.

51. Smith to Vorontsov, 16 March 1815, *ibid.,* ll. 10.

52. According to Dashkov, there were up to 359 newspapers and journals published in the United States (see "Note sur les gazettes Américaines," 1812, in AVPR, f. Kantseliariia, d. 12168, l. 13-14; TsGAOR, f. 907, op. 1, d. 66, l. 1).

53. *Correspondence respecting Russia, between Robert Goodloe Harper, esq. and Robert Walsh, Jun.* (Philadelphia, 1813).

54. Walsh to Harper, 27 July 1813, *ibid.*, p. 30.

55. *Ibid.*, pp. 32, 61, 107.

56. J. Shulim, "The United States Views Russia in the Napoleonic Age," *PAPS*, 102:155 (April 1958).

57. Harper to Walsh, 7 Aug. 1813, in *Correspondence respecting Russia*, pp. 40-41.

58. A. Eustaphieve, *Strictures on "The Correspondence respecting Russia": Published as a supplement to P. Tchouykevitch, "Reflection on the War of 1812"* (Boston, 1813), which was translated into English by Evstaf'ev. In analyzing these polemics, one must take into account that in a number of cases Walsh's critical remarks were essentially just (i.e., on serfdom, on the hard conditions of the peasants' life, on the primitive state of agriculture, etc.), although they were insulting in their form and obviously exaggerated. In contradicting them Evstaf'ev was made to appear an adherent of serfdom and a propagandist of its advantages, although in reality he was neither. His characteristic admission is not accidental: "I am not an advocate of slavery in any form, and I do not possess any slaves in Russia" (*ibid.*, p. 110).

59. Shulim, "The United States Views Russia," pp. 154, 156, 159. See Kozlov to Rumiantsev, 14 Jan. 1813, in AVPR, f. Kantseliariia, d. 2585, l. 2; Dashkov to Rumiantsev, 16/28 Jan. 1813, *ibid.*, d. 12170, ll. 24-25; Dashkov to Rumiantsev, 19 June/1 July 1813, *ibid.*, ll. 254-256.

60. William E. Nagengast, "Moscow, the Stalingrad of 1812: American Reaction toward Napoleon's Retreat from Russia," *The Russian Review*, 8:310 (October 1949).

61. See Dashkov to Monroe, 26 April 1813, with the enclosure of Evstaf'ev's letter of 17 April 1813 in NA, Russia: Notes, 1:102, 103; Monroe to Dashkov, 27 April 1813, in AVPR, f. Po-vo v Vashingtone, d. 6, l. 79.

62. Jefferson, *Writings*, 11:291-292; Shulim, "The United States Views Russia," pp. 149-150.

63. J. Q. Adams to T. B. Adams, 14 July 1812, in Adams, *Writings*, 4:375.

64. To Monroe, 16 Dec. 1812, *ibid.*, pp. 422-423.

65. To Monroe, 2 Feb. 1813, *ibid.*, p. 432.

66. It is characteristic that a sharp anti-Russian letter, "Europe's Liberators," printed in the pages of the *National Intelligencer* (Aug. 1, 1815), evoked a reply in the name of the *United States Gazette*, pointing out the friendly ties between Russia and the United States and condemning the position of Washington officialdom during the war as "only a weak echo of the French *Moniteur*" (AVPR, f. Kantseliariia, d. 12174, ll. 53-54).

67. *Ibid.*, d. 12166, ll. 5-52.

68. See Dashkov's personal file in TsGAOR, f. 907, op. 1, d. 50, 52, 66, 68-69, 73, 79, 91-92, 98, 107, 125, and others. Without dwelling in detail on this material (much of which deals with the period after 1815), I would call attention to an interesting note about the society "for colonization of free Negroes" which is erroneously entitled in the archive as a note on the "composition of population in Philadelphia." "A respect for the rights of human beings and admission that Negroes should not be deprived of them only because they were born in other climes and their skin color is darker than ours could be found in America even at the time when the colonies were still subject to the English government," Dashkov wrote justly, and pointed further to the example of the Quakers. The Minister was able to penetrate the real designs of the organizers of the American Colonization Society, pointing out that the main aim of carrying "free Negroes" from the United

States consisted in "affirming still further the right of property over the slaves and strengthening their chains for a long time to come" (see TsGAOR, f. 907, op. 1, d. 69, l. 1).

69. Touching on the history of his work, Svin'in wrote: "I had some flattering offers to publish my drawings and sketches with descriptions of America, from England where everything new and curious is received by the public with special encouragement; but the thought that I would be obliged to write in a foreign tongue, and often against the commands of my heart, my views, and justice—not the way I feel, but as England's policy might demand, or as the editors of my work might wish, who might perhaps use me as a tool of their hatred toward the United States—finally, the thought that my labors would be put into the hands of foreigners, that their first fruit would not be reaped by my own country . . . made me reject all the advantages offered and undertake the description of my colorful voyage in the United American Regions in my own language" (*Opyt,* pp. 2-3).

70. In 1811 Poletika had compiled an extensive note for the tsarist government on internal conditions in the United States and their relations with Russia (AVPR, f. Kantseliariia, d. 7697, ll. 2-17). Having collected an extensive amount of data, he already at that time was planning to publish a statistical survey of the United States and mentioned this plan during his encounter with J. Q. Adams in St. Petersburg in 1812 (Adams, *Memoirs,* 2:406). Unfortunately, Poletika was not able to realize his plans in the near future; his work was finished only in the spring of 1823, after his return from his post as Minister to the United States. A French edition was published anonymously in London and translated in the United States (*A Sketch of the Internal Conditions of the United States and Their Political Relations with Europe. By a Russian* [Baltimore, 1826]). In 1830, through Pushkin's services, an article of Poletika's, "Sostoianie obshchestva v Soedinennykh Shtatakh" (The Condition of Society in the United States of America) was published in *Literaturnaia gazeta.*

71. *A Sketch of the Internal Conditions,* Publisher's Preface.

72. *Ibid.,* pp. 21, 106-111. We can thus see that Poletika had worked out in some detail the theory of colonization and frontier before Hegel, de Tocqueville, and Loria, not to mention Turner. See N. N. Bolkhovitinov, "O roli 'podvizhnoi granitsy' v istorii SShA (Kriticheskii analiz kontseptsii F. D. Ternera)" (On the Role of the Frontier in the History of the United States [A critical Analysis of Turner's Concept]), *Voprosy istorii,* 1962, no. 9, pp. 57-74. An English translation appears in *Soviet Studies in History,* 2:2, 50-66 (Fall 1963).

73. *A Sketch of the Internal Conditions,* pp. 29, 40-41, 121ff.

Conclusion

1. A. Gamil'ton, *Otchet general-kaznacheia A. Gamil'tona, uchinennyi Amerikanskim Shtatam 1791 g. o pol'ze manufaktur v otnoshenii onykh k torgovle i zemledeliiu* (Report of Treasurer-General A. Hamilton, Presented to the United States in 1791, on the Usefulness of the Manufactories in Relation to Trade and Agriculture, St. Petersburg, 1807), p. 1.

Appendix: Writings and Sources

1. Thomas A. Bailey, *America Faces Russia: Russian-American Relations from Early Times to Our Day* (Ithaca, N.Y., 1950). In 1964 this book was reissued by the author, unfortunately without any changes.

2. Clarence A. Manning, *Russian Influence on Early America* (New York,

1953); Erwin Hölzle, *Russland und Amerika: Aufbruch und Begegnung zweier Weltmächte* (Munich, 1953); Victor Aleksandrov, *L'Ours et la baleine: L'histoire des rélations extraordinaires russo-américaines* (Paris, 1958).

3. Manning, *Russian Influence*, p. vii.

4. Hölzle, *Russland und Amerika*, pp. 81-150, 163-166, *passim*.

5. Oliver Jensen, ed., *America and Russia: A Century and a Half of Dramatic Encounters* (New York, 1962), p. 11.

6. *Ibid.*, pp. 12, 40-62.

7. Oscar S. Strauss, "The United States and Russia: Their Historical Relations," *The North American Review*, 181:237-250 (Aug. 1905).

8. Robert Walsh, *Correspondence Respecting Russia between Robert Goodloe Harper and Robert Walsh, Jr.* (Philadelphia, 1813).

9. Alexandre Tarsaidze, *Tsars and Presidents: The Story of a Forgotten Friendship* (New York, 1958), pp. v-vi.

10. John C. Hildt, *Early Diplomatic Negotiations of the United States with Russia* (Baltimore, 1906), series 24, nos. 5-6 in *Johns Hopkins University Studies in Historical and Political Science.*

11. Henry Adams, *A History of the United States of America during the Administrations of Jefferson and Madison* (9 vols., New York, 1931). It is strange that with all the sources available to him, the author utilized perhaps least of all the Adams family manuscripts; in his study there are practically no references to this extremely rich source.

12. I do not touch upon the extensive literature on the various problems of international relations from 1775 to 1815, the foreign policies of the United States and Russia, their internal situation, economic conditions, etc. Naturally, it has been necessary in each concrete case to take advantage of the various specialized studies of foreign as well as Soviet authors. Some examples are the well-known works of Academician E. V. Tarle, in particular his basic monograph on the Continental Blockade, *Sochineniia* (Works, Moscow, 1958), vol. 3; the extensive research by Isabel de Madariaga on the Armed Neutrality of 1780, *Britain, Russia and the Armed Neutrality of 1780* (New Haven, 1962); the books of Bradford Perkins on Anglo-American relations: *The First Rapprochement* (Philadelphia, 1955); *Prologue to War* (Berkeley, 1961); *Castlereagh and Adams* (Berkeley, 1964); etc. Nor must one fail to mention the numerous works by Samuel Flagg Bemis, the chief specialist in American foreign policy during the period under review: *The Diplomacy of the American Revolution* (New York, 1935; rev. ed. 1957); *Pinckney's Treaty* (New Haven, 1960); *John Quincy Adams and the Foundations of American Foreign Policy* (New York, 1949); etc.

13. Max Laserson, *The American Impact on Russia, 1784-1917* (New York, 1950), p. vii.

14. This mistake is carried over into the new, posthumous edition of Laserson's book; see *The American Impact on Russia 1784-1917* (New York, 1962), p. 7.

15. Avrahm Yarmolinsky, *Russian Americana: Sixteenth to Eighteenth Centuries: A Bibliographical and Historical Study* (New York, 1943), pp. 36-37, 43.

16. Anna M. Babey, *Americans in Russia, 1776-1917: A Study of the American Travelers in Russia from the American Revolution to the Russian Revolution* (New York, 1938).

17. John Ledyard came to Russia, not in 1785, but two years later, in 1787. Harris, on the other hand, was already in Russia in the autumn of 1803, not 1804, as Babey indicates (*ibid.*, pp. 3, 6-7).

18. *Ibid.*, pp. 127-169.

19. G. P. Kuropiatnik and I. A. Beliavskaia, "Sovetskaia literatura po istorii SShA (Soviet Literature on the History of the United States), *Sovetskaia istoricheskaia nauka ot XX k XXII s'ezdu KPSS: Istoriia Zapadnoi Evropy i Ameriki* (Soviet Historical Sciences from the 20th to the 22nd Congress of the CPSU: The History of Western Europe and America, Moscow, 1963), pp. 149-150.

20. See A. V. Efimov, *Ocherki istorii SShA: Ot otkrytii Ameriki do okonchaniia grazhdanskoi voiny* (Essays on the History of the United States: From the Discovery of America to the Conclusion of the Civil War, Moscow, 2nd ed., 1958); *Istoriia diplomatii* (The History of Diplomacy, Moscow, 2nd ed., 1959), 1: 382-403, 503-525, 670-690.

21. A. V. Efimov, *Iz istorii velikikh russkikh geograficheskikh otkrytii* (From the History of the Great Russian Geographical Discoveries, Moscow, 1950), p. 233.

22. The earliest information concerning America in Russian sources originates in the sixteenth century. The passage to this effect from the work of Maxim Grek, dating approximately to 1530, has been repeatedly subjected to a careful analysis. The learned monk, commenting on one of the "puzzling expressions" of Grigori Bogoslov, Patriarch of Constantinople, cities some extremely general information concerning the discovery of "the new world," and even mentions "a most vast land, called Cuba, the limits of which people living there do not know." More detailed, although far less reliable information concerning the new continent is found in the compilation *Khronika vsego sveta* (Chronicle of the Whole World) by M. Belsky, whose Russian translation is dated 1584. It is in this manuscript that the term "America" as the name of "a great island," discovered in the voyage of Americus Vespucci, is first used in the Russian language. For more details see Yarmolinsky, *Russian Americana*; L. S. Berg, *Ocherki po istorii russkikh geograficheskikh otkrytii* (Essays in the History of Russian Geographical Discoveries, Moscow and Leningrad, 1949), pp. 72-79; N. Lazarev, "Pervye svedeniia russkikh o Novom mire" (The First Information by A Russian Concerning the New World, *Istoricheskii Zhurnal* (The Historical Journal), 1943, no. 1, pp. 72-75.

23. Eufrosina Dvoichenko-Markov, "William Penn and Peter the Great," *PAPS*, 97:12-25 (Feb. 1953); for the text of a letter from Penn to Peter I, see *ibid.*, pp. 16-17.

24. See Jacob Myron Price, *The Tobacco Adventure to Russia: Enterprise, Politics, and Diplomacy in the Quest for a Northern Market for English Colonial Tobacco, 1676-1722* (Philadelphia, 1961); Efimov, *Iz istorii velikikh russkikh geograficheskikh otkrytii*, pp. 221-224; Raymond A. Mohl, "America Discovers Russia and Peter the Great," *Journalism Quarterly,* 44:659-666 (Winter 1967).

25. I have dwelt in so much detail on the foundations of a chronological framework because, in actuality, there exists no definite opinion on this question in historical writing, and investigators are often guided by rather haphazard and secondary considerations. To a certain extent, this can be said about the work of N. M. Gol'dberg, "Russko-amerikanskie otnosheniia v nachale XIX veka: 1801-1815" (Russian-American Relations at the Beginning of the Nineteenth Century: 1801-1815, unpub. diss., Leningrad State University, 1947), which is as yet the only qualifying dissertation devoted to the history of early Russian-American contacts.

26. A. I. Startsev, "Veniamin Franklin i russkoe obshchestvo XVIII veka" (Benjamin Franklin and Russian Society of the Eighteenth Century), *Internatsional'naia literatura* (International Literature), 1940, nos. 3-4; "O zapadnykh sviaziakh Radishcheva" (On Radishchev's Western contacts), *ibid.*, 1940, no.

7/8, pp. 256-265; "Amerika i russkoe obshchestvo" (America and Russian Society), *ibid.*, 1941, no. 9. Subsequently, Startsev published some interesting information about F. V. Karzhavin and his American journey (*Istoriia SSSR* [History of the USSR], 1960, no. 3), and a new study of Radishchev, *Radishchev v gody "Puteshestviia"* (Radishchev in the Years of his "Journey," Moscow, 1960).

27. A. I. Startsev-Kunin, "Amerikanskaia revoliutsiia, Radishchev i russkoe obshchestvo XVIII veka" (The American Revolution, Radishchev, and Russian Society of the Eighteenth Century, unpub. diss., Moscow State University, 1946).

28. *Ibid.*, p. 3.

29. *Ibid.*, pp. 130ff.

30. See Chapter V.

31. *Uchenaia korrespondentsiia Akademii nauk XVIII veka: 1766-1782* (The Scholarly Correspondence of the Academy of Sciences of the Eighteenth Century: 1766-1782, Moscow and Leningrad, 1937), p. 23.

32. E. Dvoichenko-Markov, "Benjamin Franklin, the American Philosophical Society and the Russian Academy of Science," *PAPS*, 91:250-257 (Aug. 1947).

33. The letter of 20 Feb. 1765 which Ezra Stiles asked to be forwarded to Lomonosov is preserved in the archives of the American Philosophical Society; thus, it would seem that Franklin did not send it to St. Petersburg (see G. M. Lester, "Znakomstvo uchenykh Severnoi Ameriki kolonial'nogo perioda s rabotami M. V. Lomonosova i Peterburgskoi akademii nauk" [Familiarity of the Scientists in North America in the Colonial Period with the Works of M. V. Lomonosov and the Petersburg Academy of Sciences], *Voprosy istorii estestvoznaniia i tekhniki* [Problems of the History of Natural Sciences and Technology, Moscow, 1962], no. 12, p. 145, with a reference to the Franklin Papers of the American Philosophical Society). By the time Stiles' letter from America reached him in London, Franklin already may have been aware of the death of Lomonosov, which occurred 4/15 April 1765.

34. Dvoichenko-Markov, "The American Philosophical Society and Early Russian-American Relations," *PAPS*, 94:549-610 (Dec. 1950).

35. M. I. Radovsky, *Veniamin Franklin i ego sviazi s Rossiei* (Benjamin Franklin and his Contacts with Russia, Moscow and Leningrad, 1958). A number of shortcomings and gaps in this book are due to the author's lack of familiarity with American literature and sources. See also his *Veniamin Franklin 1706-1790* (Moscow and Leningrad, 1965), pp. 228ff.

36. P. Tikhmenev, *Istoricheskoe obozrenie obrazovaniia Rossiisko-amerikanskoi kompanii i deistvii ee do nastoiashchego vremeni* (A Historical Survey of the Creation of the Russian-American Company and Its Activities to the Present Time, 2 vols., St. Petersburg, 1861-1863), 1:iii-iv.

37. S. B. Okun', *Rossiisko-amerikanskaia kompaniia* (The Russian-American Company, Moscow and Leningrad, 1939), p. 8.

38. See, in particular, A. Trachevsky, ed., *Diplomaticheskie snosheniia Rossii s Frantsiei v epokhu Napoleona* (Russia's Diplomatic Relations with France in the Era of Napoleon), 4 vols., published in *SbRIO* (St. Petersburg, 1890-1893), vols. 70, 77, 82, 88; Grand Duke Nikolai Mikhailovich [Romanov], *Diplomaticheskie snosheniia Rosii s Frantsiei po doneseniiam poslov imperatorov Aleksandra i Napoleona: 1808-1812* (Diplomatic Relations between Russia and France through the Reports of the Ambassadors of Emperors Alexander and Napoleon: 1808-1812, 6 vols., St. Petersburg, 1905-1914); A. A. Polovtsov, ed., *Doneseniia frantsuzskikh predstavitelei pri russkom dvore, i russkikh predstavitelei pri frantsuzskom dvore* (Reports of French Representatives at the Russian Court and

Russian Representatives at the French Court: 1814-1820), in *SbRiO* (St. Petersburg, 1901-1908), vols. 112, 119, 127, *et al.*

39. *Arkhiv kniazia Vorontsova* (Archives of Prince Vorontsov, 40 vols., Moscow, 1870-1895). A helpful guide facilitating the use of this collection is *Rospis' soroka knigam arkhiva kniazia Vorontsova* (A Register to the Forty Books of the Archive of Prince Vorontsov, Moscow, 1897).

40. A. L. Narochnitsky and others, eds., *Vneshniaia politika Rossii XIX i nachala XX veka: Dokumenty rossiskogo ministerstva inostrannykh del. Seriia pervaia, 1801-1815 gg.* (Russia's Foreign Policy in the Nineteenth and Beginning of the Twentieth Centuries: Documents of the Russian Ministry of Foreign Affairs: First Series, 1801-1815, Moscow, 1960-1965), vols. 1-4, 6. In the selection of documents, special attention was devoted to the most important instructions and rescripts to Russian diplomats abroad, the reports of ministers, proceedings of meetings of highest state officials, as well as official diplomatic acts (treaties, most important notes, declarations, etc.). Alongside the diplomatic documents there are also included materials illuminating various aspects of Russia's military, trade, and financial policy in their connection with international relations. Since 1965 three volumes have been published, thus completing the first series covering the period from 1801 to 1815 (7 vols., Moscow, 1960-1972).

41. F. Snosheniia Rossii s SShA, 1783 g., d. 1-3.

42. F. Kantseliariia, d. 3325-3349.

43. *Ibid.*, d. 6033-6034.

44. *Ibid.*, d. 12160-12174, 9235-9245, 2585, 7698, 13405, and others.

45. F. Posolistvo v Vashingtone, op. 512/3, d. 1-9.

46. *Ibid.*, d. 1-6.

47. The following materials were of particular significance: f. Snosheniia Rossii s Angliei, op. 35/6, 1774 g., d. 261, 1775 g., d. 36-37, 266-267, 1776 g., d. 274, 1777 g., d. 282, 1778 g., d. 288, 295, 298, 595-596, 1779 g., d. 599-600, 1780 g., d. 312, 1781 g., d. 319, 320, 323, 604, 1782 g., d. 73, 331-333, 1783 g., d. 341; f. Londonskaia missiia, op. 36, 1779-1781 gg., d. 345, 1781 g., d. 357; f. Snosheniia Rossii s Frantsiei, op. 93/6, 1775 g., d. 303, 1776 g., d. 312, 1777 g., d. 323, 1778 g., d. 333, 1779 g., d. 343-345, 1780 g., d. 354, 1782 g., d. 386, 1783 g., d. 393-394, 397; f. Parizhskaia missiia, op. 941, 1781 g., d. 4, 1782 g., d. 1, chast 1, 1783 g., d. 1; f. Snosheniia Rossii s Gollandiei, 1780 g., d. 207-208, 1781 g., d. 218, 223, 1782 g., d. 28, 236-237; f. Snosheniia Rossii s Ispaniei, op. 58/1, 1780 g., d. 388, *et al.*

48. F. Snosheniia Rossii s Gollandiei, 1784 g. d. 268, 271; f. Snosheniia Rossii s Angliei, 1799 g., d. 507-509.

49. F. Snosheniia Rossii s Frantsiei, 1784 g., d. 411.

50. See in particular f. Kantseliariia, d. 6807-6810, 6820-6822, 6829, 6831, 6834-6835, *et al.*

51. F. Kantseliariia, d. 111 (Konstantinopol'); *ibid.*, d. 10825-10827 (Stokgolm), etc.

52. In this f. I examined in particular d. 36, 68, 105, 130, 153, 172-174, 177, 178, 183, 192, 207, 215, 219, 284, 419, 963, *et al.*

53. TsGAOR, f. 907, op. 1, d. 47, 49, 51, 54-57, 59, 64-69, 71-75, 78, 79, 83, 84, 88, 90-94, 96-98, 102-105, 107, 108, 115-118, 120, 123, 125, 138, 142, 154, 159, 161, 163, 170, 172, 173, 175, 176, 182, 183, 193, 262-263, 276, 300, 304, 312.

54. TsGADA, f. 276, op. 1, d. 675; TsGIA, f. 1329, op. 3, d. 310, 301; f. 13, op. 2, d. 1408. *et al.*

55. See TsGAVMF, f. 272, op. 1, d. 99, 349; f. 197, op. 1, d. 52, 67, 77; f.

223, op. 1, d. 63; f. 227, op. 1, d. 51, 53; f. 245, op. 1, d. 16, 17, 22; and TsGADA, f. 168, d. 166; f. XXIV, Gosarkhiv, op. 1, d. 62, chast' II and III.

56. TsGIA, f. 560, op. 22, d. 1; f. 13, op. 2, d. 777, 1128, 1156, 1417, 1629, 1645, 1702, 1445; TsGADA, f. 19, op. 1, d. 262, ch. 11-13 *et al.*; f. 246, op.1, d. 668; f. 19, d. 360, *et al.*

57. TsGIA, f. 1263, 1148.

58. ROIRL, f. 93, op. 2, d. 100-103.

59. Archive of LOII, f. 238, karton 146, d. 1-26.

60. See *ibid.*, f. 36, op. 1, d. 543/520, 544/190, 545/191, 546/623, 547/418, 548/434, 550/196, 551/1033, 556/426, 563/840, 564/570, 578/342, 586/83; f. 36, op. 2, d. 205.

61. GBL (otdel rukopisei), f. 204 (OIDR), k. 32, d. 1-20, 24-26, 34, 35, 37, 39, 40; f. 255 (Rumiantsev), k. 15, d. 29, 32, 33, 34, 35. For a survey of Russian materials concerning California see L. A. Shur, "Putevye zapiski i dnevniki russkikh puteshestvennikov kak istochnik po istorii Kalifornii (Pervaia polovina XIX v.)" (Travel Notes and Diaries of Russian Explorers as a Source for the History of California [First Half of the Nineteenth Century]), *Amerikanskii ezhegodnik 1971* (The American Yearbook, 1971), pp. 295-319.

62. V. I. Lenin, *Polnoe sobranie sochinenii* (Complete Works, Moscow, 1958-1970), 1:301.

63. *Ibid.*, 7: 136-137.

64. *Ibid.*, p. 135.

65. For the original of this secret report with the signatures of Panin, Osterman, and the Bakunin brothers see AVPR, f. Sekretnye mneniia, 1725-1798, d. 597, ll. 100-114.

66. Together with the materials in the appropriate sections of the present work see my articles in the journals *Istoricheskii arkhiv* (Historical Archive), 1962, no. 3, and *Novaia i noveishaia istoriia* (Modern and Contemporary History), 1961, no. 4.

67. *Guide to Materials for American History in Russian Archives,* 2 vols. (Washington, 1917, 1937).

68. *Ibid.*, 1:149-50.

69. Frank A. Golder, "Catherine II and the American Revolution," *AHR,* 21 (1915): 92-96.

70. NA, Diplomatic Instructions: All Countries, vols. 6-7; see also the bibliography.

71. NA, Diplomatic Despatches: Russia, vols. 1-2.

72. NA, Russia: Notes, vol. 1.

73. NA, Consular Despatches: St. Petersburg, vol. 1.

74. See Hubert H. Bancroft, *History of Alaska, 1730-1885* (San Francisco, 1886), p. 223.

75. NA, Records of the Russian-American Company, 1802-1867, 1:6.

76. *American State Papers: Documents, Legislative and Executive, of the Congress of the United States* (38 vols., Washington, 1832-1861) (the Saltykov-Shchedrin Public Library in Leningrad has a complete edition of this). *The Debates and Proceedings in the Congress of the United States: March 3, 1789—May 27, 1824* (42 vols., Washington, 1834-1856). Better known in historical writing as *Annals of Congress of the United States*, it was thereafter published as *Register of Debates, Congressional Globe*, and, finally, *Congressional Record.*

77. *American State Papers: Foreign Relations (1789-1828)* (6 vols., Wash-

ington, 1832-1859); hereafter cited as *ASPFR.*

78. *Papers Relating to the Foreign Relations of the United States* (Washington, 1862 to the present).

79. *Journals of the Continental Congress, 1774-1789* (34 vols., Washington, 1904-1937); hereafter cited as *JCC.*

80. *The Diplomatic Correspondence of the United States of America from the Signing of the Definitive Treaty of Peace, 10th September, 1783 to the Adoption of the Constitution, March 4, 1789* (7 vols., Washington, 1834).

81. Francis Wharton, ed., *The Revolutionary Diplomatic Correspondence of the United States* (6 vols., Washington, 1889), hereafter cited as Wharton, *Correspondence.* The Saltykov-Shchedrin Public Library has volumes 1-3, 6; the other two were obtained from the Library of Congress in Washington.

82. A knowledgeable survey of materials in the Adams family manuscripts as they relate especially to Russia was compiled recently by Marion Mainwaring; see *John Quincy Adams and Russia: A Sketch of Early Russian-American Relations as Recorded in the Papers of the Adams Family and Some of Their Contemporaries* (Quincy, Mass., 1965).

83. According to the evaluation of the Commission, the Adams family papers, as far as private materials go, have no equal in the world for significance; see *A National Program for the Publication of Historical Documents: A report to the President by the National Historical Publications Commission* (Washington, 1954), p. 18; S. F. Bemis, "The Adams Family and Their Manuscripts," *American Foreign Policy and the Blessings of Liberty* (New Haven and London, 1962), pp. 289-303.

84. Lyman H. Butterfield, ed., The Adams Papers: A Prospectus (Harvard University Press, 1961), p. 5.

85. L. H. Butterfield, "The Papers of the Adams Family: Some Account of Their History," *Proceedings of the Massachusetts Historical Society*, 71 (1953-1957): 349.

86. *Memoirs of John Quincy Adams, Comprising Portions of His Diary from 1795 to 1848* (12 vols., Phila. 1874-1877), esp. vols. I and II; (hereafter cited as J. Q. Adams, *Memoirs*). Allan Nevins republished Adams' diary: *The Diary of John Quincy Adams, 1794-1845* [New York, 1928]).

87. Worthington Chauncey Ford, ed., *Writings of John Quincy Adams* (7 vols., New York, 1913-1917); hereafter cited as J. Q. Adams, *Writings.*

88. *A National Program for the Publication of Historical Documents*, p. 9.

89. Elizabeth Donnan, ed., *Papers of James A. Bayard, 1796-1815* (Washington, 1915), in *American Historical Association, Annual Report*, 1913, v. II; Henry Adams, ed., *The Writings of Albert Gallatin* (3 vols., Philadelphia, 1879), vol. 1:1788-1816 (hereafter, Gallatin, *Writings*).

90. Albert H. Smyth, ed., *The Writings of Benjamin Franklin* (10 vols., New York, 1907); hereafter cited as Franklin, *Writings.*

91. Jared Sparks, ed., *The Works of Benjamin Franklin* (10 vols., Boston, 1840); hereafter cited as Franklin, *Works.*

92. Leonard Woods Labaree, ed., *The Papers of Benjamin Franklin* (New Haven, 1959-); hereafter cited as Franklin, *Papers.*

93. Julian P. Boyd, ed., *The Papers of Thomas Jefferson* (Princeton, 1950-); hereafter cited as Jefferson, *Papers.*

94. See "General View of the Work" (1:vii-xx) and, especially, "Editorial Method" (1:xxv-xxxviii).

95. The total edition is estimated at fifty-two volumes. Up to now eighteen volumes, encompassing documents to the early 1790's, have appeared.

96. Hezekiah Niles, *The Weekly Register, Containing Political, Historical, etc. Documents, Essays and Facts* (75 vols., Baltimore, 1811-1849); vols. 1-8 cover the years 1811-1815.

97. *Izvestie v Amerike o seleniiakh aglitskikh, v tom chisle nyne pod nazvaniem Soedinennykh Provintsii, vybrano perechnem iz noveishikh o tom prostranno sochinitelei* (News of the English Settlements in America, Including Those Now Known as the United Provinces, Selected from the Latest Detailed Writings on the Subject, St. Petersburg, 1783).

98. P. Svin'in, "Vzgliad na respubliku Soedinennykh Amerikanskikh oblastei" (A View of the Republic of the United American Provinces), *Syn otechestva* (Son of the Fatherland), 1814, pts. 17-18; and *Opyt zhivopisnogo puteshestviia po Severnoi Amerike* (The Experience of a Picturesque Journey through North America, St. Petersburg, 1815, 2nd ed., 1818).

99. *A Sketch of the Internal Conditions of the United States and of Their Political Relations with Europe. By a Russian* (Baltimore, 1826).

100. Nebolsin *Statisticheskie zapiski o vneshnei torgovle Rossi* (Statistical Notes on the Foreign Trade of Russia, St. Petersburg, 1835), pts. 1-2; Timothy Pitkin, *A Statistical View of the Commerce of the United States of America* (New Haven, U.S. Bureau of Census, *Historical Statistics of the United States:* 1835); *Colonial Times to 1957.*

101. N. N. Bolkhovitinov, "Stanovlenie russko-amerikanskikh otnoshenii, 1775-1815 gg." (2 vols., diss., Institute of History, Academy of Sciences, Moscow, 1965).

102. With deep sorrow I must mention here the death in 1971 of both Academician A. A. Guber and corresponding member of the Academy of Sciences, Professor A. V. Efimov.

103. "An Exchange of Microfilms for Historical Research," Library of Congress, *Information Bulletin,* 25(1966):162-163.

104. AP, Letters Received and Other Loose Papers, August 1809 - April 1814, reels 408-417; N. N. Bolkhovitinov, "Dzhon Kuinsi Adams i Rossiia" (John Quincy Adams and Russia), *Istoriia SSSR* (History of the USSR), 1968, no. 4, pp. 206-207.

105. A. Rasch, "American Trade in the Baltic, 1783-1807," *Scandinavian Economic History Review,* 13 (1965):31-64; Alfred W. Crosby, *America, Russia, Hemp, and Napoleon: American Trade with Russia and the Baltic,* 1783-1812 (Columbus, Ohio, 1965). For my detailed review of these works see *Novaia i noveishaia istoriia,* 1967, no. 4. S. G. Fedorova, *Russkoe naselenie Aliaski i Kalifornii. Konet XVIII veka-1867* g. (The Russian Population in Alaska and California: From the Late Eighteenth Century to 1867. Moscow, 1971); Dieter Boden, *Das Amerikabild in russischen Schriftern bis zum Ende des 19, Jahrunderts.* Hamburg, 1968; Ekkehard Völkl, *Russland und Lateinamerika 1741-1841.* (Wiesbaden, 1968); David M. Griffiths, "Nikita Panin, Russian Diplomacy and the American Revolution," *Slavic Review,* 28:1-24 (March 1969), "American Commercial Diplomacy in Russia, 1780 to 1783," *William and Mary Quarterly,* 27: 379-410 (July 1970).

Recent writings by N. N. Bolkhovitinov relating to Russian-American relations, 1775-1815

"V arkhivakh i bibliotekakh SShA: nakhodki, vstrechi, vpechatleniia" (In the U.S. Archives and Libraries: Findings, Meetings, Impressions), *Amerikanskii ezhegodnik: 1971*, pp. 329-341.

"Novye materialy po istorii russko-amerikanskikh otnoshenii XIX-nachala XX velca" (New Materials on the History of Russian-American Relations in the Nineteenth and Early Twentieth Centuries). *Materialy pervogo simpoziuma sovetskikh istorikov-amerikanistov (30 noiabria-3 dekabria 1971 g.)*, pt. 2, Moscow, 1973, pp. 101-137.

"B. Franklin i M. V. Lomonosov" (B. Franklin and M. V. Lomonosov), *Novaia i noveishaia istoriia*, 1973, no. 3, pp. 77-81.

"Iz istorii russko-amerikanskikh nauchnykh sviazei v XVIII-XIX vekakh" (From the History of Russian-American Scientific Ties in the Eighteenth and Nineteenth Centuries), *SShA—ekonomika, politika, ideologiia*, 1974, no. 5, pp. 17-25.

"Russko-amerikanskie torgovye sviazi v period voiny SShA za nezavisimost' " (Russian-American Trade Relations at the Time of the American War of Independence), *Voprosy istorii* (Problems of History), 1975, no. 1, pp. 49-57.

"Novye dokumenty o mirnom posrednichestve Rossii v voine SShA za nezavisimost' (1780-1781)" (New Documents on Russia's Peace Mediation in the American War of Independence, 1780-1781), *Amerikanskii ezhegodnik: 1975*, pp. 231-245.

INDEX

Academic News (Akademicheskie Izvestiia), 33, 34, 36, 380

Academy of Sciences (St. Petersburg), 335, 378; contacts between American Philosophical Society and, 123-124, 126-128, 137-138, 352, 366; early contacts between American Academy of Arts and Sciences and, 128-130; *Transactions* of, 336

Adams, Abigail, 241

Adams, Charles Francis, 213, 377

Adams, Henry, 205, 232, 285, 291; on War of 1812, 307, 312, 317; on administrations of Jefferson and Madison, 361; on John Quincy Adams, 377

Adams, John, 14, 23-24, 212, 313; and Golitsyn, 16, 28; on Declaration of Armed Neutrality, 18, 19; *Moscow Gazette* on, 43; and development of early Russian-American trade, 94-95; and Gouverneur Morris, 105; and American Academy of Arts and Sciences, 128; presidency of, 350; papers of, 377

Adams, John Quincy, 304, 309, 362, 370; his visit to Russia, 24-25, 75; and Russian-American relations, 107-108; and American Philosophical Society, 137; his appointment as minister to Russia, 205, 211-214; and Russian-American

trade, 224, 239-241; and Danish seizure of American ships, 229-232; and rights of neutral navigation, 233-234, 237; success of his Russian mission, 238, 253-254, 354; and Spanish-American question, 242-243, 244-245, 246-247; and appointment of Pahlen, 248, 249; and relations in northwest America, 261-263; and War of 1812, 298, 307, 310, 311, 313, 315, 319-333 *passim*; and Rumiantsev, 326-327, 328, 377; and expansion of cultural contacts, 334, 335-337; and Russian War of 1812, 346, 355; papers of, 377-378, 383

Adams, Louisa, 241

Adams, William, 330

Adelung, Friedrich, 126, 137-138

Alekseev, M. P., 57, 65

Alembert, Jean Le Rond d', 31

Alexander I, Tsar of Russia, 145, 353, 354, 360, 369; and Russian-American trade connections, 107-113 *passim*; and public education, 138; correspondence with Jefferson, 139-144, 187, 188, 352, 370; and Russian-American Company, 169, 184; and establishment of Russian-American diplomatic relations, 195-197, 214-217; on appointment of Dashkov, 202; and appointment of Pahlen, 206-207; and J. Q. Adams, 213-214, 377;

and Danish seizure of American ships, 230, 231, 232; and conflict between Russia and France, 234-235, 237, 238-239, 280; and Spanish-American question, 245-246; and relations in northwest America, 268; and Russian mediation in War of 1812, 309, 311, 319-323, 330-331, 333; and Rush, 336; and expansion of cultural contacts, 338; and Rumiantsev, 374

Alexandrov, Victor, 358

Allen, Jeremiah, 91

Alopeus, M. M., 195-196

American Academy of Arts and Sciences, 335, 336; contacts with Russian Academy of Sciences, 128-130

American Fur Company, 272, 353; creation of, 258; negotiations between Russian-American Company and, 259-261, 263-268; and Agreement of 20 April/2 May 1812, 268-269, 368

American Philosophical Society, 138, 335, 336, 338; contacts with Russian Academy of Sciences, 123-124, 126-128, 137-138, 352, 366

Andreyev (Andreev), A. I., 147, 164, 375

Anfilatov, K. A., 92, 111-114

Anmours, Chevalier d', 58

Aptheker, Herbert, 1

Arakcheyev (Arakcheev), A. A., 246, 328

Argüello, José Darío, 178

Armed Neutrality, Declaration of, 12-19, 20, 21, 26, 29, 350

Armstrong, John, 204

Arrillago (Arrilaga), José Joaquin de, 177, 277

Astor, John Jacob, 85, 272-273, 314, 353; creation of fur company in American northwest by, 258-259; Russian contacts with fur company of, 259-261; and negotiations with Russian-American Company, 259-261, 263, 264, 265, 267; and Agreement of 20 April/2 May 1812, 269, 354, 368

Aurora (Philadelphia), 340, 346, 354

Ayres. *See* Eayrs, George Washington

Babey, Anna, 362

Bailey, Thomas A., 358

Bakadarov (attorney), 276

Bakunin, Petr, 15

Bakunin brothers, 11

Balashov, A. D., 280

Bancroft, Hubert H., 162, 375

Baranov, A. A., 178, 353; role of in colonization of American northwest, 165-166, 172; and Russian-American Company, 170, 171; commercial contacts with American shippers, 181-184, 201, 269-276; correspondence with Kuskov, 183, 372; and exploration of Columbia River, 263; and problem of illegal trade in Russian possessions, 266

Barber, Captain, 172

Bariatinsky, I. S., 7-8, 19, 23-24, 28; and early Russian-American trade, 95; and foreign vessels near "Chukotski Cape," 148, 151

Baring, Alexander, 318, 320, 321

Barlow, Joel, 140-141

Barton, Benjamin Smith, 126

Bayard, James A., 297-298, 327; and Russian mediation in War of 1812, 313, 314, 319-320, 324, 326; papers of, 377, 378

Bazhenov, V. I., 59, 62

Bellingham (assassin), 287

Bellini, Carlo, 62, 63

Bem, M., 150

Bemis, Samuel Flagg, 2, 230, 360

Benningsen, L. L. 189, 280

Benson, Adrian, 362

Bentzon, A. B., 265-266, 267-268; and Russian-American Company, 261, 263-268

Benyowski, M., 149-151, 152

Berg, L. S., 146, 147

Bergbohm, Carl, 13

Bering, Vitus, 146, 147, 148

Berkh, V., 148

Bernadotte, Prince, 307-308

Bernstorff, Count, 14, 229

Betancourt, General, 335

Bezborodko, A. A., 22, 27, 154, 165; and J. P. Jones, 71, 73; and Ledyard's voyage, 158, 159, 160

Bielke, Madame, 6

Billings, Joseph, 154, 157, 158, 161
Blanchard, William, 272
Blome, Baron de, 231
Bobrov, S., 136
Bobukh, Zakhar, 77
Bogaevsky, Ivan, 33
Bogart, John, 251
Bogdanovich, I. F., 36
Bogdanovich, P. I., 34, 36
Bolotov, A. T., 41
Bond, Thomas, 128
Born, I., 136
Bossu, Jean Bernard, 33
Boston Gazette, 340, 341, 342, 355
Bowditch, Nathaniel, 335
Bowdoin, James, 120, 129
Boyd, Julian P., 379
Bradley, Stephen, 204-205
Braiko, G. L., 36
Brandenburg, F., 88
Braun, Joseph-Adam, 120, 121, 122, 123
Brillon, Madame, 132
Brooke, Arthur, 299
Buchanan, James, 75
Buckingham, Lord, 5
Budberg, A. Ia., 142, 189
Buffington, Nehemiah, 95
Buldakov, M. M.: and Russian-American Company, 169, 170, 184; and trade between Russian settlers, 179-180, 275; and American Fur Company, 263, 265, 266; and Agreement of 20 April/2 May 1812, 268
Burgoyne, John, 7, 8, 40
Butterfield, L. H., 377

Cabot, George, 91
Calhoun, John C., 284, 289, 377, 378
Campenhausen, B. B., 233, 234, 237
Canada, during War of 1812, 284-286, 289-295, 303
Canning, George, 330
Castlereagh, Lord (Robert Stewart), 377; and War of 1812, 286-287, 288, 295; and Russian mediation in War of 1812, 311, 315-326 *passim*, 329, 330, 331
Castries, Marquis de, 153
Cathcart, Lord: and Russian mediation in War of 1812, 310, 317-328 *passim*

Catherine II, Empress of Russia, 2, 29, 360, 369, 381; and American Revolution, 5-6, 10-11, 30; hostility to Franklin, 9; and Declaration of Armed Neutrality, 13, 14, 15, 16, 18, 19; and Dana's mission, 26, 27; "liberalism" of, 31-32; on Raynal, 34; on *Moscow Gazette*, 46; and J. P. Jones, 66, 67, 68, 73, 74; and early Russian-American trade, 92-93, 95; plan for dictionary, 124-126, 352; and appearance of foreign vessels near "Chukotski Cape," 148-149; and Ledyard's journey, 154-155, 158, 160-161; refusal of proposal to establish company in America, 163-165; and Russian colonization of American northwest, 166
Caulaincourt, Armand Augustin Louis de (Duke de Vicence), 227, 235, 236, 238, 240, 377
Chernyshev, A. I., 235, 238
Chernyshev, I. G., 5, 8
Chernyshev brothers, 6
Chernyshevsky, N. G., 53
Chipman, Nathaniel, 140
Chirikov, A., 146-147
Churchman, John, 127
Clark, E. D., 337, 338, 339
Clay, Henry: and War of 1812, 284, 286, 289, 330; papers of, 377, 378
Cobbett, William, 340, 341, 342
Cochrane, Alexander, 295-296
Cockburn, George, 296
Commager, Henry Steele, 376
Concepción, María de la, 178-179
Condorcet, Marquis de, 133
Constantin, Grand Duke, 189
Continental Blockade, 230, 231, 237, 243, 251, 254; signing of, 189-190; and Orders-in-Council, 191; effect on Russian economy, 219, 226, 228-229; and Russian-American trade, 222; and Trianon tariff, 225, 232-233; Russia's joining of, 226, 227, 229; and Napoleon's attack on Russia, 235-236
Cook, Capt. James, 151-153, 154, 157, 158-159, 258
Cooper, Thomas, 139, 140
Cornwallis, Charles, 22

Crawford, William, 330
Cresson, William, 2, 360
Crosby, Alfred W., 102, 224, 384
Custis, George, 343
Cutler, James, 340
Czartoryski, A. A., 109, 110, 138, 189, 192-193, 369

Dallas, George, 75
Dana, Francis, 19, 61, 67, 212; mission to St. Petersburg, 2, 24-28, 56, 75, 362, 370, 376; and Russian-American trade, 91
Danevsky, V., 14
Danilevsky, V. V., 81
Dashkov, A. Ia., 97, 100, 115, 216, 354; appointment as consul-general, 143, 197-198, 199-200; appointment as correspondent of Russian-American Company, 197, 198-199, 200-203; sojourn in Washington, 208-210; on conditions in U.S. 210-211; correspondence with Jefferson, 211; and appointment of J. Q. Adams as minister, 211-212; on American trade with Russia, 223, 224; appointment as minister, 249, 251, 252, 253; and relations in northwest America, 255-258, 259, 269, 272; and Anglo-American War of 1812, 290-291, 292, 296, 300-301, 302; on effect of 1812 War on Russian-American trade, 304-305; and Russian mediation in War of 1812, 309-310, 311, 313, 314, 317, 325, 329; and expansion of cultural contacts, 334, 338, 347; on American attitude toward Russian War of 1812, 342, 343, 345; papers of, 372
Dashkov (Dasshkaw), Princess Catherine, and Franklin, 31, 126-127, 129-130
Dashkova, Princess E. R., 8, 381
David, Henry, 303
Davidson, Marshall, 359
Davis, John, 335
Davydovsky (contributor to *Moskovskie vedomosti*), 41
Dearborn, Henry, 293
Delarov, E., 170

Denmark, seizure of American ships by, 229-232
Derby, Elias Hasket, 85, 95-96
Derzhavin, G. R., 148, 337
Dezhnev, Semen, 146, 147
Dickinson, John, 52
Diderot, Denis, 16, 31, 40, 43
Dixon, George, 153
Dohm, C. W. von, 14, 377
Duane, John, 19
Duane, William, 340, 341, 342, 345; Jefferson's letter to, 193, 346
Dubourg, Barbeu, 121
Dulles, Foster Rhea, 360
Dulles, John Foster, 358
Dumas, C. W. F., 16, 18, 19
Du Ponceau, Peter S., 126
Durov, N. P., 56
Dvoichenko-Markova, E. M., 126, 365-366; on Karzhavin, 57, 58, 60; on contacts between scientists, 121, 122, 129; on Ledyard's journey, 158
D'Wolf, John, 181-182

East India Company, 170
Eayrs (Ayres), George Washington, 183, 272, 276
Ebbets, John, 269, 270
Effendi, Reis, 109
Efimov, A. V., 147, 363-364, 383
Eliott de Castro, John, 277
Embargo: introduction of, by U.S., 191-192, 218-219, 227, 305-306; explanation of, to Alexander I, 203
Engels, Friedrich, 13, 100, 188, 237, 368
England: and the American Revolution, 3-4, 6-7, 22-23; relations with Russia, 4-6, 9-12, 15, 20-22; Russian trade with, 81-82; and commercial treaty with U.S., 83; role of early Russian-American trade, 100, 101, 103; and U.S. embargo, 218-219; and declaration of War of 1812, 280-281. *See also Chapters X, XI*
Epinus, F.U. 15, 119, 120-121, 123, 352, 382
Erving, George, 231-232
Eton, William, 88
Etter, Karl, 335
Euler, Johann-Albrecht, 128, 130, 137

Euler, Leonard, 116, 127, 128-129, 133, 352
Europe's Messenger (Vestnik Evropy), 134-135, 380
Everett, Alexander Hill, 75, 213, 336, 337, 343
Evstaf'ev, Alexei G.: appointment as consul, 202, 208; and expansion of cultural contacts, 334, 337, 338-339; and Russian War of 1812, 342-343, 345
Exports, 219-222, 224-227

Faraday, Michael, 119
Farragut, David G., 75
Fauchille, P., 13
Faulkner, Harold, 303
Fedorov, I., 146
Fischer, Gotthelf, 335, 352, 383
Florida (Spanish), 284, 285, 286, 292
Foner, Phillip, 1
Fonton, K. K., 199
Fonvizin, D. I., 8-9, 54, 131, 150, 381
Ford, Paul, 379
Ford, Worthington C., 378
Foster, Augustus J., 281, 287, 288
Foster, William Z., 1, 284, 297
Fouché, Joseph, 236
Fox, Charles J., 42
France: and American Revolution, 7-9; Russian trade with, 82; and U.S. embargo, 218-219; attitude, toward American trade in the Baltic, 232-233; conflict with Russia, 234-239, 279-280, 312, 339-346
Franklin, Benjamin, 9, 56, 65, 145; sent to France to negotiate treaty, 7; correspondence with Golitsyn, 16; on Armed Neutrality, 18; and negotiations with Bariatinsky, 19, 23-24, 28; compared with Francis Dana, 27; and Princess Catherine Dashkov, 31, 126-127, 129-130; Russian attitude toward, 32, 39-40; Russian press on, 43, 133; and development of early Russian-American trade, 94-95; and G. Morris, 105; and scientific experiments and scientists, 116-124, 129-130, 137, 352; and Catherine II's plan for dictionary, 124-126, 352; works published in Russia,

130-132; and foreign vessels near "Chukotski Cape," 148-149, 151-152, 153; and Benyowski, 150-151; and Russian War of 1812, 355; Laserson on, 361; Startsev on, 365; and, Lomonosov, 366; papers of, 377, 378
Frederick II, King of Prussia, 14
"Free Society of Lovers of Letters, Science, and Arts," 136, 137
Friedrich-Wilhelm III, 188
Fulton, Robert, 334, 383
Fuss, Nicholas, 137, 335, 352

Gage, Thomas, 38, 39
Gallatin, Albert, 75, 191-192, 304, 327, 337; and Russian mediation in War of 1812, 313-314, 318, 319-321, 324, 326, 330-331; papers of, 377, 378
Gambier, Lord, 330
Gannet, Caleb, 129
"Genêt, Citizen," 105
George III, King of England, 4, 5-6, 15, 117
Gérard, Conrad Alexandre, 58
Ghent peace treaty, 332-333
Girard, Stephen, 85, 314
Gnedich, Nicholas, 136
Goertz, Count, 14, 377
Golder, Frank A., 2, 147, 360, 374-375
Golikov, Ivan, 163, 164, 165-166, 167, 374
Golitsyn, D. A., 16-17, 19, 20, 21, 28; and Karzhavin, 62; and Franklin's experiments, 119-120
Golitsyn, D. G. (Father Augustine), 77
Gonionsky, S. A., 383
Gorchakov, A. M., 360
Gordon, William, 129
Goriainov, S., 369
Goulborn, Henry, 330
Gower, Lord, 287
Gray, Francis Calley, 213
Gray, Robert, 258
Gray, William, 85, 212, 213
Grenville, Lord, 83, 330
Grey, Charles (Lord Howick), 191
Grimm, Baron Melchior, 31, 34, 74, 154, 381

Grosche, John Gottlieb, 127
Grundy, Felix, 284, 285-286
Guber, A. A., 383
Gülich, Gustav von, 100
Gunning, Robert, 6
Gur'ev, D. A., 233, 234, 235, 266-267, 268; and Spanish-American question, 244; and Hamilton's paper, 352

Hacker, Louis, 303
Hagemeister, L. A., 177
Hale, William, 359
Halliday, E. M., 359
Hamilton, Alexander, 19, 84, 105, 140, 352
Harper, Robert G., 284, 297, 343-344, 345
Harris, James (Lord Malmesbury), 9-10, 15, 22, 24, 377
Harris, J. L. 311
Harris, Levett, 142, 199, 256, 362, 370, 375; appointment as consul, 108-109, 115, 350; and American Philosophical Society, 137; letter from Jefferson, 144; and Russian-American Company, 185; and Czartoryski, 192-193; and establishment of diplomatic relations, 196, 197; and Short, 203; and Pahlen's appointment, 207; and appointment of Adams as minister, 213; and U.S. embargo, 219; and trade, 224; and rights of neutral navigation, 233-234; and Spanish-American question, 243, 246, 247; and Russian mediation in War of 1812, 324, 331, 332; and expansion of cultural contacts, 334, 335, 336
Hart, Albert Bushnell, 376
Hartley, David, 23, 24
Harvard University, 335, 336
Hazard, Samuel, 224
Heckewelder, John, 126
Helvétius, Claude A., 16, 31
Hermann, B. F. J., 137, 335
Hildt, John C., 95, 307, 325, 360, 361
Hölzle, Erwin, 358
Hopkinson, Joseph, 341
Hoskins, John, 251
Hubbel, Ezekiel, 181
Huebner, Max, 14

Hull, William, 293
Humphrey, David, 95
Hunt, Wilson P., 261, 270, 273
Huntington, Samuel, 19
Huygens, Christian, 116

Iatzunsky, V. K., 228
Indians, American, Russian attitudes toward, 52-53, 54, 64, 134, 136
Ioasaf, Archimandrite, 166, 175
Italinsky, A. Ia., 109, 332
Iturrigaray, José, 179
Ivanov, Fedor, 207, 248
Izmailov, A. E., 136
Izmailov, Gerasim, 152, 366

Jackson, Andrew, 286, 289, 301, 377
Jacoby, I. V., 156, 158-162, 163
Jay, John, 83, 95, 140
Jefferson, Thomas, 62, 214, 259; and Jones, 67, 71, 72, 75; and early Russian-American trade, 94-95, 111; and Morris, 105; Karamzin's *Vestnik Evropy* on, 134-135; correspondence with Alexander I, 139-144, 187, 188, 352, 370; Pahlen's visit to, 143-144; and Ledyard's journey, 153-155, 156; and embargo, 191-192; letter to Duane, 193, 346; and establishment of diplomatic relations, 195-196; and Dashkov, 198, 211; and nomination of Short as minister, 203-205, 206, 210; and Lewis and Clark Expedition, 258; H. Adams on, 361; papers of, 377, 379
Jensen, Oliver, 359
João, Prince-Regent, 205
Johnson, Catherine, 213
Johnson, Gerald White, 65-66
Johnson, Richard M., 284
Jones, John Paul, 74, 97, 377; sojourn in Russia, 56, 65-75, 351, 362, 372, 382

Kafengaus, B. B., 81
Karamyshev, Alexander, 155, 160
Karamzin, N. M., 41, 337, 381; on Franklin's *Autobiography*, 130-131; his journals, 133, 134-135, 380; influence of, 136; *Pantheon of Russian Writers*, 338

Karzhavin, Fedor Vasil'evich, 76, 77, 372, 381; sketch of, 56-57; travels to America, 57-65, 74, 351, 382; role in cultural contacts, 339

Kazakevich, V. D., 378

Khlebnikov, K., 173, 271-272

Khmelnitsky, Iv. Parf., 34

Khotinsky, N. K., 150

Khvostov, N. A., 177

Kimball, Oliver, 183

King, Rufus, 105-106, 107, 115, 350

Klichka, Governor, 148, 151, 153

Klingstädt, Baron Timotheus von, 124, 128

Kochubei, V. P., 104, 111

Kolychev, S. A., 28

Korf, Baron, 4

Koshelev, R. A., 245-246, 328, 374

Kotzebue, August, 136

Kovalevsky, M., 361

Kozlov, N. Ia., 66; on Russian exports to US, 221; appointment as consul-general, 250; and consular agent to Cuba, 251-252; and War of 1812, 290, 293, 294, 298, 299-300, 301-302, 314; and Russian War of 1812, 305, 306, 342, 345; and cultural contacts, 334

Kozodavlev, O. P., 228, 266, 267

Kraft, A. Iu., 127

Kramer, Venedikt, 184, 268

Krüdener (Kruedener), Baron A. I., 67, 107

Kruzenshtern (Krusenstern, A. J. von), I. F., 177, 335, 336

Krylov, I. A., 337

Kurakin, A. B., 189, 223, 327; and Napoleon's war with Russia, 235, 279, 280; and War of 1812, 304

Küsel, F., 108

Kuskov, I. A., 172, 274, 275-277; correspondence with Baranov, 183, 372

Kutuzov, M. I., 342, 343

Labaree, Leonard Wood, 378

Ladygin, D. M., 33, 89, 382

Lafayette, Marquis de, 10, 43, 75, 330; and Catherine II's dictionary, 124-125, 352; and Ledyard's journey, 154, 155

La Harpe, Frédéric, 139, 140

Laksman, Eric, 155

La Pérouse, Comte de, 153

Laserson, Max, 361-362

Lauriston, Marquis de, 238, 280

Lazarev, M. P., 277

Ledyard, John, 56, 75, 152, 258, 362; journey across Russia, 153-157, 351, 366, 372; deportation, 157-162

Lee, Arthur, 19

Lenin, V. I., 1, 9, 81, 368, 373

Leshkov, V., 14

Lesseps, Ferdinand Marie de, 153

Lewis and Clark Expedition, 153, 256, 258

Lieven, Christopher, 311, 316-326 *passim*

Likhonin (contributor to *Moskovskie vedomosti*), 41

Lincoln, Abraham, 65

Lisiansky, Yu. F., 173, 177

Little, Daniel, 129

Little, John, 96

Littlepage, Lewis, 75

Liverpool, Lord, 287, 315, 325, 331

Livingston, Robert, 18, 26, 91, 110

Lizakevich (Lizakewitz), V. G., 6, 230

Lloyd, James, 300

Lobanov-Rostovsky, D. I., 189, 327

Lomonosov, M. V., 32, 116, 145, 337, 378, 381; experiments of, 118-119; American press on, 120; and contacts between scientists, 121-123, 352; founding of Moscow University by, 138; Svin'in's translation of essay, 338; and Franklin, 366

López Mendez, Luis, 246, 247

Lopukhin, P. V., 170

Lowell, John, 291

Lynch, Antonio, 251-252

McClellan, George, 75

MacKenzie, Donald, 261

McNeill, Daniel, 91

Madariaga, I. de, 13

Madison, Bishop James, 62, 63

Madison, James, 15, 19, 111, 232, 239, 250; *Federalist* papers of, 140; and Dashkov, 143, 208-210, 211; and Russian-American Company, 185; and embargo, 192, 305; and nomination of Short as minister,

203, 205, 206; Alexander I on, 214; and J. Q. Adams' mission, 241; on Russian-American relations, 253; and relations in northwest America, 256, 258; and War of 1812, 280-281, 283, 286, 289, 291, 296; and Russian mediation in War of 1812, 311, 312, 320, 330; H. Adams on, 361; papers of, 377
Magellan, John Hyancinth de, 9
Malinovsky, V., 41, 352
Malkin, M. M., 363
Manning, Clarence, 358
Maria Fedorovna, Dowager Empress, 169
Marklovsky, Commandant, 158, 160
Martens, F., 15, 369
Martens, G. F. von, 376
Martin, Joshua, 202
Marx, Karl, 82, 170, 191, 283, 368
Maxwell, James C., 119
Mazzei, F., 62
Meares, Captain, 153
Medico-Surgical Academy (St. Petersburg), 335, 336
Medvednikov, V., 172
Meek, Thomas, 272
Mercier de la Rivière, Paul Pierre, 16
Mercy, Count de, 23, 24
Metternich, Prince, 318, 377
Miller, David Hunter, 376
Miller, G., 152
Minikh, Kh., 163
Mining industry, in Russia, 80-81
Monroe, James, 244, 247, 253, 330, 377; and Russian-American diplomatic relations, 195, 309; and trade, 224; and War of 1812, 281, 288, 296, 309; and Russian mediation in War of 1812, 311, 312-314, 325, 329; and Russian War of 1812, 345
Montesquieu, 31, 43
Montolivet, Count, 244
Moore, John Bassett, 376
Mordvinov, N.S., 169
Morison, Samuel Eliot, 91, 272
Morkov, A. I., 21, 22, 24, 110
Morris, Gouverneur, 74, 104-105
Morris, G. M., 1
Moscow Gazette (Moskovskie vedomosti), 32, 35, 36-39, 42-43,

365, 380; and Novikov, 40-41, 351; commentaries on well-known Americans, 43-44; on American Revolution, 44-45, 133; Supplement to, 45-46; on Shays's Rebellion, 47
Moscow Journal (Moskovskii Zhurnal), 133, 380
Moscow University, 138
Mulovsky, G. I., 154
Murav'ev, Nikita, 48
Musin-Pushkin, A. S., 3-4, 7, 12
Myl'nikov, A., 147, 169

Nagibin, P., 147
Napoleon I, 241, 286-287, 292, 307, 308, 377; his defeat of Prussia, 188; inclination of, toward peace with Russia, 189; and Danish seizure of American ships, 230, 231, 232; and Trianon tariff, 233; and Statement on Neutral Trade, 235; and conflict between Russia and France, 236, 238-239; domination of Europe, 279; attack on and defeat in Russia, 279-280, 289, 312, 339, 355; fall of, 293-294, 326; battles at Lützen and Bautzen, 318; last great victory of, 321; and Franco-Russian War of 1812, 339, 340-346
Narbonne, Count, 279
Nassau-Siegen, Prince Charles de, 66, 68, 69, 70
National Intelligencer (Washington), 340, 345, 354, 379
Nebolsin, G., 81, 92, 382; on Russian-American trade, 98-100, 226
Nelson, Lord, 292
Nesselrode, K. V., 235, 354, 369, 374; and Russian mediation in War of 1812, 309, 319, 321, 322-323, 326, 331; and Rumiantsev, 328
Netherlands, The, 17, 21, 45
Nettels, Curtis, 303
Newton, Sir Isaac, 116
Niemcewicz, J. U., 138
Nikolai, P. A., 308, 309, 310, 315-316, 325
Niles, Hezekian, 302, 343, 380
Non-intercourse Act, 218
North, Lord, 37, 39, 41
Northern System, 4-5, 11-12

Norwood, Captain, 91
Novikov, N. I., 33, 36, 37, 53, 381; and *Moscow Gazette*, 40-41, 44, 45, 350, 365, 380; political journal published by, 45-47, 54; on Shays's Rebellion, 47; and Karzhavin, 59, 63; arrest of, 103; on Negro slavery, 135
Novosiltsov, N. N., 189

O'Cain, Joseph, 181, 182
Ogden, Adele, 271-272
Okun', S. B., 147, 164, 167, 367, 375
Onís, Luis, 251
Orders-in-Council, 191-192
Orlov, Aleksei, 6
Orlov, Grigori, 31
Oster, Martin, 58
Osterman, I. A., 7, 11, 16, 21, 22; and Dana's mission, 25, 26; and J. P. Jones, 71-72, 73, 74, 97
Ostrogorsky, M., 361
Otis, Harrison Gray, 300, 343

Pahlen, F. D., 241, 251, 354; visit to Jefferson, 143-144; appointed minister, 206-208, 214, 215-216, 217; appointed ambassador, 248-249, 250, 252; and relations in American northwest, 255, 259, 260-261; and expansion of cultural contacts, 334, 347
Pakenham, Sir Edward, 301
Pallas, Peter Simon, 127-128, 142, 336, 352; and Ledyard's journey, 155, 160
Panin, N. I., 3, 4, 19, 28; on American Revolution, 6-7, 20, 22; and Fonvizin, 8; on alliance between Russia and England, 10; and Russia's foreign policy, 11; and Declaration of Armed Neutrality, 14; and Golitsyn, 16-17; removal of, 27; and foreign vessels near "Chukotski Cape," 148-149, 151
Panin, P. I., 8
Parish, David, 314
Parker, Courtland, L., 243, 247
Passek, P. B., 160-161
Paul I, Tsar of Russia, 103, 106-107, 168
Penn, William, 364

Perceval, Spencer, 191, 287
Peter I, Tsar of Russia, 87, 146, 147, 338, 364
Petrov (contributor to *Moskovskie vedomosti*), 41
Phillips, James Duncan, 91, 96
Pickering, Timothy, 107, 300
Piel, I. A., 375
Pinckney, William, 196
Pitkin, Timothy, 99, 224-225, 382
Plotnikov, A., 172
Pnin, I., 136
Poinsett, Joel, 362
Pokrovsky, M. N., 227, 228
Pokrovsky, S. A., 227
Poletika, P. I., 207, 248, 251, 330, 382; and Russian-American cultural contacts, 334, 337, 338, 339, 347-348
Political Journal (Politicheskii Zhurnal), 36, 133, 380
Polovtsov, A. A., 369
Popov (merchant), 41, 156
Popugaev, V., 136, 137
Porter, Peter B., 284
Portlock, Captain, 153
Potemkin, G. A., 6, 14, 66, 75; and J. P. Jones, 68, 69-70, 71, 72; and Catherine II, 155, 164-165
Potemkin, Pavel, 31
Pototcki, Jan, 142
Pratt, Julius, 285
Predtechensky, A. V., 228, 229
Press: Russian, on American War of Independence, 35-47, 379-381; American, on Russian War of 1812, 340-343, 354-355
Prevost, Sir George, 291-292, 299
Priestley, Joseph, 139, 140, 141
Pringle, John, 117
Pugachev, Emelian, 6, 31, 47, 54, 351
Pulaski, Casimir, 150, 151
Pushkin, A. S., 31, 53, 138, 337, 365

Radishchev, Aleksandr, 134, 137, 365; ode to "Liberty," 47-51, 54-55, 350, 366, 381; *A Journey from St. Petersburg to Moscow*, 51-53, 54-55, 116, 350, 366, 381; and Russian-American trade, 93; repression of, 103, 136; on Franklin and Lomonosov, 116, 366

Radovsky, M. I., 366
Randolph, John, 285
Rasch, A. A., 102, 383
Rasumovsky, Konstantin, 31
Raynal, Abbé, 31, 365; *Histoire des deux Indes*, 34-35, 137; *Moscow Gazette* on, 43; influence on Radishchev, 48, 49; on disintegration of Russian Empire, 51
Renaut, Francis P., 2, 360
Rezanov, N. P., 180, 274; and Russian-American Company, 169, 172-173, 174, 175, 176; and negotiations between Russian settlers, 177-179; death of, 178; and commercial contacts between Russian settlers and American shippers, 181, 183
Richardson, James Daniel, 376
Richmann, Georg Wilhelm (Rikhman, G. V.), 118, 120, 350, 381
Ricketson (doctor), 336
Robertson, William, 33
Rodde, Christian, 108
Romanov, N. M., 369
Romme, Gilbert, 104
Roosevelt, Franklin Delano, 65
Ross, Robert, 296, 299
Rousseau, Jean Jacques, 31
Rozhkova, M. K., 227
Ruis, Manuel, 276
Rumiantsev, N. P., 142, 143, 223, 299, 334, 360; and Russian-American trade, 97, 100-101, 107, 111, 112-114, 115, 187-188, 224, 226, 227; and appointment of Harris as consul, 108; and Russian-American Company, 169, 174, 175-176, 180, 184-185; becomes Minister of Foreign Affairs, 189; and establishment of diplomatic relations, 196-197; and appointment of Dashkov as consul-general, 199; and Short, 204, 206; and appointment of Pahlen as minister, 207, 216; and appointment of J. Q. Adams as minister, 213, 214; and American embargo, 219; and J. Q. Adams, 229-231, 233, 234, 239-241, 377; on Napoleon, 241; and Spanish-American question, 242-248; and appointment of Pahlen, 248, 249;

and Russian consular agents, 250, 251, 252-253; and relations in American northwest, 255-268 *passim*, 275; and War of 1812, 290, 305; and Russian mediation in War of 1812, 307-325 *passim*; evaluation of his role, 326-328, 353, 374; and American attitude toward Russian War of 1812, 345; resignation of, 354
Rush, Benjamin, 336, 383
Rush, Richard, 333
Russell, John Miller, 107
Russell, Jonathan, 288, 330
Russian-American Company, 217, 255, 256, 272-276; formation of, 167-168; sphere of activity of, 168-169; vis-à-vis Russian government, 169-170; problems of, 171-176; and negotiations with California, 177-181; and commercial contacts with American shippers, 181-184, 353; and illegal trade in Russian possessions, 184-186, 188, 201, 352-353; Dashkov as correspondent of, 197, 198-199, 200-202; and support of Pahlen, 216; negotiations with American Fur Company, 260-261, 263-268; and Agreement of 20 April/2 May 1812, 268-269, 368; studies of Tikhmenev and Okun' on, 367
Ryerson, Stanley B., 283
Rykachev (contributor to *Moskovskie vedomosti*), 41
Ryleev, Major General, 66

Saltykov, A. N., 280
Sarychev, G. A., 158
Sauer, Martin, 157, 158
Sayre, Stephen, 56
Schubert, F., 335
Schults, Theodor, 126
Scott, John Brown, 13
Scott, General, 76
Ségur, Count Louis Philippe, 66, 161
Semennikov, V., 48, 50, 365
Sérurier, J. M. P., 345
Severin, Andrey, 268
Shannon, Fred, 303
Shelikhov, Grigori, 148, 169, 375; on Ledyard, 156-157, 159, 161, 162;

role in Russian colonization, 162-163, 165-167; and Catherine II's refusal to establish company, 163-165, 374; death of, 167
Shelikhov, I., 169, 170, 175
Shelikhova, Anna Grigor'evna, 178
Sherman, William, 75
Shilder, N. M., 369
Short, William, 143, 203-205, 206, 207, 208, 210, 217
Shprygova, M. N., 36, 37
Shtelin, Ya., 152
Shulim, J., 344
Shuvalov, Count A. P., 8
Shvetsov, Commandant, 181, 183
Simolin, I. M., 10, 12, 20, 21, 23, 24; and J. P. Jones, 67; and Ledyard's journey, 153
Slavery, Negro, 46, 52-53, 54, 64, 134, 135, 136
Slobodchikov, Captain, 182
Smith, Adam, 111
Smith, J. Allen, 75-76, 344, 362
Smith, John Spear, 212
Smith, Robert, 232, 241; meeting with Dashkov, 208-209, 210; and relations in American northwest, 256, 257, 262
Smith, Samuel, 298
Smith, William Stephens, 155
Smith, William Steuben, 212
Smyth, Albert H., 378
Snell, Karl, 89-90
Society of Natural Sciences (Moscow), 335
Soimonov, P. A., 154, 163
Sokhatsky, P. A., 36, 380
Son of the Fatherland (Syn otechestva), 347, 380, 382
Sorel, Albert, 190
Soule, Cornelius, 270
Spanish America, 242-252
Sparks, Jared, 155, 158, 378
Speransky, M. M., 139, 145, 244, 245, 246, 328
St. Petersburg Gazette (Sankt-Peterburgskie vedomosti), 32, 35, 36-39, 42, 365, 379, 380; on American Revolution, 44-45; on Shays's Rebellion, 47; on Franklin's experiments, 117-118
Stanford, Richard, 285

Stanislavskaia, A. M., 383
Startsev, A. I., 36-37, 52-53, 365, 366; on Karzhavin, 57, 58, 61-62; and Russian-American Company, 169
Statement on Neutral Trade, 235, 268
Stepanov (contributor to Moskovskie vedomosti), 41
Stiles, Ezra, 120-123
Stone, John Hurford, 139, 140
Stormont, Lord, 24
Strauss, Oscar, 359
Stroganov, G. A., 180
Stroganov, Pavel, 104, 369
Strong, Caleb, 300
Stroynowski, J., 138-139
Strumilin, S. G., 80-81
Suchtelen, P. K., 307-308, 309
Sumarokov, Aleksandr B., 32, 53
Suvorov, A. V., 67, 68, 70-71
Sverchkov (mission adviser), 249, 314
Svin'in, P. P., 84, 372, 382; on Russian exports, 219-221; on American ships, 224; on American exports, 225; appointment as secretary to consul-general, 250; on War of 1812, 295; and cultural contacts, 334, 337, 338, 339, 347, 348
Swift, Benjamin (captain), 183

Talleyrand, 189, 235
Tarakanov, V. P., 183
Tarle, E. V., 80, 82, 190, 225-226
Tarsaidze, Alexander, 360
Taube, F. B., 33
Téroigne de Méricourt (pseud. of Anne Terwagne), 104
Thiel, Charles (Charles Cist), 76
Thornton, Edward, 307-308, 309
Tikhmenov, P., 167, 176, 272, 273, 367
Tilesius, V. G., 335, 336
Tolstoy, Alexei, 170
Tolstoy, Leo, 131
Trachevsky, A., 369
Tracy, Marquis de, 323
Trade: Russian foreign, 79-82, 87; U.S. foreign, 82-87; development of early Russian-American, 87-90. See also Chapters IV, VIII
Tresket, Captain, 181
Trianon tariff, 225, 233

Tugan-Baranovsky, M. I., 227, 228, 361
Turgenev, A. I., 131

Ubri (Oubril), P. Ia., 110-111
Ulrich, Franz, 119
Uukovsky, S. Ia., 277

Valnais, Joseph de, 58
Vancouver, George, 152
Vandal, Albert, 190
Vaughan, John, 137
Vedemeier, I. A., 169, 331, 332
Vérac, Marquis de, 20, 22, 24, 27, 213
Vergennes, Comte de, 7, 14, 23, 24, 28
Vernadsky, George, 144
Viazemsky, P. V., 9, 150
Vicence, Duke de. *See* Caulaincourt, Armand Augustin Louis de
Vicente de Solá, Pablo, 277
Villie, Ia. V. (James Wylie), 336
Voltaire, 16, 31, 32, 40, 43
Vorontsov, A. R., 32, 88, 104, 163; and Russian-American trade, 96; and appointment of Harris as consul, 108-109; on foreign competition in the Pacific North, 154; Catherine II's attitude toward, 165
Vorontsov, S. R., 16, 72, 170; and Morris, 104-105; and King, 105-106, 107, 115, 350
Vorontsov family, 75-76, 93, 344, 369, 372
Voskresensky, T., 133
Vostokov, A., 136

Walpole, Lord, 321, 324-325, 328
Walsh, Robert, 344-345, 359
Warren, John Borlase, 288, 295, 314, 315, 324-325
Washington, George, 10, 65, 84, 230, 350, 355; on Armed Neutrality, 18; mentioned in Russian press, 43-44, 133; and Catherine II's dictionary, 124-126, 352; papers of, 377
Watrous, Stephen D., 155
Weekly Messenger, 340-341, 355
Weekly Register (Baltimore), 302, 343, 354, 379, 380
Wellesley, Marquis of, 286, 330
Wellington, Lord, 292, 294, 346
Wetter von Rosenthal, Gustave Heinrich, 76-77
Wharton, Francis, 2, 376
Whittemore, Isaac, 272
Whitworth, Charles, 87
Wilkinson, James, 293
Willard, Joseph, 128, 129, 335
Williams, Jonathan, 127
Williams, William A., 360
Williamson, Hugh, 124
Wilson, Benjamin, 117
Winder, William H., 296
Winship, Jonathan, 182-183
Winthrop, John, 120, 121
Wistor, Casparo, 336
Witherspoon, John, 19
Wittfooth, Arvid (A. Vitfot), 92-94, 114
Wolf, Bertram, 359
Wright, Robert, 286
Wythe, George, 62, 63

Yarmolinsky, Avrahm, 362

Zamiatin, G. A., 113
Zea Bermúdez, Franciscu de, 245, 276
Zhukovsky, V. A., 337